TAMING MEGALOPOLIS

VOLUME II

How to Manage an Urbanized World

TAMING MEGALOPOLIS

Volume II

How to Manage an Urbanized World

EDITED, WITH A PREFACE AND HEADNOTES,
BY H. WENTWORTH ELDREDGE

Anchor Books
Doubleday & Company, Inc.
Garden City, New York

The Anchor Books edition is the first publication of *Taming Megalopolis: Volume II, How to Manage an Urbanized World*

Anchor Books edition: 1967

Library of Congress Catalog Card Number 67–12878

CONTENTS

VOLUME II

VOLUME I

PART THREE. HOW TO MANAGE AN URBANIZED WORLD

Chapter 13

PLANNING AS A PROFESSION

Whether "planning is too important to be left to planners" is still an open question. Responsible and irresponsible public officials since time immemorial have planned by marshaling and allocating resources in order to reach goals arrived at by various methods for measuring the "popular will." Private persons in the United States in any case will continue relatively unfettered to make the majority of plans: that is, private plans with public consequences. But now with the American Institute of Planners (AIP) and elsewhere throughout the world (The Town Planning Institute in Great Britain, for example), there is a regular guild of planners who have set themselves up as *the* planners of urban society. Or have they actually done so? In matter of actual fact, the AIP after lively debate has just opened its doors to persons not specifically trained in traditionalistic "city planning" as heretofore conceived. This is a very considerable step for a profession grounded originally in architecture and still addicted to urban physical design. Undoubtedly it is a belated recognition intellectually of the increasing dimension of urbanism and the urbanization process—and realistically of the rising competition from activist-oriented urban studies training going on in political science, social work, sociology, anthropology, geography, and in schools of law, journalism, public administration and public health. Finally, one perforce must inquire whether our knowledge can keep up with the cascading rush of urbanization and whether any one man—a generalist, that is—can keep up with all that knowledge.

William Alonso has in a mordant article analyzed the present planning profession as it strives mightily to keep up with social change; he points out its middle class and intellectual roots and takes note of its continuing limiting biases. The particular qualities of our practitioners show up in the works done for their clients—the politicos and generally upper and upper-middle class segments of our society, as expressed through government and private decision. Hitler's and Napoleon III's grandiose dreams received expression in Berlin and Paris respectively; Stalinist paranoia is reflected in Moscow University's wedding cake style; our cluttered urbanization reflects our pluralistic selves and our planners. No one seems to be in control of our big picture as the confusion of values explored in Chapter 6, "Goals for Democratic Planning," seems to indicate. Are the present breed of Western planners, or for that matter socialist/communist planners, "broad gauge" enough to build an urban civilization with all that word implies? If, however, our urban planners are not ready,

willing and able to do the job of total environmental planning including its social and economic dimensions, the job will most certainly be attempted by some overarching profession "above" them,
as yet unnamed, much less trained. For the record, even the engineers
have pretensions in this direction; the opportunity is that juicy; and
the need is that obvious.

Facing the client—especially the disadvantaged client—problem
squarely, Paul Davidoff has outlined a fresh conception of city planning as a lively part of the political process. Here different interest
groups of our multigroup society contend each with their own planning schemes and planning advocates (much as lawyers) in the open
arena of public adversary action. Planning, he points out, is not a
simple technical process nor does quantified cost/benefit analysis reveal ultimate truth; it merely builds on hidden values. He calls both
for a re-examination of present planning administrative mechanisms
and for a revised planning education, flatly contending that planning
should join the thrusting main stream of contemporary social change
moving on toward social justice. This, of course, is in keeping with
the growing school of "populist" as opposed to "elitist" planning.

Cities and City Planners

WILLIAM ALONSO*

The city planning profession, like most adolescents, is self-
conscious. It worries about its appearance, it strikes poses, it
adopts and discards heroes, it revolts against its parents while
depending on them. It tries, in short, to establish its own
identity. This identity is the product of its intellectual ancestry and of its early development, of its current situation
and, perhaps to a greater extent than other professions, of the
appearances and realities of the object of its concern, which
is the city. It is a profession in rapid change, full of contradic-
tions and given to excesses. Such a subject cannot be portrayed
at rest and separately from its object, and so we will consider

* Associate Professor of Regional Planning, Graduate School of Design, Harvard University, from which he received his B.A. and M.C.P.
degrees. He is a Ph.D. in Regional Science from the University of
Pennsylvania and carries on a consulting practice in city and regional
planning, having served the Ford Foundation, and as Technical Assistance Expert for the United Nations. In addition to journal articles,
he is the author of *Location and Land Use* (Cambridge: Harvard
University Press, 1964) and with John Friedman edited *Regional Development and Planning* (Cambridge: M.I.T. Press, 1964). Reprinted
by permission from *Daedalus,* published by the American Academy of
Arts and Sciences, Brookline, Massachusetts. Vol. 92, No. 4, *The Professions,* Fall 1963.

some of the forces that have made it what it is, but principally we will consider some of the issues that confront it and how it is coping with them, for it is in action that the importance and the weaknesses of the profession can be seen.

City planning in the United States stems from several roots, of which the earliest is architectural. The 1893 Columbian Exposition in Chicago dazzled Americans with the classic magnificence of the fairgrounds, and many visitors returned to their communities eager to ennoble their appearance in a movement called City Beautiful. The common manifestation of this movement was a superficial playing with boulevards, waterfronts and neoclassical architecture, but some of the writings of the period show a sensitive awareness of the society and the economy to be housed in this splendid container. The City Beautiful faded gradually out of American planning. Aesthetic concern for three-dimensional design returned with vigor only after World War II, and then largely as a result of European influences such as the Congrès International de l'Architecture Moderne (CIAM), of which Le Corbusier was the principal figure. However, those who now practice in this vein owe their first allegiance to architecture rather than to city planning, and they often call themselves urban designers.

Other seminal influences are harder to differentiate from one another. The muckrakers and other early reformers focused interest on the housing of workers, considering finances, family life and social organization as well as design. The development of urban sociology, mostly in Chicago in the 1920's and 1930's, served to document the conditions of urban living and shifted attention from the aesthetic of urban form to an analytic geography concerned with the social and economic landscape of the city. The New Deal provided funds and a national program for reform, emphasizing slum clearance and public housing. The naive social darwinism popularized by Herbert Spencer had held that poverty and slum conditions were the just deserts of the inferior and necessary conditions for social progress. It now became an article of faith that slums and bad housing were the cause of ill health, criminality, illegitimacy and other social evils. Consequently there was as much effort directed to tearing down slums as to providing new housing for those displaced. Today this seems a gallant charge against windmills. We have learned, for instance, that the slum is often a tightly knit social fabric that provides security and gradual acculturation to urban life, and that moving its inhabitants to antiseptic piles of brick can be cruel. We have learned that slums are often manifestations of racial as well as of class inequality, but we have not learned much about solving this thornier problem. This does not mean that nothing need be done about slums, but that the brave solutions that had seemed so evident have proved inadequate, and that learning advances slowly and painfully.

Advocates of city planning, as most urban reformers, were deeply suspicious of corrupt municipal governments, and they advocated the use of appointed commissions that could keep their hands clean of the filth of politics. From the 1920's to World War II untold planning commissions were organized, and each would hire a planner to produce a Master Plan. This consisted of proposals for parkways, a waterfront improvement, a new city hall and other items, and, always, a zoning ordinance. Public works, for obvious reasons, could often be sold by the commission to the city government. The zoning ordinance, stating what land could be used for what purposes, was often adopted, but it tended to degenerate. Seldom prepared with sufficient understanding of structural relationships, its administration consisted of a joyful or reluctant granting of variances and exceptions, so that it soon became riddled with holes. The planning commission in a social sense, and the zoning ordinance in a real estate sense, represented middle and upper class values and were too often holding operations against the forces of change. Since zoning combined conservatism with the planning advocated by the progressives, it often enjoyed considerable support together with indifferent success.

Faith that technical analysis is superior to the political process as a means of arriving at decisions has been another fountainhead of planning, at least since Hoover's 1920's. Techniques have improved by leaps and bounds in recent years in such areas as the estimation of the demand for housing, offices and highways and the calculation of the impact of particular measures. Many questions have thus been validly removed from the politician to the analyst, and this has given strength to the apolitical view of planning.

But there is a strong counter-current, and in many cases planning is moving closer to politics with the realization that what is needed is not so much a plan as a planning process. That is to say, the Master Plan, reflecting its architectural ancestry, presented a picture of an ideal final stage, much as the plans for a building represent the completed building, and the only question was how to carry it out. Today it is clear that in the nature of things every plan is tentative, both because information is imperfect and because there is no final stage: there is always a future beyond the stage projected. What is needed is continuing planning, which produces every year a plan for the next few years, and every few years a plan for the next two or three decades, so that the next steps and the distant goals are known at all times. With this concept, plans have become the companions of policy and the planner has moved inside government into a position similar to that of a general staff in an army. When plans are statements of policies the emphasis shifts from the solution of particular problems through particular projects to a view of the city as a complicated system to be guided as well as corrected.

These are the architectural, the reformist and the technocratic roots of planning. Other influences might be mentioned, such as the utopian movements with their long and colorful history, or the paradoxical importance of the romantic anti-urban attitudes in England and America, of which Lewis Mumford is a representative. There is also the British version of city planning, which is called town planning, and the continental versions, which are often called urbanism. Suffice it to say that they are closer to physical design and further from the social sciences than is American city planning.

Training for the profession is offered in the United States and Canada at some three dozen accredited schools of planning, almost all offering postgraduate programs only, two to three years long and leading to the degree of Master of City Planning. People are attracted into the profession from many fields. Students from an architectural background are now only a modest plurality. Most of the others come from liberal arts and the social sciences, some from law and the natural sciences. Their motives for entering planning are mixed. Because of the great shortage of planners, good wages and rapid promotion are certain to attract people. But altruistic motives are also important: a desire to improve our environment, to help make the good life possible in cities. Some people, although very few now, are dedicated to particular ideologies, from New Deal liberalism to several forms of socialism. The majority are apparently not interested in political ideas. Rather they feel good will toward their fellow man and, in a general way, they wish to improve his lot.

In recent years doctoral programs have gained in importance. These are offered by half a dozen universities, and they direct their training to research and teaching rather than to professional practice. Their development has raised again the question of whether the field has a valid body of knowledge or of expertness. No clear answer emerges. Certain topics interest planners principally, and others fall within traditional academic disciplines. Perhaps the answer is that the planner brings a point of view, an area of concern or a set of questions that he must answer as best he can because of the urgent problems of cities. The approach is eclectic in that it takes much from others, but the pressure of responsibility for action rather than of knowledge for its own sake forces a shifting synthesis which, whatever its intellectual inadequacies, goes to the issues and does not trouble itself with the territorial rights that tradition has established between, let us say, economics and geography. Had city planning the self-confidence, it might paraphrase the well-known definition that mathematics is what mathematicians do.

The situation of planners in this respect is very similar to that of medicine some time ago. Medicine is also a goal-oriented activity that makes use of other academic fields such as chemistry and biology. It uses their tools and findings and raises questions which may be explored by people in the field itself or in related fields. In the same way, in recent years, planning has produced a great deal of research activity under a variety of labels, including that of planning. There has resulted an explosion of knowledge and, unfortunately, a greater flood of literature with which no one person can hope to keep up, leading to the paradox of specialization in a profession that a decade ago prided itself in producing generalists in an age of specialists.

The naming of the planning association, which was founded in 1917, stimulated a revealing debate in choosing between American Institute of Planners or American Institute of Planning. The issue at stake was whether the organization should represent the activity of planning, in which anyone can participate by thinking intelligently about the future, or whether it should represent a particular body of men who labeled themselves city planners. The second alternative was chosen, and today the American Institute of Planners follows a policy of professional closure. It has persuaded agencies to write into their job specifications educational and experience requirements, and it has been discussing the establishment of registration examinations. The British Town Planning Institute, unconcerned with the semantics of its name, has had such examinations for years.

This is the profession that is trying to meet the challenge of urban change. By and large, it is right and sensible to train people to deal with urban problems and to permit them to advise the public and the authorities on these matters. It is true that our knowledge of urban phenomena is rudimentary, comparable perhaps to the knowledge of the human body at the time of Harvey's discovery of the circulation of blood. That is to say, we know a great deal, not nearly enough and much of it wrong. Still, the problems are there and decisions must be made. The advice of a good planner is probably the best available, but it is likely that in ten or fifteen years our understanding will have advanced through research and experience to where the advice of the average planner will be better than that of the best today, just as today's planners are better than those of one or two decades ago.

Knowledge is inadequate and solutions shallow, and to improve this situation it is right to be impatient with the profession. It has attracted as yet relatively few first-rate minds, and these must be prodded to produce their best. The apostolic zeal of the aesthetic and reformist heritages and many years of frustration still manifest themselves in a crusading attitude of yea-saying and a distrust of criticism. City planners are more influential than ever before, and there is a danger that power may corrupt, that mistakes will be repeated and justified rather than teach how things may be better done. Success can too easily be measured by activity and expenditure.

Perhaps these dangers to the profession can best be made clear by considering the urban situation today and by showing the inadequacy of the more popular solutions. A modern city is the most complex social and economic system that has ever existed, and, to keep from getting lost, we will focus on the interplay between size and structure of cities as the background for current planning practice.

When things change in size, they tend to change in structure. A grown man is not, at least physically, merely a very large baby. Science fiction to the contrary, being a fly implies being neither bigger nor smaller than the usual size of flies. A mutant the size of a freight car is impossible: it could not fly, its legs would buckle if it tried to walk, and, anyway, it would die of asphyxiation, since its breathing mechanism can serve only bodies a fraction of an inch in diameter. Size and structure depend upon each other. The critical relation between size and structure applies as well to social organisms such as nations and cities. But while the relation is easily accepted by most people in the biological realm, for some reason we seem to have difficulty in understanding it in the social realm, and this often leads to trouble. The fact is that, with economic development, cities and countries tend to grow, and as their size increases, their structure changes.

Looking at it from the other side, a change in structure tends to demand a change in size. Economic development is a continuing change in the structure of a society. With economic development the size of cities has changed. In the eighteenth century, a city of a few tens of thousands was a large and important city, and a few hundred thousands made a very large city in the nineteenth. In the twentieth century we have seen the city of a few millions emerge as the dominant form. Of course, this many people simply do not fit into the municipal boundaries which had been established for the earlier, smaller cities. The population has spilled over, and the urban mass covers a number of municipal units, in many cases in the United States straddling two and even three states. This urban mass, which we call by the awkward names of metropolitan area or metropolis, is the true city of today. We still refer to parts of the metropolis as "cities" or "towns," and these parts maintain their existence as municipal corporations, but they are no longer true cities in the sense of a geographic community of work and home. The facts have changed, but our thinking—much less our system of government—has not kept up with them.

But the metropolis is no mere large-scale model of the older city any more than the *Queen Mary* is a large-scale model of the *Santa María*. It is well known that economic development has brought specialization to the work of men. It has also brought about the specialization of space for men's activities. Work, home, shopping and recreation are more separated than they have ever been. Vast areas of homes specialize by race, income, family, size, age and tastes of residents. Shops cluster and separate according to price, style, variety and type of goods offered, and according to whether they are reached on foot, by car or by mass transit. Factories and offices gather and separate in complicated rhythms of their own. The great variety of indoor and outdoor amusements distribute themselves in this space according to the markets they serve.

Those who disparage the monotony of our metropolitan areas see only half the picture. There are in fact more things under the sun than there used to be, but these things are usually grouped together rather than mixed. There is therefore little variety in any one place, although there is more variety to the whole. Curiously, those who complain of monotony often also complain of the chaos of our urban areas. This apparent contradiction disappears if we think of these critics as on foot in the first instance and in a car in the second. If one is walking, the immediate area seems large and unchanging. But if one is in a car, one travels much faster and sees more things in a short time, and then the great variety of the city may become bewildering.

Bewildering, yes; but is it chaos? Chaos is only the absence of order, and order is nothing but the understanding of structure. There can be no question that our metropolitan areas have a structure, and that serious students of cities understand it fairly well, know how it got to be that way, and how it is likely to develop. The chaos of which the critics complain, then, refers not to the lack of structure but to the difficulty of perceiving it; and the problem is not one of restructuring but one of making understanding easier. A person moving through a city must be given visual clues and explanations of where he is and where he is going, of what these places are and of how they are related to each other. Many suburban residential areas should be given a more intense focus and clearer edges. Adjacent areas, such as the financial and the commercial in most downtowns, should be differentiated and articulated. People must be given a clearer image of the structure of urban areas while preserving variety and surprise within the elements of that structure. This is a very recent way of looking at urban design, but it should have considerable impact, taking the aesthetics of city planning beyond the architectural consideration of groups of buildings to the treatment of urban form as such.

The bigger pieces making up the mosaic of the metropolitan structure have also been criticized on grounds other than aesthetic. That side of sociology that used to be called social philosophy has attacked the social monotony of the suburbs, and most planners have concurred. The organization man, the member of the lonely crowd, seeks status in the endless urban sprawl by living in a house with a picture window which is usually cracked. These critics deplore the anonymity, the dullness, the conformism and the shallowness of suburban living, and they point out how short the suburbs fall of that pastoral ideal which they question in the first instance. Children brought up in this synthetic environment know nothing of the real world outside, meet only children of families exactly like their own, and grow up to be intolerant, uninteresting, ignorant conformists. The meeting place for men is the town dump, which is lacking in dignity. The women lead lives of intolerable loneliness and boredom or of frantic activity as charwomen, chairwomen, nursemaids, or hostesses, according to whom one reads.

These portraits or caricatures have proliferated recently. Some of the strokes in these portraits may be questioned, such as the relative ranges of experience of central city and suburban children, but the distaste of the authors for this suburban way of life is what is important. These critics are not just reporting on a way of life: they are judging it. By the skillful use of language they are criticizing and trying to change the tastes of their readers to have them see the suburban way of life in a new and most unflattering light. The fact, the evidence shows, is that this way of life is what most Americans want, that they are getting it and that they feel, and are supported by any reasonable comparison, that they never had it so good. Whether these people are instances of ensnared *Boobus americanus* or latter-day Candides happily tending their gardens depends on one's viewpoint. In my opinion, they are achieving their ideal, however imperfectly. Various city planners have proposed alternative modes of considerable merit and ingenuity, but their schemes have had only local and partial success. If there is to be any fundamental change, it will have to be by an extraordinary innovation in the field of taste, offering an alternative type of housing and manner of living which is as deeply rooted in the traditions and feelings of our society as is the present suburban house. What this alternative may be, if there is one, we will not know until it succeeds.

The changes in size, and therefore in structure, of cities have affected their centers as well as their edges. While the suburbs have continued to grow very fast, virtually every central city has lost population in the last decade. This has brought about a strange alliance between the intellectual—usually liberal—critics of the suburbs and those businessmen—usually conservative—with an interest in central city real estate. Their combined argument runs: the city (the central city is meant) is dying; the city is the focus of our economy and the center of our culture; therefore, unless something is done, our economy is endangered and our culture is weakened. This, of course, is nonsense. The city today is the metropolitan area, and it is growing lustily. As it grows it is developing and changing in structure, redistributing people and activities. What is in fact happening is that, as a result of this redistribution, businesses and people are shifting out from the center. This hurts some downtown businesses, though it benefits business at other locations, where new centers are forming. Like all transitions, it has its costs and dangers, but to argue that it imperils the economy as a whole would be like arguing that the development of the automobile hurt the horseshoe and buggywhip industries, and that therefore it imperiled the economy. On the cultural side as well, the argument is weak. People can move about very rapidly (this is what has made the suburbs possible), and can attend lectures, concerts, museums or the theater regardless of where they live. It may be that the suburbanite prefers to watch television, but that is a fundamental problem of our culture's tastes and attitudes, not of geographic location. If he were somehow dragged back, kicking and screaming, to the central city, once he quieted down a bit he would presumably turn on his television set.

In the past few years there has been a great deal of effort to put new life into the central cities, spearheaded by the federal Urban Renewal Program and generally endorsed by city planners. This program has much good in it, but the obsolete fractioning of our metropolitan areas into many different tax units has perverted local motives and has resulted in many futile and very expensive projects. Suppose, for instance, that a central city has a slum area. It is a well-documented fact that slum areas cost a city, in terms of police and fire protection, welfare payments, schools and other expenses, much more than they pay in taxes. On the other hand, an area of wealthy residents in apartments pays into the city much more than it takes out in municipal services. A city is, in legal terms, a municipal corporation, and like any other corporation it will be anxious to exchange a losing line for a profitable one. In other words, any municipality will gladly trade its poor for some other municipality's rich.

Under the Urban Renewal Program, a city may do just that. It may acquire a slum area under eminent domain, clear it of its buildings and sell it to a developer. No one today can afford to build for the poor without subsidy. On expensive central land it is nearly impossible to build at all except for the rich, and even that must be done at high density by means of apartment towers. On central land, the city can be quite certain that it is exchanging the poor slum-dwellers for wealthy apartment-dwellers. The cost of this operation to the city is one third of the difference between what it paid for the area to its previous owners and what the developer pays the city for it. The federal government pays the other two thirds. The profits to the city will be the increased tax revenue resulting from newer and more expensive property plus the savings in city services. This is likely to prove profitable to the municipal corporation. For instance, one large recent project cleared an area where the average income of families was $234 per month and built there apartments with an average rent of $200 per month. Only families with a monthly income of $1000 or more would normally pay such rents.

But if this type of renewal eliminates slums in an area and improves municipal finances, what is wrong with it? The answer is simple. One must look not at areas but at people; not at the finances of one tax unit but at the finances of the metropolitan area. The poor who lived in the slum have simply moved elsewhere, and the municipality hopes that they have moved to some nearby municipality, which will then be obliged to contend with their money-losing presence. Usually, the poor not only receive no direct benefit, but the clearing of the slum may reduce the housing supply for their income group, making higher rents and more crowding likely in the low-rent housing market. The high-income groups could have had housing, new or old, elsewhere, probably in the suburbs. What has happened is that the various tax units in the metropolitan area are playing an expensive game of musical chairs with the poor and the rich for tax dollars. The poor that one city has got rid of go to another city; the expensive housing that one city has gained has been gained at the expense of another city, and there is no net gain for the metropolitan area.

The federal government is playing an equivocal role with respect to metropolitan structure. With its right hand, the Urban Renewal Program, it is trying to breathe new life into the centers of metropolitan areas, counter to the ongoing structural trends. With its left, however, it is reinforcing these trends and weakening the center. It does this with its F.H.A. mortgage insurance policies and its income tax policies, which permit the homeowner to deduct the interest on his mortgage and the property tax on his home, while the renter can deduct no part of his rent. This makes owning much more attractive financially than renting and provides a powerful extra push to the suburbs. Suburbanization is the basic trend of large cities, deeply rooted in taste and the economics of land. It would take government intervention and controls of a different order of magnitude than the current Urban Renewal Program to reverse these trends, even without contradictory policies.

Meanwhile, preserving the fiction that the metropolis is composed of independent parts makes the process of growth more painful for the suburbs as well as for the center. While central cities worry because they are losing the middle and upper classes and are left only with the poor, who tend to be minorities such as Negroes, Puerto Ricans, or Mexicans, the suburbs pretend that these poor are not *their* poor, and that the suburban population is not made up of stockbrokers, professionals and insurance men but rather of homesteaders and Jeffersonian farmers conducting their affairs in a small, self-contained community not affected by the problems in the central cities. But the suburbs have their problems too, both social and financial. Because they are composed of families with children, one third to one half of their population is in the public schools; because they are absorbing most of the population growth of the nation, they need new streets, sewers and other facilities; and much of their energy is spent in anxious battle to keep out people with incomes lower than their own as well as others who would not "fit." Every part of the metropolis is encouraged to beggar its neighbor, and the egoism and short-sightedness of fictional independence serve only to create new problems.

Business and industry as well as population are also being redistributed, and Urban Renewal is also trying to preserve these activities in the central city. But again, the geographic fragmentation of an obsolete governmental structure tends to distort and pervert the renewal decisions. A recent federal publication, trying to show that the renewal of commercial and industrial areas makes economic sense, presented approvingly the case of a central city in which renewal had resulted in $180,000,000 of new construction and an increase of $200,000 in yearly property taxes to the city. This makes no economic sense to me: the increased tax revenue is only about one tenth of 1 per cent of the total investment, not big enough to be a justifying factor. Furthermore, from the point of view of the private investor, taxes are an expense, not a profit. When we look at the public share of the investment we can understand what has happened. The federal government contributed $8,000,000 and the city, $4,000,000. The new taxes represent 5 per cent on the city's investment. This is a reasonable return on the city's investment of $4,000,000; but to base the economic sense of an investment forty-five times as big on a reasonable return to the city is akin to basing the decision to have a major operation on the attractiveness of his fees to the surgeon. Such things happen, but they are not often considered desirable. They are, in fact, unethical and immoral.

The important questions are whether the total private and public investments are an efficient use of capital, profitable by ordinary business standards; and whether the total public investment to have the development take place in the central city is productive when compared with the efficiency of development elsewhere or of no development at all. This is a difficult question, but it is seldom asked by city planners, let alone answered. It may be that such an investment is wise, but we do not know that it is.

The ordinary investment criteria are not the only ones that apply in such cases. There are important qualitative changes which do not appear in any balance sheet, but which nonetheless may benefit every inhabitant of the metropolis. Without positive action the urban center may wither, and the metropolis may become a vast, amorphous, headless amoeba. A strong center is needed socially, economically and psychologically, for it is here that urban life is lived in full, and virtually all activities in the metropolitan area focus towards it. Here is the center of power, where a new enterprise may be conceived over lunch; here a woman may shop at a department store, look at expensive merchandise in exclusive shops, have dinner in a fine restaurant, and then go to the theater; here one may find a shop that specializes in stringed instruments or clothing for six-foot women, a man who can repair jade or ivory, someone who is an expert in importing from Hong Kong, an agency that can supply the names and addresses of a few thousand street railway enthusiasts or likely opponents of the death penalty. But this variety and richness is possible only because there are enough things and enough people downtown to attract more things and more people. Let the size of the downtown area drop below the necessary critical mass, and dissolution will follow. There will not be enough six-foot girls coming downtown for there to be a shop especially for them. There will not be enough lunch-time demand to keep a fine restaurant going, and if there are no restaurants, the theaters will suffer. Unless downtown is big enough, there will be no downtown. Some activities will move to the suburbs, but many will die or will never come into existence. Life will become much duller and more homogenized.

But why, if metropolitan areas are getting bigger, should the downtown area be in any danger? Once again, it is a matter of critical size. The suburbs have grown enough, and are far enough away from the old center, for there to be enough local demand to justify local department stores, lawyers and architects, fashion and furniture stores, and other services. Of course, these do not have the variety and size of their downtown equivalents, but they have grown largely at the expense of the downtown area. Industry has been shifting from railroads to trucks, and increasingly it prefers one-story buildings with ample parking, leading, of course, to suburban locations; and industry pulls related activities along with it. Even some large offices have tried moving to the suburbs, but with indifferent success.

These changes in metropolitan structure have indeed placed the downtown area in danger, for each move reduces its size and its attractiveness. But is this a short-run danger or a long-run destiny? Consider the trends that favor downtown. The employment composition of every country, as it develops, shifts increasingly to white collar jobs, and these are typically downtown jobs. Automation and rapid communication not only increase the proportion of "head" over "hand" workers; they permit their spatial separation. As physical production is automated and depersonalized, and as communications improve, managers and supervisors can send impersonal orders to a more distant production line and still be downtown for the advantages of personal contact with other decision-makers. Therefore, although the physical production part of industry may continue to become suburban, the management of that production may become more centralized. And as our population becomes richer and better educated, it seeks the luxurious, the sophisticated and the specialized, which are the major attractions of downtown. In short, then, there are very powerful forces which in the long run will mean a resurgence of the downtown area. It will be a different downtown in that it will be a more purely distilled essence of what we have today; but it will be all the better for that.

Is Urban Renewal in the downtown area a holding operation to counteract the short-run forces which are endangering the urban center until these long-run trends establish themselves? The answer is yes and no. Urban Renewal is for the preservation of the downtown area, but it uses short-run arguments and short-run thinking. It uses subsidies to create new and glamorous buildings without asking how these buildings will be used in thirty years. For instance, most of our important metropolitan areas were founded next to water, and downtown was based on proximity to the port on the edge of the urban area. But, as the port decreases in relative importance (which it almost universally has), and the urban area increases in size, downtown tends to seek the center of the urban mass. It creeps away from the water, at a rate of perhaps one-half mile every twenty years. Are not many of today's projects in the older parts of downtown trying to re-create a center on land that is fated to be an edge? Are they not trying to bring an old center back to life, rather than being midwives to the birth of a new and more viable center?

It makes excellent sense to subsidize the center if the danger to its critical size is a temporary one and a return to health is likely in the long run. But it is less than wise to pour money into glamorous architectural groupings looking with admiration and civic pride only to the size of the capital investment, the increased tax base and the added floor space. If the urban centers are shrinking, their immediate problem is overcapacity, and adding floor space will not solve it; if rents at the center are too high, so that suburban locations are more attractive by comparison, expensive buildings, strongly assessed and paying high taxes, are unlikely to be the solution. It cannot be denied that new and well-designed buildings have a glamor that attracts businesses and customers, and that they may give the downtown area a feeling of effervescence and restore confidence. But new buildings get old very quickly.

To save the downtown area, what is needed is a downtown that works well. Many of the new downtown projects are composed mostly of free-standing buildings, handsomely set about in open space, designed as sculpture on a grandiose scale. The emphasis is put on the project as such, not on the downtown area as a part of the urban system. Not enough attention is paid to the way one element relates to another. For instance, most downtowns have evolved with buildings standing side by side, filling up the blocks, with the streets as channels between them. According to their economic strength and ability to pay rent, activities take locations on the main street, on the side streets, or on the back streets, all close to each other and dependent on each other. Most of the new developments place their buildings standing free *within* the block, and little or no provision is made for those businesses that would go on side and back streets because they cannot pay prime rents. Yet many of these smaller businesses are the lubrication and the ball bearings needed for the smooth operation of the larger businesses, and many of them, such as restaurants, bars and book and specialty stores, make downtown interesting and human. The downtown area is the brain tissue of the metropolis, a complex, evolving, and little understood organ. If it is sick, it may require surgery, but this surgery should be done with sensitive fingers, with the finest surgical instruments, and with the closest attention to what is in fact being done.

In the past half-century our cities have outgrown our concepts and our tools, and I have tried to show how the lagging understanding of the changes in kind that go with changes in size has led us to try remedies which are unsuited to the ills of our urban areas. In this sense, I have been writing mostly about the past and present. What about the future? For the past few years there has been growing professional and popular interest in the step beyond the metropolis, even though we have yet to digest the present reality. The words *megapolis* and *megalopolis* are being heard with increasing frequency, usually applied to an almost continuous string of cities running from Washington, D.C. to Boston. And once this idea is launched, similar patterns are seen emerging on the West and Gulf Coasts, in Argentina and Venezuela, in Indonesia and in Europe.

The pattern does not consist of a string of metropolitan areas standing shoulder to shoulder, fighting for space like a crowd in a subway, but of metropolitan areas in a functioning group, interacting with each other. In the same manner that economic development has made the size of the typical nation inadequate and has called for super-nations, it seems that soon—at least in historical time—urban units will go beyond the scale of the metropolis to the scale of the megapolis. And just as the metropolitan area is not made up of an accumulation of little cities complete in themselves but on a system of specialized and therefore dissimilar areas, the various metropolitan units of megapolis will specialize and become more different from each other than they are today. No one knows with any certainty what the fields of economic specialization will be, or how the social specialization which occurs in metropolitan areas will reappear at the megapolitan scale, though comparisons between Washington, New York, Boston, and other cities are quite suggestive. It does seem likely that history may continue to outpace our ability to grasp and deal with our urban problems, and that, like generals, city planners may be fated always to fight the day's battles with the outworn ideas of their last war.

But even today, at the level of metropolitan development, perhaps the ultimate question is who is to be the planner's client. Is it the commission, the mayor, the council or the voters? Is it only the residents of the city, or future residents, or those who work there but live elsewhere? Should consideration be given to the interests of the region and the nation when they run counter to the city's? When we say a plan is good and desirable, who will benefit and who wants it? I have emphasized the effects of the municipal fragmentation of urban areas. Most city planners are in favor of metropolitan government but work for a particular municipality. What is their responsibility and who is their public? Questions of goals and clients are particularly difficult for city planners, but ultimately it is these questions of ethics and responsibility that distinguish a profession from other occupations.

Advocacy and Pluralism in Planning

PAUL DAVIDOFF*

The present can become an epoch in which the dreams of the past for an enlightened and just democracy are turned into a reality. The massing of voices protesting racial discrimination have roused this nation to the need to rectify racial and other social injustices. The adoption by Congress of a host of welfare measures and the Supreme Court's

* Professor of Urban Planning and Chairman, Hunter College Program in Urban Planning. He was formerly associated with Voorhees, Walker, Smith and Smith; and served as Town Planner, New Canaan, Connecticut and Associate Professor of City Planning at the University of Pennsylvania, where he received an LL.B. in 1961 after an M.C.P. in 1956. He is the author of a number of professional articles. This article is reprinted with permission from the *Journal of the American Institute of Planners*, Vol. XXXI, No. 4, November 1965.

specification of the meaning of equal protection by law both reveal the response to protest and open the way for the vast changes still required.

The just demand for political and social equality on the part of the Negro and the impoverished requires the public to establish the bases for a society affording equal opportunity to all citizens. The compelling need for intelligent planning, for specification of new social goals and the means for achieving them, is manifest. The society of the future will be an urban one, and city planners will help to give it shape and content.

The prospect for future planning is that of a practice which openly invites political and social values to be examined and debated. Acceptance of this position means rejection of prescriptions for planning which would have the planner act solely as a technician. It has been argued that technical studies to enlarge the information available to decision makers must take precedence over statements of goals and ideals:

> We have suggested that, at least in part, the city planner is better advised to start from research into the functional aspects of cities than from his own estimation of the values which he is attempting to maximize. This suggestion springs from a conviction that at this juncture the implications of many planning decisions are poorly understood, and that no certain means are at hand by which values can be measured, ranked, and translated into the design of a metropolitan system.[1]

While acknowledging the need for humility and openness in the adoption of social goals, this statement amounts to an attempt to eliminate, or sharply reduce, the unique contribution planning can make: understanding the functional aspects of the city and recommending appropriate future action to improve the urban condition.

Another argument that attempts to reduce the importance of attitudes and values in planning and other policy sciences is that the major public questions are themselves matters of choice between technical methods of solution. Dahl and Lindblom put forth this position at the beginning of their important textbook, *Politics, Economics, and Welfare:*[2]

[1] Britton Harris, "Plan or Projection," *Journal of the American Institute of Planners*, XXVI (November 1960) pp. 265–272.

[2] Robert Dahl and Charles Lindblom, *Politics, Economics, and Welfare* (New York: Harper and Brothers, 1953) p. 3.

In economic organization and reform, the "great issues" are no longer the great issues, if they ever were. It has become increasingly difficult for thoughtful men to find meaningful alternatives posed in the traditional choices between socialism and capitalism, planning and the free market, regulation and laissez faire, for they find their actual choices neither so simple nor so grand. Not so simple, because economic organization poses knotty problems that can only be solved by painstaking attention to technical details—how else, for example, can inflation be controlled? Nor so grand, because, at least in the Western world, most people neither can nor wish to experiment with the whole pattern of socio-economic organization to attain goals more easily won. If for example, taxation will serve the purpose, why "abolish the wages system" to ameliorate income inequality?

These words were written in the early 1950's and express the spirit of that decade more than that of the 1960's. They suggest that the major battles have been fought. But the "great issues" in economic organization, those revolving around the central issue of the nature of distributive justice, have yet to be settled. The world is still in turmoil over the way in which the resources of nations are to be distributed. The justice of the present social allocation of wealth, knowledge, skill, and other social goods is clearly in debate. Solutions to questions about the share of wealth and other social commodities that should go to different classes cannot be technically derived; they must arise from social attitudes.

Appropriate planning action cannot be prescribed from a position of value neutrality, for prescriptions are based on desired objectives. One conclusion drawn from this assertion is that "values are inescapable elements of any rational decision-making process"[3] and that values held by the planner should be made clear. The implications of that conclusion for planning have been described elsewhere and will not be considered in this article.[4] Here I will say that the planner should do more than explicate the values underlying his prescriptions for courses of action; he should affirm them; he should be an advocate for what he deems proper.

[3] Paul Davidoff and Thomas Reiner, "A Choice Theory of Planning," *Journal of the American Institute of Planners,* XXVIII (May 1962) pp. 103–115.

[4] *Ibid.*

Determinations of what serves the public interest, in a society containing many diverse interest groups, are almost always of a highly contentious nature. In performing its role of prescribing courses of action leading to future desired states, the planning profession must engage itself thoroughly and openly in the contention surrounding political determination. Moreover, planners should be able to engage in the political process as advocates of the interests both of government and of such other groups, organizations, or individuals who are concerned with proposing policies for the future development of the community.

The recommendation that city planners represent and plead the plans of many interest groups is founded upon the need to establish an effective urban democracy, one in which citizens may be able to play an active role in the process of deciding public policy. Appropriate policy in a democracy is determined through a process of political debate. The right course of action is always a matter of choice, never of fact. In a bureaucratic age great care must be taken that choices remain in the area of public view and participation.

Urban politics, in an era of increasing government activity in planning and welfare, must balance the demands for ever-increasing central bureaucratic control against the demands for increased concern for the unique requirements of local, specialized interests. The welfare of all and the welfare of minorities are both deserving of support; planning must be so structured and so practiced as to account for this unavoidable bifurcation of the public interest.

The idealized political process in a democracy serves the search for truth in much the same manner as due process in law. Fair notice and hearings, production of supporting evidence, cross examination, reasoned decision are all means employed to arrive at relative truth: a just decision. Due process and two- (or more) party political contention both rely heavily upon strong advocacy by a professional. The advocate represents an individual, group, or organization. He affirms their position in language understandable to his client and to the decision makers he seeks to convince.

If the planning process is to encourage democratic urban government then it must operate so as to include rather than exclude citizens from participating in the process. "Inclusion" means not only permitting the citizen to be heard. It also means that he be able to become well informed about the underlying reasons for planning proposals, and be able to respond to them in the technical language of professional planners.

A practice that has discouraged full participation by citizens in plan making in the past has been based on what might be called the *"unitary plan."* This is the idea that only one agency in a community should prepare a comprehensive plan; that agency is the city planning commission or department. Why is it that no other organization within a community prepares a plan? Why is only one agency concerned with establishing both general and specific goals for community development, and with proposing the strategies and costs required to effect the goals? Why are there not plural plans?

If the social, economic, and political ramifications of a plan are politically contentious, then why is it that those in opposition to the agency plan do not prepare one of their own? It is interesting to observe that "rational" theories of planning have called for consideration of alternative courses of action by planning agencies. As a matter of rationality it has been argued that all of the alternative choices open as means to the ends sought be examined.[5] But those, including myself, who have recommended agency consideration of alternatives have placed upon the agency planner the burden of inventing "a few representative alternatives."[6] The agency planner has been given the duty of constructing a model of the political spectrum, and charged with sorting out what he conceives to be worthy alternatives. This duty has placed too great a burden on the agency planner, and has failed to provide for the formulation of alternatives by the interest groups who will eventually be affected by the completed plans.

Whereas in a large part of our national and local political practice contention is viewed as healthy, in city planning where a large proportion of the professionals are public employees, contentious criticism has not always been viewed as legitimate. Further, where only government prepares plans, and no minority plans are developed, pressure is often applied

---

[5] See, for example, Martin Meyerson and Edward Banfield, *Politics, Planning and the Public Interest* (Glencoe: The Free Press, 1955) p. 314 ff. The authors state "By a *rational* decision, we mean one made in the following manner: 1. the decision-maker considers all of the alternatives (courses of action) open to him; . . . 2. he identifies and evaluates all of the consequences which would follow from the adoption of each alternative; . . . 3. he selects that alternative the probable consequences of which would be preferable in terms of his most valued ends."

[6] Davidoff and Reiner, *op. cit.*

to bring all professionals to work for the ends espoused by a public agency. For example, last year a Federal official complained to a meeting of planning professors that the academic planners were not giving enough support to Federal programs. He assumed that every planner should be on the side of the Federal renewal program. Of course government administrators will seek to gain the support of professionals outside of government, but such support should not be expected as a matter of loyalty. In a democratic system opposition to a public agency should be just as normal and appropriate as support. The agency, despite the fact that it is concerned with planning, may be serving undesired ends.

In presenting a plea for plural planning I do not mean to minimize the importance of the obligation of the public planning agency. It must decide upon appropriate future courses of action for the community. But being isolated as the only plan maker in the community, public agencies as well as the public itself may have suffered from incomplete and shallow analysis of potential directions. Lively political dispute aided by plural plans could do much to improve the level of rationality in the process of preparing the public plan.

The advocacy of alternative plans by interest groups outside of government would stimulate city planning in a number of ways. First, it would serve as a means of better informing the public of the alternative choices open, *alternatives strongly supported by their proponents*. In current practice those few agencies which have portrayed alternatives have not been equally enthusiastic about each.[7] A standard reaction to rationalists' prescription for consideration of alternative courses of action has been "it can't be done; how can you expect planners to present alternatives which they don't approve?" The appropriate answer to that question has been that planners like lawyers may have a professional obligation to defend positions they oppose. However, in a system of plural planning, the public agency would be relieved of at least some of the burden of presenting alternatives. In plural planning the alternatives would be presented by interest groups differing with the public agency's plan. Such alternatives would represent the deep-seated convictions of their proponents and not just the mental exercises of rational planners seeking to portray the range of choice.

[7] National Capital Planning Commission, *The Nation's Capital; a Policies Plan for the Year 2000* (Washington, D.C.: The Commission, 1961).

A second way in which advocacy and plural planning would improve planning practice would be in forcing the public agency to compete with other planning groups to win political support. In the absence of opposition or alternative plans presented by interest groups the public agencies have had little incentive to improve the quality of their work or the rate of production of plans. The political consumer has been offered a yes-no ballot in regard to the comprehensive plan; either the public agency's plan was to be adopted or no plan would be adopted.

A third improvement in planning practice which might follow from plural planning would be to force those who have been critical of "establishment" plans to produce superior plans, rather than only to carry out the very essential obligation of criticizing plans deemed improper.

THE PLANNER AS ADVOCATE

Where plural planning is practiced, advocacy becomes the means of professional support for competing claims about how the community should develop. Pluralism in support of political contention describes the process; advocacy describes the role performed by the professional in the process. Where unitary planning prevails, advocacy is not of paramount importance, for there is little or no competition for the plan prepared by the public agency. The concept of advocacy as taken from legal practice implies the opposition of at least two contending viewpoints in an adversary proceeding.

The legal advocate must plead for his own and his client's sense of legal propriety or justice. The planner as advocate would plead for his own and his client's view of the good society. The advocate planner would be more than a provider of information, an analyst of current trends, a simulator of future conditions, and a detailer of means. In addition to carrying out these necessary parts of planning, he would be a *proponent* of specific substantive solutions.

The advocate planner would be responsible to his client and would seek to express his client's views. This does not mean that the planner could not seek to persuade his client. In some situations persuasion might not be necessary, for the planner would have sought out an employer with whom he shared common views about desired social conditions and the means toward them. In fact one of the benefits of advocate planning is the possibility it creates for a planner to find employment with agencies holding values close to his own. Today the agency planner may be dismayed by the positions affirmed by his agency, but there may be no alternative employer.

The advocate planner would be above all a planner. He would be responsible to his client for preparing plans and for all of the other elements comprising the planning process. Whether working for the public agency or for some private organization, the planner would have to prepare plans that take account of the arguments made in other plans. Thus the advocate's plan might have some of the characteristics of a legal brief. It would be a document presenting the facts and reasons for supporting one set of proposals, and facts and reasons indicating the inferiority of counter-proposals. The adversary nature of plural planning might, then, have the beneficial effect of upsetting the tradition of writing plan proposals in terminology which makes them appear self-evident.

A troublesome issue in contemporary planning is that of finding techniques for evaluating alternative plans. Technical devices such as cost-benefit analysis by themselves are of little assistance without the use of means for appraising the values underlying plans. Advocate planning, by making more apparent the values underlying plans, and by making definitions of social costs and benefits more explicit, should greatly assist the process of plan evaluation. Further, it would become clear (as it is not at present) that there are no neutral grounds for evaluating a plan; there are as many evaluative systems as there are value systems.

The adversary nature of plural planning might also have a good effect on the uses of information and research in planning. One of the tasks of the advocate planner in discussing the plans prepared in opposition to his would be to point out the nature of the bias underlying information presented in other plans. In this way, as critic of opposition plans, he would be performing a task similar to the legal technique of cross-examination. While painful to the planner whose bias is exposed (and no planner can be entirely free of bias) the net effect of confrontation between advocates of alternative plans would be more careful and precise research.

Not all the work of an advocate planner would be of an adversary nature. Much of it would be educational. The advocate would have the job of informing other groups, including public agencies, of the conditions, problems, and outlook of the group he represented. Another major educational job would be that of informing his clients of their rights under planning and renewal laws, about the general operations of city government, and of particular programs likely to affect them.

The advocate planner would devote much attention to assisting the client organization to clarify its ideas and to give expression to them. In order to make his client more powerful politically the advocate might also become engaged in expanding the size and scope of his client organization. But the advocate's most important function would be to carry out the planning process for the organization and to argue persuasively in favor of its planning proposals.

Advocacy in planning has already begun to emerge as planning and renewal affect the lives of more and more people. The critics of urban renewal[8] have forced response from the renewal agencies, and the ongoing debate[9] has stimulated needed self-evaluation by public agencies. Much work along the lines of advocate planning has already taken place, but little of it by professional planners. More often the work has been conducted by trained community organizers or by student groups. In at least one instance, however, a planner's professional aid led to the development of an alternative renewal approach, one which will result in the dislocation of far fewer families than originally contemplated.[10]

Pluralism and advocacy are means for stimulating consideration of future conditions by all groups in society. But there is one social group which at present is particularly in need of the assistance of planners. This group includes organizations representing low-income families. At a time when concern for the condition of the poor finds institutionalization in community action programs, it would be appropriate for planners concerned with such groups to find means to plan with them. The plans prepared for these groups would seek to combat poverty and would propose programs affording new and bet-

[8] The most important critical studies are: Jane Jacobs, *The Life and Death of Great American Cities* (New York: Random House, 1961); Martin Anderson, *The Federal Bulldozer* (Cambridge: M.I.T. Press, 1964); Herbert J. Gans, "The Human Implications of Current Redevelopment and Relocation Planning," *Journal of the American Institute of Planners*, XXV (February 1959) pp. 15–26.

[9] A recent example of heated debate appears in the following set of articles: Herbert J. Gans, "The Failure of Urban Renewal," *Commentary* 39 (April 1965) p. 29; George Raymond "Controversy," *Commentary* 40 (July 1965) p. 72; and Herbert J. Gans, "Controversy," *Commentary* 40 (July 1965) p. 77.

[10] Walter Thabit, *An Alternate Plan for Cooper Square*, (New York: Walter Thabit, July 1961).

ter opportunities to the members of the organization and to families similarly situated.[11]

The difficulty in providing adequate planning assistance to organizations representing low-income families may in part be overcome by funds allocated to local anti-poverty councils. But these councils are not the only representatives of the poor; other organizations exist and seek help. How can this type of assistance be financed? This question will be examined below, when attention is turned to the means for institutionalizing plural planning.

THE STRUCTURE OF PLANNING

Planning by Special Interest Groups

The local planning process typically includes one or more "citizens" organizations concerned with the nature of planning in the community. The Workable Program requirement for "citizen participation"[12] has enforced this tradition and brought it to most large communities. The difficulty with current citizen participation programs is that citizens are more often *reacting* to agency programs than *proposing* their concepts of appropriate goals and future action.

The fact that citizens' organizations have not played a positive role in formulating plans is to some extent a result of both the enlarged role in society played by government bureaucracies and the historic weakness of municipal party politics. There is something very shameful to our society in the necessity to have organized "citizen participation." Such participation should be the norm in an enlightened democracy. The formalization of citizen participation as a required practice in localities is similar in many respects to totalitarian shows of loyalty to the state by citizen parades.

Will a private group interested in preparing a recommendation for community development be required to carry out its own survey and analysis of the community? The answer would depend upon the quality of the work prepared by the

---

[11] The first conscious effort to employ the advocacy method was carried out by a graduate student of city planning as an independent research project. The author acted as both a participant and an observer of a local housing organization. See Linda Davidoff, "The Bluffs: Advocate Planning," *Comment*, Dept. of City Planning, University of Pennsylvania, (Spring 1965) p. 59.

[12] See Section 101(c) of the United States Housing Act of 1949, as amended.

public agency, work which should be public information. In some instances the public agency may not have surveyed or analyzed aspects the private group thinks important; or the public agency's work may reveal strong biases unacceptable to the private group. In any event, the production of a useful plan proposal will require much information concerning the present and predicted conditions in the community. There will be some costs associated with gathering that information, even if it is taken from the public agency. The major cost involved in the preparation of a plan by a private agency would probably be the employment of one or more professional planners.

What organizations might be expected to engage in the plural planning process? The first type that comes to mind are the political parties; but this is clearly an aspirational thought. There is very little evidence that local political organizations have the interest, ability, or concern to establish well developed programs for their communities. Not all the fault, though, should be placed upon the professional politicians, for the registered members of political parties have not demanded very much, if anything, from them as agents.

Despite the unreality of the wish, the desirability for active participation in the process of planning by the political parties is strong. In an ideal situation local parties would establish political platforms which would contain master plans for community growth and both the majority and minority parties in the legislative branch of government would use such plans as one basis for appraising individual legislative proposals. Further, the local administration would use its planning agency to carry out the plans it proposed to the electorate. This dream will not turn to reality for a long time. In the interim other interest groups must be sought to fill the gap caused by the present inability of political organizations.

The second set of organizations which might be interested in preparing plans for community development are those that represent special interest groups having established views in regard to proper public policy. Such organizations as chambers of commerce, real estate boards, labor organizations, pro- and anti-civil rights groups, and anti-poverty councils come to mind. Groups of this nature have often played parts in the development of community plans, but only in a very few instances have they proposed their own plans.

It must be recognized that there is strong reason operating against commitment to a plan by these organizations. In fact it is the same reason that in part limits the interests of politicians and which limits the potential for planning in our society. The expressed commitment to a particular plan may make it difficult for groups to find means for accommodating their various interests. In other terms, it may be simpler for professionals, politicians, or lobbyists to make deals if they have not laid their cards on the table.

There is a third set of organizations that might be looked to as proponents of plans and to whom the foregoing comments might not apply. These are the ad hoc protest associations which may form in opposition to some proposed policy. An example of such a group is a neighborhood association formed to combat a renewal plan, a zoning change, or the proposed location of a public facility. Such organizations may seek to develop alternative plans, plans which would, if effected, better serve their interests.

From the point of view of effective and rational planning it might be desirable to commence plural planning at the level of city-wide organizations, but a more realistic view is that it will start at the neighborhood level. Certain advantages of this outcome should be noted. Mention was made earlier of tension in government between centralizing and decentralizing forces. The contention aroused by conflict between the central planning agency and the neighborhood organization may indeed be healthy, leading to clearer definition of welfare policies and their relation to the rights of individuals or minority groups.

Who will pay for plural planning? Some organizations have the resources to sponsor the development of a plan. Many groups lack the means. The plight of the relatively indigent association seeking to propose a plan might be analogous to that of the indigent client in search of legal aid. If the idea of plural planning makes sense, then support may be found from foundations or from government. In the beginning it is more likely that some foundation might be willing to experiment with plural planning as a means of making city planning more effective and more democratic. Or the Federal Government might see plural planning, if carried out by local anti-poverty councils, as a strong means of generating local interest in community affairs.

Federal sponsorship of plural planning might be seen as a more effective tool for stimulating involvement of the citizen in the future of his community than are the present types of citizen participation programs. Federal support could only be expected if plural planning were seen, not as a means of combating renewal plans, but as an incentive to local renewal agencies to prepare better plans.

The Public Planning Agency

A major drawback to effective democratic planning practice is the continuation of that non-responsible vestigial institution, the planning commission. If it is agreed that the establishment of both general policies and implementation policies are questions affecting the public interest and that public interest questions should be decided in accord with established democratic practices for decision making, then it is indeed difficult to find convincing reasons for continuing to permit independent commissions to make planning decisions. At an earlier stage in planning the strong arguments of John T. Howard[13] and others in support of commissions may have been persuasive. But it is now more than a decade since Howard made his defense against Robert Walker's position favoring planning as a staff function under the mayor. With the increasing effect planning decisions have upon the lives of citizens the Walker proposal assumes great urgency.[14]

Aside from important questions regarding the propriety of independent agencies which are far removed from public

---

[13] John T. Howard, "In Defense of Planning Commissions," *Journal of the American Institute of Planners*, XVII (Spring 1951).

[14] Robert Walker, *The Planning Function in Urban Government;* Second Edition (Chicago: University of Chicago Press, 1950). Walker drew the following conclusions from his examination of planning and planning commissions. "Another conclusion to be drawn from the existing composition of city planning boards is that they are not representative of the population as a whole." p. 153. "In summary the writer is of the opinion that the claim that planning commissions are more objective than elected officials must be rejected." p. 155. "From his observations the writer feels justified in saying that very seldom does a majority of any commission have any well-rounded understanding of the purposes and ramifications of planning." p. 157. "In summary, then, it was found that the average commission member does not comprehend planning nor is he particularly interested even in the range of customary physical planning." p. 158. "Looking at the planning commission at the present time, however, one is forced to conclude that, despite some examples of successful operations, the unpaid board is not proving satisfactory as a planning agency," p. 165. ". . . (it) is believed that the most fruitful line of development for the future would be replacement of these commissions by a department or bureau attached to the office of mayor or city manager. This department might be headed by a board or by a single director, but the members or the director would in any case hold office at the pleasure of the executive on the same basis as other department heads." p. 177.

control determining public policy, the failure to place planning decision choices in the hands of elected officials has weakened the ability of professional planners to have their proposals effected. Separating planning from local politics has made it difficult for independent commissions to garner influential political support. The commissions are not responsible directly to the electorate and in turn the electorate is, at best, often indifferent to the planning commission.

During the last decade in many cities power to alter community development has slipped out of the hands of city planning commissions, assuming they ever held it, and has been transferred to development coordinators. This has weakened the professional planner. Perhaps planners unknowingly contributed to this by their refusal to take concerted action in opposition to the perpetuation of commissions.

Planning commissions are products of the conservative reform movement of the early part of this century. The movement was essentially anti-populist and pro-aristocracy. Politics was viewed as dirty business. The commissions are relics of a not-too-distant past when it was believed that if men of good will discussed a problem thoroughly, certainly the right solution would be forthcoming. We know today, and perhaps it was always known, that there are no right solutions. Proper policy is that which the decision-making unit declares to be proper.

Planning commissions are responsible to no constituency. The members of the commissions, except for their chairman, are seldom known to the public. In general the individual members fail to expose their personal views about policy and prefer to immerse them in group decision. If the members wrote concurring and dissenting opinions, then at least the commissions might stimulate thought about planning issues. It is difficult to comprehend why this aristocratic and undemocratic form of decision making should be continued. The public planning function should be carried out in the executive or legislative office and perhaps in both. There has been some question about which of these branches of government would provide the best home, but there is much reason to believe that both branches would be made more cognizant of planning issues if they were each informed by their own planning staffs. To carry this division further, it would probably be advisable to establish minority and majority planning staffs in the legislative branch.

At the root of my last suggestion is the belief that there is or should be a Republican and Democratic way of viewing city development; that there should be conservative and liberal plans, plans to support the private market and plans to support greater government control. There are many possible roads for a community to travel and many plans should show them. Explication is required of many alternative futures presented by those sympathetic to the construction of each such future. As indicated earlier, such alternatives are not presented to the public now. Those few reports which do include alternative futures do not speak in terms of interest to the average citizen. They are filled with professional jargon and present sham alternatives. These plans have expressed technical land use alternatives rather than social, economic, or political value alternatives. Both the traditional unitary plans and the new ones that present technical alternatives have limited the public's exposure to the future states that might be achieved. Instead of arousing healthy political contention as diverse comprehensive plans might, these plans have deflated interest.

The independent planning commission and unitary plan practice certainly should not co-exist. Separately they dull the possibility for enlightened political debate; in combination they have made it yet more difficult. But when still another hoary concept of city planning is added to them, such debate becomes practically impossible. This third of a trinity of worn-out notions is that city planning should focus only upon the physical aspects of city development.

AN INCLUSIVE DEFINITION OF THE SCOPE OF PLANNING

The view that equates physical planning with city planning is myopic. It may have had some historic justification, but it is clearly out of place at a time when it is necessary to integrate knowledge and techniques in order to wrestle effectively with the myriad of problems afflicting urban populations.

The city planning profession's historic concern with the physical environment has warped its ability to see physical structures and land as servants to those who use them.[15]

[15] An excellent and complete study of the bias resulting from reliance upon physical or land use criteria appears in David Farbman, *A Description, Analysis and Critique of the Master Plan,* an unpublished mimeographed study prepared for the University of Pennsylvania's Institute for Urban Studies, 1959–1960. After studying more than 100 master plans Farbman wrote:

Physical relations and conditions have no meaning or quality apart from the way they serve their users. But this is forgotten every time a physical condition is described as good or bad without relation to a specified group of users. High density, low density, green belts, mixed uses, cluster developments, centralized or decentralized business centers are per se neither good nor bad. They describe physical relations or conditions, but take on value only when seen in terms of their social, economic, psychological, physiological, or aesthetic effects upon different users.

The profession's experience with renewal over the past decade has shown the high costs of exclusive concern with physical conditions. It has been found that the allocation of funds for removal of physical blight may not necessarily improve the over-all physical condition of a community and may engender such harsh social repercussions as to severely damage both social and economic institutions. Another example of the deficiencies of the physical bias is the assumption of city planners that they could deal with the capital budget as if the physical attributes of a facility could be understood apart from the philosophy and practice of the service conducted within the physical structure. This assumption is open to question. The size, shape, and location of a facility greatly interact with the purpose of the activity the facility houses. Clear examples of this can be seen in public education and

---

"As a result of the predominantly physical orientation of the planning profession many planners have fallen victims to a malaise which I suggest calling the "Physical Bias." This bias is not the physical orientation of the planner itself but is the result of it. . . . "The physical bias is an attitude on the part of the planner which leads him to conceive of the principles and techniques of *his profession* as the key factors in determining the particular recommendations to be embodied in his plans. . . .

"The physically biased planner plans on the assumption (conviction) that the physical problems of a city can be solved within the framework of physical desiderata; in other words, that physical problems can be adequately stated, solved and remedied according to physical criteria and expertise. The physical bias produces both an inability and an unwillingness on the part of the planner to 'get behind' the physical recommendations of the plan, to isolate, examine or discuss more basic criteria. . . ."

". . . There is room, then, in plan thinking, for physical principles, i.e., theories of structural inter-relationships of the physical city; but this is only a part of the story, for the structural impacts of the plan are only a part of the total impact. This total impact must be conceived as a web of physical, economic and social causes and effects." pp. 22–26.

in the provision of low cost housing. The racial and other socio-economic consequences of "physical decisions" such as location of schools and housing projects have been immense, but city planners, while acknowledging the existence of such consequences, have not sought or trained themselves to understand socio-economic problems, their causes or solutions.

The city planning profession's limited scope has tended to bias strongly many of its recommendations toward perpetuation of existing social and economic practices. Here I am not opposing the outcomes, but the way in which they are developed. Relative ignorance of social and economic methods of analysis have caused planners to propose solutions in the absence of sufficient knowledge of the costs and benefits of proposals upon different sections of the population.

Large expenditures have been made on planning studies of regional transportation needs, for example, but these studies have been conducted in a manner suggesting that different social and economic classes of the population did not have different needs and different abilities to meet them. In the field of housing, to take another example, planners have been hesitant to question the consequences of locating public housing in slum areas. In the field of industrial development, planners have seldom examined the types of jobs the community needed; it has been assumed that one job was about as useful as another. But this may not be the case where a significant sector of the population finds it difficult to get employment.

"Who gets what, when, where, why, and how" are the basic political questions which need to be raised about every allocation of public resources. The questions cannot be answered adequately if land use criteria are the sole or major standards for judgment.

The need to see an element of city development, land use, in broad perspective applies equally well to every other element, such as health, welfare, and recreation. The governing of a city requires an adequate plan for its future. Such a plan loses guiding force and rational basis to the degree that it deals with less than the whole that is of concern to the public.

The implications of the foregoing comments for the practice of city planning are these. First, state planning enabling legislation should be amended to permit planning departments to study and to prepare plans related to any area of public concern. Second, planning education must be redirected so as to provide channels of specialization in different parts of public planning and a core focussed upon the planning process.

Third, the professional planning association should enlarge its scope so as to not exclude city planners not specializing in physical planning.

A year ago at the AIP convention it was suggested that the AIP Constitution be amended to permit city planning to enlarge its scope to all matters of public concern.[16] Members of the Institute in agreement with this proposal should seek to develop support for it at both the chapter and national level. The Constitution at present states that the Institute's "particular sphere of activity shall be the planning of the unified development of urban communities and their environs and of states, regions and the nation as *expressed through determination of the comprehensive arrangement of land and land occupancy and regulation thereof.*"[17]

It is time that the AIP delete the words in my italics from its Constitution. The planner limited to such concerns is not a city planner, he is a land planner or a physical planner. A city is its people, their practices, and their political, social, cultural and economic institutions as well as other things. The city planner must comprehend and deal with all these factors.

The new city planner will be concerned with physical planning, economic planning, and social planning. The scope of his work will be no wider than that presently demanded of a mayor or a city councilman. Thus, we cannot argue against an enlarged planning function on grounds that it is too large to handle. The mayor needs assistance; in particular he needs the assistance of a planner, one trained to examine needs and aspirations in terms of both short and long term perspectives. In observing the early stages of development of Community Action Programs, it is apparent that our cities are in desperate need of the type of assistance trained planners could offer. Our cities require for their social and economic programs the type of long range thought and information that have been brought forward in the realm of physical planning. Potential resources must be examined and priorities set.

What I have just proposed does not imply the termination of physical planning, but it does mean that physical planning be seen as part of city planning. Uninhibited by limitations on his work, the city planner will be able to add his expertise to

[16] Paul Davidoff, "The Role of the City Planner in Social Planning," *Proceedings of the 1964 Annual Conference*, American Institute of Planners (Washington, D.C.: The Institute, 1964), pp. 125–131.

[17] Constitution of AIP, Article II "Purposes," in *AIP Handbook & Roster—1965*, p. 8.

the task of coordinating the operating and capital budgets and to the job of relating effects of each city program upon the others and upon the social, political, and economic resources of the community.

An expanded scope reaching all matters of public concern will make planning not only a more effective administrative tool of local government but it will also bring planning practice closer to the issues of real concern to the citizens. A system of plural city planning probably has a much greater chance for operational success where the focus is on live social and economic questions instead of rather esoteric issues relating to physical norms.

THE EDUCATION OF PLANNERS

Widening the scope of planning to include all areas of concern to government would suggest that city planners must possess a broader knowledge of the structure and forces affecting urban development. In general this would be true. But at present many city planners are specialists in only one or more of the functions of city government. Broadening the scope of planning would require some additional planners who specialize in one or more of the services entailed by the new focus.

A prime purpose of city planning is the coordination of many separate functions. This coordination calls for men holding general knowledge of the many elements comprising the urban community. Educating a man for performing the coordinative role is a difficult job, one not well satisfied by the present tradition of two years of graduate study. Training of urban planners with the skills called for in this article may require both longer graduate study and development of a liberal arts undergraduate program affording an opportunity for holistic understanding of both urban conditions and techniques for analyzing and solving urban problems.

The practice of plural planning requires educating planners who would be able to engage as professional advocates in the contentious work of forming social policy. The person able to do this would be one deeply committed to both the process of planning and to particular substantive ideas. Recognizing that ideological commitments will separate planners, there is tremendous need to train professionals who are competent to express their social objectives.

The great advances in analytic skills, demonstrated in the

recent May issue of this *Journal* dedicated to techniques of simulating urban growth processes, portend a time when planners and the public will be better able to predict the consequences of proposed courses of action. But these advances will be of little social advantage if the proposals themselves do not have substance. The contemporary thoughts of planners about the nature of man in society are often mundane, unexciting or gimmicky. When asked to point out to students the planners who have a developed sense of history and philosophy concerning man's situation in the urban world one is hard put to come up with a name. Sometimes Goodman or Mumford might be mentioned. But planners seldom go deeper than acknowledging the goodness of green space and the soundness of proximity of linked activities. We cope with the problems of the alienated man with a recommendation for reducing the time of the journey to work.

CONCLUSION

The urban community is a system comprised of interrelated elements, but little is known about how the elements do, will, or should interrelate. The type of knowledge required by the new comprehensive city planner demands that the planning profession be comprised of groups of men well versed in contemporary philosophy, social work, law, the social sciences, and civic design. Not every planner must be knowledgeable in all these areas, but each planner must have a deep understanding of one or more of these areas and he must be able to give persuasive expression to his understanding.

As a profession charged with making urban life more beautiful, exciting, and creative, and more just, we have had little to say. Our task is to train a future generation of planners to go well beyond us in its ability to prescribe the future urban life.

Author's Note:
The author wishes to thank Melvin M. Webber for his insightful criticism and Linda Davidoff for her many helpful suggestions and for her analysis of advocate planning. Special acknowledgment is made of the penetrating and brilliant social insights offered by the eminent legal scholar and practitioner, Michael Brodie, of the Philadelphia Bar.

Chapter 14

HARD DATA RESEARCH AND COMPUTER MODELS

There seems little question that the massive *novelle vague* in planning is the use of hard data managed through computer information storage systems, or data banks, and put to work by various types of mathematical simulation models in computer language for predictive purposes and for aid in decision-making. *The New Utopians*, as Robert Boguslaw* has named the "system engineer, computer manufacturer, operations researcher, computer programmer, data systems specialist, or, more simply, system designer," have rushed in to cope with the unbelievable mass of almost unmanageable information collected and needed by urban planners today. Contemporary education for graduate degrees in planning laps at this technology and numerous summer institutes struggle to retread the operating planner in these new synthesizing, intellectual tools. Admittedly they still have a long way to go, as Melvin Branch has so aptly phrased it, "to become an analytical extension of the human mind," but they already threaten to make traditional planning obsolete—at least obsolescent.

Seemingly urban planners must join with systems engineers wholeheartedly—if there is to be an urban future of style and quality. As it now stands, the urban milieu is fast approaching the limits of the existent planning bag of tricks; it would be a human tragedy if the hard data computer specialists—often inadequately trained in such as yet-unquantifiable fuzzy fields (social "well-being," communication, mental health, community, aesthetics, etc.)—were to dominate planning decision-making and skew our urban society in the direction of cost accounting and acreage by input-output analyses measured in the Philistine, if basic metric of dollars, tons, unit things and unit people. Specifically simulation models in computer language measure too few things too specifically—they are truncated/slanted and unconvincing at the same time and must be delicately handled in this their initial stage by responsible public and private officials, if we would upgrade our urban civilization. Conversely, without empirical facts, computer-stored and symbolically manipulated, we will continue to flounder in the ever-deepening morass of super-complex urbanism.

The three articles that follow should be read as a unit. See also

* Englewood Cliffs, N.J.: Prentice-Hall, Inc., 1965, p. 1.

The San Francisco Community Renewal Program: A Summary by Louis K. Lowenstein and Cyril C. Herrmann in Chapter 17. Invited by the American Institute of Planners to serve as guest editor for a special issue of its *Journal* on *Urban Development Models*, Britton Harris presents an overview. At his suggestion, another basic article from that issue is included: Wilbur A. Steger's application of analytic techniques to the *Community Renewal Program*. Carrying further the indispensable data collection function on which urban development models rest, Melvin M. Webber, planner, explores below the infiltration of new thoughtways into our understanding of the urban system and the urban planning process. To quote the *Journal of the American Institute of Planners'* summary of his article:

> "In response to the growing demand for good information that might support rational developmental decisions, 'intelligence centers' are proposed, operating with an interim programming strategy. These centers would serve the multiplicity of groups in the urban areas, supplying improved inventories and forecasts; and they would serve governmental investors by designing targets, programs and strategies for public action. They would inevitably be engaged in politic and action, but they would bring the scientific morality into urban affairs—a new ingredient in the urban political scene. They are proposed as the effective city planning agencies for this era of flux."

Urban Development Models: New Tools for Planners

BRITTON HARRIS*

A model is in general a somewhat simplified abstraction from the real world. This is true of models of all types, from the simplest architectural model to highly abstract mathematical formulations of problems. No model directly implies the use of a computer. However, it happens that urban metropolitan phenomena are so complex and so resistant to abstraction in any simple terms that computer solutions to them come

* Professor of City and Regional Planning at the University of Pennsylvania, and formerly research coordinator of the Penn-Jersey Transportation Study. He has been associated with the Chicago Housing Authority, the Economic Development Administration of Puerto Rico, and the Ford Foundation Delhi Master Planning Team. Among his publications are *Industrial Land and Facilities for Philadelphia* (1965) and "Problems in Theory of Intra-Urban Location," *Operations Research*, IX (September-October 1961), pp. 695–721. This article was reprinted with permission from the *Journal of the American Institute of Planners*, Special Issue, Vol. XXXI, No. 2, May 1965 in the version that appeared in *Ekistics*, September 1965.

to have an appealing simplicity by comparison with the difficulties of mechanical (analog) models on the one hand and analytical solutions on the other hand. Newton's law of gravitation, together with his laws of motion, are a good example of a model of elegant simplicity for which analytical solutions are readily available in the case of the two-body problem, and for which computer calculations are unnecessary. When, however, these laws are applied to problems involving three or more bodies in motion, the simple analytical solutions do not exist except in special cases, and approximate solutions involve huge amounts of computation which are best handled on a computer. Experience so far accumulated and amply displayed in this issue of the *Journal* tends to suggest that the problems of metropolitan growth and development are «many-body» problems which are best handled through extensive computations on high-speed computers.

The use of computers to simulate in an abstract way what happens in the real world may be contrasted with the use of computers for the management of large data files. This second use of computers is one with which planners are becoming increasingly familiar and with which in general they tend to feel more comfortable and at home. Data management makes use of the large capacity of modern digital computers and of their very great reliability and accuracy. However, it does not require the high-speed arithmetic capabilities which scientific computers are designed to provide. This difference between simulation and analysis on the one hand, and data management on the other, leads to differences in programming requirements, in machine requirements, and even in management attitudes.

COMPUTERS AND THE PLANNING PROCESS

There are two major problems in which the assistance of a computer and computerized models can successfully be enlisted. Most of the problems of comprehensive metropolitan planning involve in the first instance very large amounts of detailed information regarding land, buildings, public services, and activities. This information must be handled and processed quickly, accurately, and consistently. It is no longer possible to do this by conventional means using tabular pads, desk calculators, maps, and charts exclusively. The problems of volumes of work and of quality control over a large clerical staff become overwhelming. Even more serious is the second characteristic of the working problem. In any realistic and total view of a large city or metropolis, the number of interrelationships among activities and between these activities and the space which they occupy becomes astronomical. While planners are becoming more and more sophisticated at specifying the nature of these relationships, no means but a computer is available for exploring them in any fair degree of detail.

These computer processes can be appropriately related to the use of models if we consider the major elements of the planning process. I would characterize these as invention, evaluation, and prediction. By far the most important of them and the most difficult to rationalize with the assistance of computer technology is the process of invention. Here the planner exerts what I consider to be his main professional capability, which is the creative one of generating new solutions to problems, including the problem of design for better living.

Next, even if the creative act of the invention of better plans is largely intuitive, it can certainly be subjected to evaluation —the ultimate forms of evaluation being political acceptance and demonstrated viability in execution. Both the process of invention and the process of evaluation are profoundly influenced by the planner's capacity to understand and interpret the values held by others in the society at large. The process of plan evaluation in the present state of the art almost inevitably involves the measurement of many different consequences of particular lines of action, the evaluation of these consequences, and the weighting of the values attached to them.

Finally, the process of prediction is intimately bound up with most steps in the planning process. I take the meaning of prediction in the sense of conditional statements about future development—statements which are conditioned by varying assumptions as to policy and external conditions. In this context, projection might be considered a prediction which assumes a certain continuation of present influences, and which is thus more limited in scope. Both prediction and projection call heavily on the planner's capability for understanding urban metropolitan development and for systematizing his knowledge. In this realm, the planner acts as an urbanist.

PREPARING AND EVALUATING PLANS

When we examine the performance of models in these three major areas of professional planning activity, we find varying evidences of progress.

Some of the most exciting and provocative material which follows deals with the problem of using the computer to assist the planner in putting together his plans. Anyone who has gone through or observed the detailed process of comprehensive planning for any large area knows that the volume of detail work rapidly becomes unmanageable. As a result, interrelations are overlooked, simplifying assumptions are made, and detailed consistency checks are abandoned—all in the interest of getting the job done. The planner's desire to impose intelligent criteria and patterns of choice in the development of a plan are frequently sacrificed to the technical complexity and frustration of the job, and he may consider himself fortunate if he is able to hold on to a few very simple design criteria. Such planning, not being adequately adjusted to the real world, may prove very difficult to implement. The entire article by Kenneth Schlager and portions of the article dealing with planning for the Pittsburgh Community Renewal Program suggest ways by which some aspects of the design process can be brought under manageable control through careful formulation of the problem and implementation of its solution on the computer.

The plan designer selects an objective which is to be maximized or minimized—for example, the reduction of substandard housing or the total cost of construction. He then formulates a number of conditions which must be met by the plan. These conditions may include budgetary restraints, land use restrictions, density limitations, accessibility considerations, and the like. Once the problem is well formulated, the computer can find feasible solutions if they exist and can improve these solutions until the best pattern or least cost has been achieved. While the solution methods are purely mechanical (and have at present certain inherent limitations), the formulation of the problem is susceptible of almost infinite variation, and finding a sound formulation is indeed an art. Such a sound formulation might require the definition of feasible policies, some likelihood of generating acceptable results, and a proper definition of objectives. The advantages of a computer formulation of this problem are, first, that the results can be generated rapidly and in much greater detail than is possible by manual methods, and, second, that given this flexibility in generating plans, the user has much more opportunity to experiment with alternative formulations, new policies, and new combinations of policies.

So long as the generation and spelling out of plans remained an arduous and slow process, opportunities to compare alternative plans were extremely limited. In this case, the evaluation of plans became largely subjective and the subjective nature of the evaluations led to many difficulties in achieving a consensus. Given the feasibility of generating larger numbers of different plans at relatively low cost, one giant step has been taken toward assuring that comparisons and evaluations of these plans may be made more objectively and on the basis of more complete information. The sketch planning methods outlined above and in Schlager's article automatically guarantee that for a given set of restraints (policies and design standards), the plan generated will meet certain standards of optimality. As between the plans resulting from different restraints, one can make direct comparisons as to cost or whatever other objective criterion has been applied.

This procedure leaves two questions unsettled. In the first place, the planner and the decision-maker may need to evaluate the worth of some of the restraints. While some of these may be based on engineering or design considerations, others may embody normative policy judgments. In either case, but especially in the second, their implications, validity, and worth are by no means self-evident. Secondly, the plan may have very many secondary consequences which are cumulatively important, but which appear nowhere in the objective function or the constraints. These effects may or may not be measured objectively by other means. A question of measurable indirect effects, for example, might be the implicit transportation costs involved in a particular set of physical arrangements. These costs could be controlled only in part by the constraints introduced in a design model. At the other extreme, considerations of amenity and livability are very difficult to measure objectively; yet there may be wide professional agreement that large differences exist as between alternative plans. One of the great advantages of working with planning alternatives and with explicit and well controlled methods of plan formulation is that the planner and the decision-maker may both become acquainted in much more detail with the tradeoffs which inevitably exist between different benefits that may be provided in different proportions by different solutions to the problem of plan design. This deepening knowledge will ulitmately improve the plan design process itself, and will make for more informed and intelligent evaluations. Even though it will never eliminate differences of opinion, it will clarify the issues on which these differences are based, and will obviate much ill-founded contention.

Both the process of designing better plans and the process of evaluating plans depend very deeply on a detailed understanding of the way in which a metropolitan area functions and grows. This is necessarily so because the consequences, direct and indirect, of planning decisions are the most important elements entering into an evaluation, while changing these consequences by changing proposed policies is the central aim of planning design. Since the consequences of public policies are not predictable in any simple way, most modeling efforts devote major attention to problems of prediction of metropolitan functioning, growth and change under the influence of varying assumptions about the real world, about external influences, and about the policies to be pursued.

Improved understanding of the consequences of assumptions and policies can enter into the design and decision process by way of two different routes described above. On the one hand, this understanding leads to a more refined cost-benefit calculus, and it is in principle possible not only to use this calculation for making judgments, but perhaps also to enter it into the objective function of a design model. On the other hand, a better understanding of how the system works may suggest to the planner new restraints to be imposed on the design problem, leading to improvements in the results.

CHARACTERISTICS OF THE MODELS

The basic and widely accepted strategy for model design which seems almost certain to carry the field is based on the concept that a large and, indeed, complete model can be built up out of intercommunicating submodels. Thus, problems of retail location, industrial location, office location, and residential choice can be stated and modeled separately, but the effects of decisions in one sphere can be elaborated in another sphere through appropriate model design.*

* There is a succinct article "A Short Course in Model Design" by Ira S. Lowry, The RAND Corporation, to be found in the *Journal of the American Institute of Planners*, Special Issue, Vol. XXXI, No. 2, May 1965.

There are several different dimensions along which it is possible to make comparisons and establish contrasts between different models. Three are of particular interest.

Although the prevalent style in model-building is toward recursive models which make stepwise projections in intervals of two, five, or ten years, there are some notable exceptions. The most important of these is the pioneering Lowry model, the first to deal successfully with the problem of making simultaneous distributions of a large proportion of metropolitan activity. A one-shot model for locating activity, such as Lowry's, has some aspects of a general equilibrium solution, and tends to answer the question of what is the best or most probable distribution of activities if historical development is left out of the picture. This question is of overwhelming interest to planners who are concerned with exploring long-term goals and bending development in some «best» direction. Recursive or stepwise models, on the other hand, tend to answer the question of how development will actually take place, considering that private decision-makers take a relatively short view and are apt to inspect closely only conditions which exist at the time of their decisions. This second type of model is of greater utility in making realistic decisions about the impacts of policy and the feasibility of plans developed on a one-shot basis. Clearly, both types of models have a role to play in the planning process.

A second dimension of differences arises out of a consideration of how changes over time are introduced into a model. One method is to use an indirect approach which introduces only major changes in employment composition, income, tastes, technology, and public policy in relation to time. These forces are considered to influence individual behavior, which is defined in such a way that it is not necessary to observe this behavior over a long period. The opposite method takes its start in the observation of aggregate behavior over longer periods of time—for example, in an observation of residential and business locational changes over perhaps a ten-year period. Models of the first type are inescapable in the case of one-shot projections which somehow define a general locational equilibrium; here trends are irrelevant. There is in addition good reason to believe that this type of model may be generally superior to a model employing trends, on the grounds that our observations of income, general expenditure patterns, and economic development extend over a much longer period of time than do our observations of detailed locational behavior.

Finally a model based on the first set of concepts can be verified independently by reproducing, say, change over a ten-year period, whereas the verification of the second type of model usually depends (owing to the absence of data) on its goodness of fit over the period on which it is calibrated. Models of the first type, however, are much more difficult to construct and require much more data in general. Much can be learned from working with models of the second type, and their construction can prove to be both useful and rewarding.

A final type of distinction between models is closely related to the preceding discussion. There is a growing feeling that models which deal in the first instance with aggregated behavioral data such as are available in the Census must ultimately yield to models which deal in the first instance with the behavior of individual decision units. My own feeling is that this is inevitably true at least at the level of analysis. I do not concur, however, in the widespread belief that realistic simulations will ultimately have to be of the Monte Carlo type with individual decision units directly represented in the computer form of the model. There may be, I believe, an intermediate step where Monte Carlo simulation will prove useful in the development of submodels, but where the form of these submodels—on the basis of research and experience—is more aggregated. Both approaches to model-building are well represented and there is, I feel, an observable convergence between the two views. Further research will undoubtedly decide the issue.

A GLOSS ON LACKLUSTRE TERMS

The objective of much model-building is *simulation*. Literally this word means imitation, and most simulations are imitations of real world processes either through a mechanical analog or through the operation of a computer process. Strictly speaking, the term simulation can be very broadly applied. Thus the formula $s = vt$ can be said to simulate uniform motion in such a way that the distances traveled can be determined. Some users restrict the term simulation to the reproduction of *stochastic* processes. These are processes in which random events, occurring as a result of chance or of unspecified causes, are considered of interest. *Monte Carlo* simulation actually generates stochastic events inside the computer by large numbers of references to a source of random numbers. It should be noted that the simulation of a stochastic process does not necessarily imply grave uncertainty as to the outcome. Repeated runs of a Monte Carlo simulation may yield results so closely clustered as to be, for all practical purposes, determinate. In this case, the simulation may be regarded as a solution method for a difficult problem.

A special sub-class of models of growing importance is oriented not to the external world which the planner hopes to control, but to the *decision process* of which he is a part. Some of these models simulate actual decision processes, but most are abstract formulations of a problem of *optimizing*— that is, finding the best solution to a problem. *Heuristic* approaches to analysis and model-building are largely descriptive and phenomenological and do not delve deeply into the detailed nature of underlying processes.

Dealing efficiently with the problems of large-scale analysis and simulation has given rise to a trade vocabulary, some of whose terms deserve brief mention. From econometrics we borrow the term *endogenous,* which refers to variables whose values are determined within the model, and *exogenous,* which refers to variables whose values are determined externally and supplied to the model. The term *parameter* is generally used to refer to any value of a coefficient which enters into a relationship between two or more variables. Parameters are thus usually constants. They may, however, themselves vary under defined conditions. As in desk work, computers store information in tables. A rectangular table is called a *matrix,* and a single column or row is called a *vector*. Well-defined and convenient operations on tables of data exist in which the tables themselves may be regarded as algebraic quantities.

Two additional concepts are of very great importance in the design and operation of simulation and optimizing models. These are *iteration* and *recursion*. Iteration may be roughly equated with the idea of successive approximations, and many problems internal to the operation of modes must be solved by this method at some cost in computer time, since direct solution methods are not available. Recursion may be equated with a step-wise solution to a problem and hence in particular with a step-wise projection or prediction. In a recursive process, the results of one step become the starting point for the next step. Unlike iteration, recursion has a substantive content; a recursive projection ordinarily will yield different results from a one-step projection because intervening changes in conditions influence the final outcome.

The fitting and testing or «*calibration*» of modes makes massive use of statistical methods and techniques. Most of the established and widely discussed techniques in this field deal with *linear* systems. These are systems in which the relationships between variables are essentially based on proportionality, or on proportionality plus a fixed constant. Such relations are clearly inadequate to explain even such simple urban phenomena as the attenuation of trips over distance, but their use is greatly facilitated by the large body of theory and existing practice in other fields.

The essential basis for linear statistics is the simple *correlation* between pairs of variables. The coefficient of correlation, r, may vary from -1 to $+1$, and the coefficient of determination, r^2, indicates the extent to which the variation in one variable may be regarded as a function of the variation in the other variable. Since in urban analysis we are frequently dealing with hypotheses of multiple causation, the variation in a dependent variable is usually regarded as a function of the variation in a number of independent variables. This case is dealt with by *multiple regression,* which proceeds from a consideration of the simple correlations between all pairs of variables and arrives at a generalized coefficient of determination R^2.

Especially in the urban context, multiple regression is plagued by the fact that many variables are spatially distributed in a correlated fashion. When a large number of such correlated independent variables are considered as a basis for explaining other phenomena, the situation gives rise to a mathematical difficulty called *collinearity* or *multi-collinearity.* The existence of collinearity casts many doubts on conventional statistical analysis, and creates severe operating problems. One approach to reducing the number of variables and the interaction between them while preserving, if desired, the influence of a large number of variables, is based on the use of *component analysis* or *factor analysis*. The actual nature of these techniques is in detail highly abstract and mathematical. In concept, however, they provide a way in which the appearance of a number of interrelated variables in the metropolitan area can be reduced to a more limited number of independent factors. In demographic analysis, for example, it has been found that a large proportion of the differences between neighborhoods in a city may be explained on the basis of only three independent or nearly independent factors which are related to status, density and family size, and segregation. Similar component or factor analyses provide a powerful means for organizing large masses of data and identifying underlying patterns of interrelations among variables. Their use is largely descriptive and does not frequently enter directly into further computations.

For purposes of further organizing knowledge gained from factor analysis and other statistical analysis, some effort has been directed toward *cluster analysis*. This technique, as yet imperfectly developed, is directed at providing systematic means for grouping areas or lines of business or population classes for further systematic treatment.

An important technique for solving certain problems in optimizing or in market behavior is called *linear programming*. This technique will find by iterative methods an *allocation* which maximizes or minimizes a linear *objective function*. The allocation may be an allocation of construction to subareas, an allocation of families to dwelling units, or of budgets to projects. The objective function would be some measure of cost or achievement determined by multiplying each allocation by an associated coefficient and summing over all cases. The solution to a linear programming problem has a dual solution which provides information about costs and benefits assignable to different aspects of the allocation arrived at. In particular, the imputed values derived from the use of resources are sometimes called *shadow prices*.

Review of Analytic Techniques for the CRP
WILBUR A. STEGER*

I. INTRODUCTION

Early Community Renewal Programs[1] attempted to implement programs of renewal action based solely on the need for treatment as determined by ratings of "physical blight." A recent review of their early recommendations and urban renewal projects has shown that these programs were only "nominal successes at best."[2] It has also been pointed out that many existing urban renewal projects are having problems, because in selecting the projects great weight has been placed on "eliminating blight," and inadequate weight given to numerous other factors which might generally be called "needs" and "resources." As a consequence, the preparation of

* President of CONSAD Research Corporation (systems research and planning) Pittsburgh, Pa. A Ph.D. in economics from Harvard, he served as a teaching fellow there and is presently Adjunct Professor of Economics and Business Administration at the University of Pittsburgh. He headed the RAND Logistics Simulation Laboratory developing methods for integrating large-scale information retrieval systems and systems simulation models for decision-making purposes. At CONSAD, he has participated in or directed simulation studies for urban renewal in Pittsburgh, land use models for the Delaware Valley Regional Planning Commission, managing the design of impact studies for the Northeast Corridor Transportation Project (U. S. Department of Commerce) and models to aid the planning process in New York City. Dr. Steger has published in the areas of simulation, systems design, systems analysis and management, logistics and transportation, tax policy and systems cost analysis. This article is reproduced with permission from the *Journal of the American Institute of Planners*, Special Issue, Vol. XXXI, No. 2, May 1965.

[1] Alfred Van Huyck and Jack Hornung, *The Citizen's Guide to Urban Renewal* (West Trenton, New Jersey: Chandler-Davis, 1962). Community Renewal Programs (CRP's) are federal Housing and Home Finance Agency programs, the overall purpose of which is to establish a long-range working program for elimination of slums and blight in cities. They are partially federally, and partially locally financed. See also David A. Grossman, "The Community Renewal Program: Policy Development, Progress, and Problems," *Journal of the American Institute of Planners*, Vol. XXIX, No. 4, Nov. 1963, pp. 259–269.

[2] These discussions are reported in *CRP Experience in Major Cities*, sponsored by the Urban Renewal Administration and by the National Association of Housing and Renewal Officials, Washington, D. C. March 9–10, 1964.

modern-day CRP's ordinarily includes a series of studies designed to identify needs and resources for urban renewal action.

In recent years, digital computers have been used in many different ways to assist in the analysis of urban problems and in the pulling together of these many diverse elements. If a review of these uses were made, it would have to cover the many uses of statistical analyses in urban and regional planning,[3] the techniques ranging from regression techniques to more sophisticated factor analyses, component factor analyses, and cluster analyses.[4] In addition, generalized statistical programs have been written for the ultimate reduction of statistical tools to more readily available and usable forms.[5] Other important aspects would be the relation to economic structure, market analyses, demographic projections, and analyses of governmental resources and requirements.[6] Still another important grouping of research is that of land use model-building activity.[7] Furthermore, during the same time that innovation

[3] Albert Mindlin, "Tract Facts and Housing Discrimination—the Use of Census Tract Data in Assessing the Need for Fair Housing Legislation," Papers presented at the Census Tract Conference, September 5, 1963, *Working Paper No. 17*, U. S. Department of Commerce, Bureau of Census; C. Bodian, E. A. Gardner, E. M. Willis, and A. K. Bahn, "Socio-Economic Indicators from Census Tract Data related to Rates of Mental Illness," *Working Paper No. 17*, op. cit. See also Health and Welfare Association, "Level of Living Index," Community Renewal Program, Pittsburgh, Pennsylvania, January 1964.

[4] Robert C. Wood and Vladimir V. Almendinger, *1400 Governments* Harvard University Press, Cambridge, Massachusetts, 1961, p. 196; David R. Seidman, "Report on the Activities Allocation Model," Penn-Jersey Transportation Study, November 1964; W. A. Steger and N. J. Douglas, *Simulation Model*, Community Renewal Program, Pittsburgh, Pennsylvania, Progress Report No. 5, January 1964.

[5] Generalized statistical analysis programs have been written for this purpose. For example, see V. Almendinger, "SPAN: A System for Urban Data Management," System Development Corporation, SP-1862, November 1964.

[6] For example, see the Center for Regional Economic Studies, "Employment, Income and Population Submodels," Community Renewal Program, Pittsburgh, Pennsylvania, January 1964; Brian J. L. Berry, *Commercial Structure and Commercial Blight*, Department of Geography Research Paper No. 85, University of Chicago, Chicago, 1963; R. F. Muth, "The Spatial Structure of the Housing Market," presented before the Econometric Society and the Regional Science Association, December 1960.

[7] For an excellent review of such models through 1962 see Traffic Research Corporation, *Review of Existing Land Use Forecasting Techniques*, Boston Regional Planning Project, Massachusetts Transportation Commission, July 1963; also, see Ira Lowry's review article in this issue

was taking place with regard to substantive knowledge of land use forecasting problems, a technological breakthrough was being made in the use of simulation. Some of the models dealt with aspects of national, regional, and urban development.[8] Other simulations, while dealing with the spatial dimension in part, were concerned with general problems of simulation methodology.[9]

The following sections explore existing urban renewal model building, or models which have evaluation of urban renewal plans as one of the basic "driving forces" along with other exogenous events (such as external population and employment factors). It is this ability to incorporate, use, and evaluate urban renewal plans (projects, programs) in some detail which makes a model an "urban renewal decision-making aid."

II. EXISTING URBAN RENEWAL (AND RELATED) MODELS

There are actually only two models designed to be used in urban renewal decision-making *per se*. These are the Pitts-

---

of the *AIP Journal*. Of particular utility to urban renewal model construction are the following land use studies: B. H. Stevens and R. E. Coughlin, "A Note on Inter-Areal Linear Programming for a Metropolitan Region," *Journal of Regional Science*, Vol. 1, No. 2, Spring 1959, pp. 75–83; H. W. Bruck, "The Simplified Distribution Model," Penn-Jersey Transportation Study, *P-J Program Review Memo No. 5*, March 20, 1963; F. Stuart Chapin, Jr., and Shirley F. Weiss, *Urban Growth Dynamics*, University of North Carolina, 1962; Ira S. Lowry, "A Model of Metropolis," RAND Research Memorandum, RM-4035-RC, August 1964; W. L. Garrison, "Toward Simulation Models of Urban Growth and Development" in Knut Norborgled, *Proceedings of the IGU Symposium in Urban Geography* (Lund, C. W., K. Gleerup, 1960), pp. 91–108; William Alonso, *Location and Land Use*, Harvard University Press, Cambridge, Massachusetts, 1964; and John S. deCani, "On the Construction of Stochastic Models of Population Growth and Migration," *Journal of Regional Science*, Volume 3, Winter 1961, pp. 1–13.

[8] For a discussion of these and related research, see Forrest R. Pitts, "Scale and Purpose in Urban Simulation Models," discussion paper prepared for the Conference on Strategy for Regional Growth, Iowa State University, Ames, Iowa, October 12–14, 1964.

[9] Kalman J. Cohen, "Computer Simulation: Some Methodological Problems," Research Memorandum, Carnegie Institute of Technology, Graduate School of Industrial Administration, Behavioral Theory of the Firm Project, *Working Paper No. 16* (November 25, 1959); see also M. A. Geisler, W. W. Haythorn, and W. A. Steger, "Simulation and the Logistics Systems Laboratory," *Naval Research Logistics Quarterly*, Vol. 10, No. 1, March 1963, pp. 23–54.

burgh and San Francisco models.[10] But other models are of distinct relevance here also: those done for the transportation study in Baltimore;[11] part of the Penn-Jersey Transportation Study;[12] Boston Regional Planning;[13] and Southeastern Wisconsin Regional Planning.[14]

These latter models are primarily constructed for regional transportation land use planning where urban renewal is only one of the considerations. They are therefore much less detailed with respect to their ability to incorporate alternative urban renewal planning treatments and projects.

The models fall, more or less, into certain categories insofar as their projection phases are concerned: (1) controlled variation of independent variables, (2) simulation forecasting models, and (3) analytic mathematical models. These are not mutually exclusive choices within a total effort, for some of the studies (such as the Pittsburgh, Penn-Jersey, and Southeastern Wisconsin efforts) are all of these in combination. They will be classified below, however, under their primary usages. Moreover, the statistical techniques used for parameter estimation (factor analysis, multiple regression, and so on) are not necessarily related to the projective technique and so can be discussed independently of these.

A. Controlled Variation of Independent Variables

Let us assume that the estimating relationships between relevant variables have been developed and are understood to the

[10] Steger and Douglas, *op. cit.*; W. A. Steger, "Data and Information Management in a Large-Scale Modelling Effort: The Pittsburgh Urban Renewal Simulation Model," CONSAD Research Corporation. Prepared for the Seminar on Models of Metropolitan Land Use Development, University of Pennsylvania, (October 1964); the San Francisco effort is described in Ira M. Robinson, *A Simulation Model of the Residential Space Market in San Francisco,* Arthur D. Little, Inc. Prepared for the Seminar on Models . . . *op. cit.*

[11] T. R. Lakshmanan, "A Model for the Distribution of Urban Activities: Formulation, Evaluation and Reformulation." Paper prepared for presentation at Seminar on Models . . . *op. cit.*

[12] David R. Seidman, *Report on the Activities Allocation Model,* Penn-Jersey Transportation Study, November 17, 1964; David R. Seidman, "An Operational Model of the Residential Land Market." Paper presented at the Seminar on Models . . . *op. cit.*

[13] Don Hill, "A Growth Allocation Model for the Boston Region— Its Development, Calibration and Validation." Paper prepared for Seminar on Models . . . *op. cit.*

[14] Kenneth J. Schlager, "Mathematical Models for Urban and Regional Planning, Land Use Plan Design." Paper prepared for Seminar on Models . . . *op. cit.*

extent that one is able to forecast the impact of a change in one or more independent variables upon the relevant dependent variables. For the purpose of aiding the planner in decision making, experimental design or alternative testing is an invaluable technique. Now, suppose that a plan is proposed and its outcome—dependent variables—are forecast. Then, the question arises as to what the outcomes might have been if certain of the inputs—independent variables—had been changed. Answers to this question can be provided by the technique of alternative testing. Further, by use of experimental design—a technique that determines ways by which one can get the greatest amount of information about the impacts of alternatives with the least amount of experimentation—this technique can be used to test the impacts of a multitude of alternative plans upon urban development.[15]

The prime examples are the Baltimore, Boston, and (portions of) the Penn-Jersey work.

The Baltimore model uses as an analytic framework "disaggregated" land users, creating "homogeneous" locational groups whose spatial preferences are estimated as a function of area characteristics through multiple regression. The dependent variable values are then treated as growth indices for the corresponding areal units and are used to prorate exogenously estimated growth for each major land use activity. The rationale of the Boston model is that (a) the development of land for population, employment, and other uses is highly interrelated, and (b) the development of land for various uses is influenced by many external "causal" factors. The Boston EMPIRIC model extensively used the statistical method of indirect least squares. This model, which demonstrated high correlations and showed a high explanation of growth and development during 1950–1960, is being prepared for use by the Boston Regional Planning Project. The Penn-Jersey work, which was originally based on a linear programming version of the economic activity of individual household locational decisions, has turned to multiple regression (in form) models which describe this same behavior in an aggregated manner "sufficiently accurately that we can use these descriptions to

---

[15] F. Stuart Chapin, Jr., *op. cit.*, with associates (particularly S. F. Weiss and T. G. Donnelly), has been the leader in developing this technique. For a recent report on this activity, see F. Stuart Chapin, "Urban Activity Systems and Land Use Models," prepared for the Seminar on Models . . . *op. cit.*

project the locational tendencies of activities in the future." All the models are capable of incorporating land use alternatives, public works, and redevelopment policies (at a gross level). The Boston and Penn-Jersey work places more emphasis on accessibilities of various types as "causal" factors. In Penn-Jersey terms, the word "accessibility" has a special and specific meaning in this context. It denotes the ease with which opportunities of a given type throughout the region can be reached from a particular subarea. It is essentially the average cost-distance travelled (that is, distance in terms of total time and operating cost) in making a trip to a given type of activity via a given mode of travel.

B. Simulation Forecasting Models

By integrating the results of statistical and substantive analyses of data for a particular city or region with various theories concerning urban growth, decline, and/or development, one can (hopefully) determine mathematical procedures for forecasting subsequent urban development. The types of models range from regression equations through various time series equations to equations based on probability of occurrence of various phenomena (based on empirical evidence), or any combination thereof. These models, combined with, and in some cases constrained by, judgments of experts in the related areas, are then combined into a sequence of equations which will take a considerable quantity of input data, evaluate the interrelationships, and produce an output of the same kind of data updated to the end of the forecasting period. One of the major features of this approach as compared with that of controlled variations of independent variables is the simultaneous development and interaction of a variety of sub-models and a structure created for integrating their outputs.[16] In models characterized as simulation forecasting models, the conditional projections of the future are based on a few predominant concepts of the underlying phenomena which account for urban activities and represent them as more or less "complete" theoretical frameworks for the relevant urban characteristics

---

[16] While sub-models of the Penn-Jersey effort are of the "controlled variation of independent variables" types, the overall model is that of a simulation forecasting model. This is brought about by the use of a sequentially run recursive "supervisory routine" through which an executive program calls in each land use sub-model in a theoretically valid manner.

under study. The Pittsburgh and San Francisco efforts are characterized by these features.[17]

In the Pittsburgh Community Renewal Program it is now possible to measure the cumulative effects of certain program decisions over a period of time. These programs include land use activity, but are not necessarily related exclusively to urban renewal and include other aspects of land use policy (broadly conceived): zoning, specialized housing for certain client groups, tax policy for development purposes, intra-urban transportation, income supplements for selected client groups, and others.[18] The simulation model pictures urban development as based on certain assumptions. The first assumption is that employment opportunities are directly or indirectly responsible for all development decisions. They are the driving force behind the model and trigger all later calculations within the model. A four-region interindustry input-output model, with varying assumptions as to export demand, unemployment, productivity, and labor force participation, is at the heart of this portion of the overall model. The second assumption is based on the distribution of this employment throughout the surface of the city. It says that various types of "site oriented" employment will gravitate to specified areas of the city based on several locational criteria, such as present employment clusters, land use policies, access by various transportation models, assessment patterns, and so forth. This portion of the model is a stochastic, heuristic simulation, the closest of all the models to the Monte Carlo simulation used in more traditional operations research. The third assumption allocates the remaining "non-site oriented" employment and measures the effect of total employment upon location of households. Households tend to locate at prescribed distances from work, and commercial service employment tends to cluster at locations within prescribed distances from households. Racial, occupational, and economic characteristics of households also constrain household location. The types of

[17] In addition, another of the Penn-Jersey sub-models has the characteristics of a simulation forecasting device. It is Penn-Jersey's Residential Space Consumption Model (Seidman, *Report on the Allocation Activities Model, op. cit.*); also Seidman, "An Operational Model of the Residential Land Market," *op. cit.* It is based on W. Alonso's *Location and Land Use, op. cit.*, and, like that model, determines residential density and land rent given a distribution of residences "considered to be optimal" based upon a theory which borrows heavily from classical economic location theory.

[18] W. A. Steger and N. J. Douglas, Jr., *op. cit.*, p. 5.

CHART I *Comparison of Systems Research Techniques*

Information Collecting Methods				Information Synthesis Methods			
Real World Observation and Measurement	Studies in Operational Settings	Field Experiments	Lab/Simulator Experiments	Abstract Simulation	Stochastic Models	Iterative Approximator	Closed Analytic Solution

Left group (arrows under Field Experiments / Lab/Simulator Experiments):

- Increasing Control →
- Decreasing Realism →
- Increasing Symbolism →
- Increasing Level of Abstraction →
- Increasing Cost →

Right group (arrows under Abstract Simulation → Closed Analytic Solution):

- Increasing Specificity of Solution →
- Decreasing Complexity of Formulation →
- Increasing Symbolism →
- High Abstraction →
- Decreasing Cost →

housing offered by the area are also constraints. In other words, given the attributes of employment located previously, households of a certain size are created within a specified distance and at predetermined locations, creating service employment again at specified distances from the households. This new employment generates new households which produce additional service employment. This process repeats itself in the model until it is approximately stabilized. In all cases, multi-variate component factor analysis has been used to retain the rich complexity of the small area economic, demographic, and social data for households, housing, land use, commercial, and industrial activity.

Unlike the Pittsburgh model, the San Francisco CRP simulation model as initially designed deals primarily with the residential sector for which data in the detail necessary are most available.[19] In the words of the designers, the model is, in effect, a replication of the land and building space market in San Francisco. The effect of public actions and controls on the market can be evaluated by introducing into the model alternative "hypothetical" public actions and controls. Analysis of these effects provides a basis for developing a long-range strategy and program for renewal. The operation of the model is based upon a matching within the computer of existing stocks of space in the city with potential "users" of the space, on the basis of the relative need or desire for particular types or categories of space by particular categories of users. When the existing supply of space is not adequate to satisfy the needs of the different users, changes in the space stock are generated within the computer to a degree sufficient to satisfy this need within the limitations of the financial feasibility of the change. Financial feasibility is determined by comparing the rent-paying ability of a prospective user category with both the cost of making the change and the anticipated future yield of the change by the type of space. If this comparison indicates that profitable development conditions exist, the computer will add an appropriate number of new housing units to the inventory of the city's housing stock. The computer will then compute the new conditions that would result from these additions: shifts in rent levels, new market values, modifications to the tax base, changes in neighborhood amenities, and so on. When all effects have been accounted for, new inputs are fed in, and the process begins again.

[19] Ira M. Robinson. *A Simulation Model of the Residential Space Market in San Francisco, op. cit.,* pp. 2, 4, 5, 9.

Since the Pittsburgh, San Francisco, and Penn-Jersey efforts have not been completed, it is not possible to describe the results. The sub-models for the Pittsburgh and Penn-Jersey efforts are fully programmed, but parameter estimation is only partially completed. They are all due for operational completion in 1965.

C. Mathematical Optimizing Models

As opposed to simulation forecasting models (which are also "mathematical models"), the models referred to in this section are more or less strategy-calculating models. That is, assuming that we have forecast various urban growth developments, how can we affect the development to best cope with undesirable outcomes? This, of course, implies that we in fact know what outcomes *are* undesirable. For instance, in the case of industrial "blight," previous analysis may have revealed that there are a few key factors which define and in fact are the "causes" of it. The problem then becomes one of eliminating these negative factors. There will probably be several alternative means of accomplishing this. The problem is to decide upon the *best method* or *best combination of methods* for the purpose. Various techniques from the field of operations research and analytical decision theory are applicable, and each application requires its own format and variations thereof. The expected results of applying these techniques will be an optimal or at least satisfactory strategy (in terms of time or cost) for accomplishing the stated objectives. We have already seen that the Penn-Jersey effort was originally based upon a linear programming formulation[20] for allocating households to land, each locating household type being assigned a "locational budget" for each zone equal to the annual amount of money it is prepared to spend there for transportation and housing. The end result of the linear programming formulation is that, within specified constraints, the households locate in such a way as to maximize aggregate rent-paying ability.[21] For various reasons, however, Penn-Jersey has turned from optimizing models like this one to models based on "controlled variation" and simulation meth-

[20] J. D. Herbert and B. H. Stevens, "A Model for the Distribution of Residential Activity in Urban Areas," Penn-Jersey Transportation Study, *P-J Paper No. 2*, 1964; B. Harris, "Linear Programming and the Projections of Land Uses," *P-J Paper No. 20*, 1962.

[21] The reader will note the similarity between this and the San Francisco model. The latter, however, is not a linear programming model.

odology. Data limitations and the multiple-goal nature of the system are the more obvious reasons for this change.

In the Southeastern Wisconsin Regional Planning work,[22] the land use plan function consists essentially of the allocation of a scarce resource, land, between competing and often conflicting land use activities. This allocation must be accomplished so as to satisfy the aggregate needs for each land use and comply with all the design standards derived from the plan objectives at a reasonable cost. The land use plan design model has as its objective assisting the land use planner in the design of a land use plan. Given a set of land use demands, design standards, land characteristics (natural and man-made), and land development costs, the model produces that plan which is the *minimal cost plan complying with the design standards*. Two related mathematical techniques were examined as possible frameworks for this land use plan design model. The first technique was linear programming. The second was dynamic programming. The model technique chosen was dynamic programming, because of "primary restrictions" inherent in linear programming. The dynamic programming version of the model is "still very experimental." The primary problem in the use of this model however, will not be the purely mathematical one (that of finding the optimizing set of Lagrangian multipliers), but the input problem of determining the suitable cost and demand functions, as well as the "design standards" constraints.

The purpose of the Pittsburgh mathematical optimizing sub-model is, similarly, to *choose* between various urban renewal treatments. This sub-model has not been run yet since it requires as inputs cost and demand functions which are being estimated by the Pittsburgh simulation forecasting model. Like the Wisconsin effort, the optimizing sub-model is designed to choose between alternatives automatically, but in neither case can this be used without elaborate input preparation, which, in the Pittsburgh case, is created through the use of simulation.

---

[22] Kenneth J. Schlager, *op. cit.*, pp. 3, 4, 13, 16, 17, 20, 21, 23. Southeastern Wisconsin is also employing simulation techniques in its regional economic forecasting work. The model, actually a dynamic interindustry input-output formulation, is described more fully in Kenneth J. Schlager, "Simulation Models in Urban Planning," The Second Annual Conference in Urban Planning and Information Systems and Programs, the University of Pittsburgh, September 1964. (No copies were available at the time this review was written.)

III. CHOICES MADE AND REMAINING IN URBAN RENEWAL MODEL BUILDING

There are several substantive areas in which general agreement has *not* been reached, although in each case one decision or another has had to be made in each of the specific model-building efforts. These areas can conveniently be grouped into three categories: (A) techniques adopted, (B) planner-model building relationships, and (C) general scope and level of detail. I shall not categorize all the models with respect to all of these attributes, but shall refer to them only where particularly appropriate.

A. Techniques Adopted

The existing models have already been classified into categories which, in turn, correspond to a hypothetical spectrum of systems research techniques,[23] shown in Chart I in the following way: the "controlled variation of independent variables" is analogous to the left-hand side ("observation and measurement") while the mathematical optimizing techniques corresponds to the right hand, with conditional (simulational) forecasts being produced by mid-spectrum techniques. Some of the comparative advantages and disadvantages of the techniques are also noted, these being considerations the model builder-analyst-planner must balance in each particular case. One notion of increasing practical importance is that of "playing the spectrum of techniques," interweaving the uses most appropriate to the general environment being simulated and the knowledge of the user or model-builder. The more one allegedly knows about the environment (including goals), the more one can turn eventually to optimization, using the relatively low-cost smaller numbers of variables peculiar to closed analytic models with single objective functions. Only where the objective functions (and constraints) are represented by fairly definitive statements (as in the case of the Southeastern Wisconsin land use control design model) or *after* the response surfaces have already been defined (as by the Pittsburgh urban renewal simulation model), do mathematical programming formulations appear highly promising in the near future. In these two uses, and also Penn-Jersey, the full complement of

[23] M. A. Geisler and W. A. Steger, "The Spectrum of Alternative Systems Research Techniques," *Management Technology* (May 1963); also M. A. Geisler, W. W. Haythorn, and W. A. Steger, *op. cit.*

techniques appears to have been examined and employed in one or more of the sub-models of the overall model. Notwithstanding, pure simulation, in which specific numerical solutions are first obtained in a step-by-step fashion after they have been translated into mathematical computer language made for purposes of numerical solution, is *not* in actuality being used.[24] To simulate the lag/lead effects, rather than overall period-by-period equilibrium (as in the San Francisco model), the Pittsburgh model establishes different potential mobility rates for each population/business class. Few of the models incorporate this feature, but all are (or are capable of being) partially recursive in time; that is, they consist of a series of sequential forecasts through time where output from one forecast is used as input for the forecast of the next point in time. As for other important technique characteristics:

1. They all utilize computers to an extent, none employing manned simulation (or "man-machine" simulation). The larger models suffer from lack of core storage size. The newer large frame, high-speed digital computers should offer significant advantages to these. Where the model contains many small geographical areas, as in the Pittsburgh case, lengthy runs of hours (on an IBM 7094 or equivalent) are necessary to run out twenty years' worth of simulated data. Of course, several million equations need to be solved in such a case.

2. We have seen that realistic behavioral components, in particular micro-components, have not been intensively used. Where a population class is involved (as in San Francisco) assumptions of rationality are frequently made. One of the Pittsburgh models does contain a realistic depiction of heuristics of industrial locators, based as it is on intensive survey data, but in the equilibrium portion (that is, the residential sub-model) of the Pittsburgh work the same general lack of knowledge of behavioral relationships is evident. Few "decision rules" for simulation "actors," as a result, have been fully implemented, although in specific areas (such as the Pittsburgh

[24] With the exception of the Monte Carlo portion of the Pittsburgh model, the stochastic distribution functions underlying the industrial location model, and the recent Chapin work, "Urban Activity Systems and Land Use Models," probability concepts are not in use. For a more complete discussion, see Guy H. Orcutt, "Simulation of Economic Systems: Model Description and Solution," presented at the IBM Conference on Simulation Models, Yorktown Heights, N. Y., December 1964. Orcutt compares various analytic and simulation models for solving microanalytic models and finds the former "attractive but unattainable" for many reasons.

code enforcement study) decision tables have been formulated and found quite usable.

3. The use of theoretical underpinnings as opposed to (in the extreme) pure statistical "curve fitting" will have no opponents conceptually. In practice, we have seen, many researchers have chosen a course similar to the latter, primarily out of a frustrated feeling that there was no theory to which they could turn. Criticisms have been made of these models based, more or less, upon the models which seek high regression coefficients based upon too little theory.[25] But the criticisms are often too certain about the (alleged) presence of a theory of urban development—which even the users of such theories (for example, the Pittsburgh and San Francisco efforts) admit *to be quite difficult to interpret and use in an operational setting.* Furthermore, there is often considerable justification advanced for those who are fitting large-scale multiple regressions for, first, calibration, and then prediction purposes.

The argument over appropriate methodology will undoubtedly continue, but increasing attention is being paid by users and model builders to the choices made and the reasons for these.

B. Planner—Model-Builder Relationships

The "care and interest of planners" is most important for the ultimate success of these efforts. It is frequently *their* methodology being implemented and made explicit through the use of the models. Further, it is *their* decision-making process which allegedly is to be enhanced. Unfortunately, few of the models have been with us long enough to permit significant amounts of experience to exist. Some efforts have devoted a considerable amount of effort to this problem area, others less. Several points should be made in connection with the subject, which itself deserves a considerable amount of deeper thought:

1. Outside of relatively clear-cut "design" situations, the *recognition* of the planner's rather vague and ill-specified multiple objectives is often a useful bridge. Nevertheless, if this recognition results (as in the Pittsburgh or Penn-Jersey work) in large numbers of output measures, the planner

[25] For example, see F. M. Fisher and Louis Lefeber, "Review and Evaluation of the Work Undertaken by Traffic Research Corporation for the Boston Regional Planning Project," a Report to the Boston Mass Transportation Committee, March 1964.

should be encouraged by the model builder: (a) to visualize these as sub-goals which "trade-off" against one another—at least insofar as resource competition is involved; (b) to specify super- and sub-goals, the latter designed to serve more as constraints which have to be "satisfied" in order to attain the super-goal(s); and (c) to search for and adopt *measures* of the super- and sub-goals which can be made acceptable to the community's (ultimate) decision-makers—as well as being, in actuality, sensitive to the manipulation of the model.

2. The model-builder must find effective ways to synthesize and display both the assumptions of each run and its consequent outputs. Computer graphics of various types are increasingly economical and simple to use in conjunction with model-building efforts. The more recent simulation languages (such as SIMSCRIPT) enable the more knowledgeable planner-user (if the model is written in that language) to call for a report—through the language's "report generator"—and cause the computer model to write its own output program (in essence). Another important factor is the relationship established between the two groups; to the extent that the methodology and theory have been accepted (or devised) by the user, the higher is the probability of successful implementation.[26]

3. A major criterion often demanded by the planner—and frequently rightfully so—is the ability of the model to incorporate in its input changes, plans, and projects specified by the planner as hypothetical patterns for testing purposes. The receptivity of the model is most important—both in terms of level of detail and in the ultimate reality of the consequences to the harnessed imagination of the planner. While the model-builder is frequently clever in his use of parametric variation to reflect intended urban renewal changes, it is important—if the model is to become part of the overall planning process—that the planner learn how to utilize the potentially enormous power of computer models to examine highly diverse alternatives thoroughly.

4. The question of validation of model results to build up planner (and ultimate decision-maker) confidence is not yet resolved. Few of the models, primarily for reasons of cost

[26] Unfortunately, the knowledgeable planner's hands are often tied with respect to ultimate decision-making, and the use of models such as those described in this review may conceivably enhance or debilitate planner-politician relationships. Experience, minor as it is, suggests that "planner-ultimate decision making" relationships can be substantively enhanced through proper use of the model as an active tool for evaluation and insight formation.

and time, have attempted to reproduce actual observed periods to any degree of tolerance, and those which have (such as the Boston Regional empiric model) are criticized for credit taken in attaining this objective, since the *true* test can only be in the future. The best parameter estimation can yield excellent "backcasts," but, of necessity, a valid theory is also necessary for long-run forecasts. Validation to enhance planners' confidence will more than likely, in specific instances, have to rest on the worst of all possible touchstones, that of *short-run* projection credibility. Several of the model-builders (as in San Francisco) have gone on record to deny the ultimate utility of this test, but it is one, nevertheless, which will be applied.

5. There is little question but that two-way interaction, planner to model-builder and vice versa, is needed. In most of the models under examination here, the ultimate user and the method of financing the project are instrumental in causing this two-way interaction. Specifically, the urban renewal models are financed by the Housing and Home Finance Agency; the more transportation-oriented are paid for by combinations of state highway departments, Bureau of Public Roads, and occasionally the Housing and Home Finance Agency. One important consideration is the active role of the planning department or agency involved and the presence on the staff of such an agency of individuals who are working in a daily relationship, training and being trained by the model-builders. The model exercises discussed above vary in this quality, ranging from relatively complete involvement to very little. In no case to date has there been, however, a *truly* daily working relationship yet established where urban renewal planners and decision makers are testing out new alternatives through the use of computer models built for them.

Not enough work has been done in examining the urban renewal planning process—either before or after the introduction of computer models—to permit further observations. Certainly, the political roles of the participants cannot be ignored, nor should the potential revolution which workable and acceptable models bring to the planning process be ignored.

C. Scope and Level of Detail

Scope and level of detail have already been touched upon with regard to the major questions; to what are these models addressed, and what are their objectives? None of the models include all aspects of the "CRP-comprehensive plan" process. For example, large-scale portions of the poverty program are omitted from the Pittsburgh model which, in scope, is among the more ambitious of the efforts. All the models deal with the residential sector and most with the industrial, fewer with the commercial. As for inputs, all include some measure of spatial dispersion or "access," few include changes in attractiveness due to community facilities available over a period of time. Many deal with a comparatively small area level of detail; that is, census tract or below. Some have developed their own areal units for specialized purposes (for example, the FRACT of the San Francisco effort or the data block of the Pittsburgh effort).

The differences are traceable to the general overall orientation of the effort as well as short-run data availability: is it primarily a city plan as opposed to a regional plan; is it employment-oriented or housing-oriented, or both; what is to be taken as exogenous (perhaps control totals, and density constraints); what degree of stratification is desired (what kind of population, industry, land use breakouts are useful in making decisions)?

Most of these revolve about the goals and objectives of the model-building effort. To an extent, the efforts to date have not had their specifications established by the ultimate user so much as by the model-builder, primarily because the "state-of-the-art" in model-building is as yet so nebulous that no rigorous specification can be established. Nevertheless, it would appear worthwhile and now possible for future efforts of this type to see the model's objectives, framework, data to be used, and resources needed discussed thoroughly and explicitly by the users and the model-builders.

The Roles of Intelligence Systems in Urban-Systems Planning

MELVIN M. WEBBER*

Among the more significant developments in the urban-policy sciences are the changes being wrought in our images of cities, urban problems, and ourselves. Rather paradoxically, in place of the conceptual order that once composed the urban system into discrete and separable parts, the clarifying images

* See Chapter 1 for a biography. This article is reprinted with permission from the *Journal of the American Institute of Planners*, Vol. XXXI, No. 4, November 1965.

are revealing blurred boundaries demarking ambiguous subsystems. In turn, these are seen enmeshed in such complex interplay as to deny us our previous conceptions of order and causation and our traditional perceptions of our roles. These new thoughtways may fundamentally reshape the character of research, planning, policy-making, and action in urban affairs.

I should like briefly to touch upon some of these revised images, and then to examine some of their implications for planning and for the intelligence systems that might support improved planning.

I. NEW IMAGES OF URBAN SYSTEMS

From Stocks to Flows

Reflecting the early literature of urban geography and human ecology, city planning has traditionally perceived the city as a discrete physical entity whose signal traits are size, shape, and density. This perception has encouraged much the same sorts of morphological measurements and classifications that typified early biology. It's only in recent years that serious attention has been directed to the interaction among city dwellers. The new studies are now leading us to a different conception of the city and of the policy issues associated with urbanization.

Recent investigations are converging to reveal an urban-system complexity we had not previously suspected. These include, most notably, the input-output studies, the tracings of interregional income and commodity flows, the studies of the interactional consequences of relatively falling transportation and communication costs, the investigations of social mobility and of changing social organization and social behavior. Alongside the neatly compartmentalized arrangements of urban settlements, such as show up in central-place maps, these findings are beginning to uncover networks of interdependent but functionally specialized social and economic communities. Each such community (whether an industry, professional group, or religious order) is composed of different sorts of people who are distributed among distant settlements and who play various roles in a great many different sorts of interest-based communities. The pattern seems to be very disparate, ambiguous, and indeterminate. Unfortunately, it is still very poorly understood. Despite all the recent work in urbanism, we still do not have even an inadequate description of the urban system's structure.

In search of some organizing principles that might give coherence to these new findings and conceptions, students of urbanism are turning their attention from considerations of form to considerations of process. That is, in an effort to find out what the urban system *is*, we are beginning to ask how it *works*. Increasingly, our preoccupation with *stocks* of people, goods, buildings, and wealth is being supplemented by a growing attention to the *flows* of money, goods, services, information, and satisfactions among the individuals and groups who inhabit cities; for it is these flows that shape opportunity and welfare.

As one result, it is less common to deal with human settlements as members of a hierarchical set of territorially defined cities and metropolitan areas—as discrete and essentially closed mechanical systems of buildings, utility lines, and roads. Instead we are finding it helpful to view settlements as but aspects of societal systems. Thus, social organization and human interaction are replacing density and place as the foci of inquiry and of political strategy. Increasingly, we are coming to see that the many *legally* discrete governments, governmental departments, and private organizations are in fact *functionally* interlocking and interdependent. And so, we are finding it useful to view local government and federal government as but aspects of each other and as continuous with the larger spectrum of authority centers.[1] In turn, we are led to search for budgetary and programmatic approaches that would integrate the activities of complementary public governments and to look for the overlaps and interdependencies among the various public and private governments that collaborate in urban development.

Our new perspective is helping to distinguish the urban subsystems by their economic and social functions—by the roles they play and the purposes they serve—rather than to define them merely by their locations or by their administrative organization. Each subsystem is being seen as open to the flows of information, money, and goods from other subsystems it

[1] Morton Grodzins, "The Federal System," in *Goals for Americans: The Report of the President's Commission on National Goals* (Englewood Cliffs, N.J.: Prentice-Hall, Inc., 1960) pp. 265–284. See also his "Centralization and Decentralization in the American Federal System," in *A Nation of States: Essays on the American Federal System* (New York: Rand McNally & Co., 1963) pp. 1–23.

depends upon. The stability, growth, and efficiency of each is being understood to depend upon the complex self-organizing and self-regulating processes through which flows between subsystems are modulated and adaptation to environmental change is accomplished.

Those who would plan for such open, self-regulating systems must confront their tasks with quite different strategies than are appropriate to the design of mechanical systems. Concomitantly, the informational demands are also quite different. And so, I shall return to a closer examination of these implications for planning.

The Merging Actors

At the same time that increased understanding of urban processes is depreciating product-perceptions of cityness and is blurring the boundaries among settlements, those boundaries that once distinguished the separate species of urbanists are becoming even more blurred. This is most clearly evident in the growing collaboration among the various breeds of social and behavioral scientists, the variously professionalized practitioners, and the more varied executives and politicians in and out of government. The traditional professional societies, long the dominant locus of rights and obligations, are finding themselves in active competition with a new crop of associations and ad hoc groups. These new groups are arising out of shared interests in social and intellectual problems, rather than out of occupational or disciplinary heritages. Their members typically admit no fealties to either economics, law, sociology, medicine, geography, political science, city planning, or any of the other institutionalized professions exclusively. The long-sought but elusive unification of the social sciences and of the practice-professions seems now to be just happening, and without the self-consciousness that marked most early searches for commonality.

A great many influences have contributed to this gradual erosion of professional boundaries, but two stand out. The first is that the accumulating refinements in theory, within each of the traditional disciplines/professions, have demanded the admission of ever larger ranges of variables, and these have made for acceptance of once-alien concepts that had been the exclusive properties of other professions. Simultaneously, the rapid improvements in analytic methods, coupled with the new computational capabilities, are making it *possible* to deal with large masses of data pertaining to large numbers of variables.

The second is the growing sense of discovery among researchers that their theory really *is* useful in dealing with contemporary social problems. In turn, this is reinforcing the growing attraction to *problem-focused* research which supports action while further building theory. In addition, the demonstrations of the social scientist's usefulness is persuading practitioners and politicians that effective action really *does* depend upon systematic analysis and upon the capacity sensitively to predict the consequences of actions. These men are now becoming major customers for the rigorous theory and method that used to interest only the academes.

As one result, the so-called "academic" types find themselves shuttling back and forth, with increasing frequency, between classroom and White House, state house, city hall, and corporation executive suite. Once admitted to these high councils, it is unavoidable that they identify to new sets of peers for whom the test of excellence is the ability to effect change in the real world out there.

In parallel manner, the "operator" types are being acculturated into academic society. It is already quite difficult to classify many a civil servant as either social scientist, practitioner, or policy-maker. He simultaneously plays all those roles, having been bred into a hybrid species of sophisticated and sometimes effective "problem solver."

One effect of these changes I've already alluded to. It has been to bring about a multiplicity of *industrial*-union-type groups, as Leonard Duhl has put it—groups composed of diverse researchers-practitioners whose interests and skills equip them to deal with specific problem situations, and who jointly undertake a common task. Operationally, although not yet formally, these heterogeneous groups are fast replacing the *craft*-union-type groupings that have been associated with the traditional academic disciplines and with the traditional practice professions.

Another effect of these changes has been to erode the dualisms and other simplistic constructs that have for so long reinforced the boundaries between groups and served to hide the complexities of the problems they've dealt with. The dualism that would polarize "academics" and "practitioners" has been paralleled by a vast array of equally devilish ones: science and art, fact and value, action and theory, public and private, individual and society, good and evil, urban and rural, politics and planning, capital budgets and operating budgets, auto and transit, and many more.

Polar distinctions of these sorts are very handy, if one wants to incite others to action or to defend a faith. But dualisms get very blurry under the fine lenses of inquiry. Indeed, the history of modern science records the destruction of one dualism after another.

In the most dramatic blows—the ones that knocked out the dualisms that had once appeared to be most indestructible— Freud's discovery of the unconscious merged body and soul as but aspects of the same phenomenon; Einstein showed that energy and matter are transformable into each other; Darwin laid the man-versus-animal dualism to rest for all time; and Dewey exposed the essential sameness of ends and means. Although these are surely the most significant scientific events of our age, they are not unique. One by one a vast array of black-white, yes-no, push-pull, either-or dichotomies have been falling, forcing us to look along the continuums, rather than to focus on the extremes.

Now, I should make it clear that nothing I've been saying about the blurring boundaries of urban systems and urban actors is intended to mean that they are becoming homogeneous. I mean just the opposite. Whatever the settlement pattern might be, locations will always be highly differentiated, and individual locators will continue to search out those spots that seem to suit their special purposes best. Social and economic communities are becoming increasingly diverse, as people regroup themselves in exploiting newly opened opportunities. The efforts to alleviate poverty, that are now being made by representatives from the health, social welfare, urban renewal, education, and the many other agencies of municipal government, are leading to new program designs that cut across traditional agency boundaries. They are making for new alignments among pieces of agencies. Rather than homogenization, the changes are toward ever-increasing diversity.

The new togetherness among the many players in the urban-policy game is by no means a sign of homogenization, either. Although many people from diverse origins are converging around specific urban problems, they are not about to lose their identities in a faceless professional mass. Quite the contrary. Each brings a somewhat different bundle of perceptions, methods, values, loyalties, and interests. Each therefore plays the game according to somewhat different rules. And, equally important, each plays an assortment of roles, such that the scientist is also politician who advocates preferred analytic methods, evidence, and conclusions; and the lobbyist is also scientist who searches for most-workable strategies and actions.

This growing pluralism among the pros is being paralleled by increasing diversity in the population at large and by ever-more complex relations among the many governments, agencies, and firms that take actions affecting those populations. That is to say, at the same time that the contributors to public decisions are becoming more varied, the publics themselves are becoming more diversified, the numbers of decision centers are increasing, the networks of influence among publics and decision centers are becoming more intricately woven; and, hence, the decision rules are getting more complicated. In this context of ever-increasing ambiguity and pluralism among open, self-organizing and self-regulating systems, then, what sort of planning strategy is most likely to work? What is the effective place for the information sciences? And what roles can the information producers profitably play?

II. STRATEGIES FOR PLANNING

There is a lively search for new urban-planning methods nowadays, for the plain fact is that we have not yet devised a workable planning method that conforms to our new conceptions of system structure and behavior, or to our new understanding of how decisions get made. We find ourselves dissatisfied with traditional methods, perplexed by some built-in paradoxes that our new images and findings erect, and groping for ways to improve our effectiveness in the face of these puzzles.

Present Goal-Setting Methods

The available and presently institutionalized methods derive from experience with systems having characteristics different from those I've been describing. They were refined in the more unitary settings of the private corporation, the engineering firm, and the single-function governmental agency; and they have proved most useful in designing and constructing machines, buildings, and similar physical objects. Because of their success with very complicated weapon and missile systems and with production processes, some systems analysts and operations researchers are now seeking to apply their sophisticated methods in municipal government. They are finding, however, that their planning strategies are not easily transferred, since they call for a measure of goal consensus, for a quality of prediction, a hierarchy of command, and a degree of control that do not exist in the normal context of public affairs.

It is true that the large corporation or the military establishment holds multiple goals, that it harbors many competing groups having conflicting interests, and that in microcosm it thus resembles the larger political arena. But the goals of the corporation or the Pentagon are nonetheless fairly clear. They are certainly simpler than those pursued by the many groups operating in a metropolitan area. Their authority systems, however diffuse, are considerably more centralized than those of the larger urban society. The establishment is thus able to direct its actions toward desired future states much more purposefully.

On the basis of completed research-and-development work and operations-research preparation, a new product can be designed for production, the tools can be cut, the production lines laid out, a work force hired and trained, and a marketing system erected—all with considerable coordination and centralized managerial control. However, because this sort of coordinated effort is seldom possible in urban affairs, the managerial and analytic techniques that have proved effective in industrial or military applications must be considerably modified before they can be adapted to the more complex urban setting.

Similarly simplistic planning methods have long been institutionalized in urban governments, however, having been introduced by professional groups skilled in designing the physical components of cities. Like those that find favor in the industrial firm, these methods call for a degree of centralized control that is more commonly associated with authoritarian organizations and/or for a concordance of values that is most typical of voluntary groups. This planning procedure revolves around sets of standards for the sizes, locations, capacities, and other physical dimensions of highways, school houses, water systems, library buildings, and the like. In turn, it relies upon long-range forecasts of demand (sometimes called "requirements"), and upon professionals' judgments of desired future conditions. It results in the declaration of a design (or "plan") for facilities that conforms to those standards and judgments and matches the expected loadings. Although the key decisions are imbedded in the standards and the professional predilections, only rarely are their origins or rationales made explicit. They are typically imbedded in the ideological heritage of the individual professional groups that market them.

To the degree that legislators accept these standards, forecasts, preferences, and designs as reflecting their own objectives and outlooks, and to the degree that their political and fiscal powers permit them to act autonomously, they can indeed approximate the behavior of well-staffed corporation executives. The accomplishments in paving city streets, disposing of sewage, and building school houses suggest that, however crude, such plans for physical structures are highly useful. Because of the long lead-times required and the obvious importance of mechanically fitting physical parts together, such long-term designs may even be necessary.[2]

But they yield no assurances that the investment payoffs would best serve the objectives being sought, that the allocations of benefits and costs are most equitable, or that the timing of construction is optimal to the intended goal. Moreover, it is highly doubtful that this planning approach facilitates adaptation to rapidly changing external conditions, that it is also suited to planning community *service* programs, or that it is relevant to the millions of market-oriented decisions and actions that are taken by agencies outside the direct authority system of the municipal corporation.

American city councils make only a small proportion of the decisions that affect the course of urban development. Of these, a smaller fraction still are made autonomously, expressing the willful choices of resolute councilmen. Even in such seemingly straightforward decisions as those affecting freeway location, park and playground design, or the installation of sewage-treatment plants, the numbers of contending actors are likely to be huge. State and federal agents have strong strings attached to funds, and they exert powerful influence on members of their own professional societies who work for local government. No matter whom they work for, the members of a professional group are likely to share beliefs on "appropriate standards" and "necessary requirements." This gives them considerable power, since laymen tend to be

---

[2] I tried to state the positive case for future-state plans in a paper entitled "Prospect for Policies Planning," in Leonard J. Duhl (ed.), *The Urban Condition* (New York: Basic Books, Inc., 1963), pp. 319–330.

awed by their superior technical knowledge and by the shared
conclusions presented by the professionals in federal, state,
and local governments. A vast array of interest groups will
direct whatever power they may have to influence the judgments of politically conscious legislators. Thus even here,
where the city legislator acts most autonomously and could
presumably act with most deliberate rationality, the decision
processes conspire against him.

Even ignoring the unsolved problems of forecasting future
demand and predicting future goals of future populations, we
are thus left with many doubts about the utility of long-term
designs of this sort. For example, land-use plans in American
cities are not designs for action, unlike those in centrally controlled New Towns and unlike construction plans for buildings, bridges, and machines.[3] They express the authors' opinion of a desirable future state, but offer few guides for getting
there, and fewer clues about the possibilities of ever getting
there. In the absence of authoritarian controls, their most important function is hortatory in character.

More important still, many of the crucial decisions affecting urban development are not influenced by even this sort of
hortatory portrait of a desired future state. Surely the most
important conditioner of urban development and of human
welfare is the state of the national and regional economies.
Industrial expansion or contraction directly affects the local
residents where it really matters. But employment and income
levels are shaped almost exclusively by decisions made by
distant governments and in a multiplicity of widely scattered
individual firms, each responding to market conditions that it
has only slight control over. Medical, educational, and the
other services that people care about most are supplied by a
wide array of nonprofit and profit-making establishments. Despite the ideological rigidity that marks these groups, their programs must constantly be adapted to changing conditions
within their respective markets.

The problems associated with race and poverty, currently
being exacerbated by the rapid pace of cybernation, are surely
the most difficult of the social issues facing the major cities.
Their origins lie largely outside the cities where they are mani-

---

[3] The contrast between city plans in the United States and town plans
in other places and times is great. Eugene Rostow has insightfully noted
that virtually all the European and Asian cities that are generally admired were designed and built under the direction and control of authoritarian rulers.

fested, however, and almost wholly outside the municipalities' influence. Unfortunately we still have very few workable ideas for dealing with this growing social dilemma. At best we can hope for some imaginative experiments to test different sorts of programs, dropping those that fail, building on those that show some promise of helping to relieve distress, feeling our way through the course of future time in an effort to improve conditions, but always uncertain of the odds. A master plan that showed some desired future state for the presently poor without also showing the methods for attaining it could scarcely command much attention.

In Search of a Programming Strategy

Many planners are therefore searching for an action-shaping approach to planning and deciding that might succeed in those fields where the traditional end-stating approaches cannot. Most of these explorations are trying to develop methods for formulating some types of programmatic, goal-directed courses of action. The by-now-classic formulation that underlies most of the current experiments was succinctly summarized in 1955 by Edward C. Banfield. He described the process of rational decision-making as comprising the following planning strategy:

1. the decision-maker considers all of the alternatives (courses of action) open to him; i.e., he considers what courses of action are possible within the conditions of the situation and in the light of the ends he seeks to attain; 2. he identifies and evaluates all of the consequences which would follow from the adoption of each alternative; i.e., he predicts how the total situation would be changed by each course of action he might adopt; and 3. he selects that alternative the probable consequences of which would be preferable in terms of his most valued ends.[4]

Banfield then goes on to recognize that one can never identify all alternative courses of action or all consequences, and that rationality is necessarily bounded, but suggests that this model represents an unattainable ideal *toward* which we nonetheless should strive.

[4] Martin Meyerson and Edward C. Banfield, *Politics, Planning and the Public Interest: The Case of Public Housing in Chicago* (Glencoe: The Free Press, 1955), "Supplement: Note on Conceptual Scheme," p. 314.

A year later, in a seminal paper presented to the American Institute of Planners, Martin Meyerson spelled out the operational framework for such a programmatic strategy.[5] His formulation of continuous market analysis, periodic reports on the state of system behavior, action programs oriented to the middle-range future, and continuous post-hoc testing of predicted consequences, has won wide acceptance in recent years. The passage of the federal Community Renewal Program (CRP) legislation followed three years later in 1959; and, by now, CRP staffs in several major cities are working to frame such developmental programs—one-to-ten-year courses of action.

In brief, these efforts are drawing upon whatever is usable in social science theory in attempting to design operational models capable of predicting the repercussions of alternative public or private actions in one subsystem on a network of other subsystems. Some experimentation is under way with decision models that would have the further capability of interpreting desirable actions from preestablished decision rules. There is some optimism abroad that we might also be able to estimate optimal timing of sequenced actions. In some circles, there is now beginning optimism that, in addition to predicting efficiency effects of alternative actions, we may also be able to predict distributions of benefits and costs to the various publics that would be affected. Surely if these methods could be made to work, legislators could better know what to *want* and more rationally decide what to *do*.

But during the past few years the growing confidences in even this sophisticated formulation have been increasingly clouded. The wave of urban politics studies began flooding the bookstores in 1961. They have essentially discredited both the popular image of a monolithic power-elite and the civics-book portrait of a deliberative and selflessly rational city council. Only rarely, it appears, is it possible for either an extra-governmental or a governmental legislature to make forthright decisions across the municipal and local-industrial board. They report that it is only rarely possible to make coordinated decisions from a central command post for even a few of the urban subsystems. Instead, these studies portray multitudes of

---

[5] Martin Meyerson, "Building the Middle-Range Bridge for Comprehensive Planning," *A.I.P. Journal*, XXII:2 (Spring 1956), 58–64. This formulation was anticipated in an unpublished paper by Harvey S. Perloff, "Form and Function of Master Planning in Puerto Rico" (mimeo.), January 1952.

separate groups, each pursuing somewhat different bundles of objectives, participating segmentally in decisions that affect their several interests.

Except for the government bureaus and private clubs that are stabilized and controlled by the professional ideologies, the groups seem to form in ad hoc fashion around each current issue, such that the membership in each, and the variable interests they reflect, merge into each other at their fuzzy boundaries. Without a single decision center, coordination of even a few municipal agencies' activities seems difficult, and hence unlikely.

Rather more serious doubts have been raised by Charles Lindblom and his associates, however. Contending that the only possible and the most effective tactic is one of "disjointed incrementalism," they reject the Banfield-Meyerson strategy that would seek to explicate alternative means in each subsystem, to trace their repercussions on the others, and then to select those means that seem most efficient in accomplishing system-wide ends. "Instead of adjusting means to ends," Lindblom observes, "ends are chosen that are appropriate to the available means. . . . Ends and means are chosen simultaneously." With Karl Popper,[6] he contends that, necessarily, "analysis and policy making are remedial; they move *away* from ills rather than *toward* known objectives," and that "the analysis of consequences is quite incomplete," thus "no attempt at comprehensiveness is made."[7]

If comprehensive analysis and decision are not feasible, then we can never hope to optimize for whole systems, and the classic program-design strategy may be no more workable than the end-state approach. But Lindblom and his colleagues are arguing, further, that even suboptimization is impossible. At best, they would contend, one can hope to take only small, marginal decisions and actions with respect to subsystems, such that each might help to relieve the most undesired conditions as they emerge through time. Thus, if Lindblom's strategy were pursued, we need not bother ourselves with either the dilemmas tied to identifying long-term goals or with the

---

[6] Karl R. Popper, *The Open Society and Its Enemies* (New York: Harper & Row, Torchbook edition, 1963), Vol. I, 158.

[7] Albert O. Hirschman and Charles E. Lindblom, "Economic Development, Research and Development, Policy Making: Some Converging Views," *Behavioral Science*, VII:2 (April 1962) 215–216. See also his more thorough development of this thesis in David Braybrooke and Charles E. Lindblom, *A Strategy of Decision* (New York: The Free Press of Glencoe, 1963).

complexities of designing coherent courses of action. Instead, each of us, in our plural roles, need deal only segmentally, on a day-to-day basis, with the fragments of problems that fall within the purview of our competences and interests—each of us promoting those ends-means chains we happen to prefer at the moment.

But an alternative approach is emerging that might answer some of Lindblom's most cutting criticisms. It is the tactic of programm*ing*, as alternative to program-making or plan-making. It calls for the installation of decision-aiding processes that might never yield a formal program for even middle-run actions. Rather, it would support the incremental, multi-centered processes of deciding and acting; but it would expand the probabilities that these decisions and actions would be taken more rationally. I shall have a word to say about this planning method shortly, for I believe it will serve us as an interim strategy until some resolutions of the inconsistencies within planning theory can be found.

However persuasive Lindblom's way of thinking, and however common incremental decision-making may be, we nonetheless know that governments, unlike even the largest corporations, *are* able to take big investment leaps. Since governments in the United States do not face bankruptcy or political overthrow, they are able to undertake larger and higher-risk projects than can some foreign governments or corporations in this country. If the project should fail to bring expected returns, it really doesn't matter much. And so, governmental planners are encouraged to think big, and to recommend actions that would induce parametric changes in the urban system. The success of the British town planners in changing the rules of city building in England, and the success of the Puerto Rican planners in helping to transform an agrarian society to industrial status in less than a generation, suggest that even though planned parametric change may be uncommon, it is nonetheless possible.

Because governmental accounting systems do not require short-run payoffs, and because many developments in cities will be generating their consequences over the long-run future, city planners have typically adopted longer-term planning horizons than have other planners. And, equally important, because the substantive concerns of general government are much more inclusive than are those of individual firms or individual governmental departments, city planners have been induced to search for higher-level optima than do those who work in agencies or firms dealing with parts of subsystems.

Despite the impossibility of rationally planning for the whole urban system, the traditions of city planning have led us to try to find optima for at least somewhat larger wholes than are typically sought elsewhere. Dyckman voiced the city planners' optimism in this respect when he said,

> there is some evidence that the city planners may, in the long run, make a contribution to urban studies as well as to the necessary social and physical engineering. For if deficient in certain techniques, the city planners, or at least the best trained of them, are equipped to ask the right questions. The synthetic, organizing role of city planning, which once might have been dismissed as "holistic" nonsense or Bergsonian mysticism, becomes, in a world of expanded technical possibilities, a valuable approach.[8]

An Interim Programming Strategy

Even though planning theory is in so unresolved a state (and I've mentioned only a few of the troublesome questions) the current experiments with program-type methods suggest that we may eventually locate some routes out of the maze. Meanwhile, even though we have growing doubts about traditional planning procedures, and even though we accept the many new warnings about the bounds of rationality, we do have some growing confidence that certain types of planning activity will return profitable payoffs. There is still a great deal that planners can now do to improve the quality of decisions and actions, even recognizing that human cognitive capacities are highly limited, that knowledge is always in terribly short supply, that our theory is still very primitive, that we still don't know how to discount future values or to estimate present benefits and costs, that we shall probably never find optima for total systems that are marked by multiple goals, and that, at best, we can hope to make only slight improvements in predictions.

Among the most valuable things we can do is just to supply better information about the current states of affairs in the various urban subsystems. William Wheaton recently argued this proposition persuasively by describing the confusions and

[8] John W. Dyckman, "The Scientific World of the City Planners," *The American Behavioral Scientist*, VI:6 (February 1963), 49.

the gross irrationalities that abound in metropolitan decision-making. In summarizing his observations of public and private investors' behavior, he concluded that

> the market facts are not widely available or widely understood, . . . [and] *this* is the *determining* factor in an overwhelming majority of decisions being made. The simple act of providing facts regarding market trends in usable form, [and] accessible to deciders, would make a real difference in our urban development rates.[9]

The readers of this *Journal* would be quick to join in his appeal and with his second-order entreaty for improved predictions of at least the short-run changes.

These simple-sounding demands are, of course, nothing of the sort. Data are terribly expensive commodities. Although the utility of good information and good analysis is coming to be widely appreciated in political circles (witness the vast sums spent by the presidential candidates last year for survey-research into voter preferences), adequate financing for urban data is still hard to come by. But that's almost the least of it. An adequate urban intelligence center would need to maintain current inventories of both stocks and flows relating to characteristics of, at least, people, property, and the activities of organized groups (such as sales, shipments, bank clearings). But *which* characteristics should be monitored depends upon the theoretic formulations we believe best explain the workings of the systems they belong to and best reflect the valuative preferences that deciders hold to.

In this light it is becoming apparent that many of the new data banks are little more than grab-bag collections of data for which no theoretic bases exist. Like the drunk who was searching for his lost keys under the lamp post because the light was better there, many of the new data banks seem to be storing data just because these specific numbers happen to be easy to get. The models that serve policy-making and action may call for very different numbers, and so we can expect that as the banks become informed by urban theory, they will turn their large storage and computing capacities to the information that might prove useful.

The relations between data selection and theory are recipro-

[9] William L. C. Wheaton, "Public and Private Agents of Change," in Melvin M. Webber and others, *Explorations into Urban Structure* (Philadelphia: University of Pennsylvania Press, 1964), p. 189. (Italics added.)

cal, or course. It is therefore equally important that an urban intelligence center be as purposefully directed to identifying potentially fruitful research and potentially effective social experiments, as it is to supplying current inventories. Such theory-oriented work will identify new types of useful data that would contribute to the next rounds of social action. In turn, the continuing processes of social action, if carefully monitored and imaginatively evaluated, can further improve the theory that effective action depends upon.

Many are thus coming to visualize an idealized urban intelligence center, that is, an effective city planning agency, as being equally oriented to improving theory and action, for we know that the dualism that would distinguish them is false. In contrast to a mere "information center," such an intelligence center would seek to describe and explain what is going on, to report on stocks and flows, and to identify cause-and-effect relations. Using simulation-type techniques, it would try to predict what would happen *if* one course-of-action were taken rather than some other, and to trace the repercussions of those actions through as many of the subsystems as our theory and data permit. By thus feeding-forward predictions of likely outcomes, the center would inevitably become an agent of change, affecting actions and subsequent outcomes. Flatly rejecting the notion that it can serve a single client, it would seek to supply information on current conditions and predictions of future conditions to many interested parties, in addition to the city council that pays its bills. In an effort to test accuracy of predictions and adequacy of the theory underlying the predictions, its monitoring stations must be set up at key junctions throughout the urban system and the signals continuously fed back. It need not presume that control is centralized at any specific decision points or that consistent courses of action will be pursued by anybody. Rather, each of the multiplicity of groups would be aided in searching out its own objectives and its own best current actions.

For those few groups whose objectives are clear and whose authority systems permit them to chart long-term and consistent programs of action, such an intelligence center could become an especially valuable resource. If predictive models were good enough, the center could help them to design targets (accomplishment levels tied to specific future dates), programs (detailed, time-sequenced steps to be taken), and pre-arranged strategies (alternative programs that say what to do when the meters indicate that anticipated events are not occurring). Some groups would never adopt such formal targets, programs, and strategies, however. For some, even the goal directions shift with changing external conditions, and if data on developing events can be continuously fed-back into the intelligence system, these deciders could better operate simultaneously as short-run opportunists and as long-run goal-seekers. Similarly, they can operate simultaneously (although segmentally, of course) as Wheaton-type informed deciders, as Banfield-Meyerson-type middle-run programmers, as Lindblom-type particularistic incrementalists, and as Dyckman-type seekers after higher-level optima. With the multiplicity of diverse groups chasing divergent goals, it is quite unlikely that they would ever behave consistently on all matters or operate collectively as members of an integrated team.

III. THE POLITICS OF INFORMATION

Nothing I have been saying is intended to imply that the men who would staff such a sophisticated intelligence center could be, in any sense, the dispassionately objective scientists of either the old Technocracy school of social engineers or the more recent schools of scientific positivism. Whether we like it or not, social science, and especially policy-oriented social science cannot be value-free science.

In a field such as astronomy, one's observations and theoretic generalizations are very unlikely to make much difference to the phenomena being observed. The remarkable discoveries in astronomy since the war have led to some striking new theories about the histories of stars and the history of the universe, but the stars and the universe are wholly unaffected by them. In the social sciences, however, as John Seeley has perceptively described it, to report one's observations is to change the phenomenon being observed.[10]

To inform a shopping-center investor about consumer travel behavior and about market potentials is to shape his decisions about shopping-center locations and tenant mix. In turn, those decisions will influence the decisions of merchants, shoppers, house-builders, bankers, and others; and they will thus affect the behavioral and market conditions that were initially observed. To supply the facts on national income distribution, as Keyserling and Harrington recently did, was to set loose a

[10] John R. Seeley, "Social Science? Some Probative Problems," in Maurice Stein and Arthur Vidich (eds), *Sociology on Trial* (Englewood Cliffs, N.J.: Prentice-Hall, Inc., 1963), pp. 53–65.

chain of responses that may yet change the distributional facts that were initially reported. The same sort of thing happens with forecasts, of course, as business-cycle theorists and stock-exchange brokers have long known.

Seemingly straightforward facts about societal things and events are seldom, if ever, value neutral. They inevitably intervene into the workings of the systems they describe. The information supplier, whatever his motives and methods, is therefore inevitably immersed in politics. The kinds of facts he selects to report, the way he presents them, the groups they are distributed to, and the inferences he invites each work to shape subsequent outcomes—subsequent facts.

The current interest in better urban information mirrors a spreading recognition that facts available to actors shape their actions, and hence the belief that better information will make for better actions. But I raise these questions because I find a misconception among some urban scientists who believe that information, per se, is nonpolitical—that as "pure scientists" they can stand outside the system and, with positivistic detachment, record and explain what they see. This perception of dualistic roles is patently distorted. The scientist, no less than the politician or the merchant, is *inside* the system, and his work affects its workings. None of us can escape the fact that our facts are instruments of change. To play the role of scientist in the urban field is also to play the role of intervener, however indirect and modest the interventions may be.

This outcome is reinforced by the large political and economic capital that information represents. Information, like money, yields power to those who've got it. And, like money, the ways in which it is distributed will determine which groups will be favored and which deprived.

Accordingly, an urban intelligence center could in no sense operate as a neutral informant. Even if it somehow *could* succeed in becoming a nonpartisan supplier of information, making its findings available to all comers, this in itself would represent a powerful intervention into economic, political, and social processes. To redistribute information-income in such fashion would dramatically change the rules of the political and economic games that are played in the metropolitan arena. To reduce secrecy would reduce the advantages that redounded to those favored few who used to be in on the secrets. To reduce ignorance among those groups that cannot now afford the high costs of good intelligence would strengthen their political and economic positions. To supply comparable information to all interested parties, would broaden the spectrum of consensus and might thereby increase the odds of mutually reinforcing actions.

Of course, nothing even approximating equality of access to information is likely, even if an intelligence center were to be established and supported by a diversified group of governments, industries, and foundations. The power that such a center would represent is already clear to many; indeed, this is one of the reasons that financing has been hard to get. As city planning agencies grow to become intelligence centers, however, we can expect a growing partisan competition to gain control over their activities and to limit outputs; for information of some types can be a very dangerous weapon. Thus, the social-scientist-types who would staff them would immediately find themselves intimately involved in internal politics over the centers' programs, mirroring the external politics of the metropolis.

Which studies should be conducted? Which models employed? Which data collected? Which variables accounted? Which analyses made? Which forecasts attempted? Which alternatives explored? Which conclusions reported? And which findings and recommendations reported to which of the competing groups? The staff may wish to believe that their science can supply the answers. But, however true that may be, it is equally true that, simultaneously, these would also be political answers of a straightforward sort.

CONCLUSION

Very few, if any, general decision rules are relevant to all the separate groups operating in an urban area. Each group seeks its own survival, its own special types of advantage, its own uniquely perceived images of self and public welfare. Thus, an elected official may promote a costly public-works project as a way of stabilizing his political position. If the analyst should fail to include these so-called "noneconomic variables" in calculating expected returns from the investment, he of course misses the main point. If he does account for them, he aligns himself with the interests of one partisan group against others. A businessmen's group may seek to redevelop a section of the central business district, ostensibly to "revitalize the city's heart" and thereby to "serve the public interest"; but unless the analyst is alert to the real motives driving the project, his information is not likely to give them the indicators of success they really want. And, again, if he should serve their purposes, he aligns himself with the project's proponents and against the opponents. I point these rather homey examples to say that the man who would pursue the urban information sciences thereby chooses a career in politics—politics in the vernacular sense, for he cannot avoid the posture of protagonist.

But he thereby also chooses a political career in its grander meaning—he becomes a policy-shaper if not a policy-maker. In playing the roles of producer of new facts, as identifier and evaluator of potential action-courses, and as prophet of the future, he thereby plays the role of planner. His position requires that he say what he thinks *ought* to happen, as well as to say what *might* happen.

By now it should be clear that I do not pose these as duals. Rather, I am saying that it is impossible to separate the "is-type" propositions from the "ought-type." To report what is, or what is expected to be, unavoidably shapes what is likely to be. In a way different from the workings of Merton's self-fulfilling prophecy, the inherent consequence of producing information is to influence actions; and, motivations aside, to say what is, and hence to affect what will be, is inseparable from saying what should be.

It is also clear that planners must perforce say what they would like to happen. With their superior knowledge of the system's structure, its processes, and the value-ranked wants of the various publics, planners who can draw upon an elaborate intelligence center might be well-equipped to design action-programs having high odds of bringing high welfare returns. Competence in the positive aspects of the sciences strengthens competence in the normative aspects.

The ablest students of human problems have often known their clients' wants better than the clients have, and they have often known better what the clients should do. (Fluoridation is an apt example here, if accounting for the paranoid need for an aggressor be temporarily suspended.) To be sure, clients are wont to ignore their counsellors, sometimes at their own loss (and again fluoridation illustrates my point). But the socially responsible student, or planner, or scientist—choose whichever name you happen to like best—has an ethical obligation to say what he thinks *ought* to be, no less than that the early atomic physicists were obligated to report their findings as best they understood them and the physician is obligated to advise his patient to submit to unpleasant therapy.

In this respect, the scientist-politician-planner may be of a peculiar breed in the political scene. Like all other political actors, he is surely a member of an interest group composed of peers who share his particular frames of reference and, hence, his social objectives. With them, he sees the world through special filters and holds vested interests in certain concepts, analytic methods, and social programs. With them, he tries to sell his particular brands of rationality and his particular images of the social welfare. Despite the weakening boundaries between professions, his beliefs and intellectual style are likely to have been shaped by the profession that reared him. He is likely still to believe that its variables are more critical than others, to believe that its thoughtways are more productive, and to value its brands of objectives more highly than others.

His special character mirrors the special character of science. To a degree far less common in other interest groups, he has learned to *doubt;* to question his beliefs, his data, and his findings; to submit his conclusions to critical evaluation by his peers; to tolerate uncertainty and ambiguity; to bear the frustrations of not knowing, and of knowing he does not know; and, by far the most important, to adopt the empirical test for validity.

As much as the improved facts, the improved modes of predicting, and the disciplined imagination that he brings, it is the new injection of the *scientific morality* into urban policy-making that makes the saturation of scientific talent into urban affairs a happy event. Partisanship, parochialism, and partial knowledge are inherent to the urban system, as they are to science. The intelligence centers can never eliminate them. The new planners must accept them as facts, no less real and valid than rents, transport costs, interest rates, and topographic conditions. By more systematically accounting for these variables, however, and by then exposing alternative action and value hypotheses to critical and systematic examination, those in the information-and-planning sciences may help to eliminate the most negative consequences of partisanship and of ignorance.

By offering their own preferred images of private-public welfares, their own perceptions of good ends-means, and their own proposals for social programs, the new hybrid species of urban planners are likely to make significant contributions to ameliorating social problems. With so many different types of professionals now converging upon city planning, and with such large public investment being made to support their efforts, we shall not have to wait long to find out if they will.

Editor's Note:
This article was presented as a keynote to the Second Annual Conference on Urban Planning Information Systems and Programs, University of Pittsburgh, September 1964. The author has gratefully acknowledged Ira Robinson's critical comments and suggestions to an earlier version.

Chapter 15

GOVERNMENT STRUCTURE FOR PLANNING

In a political democracy, especially under federalism with its splintered three-tiered maze of government, how can the sprawling metropolis be managed? Many have been tempted in the recent past, seeing that the political city was not remotely the functional city, to stretch the body politic to some sort of metro government. This interjected new level would presumably fit—at least for the moment—the urbanized area, regarded as more or less a functioning system. Intellectually satisfying as a means for tidying up the jurisdictional mess, metro government ideas have had scant success to date, foundering on the bleak realities of local politics and generally reluctant suburbia. Private and public investments of both major and minor scale come tumbling one on top of another as the great urban "wens" spread over the land—thus bringing up the quite fascinating exercise of planning without government. Failing metro government, how can we plan and program in a reasonable fashion for the metropolitan area (as a preliminary exercise to handling megalopolis)?

There are naturally a variety of views on this matter and several will be explored here. Frank Smallwood, political scientist and student of comparative urbanism, steeped both in the American metro story and in London's complex attempt to force certain governmental functions to a metropolitan level, has given a cool look at the much-touted Toronto Metro on its tenth anniversary and thereafter. He concludes that it has solved certain crisis situations of water supply, sewerage system, and schools, but (a) in no way dared to tackle the sensitive social problems which now thrust themselves into the forefront of planning or (b) to still parochial suburban howls about the imbalance of tax burdens. The "steam shovel" approach of visible public works under a tough, charismatic metro boss got the job started, but in no way provided an easily transferable, Grade A model to be followed elsewhere. Three knowledgeable people: William Nash, Harvard planner; Edward C. Banfield, Harvard political scientist, and Harvey Perloff, economically oriented urbanist from Resources from the Future Inc., set their minds to the problems of the almost powerless Boston Metropolitan Area Planning Council, at its request, to explore various avenues for advancing some order in this area lacking metro government. What pre-government steps might be initiated to forward the area's well-being irrespective of whether a metro government did emerge in the foreseeable future?

Nash, after exploring the 126 metro planning bodies covering 142 of the 212 SMSA[1] of 1963, concludes in a somewhat similar fashion to Smallwood's findings, that so long as tough controversial problems are avoided, at least something can be done to cope with area-wide problems. But generally financially starved and lacking jurisdictional authority to do anything, there is no wonder that metropolitan planning bodies produced no spectacular results. He sees the careful collection of reliable information on an area scale, which can influence decision and can educate the public to back such discussions as they are brought into the open form of public debate, as an important initial step. Banfield, less optimistic about possibilities for action and somewhat scornful of naming information-gathering "planning," addresses himself directly to metro planning in the *absence* of metro government. Discounting our abilities to look ahead more than five years, he sees no possibility of arriving at common metro goals even at the "vague generality" level, much less political action level, contending that no one could reach such goals in any case. The Boston Metropolitan Area Planning Council should limit itself to certain few problems of areawide development: (a) design of a transportation system, (b) taxation to equalize burdens and resultant service, and (c) the provision of water supply, sewage disposal, air pollution control and outdoor recreational facilities. Since metropolitan Boston is in one state he believes that strengthening the office of governor (and his Council) is the most useful preliminary exercise in building up metro planning. Harvey Perloff summarizes areas of agreement and disagreement in Nash's and Banfield's papers by listing common metro functions: (a) *flow systems* (water, electric power, etc.); (b) *natural resources or environmental setting items* (terrain, air and water bodies, etc.); (c) *specialized services and facilities* (education and hospitalization of areawide scope); (d) *cooperative items* (saving by increase in scale—such as garbage collection); (e) *equity questions* (tax equalization). He stresses the theme that the metro planning agency is in a useful position to help manufacture that golden consensus which can lead eventually to the definition of areawide interests, a plan and its implementation—metro government or not.

Unquestionably we are beginning to delineate the capabilities of metro planning without metro government, especially with a financially benevolent federal government funding research, planning, and facilities differentially favorable to metro areas organized to plan.

[1] Standard Metropolitan Statistical Areas.

Metro Toronto: A Decade Later

FRANK SMALLWOOD*

. . . At the time of its inception in 1953, Toronto's Metropolitan Council was given exclusive jurisdiction over only a limited number of basic services, most notably assessment, borrowing and major arterial highways.

The area's thirteen local municipalities were also given exclusive jurisdiction over only a limited number of services such as police, licensing, fire protection, libraries, and local tax collection.

The great majority of major services were shared between the Metropolitan Council and the local municipalities, or between a number of quasi-independent boards and the local municipalities. Services shared between Metro and the local municipalities included planning, parks and recreation, water supply, sewage disposal and welfare. Responsibility for public housing was divided between a number of special housing boards and the thirteen municipalities, while the educational services were shared between a new Metropolitan School Board and a group of locally elected school boards.

Finally, another new quasi-independent group, the Toronto Transit Commission, was given exclusive control over all forms of public transportation, exclusive of railroads and taxis.

The essence of this original scheme was that Metro was to perform a "wholesaler" role in such service fields as water supply, sewage disposal and the like, while the local municipalities were to perform a "retailer" role in these same fields. Above all else, through its exclusive control over borrowing for all local government agencies (i.e., itself, the thirteen local municipalities, the quasi-independent boards, and the Toronto Transit Commission), Metro was designated to

* Associate Professor of Government and Chairman of the City Planning/Urban Studies Program at Dartmouth College. A Ph.D. from Harvard, he served four years with the Atomic Energy Commission. He is the author of the widely praised *Greater London: The Politics of Metropolitan Reform* (Bobbs-Merrill Co., Inc., 1965). The following in abridged and updated form is reprinted with the kind permission of the Bureau of Municipal Research, Toronto, Canada, from the original publication of the same title which appeared in 1963.

serve as the central capital works agency for the entire Greater Toronto complex. In effect, it was expected to provide the means, both financially and jurisdictionally, to carry out the major public works projects which were so badly needed throughout the Toronto metropolitan area.

The basic allocation of powers has remained essentially intact during Metro's first decade, although three significant changes were made following a Provincial review of Metro's operations in 1957. At that time Metro was given exclusive jurisdiction over the police and air pollution services, while licensing was moved up into the "shared" services category.

While the initial allocation of responsibilities between the two tiers of government involved some difficult problems of accommodation, the representative arrangements that went into the making of the new Metropolitan Council presented an issue of even more controversial political overtones.

The 240-square-mile Toronto metropolitan area contains thirteen local municipalities that fan out from the north shore of Lake Ontario in three concentric rings. At the very center of the area is the City of Toronto, which although by far the largest of the thirteen local governments, was experiencing a slight population decline during the immediate postwar period.

A second "inner ring" consists of nine suburban municipalities adjacent to, and encircling, the central city. While each of these nine municipalities had experienced some population growth during the postwar period, this growth was relatively small in absolute numbers, since all nine were reasonably well developed by the time of Metro's inception.

Finally, there is a third, "outer ring" of three large suburban communities: Etobicoke to the west, North York to the north, and Scarborough to the east. These three units, which were largely undeveloped in 1953, occupy a huge land area, and they were already experiencing a massive population boom.

In devising a formula to provide for the representation of these thirteen municipalities on the new Metropolitan Council, the major problem related to the realization of an equitable balance between the central city and the twelve suburbs taken as a whole. . . . In "Bill 80" (the final legislation actually establishing Metro), the Ontario Provincial Legislature . . . provided for a twenty-five-man council: twelve representatives from the City; one representative from each of the twelve suburbs; and an independent chairman, to be designated for the first two years by the Province, and elected annually thereafter by the Metropolitan Council.[1]

The effect of this formula was not so much to distort the representative balance between the City and the twelve suburbs taken as a whole, as it was to produce gross inequalities in representation between individual suburban municipalities. Swansea, for example, with 8,300 population was given one Council member, while North York, with 110,000 population, also received one representative on the Council. These initial inequalities were destined to increase dramatically during the ensuing decade.

The above division of powers and representative arrangements were the major influences shaping the initial organization of Toronto's new metropolitan government. In appraising this government's performance during its first ten years, a certain degree of speculation is inevitable, due to the fact that while relevant comparisons can be made between the pre-Metro years before 1953 and the Metro performance in 1963, it is impossible to make the most meaningful comparison of all. This is, of course, an analysis of Metro Toronto as it actually exists in 1963 with its established metropolitan government, and Toronto as it would be in 1963 if this government had never been created.

The lack of any such comparative data poses especially difficult problems when one attempts to compile the debit side of Metro's ledger. Some of the problems noted in the ensuing analysis are as much an outgrowth of the environmental pressures which have accompanied Toronto's growing pains during the past ten years as they are the result of any actions, or lack of actions, on the part of Metro itself. While objectivity requires repeated emphasis of this fact, enough data is now available to provide a meaningful base for an analysis of Metro's major achievements, and limitations, in an effort to determine how well this governmental organization has fulfilled its original expectations.

METRO'S MAJOR ACHIEVEMENTS

Although Toronto's Metropolitan Council can point to a wide variety of accomplishments since 1953, three particular achievements stand out as being especially significant in terms of the challenges that Metro was designed to meet, and the

[1] In this article, superscript numbers refer to bibliographic References appearing at the end.

environmental considerations that surrounded its original creation. These are: the realization of a strong base of public and political support for the metropolitan government concept; the resolution of a series of specific service crises; and the provision of a capital financial capability that has helped the Toronto metropolitan area meet the demands of its burgeoning population growth.

1. *Securing Its Political Base*

The first, and in many aspects the foremost, accomplishment of the Metropolitan Council has been the realization of a solid expression of support for the general concept of metropolitan government in the Toronto area . . .

The most crucial difficulty the new Council had to face was the widespread suspicion, if not acrimony, with which the existing municipalities greeted its initial establishment. Neither the central city nor the twelve suburban communities had realized their basic objectives in the final Metro compromise, and in 1953 it was by no means certain that they would not attempt to gang up on the new metropolitan government in an attempt to undermine its very survival . . .

Three factors enabled Metro to meet this challenge—the force of personality; the political significance of the representative formula utilized in determining the Metro Council membership; and the specific nature of the program priorities that Metro has elected to push the hardest.

The first of these three factors—the force of personality—highlights the crucial role of Metro's original chairman (1953 to 1961), Frederick Goldwin Gardiner.

To say that Gardiner—a highly successful, tough and dynamic Toronto corporation lawyer—ran a taut ship during his crucial tenure as Metro's chairman would classify as the understatement of this, or any other, year. Locally known as "Big Daddy" after the domineering character in Tennessee Williams' *Cat on a Hot Tin Roof,* Chairman Gardiner provided a number of key ingredients that went into the making of Metro's initial success.

First, as a former Reeve (i.e., Mayor) of wealthy, suburban Forest Hill Village and as a successful lawyer of considerable personal means, Gardiner provided the Metro program with a symbolic aura of prestige, integrity, and honesty. In addition, he transferred to this program his tremendous sense of personal drive, self-confidence, and determination to "get things done." Third, as the former Vice-President of the Ontario Conservative Association, he was on very close terms with the then-Provincial Premier, Leslie Frost, and the personal liaison he established between Metro and the Provincial government was so close as to be characterized as a "Family Compact." Finally, and of most telling significance, Gardiner possessed an understanding of, and a willingness to utilize, his personal prestige and power to keep his potentially explosive Council from flying apart.

All four of the above elements are evident in Gardiner's terse explanation as to why he accepted the Metro chairmanship at Premier Frost's personal urging: "Hell, I knew what it was all about. I didn't want the job, but I knew someone would have to head it up—someone with the qualifications and who could afford it."[2]

Despite more than occasional grumblings within Metro that Gardiner ran the organization as a tyrant, he was re-elected Chairman by the Metro Councillors for seven successive years, from 1955 through 1961. His tough, abrasive, pragmatic approach to the Council's problems attracted widespread support throughout the Toronto area. He provided the dramatic flair, and the symbolic sense of 'no-nonsense' accomplishment that created a favorable image for the Metro operation.[3]

It is important to observe, however, that Metro has paid a price for Chairman Gardiner's forceful approach to leadership. In essence, Gardiner became so closely identified with the entire Metro operation that it was often difficult to determine where he left off and where Metro began. The perspective of hindsight now indicates quite conclusively that much of Metro's original sense of purpose was actually embodied in the dynamic personage of its first chairman, rather than in any independently conceived central philosophy. This fact has become increasingly obvious in the past two years, now that Gardiner has left the Council. Paradoxically, Gardiner's forceful brand of leadership played a crucial role in the successful launching of the Metro enterprise during the Council's formative years, yet once he had stepped down from his chairmanship post, he left a void that threatened to undermine the subsequent success of the Metro operation during more recent years.

The second consideration contributing to Metro's successful political inauguration was also another paradoxical mixture of strength and potential weakness. This was the representative formula that went into the formation of the new Metropolitan Council.

The advantages of this formula were to be found in the fact that the mayors and other local political leaders in the area were automatic members of this new Council by virtue of their constituency positions in their local municipalities. As Council "insiders," they helped to formulate the new Metro program. Such an arrangement had the practical effect of diverting potential political attacks away from a wide-open, external assault against the basic concept of the new metropolitan governmental program. Instead, Metro's initial controversies were limited to a more restricted display of political in-fighting within the confines of Metro's council chambers. While the area's local political leaders may not have been in agreement with all of the Council's policies, they were hesitant to undermine the entire Metro operation, and in the process, do themselves out of a new job which carried considerable prestige and importance . . .

Hence Metro has been relatively immune from external political attack largely due to the inclusion of local political leadership on its Council. However, it is important to recognize that, while this representative formula may have helped initially to solidify the new government's early political base, it has not been without some very definite liabilities which, again, have become more apparent during recent years.

The third factor that influenced the realization of a strong base for support for Toronto's metropolitan government was the Council's emphasis on public works' priorities.

To a large extent, this was an inevitable response to a number of very serious crises, coupled with the capital financing mandate that Metro was given at its inception. Yet the observation should be made that Metro's emphasis on large physical projects has not been totally divorced from its continued political well-being.

An analysis of *gross*** cumulative capital and current expenditures from 1953 through December 31, 1962 (exclusive of education which is handled as a special account by the Metropolitan School Board) reveals quite clearly the nature of Metro's programmatic priorities:

* The figures are gross expenditures, exclusive of Provincial grants, etc., in an effort to give the clearest picture of how Metro felt it should expend its total resources.

TABLE I

METRO'S CUMULATIVE GROSS EXPENDITURES: 1953-1962[4]

Program	Capital Expenditures	Current Expenditures (Excluding Debt Charges)	Total	% of Total
Roads	$159,311,362	$ 45,964,774	$205,276,136	26.3
Adm. of Justice & Protection	8,257,919	136,784,068	145,041,987	18.6
Welfare & Housing	24,488,228	91,711,586	116,199,814	14.9
Sewage	80,179,880	23,360,202	103,540,082	13.3
Waterworks (Self-Liq.)	59,822,745	41,970,482	101,793,227	13.0
Misc. & Gen. Admin.	1,028,436	43,488,900	44,517,336	5.7
Toronto Transit Comm. (Metro Share only)	37,835,783		37,835,783	4.9
Parks, Rec. & Conservation	14,973,811	10,933,716	25,907,527	3.3
Totals	$385,898,164	$394,213,728	$780,111,892	100

It is significant to note that three services—transportation, water supply and sewage disposal—have taken up over 50 per cent of all Metro's cumulative expenditures (capital plus current) since the Council's inception in 1953. While each of these three services required huge capital outlays to alleviate desperately inadequate conditions that were fast approaching a crisis stage, it is also worth noting that Metro's expenditure pattern had some very direct political consequences.

In large measure, this pattern reflects the philosophy that Frederick Gardiner brought to the job of Metro Chairman. In his 1961 inaugural speech to the Metropolitan Council, when he announced his pending retirement and attempted to outline Metro's major achievements under his leadership, Gardiner made the telling observation that Metro's early years represented "a time when imagination had to be translated into physical accomplishments to prove that the first metropolitan government on the North American continent would work."[5]

Gardiner reiterated this philosophy when he visited Winnipeg later in 1961, and in commenting on the problems of the embattled Winnipeg government, he observed, "the main thing is to get your plans, work out a system of priorities, and then put the steam shovels into the ground."[6]

The political payoff that comes from putting "the steam shovels into the ground" is, of course, obvious. One need look no further in the United States than to the power positions of Robert Moses and the Port of New York Authority to see the role that tangible physical achievements can play in solidifying a position of political strength. Today, the direct evidence of many of Metro's most important accomplishments can be found throughout the metropolitan area, and this evidence ranges from a now adequate water supply system to the massive Frederick G. Gardiner expressway project taking shape on the north shore of Lake Ontario.

When Metro faces the challenge of explaining what it has been able to accomplish, there is a literal display of concrete evidence to justify its continued existence. As Professor John Grumm has noted, the policy "has been to place emphasis on tangible public works and to attack those problems where results could be immediate, concrete and apparent."[7]

Whether this aspect of the Metro success story has also contained corresponding elements of potential liability is a difficult question to answer. Obviously, any governmental organization is limited to a definite amount of resources, and it can emphasize one type of program only at the expense of others. Existing evidence, shown later, does indicate that Metro has tended to underplay certain key responsibilities. Yet the point remains that the nature of existing needs, and the nature of Metro's original capital financing mandate, indicated that the large public works projects would receive priority attention in the Council's new program.

In essence, Metro has been able to consolidate its base of support through the triumvirate of personality, political accommodation (in its Council representation formula), and an emphasis on physical priorities. The fact that some or all of these factors have created subsequent problems for the new government should not detract from the magnitude of this very basic initial feat.

2. Resolving Specific Service Crises

The significance of a second major Metro achievement can best be understood through reference to the widely quoted local adage that Toronto's new government was "the product of desperation, rather than inspiration."

While this desperation was becoming more obvious on a wide variety of fronts, it was particularly apparent in the water supply, water pollution control, and education services. By

1953 the rapid postwar expansion of Greater Toronto was producing unprecedented demands on all three of these services, with the most extreme crisis conditions buffeting the "outer ring" communities of North York, Etobicoke and Scarborough.

As was indicated in Table I, the Metropolitan Council has thrown its major energies into these crisis situations with spectacular results. During the past ten years water supply capacity has increased by 45 per cent to 345 million gallons per day, while trunk distribution mains have jumped from 85 to 207 miles. A comparable record has been established in sewage disposal, where total treatment capacity has risen to 192 million gallons per day, a 70 per cent increase over ten years ago.[8] School construction represents a third area of equally impressive accomplishments. Under the guidance of the Metropolitan School Board, an ambitious building program has been able to handle a 46 per cent area increase in public elementary enrollment, and a 92 per cent increase in secondary enrollment.[9] Since 1954, the metropolitan area has witnessed the construction of some 175 new schools and 293 additions, at a capital cost of nearly $225 million. The result has been an increase of 166,055 pupil spaces in school accommodations.[10]

In highlighting these achievements, it should be emphasized that water supply, sewage disposal and school construction do not constitute the only Metro accomplishments during the past ten years. Since 1953, the new government has established a 4,800-acre metropolitan parks system; it has pursued a highly ambitious (if again somewhat controversial) program of expressway construction and road improvements; it has provided a unified system of police administration throughout the area; and it has discharged a host of other responsibilities.

However, of all the service activities it has undertaken, water supply, sewage disposal and school construction are of primary importance. Indeed, Metro was established in the first place precisely because these services had reached the crisis stage, and the fact that these crisis situations have been resolved represents a highly notable accomplishment on the part of the new metropolitan organization.

3. Provision of Capital Finances

Metro's third major achievement—the provision of the capital financing necessary to meet steadily expanding local demands within Greater Toronto—represented another crucial consideration that led to the original establishment of the new governmental program. The fact that the new Council was given exclusive jurisdiction for assessment and capital borrowing for itself, for the area's special boards and commissions, and for the thirteen local municipalities provides the most striking evidence of the high priority that Metro's creators placed upon this particular responsibility.

In considering Metro's capital financing record, one enters an area of some disagreement and controversy. To begin with the least controversial aspect of this record, there is no doubt that the new governmental organization has realized considerable savings in the interest rate charges it has paid for capital borrowing undertaken during the past decade.

Although Metro was not established with the primary objective of saving money, in the field of capital financing it has been able to do just that. It was the Metro Commissioner of Finance who first described the nature and magnitude of such savings in his presentation to the first Provincial Commission inquiring into Metro's affairs in 1957. At that time, the Commissioner estimated that the total savings in interest costs on bonds issued during the first four years of Metro's life approximated $21,500,000.[11]

If the Commissioner's same formula is applied to Metro's debenture position through 1962, it indicates that the total savings on interest charges to date have exceeded $50,-000,000.

. . . A second, reasonably non-controversial aspect of the Metro record relates to the continued rate of growth in Metropolitan Toronto's assessment base that has supported Metro's capital borrowing program during the past ten years.

An evaluation of the value of building permits issued in the metropolitan Toronto area indicates an average annual increase of $166,005,000 during the period 1947 to 1953.[12] Subsequently, the value of such permits has jumped to an average increase of $352,775,000 during the period 1954 to 1961.[13] While both inflation and the population increases accompanying a new surge of immigration help to explain this annual rise in building permit values, the figures do indicate the dramatic growth that the metropolitan Toronto area has been experiencing since the inception of Metro some ten years ago.

. . . In the field of capital financing, inequalities between the different municipalities may well have taken place during the past ten years, but these may have been primarily the result of factors external to Metro, rather than any major actions on the part of Metro itself. The significance of Metro's achievement derives from the fact that it has enabled the municipalities to continue to borrow for their growing needs despite such external pressures. It has done this first, by acting as the debenture agent for these municipalities; and secondly, by assuming a variety of capital costs that the various municipalities previously had to meet on an individual basis.

Metro was established originally to provide the capital financing necessary to meet exploding growth problems throughout metropolitan Toronto, and in the past decade it has done just this. The fact that certain inequities have resulted begs the question of whether the original metropolitan federation concept has perhaps been too weak, rather than too strong, to permit the discharge of such responsibilities in an equitable fashion.

METRO'S MAJOR DIFFICULTIES

The three most difficult problems Metro has faced during its first decade have been quite closely interrelated. . . . These problems are: the development of a growing imbalance in the economic resources, and burdens, between Metro's member municipalities; the failure to achieve a cohesive spirit of metropolitan unity among these members; and the reluctance on the part of Metro and its members to deal decisively with a number of important commitments and responsibilities.

1. *The Problems of Economic Imbalance*

Since Toronto's Metro organization represented a very deliberate attempt to preserve a considerable degree of local diversity within the general framework of a larger metropolitan unity, it never promised to balance out all of the financial inequalities that existed between the various municipalities in the metropolitan Toronto area. Certainly, for example, this scheme was not designated to produce a completely uniform tax rate for all thirteen local communities.

. . . Yet, it is fair to say that, in 1953, the new metropolitan government was created with the expectation that it would at least help to alleviate, if not eliminate, existing financial inequities between its thirteen member communities. Indeed, one of the key problems the "Cumming Report"† referred to in an effort to justify the new governmental program was the existence of an "inadequate and inequitable distribution of existing or potential taxable resources."[14]

There were two ways in which Metro might reasonably have been expected to relieve this situation. First, on the expenditure side, by providing the means through which the local municipalities could share the costs of certain area-wide services, Metro could help to balance out some of the existing inequalities between these municipalities. Second, on the revenue side, through a vigorous exercise of its planning and development powers, Metro might help to achieve a more equitable assessment base (i.e., a more favorable industrial/commercial to residential balance) between these same municipalities.

Considerable care must be exercised in any evaluation of Metro's performance in this respect due to the basic comparative problem noted in the previous analysis on capital financing. Once again, the most meaningful comparison is not that of 1953 to 1963 under Metro, but rather what 1963 would look like with, and without, Metro. Yet the very important question still remains as to how much relative improvement has been made during the past ten years under the Metro scheme.

Two basic assumptions can serve as significant guidelines for any such evaluation. The first is that the financial inequities that existed between municipalities in 1953 should be less severe now than they were a decade ago. The second is that with the passage of time, this situation should be improving rather than deteriorating. The indications are, however, that neither assumption is being met at the present time. Instead, there is considerable evidence to indicate that the financial inequities between the local municipalities are more pronounced today than they were in 1953, and that this situation appears to be deteriorating with the passage of time.

A number of factors help to explain this unforeseen development. First, the local performance of specific service responsibilities has tended to vary more widely between the individual municipalities than originally anticipated; second, in certain key areas, Metro's relative share of service costs

† This was the report of the Ontario Municipal Board, under the chairmanship of Lorne R. Cumming, which originally recommended the creation of the new metropolitan government in 1953.

has failed to keep pace with the increasing burdens that have been carried by the local municipalities themselves; and third, there has been no real equalization of the basic resources (i.e., assessment base) of the thirteen local municipalities. . . .

2. The Problems of Metropolitan Unity

When the "Cumming Report" was issued in 1953, it noted the "serious cleavage of interest" that existed between the City of Toronto and the twelve other municipalities, and expressed the hope that a "better spirit of metropolitan unity" would be realized in future years.

Perhaps if one of the Report's major organizational recommendations had been followed, the development of this spirit of unity could have been expedited. The Report proposed that the City of Toronto should have four members on the new Metropolitan Council, while the twelve suburbs should have an equal number of members drawn from four suburban "divisions," each of which would appoint one councillor. Although this arrangement would not have alleviated any potential city-versus-suburbs split, it at least represented a step in the direction of breaking down narrow local identities within the suburban community. When the Provincial Legislature rejected this proposal in favor of a twenty-four-member constituency-unit system of representation (i.e., one representative for each of the twelve suburban municipalities plus twelve for the City of Toronto), it both helped and hindered the future development of the new metropolitan government.

As previously argued, the help came from the fact that such an arrangement tended to minimize the potentialities of an external attack upon the new governmental body by local political leaders. Because these leaders were involved in the formulation of Metro policies, they understood what these policies were all about, and they were in a position to translate the significance of the policies to their local communities. In essence, the Toronto arrangement provided the means for a close liaison between the new Metro Council and the existing local municipalities. Yet the price the Council has been forced to pay for such potential liaison has been a very severe one.

In effect, the representative arrangements adopted by the Province have tended to turn the new metropolitan government into a very real "Assembly of Sovereign States." Since the Metro Council members are the actual Mayors, Reeves or other local political leaders of their constituent councils,‡ it has been virtually impossible for these members to ignore parochial interests in approaching their Metro responsibilities. Under the circumstances, Council deliberations can easily turn into bargaining sessions, in which local representatives tend to place more emphasis upon their respective constituencies than upon the larger needs of the metropolitan community taken as a whole.

The appearance of such a conflict is not a new problem unique to the Toronto Council. Despite Edmund Burke's historic plea for the broad exercise of representative judgment, political man has always experienced considerable difficulty reconciling the tug of local demands with some larger concept of community interest, even under the very best of circumstances. Yet by placing local leaders (who have been elected to oversee the interests of their individual communities) upon its Council, Toronto's metropolitan government has tended to magnify this already difficult problem to the breaking point. It is hard enough to serve one master well, much less two, and perhaps the best insight that can be gained into the true nature of the Toronto Councillors' dilemma is to visualize a Canadian Parliament made up solely of Provincial Premiers, or a United States Congress consisting of fifty State Governors.

This potential drift toward parochialism has been reinforced by the pattern of the area's population growth during the past ten years:

TABLE II
POPULATION GROWTH (1953–63)[15]

	1953	1963	% Increase
City of Toronto	665,502	644,358	— 3.2
"Inner Ring"			
York	100,463	126,511	+ 25.9
East York	65,736	71,300	+ 8.5
Forest Hill	17,719	21,513	+ 21.4
Leaside	15,910	18,853	+ 18.5
Mimico	12,301	17,989	+ 46.2
New Toronto	11,190	12,924	+ 15.5

‡ In the case of the City of Toronto, the twelve members are the Mayor, the two City Councillors with the highest popular vote, and nine City Aldermen. The member for each suburban municipality is the Reeve or the Mayor.

Long Branch	9,140	11,091	+ 21.3
Weston	8,374	9,832	+ 17.4
Swansea	8,344	9,249	+ 10.8
"Outer Ring"			
North York	110,311	286,446	+160
Scarborough	78,803	230,338	+192.3
Etobicoke	70,209	165,001	+135
Totals	1,174,002	1,625,405	+ 38.4

The basic result of this growth has been to increase further the population inequities of a previously inequitable representative arrangement. By 1963, North York, with some 17 per cent of the area's total population, had one representative on the Metropolitan Council, while Swansea, with considerably less than 1 per cent of the population, also retained its one member. The seven smallest municipalities contained only 5 per cent of the total area population but almost 30 per cent of the seats on the Council. A similar, although not as dramatic imbalance was becoming apparent with respect to the City's position. Whereas in 1953, the City had to be given half the Council seats on the grounds that it contained 57 per cent of the area's total population, by 1961 the City had dropped to 40 per cent of the area's total population, yet it still retained its twelve Council seats.

While the most obvious implication of this situation has been a growing representative imbalance on the Council, its more subtle manifestation has taken the form of a more parochial approach toward Council deliberations. Representatives of the smaller municipalities, realizing that they are the beneficiaries of a representative system that defies any logical justification, can hardly help being tempted to adopt an increasingly defensive and protective attitude toward their existing position. Representatives of the larger suburban units, looking on themselves as the victims of an injustice, are equally tempted to adopt an increasingly more aggressive pursuit of their own local interests. These psychological attitudes have tended to split the smaller and the larger suburban communities on a number of issues. Yet, the Council has always operated under the threat that the twelve suburbs would, in fact, be able to realize a total alignment of forces and thus produce a complete deadlock in the form of a basic city-versus-suburbs split.

During earlier years, the appearance of any such division

was forestalled by Chairman Gardiner's forceful leadership, coupled with the ability of the twelve City representatives to organize themselves as a unit, and thus carry the day by picking up one or two "strays" from the initially disorganized suburbs. As a result, the only serious early City-suburban break occurred in the form of a bitter fight over water rate charges, with the issue not being resolved until Chairman Gardiner had twice cast his tie-breaking vote. A second major break threatened to occur in late 1961 when Toronto Mayor Nathan Phillips made a major push for his total amalgamation scheme, but the Council rejected this idea decisively by an 18 to 5 vote, with six of the City representatives deserting their Mayor.

Yet, while surface appearances may have indicated a relatively mild degree of City-suburban infighting, beneath this surface tensions were building up to a point where only a very slight nudge was needed to split the Council wide apart. Such a nudge appeared in the 1963 session in the form of the Toronto Transit Commission subsidy issue, and the basic stakes were largely economic in their underlying impact. . . .

During the early winter months of 1963, it became obvious that the Commission was destined to go far into the red in its projected current year budget, and it announced that, unless it received outside financial assistance, it would increase fares again on May 1. The Metropolitan Council held a preliminary debate on the question in March, with two virtually solid phalanxes emerging. The City favored a T.T.C. subsidy (the subway lines are located wholly within its boundaries), and the suburbs were against it (unless there was a new fare structure that would, in effect, give cheaper rides to suburban residents). The division was clear-cut and simple; so simple, in fact, that Toronto's new Mayor, Donald Summerville, complained, "Metro Toronto is getting like a kindergarten."[16]

Although Toronto's three daily newspapers, *The Star, The Globe and Mail,* and *The Telegram*§ warned that "The Metro Split Widens," little could be done to head off the impending clash that lay ahead. The die was cast when the Provincial Legislature removed all previous restrictions on the Council, permitting it to grant direct operating subsidies to the T.T.C. if it elected to do so. The Council considered the issue in late April and although a majority of its members supported a

§ All of whom are critical of the current federation concept and favor some form of complete amalgamation of the thirteen municipalities into one united metropolitan city.

$2.5 million T.T.C. subsidy, it failed to secure the necessary two-thirds vote. The final count was 13 to 11, with all twelve City representatives (plus one suburbanite) supporting the subsidy and the remaining eleven suburban members lined up solidly against it. The City's reaction was immediate and bitter, with Mayor Summerville charging that Toronto was being milked by the suburbs through metropolitan government.[17]

On May 1 the Transit Commission raised its fares, thus setting into motion a further series of bewildering procedural and parliamentary maneuvers that defy easy description. The net result was that the Metropolitan Council once again reconsidered the issue at a series of meetings in early May, before finally approving the $2.5 million subsidy.

If the City's previous reaction to its initial defeat had been bitter, its reaction was mild compared with the explosion that marked the suburbs' approach to this second switch in policy. Indeed, two of the "outer ring" giants, North York and Etobicoke, were so incensed as to set off a chain of events that may well lead to the disintegration of the basic metropolitan federation concept as it is presently organized.

Spearheaded by North York's Reeve, Norman Goodhead, these two communities filed suit against the Metropolitan Council, challenging the legality of its action and attempting to have the subsidy declared null and void. Both sides have retained special counsel to handle their cases and the litigation promises to be both protracted and bitter.

This latest action has had a two-fold impact on Metro. First, it has represented a new phase in the deterioration of relations within the Council itself. For the first time two of the Council's more powerful members have launched a direct and massive assault upon the metropolitan body, and in the words of the Council's new Chairman, William R. Allen, there can be "no real winners" in the legal battle that lies ahead.

In addition, the Council's handling of the entire subsidy issue appears to have tarnished its public image quite severely. The newspapers, in stepping up their campaign for total metropolitan amalgamation, have launched especially vitriolic attacks upon the current organization—witness the following sample from *The Telegram*.[18]

. . . Ad hocery, government by gimmick, decision by intrigue, policy-making by playing one faction against another, back scratching and saw-offs—these are the built-in weaknesses of Metro politics . . . Metro is a balkanized state where each municipality subordinates the interests of the whole to its own interests. . . .

Whether or not it survives its current political and legal woes, it is obvious that Toronto's federated government is now in deep trouble. Whatever else it may or may not have been able to accomplish in the past decade, the federation approach has made very little headway toward the realization of the "spirit of metropolitan unity" that the "Cumming Report" so wistfully contemplated some ten years ago. Indeed, the most alarming aspect of the whole situation is that the relations between Council members appear to be growing worse, rather than better, with the passage of years.

3. The Problems of Indecisiveness

The parochial strains within Metro have tended to inhibit the Council's program in a number of distinct ways. First, there have been occasions when the more affluent municipalities have demonstrated a reluctance to share their wealth with the area's less fortunate communities. The resistance encountered in raising the level of maintenance assistance grants in the field of education serves as an apt illustration of this development.

Second, and on the opposite side of the coin, there have also been cases where the less wealthy communities have balked against accepting increased responsibilities on the grounds that it would further jeopardize their already precarious financial positions. The field of public housing provides a dramatic example of this problem. . . . Despite the proliferation of housing authorities throughout the metropolitan area, metropolitan Toronto has witnessed the completion of only 5,000 units of public housing during the past decade.[19]

While much of this delay must be blamed on the problems of red tape and intergovernmental confusion resulting from the complicated housing organizational structure, another problem has been the marked reluctance on the part of local municipalities, most especially the three "outer ring" suburbs, to absorb additional public housing programs. . . .

. . . If public housing is to move forward in metropolitan Toronto, it will have to depend upon the co-operative support of the three "outer ring" suburbs since these three communities contain the only major blocs of undeveloped land remaining within the present Metro boundaries. Yet resistance to accept such housing has characterized the attitude of all three communities, with Scarborough arguing most adamantly that its present financial problems preclude the absorption of additional housing projects. Scarborough's attitude serves as a fitting illustration of the second limitation which has affected Metro's growing inability to act decisively—the reluctance of the less wealthy communities to accept increased responsibilities for major new projects on the basis that such action would further jeopardize their already difficult financial problems.

The third sphere where Metro has displayed considerable indecision is not solely economic in its underlying origins. Instead, it appears to be the outgrowth of a highly pragmatic leadership philosophy that has shaped the Metro operation from its very inception.

There is little doubt that Metro's great leadership strength to date has been in its response to the more dramatic physical service crises that have exerted the loudest demands for immediate and sustained attention. Metro has realized its greatest accomplishments in tackling such drastic situations as those that were to be found in the water supply, sewage disposal, school construction, and transportation services. Although this effort has required a massive organizational and financial capability, it has not placed too many subtle, or even controversial, demands on the Metro Council members because both the nature of these problems and the nature of the actions necessary to realize their solution have been relatively obvious. During its formative years, Metro's basic *raison d'être* has been reasonably apparent to all. Faced with a staggering backlog of previous neglect in a variety of public areas, the Metropolitan Council has had little choice but to emphasize the 'steamshovel approach' to its job in order to build the miles of new sewers and the myriad of new schools necessary to preserve metropolitan Toronto as a going, and growing, concern.

Largely as a result of the pragmatic nature of this initial mandate, the Council has tended to adopt a highly pragmatic approach to all spheres of its operations that has meshed very closely with the personal philosophical orientation of its first chairman, Frederick Gardiner. Stated quite simply, Metro has often been inclined to operate more as a business than as a governmental organization—the more as a gigantic construction company operating under a metropolitan-wide mandate than as a political body responsible for a wide range of social, as well as physical obligations. Ten years' cumulative experience indicates that the Metropolitan Council has been consistently aggressive in tackling the so-called "hard core" problems where results are concrete and obvious, and considerably less assertive in meeting some of the "softer," more socially oriented issue areas where results are usually less tangible and more controversial. An analysis of some of the particular fields where Metro's record of response has not been particularly aggressive indicates the true nature of this dichotomy.

Three such fields are public housing, planning and the publicity and information functions that are involved in carrying Metro's story to the public. The lack of assertiveness that has characterized the field of public housing has already been described in enough detail to indicate that Metro's record of accomplishments here falls far short of its more spectacular achievements in the water supply, water pollution control and related public works fields.

Planning represents another field where a disturbing lack of resolution has tended to characterize the Council's position. This is not to assert that Metro has suffered from any lack of adequate planning guidance at the staff level. The Metropolitan Toronto Planning Board and a second quasi-independent body, the Metropolitan Toronto and Region Conservation Authority, have both formulated some excellent open-space, recreational and general planning proposals that promise to add a great deal to the future well-being of the metropolitan Toronto area. Yet it is significant to note that while the Planning Board has prepared a general master plan for Metro Toronto, this plan still remains in the draft stage. During ten years of existence, the Metropolitan Council has never got down to the difficult business of approving a formal Official Plan to guide the growth of the metropolitan Toronto area.

While it might be argued that the existence of a draft master plan makes any such formal action unnecessary, this is a debatable contention at best. A plan is not only designed to serve as a guideline for future growth, but also as an official policy commitment on the part of its sponsoring agency. Through the adoption of a formal Official Plan, Toronto's Council would actually be forcing itself to hammer out its future development policies and priorities for the entire metropolitan area. In the process it would be formulating a comprehensive guideline that could help to provide a sense of central cohesion to the entire Metro operation. This is precisely the task which the new Winnipeg Metropolitan Corporation has viewed as constituting its primary obligation. Yet while the Winnipeg Corporation is attempting to work out its long-range planning projections as its first order of business, the Toronto Council has permitted ten years to pass without bothering to adopt a formal plan. The Council's record here has been far from decisive.

A comparable lack of decisiveness has characterized the Council's approach to its public information responsibilities. In all fairness, it must be noted that Metro's new Chairman, William Allen, has been making a major effort to emphasize Metro's public education role during the past two years through an increasingly heavy program of speaking engagements and other public commitments. Yet it is highly questionable whether one man's efforts can fill the organizational void that exists in this area. During more recent years, Metro's major public information document has been an attractive annual brochure which summarizes the Council's key achievements to date. It is interesting to note, however, that responsibility for producing this brochure has been assigned to an already busy operating unit, the Metropolitan Planning Board. In effect, the Metropolitan Council has viewed its public information effort as an "added chore" that is to be relegated to an existing operational unit that is already attempting to discharge a full-time responsibility of its own. As is the case with its research and central intelligence responsibilities, which have been relegated without any major staff commitment to the Treasury Department, the Metropolitan Council has not regarded its public information role as being of enough importance to warrant its own central staff organization.

This general lack of decisiveness in the planning, the research, and the public information fields becomes highly relevant if one views the major components of the political leadership role in its totality. In addition to its responsibility to respond to existing crisis situations, any strong leadership agency must be prepared to anticipate future developments and to educate the public with regard to their implications. This is especially true in a democratic society which places a high premium on the existence of an informed public opinion. Metro's forte to date, however, has most decidedly been an emphasis upon response to already apparent crisis situations to an extent where the other components of the leadership process, most especially public information and education, have been largely ignored.

Perhaps the Toronto Council has not been unique in this regard. Urban America's current unpreparedness to deal with a rising civil rights crisis that has been a long time in the making serves as another telling indication of the tendency of our political institutions to limit themselves to the rudimentary elements of a basic stimulus and response pattern—in short, these institutions are all too often unable, or unwilling, to act until after obvious crisis situations are already crashing about their ears. Yet this is a rather dismal picture at best, and indeed, tell-tale signs are now emerging in the Toronto area that raise the question of whether the Metropolitan Council can follow any such course in the future.

These signs are the outgrowth of some basic environmental changes that are now taking place in Metropolitan Toronto, many of which appear to be the result of Metro's own initial successes. As this new governmental organization has resolved many of the most immediate crisis problems that have plagued Greater Toronto in the past, the area's basic service demands have been shifting gradually from the larger public works' priorities of the past to the considerably more complex, and subtle, considerations of social and economic accommodation. Metro itself, or at least the Metropolitan Planning Board which prepared the Council's Tenth Anniversary Report, has begun to indicate a fundamental awareness of this changing environmental context:

> The changing nature of the metropolitan problem is perhaps best reflected in the shifting focus of metropolitan concern. Where emphasis in the first 10 years has of necessity been largely on the basic and essential physical services, that of the next 10 years will be increasingly on social and community welfare. In the first 10-year capital works program adopted by Metro in 1955, the projected expenditure . . . was allocated on the basis of 76% to roads, sewers and water supply; 21% to education; and only 3% to all of the other services and facilities, such as housing, welfare, conservation and parks, and the administration of justice.
>
> The 10-year capital program adopted in 1963 . . . presents a far different picture: 36% on roads, sewers and water; 28% on education; 30% on public transit; and 6% on the other Metropolitan services.[20]

Although the major forces of change at work here have been largely self-generating (i.e., Metro, through its own initial successes, has been working itself into new jobs), certain external factors have tended to magnify the impact of these shifting priorities. The most dramatic of these factors has been a very high degree of foreign immigration into the metropolitan area during the past decade. The City of Toronto Planning Board estimates that Metropolitan Toronto has absorbed some 385,000 immigrants between 1951 and 1960. While English, Germans, and Italians comprise the major portion of this new influx, the Planning Board lists no less than thirty different nationalities as migrating to the Toronto area in the past ten years.[21] Although this changing cosmopolitan population contains the promise of a rich mixture of cultural vitality, it also contains difficult challenges of social adjustment, as efforts are made to integrate these groups fully into the daily patterns of metropolitan life. Here, once again, there is a strong indication that Metro's mandate is now shifting from the physical to the social challenges of urban living. Under the circumstances, the Metro organization will have no choice but to pay increasing attention to some of the less glamorous problems of social accommodation that it has tended to subordinate to its higher priority public works goals of the past.

It is this final observation that relates back to the earlier analysis of the widening economic inequalities that are now becoming more apparent in the original metropolitan federation framework as it was first devised in 1953. During its formative years, one of the reasons Metro has been able to achieve a considerable degree of consensus among its member municipalities is due to the fact that the basic problems that have represented its primary fields of concern have been relatively obvious in their priorities and relatively non-controversial in their implications. While these different member municipalities may have been subjected to widely divergent fluctuations in their own local resources, it was hardly difficult for them to agree that a modern metropolitan community must have an adequate water supply system if it is to survive. As Metro now places increasing emphasis on such fields as welfare, housing, recreation and the like, the considerably more contentious nature of these newer priorities (complete with all their implications of "unnecessary frills") promises to place increasing strains upon the original federation framework. In short, Metro has been suffering from a growing lack of resolution during its first decade in precisely those fields that will demand an increasing amount of its attention during the next decade. It is highly debatable whether the existing Metro municipalities will be able to achieve a degree of consensus on these newly emerging issues of social reform that will be comparable to the degree of consensus they have been able to achieve in the past when considering the more tangible, "hard core" problems that have monopolized Metro's first decade.

Such an observation argues that there may well be political as well as economic forces of fragmentation at work that justify the consideration of some basic changes in the original Toronto federation framework as it was first devised in 1953. . . . The environmental changes which have taken place during the past decade indicate that a basic review of the entire Metro program is, indeed, highly desirable. The new Royal Commission which will now conduct just such a review¶ can consider a variety of alternative changes in the existing Metro organization. Much local press and central city political sentiment appear to favor a total amalgamation of all thirteen local municipalities into one large metropolitan city.[22] A second alternative, and one worthy of thoughtful consideration, was proposed by the Gathercole Report in 1961. This group pointed out that it might well be feasible to preserve the essence of Toronto's original metropolitan federation concept by rationalizing the existing second-tier structure through consolidation of the thirteen existing local municipalities into four, or five, enlarged and more equalized boroughs.[23] This basic theme has subsequently been picked up by a number of suburban leaders.

There is one alternative, however, that lies beyond the bounds of political feasibility. This is the complete abandonment of the basic metropolitan government approach in favor of a reversion to conditions as they existed prior to 1953. No significant group, either inside or outside of Metro, has come out in favor of such a course of action. This fact, in and of itself, serves as the most telling commentary on Metro's first decade. Despite any of its shortcomings, Toronto's metropolitan government, when evaluated in terms of the totality of its

¶ In June 1963 Ontario's Provincial Premier, John Robarts, announced that a Royal Commission headed by a lawyer-economist from Montreal, H. Carl Goldenberg, would conduct a full-scale inquiry into Metro's operations to determine what changes, if any, should be made to strengthen Toronto's metropolitan government in future years.

achievements, has compiled an exceedingly impressive record during its first ten years of existence. It is now the responsibility of its parent body, the Provincial Government, to make any adjustments that may be necessary to assure that this will again be true at the completion of Metro's second decade of operations.

POSTSCRIPTS

(EDITOR'S FIRST NOTE: In June 1965, the Goldenberg Royal Commission on Metropolitan Toronto issued its final report. The following is a summary of the Commission's major proposals.) *

Metropolitan Toronto's thirteen municipalities should be amalgamated into four new cities.

This is the major recommendation to emerge from the Royal Commission report of H. Carl Goldenberg released in June. The proposed new cities under Toronto's metropolitan government (i.e., Metro) would look as follows:

City of Toronto (900,513 population; 54 sq. mile area) composed of Toronto, York Township, East York, Forest Hill, Leaside and Swansea;

City of North York (351,891 population; 69.1 sq. mile area) taking in North York and Weston;

City of Etobicoke (238,635 population; 47.9 sq. mile area) consolidating Etobicoke, Long Branch, New Toronto and Mimico;

City of Scarborough (253,292 population; 70 sq. mile area) remaining as is.

If the Goldenberg recommendations are adopted, the Metro Council will increase in size to 26 members (it presently has 24 members plus a chairman) under a new electoral formula which will allocate 13 seats to the City of Toronto, 5 to the City of North York, and 4 apiece to Etobicoke and Scarborough. Each city will be represented on Metro by its mayor, elected at large, and by metropolitan councillors elected by wards. These councillors will serve on both Metro and their respective city councils. Under another of the report's recommendations, the terms of office for all Metro and local councillors would be increased from two to three years.

* Reprinted from F. Smallwood, "News in Review: Metropolitan Areas," *National Civic Review*, Vol. LIV, No. 8, September 1965.

While the report does not propose any major extension of Metro's boundaries, it does recommend that the City of North York should annex adjacent territories without delay if satisfactory arrangements are not made to provide required water and sewage facilities for the area's northern fringe.

Other highlights of the Goldenberg study are as follows:

• Metro's planning powers should be strengthened to provide more explicit responsibility for basic zoning standards, redevelopment, renewal and uniform building by-laws. A Metropolitan Official Plan for the entire area should be adopted "without undue delay";

• Metro should exercise more formal co-ordination over transportation policy, including arterial roads, traffic engineering and parking. Metro's Chairman should be ex officio a full member of the Toronto Transit Commission;

• Metro should have responsibility for an area-wide emergency ambulance service, and should have increased powers over waste disposal and the development of lakefront parks and recreation;

• The four new cities should retain basic responsibilities for fire protection, licensing, libraries, and important aspects of the health and welfare services. A Juvenile and Family Court should be set up in each of the cities to be financed by immediate increases in Metro's budget;

• The education system should be reorganized under eleven school districts administered by Local District Education Councils, with central co-ordination being provided by an elected Metropolitan Toronto Board of Education. A uniform municipal tax levy for education should be applied on an area-wide basis;

• The Ontario Housing Corporation should act as a single agency for both the federal and provincial governments in dealing with all metropolitan low-rental housing developments, with Metro assuming the remaining municipal financing responsibility for such housing.

It is obvious that Commissioner Goldenberg's major objective was that of alleviating the basic inequities between Toronto's local municipalities that had become so apparent during Metro's first decade. The proposed four-city plan would provide for a more even distribution of financial resources and burdens between Metro's new member municipalities, and a more balanced system of representation on the Metro Council, itself.

While recognizing this fact, the local Toronto press did not greet the major Goldenberg proposals with open enthusiasm. The *Globe and Mail* editorialized:

> If the four city plan is introduced, it undoubtedly will bring into ever sharper focus the desirability of making this a single municipality. That may come in the seventies. For the present, however, the prospect is consolidation—a word which, at quick glance, could be mistaken for conciliation.

Ron Haggart, the Toronto *Star* local correspondent, was even more pointed in his criticism of the report's failure to recommend an enlargement of Metro's territorial boundaries, and he termed the report's education proposals as "beyond belief":

> His (i.e. Goldenberg's) idea of 11 local School boards (the same number as now but representing new and artificial constituencies) is a contrived paste-up, a useless redundancy.

(EDITOR'S SECOND NOTE: In June 1965, the Goldenberg Royal Commission on Metropolitan Toronto issued its final report, which proposed a new "four city" Metro plan for Toronto. This plan was later modified by the Ontario Provincial Government and a new Metro Act was passed in June 1966 to take effect on January 1, 1967. The following is a summary of the major provisions of this Act.)*

Following a lengthy review of the June 1965 Goldenberg Royal Commission Report, Ontario's Premier John Robarts announced a basic modification which increased Goldenberg's proposed four-city Metro into a new six-city plan. This modified plan, as adopted by the provincial legislature, provides for the amalgamation of Toronto's existing thirteen localities into the following new metropolitan municipalities:

1. City of Toronto (population 681,500), composed of Toronto, Forest Hill, and Swansea;

2. Borough of Etobicoke (239,000), consolidating Etobicoke, Mimico, New Toronto, and Long Branch;

* Reprinted from F. Smallwood, "News in Review: Metropolitan Areas," *National Civic Review*, Vol. LV, No. 10, November 1966.

3. Borough of York (138,000), consisting of York and Weston;

4. Borough of North York (341,000), to remain as is;

5. Borough of East York (90,700), taking in East York and Leaside; and

6. Borough of Scarborough (253,000), to remain as is.

Under the new plan, the former 24-member metropolitan council has been increased to 32, divided according to the following representative formula: City of Toronto, twelve; North York, six; Scarborough, five; Etobicoke, four; York, three, and East York, two. Thus, although the city still retains the largest number of council members, it no longer controls 50 per cent of the seats.

In keeping with previous practice, there is no direct election of the new Metro council members. Instead, the mayors and other designated elective officials of the six member municipalities continue to perform double duty on the metropolitan council. The council elects as its chairman one of its own members, "or any other person," and the terms of the members and chairman have been increased from two to three years.

In a second major modification of the Goldenberg report, the provincial legislature reduced the existing (and proposed) eleven local school boards into six new boards of education which are coterminous with the six new municipalities. The new legislation took effect on January 1, 1967.

REFERENCES

1. Ontario Municipal Board, p. 83, and Statutes of Ontario, 2 Elizabeth II, Chapter 73 (assented to April 2, 1953).

2. Alden Baker and Michael Graham, "Big Daddy," *The Globe Magazine,* October 21, 1961, p. 4.

3. *Ibid.,* p. 21.

4. Financial Statistics, Treasury Department, Municipality of Metropolitan Toronto.

5. Frederick G. Gardiner, Address at the Inaugural Meeting of the Metropolitan Toronto Council, January 13, 1961, p. 2.

6. J. Hayes, "Embattled Metro Gets Cheery Word," *Winnipeg Tribune,* November 2, 1961.

7. J. G. Grumm, *Metropolitan Area Government: The Toronto Experience* (Univ. of Kansas Publications: Gov-

ernmental Research Series No. 19, Lawrence, 1959), p. 33.

8. "Metropolitan Toronto 1953–1963: 10 Years of Progress," Annual Brochure issued by the Metropolitan Toronto Council, June 1963, pp. 28–31.

9. "1962 Metropolitan Toronto," Annual Brochure issued by the Metropolitan Toronto Council, June 1962, pp. 26–29.

10. R. Henderson, "School Building Boom," *Toronto Daily Star*, May 8, 1963, p. 7, and "Metropolitan Toronto 1953–1963: 10 Years of Progress," *op. cit.*, p. 33.

11. Submission of Metropolitan Council to Provincial Commission of Inquiry, June 15, 1957, pp. 2–3.

12. Data prepared by Toronto Bureau of Municipal Research.

13. *Ibid.*

14. *Ibid.*, p. 17.

15. "Metropolitan Toronto 1953–63: 10 Years of Progress," *op. cit.*, p. 11.

16. Quoted in "The Metro Split Widens" (edit.), Toronto *Daily Star*, March 19, 1963.

17. Quoted in Toronto *Globe and Mail*, April 30, 1963, p. 5.

18. Toronto *Telegram*, "Metro's Ad Hocery" (edit.), May 8, 1963.

19. Data on numbers of housing units taken from "Metropolitan Toronto 1953–63: 10 Years of Progress," *op. cit.*, pp. 37–40.

20. "Metropolitan Toronto 1953–63: 10 Years of Progress," *ibid.*, pp. 5–6.

21. City of Toronto Planning Board, A Report on the Ethnic Origins of the Population of Toronto, September 12, 1961, p. 4.

22. For an interesting expression of the opposing viewpoint see: Albert Rose, "The Case Against Total Amalgamation in Metropolitan Toronto," Public Affairs Report, Bulletin of the Institute of Governmental Studies, University of California (Berkeley), Vol. 4, No. 2, April 1963.

23. The Ontario Department of Economics, A Report on the Metropolitan Toronto System of Government (Toronto: November 1961).

*Metropolitan Planning: The Past and the Future**

Part 1. *The Effectiveness of Metropolitan Planning*
WILLIAM W. NASH, JR.

Part 2. *The Uses and Limitations of Metropolitan Planning in Massachusetts*
EDWARD C. BANFIELD

Part 3. *Metropolitan Planning: Comments on the Papers by Nash and Banfield*
HARVEY S. PERLOFF

The Effectiveness of Metropolitan Planning

WILLIAM W. NASH, JR.†

The role of metropolitan planning is to present in a systematic way the choice that a population can make in guiding the development of the metropolis.[1]

* Originally presented by the Joint Center for Urban Studies of the Massachusetts Institute of Technology and Harvard University in cooperation with the Urban Renewal Administration of the Housing and Home Finance Agency to the Metropolitan Area Planning Council of the Commonwealth of Massachusetts, June 18, 1965. Of the original four articles, one has been omitted: Nash's has been entirely rewritten and updated; Banfield's stands without change and Perloff's has been entirely rewritten, in each case by the respective author.

† Professor in City Planning and chairman, City and Regional Planning Department, Harvard Graduate School of Design. A Research Associate and member of the Faculty Committee of the Joint Center for Urban Studies for M.I.T. and Harvard, he has been responsible for a number of significant research projects for the Federal government and various city governments in metropolitan planning, transportation and housing. Practicing as a planning consultant, he has conducted his own firm and been associated with Arthur D. Little, the Ford Foundation, and UNTAB as Technical Advisor to the School of Regional and City Planning, Bandung Institute of Technology, Indonesia. A Ph.D. in City Planning from the University of Pennsylvania, he is the author of *Residential Rehabilitation: Private Profits and Public Policy* (New York: McGraw-Hill Publishing Company, 1959) and *Report on Metropolitan Planning Organization* (Cambridge: Joint Center for Urban Studies, 1964) with Charles Haar and Bernard G. Frieden, as well as a number of professional papers.

[1] Robert C. Weaver, *The Urban Complex*, Garden City, New York (Doubleday & Company), 1964, p. 149.

In the summer and fall of 1963, a team at the Joint Center for Urban Studies, under the direction of Charles Haar of the Harvard Law School, prepared a report on metropolitan planning. In it we were seeking prescriptions for effective metropolitan planning as the basis for federal legislation then being drafted by Senator Muskie of Maine.[2] After examining existing and proposed state enabling legislation, questionnaires sent to metropolitan planning agencies, all pertinent writings, and, in addition, conducting interviews ourselves with representative agencies, we were led to one overriding conclusion. Agencies which deal with metropolitan problems are patiently and painstakingly made effective by their members and staffs, not instantaneously born by brilliantly drafted legislation. After briefly summarizing the facts that led us to this conclusion, the findings will be interpreted to develop an operating strategy for the Boston Metropolitan Area Planning Council.

THE NATIONAL STATUS OF METROPOLITAN PLANNING

In 1963 there were 126 metropolitan planning agencies, covering 142 of the 212 Standard Metropolitan Areas in the United States. Of these, thirty-eight served multiple jurisdictions (as does Boston's Metropolitan Area Planning Council), two-thirds covered areas with populations in excess of 500,-000 persons, and more than half were empowered to extend their boundaries by simple agreement among their participants. State representation is found on about 40 percent of the large multijurisdictional commissions, indicating the growing involvement of states in the affairs of their urban centers.

The annual operating budget averaged $433,200 for agencies dealing with populations of one million or more. These funds were derived from federal, state and city sources in that order. Only four of all the 104 agencies reporting on their finances were supported, in part, by a direct agency tax, and two of these were large, multijurisdictional agencies. The staffs of the large agencies averaged twenty-five persons, approximately half of whom were trained professionals. Of

[2] Joint Center for Urban Studies of M.I.T. and Harvard University, *The Effectiveness of Metropolitan Planning.* Prepared for the Senate Subcommittee on Intergovernmental Operations of the Committee on Governmental Operation, Washington, D.C. (U. S. Government Printing Office), June 30, 1964, 209 pp.

course this figure is somewhat misleading, since typically about 5 percent of the annual operating budget went to consulting services.

Because most agencies have neither the funds nor the statutory authority to perform actual functions influencing regional development, they concentrate on population studies, economic analysis, and traditional land use planning. Only fifteen of the thirty-eight largest agencies have undertaken comprehensive transportation plans of the kind currently under way in Boston. Surprisingly, only twelve of all reporting agencies saw transportation planning as vital to the development of their areas.

Less than half of the thirty-eight multiple jurisdictional agencies had completed a general comprehensive plan in spite of the fact that all of them were required to do so. Nineteen were offering technical services to local governments by providing data, undertaking research, and offering advice rather than by actually preparing local plans. In most areas, these same services were offered to such non-planning units as water boards and transportation agencies.

Once their studies have been completed and recommendations have been developed, most metropolitan planning agencies must depend upon persuasion through public relations to gain acceptance of their views. Sixty-one percent of the multijurisdictional agencies issue press releases and more than half publish a regular newsletter. Except for the two agencies serving some form of metropolitan government,[3] agencies must rely upon review powers to gain acceptance for their plans. However, only 24 percent of the multijurisdictional agencies have the power to review actual development projects, and an even smaller number, seventy-five agencies, have mandatory referral powers over local plans. Their reviews, therefore, must be largely informal, and their conclusions aired through their own public relations outlets.

Mixed reactions can be found to the implementation power derived by providing consulting services to local planning agencies. In general, the older, often more respected agencies view local extension services as a means of inserting a metropolitan overview in local development decisions. Other agencies, less strongly entrenched, see local services as a source of potential conflict which could rock their tenuous foundations within the metropolitan area's decision-making structure.

---

[3] Dade County, Miami and Nashville, Tennessee.

The depth interviews with leaders in fifteen metropolitan areas suggested the essential fact that the effectiveness of a metropolitan planning agency increased with its age, provided it carefully nurtured and cemented its relationships with the older, existing agencies. This was particularly true if the agency had assured sources of financial support and the good wishes of suburban forces which recognized the importance of shoring up the area's struggling center-city. New agencies, acting on the principle that discretion is the better part of valor, usually remain silent on controversial issues. Minority group problems, tax questions, and many delicate site location controversies are avoided in favor of simple data gathering, the ardent advocacy of more open space, and the provision of statistical services to other planning or operating agencies.

Perhaps the most significant finding of the total study was that an effective agency provided a means for local and state leaders to reach consensus on metropolitan matters. This led to the study's concept of metropolitan planning:

> The metropolitan planning that is envisioned is . . . of a representative body working with a competent technical staff to provide a factual context for the consideration of policy questions, to study the implications of alternative development choices, and to promote consideration of two currently neglected points of view . . . the area-wide rather than the local, the long-range rather than the immediate.[4]

Our concluding recommendations concerning how to organize an effective metropolitan planning agency were that it should have responsibility, flexibility, and be able to accommodate to changing circumstances; on accommodation, the agency should voice metropolitan objectives without smothering existing concerns or "the legitimate expectations of private interest";[5] on flexibility, the agency's powers and role should not be too strictly determined at the time of its formation; on responsibility, the agency should be required to prepare a comprehensive plan as the basis for its judgment on all major development issues.

The present resistance to preparing a comprehensive plan probably stems from the uncertain stability of most existing

[4] *Op. cit., The Effectiveness of Metropolitan Planning*, p. 1.
[5] *Ibid.*, p. 121.

metropolitan planning agencies. They are not established strongly enough to issue a document containing a bundle of specific policies accompanied by the usual map or maps indicating their possible physical consequences. Our report suggested that if the appropriate functions of a metropolitan agency could be determined and universally agreed upon, a plan restricting itself to these functions should be received with less controversy. Therefore, following Luther Gulick's lead of "particularization,"[6] the report listed the detailed aspects of each large function usually considered of metropolitan concern such as transportation, to identify those parts of them which would profit from a metropolitan overview. Even assuming the nature of a metropolitan plan was derived through careful study rather than the present pattern of trial and error, protracted negotiations among all interested parties doubtless would continue to delay the appearance of a useful plan.

IMPLICATIONS FOR BOSTON'S METROPOLITAN AREA PLANNING COUNCIL (MAPC)

The MAPC is fortunate in having the basic structural elements demanded of a forceful agency. It has sufficient assured funds to employ a well-trained staff. It represents enough local and state interests to lend force to any recommendations growing out of its debates. Its seventy-nine city and town planning area is a reasonable, though not perfect, representation of the "urban and urbanizing" areas of Greater Boston.[7] Its growing membership should command the attention of the mass media in publicizing its contributions to the region's development. Finally, it is assisting the Boston Regional Planning Project (BRPP) in preparing a comprehensive plan to be completed in the near future and used thereafter as the yardstick for measuring the worth of the area's many development projects.

Given this promising structure, however, there remain several critical issues to be decided at an early date concerning

[6] Luther Gulick, "Notes on the Theory of Organization." In Luther Gulick and L. Urwick (eds.), *Papers on the Science of Administration,* Institute of Public Administration, New York, 1937. See also *op. cit. The Effectiveness of Metropolitan Planning,* Appendix B.

[7] Although its official boundaries may be further expanded in time, studies undertaken now underlying a metropolitan plan for the present area necessarily will have to consider a much larger area that is influenced by, and influences the central portion of the greater region.

its functions. These are: its role and objectives in the area's development; the nature of the issues it should examine, and its manner of doing so; and the communication links it should develop with other agencies and the general public to forward its views.

MAPC ROLE AND OBJECTIVES

The MAPC is not the sole agency[8] concerned with developments in the Boston region and representing larger-than-local interests. Duplication should be avoided if the MAPC is to find a distinctly useful role which will crystallize its place in the community. A brief examination of the more important existing agencies should block out the potential contribution of the MAPC.

The Metropolitan District Commission was established in the last century to be responsible for much of the area's water and sewer services, its major parks and recreational facilities, and its network of parkways (which have become an important part of the commuter network). In fact, it was engaged in a form of comprehensive planning from 1923 through 1941.[9] Its constituency is now smaller than the Council's, and its planning responsibilities are limited to the functions it performs.

The Massachusetts Bay Transportation Authority, created in 1964 with wider powers than the MTA it supplanted, has a growing planning division. This division is displaying increasing interest in suburban land use developments because they affect potential ridership on its proposed mass transit extensions. It should also become vitally concerned with suburban zoning, open space acquisition, and highway development plans as the role of mass transit expands. However, the MBTA's interests will be concentrated on their implications for transit ridership rather than broadened to deal with the style of life the area's structure provides its residents.

The State Department of Public Works, with a long-standing responsibility for highway location and design, has recently developed cooperation agreements with most of the area's cities and towns, to assist in mediating the locations of

---

[8] Several of the agencies are the MDC, the MBTA, the State Department of Public Works, the Port Authority and the State Department of Commerce and Development.

[9] Charles W. Eliot, *Planning in the Boston Area.* Paper prepared for the American Society of Planning Officials, 1964 Conference.

future regional highways. This, together with the subregional policy groups established by the Boston Regional Planning Project to participate in the development of its 152-community comprehensive transportation and land use plan, represents local interests over a much larger and more realistic area than that of the MAPC. Again, the main conceptual overview focuses on moving people and goods.

Although the Massachusetts Port Authority's facilities are located in the central city, its search for cargoes involves it in the industrial affairs of the entire region and beyond. Its studies include ones of land transportation to and from the port, regional economic development, the state of the area's financial community, and the Boston Redevelopment Authority's reuse plans for waterfront land use. The Port Authority, as in the case of the Massachusetts Turnpike Authority, performs limited functions but with area-wide significance.

One of the agencies potentially most important to the area's development is the recently reorganized State Department of Commerce and Development. Its five Divisions[10] are headed by Deputy Commissioners whose statutorily broad responsibilities and activities will be coordinated by the Commissioner. Although it is too early to determine the Department's future effectiveness, the Governor is requesting additional funds for the Division of Planning, and the Commissioner is applying for federal training grants under both Title VIII of the Housing Act and the proposed Higher Education Act, Senate 600. With these clear indications that the Commonwealth intends to expand aggressively state planning, it is natural to assume that much of the Commonwealth's energies will be expended in the Boston area where most of its citizens live.

All these agencies, along with many semi-public and private institutions such as the utility companies, the Federal Reserve Bank, and construction corporations, are partners in the area's long-range development. Yet none of these agencies have both the same broad community representation and the obligation to examine all development issues individually and comprehensively with a far-ranging perspective as does the MAPC.

The clients of the MAPC, then, are not just the area's present citizens but its future citizens. The current issue may be the extension of a single mass transit line, but the recommendations of the Council should be based at least in part

[10] The Divisions of Housing and Urban Renewal, Transportation, Tourism, Economic Development, and Planning.

upon the future style of life such an extension would bring to that sector's population. The hurly-burly of present politics should not cloud the Council's vision to the point where it issues expedient recommendations. Its objectives, given this larger vantage point, should be (1) to help clarify the separate roles of the several local jurisdictions in its area, (2) to hasten or retard land developments, whether sponsored by public or private interests, in accordance with a long-range comprehensive plan, and (3) to provide an effective arena for the debate of different and often conflicting views on larger-than-local development issues.

An agency devoted to these ends is notably lacking in the Boston area, and with some care, the MAPC can now fill this long-neglected void.

THE TECHNICAL FUNCTIONS OF THE MAPC, INCLUDING ITS PUBLIC RELATIONS

Recalling the warning our national study provided, critical or "delicate" issues are supposed to be ignored when the survival of a planning agency is at stake in its early days. At the same time, these issues cannot and should not be avoided. I would like to suggest that any issue important to the metropolitan area's development can be usefully handled by one of three service areas, each of which has important time dimensions insuring an agency's survival. These are, first, the immediate provision of information to other agencies; second, the undertaking in private and over a period of months, or even years, of basic studies of complex problems which will yield the solid evidence needed in the Council's debates; and third, the broad dissemination of timely reports about important issues.

Certainly regular releases of land-use inventories, transportation data, population and economic statistics would not only secure good relationships with other agencies but do so with extremely useful, non-controversial data. On the other hand, issues which too often trigger hasty political conclusions should be studied with care before the Council issues its judgments. Such proposals as Edward Logue's recent suggestions to bus Negro schoolchildren to the suburbs for the sake of overcoming de facto segregation could be studied by some of the Metropolitan Area's academic centers with questions of practical application analyzed by the Council's staff in preparation for their debates.

Undoubtedly the more sensitive the issue the longer it would take for the Council to reach a consensus based soundly on the best factual studies available. No public dissemination of any recommendation should occur until after the Council members are certain that it represents their best judgment concerning the issue at hand. Therefore, factual information would constitute the bulk of the early press releases or newsletters, while policy statements could be reasonably delayed.

The Council's allocation of staff resources among these service areas will do much to influence the tone the agency sets for the outside world. An agency devoted solely to data gathering and dissemination may be useful but cannot be considered as a responsible decision-making entity any more than a salad cook can claim to be a master chef. Similarly, complex problems can be studied until their final conclusions meet with apathy; public information programs must have meaningful content or suffer the fate of most third-class mail. Several examples of the possible treatment of some of the Boston area's most critical development problems might suggest how to skirt these pitfalls.

Perhaps the most sensitive issue facing the area is that of civil rights. Civil rights organizations currently are pressing for free access to the suburban housing market, equal job opportunities, and the elimination of de facto school segregation. Some civil rights leaders argue that suburban housing will help solve the school issue and establish cordial contacts with the white community leading in turn to equal treatment at hiring offices. Other more militant voices suggest that such Negro dispersion might be folly because the loss of physical cohesion will result in a diminution of organized function and political effectiveness for the Negro community. These differences in civil rights strategy are reflected in the tepid support or outright indifference of various minority group leaders to the suburban Fair Housing movement, in differential reactions to the Willis Report, and in the recent criticisms of the Massachusetts Commission Against Discrimination.[11]

A cursory analysis suggests that these differences in strategies within the civil rights movement boil down to disagreements over the time schedule for complete integration, and varying degrees of skepticism over the acceptance Negroes

[11] *Permission to Discriminate* (An Evaluation of the MCAD), Massachusetts Freedom Movement, 41 Winthrop St., Roxbury, Mass., October 1964, 9 pp. (mimeo).

might expect in the majority community even if they obtained free access to the suburbs.

Obviously the MAPC must eventually play a decisive role in civil rights, an issue which directly affects 3 percent of the area's present population and indirectly influences the entire population's present and future economic and social prospects. While this issue cannot be avoided, it can be handled forthrightly and constructively without destroying the Council's growing authority within the community. First, the existing facts as to the Negroes' relative share in the area's prosperity could be assembled quite easily for the Council members. Most of the facts are readily available which are essential to sound debate.[12]

Research on more fundamental questions could be outlined by the Council's staff and sponsored by the Council as doctoral theses or research studies by qualified scholars within the area's colleges and universities. Many issues require careful investigation, such as the following possibilities: the appropriate aims of welfare programs for the Negro community;[13] the opportunities for political participation given various patterns of residential dispersion; the conditions and degree of social acceptance accorded the area's Negroes presently living in suburbia; the effectiveness of the Commonwealth's current civil rights laws; and the possible economic and social impacts upon public facilities and services should the Negro find full entry into the suburbs. The findings of these studies as well as the immediate facts assembled by the staff should be regular agenda items, of which one aspect should be the decision concerning materials to be prepared for public release.

Another broad issue, not entirely unrelated to the question of civil rights, is that of transportation improvements. The broad lines of a regional transportation plan will soon be made available by the Boston Regional Planning Project. Probably this will consist of the presently planned interstate system together with contemplated mass transit extensions. It should include recommendations concerning the sequence of construction or improvements of all major arterials, interchanges and terminals. These plans will probably be placed in the

[12] See the papers prepared by the Housing Advisory Research Committee of the Massachusetts Commission Against Discrimination in Housing, the Willis Report, Leon Mayhew's Harvard doctoral dissertation, *Law and Equal Opportunity*, 1962, etc.

[13] See *Youth in the Ghetto: A Study of the Consequences of Powerlessness* (Harlem Youth Opportunities Unlimited, Inc.), 1964.

hands of the Council along with the tacit responsibility to nudge the operating agencies and recipient communities into decisive action. The past few years make it quite apparent that some elements in the plan will be vigorously resisted. The extension of Route 2 and the Inner Belt highway in Cambridge, the extension of the Southwest Expressway from Route 128 to the Inner Belt in Boston,[14] the extension of an integral MBTA line to the South Shore are all issues that continue to ignite much heated opposition. Inevitably these carefully conceived plans will continue to generate debate in the center of which the Council should find itself before its position in metropolitan affairs is completely secure.

Constructive studies may be demanded to identify properly the underlying reasons behind opposition statements. Cambridge's reluctance to sponsor highway construction may be politically inspired at the present time, but it rests on much more solid ground. A study of whether the potential relocation burden can be responsibly handled, given the heavy volume of displacement from other cities in the Metropolitan Area, and an investigation of its effects on Cambridge's tax rolls in the context of other developments in the community, could set the issue in a more balanced perspective for the Council's discussion. Similarly useful would be studies of the impact of projected traffic volumes carried by the Southwest Expressway on the Massachusetts Turnpike Authority's bond redemption schedule, and the socio-economic characteristics of population increments in suburban communities following transit extensions.[15]

This is by no means exhaustive of the useful studies that could be undertaken with respect to transportation. Certainly the Council's staff could suggest many other, and perhaps more timely, studies. To avoid being accused of unnecessary

---

[14] The author estimated that at least twenty-three thousand families would be displaced by presently proposed highway construction and urban renewal clearance in the Boston Metropolitan Area within the next decade. This does not include possible displacement caused by rehabilitation under public renewal, other public construction, or private activities. Resistance to highway construction in dense urban areas, therefore, is not surprising in a housing market with less than 2.5 percent vacancies. *The Impact of Public Programs on the Low-income Housing Market in the Boston Metropolitan Area,* Massachusetts Commission Against Discrimination in Housing, 1963 (mimeo).

[15] Some observers have suggested that the South Shore wants a separate monorail system so that Negro families displaced from Roxbury will find it more convenient to live elsewhere.

delaying tactics, the Council will have to press quickly for the enactment of non-controversial proposals and publicize properly the available facts. This should provide breathing space to either sponsor, or to have its staff undertake more fundamental studies clarifying the more debatable elements in the plan.

Proposals for additional local taxes are another major issue calling for a definite stand by the Council. The comparative bundles of community services offered by Boston and the surrounding communities in return for a given level of taxation will determine their share of the area's economic growth and related population. Reports of the potential yields to different communities of the several current tax proposals have already appeared. While scattered comments on the prospective burden of taxation have already been made, as yet there is no comparative analysis of the probable long-run effects of either the final incidence of the proposed taxes or of their implied benefits in terms of the community facilities and services they afford.

Many other questions are raised by the tax issue. Among others, how much, and where should additional regional parks and open-space preserves be established? What is the effect of industrial overzoning given their locational requirements? What is the preferred distribution of support for the area's medical and cultural facilities? What are the revenue implications of the area's changing population?[16] What are the potential social and fiscal effects of the Home Builders' Association's perennial proposal to restrict lot size? Are goods distribution costs rising as the population density of the metropolitan population declines and, if so, what other expenditures are declining?

It should be readily apparent that most of these topics are interrelated since they all influence the distribution potential of population and employment, resulting land-use developments, and the whole nexus of community service responsibilities as well as their several capacities to pay. It should be equally apparent that although much scattered information is readily available on some facets of all these questions, no agency is systematically and comprehensively collecting, reviewing, analyzing, discussing, and publicizing these facts or even initiating supplementary studies. These are desperately needed services if the Boston area is to compete effectively

[16] See Federal Reserve Bank of Boston, "Changing Specialization and Bay State Growth," *New England Business Review*, April 1965.

for its share of the nation's wealth by developing as an harmonious and satisfying environment for its businesses and people. Discovering the proper blend for a comprehensive metropolitan plan should be both a first order of business and a continuing challenge.

To recapitulate the steps toward effectiveness, the MAPC should embrace a double role as the Boston region's primary forum for debate and its clearinghouse for development information. While accepting the challenge of every issue, it should act warily in its early days by feeding these issues into technical pipelines of different length, thus assuring that its public statements will be supported by the best possible information, tempered by thoughtful discussion among the representatives of the area's community and development interests. It should call upon the many public and private operating agencies and the academic resources of the area to contribute facts and investigative talents to the continuing reassessment of development trends, policies, and their implication.

This is no easy undertaking. There are no easy prescriptions for survival and success. It will not be easy for the Council and its staff to strike a balance between collecting information for debate and issuing public declarations. The measure of the MAPC's ultimate effectiveness, however, will be its capacity to deal with the so-called "delicate" issues outspokenly and with accelerating dispatch. This will be a sure sign that it is using the right facts to gain a consensus on the area's most critical development problems.

The Uses and Limitations of Metropolitan Planning in Massachusetts

EDWARD C. BANFIELD*

Metropolitan planning bodies serve several quite different functions. Some are essentially data collecting agencies. Others are mainly engaged in giving technical assistance of one kind and another to local planning bodies. Others plan projects, or

* Henry Lee Shattuck Professor of Urban Government, Harvard University. He holds a Ph.D. from the University of Chicago and was on the faculty of that institution as well as with the U. S. Forest Service and the Farm Security Administration. He is the author with Martin Meyerson of *Politics, Planning and the Public Interest* (Free Press,

assist in planning projects, involving several local jurisdictions. Still others deal with problems of an area-wide character.

I shall not discuss the first three of these functions. Doubtless they are worthwhile. But to my mind it seems something of a misnomer to call them metropolitan planning. The question I want to consider is what part a planning body can play in coping with problems that pertain to the metropolitan area as a whole rather than to parts of it. If we had all-purpose metropolitan area governments in this country, planning would surely be one of their functions. The interesting question for me is, in what manner and to what extent can this function be performed in the *absence* of metropolitan government.

I should say at the outset that I believe that a metropolitan planning body can make an important contribution here in the Boston area at the present time. But I believe that it is likely to make one only if it recognizes the limitations that the situation imposes upon it and finds ways of working within these limitations. If it allows itself to be carried away by visionary notions of what planning ought to be, it will waste its time and money.

The visionary notion is that planning should be comprehensive. A planning body should take into account all of the principal factors that influence land use significantly—demographic, technological, economic, cultural, and so on—and it should clarify the goals of the community and arrange them according to relative priorities. Then it should lay out courses of action, within the bounds of the possible, so as to attain the goals over a period of 20 to 30 years. The comprehensive plan is therefore a conception of the future as it ought to be and as it can be made. Its function is to help policymakers choose wisely among present alternatives by making apparent the wider and more long-range effects of their choices. It shows how actions in some spheres will affect others in other spheres and how they will affect the situation as a whole—i.e., the general design, or conception, which the community wants to realize. For example, if people want to live spread out over the countryside in relatively low density settlements 20 or 30 years from now, transportation lines must be laid down now with that in mind, outdoor recreation space must be reserved with that in mind, industrial location must be guided with that

---

1958); *Political Influence* (Free Press, 1960); Editor of *Urban Government: a Reader* (Free Press, 1960); with James Q. Wilson, *City Politics* (Harvard University Press, 1963); and with Martin Meyerson, *Boston: The Job Ahead* (Harvard University Press, 1966).

in mind, and so on. If we have a comprehensive plan that shows where people will be living 20 or 30 years from now, we can avoid mistakes some of which may be irremediable. Without a plan we cannot.

That is the theory, and it is a very appealing one. The trouble is that it does not take account of reality. I should like to list four obstacles in the way of comprehensive metropolitan planning in the United States at the present time. Any one of these obstacles should be enough to give the would-be comprehensive planner pause. Taken all together, they should stop him in his tracks.

1. Change occurs so rapidly in our society that it seldom makes sense to try to look ahead more than five years. The importance of technological change is obvious: just one invention may drastically change the pattern of metropolitan growth. (For example, what will be the effect of the vertical take-off plane on the cities?) But changes in consumer tastes and in public opinion occur just as fast and may be even more important. (Who even five years ago predicted the civil rights revolution? And who will say what the relations between the races will be five years from now?) It is impossible to provide now for the future as people will want it 10, 20, or 30 years from now if we have no way of knowing what they will want. If we assume that there will be no depression and no war (both large assumptions) we can make some plausible guesses as to average per capita income 10 or 20 years hence. But what part of that income will people choose to take in the form of leisure? And how will they use their leisure? Will they prefer indoor recreation or outdoor? Will they want still lower densities in the suburbs and exurbs or still higher ones downtown? Except as we have answers to such questions we cannot plan. And we cannot have answers that are worth anything.

2. A metropolitan area (or for that matter a city) has no goals. Planners cannot discover a set of "public purposes" toward the realization of which their plans can be directed because there are none. To be sure, within a metropolitan area there is consensus on many values. Everybody agrees, for example, that it is desirable that people be self-supporting rather than on welfare and that everyone have at least a minimum support whether or not he can provide for himself.[1] But such "goals" are so very general that they beg all of the questions that have to be settled. (Should ADC mothers be expected

[1] Cf. Harvey S. Perloff in L. J. Duhl, ed., *The Urban Condition*, 1963, p. 335.

to work? Should the minimum wage be raised or abolished? What is a reasonable "minimum" support?)

Not only does consensus exist only at the level of "vague generality," it is often statable only in negative terms—it refers to what the public wants to avoid, not to what it wants to bring about or achieve.

3. With respect to all of the most important policy questions there are profound differences of opinion and interest within the metropolitan area. (Should rapid transit be encouraged at the expense of the automobile? Should housing for the poor and for members of minority groups be provided in the better suburbs?) Our political system, moreover, is highly decentralized, a circumstance which offers opportunity and incentive to all those who have a stake in a public question to get and use political power in order to affect the settlement of it. This is the American version of the democratic way, of course, but it leads very often to stalemate or to compromise, both of which are the antithesis of comprehensive planning.

It is true that technicians have more authority than they did a generation or so ago. They are not immune to political pressures, however; they have to take account of the maintenance needs and enhancement of their departments and agencies and this makes them responsive to pressures of various sorts. The important questions are settled ultimately by elected officials (politicians) whose decisions are normally more by-products of their competitive struggle to get and keep office. No competent politician will sacrifice votes that may be needed in the next election for gains, however large, that may accrue to the public 10, 20, or 30 years hence. (It is not cynical to say this. Our political system is designed to work this way, and on the whole it works very well.)

All of this means that democracy as we Americans practice it is radically incompatible with comprehensive planning. (If anyone thinks that we can decide now on grounds of "the public interest as it will be 20 years from now" into which suburbs Negroes should be assisted to move, let him run for office on that platform. A comprehensive plan must deal with the question of where the Negro is to live and work. If it cannot be dealt with on its merits, comprehensive planning is impossible.)

4. Finally, even if the metropolitan area had goals that everyone agreed upon, no one would know what to do to realize them. We do not at present know how to solve any of our more pressing social problems, and some of our problems

we may never know how to solve. We do not know how to educate slum children. We do not know how to prevent the growth in the big cities of great ghetto-like enclaves of the poor and the alienated. We do not know how to build a beautiful city. We do not know what physical form of the city, if any, is implied by one or another social ideal—say, Christianity. "Students of the city," writes Melvin Webber, "are still unable to agree even on the nature of the phenomena they are dealing with."[2] If this is the case, how can they make comprehensive plans?

These arguments would lose most of their force if someone could point to an example of successful comprehensive planning in the United States. I do not believe anyone can. "There is no instance anywhere," a recent publication of the Twentieth Century Fund says, "of successful, comprehensive planning of a wide urbanized region."[3] This is not for lack of trying. The Detroit, Chicago, and New York metropolitan areas, among others, have made elaborate efforts at metropolitan planning for a good many years.

What this report says of comprehensive planning for a region can as well be said of comprehensive planning for a single city. Most so-called comprehensive city plans are not really comprehensive (I doubt any of them takes account of the Negro and of the fact of race prejudice, for example); many are mere projections, or Utopian visions, rather than plans. Of the few that really are comprehensive plans, none, so far as I have been able to discover, can be called successful. Most have been ignored by policymakers, and we have it on the authority of the late Henry S. Churchill that this is just as well. "Some cities," Churchill wrote, "have had three or four official proposed plans. They are instructive because nearly always they show a lot of things that fortunately were never done."[4]

Lately practically all cities have been making comprehensive plans. This is because the Housing and Redevelopment Act was amended in 1954 to require that a city applying for assistance produce a "workable" program and, as soon as feasible, a comprehensive plan. Most cities, apparently, go

---

[2] Melvin M. Webber, in Lowdon Wingo, Jr., ed., *Cities and Space,* Johns Hopkins University Press, 1963, p. 23.

[3] Wolf Von Eckardt, *The Challenge of Megalopolis,* The Macmillan Company, 1964, p. 121.

[4] Henry S. Churchill, *The City Is for People,* Second Edition.

through the motions of making plans merely to get federal money. ("Too many communities," Dennis O'Harrow, the Executive Director of the American Society of Planning Officials, told a Congressional committee, "treat the existing workable program requirements merely as a bit of redtape between themselves and all that Federal money.")[5] My guess is that plans made to meet federal requirements are rarely discussed by city councils, newspapers, and candidates for office, that they seldom reflect the intentions of the principal actors on the local scene, and that their provisions are generally unknown to the policymakers who are supposed to be guided by them.[6]

This is not simply because there is a temporary shortage of competent planners and the cities meanwhile must get on with the job. It is true that only a handful of planners had ever attempted to make comprehensive plans before the federal government began to require them; even now most planning schools do not give courses on how to make comprehensive plans. This lack of trained personnel would be unaccountable, however, if it were not that in the American political system the making of comprehensive plans, as distinguished from the manufacture of documents to satisfy federal requirements, has never been a real possibility.

If comprehensive planning is not practicable within a single city, what chance has it within a metropolitan area? Within the city there is a general-purpose government, albeit perhaps a very weak one, capable, at least in principle, of laying down some general lines of policy. The metropolitan area, by contrast, is a political no-man's land into which a planning body ventures at its peril.

This is one reason, I suppose, why so many metropolitan planning bodies have confined themselves to collecting data, helping local planning bodies, and other such innocuous and largely futile tasks. Without some political direction, a planning body cannot even make a stab at comprehensive planning. Consider the example of the Boston Regional Planning Project, one of the most competent and heavily financed undertakings that has yet gone under the name of planning anywhere. The Project's endeavors are called planning, but only

[5] U. S. Senate, *Metropolitan Planning*, Hearings before the Subcommittee on Intergovernmental Relations of the Committee on Government Operations, 88th Cong. 1st Sess., May 21, 1963, p. 11.

[6] For an account of plan making in St. Paul, see E. C. Banfield and J. Q. Wilson, *City Politics*, Harvard University Press, 1963, pp. 192–96.

because the federal laws under which it is financed require the use of that word. In fact, its product so far at least has been projections, not plans. These show the situation that will exist at various future times (5, 10 and 20 years hence) if the many local plans affecting transportation are carried out. No one believes that they will be carried out. In any case, no one can tell from the projections how any particular local plan should be changed in order to improve the future situation of the region. And even if it were possible to say how the local plan should be changed, no one has authority to require the changes.

Poor as its record is, comprehensive planning nevertheless seems to be regarded by many as *the* solution, or at any rate as an essential ingredient of the solution, to the problem of the metropolitan area organization. Senator Muskie and others are pressing hard for legislation requiring the making of comprehensive metropolitan plans as a condition for receiving Federal assistance. The intention is of course to secure a greater amount of coordination among the many local, state, and federal agencies that are active within the metropolitan areas. No one can deny that a successful comprehensive plan would serve this purpose. The catch is that the making of a plan is precluded by the very problem—lack of coordination—that the plan is supposed to help solve.

I believe that metropolitan planning will serve a useful function if it limits itself to a very few problems of area-wide development that are not being worked on by other agencies and tries to clarify these and prepare them for action by the appropriate political authorities.

In some discussions it seems to be assumed that *all* urban problems are essentially metropolitan in nature and that there exists *no* governmental machinery for dealing with them. In fact, it seems to me, there are very few matters that require being dealt with on a metropolitan basis. Some matters involve two or three or more local governments; these call for inter-governmental cooperation, but not necessarily for management by a metropolitan body. If the General Court gave local governments more freedom to work out cooperative arrangements among themselves (to buy and sell services from each other at prices they set, for example), some needs could be perfectly well met by local action.

The main functions that cannot be well performed on less than a metropolitan basis (and perhaps the only ones in some metropolitan areas) seem to be these: 1) the design of a transportation system, including the routing of major highways, the location of major truck terminals, and the provision of mass transit; 2) the taxation of real estate so that the local service level need not depend upon the local tax base; 3) the provision of the principal facilities for water supply (including storage and treatment), sewage disposal, and water pollution control; 4) the control of air pollution; and 5) the development of major outdoor recreation areas.

Most metropolitan areas have some instrumentalities for dealing with these matters. The Boston area, with the Massachusetts Bay Transportation Authority and the Metropolitan District Commission, is particularly well provided with them. (The MDC has more than once been a model for the establishment of similar districts elsewhere.) If the MBTA and the MDC are not planning, the fault lies with them and it will not be corrected by having an independent body do it for them.

Some planning beyond what these agencies are doing (or might do) is needed, however, in order to take care of certain matters that lie outside of their jurisdiction and in order to assure coordination of their plans with each other and with those of local, state, and federal bodies. As Bernard Weissbourd, a developer with wide practical experience, has written, "What each region now needs is a plan covering all of the agencies already involved in the expenditure of public funds, which states where and when the public will spend its money for water systems, sanitary and storm sewers, highways and rapid mass transportation, and in what areas subsidies will be available for housing. Regional growth can thus be controlled, with private enterprise left to develop variety within the overall framework of the plan. The agencies that decide on the location of public buildings, such as federal office buildings and state college campuses, should also be involved in this planning, because where these buildings are placed greatly influences the direction of regional growth."[7]

Coordinative planning of this sort cannot be carried on without a political base, however. The Governor must be in effect the chief executive in metropolitan area matters (but not, of course, in purely municipal ones), not only for the Boston area but for the whole state. To be effective, metro-

[7] Bernard Weissbourd, *Segregation, Subsidies, and Megapolis*, Occasional paper No. 1 on The City, Center for the Study of Democratic Institutions, Dec. 1964, p. 10.

politan planning must be a part of his general executive functions.

The way to bring about coordination in metropolitan affairs is to strengthen the office of Governor. Some steps in this direction have been taken recently: the powers of the Governor's council have been curtailed and the term of office of future Governors has been increased. In order to make the Governor fully effective, however, additional measures are needed. He should have the final say within the MBTA and the MDC. He should have enough patronage to assure him a powerful bargaining position in the legislature. And he should have a staff that is large enough and technically competent enough to advise him adequately. So long as he must depend for technical advice upon the departments, independent agencies, and interest groups, he is bound to be their prisoner.

A powerful and well-staffed Governor—and probably only he—could force the federal agencies to coordinate their activities with those of state and local bodies. In theory nothing prevents the General Court from giving the Governor powers equal to or greater than those that the Muskie bill would confer. In practice, however, a powerful Governor would probably not need such formal powers. The federal agencies would generally defer to the Governor's wishes out of timidity and fear of "bad publicity."

In emphasizing that the Governor should have the paramount role in metropolitan planning, I mean to emphasize also that the Metropolitan Area Planning Council should have only a very subsidiary role. It cannot take the Governor's place, or share his place, as a maker and coordinator of metropolitan policy because it does not have, and cannot have, political weight. It cannot win elections, and that in our system is the basis of power.

It may be thought that in calling for the strengthening of the Governor's office and for his assumption of the role of chief metropolitan planner I am being as Utopian as the believers in comprehensive planning whom I criticized. Frankly, I do not feel at all sure that these developments will occur; I would be surprised if the Governor's office were much engaged in metropolitan planning ten years from now. But I can see some forces that are tending in that direction. And certainly there is not *in principle* anything to prevent the people of Massachusetts from strengthening the office of Governor to anything to prevent a Governor from concerning himself more with the coordination of policies that affect the metropolitan area. On the other hand, there are, as I tried to show, difficulties *in principle* with the idea of comprehensive planning.

When the Governor's office has fully evolved—I should say, *if* it fully evolves—there should be no need for the Council. At present, however, there is a need for it. It can help to make up for the deficiencies of the Governor's office as it now exists and it can prepare the way for the eventual development of the planning function within it.

The structure of the Council is well suited for these interim purposes. Being formally independent, the Council can offer itself as neutral ground, so to speak, on which the various more or less competing political leaders (especially the Governor, the Mayor of Boston, and leaders of the General Court) can meet. It can serve as a communications link between these political leaders on the one hand and the press and public of the metropolitan area on the other. Through its technical staff, it can prepare the way for eventual political decision of matters that would otherwise be ignored or neglected.

If it is to make use of these opportunities, however, the Council must remember that the center of political gravity is the Governor's office. It must work on problems which a Governor thinks important. And it must work towards solutions which he will find constructive and practical. To some extent it will have to decide for him what these problems are.

Planning differs from administration in general in the emphasis that it places upon anticipating the future and providing for it in advance. If the Council can see even a little farther ahead than can the political authorities, whose eyes are necessarily on the next election, it may prove its value to them and to the people of the metropolitan area.

Metropolitan Planning: Comments on the Papers by Nash and Banfield

HARVEY S. PERLOFF[*]

The Nash and Banfield papers serve to highlight the fact that there is no one accepted view of what metropolitan planning is or ought to be. This is not at all strange or unexpected.

[*] Director, Program of Regional and Urban Studies, Resources for the Future, Inc. Formerly Economist, Federal Reserve Board; Consultant, Government of Puerto Rico; Professor of Social Science and Head,

Metropolitan planning is at an early stage of development; the concept has not been carried very far either intellectually or practically. There is another reason for the differences: city planners and political scientists tend to view "reality" through different glasses.

Yet, there are also some significant areas of agreement.

One is that metropolitan planning should concern itself only with *area-wide* problems, leaving local problems to the local jurisdictions. Both authors refer to some of the functions that are of area-wide interest and importance, such as transportation, water and sewerage, open space, and taxation. But why these particular functions? Neither has tried to provide a rationale for what is appropriately area-wide in scope. It seems to me that such a rationale is necessary in order to provide a basis for agreement between the metropolitan view and the local view and to provide an element of legitimacy for the functions which a metropolitan planning agency takes on.

I would like to make some suggestions along these lines.

Metropolitan-wide functions logically encompass those in which efficiency and/or equity are substantially increased through region-wide activity. First are those items that are of central importance to what might be called "functional efficiency"—i.e., the operational efficiency and the viability of the metropolitan region. An important consideration here—one that is just coming into the consciousness of the people of the United States—is the strength of the underlying economic base of the region and the ability to attract and hold high-wage industries and other desired economic activities. Activities that are essential to strengthening the regional economy reasonably fall into the metropolitan category.

As far as public service functions are concerned, a useful distinction can be made between what might be called the *skeletal* items and the *cellular* items. The skeletal items are those that hold a region together as a unit of interrelated functions. The cellular items are those functions which are associated with given sizes of population and are repeated over and over again, such as elementary and secondary schools,

Planning School, University of Chicago; Consultant, President's Water Resources Policy Committee and Tennessee Valley Authority; United Nations Missions to Turkey and to Israel; member Committee of Nine, Alliance for Progress. He is the author of *State and Local Finance* (1944), *Puerto Rico's Economic Future* (1950), *Education for Planning —City, State and Regional* (1957), *Regions, Resources and Economic Growth* (1960), *Planning and the Urban Community* (1961), *How a Region Grows* (1963).

fire and police services, local hospitals, and the like. The skeletal items are essentially of a utility type or a systems-flow type, including transportation, communications, water, sewerage, electric power, and the like. Incidentally, I suspect that over time a new theory about planning is going to grow up around the question of how to hand flow systems over a wide and diverse area.

A second major category are the *natural resources* or *environmental-setting* items. These cover the watershed and "airshed" of the area, involving problems of large-scale water supply, flood control, air and water pollution. If anybody has any doubt that these are really good regional issues, he should visit New York to see how people feel about water and Los Angeles to get a reading on the issue of air pollution. (Incidentally, the water problem in New York is a direct result of a lack of regional planning over the last fifty years. They're just reaping the harvest now.) Other environmental questions center on open space and space-consuming recreational areas.

In the third category are the *highly specialized services and facilities* that can be supported only on an area-wide basis. These include higher education, specialized hospitals, and the specialized cultural and recreational activities which are distinctly area-wide in scope. In modern terms, these are critical for the viability and the attraction of the metropolitan region.

In another category are the activities that provide efficiency and savings through *cooperation,* as in the case of certain local public services, such as specialized police services or cooperation with regard to the collection of garbage.

Those functions which are legitimately of a basic "skeletal" regional nature can be said to be a logical concern of metropolitan authorities.

In addition to the search for efficiency, metropolitan planning can legitimately concern itself with *equity questions* where jurisdictional elements are key to the achievement of equity. This category encompasses the issues stressed by Nash, including the "civil rights" question, the question of the level of public services which are important in achieving equality of opportunity, as well as the question of tax equity and tax advantages.

The key point I wish to stress is that it is important to provide a sensible rationale for regional as against local functions so that an understandable base can be established. Only such a base can enable an agency such as MAPC to move ahead stage by stage with full local support.

Another area of agreement among the authors is to the effect that a metropolitan planning agency can and should provide an arena for the working out of a consensus on important metropolitan matters to form a firmer basis for metropolitan action. If this is recognized as a central function of metropolitan planning, it provides a standard for judging organization and strategy. An important test, then, is whether or not the regional organization and the tools employed are or are not useful for working through to a consensus on metropolitan planning. It seems logical to follow through as to what this implies for some of the problems that the authors have raised. A substantial amount of disagreement appears around the question of comprehensive plans. There is some logic in Banfield's aversion to the use of the term *comprehensive*. Genuine comprehensiveness is unachievable on the face of it. Professor Nash overstates the case when he suggests that a comprehensive plan is the basis of a metropolitan agency's judgment on all major development projects or issues or that a comprehensive plan is the yardstick against which to measure the worth of the area's development problems.

It seems to me that inevitably quite a few other yardsticks are needed, including partial plans and some rather general policy statements and, most of all, performance standards and procedures. We have to face the fact that we simply do not know how to evolve comprehensive plans that provide a sound framework for decisions about facilities that will last for a very long period of time. This is so particularly since it is not at all clear as to what type of metropolitan physical structure would be most satisfactory and most efficient. Here the reaching out for an area-wide view rather than a miscellaneous collection of local views and the reaching out for the long-range rather than the immediate, as Nash points out, is critical.

Banfield does not escape the central problem of "comprehensiveness," however, when he shifts the focus of activities to functional planning. The same problem appears even if the concern is only for, say, regional transportation. The difficulties are quite similar. For example, there are very rapid changes in taste and technology which Banfield points out as being severe limitations in trying to do comprehensive planning. Certainly, changes in taste and technology in transportation are extremely rapid. Also you have to agree on goals in the case of transportation, since you have to decide what purpose the transportation system is to serve, and you have to reconcile very sharp differences of opinion, that is, you must work out some sort of consensus. In other words, the problems of transportation are every bit as tough as the examples he uses for more general planning. What is involved in transportation planning is nothing other than a lower order problem of comprehensiveness. The key question remains the same. We have to learn how to interrelate the major items in some sort of a sensible framework.

That the issue of comprehensive planning is extremely complex can also be highlighted by the problem of interagency and interjurisdictional coordination of plans. In his paper, Banfield warmly approves Mr. Bernard Weissbourd's view of the need for plans covering all of the agencies already involved in expenditure of public funds. This, I agree, is needed, but it is well to note at the same time that it involves more "comprehensiveness" than any existing metropolitan plans have tried to achieve to date. The point is that the game we're talking about is the *search* for consensus on developmental direction and on policy issues, the *search* for more coordination among agency and jurisdictional activities, the *search* for clarity of both goals and means, and, finally, the *search* for some sense of comprehensiveness—fully aware that we can't even come close to ever being really comprehensive.

As far as procedural strategy is concerned, there is general agreement between the authors. Both stress the necessity for crawling before walking, and certainly before running. They agree that a metropolitan planning agency should attempt to be useful to others, while trying to fulfill a unique function for itself and thus avoiding duplication as much as possible. I believe there is great wisdom in Nash's suggestion that ticklish issues should be fed into "technical pipelines of different length" (that's a nice phrase), thus assuring that the agency's public statements will be supported by the best possible information. Good sound information is a very important ingredient for consensus. (Other things are also needed for consensus, including good sound politics.)

Finally, there's the question of organization. In true Banfieldian fashion, Banfield gives the Council a limited, secondary role, suggesting that it ought to defer to the leadership role of the Governor. But there is a surprising omission. He leaves out of consideration the rather central question of the competition between the state and the metropolitan areas. The difference between a state-wide view and a metropolitan view is every bit as real as the one he acknowledges as existing between the metropolitan view and that of the localities. There will always be a need, it seems to me, for a metropolitan planning unit to reflect a specific metropolitan view, even when there is a powerful office of the Governor. In California, for example, the local interests are so strong that some local groups are ready to split the state in two in order to achieve their interests.

Metropolitan planning is an accommodation to a new situation calling for an adjustment within our Federal system to provide the protection and promotion of a new kind of broadened "local" interest; namely, the area-wide interest of a highly interdependent, metropolitan region. Not the least of these interests is the obtaining of Federal funds for the region. The functions, strategy and organization of the metropolitan planning unit must aim directly at achieving this kind of protection and the promotion of this new kind of interest. It may not have a very solid governmental structure, but the area-wide interest has reality nevertheless. The job of the MAPC, as I see it, is to make this a reality for the Boston region.

Chapter 16

NEW TOOLS FOR ANALYSIS AND CONTROL

In addition to the intelligence system or data bank discussed by Melvin M. Webber in Chapter 14 and to the computer-based, mathematical model as a possible quantum jump in planning technology, there are a number of other recent suggestions for both devising and administering plans and building planning policies. Increasingly, the truism becomes more obvious in urban planning that *means* as well as *ends* are important and that *ends*, often tacit, must be spelled out more thoroughly and precisely as was explored in Chapter 6, "Goals for Democratic Planning." A most comprehensive bag of research and organizational tricks must be readily available on the planner's shelf—as well as much more knowledge about man and society—in order to manage the rapidly expanding urban space and rapidly complicating urban social* structure. Inventiveness, experimentation by the employment of empirical testing (where possible), sensitivity to social externalities and the constant assessment of past efforts are required to guide operational planning. Every planned change in physical form or social structure should be regarded and treated as an experiment, important as a resource to guide future actions.

F. Stuart Chapin, Jr., planner, takes stock of our planning techniques and policies with an eye to a systems approach as the only feasible method of guiding increasing urban complexity. He sees five subsystems, all interrelated and each with a dynamic of its own. The basic guidance system is an operations plan which by modern systems analysis can to an extent (modified by political realities) be employed to cope with the five subsystems which are themselves bundles of techniques. John W. Reps, in his prestigious Pomeroy Lecture before the American Society of Planning Officials conference of 1964, purposely takes a provocative stance in attacking the sacred zoning cow for controlling urbanization, contending that more positive devices of incentive and public investment are needed. *Cookies* rather than *whips* will encourage the private decision-maker to foster the public good; planning should not be remedial and negative, but positive and constructive. Dennis O'Harrow rises to Reps's bait and defends the basic zoning ordinance as one of the tested devices for returning to the citizenry not so obvious external economies and external human rewards.

* This term is used in its behavioral science sense to include political and economic as well as social.

Existing Techniques of Shaping Urban Growth
F. STUART CHAPIN, JR.*

The steady drift of population to urban regions, coupled with trends toward larger families and an extended life span are clearly changes of great importance for city planning. Certainly the take-off base for this growth is incontrovertible: there is no mistake about the expansion under way in metropolitan areas today. What proportions this build-up will reach one, two, or three decades ahead is anybody's guess, but under the most conservative view, the physical impact is likely to be staggering. How well equipped is the planning profession for the task ahead? Quite apart from the never-ending quest for new and improved techniques, what tools do we now have for shaping growth, and are we getting optimal performance out of them?

This paper seeks to take stock of the situation by reviewing the range of techniques available to urban planners today and then exploring ways of making more effective use of them. "Techniques" is used to refer to means for prescribing, regulating, or in other ways influencing the course of events in urban areas so as to produce an intended pattern of land development. Urban growth or expansion is taken to mean the physical extension of urban areas by growth. Though related to urban growth, the renewal of developed areas is not specifically treated here.

In focusing on techniques, this discussion by definition is not directly concerned with goals. Yet in some respects, a goal

* Professor, Department of City and Regional Planning, and Director, Center for Urban and Regional Studies at the University of North Carolina, Chapel Hill. He has served as Community Planner for the Tennessee Valley Authority, Director of Planning at Greensboro, N.C., and past President of the Association of Collegiate Schools of Planning. He has contributed to a half dozen books and is the author of *Urban Land Use Planning* (University of Illinois Press, Second Edition, 1965), co-editor and contributor, *Urban Growth Dynamics* (John Wiley & Sons, 1962) as well as author of various journal articles and research monographs. The following article has been adapted and reprinted with permission from the *Journal of the American Institute of Planners*, "Taking Stock of Techniques for Shaping Urban Growth" in the May 1963 issue which was based on a paper appearing in *Urban Expansion—Problems and Needs*, The Administrator's Spring Conference, Housing and Home Finance Agency, June 1962.

image of the form of the city as it may develop and assume a semblance of reality in the consciousness of the community constitutes a technique in itself—in the long run, perhaps the most powerful technique of all. The Center City image of Philadelphia indicates how an idea can achieve momentum of this kind. While there is thus power to an idea that in effect makes it a technique, for purposes of this discussion goals per se are not considered.

BACKGROUND

Techniques in use in urban areas today are a curious patchwork of devices, many an outgrowth of special-purpose efforts to meet particular problems and needs of their time, and many bearing the mark of the fragmented governmental situations that have prevailed during the period when the techniques evolved. We do not have to look far to see that urban growth problems have been with us for some time, but only in the post-World War II period of growth have we begun to see the serious proportions that these problems can reach in the years immediately ahead. Until recently it was common to find techniques developed and administered on an individual basis, each serving a purpose with respect to a problem or need and each treated unilaterally for that purpose alone. The "Balkanization" of governmental jurisdictions in metropolitan areas has greatly complicated the situation, and until improved mechanisms of intergovernmental collaboration are developed and put into practice, this situation is likely to continue to be a source of difficulty and confusion.

Many of the techniques were pioneering developments of their time and came into being with much travail. The persistence of a technique—its ability to weather change and resist attack through the ensuing years and, indeed, repel modernization and readaptation—appears to bear some relationship to the extent of baptismal fire it faced in the beginning. Zoning offers a classic illustration of a war horse which has achieved great strength by dint of the battles it has been through. Acceptance was slow to develop, and even after its initial validity as a technique was established, it went through many tests. To survive, therefore, techniques such as zoning have become so thick-skinned that they seem to have an immunity to reevaluation and modification. Families and businesses which made location decisions on the basis of these measures view their modernization with suspicion—sometimes with justification. Further, the custodians of these techniques sometimes add to the climate of resistance. Local officials frequently are unable to free themselves from the memories of the battles encountered in getting acceptance of the technique and behave in ways which slow up the readaptation of old techniques to mesh with new ones.

Thus the evolution of techniques one at a time and in segmented jurisdictions, and the resistance to change that goes with the hard-won acceptance of a technique, have all contributed to the patchwork inheritance we have today. But in a changing society where values, modes of behavior, and their governing precepts are shifting rapidly, there is constant pressure to modify techniques of shaping urban growth. Now that the magnitude of growth and the outlines of the problems that lie ahead can be seen more clearly, there is a willingness to try new techniques which were unheard of before World War II. There is also a greater emphasis on positive measures, a deepening interest in pinning down goals of urban growth and expansion and in defining alternative land development and transportation patterns for fulfillment of these goals. To reach decisions where choices must be made forces local officials and groups into a wider scope of approach to problems and needs of expansion. This enlarged perspective in turn makes for a more favorable climate for acceptance of new techniques and adaptation of old ones. It permits an approach that looks beyond the present or even the decade ahead, and views urban expansion in terms of a whole sequence of growth stages where techniques are utilized in varying matched combinations at different points in time. This dynamic approach is fundamental in evaluating techniques for guiding urban development.

What are the techniques that have been used to date in regulating, directing, or in other ways influencing urban expansion, and what are the objectives implicit in each? How might they be used with greater effectiveness? Techniques in use today might be classified in any number of ways, but for purposes of this discussion they are listed on a basis that will fit into the guidance system approach proposed at the end of this paper:

1. A general plan for the metropolitan region
2. The urban development policies instrument
3. A metropolitan area public works program

4. An urban development code
5. An informed metropolitan community

Implicit in this listing is an over-all organizing force which is customarily embodied in the general plan. But in performing this organizing role, the plan functions as a technique through the medium of the other techniques which succeed it on the list. Also implicit is the mutual reinforcement that the last four groups of techniques supply to one another and the notion that techniques can be employed in strategic and linked combinations. These interrelationships among techniques will be taken up in the last part of this paper.

1. *A General Plan for the Metropolitan Region*

The general plan—variously known as the comprehensive plan, master plan, guide plan, development plan—is perhaps the oldest of the techniques for guiding urban expansion in use today. The use of a plan for organizing the structure and form of urban settlements goes back well before the Christian era. In recent times, especially in the Western World, the effectiveness of a plan in guiding development has been dependent on how well-related it is to the decision-making process of governing bodies. This dependence has given rise to the emphasis that today is placed on the planning process and the function of planning in government.

Acceptance of the general plan concept is not universal. Indeed, the concept has been under heavy attack in the past few years. Much of the criticism can be expected as a normal outgrowth of the first large-scale test of the concept, for until the 701 Program came along, the instances where the general plan was used as an instrument of decision-making by local governments were not many. Under the spotlight, the fly specks of the general plan suddenly assume enormous proportions. There are also whole new legions of "experts" on the scene who provide a considerable claque in the politics of finding fault with a concept. But with all the growing pains of a concept undergoing its first widespread test, it is well to note some of the more basic criticisms that lie beneath the smoke.

There are many worthy of note. Perhaps the most fundamental criticism in recent time is the inadequate attention given to the human and social issues as they relate to the general plan—the values and behavior patterns of urban society differentiated as to their legitimacy to serve as social norms of the day. While the economic basis sustaining urban life has long been respected in plan-making, city planning has had less to do with social structure and social interaction. More and more today we see emphasized that planning must take into account the security of the individual and the group, their social as well as physical well-being and their opportunities for social interaction as well as economic advancement. Besides focusing on the physical environment, the plan is more and more seen as an instrument for defining a whole range of needs connected with urban life.

Another very fundamental and often repeated criticism is the Rip Van Winkle history of the general plan concept in many communities—a failure to follow through on the original legislative grant of authority to develop and adopt the general plan, often resulting in a decimation of the concept by the use of such techniques as zoning and subdivision control without first preparing the plan on which they were supposed to be based. Indeed, the traditional concept of a plan consisting of a mapped presentation of spatial relationships has been found wanting. Having found a long history of ineffectual use of plans in traditional map forms, Charles M. Haar suggests the use of "land development plan" as a more precise term for the subject matter presented in plans and proposes putting the main emphasis on the enunciation of policies and standards rather than on a map of proposals.

A whole series of criticisms focus on the nature of the plan itself. One of these sources of criticism points to the mechanistic and unimaginative character of plans, a complete blackout in the area of urban design. Another points to the absence of any consideration of attitudes and preferences of people living in the urban area, and another singles out the blind spot in plans with respect to the tensions and pace of modern-day living patterns, a seeming lack of consideration of their adverse effects.

Another group of criticisms is leveled at some of the old concepts of planning. For example, the neighborhood unit concept came under fire in the early 'fifties on grounds that it had become an over-romanticized concept being perverted to selfish ends and used as an instrument of segregation. Now, fifteen years later, still in a cloud of doubt, the concept is under attack on other grounds. The new criticism maintains that the concept is rendered obsolete by technological change and altered living patterns, and suggests that not only are many neighborhood concepts obsolete but that many other long-

accepted principles and standards of planning must be re-
examined and adapted to the present-day character and locus
of activities of the average metropolitan area household. It is
pointed out that these changes have stretched out distances
and changed the whole scale of the general plan. Such criticisms indicate some of the pressures that the planning field
is facing in updating the general plan concept and keeping it
in a central position as a technique for shaping urban growth.

These very criticisms indicate an underlying strength that
the general plan concept possesses, and this strength will undoubtedly increase as more research and study are focused
on these problems. The strength of the general plan as a
technique derives from the perspective it gives of the interrelationships between functional, time, and spatial components
of urban development. In a functional context, it provides an
overview of the structural relationships among land use, transportation, and community facilities and services. In a time
context, it provides for sequence or scheduled progression of
public action in relation to urban expansion, and in a spatial
context it establishes the pattern and form of urban expansion.

In recent years there has been a tendency for the general
plan to be set forth in three levels of detail. First, there is the
"horizon" concept of urban expansion in the larger region,
usually expressed in a very generalized pattern as a "goal
form" for growth and development. It has no time schedule
and no price tag attached. Second, there is the traditional version of the plan—a coordinated set of proposals for development over a 20- to 25-year period, with its recommended
general priority schedule, financial program, and various actions needed in effectuating the plan. As a plan which may be
formally adopted, it frequently focuses on a particular jurisdiction. The third concept involved in the general plan is short-
term, often a five-year scheme, essentially a first stage to the
20-year plan which becomes the basis for the capital budget of
the governing body. A more extended form of this kind of
improvement program, called the "Community Renewal Program," has been stimulated by federal aid in recent years.

Implicit in the general plan concept is the necessity for relating plans to the flow of time and for progressive refinement
of the more distant-horizon proposals so that they may be
introduced into the decision-making process at the proper
time and carried forward from the 20-year docket to the five-
year schedule. There is also the necessity for re-evaluation of

proposals in the pipeline against the unpredictable changes that emerge and alter the validity of the basic premises of the general plan.

While the concept is therefore well defined, this does not insure that the plan will be used to guide growth. There are several fundamental requirements which must be fulfilled if the plan is to have force and effect. First, the effectiveness of the general plan as a technique is dependent on the imaginativeness of the plan itself and its power to inspire wide support. Second, it is dependent on the technical practicability of the plan and its power to inspire confidence. Finally, it is dependent on the extent to which planning is in the mainstream of decision-making.

The imaginativeness of the plan is directly related to its success in dealing with the living qualities of cities, the extent to which it recognizes how the city affects man's sense and his satisfactions with his surroundings, and thus his outlook and behavior generally. Few general plans have been based on considerations that go deeply into livability and the psychological adjustments that residents must make to emerging forms of urban society; few have given much consideration to the ways in which urban design may serve to alleviate stress in day-to-day activities and make the urban environment more satisfying. To remedy this situation a great deal more attention must be given to carrying the general plan beyond the somewhat mechanistic functional stage that has characterized plans in the past, to a conception of the city as it may be experienced by residents once proposals take form on the ground. Not only must studies of livability and the follow-through in urban design be an integral part of the general plan preparation, but they must be a continuing part of the planning activity.

The practicability of the plan is a function in part of how feasible the proposals are and in part of how competent they are. Feasibility is usually measured in terms of the financial reasonableness of proposals and how sensitive they are to human considerations and the overriding political factors. Boldness and imagination do not mean that a plan is unfeasible. Indeed, a plan may be unfeasible unless it is bold and imaginative. But even with the widespread appeal that comes with a truly creative plan, the cost-benefit aspect of the proposals contained in the plan cannot be slighted.

The technical competence of the general plan must be judged by the extent to which the plan considers underlying interrelationships among the structural elements of the city—relationships over time and in space between activity centers, movements of people and goods between these centers, an availability of essential facilities and services for the various activities. As the plan becomes a greater force in decisions, pressures for improving techniques of analyzing these relationships will increase. More and more, planning agencies in large metropolitan areas will turn to machine methods of data handling and systems analysis approaches in their analytical work. Until recently most metropolitan planning agencies were still struggling with obsolete techniques of a craftsman's era, totally inadequate for the kinds of demands which urban areas are even now experiencing. In this respect, research is of crucial importance in updating planning techniques so that the general plan can assume a more effective role as an instrument for organizing urban growth.

Yet advances in design and analysis are not enough to insure that the general plan will become an organizing force in urban expansion. To be a force, it needs to be something more than a phrase in the enabling legislation or a collection of proposals in a handsome spiral-bound report with fold-out color maps and acetate overlays. The general plan is a politically dynamic concept, influencing the governmental decision-making process and responsive to it. No matter how imaginative and well-conceived the plan may be, it is unlikely to achieve success as an organizing force unless planning is a well established and an astutely directed function of local government, situated in the mainstream of the decision-making process. For planning to be effective at the metropolitan level, governmental arrangements are needed which give planning direct access to decision-making channels encompassing the entire urbanizing region. In sum, a well-conceived plan has a greater chance of becoming an organizing force when there are established channels for handling plan proposals on a metropolitan-wide basis and when proposals introduced into these channels are imaginative and practical.

2. *The Urban Development Policies Instrument*

It is increasingly recognized that where public policy is closely keyed to the general plan, it can be an extremely effective technique for guiding urban expansion. "Public policies" is considered here to refer to consciously derived guides that governing bodies, commissions, or administrative officials of government develop to achieve consistency of action in the pursuit of some public purpose or in the administration of particular public responsibilities. In this sense, policies may exist in a great many spheres of urban affairs not directly or even indirectly germane to urban expansion. However, a great many policies do have significance for the physical setting of cities, and it is this sphere of policy formulation that is of concern here.

Illustrative examples come to mind. Policy on the degree of commitment by city administrations to support various forms of transportation is an illustration. The establishment of a sewer extension policy or the adoption of an annexation policy are familiar examples of policies that city councils may develop to insure a consistent and equitable approach in actions they take on these needs as they arise from time to time. Although not covered here, tax policy should certainly be listed as a policy area of profound importance to urban expansion. Many other examples could be mentioned.

The potentialities of using public policies as instruments for guiding expansion have passed virtually unnoticed until relatively recently. But public bodies are beginning to recognize the cumulative impact that consistency of action can have in achieving particular goals: planning and transportation agencies, for example, are increasingly concerned with the impact that various public policies may have on the patterns of urban growth. There is rising interest in the effect that the service level policies for water and sewerage systems, expressway and transit systems, and schools and recreation systems may have on patterns of land development. Similarly state policies on such matters as stream sanitation, air pollution, reforestation, and other state resource-use programs may exert direct or indirect influences on patterns of urban expansion.

The impact of federal programs on localities is a particularly critical area of policy co-ordination. Federal grants and loans for various public works have long been recognized as a force that directly or indirectly influences local decisions on growth and development. The policies that are established in administering mortgage insurance, small business loans, defense plant location, programs aimed at overcoming poverty and for upgrading Appalachian-type distressed areas, or programs relating to such national resources as land, water, and forests all may have an indirect effect on the form of urban development. Thus, if FHA policies are administered so that in addition to enforcing underwriting standards they provide for direct and continuous co-ordination with local land use objectives, these policies, in unison with local public works policies, can be expected to complement and reinforce local efforts at guiding land development. Similarly, policies on small business loans and assistance in poverty programs and to distressed areas can become positive influences when fitted to a policies instrument at the local level. The accelerated tax amortization incentives for defense plants which meet certain local criteria have been used in the past to implement certain defense policies. Water control policies for drainage and protection against floods, soil conservation, or recreation, all may profoundly affect the patterns of urban expansion. If systematically co-ordinated with local public works and other policies, such federal policies can be made to function in concert with local techniques for guiding urban growth.

So long as policies grow out of one responsible agency there is some likelihood of deliberation and reasoned co-ordination. The farther removed the administration of policy is from the point of application, the less likely it is that policies relating to urban expansion will be enmeshed in one coordinated policies instrument on any spontaneous basis. State policies are likely to be unilateral in their application in urban areas, each administered for the special purpose for which it was established, often without reference to other state policies or to local policies. The same may be said of federal policies. In programs where grant and loan provisions call for administrative co-ordination at the point of application—such as the workable program requirement for HHFA housing and renewal assistance and to some extent the Highway Act of 1962 relative to coordinating federal aid highway proposals with local urban area plans—substantial progress is being made to relate public policies that impinge on urban expansion at the local level. But as yet there is no comparable mechanism to insure that all relevant state and federal programs are co-ordinated with local development policies at the point of impact in local areas.

Clearly the effectiveness of policies as a means for shaping urban growth is dependent on whether the relevant policies can be brought together in one *modus operandi*—a framework for steering public policy—and whether such a framework becomes a recognized basis of co-ordinated action by all levels of government in policy decisions relating to urban development. What is suggested here is a follow-through on the notion that Henry Fagin advanced a few years ago for codifying urban policies in one *urban development policies instrument*.[1]

As noted above, individual policies are often adopted initially for quite different purposes. But if a policy is adopted to achieve some consistency and equitableness in the expenditure of public funds for sewer extensions and to keep expenditures in this area within the fiscal capabilities of local government, conceivably it could at the same time take into account *where* the sewers are extended and the implications this may have for water-main extension, street improvements, and school construction. The thought here is to achieve coordination in policy formulation and thereby accomplish a sounder result from an over-all fiscal point of view and achieve a better pattern of growth in the bargain.

For the urban development policies instrument to be an effective technique, it must be sufficiently concrete and acceptable to the governing bodies concerned to be adopted by resolution. Whether it is adopted initially may be dependent on political considerations—and it is beyond the scope of this paper to go into problems of intergovernmental relations—but ultimately there will need to be a formal statement of policy with concurrence by all participating metropolitan area governing bodies. This kind of collateral action is beginning to develop on a formal basis (for example, the Metropolitan Regional Council in the New York area), and there are numerous instances of informal understandings between units of local government. Such an instrument could become quite common if formal joint agreement on an urban development policies instrument were a requirement in order to qualify for various federal and state financial aids.

The exact content of the instrument will be determined in each metropolitan area from the general plan, its guiding statement of goals for urban expansion, the proposals set forth for achieving these goals, and the timing of the development

---

[1] See Henry Fagin, "Organizing and Carrying out Planning Activities Within Urban Government," *Journal of the American Institute of Planners*, XXV (August, 1959), 109–14, and his more recent statement, "The Policies Plan: Instrumentality for a Community Dialogue," Eleventh Annual Wherrett Lecture on Local Government at the University of Pittsburgh, 1965.

Note the suggested term "urban policies instrument" as opposed to Fagin's "policies plan." The purpose of this distinction is to narrow the area of concern to a more pragmatic usage of "policy," to limit the focus to land development policies within the full gamut of public policies, and to get away from a potential source of confusion for planners in attempting to explain to local groups the difference between a "policies plan" and a "general plan."

proposals. In implementation of these concepts, the policies instrument brings together relevant existing policies that impinge on urban expansion, identifies appropriate new ones, and ties the old and new into a related series of statements. Thus it considers current policies for transportation, utilities, schools, recreation, fire and police protection, and other public services to insure that such matters as levels and intensity of service, areas to be served, and method of financing are working in harmony and not at cross purposes with the general plan. In addition, tax policies, debt policies, annexation policies, and so on, would be examined as they affect land development. Similarly, policies on which regulatory measures are based would be taken into account.

Along with content, timing is important. The policies instrument will need to recognize general growth stages identified in the plan. Accordingly, it may group policy positions into a graded series of "policy bundles" consonant with particular growth stages. Under such an approach, policy bundles may be organized according to the extent of emphasis on development called for during a particular period of time. To take a very simple illustration, policies conceivably could be grouped into these four bundles: Condition I bundle might contain policies which would tend to inhibit development; Condition II bundle, policies which would tend to postpone development; Condition III bundle, policies which would tend to initiate development; and Condition IV bundle, policies which would tend to push development. Such policy bundles might then be applied to particular planning or development areas identified in the general plan (see Element 2 in Figure 1). The foregoing example is hypothetical, for it is clear that how these bundles are actually organized and what is finally set down in statement form within each bundle will vary with every metropolitan area.

Finally, recent research on land development models has made it possible to test the implications for land development of putting into effect different policy combinations. Much more research is needed, but studies made to date suggest that it is possible to establish a connection between a particular mix of public policies and particular patterns of land development. These relationships are complex. It is difficult to isolate the impact of policies from other forces that influence the direction and intensity of land development, and it is difficult to evaluate the lag differentials and take into account technological factors that will modify the effect of policy combinations. But this work suggests that an urban development policies instrument, especially when it is coupled with public works programming, has great potentiality as a technique for guiding development.

3. A Metropolitan Area Public Works Program

Public policy formulation and public works programming go hand in hand. While public policy establishes the conditions under which public facilities and services will be extended, the public works program constitutes a means of follow-through once a policy has been adopted. It identifies specific improvements for specific locations and gives them a priority. If day-to-day decisions of governing bodies can be related through a policies instrument to achieve a more rational pattern of urban expansion, a public works program related to the general plan and attuned to the policies instrument can have an infinitely stronger influence on urban development.

Somewhat parallel to the situation with respect to policy formulation, there are three problems in making public works programming an effective mechanism for shaping urban growth: 1. co-ordination among functional elements of the over-all public works program, 2. co-ordination of public works programming among local governmental jurisdictions, and 3. co-ordination of federal and state with local programs. The first kind of co-ordination is typically achieved through the public works and the capital budgeting mechanism. The second is a metropolitan area problem, requiring some form of intergovernmental collaboration within the metropolitan area and the surrounding region. The third requires mechanisms for intergovernmental co-operation in the planning and the scheduling of state and federal works which are to be constructed in or near metropolitan areas.

The programming of public works properly grows out of the general plan and is an important link between planning and the decision-making process. As a mechanism for guiding growth, the scheduling of public works provides a means of influencing the location, timing and intensity of development in an urban area. The development of an expressway system in a particular quadrant of the metropolitan area will draw growth into this quadrant and along tributary systems of major streets that feed into this expressway. If properly co-ordinated with the construction of sewage disposal facilities and trunk sewer lines, expansions in the water treatment plant and water mains, and the development of school facilities in this sector, these measures can have considerable cumulative effect in channeling growth to particular areas, and in dispersing or concentrating it. Therefore, to insure that these facilities are located and timed in harmony with other techniques used in shaping urban growth, the programming of public works will need to be done in project combinations, probably with the make-up of these combinations changing with each growth stage (see Element 3 in Figure 1).

But public works programs frequently involve decisions made at other levels of government. If HUD's Community Facilities Administration makes loans to local sanitary districts without consideration of the metropolitan-wide water and sewerage problem, and of the effect that unco-ordinated small systems may have on a metropolitan land policy, an important means of guiding urban expansion will be dissipated. As recognized in the Highway Act of 1962, the importance of co-ordinated programming is particularly critical in the transportation field. Programs for improvement in commuter and mass transportation fully co-ordinated with expressway building programs constitute a powerful technique for shaping the growth patterns of cities.

The list of public works that involve intergovernmental patterns of co-operation extends to many other fields of concern —urban renewal, public housing port development, river and harbor improvements, airports, and including soon in all likelihood, public school and college facilities. Can any one decision be divorced from other public works decisions? If the intent is to exercise some consistent and rational guidance over urban expansion, logic will surely argue for some form of co-ordinated public works programming in an intergovernmental framework for joint action.

4. An Urban Development Code

While policy direction and public works spending have been underused as tools for guiding urban expansion, control by regulation has been widely used, often overworked, as a technique for steering urban growth. Here too, we encounter problems resulting from the fragmented governmental situations that often prevail in large metropolitan areas. Under zoning, there is frequently an absence of uniform criteria for the establishment of zoning districts and a lack of uniform standards for use, density, and bulk requirements from one municipality to another in a metropolitan area. Enforcement practices may also vary considerably. Moreover, within single jurisdictions, a problem results from the proliferation of regulatory measures that have been adopted one by one without being related to regulations already on the books.

So far there has been no extensive involvement of the federal government in regulatory measures and only limited involvement of state governments. Indirectly, through HUD's workable program requirement, for example, the federal government has sought to strengthen the effect of urban renewal programs by requiring as a condition for federal aid that localities put into effect or upgrade such regulatory measures as zoning, housing, and building codes. Up to the present time, the state has entered the picture mainly in providing enabling legislation, in enforcing statewide standards in certain areas (building codes, stream sanitation requirements), and in providing assistance in drafting ordinances. However, as metropolitan areas spread territorially and coalesce from one part of a state to another and across state lines, we can expect an increasing state participation in regulatory activity.

To achieve a broader approach to urban expansion and to insure more effective and expeditious regulation, metropolitan areas increasingly will need to devise and experiment with new ways of collaborating on a metropolitan-wide basis. Such ordinances as zoning, subdivision control, building, housing, fire and other similar codes, regulation of open space easements and airport approaches, and rules governing mapped streets and future transportation corridors will need to be brought together and reorganized into one *urban development code*.

The urban development code would reorganize and codify in one metropolitan area instrument the regulations presently scattered through different ordinances in each jurisdiction that relate to land development and the construction, use, and occupancy of structures on the land. Such a code would also include controls in the use of land, water, and air in the larger region. If the image of the general plan for urban growth in an entire metropolitan area is to become an effective consideration in the thinking of the many households, firms, and institutions that take up the land and develop it, a single metropolitan code with some measure of order and simplicity is essential. Developers work in many jurisdictions, and individual location decisions are constantly made without reference to municipal or county boundaries. With the profusion of regulatory measures and the continual tinkering with these ordinances, even the most imaginative metropolitan area plan loses its organizing force and the image becomes blurred in skirmishes with the rules.

Simplification is needed to make regulatory requirements intelligible to the general public as well as easy to administer. In the process of codifying, parts of ordinances dealing with similar matters would be brought together. Thus, site planning features of group housing developments might be brought together in one place in the code, construction requirements in another, and the occupancy requirements in still another. Parts of ordinances which define districts (building use zones, fire zones, density zones) might be brought together so as to minimize confusion for the citizen as well as for the administrator.

In addition to the emphasis on co-ordination and simplification, the urban development code would be designed to function as a positive influence in shaping growth. Assuming legislative authorization for development timing, the code would seek to define in matched combinations varying development requirements corresponding to particular development stages identified in connection with the policies instrument discussed above. Thus, for the newly developing areas, one set of requirements may be featured; and for older established areas, another combination may be employed (see Element 4 in Figure 1). Over time, according to some kind of performance criteria, the combination of requirements would be modified. This kind of flexibility might well be a built-in feature of the code.

5. An Informed Metropolitan Community

This final technique relies on the persuasive power of a sound and logical approach to urban expansion. It depends on a broad and continuing program of civic education and assumes that the residents of the metropolitan area—the households, the industrialists, the businessmen, and the institutional groups—will see the wisdom of planned urban expansion. While other techniques seek to guide the location decisions of these groups by plans, policies, public works, and regulation, this is a direct-appeal technique built around the notion of keeping people informed about the general plan and of achieving public objectives of urban expansion through the cumulative effect of general adherence to sound principles and standards of land development.

While directed to many of those whose decisions to move or locate in the future will account for a substantial part of

the expected urban expansion, civic education is an extremely
elusive guidance technique. A broadly conceived and continuing program of civic education utilizing a variety of communications media will probably exert some influence on location decisions of households, firms, and institutions over
time, but there is unlikely to be a groundswell of spontaneous conformance without some reinforcement from other
techniques.

There are at least four complementing areas of emphasis
in a civic education program. One is more direct than the other
three and is the most familiar of the civic education techniques.
It involves a carefully worked-out continuing program of public information, reporting on problems and needs and the
steps necessary to meet them as they arise in the future. It
utilizes mass media of all kinds—the press, radio, television,
public forums, illustrated talks, exhibitions, printed brochures,
leaflet reminders. A second technique of civic education utilizes the principle of participation to inform individuals and
groups. It seeks to guide actions by developing a sense of
responsibility. Thus, technical and citizen advisory committees
assist in various ways in studying, advising, and publicizing
approaches to such problems as traffic, housing, and stream
or air pollution. A third technique seeks to educate through
demonstration projects of self-help and mutual co-operation.
This technique has been successfully used in urban renewal
programs in several cities, showing how private effort can be
related to public actions in upgrading residential areas. The
fourth technique is directed to school children and, by means
of field studies and school projects, seeks to develop interest
and understanding on the part of children through group investigation and study of their community. Such a technique
has a dual role—it reaches the parents through the child's
interest in local problems, and it has long-range implications
in developing a more informed citizenry for the 10- to 20-year
pull ahead.

Like policy planning and public works programming, civic
education is a relatively underdeveloped technique in most
metropolitan areas today. Direct media such as newspapers,
radio, television, and printed reports have been used widely,
but much more can be done in relating these efforts to a carefully structured continuing program of civic education. To
achieve maximum effectiveness in the use of these four civic
education devices, a general long-range civic education program would need to be organized and timed in close relation-

ship to the other techniques, and to key stages in the general plan.

The individual civic education techniques would need to be used in differing combinations, with some designed for use in particular stages during the preparation of the general plan and others for particular stages in implementation of the plan, in effect backstopping other techniques. Some combinations may be grouped for use in particular areas to deal with particular stages of growth (see Element 5 Figure 1). Thus the civic education program, like the other techniques, has possibilities for much wider application in guiding urban growth.

CO-ORDINATED USE OF TECHNIQUES:
A GUIDANCE SYSTEM

So far, emphasis has been placed on a broadened approach and a fuller use of existing techniques. I have suggested that by making better use of the techniques we have, we can make urban expansion follow more rational patterns. We may also hope to achieve greater economy, convenience and attractiveness of development through the conscious and purposeful use of these techniques. But I have also tried to stress the fact that much of the positive benefit to be gained from these techniques will depend on how well co-ordinated they are, whether they augment or work at cross purposes with one another. Thus we come finally to the notion of *urban development guidance systems*. The terminology is used advisedly. While this is obviously an area where methods of systems analysis can be introduced to advantage, the term is also being used in a pragmatic sense. Thus, each of the five classes of techniques that have been discussed may be viewed as a subsystem to the larger guidance system.

The concept is a simple one. A guidance system draws upon the general plan of the metropolitan area for the underlying rationale in the location and timing of urban expansion —land development, the construction of essential links in the transportation networks, and the provision of required community facilities. Call it a land development plan, a master plan, or a comprehensive plan, it is a schematic representation of spatial relationships and a reference map for points where specific standards are to be applied as spelled out in the text of the plan—standards designed to give an essential balance, order, and relatedness to the functions performed in the metropolitan area. In serving as an organizing force, the general plan thus becomes a key technique for steering both public and private actions so that they produce the desired pattern of development in the metropolitan landscape. But at the same time an urban development policies instrument that specifies under what conditions public services will be extended to new areas of development, and a public works program that sets forth the schedule under which facilities will be built in order to supply these services, become the key techniques for formalizing actions in the public sector. By the same token, an over-all urban development code and a broad-

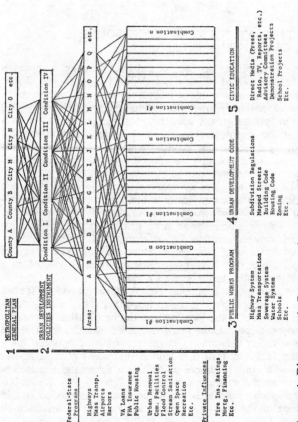

FIGURE 1. Diagrammatic Representation of the Elements of an Urban Development Guidance System

gauge civic education program become key techniques for regulating and insuring more informed action in the private sector. Thus the techniques we have been reviewing are interrelated, and if they are to achieve their fullest potential their relationships must be recognized and given conscious direction through one co-ordinated framework.

Figure 1 is a crude attempt to outline such a framework. In this chart the metropolitan area general plan for a series of counties and cities in the larger urbanizing region sets forth in specific locations in a specific time sequence a series of proposals for achieving certain pre-established goals of urban development. The urban development policies instrument identifies particular bundles of policies which will tend to regulate growth according to the plan. One bundle may apply to a situation where the plan calls for postponement of full development; another may apply in a situation ripe for immediate full development. The bundle appropriate to each development area in the plan is established and applied by collateral action of the proper governing bodies and local officials. The policies applied to particular areas are reinforced by selected combinations of public works suited to the placement and timing of development planned for these areas. Concurrently particular combinations of urban development regulations are applied and particular combinations of activities in the civic education program are launched.

Figure 1 is also suggestive of the complexity of interrelationships among the five subsystems. In suggesting a pattern of over-all organization to a guidance system, it also indicates that each subsystem has a special and unique contribution to make which sets it apart from the others. There is also a dynamic aspect to such a system, not easily portrayed in a chart. In a time sense, techniques organized in a fashion suggested in Figure 1 will provide an impact on urban growth which will produce feedback. In a dynamic system, feedback can be made to lead to systematic readjustments in combinations of techniques employed in the next stage. In other words, Figure 1 is equivalent to one frame in a film-like sequence. Functioning through changing combinations in the subsystems, the guidance system produces a whole sequence of linked frames constantly adapting to urban expansion.

In the abstract, then, the guidance system is an operations plan. Theoretically, modern systems analysis techniques can cope with such a complex of techniques. In practice, there may be strong political reasons that would militate against utilizing it in any complete sense of the meaning suggested above. Regardless of the degree to which such a systems approach is achievable, the underlying principles have an urgent and immediate applicability. This is no long-range proposal. Both public and private decisions are being made today which require the organizing force of a well-conceived plan and a programmed use of techniques aimed at shaping urban growth. Without a guidance system to give urban expansion patterns a more rational form, metropolitan areas face problems which will be truly staggering by today's standards.

Requiem for Zoning

JOHN W. REPS*

The year 1966 will be a significant one for American Planning. It marks two anniversaries: the beginning of the fifth century of the oldest city in the United States and the ending of the fifth decade of comprehensive zoning. It is a nice question which is less obsolete—the St. Augustine plan of 1565 or the comprehensive zoning ordinances of this country based on the New York City Zoning Resolution of 1916. The quaint, narrow streets of the old Spanish town serve at least to attract the tourist dollar; the quaint, narrow provisions of our zoning ordinances, judging from current comments, attract only the lawyers.

Zoning is seriously ill and its physicians—the planners—are mainly to blame. We have unnecessarily prolonged the existence of a land use control device conceived in another era when the true and frightening complexity of urban life was barely appreciated. We have, through heroic efforts and with massive doses of legislative remedies, managed to preserve what was once a lusty infant not only past the retirement age

* Professor, Department of City and Regional Planning, Cornell University and formerly Chairman of the Department (1952–64). He has been engaged as a planning consultant since 1951 and was Cornell University's Planning Director (1947–50) as well as a member of Broome County, N. Y., Planning Board. He headed the American faculty at the Salzburg Seminar in American Studies on "Planning and Development of the Urban Community" in the spring of 1965; was a Guggenheim Fellow (1958), an Eisenhower Exchange Fellow (1959) and a Fulbright Research Scholar (1965–66). He has published numerous articles in journals both here and abroad. This article, The Pomeroy Memorial Lecture for 1964, is reprinted with permission from *Planning, 1964,* American Society of Planning Officials, Chicago, Illinois, 1964.

but well into senility. What is called for is legal euthanasia, a respectful requiem, and a search for a new legislative substitute sturdy enough to survive in the modern urban world.

The powers of zoning and all of our other techniques for controlling urban development appear grossly inadequate when measured against the often radically different development patterns which modern metropolitan plans propose. I am not here judging the desirability of such alternative urban configurations as advocated by the Dutch in their Rim City plan, the Danes in their finger plan for Copenhagen, the British in their satellite city and greenbelt design for Greater London, or the radial corridor scheme for Washington, D. C. I am contending only that our existing system of development guidance permits us to hope for nothing better than partially controlled sprawl and that such bold plans now have little chance of success.

My concern today is with only one of the means of planning implementation, but it is necessary first to view its position in the matrix of urban shaping devices. In another context I have suggested, as have others, that the mechanisms for directing the urban pattern might be regarded as a guidance system.[1] Like the components of the machinery that places a satellite into a planned orbit, this urban guidance system comprises a number of subsystems that can be used to steer a metropolis through time to a predetermined goal.

Also, like the guidance system of missiles or satellites, mine takes its name from the acronym formed by the initial letters of its four groups of components. The word thus formed—ACID—is unfortunately not very inspiring, but it does tend to burn itself in one's memory.

What do those letters stand for? What are these methods by which the patterns of urban growth and change can be shaped? I suggest that all of our activities in this direction can be classified under one of the following: advice, controls, inducements, and development. The order in which I have listed them is roughly the order in which they have been employed in our attempts to assert greater public leverage in constructing urban patterns.

When the first public planning agencies were created, their

[1] John W. Reps, "Mechanisms for Directing and Controlling Future Development Patterns," Barclay Jones and Burnham Kelly (eds.), *Long-Range Needs and Opportunities in New York State* (Ithaca: Cornell University Center for Housing and Environmental Studies, 1962), pp. 306–337.

sole power was that of advice: advice to governmental departments and officials, to other levels of government, to civic organizations, to individuals. Advice, and the closely related techniques of persuasion and inspiration, still play important roles in guiding development. Indeed, at the metropolitan scale this is the chief technique on which we rely. But the power of advice necessarily has its limits, especially where advice runs even faintly counter to the dictates of the marketplace.

Next in point of time came our inventions of various kinds of control devices—zoning, subdivision regulations, official map techniques, and building, housing, and sanitary codes. But controls are negative instruments—they can prevent but they cannot compel, and their usefulness proved limited.

We then turned to various types of inducements or incentives as a method of attracting private building of types and in locations and under conditions that contributed to the public good. Through low-interest loans, tax exemptions, aids in land acquisition, direct subsidy payments, guarantees against financial loss, and other techniques, public bodies began to influence the urban pattern by combining the carrot of inducements with the lash of controls. Early redevelopment projects resulted from programs extending such financial incentives. The cluster subdivision concept provides another example.

Finally, direct public development has now taken its place as an urban forming force. In one sense, of course, this is nothing new. Vast public construction of streets and utilities in advance of need during the 1920's made possible the land boom of those wild years and certainly influenced the form of cities. But acquiring, planning, and selling land in central redevelopment areas to reshape the city's core is employing public development powers in a new way. Expressways, rapid transit routes, trunk utility lines, and major public buildings have powerful influences on the growth patterns of cities, and coordinated planning of these and other city-shaping elements offers great promise as an effective guidance mechanism.

I would go much farther in the direction of public development and use some modification of redevelopment techniques at the urban fringe. To be specific, some public agency with metropolitan jurisdiction might acquire raw land, plan it, provide street, utility, park, and other needed improvements, and then convey lots, blocks, or neighborhoods to private builders for development as planned and as controlled by deed restrictions. This would accomplish three things: it would provide a public yardstick operation against which purely private land development activities could be measured, it would establish a more precise tool of environmental control and guidance, and it would, paradoxically enough, aid private enterprise and the competitive market by making it possible for small builders who cannot afford the uncertainties and costs of the modern scale of land development to stay in business.

I hope my position is clear that the incentives and public development components of the urban guidance system need much further examination and expansion. I am convinced that in the long run these are the areas in which much of our intellectual resources should be invested. It should also be clear that what I shall now have to say about zoning and its future deals with a minor, although far from unimportant, aspect of urban planning implementation.

Having narrowed the subject for discussion while at the same time placing it in its larger context, let me now attempt a working definition of zoning for purposes of analysis. I suggest the following: zoning is a police power measure enacted by units of local government under permissive state legislation. Zoning regulations establish, in advance of applications for development, groups of permitted uses that vary from district to district. These regulations are not necessarily related to other regulatory devices or to any community plan. They are administered by officials having only limited discretionary powers. Ultimate review of the regulations and the actions of administrative officials under them is by appeal only and is a judicial function.

Now let me challenge the wisdom of zoning as so defined. This is, frankly, an effort to free your minds of whatever convictions you may have that our present system of zoning is somehow the only or the best method for controlling the bulk, use, intensity, location, and density of development. The sanctity of half a century of tradition stands between me and this goal, but let me make the attempt. A number of propositions will elaborate on the elements of my definition, against each one of which I will pose a question for your consideration.

One: Zoning is a police power measure. It follows that the impact of zoning regulations must be reasonable and that their effect must not be so burdensome that they amount to a taking of property instead of a mere restriction in the interests of protecting or promoting the public health, safety, morals, or general welfare. Regulations found to be unreasonably burdensome are invalidated by court action. Constitutional rights are protected, but the community is stripped of this power to guide land development, and the public at large may suffer unfortunate consequences from the assertion of private rights in land. *Question:* Would it not be desirable to introduce a system of compensation to supplement the police power where severe limitations on land use are deemed essential or desirable to shape and guide community development?

Two: Zoning is permissive. While much state legislation requires municipalities to carry out specified services or to provide certain facilities, the choice of regulating or not regulating land use is optional under American enabling statutes. *Question:* Would it not be desirable for state legislation to require all communities or those having certain characteristics to enact such regulations?

Three: Zoning is enacted by units of local government. Zoning regulations are intensely parochial. Standards required in any single metropolitan area may vary enormously depending on the whims of local legislators. We make much of the principle that land similarly located must be similarly zoned within a given municipality, but this concept is cruelly violated when a homogeneous area is zoned for industry on one side of a municipal boundary line and for high-class, low-density residential uses on the other side. Standards of enforcement vary equally widely. The possibility of achieving coordinated and balanced metropolitan development under such a situation, insofar as land use regulation is effective at all, can be written off as a mere fiction. *Question:* Would it not be desirable to deny zoning powers to the smaller units of government and place this responsibility at the county level, or as a duty of some metropolitan government or agency, or as a function of the state government?

Four: Zoning establishes regulations in advance of applications for development permission. As Daniel Mandelker has so well put it, "One difficulty with American legal techniques is that they borrow constitutional trouble by making land-use decisions with constitutional impact before the fact. Thus, exclusive agricultural zoning is restrictive immediately upon its enactment. It immediately raises a constitutional issue throughout its area of application regardless of the fact that many affected landowners would be quite happy with an exclusive agricultural restriction. But under the present system, an attack by a few will affect the entire ordinance."[2] *Question:* Would it not be desirable to have a method of control which avoided this difficulty and left the issue of legal validity to be raised when dealing with each application to develop land or to change its use?

Five: Zoning establishes groups of permitted uses that vary from district to district. In our understandable attempt to simplify in a complex and bewildering world we have done three things. We have attempted to prepare detailed standards for development which are supposed to cover all conceivable situations. We have Balkanized our cities into districts with precise and rigid zone boundary lines. We have established categories of uses that have segregated rather than integrated functional portions of cities and which have often disregarded the interrelationships between rather widely separated categories of uses. *Question:* Would it not be desirable to do away entirely with, or at least place far less emphasis on, the creation of districts and lists of supposedly compatible uses?

Six: Zoning is not necessarily related to other regulatory devices. Forget the theory here, and look at the facts. There is a multitude of regulatory measures—zoning, subdivision regulations, building codes, sanitary restrictions, housing ordinances, official map regulations, and others—enacted at different times, often by different bodies, enforced by different sets of officials, and reviewable by different administrative tribunals or courts. It is a rare zoning ordinance that does not in several ways conflict with the community subdivision regulations. It is a rare community that has not omitted some vital provision from both. It is a common necessity for the developers of all but the most routine and standardized projects to deal with several boards or officials and to secure amendments, approvals, waivers, or variances from the provisions of a number of ordinances and codes in order to proceed. *Question:* Would it not be desirable to consolidate all or most regulations dealing with control of urban growth into a single development ordinance that provided a sensible and

[2] Daniel L. Mandelker, "What Open Space Where? How?," American Society of Planning Officials, *Planning 1963* (Chicago: ASPO, 1964), p. 25.

efficient system of administration and enforcement, and which was purged of ambiguities, conflicting provisions, and redundancies?

Seven: Zoning is not necessarily related to any community plan. Again, forget the theory and look at the facts, including the depressing but understandable record of judicial review on this point. There are few communities that can claim with much justification that their regulations stem directly from any comprehensive, long-range plan. Charles Haar has demonstrated, in perhaps the most frequently court-cited law review article on zoning ever written, that whatever we think state legislation says about the necessity to ground zoning in a well-considered or comprehensive plan, the courts by and large have interpreted such a plan to be the zoning map itself.[3] This circular reasoning will prevail until new legislation changes the rules of the judicial game. *Question:* Would it not be desirable for statutes to require any local development regulations or discretionary administrative decisions reached on development proposals to be clearly based on a community plan, expressed graphically and/or as meaningful statements of development policy?

Eight: Zoning is administered by officials with limited discretionary powers. I am not here concerned with the scandal of unwarranted discretionary decisions by boards of appeals or such comparative novelties as floating zones or site plan approval procedure, but with the amount of discretion normally exercised by administrative officials in reviewing applications for zoning or building permits. It is in the nature of controls by districts, use lists, and bulk and density standards that present administrative review is essentially mechanical and requires only a check-list mentally. *Question:* Would it not be desirable to construct a system of development controls in which, as is the case of subdivision review, informed discretionary judgment plays the dominant or at least a much larger role in the process of reviewing applications to build or develop?

Nine: Ultimate review of the regulations and the actions of administrative officials under them is by appeal only. Only a person who feels aggrieved and who has the ambition, time, and money to appeal can obtain some kind of review of the

[3] Charles Haar, "In Accordance with a Comprehensive Plan," 68 *Harvard Law Review* 1154 (1955).

wisdom or legality of a zoning enactment or administrative decision. State governments, which have conferred regulatory powers on localities, have failed to provide any form of central review of the regulations as originally established or as amended or of administrative actions taken under them. There is no county or metropolitan review of local regulatory activities except the most peripheral. *Question:* Would it not be desirable to establish a system of state or metropolitan review of zoning-type regulations that could insure conformity with state or metropolitan development objectives and, in the case of local appeals situations, conformity with standardized fair procedures that would insure adequate attention to due process requirements and would curb both excessive restrictiveness and undue liberality on the part of administrative officials exercising wide discretionary powers?

Ten: Ultimate review of zoning regulations and administrative action is a judicial function. Courts are more and more being called on to decide issues which are increasingly technical and complex. Most courts have taken refuge in the doctrine of the presumption of legislative validity, but as the thrust of regulations becomes more vigorous it is unlikely that courts can refuse to decide issues on their merits. Yet, courts are ill-equipped to make decisions on technical matters, and it is far from clear that the adversary system provides the best approach to decision-making. *Question:* Would it not be desirable to create state administrative tribunals, assisted by an expert staff, authorized to obtain evidence in a variety of ways, and empowered to decide appeals or claims arising from the application of land use controls?

For my purposes I am now going to assume that the answers to the foregoing questions are in the affirmative. What would be the broad outlines of that portion of a development guidance system replacing our present system of zoning? How would we approach the control of bulk, use, intensity, location, and density?

First, I think it highly desirable to combine such zoning-type restrictions with other related public controls into a set of what might be called Development Regulations. From the standpoint of procedure we have already moved some distance in this direction. The use of floating zones, increased reliance on special exception or conditional use devices, and the requirements of site plan review as a condition of zoning permit approval, to name three among several methods that are currently employed, have all brought the procedure for securing permits under the zoning ordinance closer to that of subdivision control. I suggest that we pursue this approach much further and require most types of proposed development to be submitted to a local agency that would administer, through discretionary review, an ordinance combining at least zoning-type and subdivision regulations. This should simplify development control. Elimination of conflicting provisions and greater convenience for both administrative officials and land developers are but two of the advantages that would result.

Second, to guide administrative officials in reaching discretionary decisions, there should be a plan for community development and a comprehensive set of development objectives and standards. This plan should be made mandatory, it should be adopted by the legislative body, and review and readoption at fixed intervals should be required. Such plans should show generalized proposed future land uses, circulation systems, population density patterns, and community facilities.

Before adoption of the plan by the legislative body, hearings would be required. After adoption, provisions of the plan would be subject to review by a state agency that would also be empowered to hear appeals submitted by those opposing details of the plan. The state review agency would have final authority to confirm or modify the plan. All discretionary review of development proposals would be guided by this plan. Appeals from local decisions could be taken to the state review agency. Further appeals to courts would be permitted only on matters of procedure or on the scope of statutory power, not on matters of substance.

I realize that in this era of "ad hocmanship," advocacy of a community plan to serve as a guide to public decision-making sounds faintly antiquarian. But the use of a plan as just described provides fresh meaning to the planning process and thrusts the general plan forward to a position of new importance.

Discretionary action limiting development in such a way as to cause severe deprivation of property rights would be accompanied by some form of compensation. This would, in Haar's words, add "the money lubricant . . . to the machinery of land use controls in order to achieve greater flexibility."[4]

Appeals to determine the amount of compensation, if an offer is declined, would lie to the state review agency. In reaching such determinations the state agency would consider the degree of regulation that would be upheld under the most severe exercise of the police power and the value of the land burdened by such restrictions. Compensation would be payable only for the difference between that value and the value of the land if further restricted as specified by the local administrative body. After the payment of compensation, the restrictions imposed would be registered as part of the title. If, in future years, more intensive development were permitted, the amount of the compensation would be repayable by the owner.

Parenthetically, I should add that a system of betterment charges should also be devised to permit public recoupment of part of any increased land value conferred by public activities. Such a system might prove unnecessarily complex if applied to all land, but as a minimum a somewhat wider view of our present benefit assessment techniques should be investigated. David Levin, in a recent exploration of offsetting compensation with betterment charges in connection with highway access limitation, suggests that this approach "could be expanded substantially, giving a much wider recognition to benefits that in fact exist."[5]

Third, while I have referred to the discretionary administrative review body as local, I envisage this body ultimately as one with a geographical jurisdiction more extensive than the present city, town or borough boundaries. The new pessimists from the left-bank of the Charles River have lately been stating that multi-purpose metropolitan government is impossible to achieve and probably undesirable anyway. Perhaps they are correct, but as they point out, *ad hoc* metropolitan working agreements, authorities, special districts, and other single-purpose arrangements or agencies will be necessary as partial substitutes.

I suggest that sooner or later the general control of land use

[4] Haar, "The Social Control of Urban Space," Lowdon Wingo, Jr. (ed.), *Cities in Space: The Future Use of Urban Land* (Baltimore: The Johns Hopkins Press, 1963), p. 216.

[5] David Levin, "Aspects of Eminent Domain Proceedings in the United States," Charles Haar (ed.) *Law and Land: Anglo-American Planning Practice* (Cambridge: Harvard University Press and the M.I.T. Press, 1964), p. 238.

should be recognized as a responsibility to be located at the metropolitan level. In the absence of voluntary local action, the state agency previously mentioned should be empowered to establish broad guide plans in metropolitan areas and certain over-all land use control objectives and standards, against which local plans and land use objectives and standards would be reviewed. The next stage would be the creation of a metropolitan planning and discretionary control agency by action of the separate units of local government. Certain classes of development review might then well be left with smaller units of government, while other categories of development would be subject to metropolitan agency scrutiny. The alternative would be the direct exercise of land use controls by some agency of state government.

Fourth, the land use regulations themselves would need to differ substantially from those presently encompassed under zoning. Except as I will mention later, no district boundaries— no zoning map—would exist. The comprehensive plan, expressed in graphic form and in statements of development objectives, would be one guide to the discretionary administrative body, which might be called the Office of Development Review. While ultimately the plan itself might be regarded as a sufficient standard or rule of conduct to guide discretionary action, probably we shall need in addition rather detailed standards enacted by legislative bodies. These would be similar to those we now find in the better ordinances which authorize floating zones, conditional uses, and site plan approval permits. I suggest that these standards need to do more than merely specify the public good as a rule of conduct. In other words, the standards should be fairly specific and should relate to defined categories of land use. Such requirements should take the form of performance standards, rather than rigid specifications. Permissible ranges of height and bulk, for example, should be expressed in such measures as floor area ratios and angles of light obstruction. Emphasis should be placed on such performance criteria as noise, traffic generation, smoke emission and air pollution, odor production, vibration, and the like. Even so, some specification standards would doubtless be needed.

Within this rather general framework of plans, goals, and standards, the Office of Development Review would exercise broad discretionary power in granting or denying or modifying requests for development permission. Such permits would be for both tract development and single buildings on individual sites. As in most current floating zone procedures, approval would be for specific uses and building designs as shown on site plans, elevation drawings and as described in supplementary text material. This procedure, then, would not be at all like present zoning, the effect of which is blanket permission for any of a wide range of uses permitted in the zoning district. The discretionary powers would be broad; the development permit would be narrow in the development rights that would be conferred.

Fifth, this type of discretionary review and control would be most appropriate at the urban fringe or applied to in-lying undeveloped areas. Some vestiges of the concept of districts might have utility. We would probably find it advantageous to establish a skeleton list of uses that would be permitted as a matter of right, along with a set of simplified district boundaries. One advantage of this approach would be to reduce the volume of detailed review that would otherwise be necessary if we relied on a wholly discretionary system. Another purpose would be to clothe the new system in some of the familiar garments of zoning to lend an air of respectability in gaining both public acceptance and judicial recognition.

In areas largely built-up, where most new construction would be on a discontinuous lot-by-lot basis, more of the present zoning techniques—district boundaries and use lists— could be retained, although modernized to incorporate many of the recent innovations in zoning.

For redevelopment areas, major reliance should be placed on deed restrictions as the chief control mechanism. Urban Renewal Commissioner William Slayton may have been only partially overstating the case when he recently asserted that zoning has no place at all in redevelopment. Since the redevelopment site passes through a period of public ownership there is an opportunity to condition the sale of such land with precise and detailed restrictions. Police power controls can safely be suspended in such areas, although held in readiness should some legal flaws develop in the system of covenants, or to be applied at the termination of the period specified in the deed restrictions.

This approach to land use controls put before you only in the broadest of outlines appears to me the most likely and desirable of several alternatives to the present system. Doubtless, many of you have recognized its similarity to the land control process operating in Britain since 1947. It thus has precedents in a country not wholly dissimilar to our own. Moreover, if I read the trends correctly, it seems to be a direction in which we are already heading. The land planning and zoning code prepared by Carl Feiss for Bratenahl, Ohio, is a first step along the lines I have suggested.[6]

Yet there are serious objections which can be raised and with which, in conclusion, I would like to deal. Seemingly this approach to land use control violates the cherished principles of certainty and predictability that are supposed to be the virtues of our present system of districts, use lists, and elaborate development standards. This theory, however, is deeply undercut by the multitude of zoning amendments, improper variances, special exception permits, floating zone approvals, and unenforced violations. What remains is the structure of certainty without the substance—a mere facade of respectable predictability masking the practice of unguided administrative and legislative discretion.

Would a system such as I have proposed, with discretionary judgments firmly based on an official plan serving as Haar's "impermanent constitution" and guided by stated development goals and standards, fundamentally reduce the degree of certainty that now prevails? I submit that it would not, and that it would be more honest to present the meat of reality rendered of its semantic fat.

Further, I suggest we have little to fear from courts reviewing the legislative basis of such an approach to land development control. The little band of radicals in 1916 pushed the judicial clock further ahead in their time when they introduced comprehensive zoning than we would do in ours by pressing for additional discretionary powers. Perhaps I betray a naive faith in judicial liberalism, but recent decisions in our higher courts seem to leave little to fear in this respect.

My reservations concerning the wisdom and practicality of adopting the system I have proposed lie in other directions. Are we planners, as those who would be charged with exercising such discretionary authority, ready to accept the responsibility inherent in such an approach to development control? Are we confident that we possess the informed judgment to make intelligent decisions when granting or withholding development permission? Are we certain that we could

---

[6] Village of Bratenahl, Ohio, *Land Planning and Zoning Code and Zone Map* (July 1962); Carl Feiss, *Bratenahl Development Report* (Washington, 1962).

withstand the inevitable political pressures that would be brought to bear on us? Does the present status of planning suggest that legislators would be willing to grant us such powers in the first place? Is there any clear evidence that the adoption of such a system would lead to development patterns significantly different or markedly better than we are currently achieving or which might be brought about by some less drastic modification in our traditional techniques?

Finally, could we produce personnel of the quality and in the quantity that would be demanded to provide careful review of development proposals in a period of rapid urban growth and change? The new breed of planners seemingly has less interest in and knowledge of the micro-physical environment than in the novelties of new analytical methods based on a computer culture, more applicable to macro-planning at the metropolitan scale. Can we safely trust site plan review to this new generation of urban scientists?

Although we may now answer these questions in the qualified negative, that does not mean we should reject the alternative control system I have described. The same questions could have been posed in 1916. The answers then would surely have been equally discouraging. Who could have predicted, for example, the almost indecent haste with which state lawmakers clutched to their legislative bosoms the Standard State Zoning Enabling Act of 1922?

While I think it extremely doubtful that that episode of almost revolutionary legislative history will be repeated, we should not lose hope in evolutionary progress. If large increments of discretionary powers seem called for eventually, we should begin now to prepare the legislative and professional basis for the future.

Fortunately, there are grounds for optimism. The last ten years have witnessed the adoption and judicial approval of many techniques to ease the rigid Euclidian bonds of zoning districts, use lists, and precise standards. There are new signs of life in the corpse of state planning that was laid to rest in the 1930's. The experiment with statewide zoning in Hawaii promises to teach us some new lessons. A committee of the American Law Institute, aided by a substantial foundation grant, is now at work on a reassessment of American planning legislation. The proposals before Congress for broadening federal aid for such programs as open land acquisition, metropolitan planning, advance provision of neighborhood facilities sites, and the development of new towns will require new legislative responses at the state and local levels.

At this stage of our urban development we badly need imaginative experimentation in our fifty legislative laboratories. Where are the states that have placed metropolitan decision-making power at the metropolitan level, that require state or metropolitan approval of local plans, that provide for state or metropolitan review of local appeal decisions, that have reorganized the fiscal systems of municipalities so that land use decisions can be freed from the shackles of tax and revenue implications, that permit zoning-type regulations based on a community plan instead of a zoning map? And where have been the planners who should have been in the front ranks of those demanding reforms at the metropolitan and state levels?

For half a century we have engaged in a kind of legislative Shintoism, worshipping at the shrine of the Standard State Zoning Enabling Act. Zoning served us well during a period when urban life was simpler and less dynamic. We should honor those who were responsible for its birth and early care —the Bassetts and the Bettmans and, later, the Pomeroys of our profession—all of whom demonstrated a fertility of intellect that we have failed to imitate. But we do these men, and ourselves as well, ultimate honor not by tending their legislative monuments at the end of the by now well-worn legal road they constructed but by carving new trails toward new frontiers to serve an emerging new urban America.

Zoning: What's the Good of It?

DENNIS O'HARROW*

There is a famous mystery story about an Invisible Man. A murder is committed at a definite time during which the victim's house—the scene of the murder—is being watched by a whole squad of policemen. The policemen swear that not a

* Executive Director of the American Society of Planning Officials. He has served as the Youngstown Comprehensive Plan Director and as private consultant to New York, Chicago, Kansas City and Pittsburgh among others. His service on committees and boards in the planning field has been extensive including Deputy President of the International Federation for Housing and Planning (The Hague) 1962– ; Public Administration Service Board of Trustees; Board of Directors, Conference on Metropolitan Area Problems; *Sociedad Interamericana de*

soul could have come near the house during the critical period. The only possibility—which is an obvious absurdity—is that the murderer was *invisible*.

The solution to the mystery is that the Invisible Man is the postman. He goes up to the door, murders the victim as he hands him a special delivery letter, and leaves. The point of the story is that the postman on his daily rounds is so much a part of the background scenery, so natural and expected, that he is invisible to the watching policemen.

Such is the position of zoning for millions of householders in the United States and Canada. It is there, but it is invisible.

Take the developer who has to get a zoning change for a 500-unit apartment building. He is very much aware of zoning, considers it at least a nuisance, if not downright unfair. The city council that makes the change also thinks zoning is a nuisance, and wishes there were some absolutes by which the merits of each request could be measured. The staff planners think the request is a nuisance because it interferes with other work they prefer to do, and they probably think the council is completely off-base in granting the change. For all of these persons, zoning is far from invisible.

But what about the people who eventually occupy the 500 apartments? What does zoning of the building site mean to them?

Perhaps a few of the first generation of tenants will have been aware of the struggle over rezoning for the new building. But in a short time, as the tenants come and go, no one in the building is aware of the zoning—it has become invisible.

So it is with persons buying houses. Perhaps one out of 20 will ask a real estate salesman about the zoning of the property. To the other 19 the zoning will be invisible. They will take zoning for granted and not even know that they are doing so.

Even to developers and councilmen and planners, there is a low visibility of zoning in those areas where there are no problems.

It therefore will come as a surprise to many people that

Planificacion Advisory Council; Sears Roebuck Foundation Fellowships Selection Committee, 1958– . He is the author of various encyclopedia articles, and reports and studies in the field of planning and zoning, including: *Performance Standards in Industrial Zoning* (1951), *Economic Analysis of Market Area for Shopping Centers* (1952), *Churches and Planning Controls* (1958), *New Techniques for Shaping Urban Expansion* (1962). The piece below is reprinted with permission from the *ASPO Newsletter*, Vol. 30, No. 7, July–August 1964.

there are cities and villages where even at this late date the question of whether or not to adopt the first zoning ordinance is being debated.

To compound the problem for the unzoned, we who work with zoning have been highly critical of it, which does little to encourage those who are fighting to get it adopted in the first place.

Because it is still a fight. Anyone who tries to get zoning introduced into his community can expect to be accused of being a Communist and of trying to tear down the Constitution. He will hear that zoning is just a step on the road to poisoning water with fluorides and clapping right-thinking people you don't like into insane asylums. He can also expect to be linked up with vivisection, urban renewal, and metropolitan government.

So it behooves those of us whose communities went through the struggle 40 to 50 years ago to say a few honest words about why we like zoning, and what it has done and can do.

In the first place, an explanation of our criticism of zoning. We are like the fond parent who is ambitious for his child and wants to make him perfect. He really loves the child dearly and would not exchange him for any other person in the world and the child psychologist tells the parent that criticism is all wrong, but Pop *does* wish the kid would keep his hair combed and stop bolting his food.

We should also own up that there has been much wishful thinking in zoning. At the beginning, zoning was seen as a device to "lessen congestion in the streets" and to "prevent the intrusion of improper uses into homogeneous areas." While some early planners thought that "districting" could be used to determine precisely the future use of outlying, undeveloped land, the job at hand, in the opinion of the early zoners, was to prevent deterioration in the built-up part of the city.

The point of current criticism of zoning is not so much that it failed in its original purpose, but that it disappointed those who saw it as *the* creative force to shape the future city. They protested loudly that zoning was not "planning," but at the same time they tried to use zoning to carry out all of their plans, an assignment it was not equipped to do.

There may be more congestion in the streets today than there was the day the zoning ordinance was adopted, but there is much less congestion than there would have been without the zoning ordinance. Zoning has done this by keeping traffic-creating uses out of residential neighborhoods and by putting them along streets better able to carry the traffic they create.

Zoning has also been effective in keeping unwanted uses out of homogeneous neighborhoods, its detractors to the contrary notwithstanding. Those of us who follow the zoning administration in our own city or the zoning decisions in the courts sometimes get the idea that all is *Sturm und Drang,* the whole structure of zoning is falling to pieces around our ears.

Our vision is warped, our hearing is defective. For every "bad" (in our opinion) ruling by the board of adjustment, 500 occupancy permits are authorized routinely and in full compliance with the zoning regulations. For each "bad" (in our opinion) decision by an appellate court, owners of 5,000 to 50,000 single-family homes relax under full zoning protection.

If you want protection for your property—and there is nothing unreasonable in such a desire—what is your alternative to zoning?

According to the opponents of zoning, the alternative is the private covenant:

a. Unless there are deed restrictions on your land *and* on that of all your neighbors within the blighting radius of a drive-in hamburger joint or used car lot or billboard, you cannot expect to start now and get those restrictions written into the deeds.

b. If you do a little research on how unreliable most private covenants have been as protective devices, and what costs there would be if you as an individual try to enforce a private covenant, you will understand why land use regulation by your own government is to be preferred.

The boil and bubble of urban building and rebuilding, the turmoil caused by population growth, migration, expanding markets, personal affluence, new technology, and a dozen other economic and social forces, has knocked a lot of holes in our zoning plans. Those who thought that zoning was forever are disappointed.

But in spite of its battle scars, community zoning is still giving millions of people the assurances they want—assurance that their city will be a place to be proud of, assurance that their neighborhood will be a pleasant, and financially secure, surrounding for their home.

No community without zoning can make the same claim. *And so far as we know there is not a single urban community with zoning that would repeal the ordinance and try to get along without zoning.*

Chapter 17

PLANNING AND DEVELOPMENT AS PROCESS

The cliché that "planning is process" does most assuredly apply to city building and rebuilding. One generation's utopias, as indicated above, turn out to be purgatories for future generations. The recognition that urban planning is a slightly rational managing of social change is fairly widespread in the relevant professions today; theory and methodology are fast forming to embody these perceptions in an efficient operational fashion. Again systems analysis and mathematical models beckon: with planned inputs eventuating in fresh outputs thereby changing the system and thus necessitating fresh planned inputs. R. W. G. Bryant's warm tale of a new Coventry recovering from historic blight and World War II bomb is in the solid tradition of British planning, where yesterday forms part of today and both will be there in the future. Reginald Isaacs, in his experienced capacity as city redeveloper, synthesizes his long experience going back to the early Michael Reese development in Chicago in suggestions given to the Puerto Rico Urban Renewal and Housing Administration for the year 2000 for a series of phased inputs broken down into four-year Capital Improvement Programs and multiples thereof. "The greater profits of the quiet approach of less drastic treatments will be in the preservation of community social qualities and in far less expenditures required of a future generation." Louis K. Loewenstein and Cyril C. Herrmann, as representatives of Arthur D. Little, Inc., under contract to the City of San Francisco, have developed an eminently "hard-nosed" approach already stored in a computer simulation model of what renewal means to that city. "The model was in effect a replication of a residential and building space market in San Francisco. It was purposely designed to be sensitive to public opinion decision and city policy problems." It was programmed by the ADL staff to be dynamic and to serve the skilled planner as a method for testing the ramifications of alternate plans prior to execution and is now regarded as one of the significant forward steps in mathematical model building, discussed above in Chapter 14, "Hard Data Research and Computer Models."

The Reconstruction of Coventry

R. W. G. BRYANT*

In the popular image, Coventry was destroyed by Nazi bombers in 1940, and is now rebuilt. That is an oversimplified view. The importance of the blitz is often exaggerated. It must be seen in its proper perspective, as only one incident in the long record of one of England's most historic cities. The damage, great as it was, was nowhere near the scale of that later inflicted on German cities, nor was there any considerable area of total devastation. All that the Nazis achieved, in physical terms, was to inflict grievous damage on the city center—a warren of antiquated buildings, sadly in need of reconstruction, blitz or no blitz—to destroy about fifty-five hundred homes, and to cause limited and temporary dislocation to the city's war production.

In the city center, the greatest loss was that of some ancient and historic buildings. The Cathedral church of St. Michael is the best-known, but there were others. Not all were destroyed. The gracious almshouse for old ladies, Ford's Hospital, was badly knocked about, but lovingly restored to its original state, and is still in use for the purpose intended by the philanthropic merchant who founded it in the sixteenth century. It is a timbered "black and white" building with a charming interior courtyard or patio surrounded by a garden. Likewise, the fourteenth-century guildhall of St. Mary's, in which the Mayor (since 1953 the Lord Mayor) has been installed with appropriate ceremony every year since 1346, has been repaired. The carved bosses on the roof timbers had been removed for safety on the outbreak of war—when the roof was repaired, they were put back, not as they had been in 1939, but expertly painted in the brilliant colors beloved of medieval craftsmen. Two gate towers remain, and fragments of the city wall dismantled in Charles II's time.

Coventry has in fact a dual personality. On the one hand,

* Associate Professor of Geography, Sir George Williams University, Montreal, and formerly Director of Research, *Institut d'Urbanisme, Université de Montréal* (1962–66) and Development Plan and Research Officer Coventry (1950–61). He holds an M.A. (Aberdeen) in Geography and Economics and an M.Sc. (London) in Geography and has made various contributions to professional publications in Canada and the United Kingdom.

it is one of the great historic cities of England. On the other, it is a thriving industrial center, bound up with twentieth-century technology.

The history of Coventry is succinctly expressed, on a great wall of marble in the foyer of the Hotel Leofric—"this hotel is named after Leofric, the Great Earl of Mercia and Captain-General of King Canute's forces, who, with his wife Godiva founded the Benedictine monastery, on which, according to the chronicler, did chiefly depend the wealth and honor that subsequently accrued to Coventry." Evidently, Leofric was not the clown that the Godiva legend makes him out to be. Be that as it may, the industrious monks provided the conditions under which town life could flourish. Coventry became a great center for making and selling woolen cloth. Early mayors were often also "mayors of the staple" at Calais, and there were close trade links with the Flemish cloth centers.

Therefore, by the middle of the fourteenth century, Coventry was indisputably the greatest city in the Midlands, and the fourth, or perhaps the third, in all England. Cities like Birmingham, eighteen miles away, which now has more than a million inhabitants, as against Coventry's 330,000, were mere hamlets, when Coventry had walls and a corporation and trade guilds and all the other appurtenances of medieval city life.

For various and complex reasons, Coventry missed the bus in the first, or steam phase, of the Industrial Revolution. It was then based on two industries—fancy ribbon weaving and watchmaking, both of which were largely carried on in small domestic workshops. Many of these "top shops" still exist, built as a third storey on the old cottages. The "dark satanic mills" are not a characteristic part of the Coventry scene. By their nature, too, both industries were hard hit by French and Swiss competition, after the introduction of Free Trade. In the 1860s, therefore, Coventry was in a poor way. There were soup kitchens for unemployed craftsmen, and the population of the city actually fell slightly between 1861 and 1871.

But the city revived. The traditional local skills were applied to sewing machines, and then to bicycles. By the turn of the century, Coventry was the bicycle metropolis of England, and the bicycle epoch paved the way for the even more important development of the automobile industry. The English Horse-less Carriage Company (now Daimler) established itself in Coventry in 1894, and since then the City has never looked back. Other automobile firms were set up, such as Alvis,

Singer, Sunbeam, Standard, Hillman, and Humber, and other industries too. Courtaulds (rayon and viscose) established themselves in Coventry in 1904, and now, the headquarters and research establishments, together with sizable manufacturing plants, maintain Coventry's ancient association with the textile industry. But the dominant employment is in engineering and vehicle-building—not only automobiles, but also machine tools, aircraft, and electrical equipment. Tractors are a major product (Massey Ferguson). The Whitley bomber, of World War II vintage, was named for the Coventry suburb where it was made. Jaguar cars are made in a plant built as a war emergency "shadow" factory for Daimlers.

The consequence of all this modern industrial development is that the population of the city has more than quadrupled since the beginning of the century, from just short of 70,000 in 1901, to 330,000 in the mid-1960s. People have streamed into the city, where work was to be had even during the prewar depression, from the distressed regions in the North of England, Scotland and Wales. It is still growing, by something like five thousand annually, though natural increase is today more significant than immigration. By American standards, such growth is nothing unusual; by British standards, it is phenomenal. It supplies the key to many of the problems facing the city, and to the quality of its life.

Moreover, the great influx of workers drastically altered the social composition of Coventry. It became essentially a city of well-paid industrial workers. The old-established local families, which wield effective power in many British cities, were swamped by the newcomers. The vested interests which might have impeded the imaginative postwar reconstruction were beaten into the ground at an early stage. The absence of deep local roots on the part of many voters gave opportunity for vigorous leadership. Up to 1938, Coventry had been governed by a normal "small-town" city council of businessmen, lawyers, and the like. But social change was reflected politically; in 1938 the Labor Party won control of the council and has been firmly in power ever since. Very fortunately, the leadership has included people equal to the challenge and the opportunity. Therefore, a new tradition has been superimposed on those of this ancient city, namely, that what Coventry does today, the rest of Britain may do some time later. This applies not only to physical planning and building, but in many other fields of civic endeavor, such as education, drama, housing, welfare, and so on. Any honest account of Coventry must insist that it is a state of mind rather than simply a city.

Replanning of the central downtown area was an urgent need, as was already recognized long before the outbreak of World War II. The old downtown had become utterly inadequate, and its narrow streets were choked with traffic, even between the wars, when there were far fewer automobiles than now. The city's equipment of public buildings, big city shops and the like, was simply not matching the growth of population. Aesthetically, it was described as one of the ugliest cities in England, and there was a publicly expressed demand for a clearance of outworn buildings to open up a view of the two noble medieval churches, St. Michael's and Holy Trinity, whose spires dominate the heart of the city, together with the lesser Christ Church spire, and give Coventry its name as the "city of the Three Spires."

Unfortunately, before the war there were no powers available to British local authorities, for comprehensive urban renewal. Slum clearance could be undertaken under the Housing Acts, but these did not apply to business premises, nor did they provide for thoroughgoing replanning. The city council had to resort to privately sponsored legislation, in order to push through two major street improvements, in 1931 and 1937. The city was feeling its way toward an inner ring highway solution for the central traffic problem, thirty years ago.

Apart from the traffic problem, the city had an inadequate library and swimming pool, no art gallery or civic auditorium. Its essential equipment had been outstripped by its rapid growth. Clearly, the city would obtain the best value for money, and the best results in the end, if all these facilities were grouped on one large site, rather than spread around on separate sites, as and when these became available. To the east of the Cathedral there was an area of poor housing, an obvious location for a new civic center. Sketch plans were prepared for this, long before the blitz, and here now stand the new museum and art gallery, the new Central Swimming Pool, and the Lanchester College of Technology.

There was much lively discussion of the proposed rebuilding, in the city council, in the local press, and in private circles, which accurately reflected two contrasting states of mind, not peculiar to Coventry. Some good citizens asked if the city could afford to do all this. Others asked if they could afford *not* to do it, given that it would inevitably be much more costly for succeeding generations.

In 1938, a young architect, now Sir Donald Gibson, Director-General, Ministry of Public Buildings and Works, was appointed as the first City Architect, to handle the growing program of municipal building, including a projected massive upswing in the number of municipal dwellings built for renting—an upswing cut short by the outbreak of war. In the event, Gibson had little chance to design buildings at this time, but he did produce a standard design of air-raid shelter that was taken up by the national government. At this time, too, he had no official responsibility for city planning—that was in the hands of the City Engineer. But Gibson and his young men took a hard look at Coventry as it was, and they fell to adding their own contribution to the stock of dream plans.

Such, then, was the state of planning in Coventry when war broke out. In May 1940, to keep up the morale of the citizens, and to show them something of what the city might become after the war, an exhibition of dream plans was held in the fourteenth-century guildhall of St. Mary. Then came Dunkirk, and in November, the blitz on Coventry.

At the very first subsequent meeting of the City Council, while the rubble was still being swept up, the old Buildings Committee was reconstituted as the Planning and Redevelopment Committee, charged with the duty of "securing both in broad outline and in detail a worthy reconstruction of the city." It is to the lasting credit and honor of Coventry that this historic instruction, written into the Council's standing orders, has been faithfully carried out, whereas some other British cities, which suffered just as much bomb damage, fumbled badly.

The high purpose of the city council was fortunately matched by equal vision and imagination on the part of Sir John Reith, then Minister of Works, and in charge of postwar reconstruction. To the civic deputation which went to London to show him some of the dream plans and to seek his advice, he said: "That is the sort of thing I want to see. Plan boldly—do not worry about financial, legal or administrative difficulties." They would be taken care of by the national government. The deputation returned to their battered city with fresh heart. Coventry would be used as a test case for the problems of blitz reconstruction. One consequence was the Town and Country Planning Act of 1944, the "Blitz and

Blight" Act, under the terms of which, for the first time, local authorities were armed with powers and funds to undertake comprehensive reconstruction of areas scheduled by the Minister as areas of extensive war damage, and the "twilight" zones of decay not covered by prewar slum clearance legislation.

Under the terms of this Act, Coventry submitted to the Minister an area of 452 acres, so damaged as to warrant wholesale reconstruction. After a public hearing lasting several days, at which hundreds of objections were heard (mostly concerned with compensation) the Minister whittled down the area to 274 acres. This is thus a "Declaratory Order Area" within which the city council has the right to make compulsory purchase orders (in American terms, "eminent domain"). It has ever since been the firm policy of the city council to acquire the whole of the area, except for certain sections such as the Cathedral site, where replanning does not involve altering plot boundaries. In fact, much of the area has been acquired by agreement. There is a joker in this—the Government of the day would not allow Coventry to acquire the whole area at one time, as was done in eminently practical Dutch fashion in Rotterdam. Separate compulsory purchase orders have to be made for relatively small sections of land. The making of each order involved an extremely cumbrous procedure, and another public hearing, at which the same objectors may be heard, who were theoretically disposed of at the main hearing in 1946. To safeguard the rights of individuals is one thing, but to tie up a great public enterprise in a jungle of red tape is another. This has undoubtedly slowed down the rebuilding. Moreover, since compensation figures are settled by the District Valuer, an official of the central government, working to rigid and complex rules, the City is now in the position of having to pay for values enhanced by its own adjacent redevelopment.

One of the keys to Coventry's successful reconstruction has been an excellent public relations policy, with citizen participation and interest maintained as fully as possible. Several public exhibitions were held after the war, and there is a permanent "showcase" on the ground floor of the city planning office. The city has always been willing to discuss particular problems with sectional interests, so that it was possible to achieve much without antagonizing individual proprietors.

While the Government was preparing its legislation, Cov-

entry was getting on with its planning. For the central downtown area, a synthesis was made of prewar plans. From the
sketch plans of this time still in existence, it is clear that many
ideas were worked over, modified, adopted or discarded. Gibson had a particular inspiration that has since proved to be a
winner. This idea was to obliterate the western arm of the
ancient crossroads, which had been the heart of the city, and
to replace it with a pedestrian precinct, or mall, of shops on
two levels. This sort of thing is common today—but in
the 1940s, it was quite revolutionary. The old Smithford
Street, very badly damaged, had been one of the main shopping streets; it was only wide enough for a double set of street-
car tracks, so that when two streetcars passed, it was definitely
a "no parking" street. On prewar Saturdays, it had been
chock-a-block with people. But to write it off as a traffic
street, to replace it by a mall, with service roads and car parks
at the rear of the shops, that was at first a big thing for public
opinion to swallow. The shopkeepers and the Chamber of
Commerce had doubts so grave that they succeeded in having
the plan modified to the extent of inserting a north–south
street, intersecting the Precinct at right angles. This was
known, unofficially, as the Chamber of Commerce road, and
it effectively ruined the conception of a traffic-free shopping
area. It actually started to get built. But when the easternmost
part of the main Precinct was complete and working, it was
possible for Arthur Ling (now Professor at Nottingham University), who had just become City Architect and Planning
Officer, to persuade the city council and the public to have
second thoughts. In 1955, this intersecting street was rede-
signed as a pedestrian mall, with negligible opposition, and
it has been completed as such. That is the genesis of the great
cross-shaped mall which is the basis of the new Coventry
downtown shopping area. It is still one of the most extensive
pedestrian shopping areas in the world. Nobody ever sat down
at a drawing board and planned a cross—it just worked out
that way. Actually, it is a very satisfactory and logical arrangement. In three of the four quadrants behind the shops there
is a multilevel garage, and the whole is bounded by a circulat-
ing traffic route, nearly all formed of existing streets. The
traffic-free area has been extended more recently by conver-
sion of yet another important street, Hertford Street, to a
pedestrian mall.

The challenge of the automobile has been recognized and
met; Coventry is pushing on with a bold program of municipal

downtown parking areas, with ten thousand car spaces inside the Inner Ring road, which is being extended around the entire city center. Parking fees are levied. The rest of the cost is borne either by the general finances of the city, or is reflected in the rents charged for shops and offices. The redesign of the north–south axis of the shopping area has enabled a whole new high-level parking system to be incorporated. It started with the Retail Market, opened in 1958. It is a great circular building, on three levels, with market stalls on the ground level, and a service basement, with ramp for truck access. On the roof, there are 250 car spaces, reached by another curving ramp. Shortly after, a three-level garage was added with the upper levels reached from the market ramp. The market roof is connected by bridges to the roofs of adjoining two-storey shops, and the final section of the pedestrian mall is covered over, so that roof parking carries right across it.

The traffic problem is by no means solved. The original Development Plan of 1951 envisaged three ring highways, the innermost of which girdles the downtown area. It involved heavy surgery on the urban tissue and is now half complete. But this ring conception, applied to a strongly radial-concentric city, was not based on scientific traffic analysis. It was "hunch" planning, soon seen to be obsolete. By 1959, national expressway planning crystallized out into an extension (M6) of the M1 expressway from London, skirting Coventry on the northern side: this obviously meant thinking again, in terms of a major north–south artery, with arms tangential to the downtown core. A properly organized traffic study carried out in 1961 came up with the same answer: a Y-shaped motorway.

Coventry is typically a city of large manufacturing plants located all over the city: the pattern of desire-lines is therefore highly complex, with much crosstown movement. Most passenger movement is still handled by the efficient municipal bus service, which operates many special trips to factory gates, but its relative importance is declining. The city must needs do all it can to maintain the attractions of public transportation; it is clearly recognized that more downtown parking areas are not the total answer. The automobile is being canalized, and wheels definitively separated from legs, where possible. This is perhaps easier than to arrange the desirable modal split as between cars and buses. To maintain an effective and popular public transportation system would be far cheaper than to revamp the highway system to handle all the cars that might come.

The finances of Coventry reconstruction are extremely complex. The city has, until recently, received "blitz" grants from the central government. But the net cost to the local taxpayers has been astonishingly small—a mere fleabite in the total city budget—and this covers the relatively early stages of the scheme, when interest charges are being met on expenditure not yet productive. In 1960, the total city revenue on central redevelopment was well over £1,000,000. The net cost of central redevelopment is no great burden to a growing city, in spite of its being hampered by official restrictions and red tape that would daunt most private developers.

How is this done? Mainly because the city council have gone into the real estate business themselves. Coventry has leased several sites to private developers on ninety-nine-year building leases, but retains the chief interest in the land, which will ultimately revert to the city. In this sort of combined effort by public and private enterprise, it is all too easy to have the profitable eyes of the job picked by developers, leaving the less profitable parts to the local authorities. Coventry has not let things happen that way.

But many notable sections of the downtown redevelopment have been carried out by private developers, working in close collaboration with the city—including the original upper half of the Precinct, with the Hotel Leofric, the tall apartment block opposite the Belgrade Theatre, the Owen Owen department store, the complex of shops and offices on the charming pedestrians-only Shelton Square, the square beside the railway station and so forth. And one must not omit the new station itself, a fine contribution by British Railways to the new Coventry. The key is harmonious collaboration within the framework of a detailed, but constantly evolving plan, "progressive planning," in fact.

But the development of the shopping center must be set in its right perspective. Coventry city council has concentrated its efforts on the revenue-earning commercial section of downtown, the better to be able to finance the non-revenue public buildings in the civic and cultural zone on the far side of the Cathedral. The cost of these cannot be charged to redevelopment—they would be required in any case. It is a matter of municipal housekeeping to decide the order of priority among projects, all urgent. And also, a matter of good public relations, to explain to the citizens that they've either got to pay for these facilities at postwar cost levels, or do without. Most British cities have a legacy of nineteenth-century public buildings whose capital cost has been paid off long since—not so Coventry. But the city's property tax level is around the average for all English county boroughs.

Nobody without inside knowledge could possibly appreciate the difficulties under which the city has labored in restoring its heart. After the war, there were dire shortages of labor, materials, building licenses, professional staff. The loss of houses by bombing accentuated the general postwar shortage of shelter. Housing was the prime need, as we shall note below, and second to housing has been schools. There are now more than twice as many children at school, as in 1946. The city has had to build schools willy-nilly, using every kind of unconventional technique, from precast concrete to aluminum. The program has been used for bold experiment both in the architectural and educational fields.

The Coventry school system is in fact one of the most notable in Britain. The Education Act of 1944 provided that on leaving the primary schools, at the age of eleven, children would sit an examination, on the results of which they are graded and selected for the kind of secondary education they would thereafter follow, grammar schools for the bright ones, secondary modern, or secondary technical, in descending order. This eleven-plus examination has come in for strong criticism on the ground that it is not right to determine the whole direction of a child's subsequent career at a relatively tender age. One of the ways of meeting this point is the comprehensive system, of secondary schools of many tracks, or streams as the British call them. These comprehensive schools necessarily must be large, to cater for all types of stream and to allow students to select among many subjects, and switch as their abilities develop, without changing schools. There are various ways of preventing these very large schools from becoming impersonal.

Some other authorities, such as London County Council and Manchester, experimented with comprehensive schools, but Coventry jumped in at a very early stage, and based its whole secondary, or "high school" system on them. Educationally, they have been highly successful. From the city planning angle, the very large areas of playing fields attached to the schools, required both by law and by British practice, means that the new comprehensive schools which are one of Coventry's proudest possessions, had to be located around the outskirts. Their broad green spaces help to define and contain the built-up area, and sometimes help to separate neighborhood units. The buildings themselves are generally outstanding examples of school plant architecture. A pioneer one (Woodlands) was designed as a demonstration project by the design team of the Ministry of Education—others by the City Architect. A particularly elegant one is Whitley Abbey, set in the grounds of a former mansion house, with its main buildings grouped around a pond, crossed by a graceful footbridge.

Downtown had to take its place in the line. The difficult part of the operation was just after the war, when there was nothing to see but a shambles of Nissen huts and patched-up ruins. It was the Dutch who helped to set the ball rolling. They offered a gift of plants, in gratitude for their liberation. Given that it was not then possible to make any serious start on central reconstruction (at that time, the city had a token allocation of an annual £100,000 worth of building licences for that purpose), it was decided to lay out the new Broadgate square, with its garden island, long before any new buildings could be started. This would also help to keep up the morale of the citizens and the demobilized servicemen, and give them an earnest of things to come. So it was—and the garden island stands today, with Godiva mounted in bronze, in the middle, and the Hollanders' trees offsetting the new buildings that have since risen around it.

Gradually, downtown Coventry has received something like adequate physical equipment to serve as the heart of a city, not only shops, and offices, but also pubs, restaurants, an intimate theater, a dance hall, and so on. Much remains to be done, to be sure. The old covered swimming pool, for example, might have been adequate for a Victorian town of a fraction of Coventry's present population. It was bombed, and for years an elm tree grew in what had been the pool. Now, it is replaced by the Central Swimming Baths, with one of the few covered Olympic-standard pools in Britain. One of the most important new things downtown is the campus of the Lanchester College of Technology. An even more important addition to the city's essential equipment is not downtown, but on the edge of the green belt, namely, the new University of Warwickshire.

The Cathedral is an essential part of the Coventry reconstruction, yet a distinct and distinctive enterprise, in no way due to the municipality. The old cathedral church of St. Michael's, an exceedingly fine example of the Perpendicular Gothic style, was destroyed by incendiary bombs. There remain only the outer walls and the noble steeple, three hundred feet high, which was and is the visual centerpiece of the city. By reason of the tremendous impact on national and even international public opinion of the bombing of this great church, its rebuilding was much more than a local Coventry matter. The new cathedral is a national monument, and the controversy which surrounded the choice of its design was a national issue. There were good sincere people who wanted the old cathedral to be restored just as it was, others who felt that a new one should be built according to the spirit and ideas of the twentieth century. All this was discussed, in the report of the committee headed by Lord Harlech, and as that report recommended, a national competition was held. The winning design by Basil (now Sir Basil) Spence, is not modern in any radical sense—it is an interpretation in contemporary form of a traditional theme.

It is at right angles to the old cathedral. The ruined walls are retained, as a forecourt. There is no need of a new tower —the lovely old steeple is still part of the cathedral. This integration of the old and the new is a stroke of inspired genius. The roofless ruin has a message which has an impact on countless visitors. It is as if one of the great ruined abbeys, like Fountains or Furness, were set in the heart of a busy city. The new cathedral is built of a similar warm red sandstone as the old, and it is a treasury of the finest craftsmanship of today, like the pairs of gloriously colored stained-glass windows. Sir Jacob Epstein's last work, "St. Michael and the Devil," is on an outer wall. The great tapestry of "Christ in Majesty," by Graham Sutherland, was woven at Aubusson, in France—the biggest job they've yet tackled.

The new structure and the old are connected by a great porch, and a public right-of-way runs between the new and the old, so that the cathedral will not be something set apart from the life of the city. Citizens coming and going on their daily occasions will see the full length of the cathedral interior through a screen of etched glass.

There is marble given by a church in China, and an illuminated address to mark the financial contribution from Theodor

Heuss, president of the Federal Republic of Germany. A brown paper parcel arrived one day from Russia—the Soviet Embassy had no knowledge of it, but in it was an ikon, the Virgin of Kazan, sent by Stalingrad Cathedral. German volunteer helpers have contributed. In return, crosses made of nails from the ancient timbers have been sent all over the world. Apart from its international significance, it forms a splendid centerpiece to the reconstructed city center, and a landmark in the entire urban composition.

But there is more to Coventry than simply a lively downtown. By far the biggest single item in the city's capital expenditure since the war has been housing. As in other British cities, municipal dwellings are built for renting, on a scale relatively far greater than in North America: there are around sixty-nine public dwellings per thousand inhabitants, as against 0.6 for all Canada.

The postwar housing situation, serious enough generally, was more difficult in Coventry because of the extreme local shortage of building labor, owing to high wages and overfull employment in the city's basic engineering industries. A perusal of the documents and files of the late 1940s makes one feel that it was a miracle that anything got built at all. Yet the city was desperately short of buildings of all kinds. It was said at the time that there was only room for a very thin man to go and live in Coventry.

The Attlee government, with the late Aneurin Bevan as minister responsible for housing, decided that local authorities would be the "chosen instrument" for building houses to meet the postwar crisis. This was inevitable in the circumstances; it was the natural development from prewar policy. For Coventry it simply meant resumption of a policy interrupted by the war.

Britain had experienced an extraordinary building boom, in the 1930s, and Coventry with its fast-growing population had attracted the attentions of the speculative builders in full measure. The fringe of prewar spec-built houses which surrounds most British cities is in Coventry a vast mantle—a horrid problem in urban renewal for our grandchildren. Houses were available for those who could afford them; the City Council intended to build on a massive scale for those who could not. The first municipal dwellings had been built as early as 1908, under the powers of the Housing Act, 1890. The following table indicates the buildup:

TABLE I

	No. of Dwellings
Housing Act 1919	715
Housing Act 1923	293
Housing Act 1924	1,697
Housing Acts 1925 and 1935 (unsubsidized schemes)	808
Housing Act 1925 (street improvements rehousing)	171
Housing Act 1930 (slum clearance)	1,211
Dwellings purchased	94
Housing Acts 1946 to 1958	14,483
Temporary prefabricated bungalows	1,093
Total (3/31/62)	21,607

The scale of this municipal housing effort is indicated by setting the above figures alongside the total number of dwellings on the tax rolls at the same date, viz., 92,696, together with 1,677 dwelling units over shops. The city owns well over a quarter of its stock of housing, and that is not much more than the national figure, which is 21 percent.

The postwar housing problem was eased to some extent by the fact that various tracts, whose development had been interrupted by the war, were available complete with roads and services. The first major contribution toward easing the postwar housing shortage was provided by 1,093 factory built prefabricated bungalows, produced on behalf of the government and sold to local authorities. These were designed for a ten-year life. As it turned out, it was out of the question to do away with them at the end of that period—as so often happens with temporary buildings. The first of the prefabs was condemned as unfit in 1960, and the city now has to relocate the occupants, and redevelop the sites.

Owing to the acute shortage of building labor, the city's permanent postwar housing has relied greatly on non-traditional methods, that is, distinct from double brick wall with cavity, standard in that region. The British Iron and Steel Federation produced a permanent prefabricated house—the B.I.S.F. house—of which several score were built soon after the war's end. They proved eminently satisfactory, and further construction was abandoned only when it became apparent that steel at that time was in even shorter supply than bricks.

Another non-traditional method of house building, extensively used in Coventry, is the "no-fines" concrete technique, wherein whole walls, complete with door and window openings, are poured between wooden forms in coarse concrete aggregate. This method requires plant beyond the resources of small jobbing builders, and Coventry "no-fines" output has been in the hands of one large national firm of contractors, Messrs. G. Wimpey and Co. In large-scale output, and successful repeat tendering, the economies of bulk production were available both to the firm and to the city. The first cost, and the annual maintenance, are more or less the same as for comparable brick structures. Now the city is proceeding with even more radical industrialization of building, and has taken part in forming a consortium of local authorities in the region, to develop joint measures of speeding house production, improving design, and obtaining value for money.

From a housing viewpoint, its untypical historical growth curve means that Coventry is fortunate in not having the massive slum problems of Glasgow, or Liverpool or the industrial north generally, for the simple reason that its period of rapid growth came after the great Public Health Act of 1875 and other measures which laid down minimum standards. Before the outbreak of war in 1939, Coventry had only about 2,000 dwellings listed as unfit by the standards of the Housing Act of 1936, and half of these were destroyed by Hitler's bombers. On the other hand, there are considerable "gray zones" around the city center, of obsolete, or obsolescent housing not really capable of being modernized; the districts of Hillfields (137) and Spon End (38) acres were included as Comprehensive Development Areas in the first Development Plan, produced in 1951, and agreed by the Minister of Housing and Local Government in 1957. It was not possible to make an early start on redevelopment—the pressing need, for years after the war, was simply for more shelter. This could be more speedily and cheaply built on the outskirts. The Comprehensive Development Areas had to wait their turn, and the first contract was not let until 1959. Now the city is pressing on with redevelopment as fast as it can, subject to finance, and the extraordinarily cumbrous statutory procedures for acquisition of land outside the city center. A single objection can cause delays of up to eighteen months.

The Development Plan of 1951 set out the main locations of the postwar municipal housing program, mainly in three great residential clusters, Bell Green to the northeast, Tile

Hill/Canley to the southwest, and Willenhall/Stoke Aldermoor to the southeast. These have been substantially completed—they are simply peripheral extensions to the built-up area. Coventry is not yet so big that it has to think in terms of detached satellite towns. These great clusters are divided into neighborhood units, with properly planned community services. Shopping centers are integrated with churches, clubs and pubs, not just set down any old how, where a developer can acquire commercially zoned land. A good deal of other municipal housing has been built on scattered "infill" sites elsewhere in the city.

Since the city owns more than a third of its area, and its housing projects are planned as an integrated whole, it has an opportunity to achieve very high standards of design—far more effectively than under zoning by-laws or development control. Coventry has mostly maintained a general standard of excellence in the design and layout of its municipal housing. A number of its projects, or "estates" in British parlance, have won awards in the annual competitions for good design, arranged by the Ministry of Housing. Conversely to the common American situation, public housing in Coventry is generally superior to the rather banal designs often produced by private enterprise. The city has also made vigorous use of its powers of development control to coax private developers into raising their standards, a difficult and delicate task but one which has met some success; some interesting private housing has been coming along.

Among municipal housing projects one might cite Tile Hill North, built in the early 1950s when difficulties were formidable—a pleasant complex of walk-ups, row houses and senior citizens' bungalows at approximately fifteen dwellings to the acre net. The neighborhood center is now complete, with its shops, pubs, churches, group health center and the like, and three eleven-storey apartment towers forming a visual focus. This was an early Coventry showpiece which wears well. A more recent prizewinner is Willenhall Wood I, on the opposite side of the city, a medium density application of the Radburn principle. There are 550 dwellings, about half row houses, half apartments, at a net density of just under twenty dwellings to the acre, built along pedestrian paths leading to a pleasant little shopping center. These pedestrian ways were carefully designed along existing hedgerows, and the trees were retained. The whole effect is better than that of many residential areas of much lower density—Willenhall Wood in a way explodes the density fetish; for it points up the fact that quality of layout is often more important than density. It is nearly all of two-storeys, with a few four-storey walk-ups for small households, on the edge of the Green Belt.

The new neighborhood center at Bell Green, on the north-eastern side of the city, is even better than the Tile Hill one— a carefully designed pedestrian shopping and social center grouped around a high-rise block giving it proper visual emphasis.

Senior citizens' housing is, as generally in Britain, an accepted responsibility of local government. In Coventry, this responsibility is divided between the Welfare Committee and the Housing Committee (apart from the hospital cases). The Welfare Committee operates a group of old people's homes, for folk who are not chronically ill, but who are not capable of fending for themselves. These homes, excellently designed and built, each accommodate around forty people—they are not so large as to be institutional, or barrackslike, and not so small as to be hopelessly uneconomic to operate. This is a straight "welfare" service, not subject to the normal factors of housing finance. The inmates pay a nominal charge based on their income—usually consisting of the normal national old-age pension—and covers only a small part of the cost. The atmosphere in these homes is rather like that of a comfortable modern hotel.

The Housing Committee provides housing for old people who can manage their own housekeeping, usually either in one-bedroom bungalows, one-bedroom flatlets, or bed-sitter flatlets. There were 3,596 of these on October 31, 1961 (included in the figures given above). These are rented at specially low rents bearing no relation to the cost of accommodation, but related to the limited incomes of most old people. In between the old people's hostels and the old people's dwellings, are the "aged persons" flatlets, that is, flatlets designed especially for single old people, affording privacy, but grouped in blocks adjoining the old people's hostels, with the supervisory staff of the latter on easy call in emergencies. Costs are shared between the Housing and Welfare Committees.

Another "extension" of housing, for particular groups of the population other than families relates to single people. By reason of its economic structure and growth, Coventry has a relatively large proportion of unattached single people. During both world wars too, large temporary workers' hostels were built to house the labor force needed for war production. During World War II, bomb damage destroyed much housing, but did not prevent enormous expansion of war production. Therefore, the government built temporary camps to accommodate something like fourteen thousand people. Most of these hutments have now been removed, and the sites used for other purposes, but the city acquired two, Stoke Hill Guildhouse (678 places), and Chace Guildhouse (1,056) and operates them as hostels for single people, within the administration of the Housing Department. These "guildhouses," to use a very distinctive Coventry name for them, are wartime temporary structures, which will doubtless be renewed as soon as possible. Manor Guildhouse, on the other hand, is a fine modern building, opened in 1959 and specifically designed for its use as a hostel for 405 single men in bed-sitting rooms. It comprises two four-storey blocks. The inhabitants do most of their own catering; cooking facilities are provided in separate rooms, communal lounges, and a tea bar. Manor Guildhouse was built to replace an old "temporary" hutted barracks built during World War I—an indication of just how "temporary" temporary buildings can be! The Guildhouse accounts are kept separately from the normal housing accounts, and the operation is self-supporting.

The City Council runs the city, acting on the normal British committee system—and nearly all the committee members are aldermen or councillors. There is no counterpart in Coventry, or in most other British cities for that matter, to the kind of citizen groups which wield effective power in many American cities. The Chamber of Commerce, for instance, would not consider it part of its function to take an active part in redevelopment. Nor is there a plethora of ad hoc authorities for specific functions. The British setup is such that there is no need for ad hoc planning housing or redevelopment authorities, only loosely connected with the city council. Decisions and policymaking rest firmly in the Council House, or City Hall. The bulk of the work is done by the various committees, such as Planning and Redevelopment, Housing, Estates and Parliamentary, and so on, co-ordinated by an all-powerful Policy Advisory Committee. It is essential to appreciate that Coventry City Council, with its seventy-two members, is a much more powerful body than most American city councils. There is no city manager either, but the senior salaried official, the Town Clerk, is chief executive and administrative officer. Much depends on effective teamwork between department heads, as in British local government generally.

The city planning office in Coventry is a division of the City Architect and Planning Officer's department. The reason for this is historical. Owing to the tremendous contribution of Gibson, as city architect, to the planning effort of the 1940s, it was natural that he should take over the planning function from the City Engineer's department, when Ernest Ford retired in 1949.

Coventry very seriously considered setting up a separate planning department in 1964, when Arthur Ling (now Professor Ling) ceased to be City Architect: they decided to retain the architect-planner setup for the time being, at least. In principle, the functions of city planning in a city of over three hundred thousand are clearly complex and important enough to require a full-time director with adequate staff. The same holds good, too, for the functions of the city architect, especially in Coventry, where the municipal building program is on a scale far greater than that of any American city of comparable size. But principle and practice need not always coincide.

Coventry is so often criticized as a city of excessively well-paid philistines, but there is much more to it than that. It is building up a new tradition, exemplified not only in physical design, but in all sorts of other ways. In 1959, Coventry completed the Belgrade Theatre—the first municipal theatre to be built in Britain. It derives its name from the gift of a shipload of timber, by the Yugoslavs. It is also the first sizable postwar theatre to be built in Britain. It is a success, architecturally, socially, artistically and even financially—the deficit is trifling. Not that this would signify—the city of Hamburg spends more each year on music and the arts than the Arts Council of Great Britain. London fumbles with the relocation of the Covent Garden wholesale market—Coventry years ago built an efficiently laid-out wholesale market, logically sited out of center in the direction whence most trucks have to come.

It has a special place in British life, not any more as the city which suffered the first big blitz outside London, but as the city which measures up, more than most British cities, to the needs and standards of the twentieth century.

The Dynamics of Urban Renewal
REGINALD R. ISAACS*

INTRODUCTION

In 1953, the American Council to Improve Our Neighborhoods defined Urban Renewal as "the total of all the public and private actions which must be taken to provide for the continuous sound maintenance and development of the urban area."[1] This definition calls for carefully articulated and continually re-evaluated processes of planning, programming and treatment.

Yet, present programs for Urban Renewal treatment usually prescribe complete change in present conditions, i.e., slum or blighted areas to be cleared and new buildings and facilities built, near-blighted buildings and areas to be rehabilitated by large private and public economic investment in major repairs and limited replacement, and middle-aged buildings and facilities to be conserved by mainly private investment through relatively minor repairs of a less costly nature. Once this work is carried out, it ordinarily is assumed that the areas so treated will remain almost permanently in their new, conserved or rehabilitated conditions with little more than careful maintenance.

This is erroneous, for it is in the nature of almost all things to age, to become obsolete and eventually to be replaced. Perhaps the best Urban Renewal treatment can do is to slow

* Charles Dyer Norton Professor of Regional Planning and formerly Chairman of the Department of City and Regional Planning at Harvard. Trained originally as an architect, he has been engaged in city planning activities in Washington, Minneapolis, Chicago, Philadelphia, San Juan and Syracuse (among others) with private, city, metropolitan and federal agencies—as well as abroad. He is well known for his pioneering work in redevelopment with the Michael Reese Hospital and the Chicago South Side Planning Board. He is the author with John Dyckman of *Capital Requirements for Urban Development and Renewal* (1960) and contributor to various professional publications. This article is adapted from a report prepared for the Puerto Rico Urban Renewal and Housing Administration and published in their *Community Renewal Program, San Juan Metropolitan Area, 1964–65.*

[1] Blucher, Walter H., in *Urban Renewal Research Program*, American Council to Improve Our Neighborhoods, New York City, November 1954.

down this cycle, to prevent repetition of the present pressing need for the total and costly treatment of large areas at one time and avoid even greater costs in the future.

However, the broad view of ACTION was not adopted and, in practice, Urban Renewal has had a more limited definition—that of monolithic project approach. In part, this approach has come about from the initial patterning of the Federal programs for renewal on the now institutionalized traditional programs for housing projects. In part, the monolithic project approach reflects a viewpoint that substandard areas are clearly definable in terms of static boundaries and that the correction of their ills is to be solved internally within these boundaries. Perhaps contributing to this monolithic project approach is the desire to identify existing, or to create new, social or physical organizations within the substandard areas as neighborhoods or communities. The project approach was necessary in the past but seems to have dominated the process because of the growth of administrative requirements which have grown up about even a single project. The project approach also was necessary in our past government systems where all public expenditures had to be clearly identifiable. But is this system consistent with the current trend toward "functional budgeting"? Now it is understood that the complex growth and change of our metropolitan areas must be matched by more improved approaches which recognize continual and inevitable change.

This brief essay reflects the thinking of a growing number of social scientists, educators, planners and governmental officials who have evidenced their concern in their searches for revision of present-day programs. Among these are William Nash, John Dyckman, and Martin Meyerson. Members of the Long-Range Planning Office of the Urban Renewal and Housing Administration of Puerto Rico and my fellow consultant, Myer Wolfe, have contributed much to the range of ideas presented here. Although it is not claimed that all or any of the above are in complete agreement with the ideas set out here, there is probably unanimity in the recognition of the need to revise public and private attitudes from those of admiration and aspiration for the conspicuous and costly, to the anonymous and economical. There is recognition that the practice of Urban Renewal, despite the universality of its best definition, must be quite different in each city, given its present economies, governmental structure, environmental factors, cultural aspects and the aspirations of its people.

THE COMMUNITY RENEWAL PROGRAM

William Nash wrote:

The community renewal program (CRP) became a Federal possibility in 1959. It was devised to help avoid Urban Renewal programs which concentrated too heavily on completing individual projects while ignoring the broader issues of comprehensive, community-wide planning. This new program would have been completely unnecessary if the requirements of the workable program, which include a comprehensive plan and "neighborhood" analysis, had been rigidly required of the participating local agencies. Admittedly, the CRP is interpreted somewhat differently in that it is supposed to integrate the several renewal project plans into a detailed comprehensive plan and program for renewal in accordance with the community "master" plan. In a sense, it is a plan for a community-wide renewal program.[2]

Under Section 405[3] of the Housing Act of 1959 Pl. 86–372, the CRP includes but is not limited to:

1. identification of slum areas or blighted and deteriorated areas;
2. measurement of nature and degree of blight and its causes;
3. determination of financial, relocation and other resources needed for the renewal of the areas;
4. identification of project areas and type of treatment; and
5. scheduling or programming of urban renewal activation.

The CRP *must* conform to the general plan. The CRP is *not* a requirement, but the federal grant (one-third local, two-thirds Federal participation) promotes its probable use in the Urban Renewal program. Nash further wrote:

Although it is suggested that Section 405 was an incentive to promote more overall comprehensive planning, it

[2] Nash, Jr., William W. *The Links Between the CRP and Metropolitan Planning,* Metropolitan Planning Study: Memo 3, an unpublished lecture, Harvard University, Cambridge, Mass., July 23, 1963.

[3] The most recent revision of Section 405, Administrative Letter #276 places even greater emphasis upon the comprehensive planning contributions of a "properly conceived community plan, the CRP." This is very much in accord with URA's *Community Renewal Program Policy,* published in October 1963.

also is useful to "plan for Urban Renewal planning." Insofar as the Urban Renewal Administration grants do not provide funds to prepare a workable program, comprehensive planning was relatively neglected. The CRP grant (not loan) has closed this gap and in many cases is being used to provide funds supporting comprehensive planning.[4]

The "workable program" is entirely at the community's expense, and it does require housing and building codes and maintenance. The problem is, therefore, also in terms of the adequacy of the administrative and enforcement means, both incentive and punitive.

In general, however, the language of the Federal program as embodied in the legislation and interpreted by the Administrator's newsletters from Washington, does contain a conceptually correct approach to Urban Renewal despite the program's housing project genesis.

THE COMPREHENSIVE PLAN

An ordinary first point of inadequacy in Urban Renewal programs or CRP's is the preparation of Comprehensive City or Metropolitan Area Plans as static Master Plans. We are told that a plan usually includes:

1. a complete analysis of "planning analysis areas," which in turn are defined as relatively homogeneous units[5] with boundaries usually coterminous with Census tracts; the indices of homogeneity may be selected from all relevant variables describing site characteristics;
2. identification of factors causing change, measurement of their magnitude and projection of future land use patterns preparatory to an evaluation of problems and possibilities in terms of the community's goals;
3. a plan specifying the proposed treatment of the entire community, with more detailed suggestions for areas made critical by their poor condition or obvious potential utility; and
4. a program of implementation including information concerning priorities, legal and administrative changes

[4] Nash, *op. cit.*
[5] These are units to be treated, both in analysis and plan, and deserving of some common consideration.

required, money needed and its sources; this last would include the Urban Renewal plans.[6]

However, the process of Comprehensive Planning must be a continuing one beyond the preparation of "Preliminary", "Comprehensive" and other stage Plans. The process must provide for constant re-evaluation and change in the plans. There must be re-evaluation of criteria and definitions utilized, of the process, as well as of the results of the Plan's recommendations when carried out.

Presently, emphasis is given to the preparation of a physical Plan for a metropolitan area for 1980; yet the Plan may be more a statement of problems of, and solutions for, the period in which it is being prepared rather than those of 1980. In other words, the Plan for 1980 may be barely more than our present-day conditions projected, corrected and made neat on paper. Long before the 1980 Comprehensive Plan could be carried out, its reorganization in terms of 1990 and the year 2000 would have to be started. Perhaps to meet needs as they may be in 1980, the Plan for the year 1990 may have to be devoted to hindsight programming and implementation.

An intelligent Comprehensive Plan *is* a plan for Urban Renewal. However, it is a rare Plan which, in practice, contains the elements necessary to obviate the need for a special program—"workable," "urban renewal," or other label. This connotes that Urban Renewal is simply a tool to carry out city planning.

URBAN RENEWAL CONSIDERATIONS

In Urban Renewal, with an immediate objective being that of improving 1964 conditions to a "modest standards level" by 1980, there must be recognition that a building or an area conserved in 1964 may require major rehabilitation by 1980. Similarly, a building or an area rehabilitated in 1964 may be ready for new rehabilitation or clearance by 1980. A new building completed in 1964, no matter how well maintained, ordinarily within twenty-five or thirty-five years, or by the year 2000, will require rehabilitation.[7] Age and condition are not necessarily the only factors to determine need for Urban Renewal treatment; social and technological obsolescence or the market may be factors of equal importance. Furthermore,

---

[6] Nash, *op. cit.*
[7] Rehabilitation or major repairs will be required to overcome the results of obsolescence and deferred maintenance.

prescribed treatment, when carried out, does not insure immortality for the building.

Further complicating these dynamics is the fact that in many areas more buildings are built as slums than those that become slums through the processes of maturation. Further community facilities, streets, and services have become completely outmoded with greatly increased densities of population and increased automobile ownership.[8] All of this has required a greatly increasing public commitment.

DESIRABLE STAGES FOR PLANNING

In view of the need to create a dynamic Plan, a very long-range ideal has to be created almost without limit of time. The year 1980, thirteen years away, provides too short a period to carry out imaginative ideas, too short a period within which to create a plan, to educate and gain the interest of citizens, and too short a period within which to devote a major share of limited resources. The year 1980 hardly permits sufficient time to correct the problems of 1967.

A twenty-five- or thirty-five-year phased Plan for 2000 would represent our best hopes for the environment of a new generation, would not be unrealistic and were it to obtain, would not restrict the decisions of that generation. As a deterrent to unrealistic planning and as a guide to re-orienting of direction as may become necessary from time to time, evaluation and shorter-term plans would be provided as part of the processes of planning.

Following the establishment of these long-range objectives, a First Stage Plan may be outlined in relationship to money and legislation immediately available and the desires of the public immediately discernible. In other words, first steps should be taken toward the wise use of existing resources, without the need to obtain new funds, new laws or to determine the will of the citizens.

A secondary or intermediate stage advisedly may be as brief as one, two or three, four-year Capital Improvement Programs. Such an intermediate stage will be held to the most

---

[8] In many areas, densities may not be substantially increased over those of relatively few years ago. However, sometimes, where no car or one car was owned then, two or even three are present now. Where activities were circumscribed by family and home, these now spill over and far beyond. Perhaps the degree of *intensity* of activities, not density, should be the measurement.

careful development through the device of annual re-evaluation of resources. The entire four-year, or multiple of the four-year period, Capital Improvement Program will serve additionally as a means of evaluation of the long-range Plan.

URBAN RENEWAL STAGING

It would appear logical to divide Urban Renewal objectives into immediate, intermediate, and long-range phases as closely as possible identical with those of the Comprehensive Plan. However, the problem of relocation of families and businesses, as well as economics and politics, would tend to delay what might be considered immediate steps in Urban Renewal treatment programs. Perhaps the minimal period would be equivalent to that of the capital improvement program budget related to the Comprehensive Plan. In many cities this is now four years. Each year this period would be advanced by an additional year through re-evaluation of entire urban area programs involving current collections of data recognizing

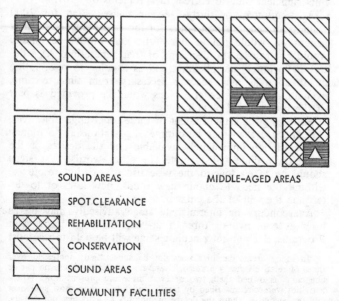

SOUND AREAS   MIDDLE-AGED AREAS

█████ SPOT CLEARANCE

▨▨▨▨▨ REHABILITATION

▧▧▧▧▧ CONSERVATION

☐☐☐☐☐ SOUND AREAS

△ COMMUNITY FACILITIES

FIGURE 1. A Suggested Staging of Urban Renewal Treatment

accomplishment and new financial opportunities. A four-year period would be a relatively logical one within which to develop forms of financing, to gain some understanding of the public, and to obtain such new legislation as may be necessary.

Somewhat lower priorities are given to sound areas prematurely requiring spot conservation treatment or to deteriorating areas with pockets of individual structures which can be conserved.

If some fifteen years are considered as a measurement of time within which the condition of a sound building or area matures to the need for conservation treatment, there would

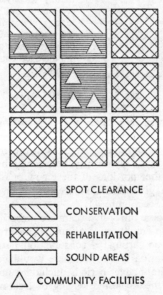

FIGURE 2. Deteriorated I and II Areas[9]

[9] ARUV has defined "deteriorating" and "dilapidated" in terms of residential housing. This definition should be expanded to describe non-residential and area aspects as well; however, it is not used in that expanded sense here.

"Deteriorating I Housing Units (with all plumbing facilities)—housing units with structural defects of an intermediate nature which need more repairs than would be provided during the course of regular maintenance. These units have all plumbing facilities, inside the structure, for the exclusive use of the occupants." (Definition by ARUV, Puerto Rico.)

be encompassed three to four capital-budget periods. Therefore, maturation to middle-aged status might occur in four stages of four years each, say A, B, C and D related to the budget periods. (See Figure 4)

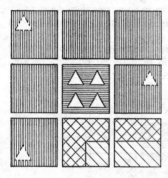

It is understood, of course, that these designations may lapse into a project approach unless they are continually integrated into areawide needs. It is also apparent that these stages relate mainly to physical, social, and economic maturation. Areas of high reinvestment opportunity for reasons of location and prestige tend to remain in the middle-aged category almost indefinitely.

FIGURE 3. Dilapidated[10] Areas.

In other words, areas of sound construction or otherwise stable condition requiring immediate spot conservation treatment would be in an A category to keep the entire area from being affected physically or psychologically by the detected deterioration. Other portions of these new or otherwise sound areas would be given tentative treatment stage assignments B through D. (See Figure 4)

Similarly, if some thirty-five years are prescribed as a period within which the condition of a building or area moves from a sound condition through a conservation period to one requiring rehabilitation treatment, there would be encompassed about eight capital-budget periods, including stages A through H indicated in the suggested staging of treatment. (See Figure 4)

The deteriorated areas containing pockets worthy of con-

"Deteriorating II Housing Units (lacking some or all plumbing facilities)—housing units with same structural condition as above, except that these units lack some plumbing facilities or its occupants share the same facilities with the occupants of other housing units." (Definition by ARUV.)

[10] "Dilapidated Housing Units—housing units which do not provide safe and adequate shelter. These units contain one or more critical defects or combinations of intermediate defects over such a large area that extensive repair or rebuilding is necessary." (Definition by ARUV.)

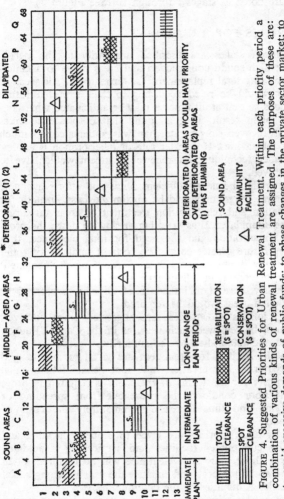

FIGURE 4. Suggested Priorities for Urban Renewal Treatment. Within each priority period a combination of various kinds of renewal treatment are assigned. The purposes of these are: to avoid excessive demands of public funds; to phase changes in the private sector market; to relate to the production abilities of the construction industry; to avoid large-scale relocation; and to establish a complete and rational dynamic system of provision and a more gradual maturation to result in a slow, eventual replacement. (See Figure 6.)

servation as well as for clearance and redevelopment treatment are noted as stages I through L. (See Figure 4)

PRIORITIES FOR TREATMENT

Seventeen stages are ascribed arbitrarily to the period within which sound construction and areas move to a condition requiring total replacement (A through Q). All areas of the city would be rated according to their expected future conditions so that at all times it may be anticipated what conditions might result. If it is found that obsolescence takes place at an even slower rate than was anticipated, so much greater the savings. If a faster rate of deterioration is experienced, then techniques for renewal treatment would have to be improved.

Meanwhile, the never-sufficient funds and efforts available for renewal programs would be maximized by utilization for conservation and rehabilitation treatment of areas far larger than the dilapidated, thus arresting or slowing down the processes of maturation and the need for total clearance, thus reducing future greater costs. The costs of total clearing and rebuilding will not be greater as a result of postponement (except, of course, in inflationary terms).

Obviously, careful maintenance of all new, conserved or rehabilitated areas would be required.

The priorities shown here are suggested ones; however, these must be reviewed each year, as in the Capital Budget, changed and established by the authorities.

Highest priorities for treatment are given to middle-aged areas requiring conservation and spot rehabilitation. Such high priority for the forms of treatment is required in order that the poor conditions be prevented from spreading or intensifying and thus increasing prematurely the costs of treatment.

Equally high priorities are given to properly locating and providing community facilities and services in dilapidated areas; for those, only spot clearance will be required. Such facilities would preserve and enhance the usually strong social organizational qualities of the communities.[11]

Somewhat lower priorities are given to sound areas prema-

[11] See, for example, *A Plan for the Transformation of the Llorens Torres Public Housing Project in San Juan,* Puerto Rico, Special Studies Section, Long Range Planning Office, Puerto Rico URA, September 1963.

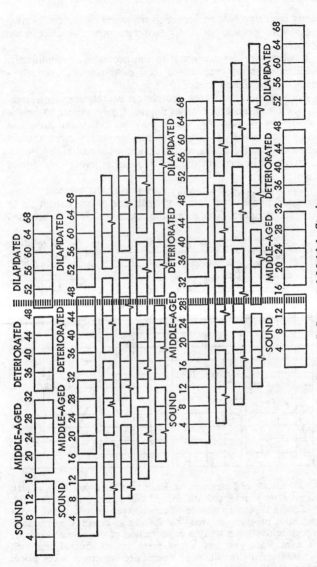

FIGURE 5. Suggested Multiple Staging

turely requiring spot conservation treatment or to deteriorating areas with pockets of individual structures which can be conserved.

Lowest priorities are given to the provision of community facilities in sound areas or to total clearance and redevelopment of dilapidated areas.

For communities which are almost completely dilapidated, complete clearance and redevelopment may appear to be the only treatment possible. There may be individual structures and pocket areas of higher qualities requiring more modest forms of renewal treatment. Such areas require high priority of treatment in terms of the low qualities of living to be found there.

However, these are the areas requiring the greatest investment and highest cost forms of treatment to bring them up to a model standard. These are the areas which have attained

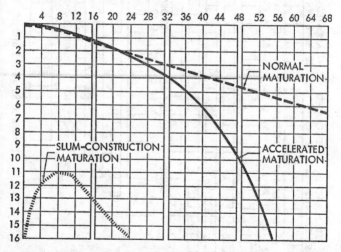

FIGURE 6. Rate of Deterioration. Each year the capital budget plan and program is reviewed and moved one year forward. (See Figure 5.) Each year a measure of renewal program is added and a cumulative program evolved, distributing as carefully as possible, through critical path study a cross section of the several kinds of treatment. Each year new sound areas are constructed and each year substantial demolition of dilapidated structures takes place. Over a period of years, a simple deaccelerating rate of deterioration would be established and result in substantial savings.

almost maximum retrogression or which were actually built as dilapidated areas or slums. These slums require containment to keep them from spreading or affecting adjacent better areas, as well as special treatment not ordinarily prescribed today on the mainland.

These areas should be given priority in planning for the future. Indeed, the provision of a future plan would allow the residents to plan their own futures, to phase out their relocation or, where applicable, through self-help programs to secure their futures as part of a planned community. Priorities for eventual clearance and rebuilding would also be established long in advance of the actual work.

Given four major categories of condition, seventeen sub-classifications of these, and ten to twelve priorities for action, linear programming and computer techniques are in order. With these, projection and prediction will provide estimates and ranges of condition and public and private investment to be required. Variables, perhaps similarly predictable, would be those in respect to policies at several levels of government and in anticipation of available funds.

In other words, the priorities treatment prescribed would be heavily oriented to less-than-total clearance and replacement. It is obvious that this approach is less dramatic than new projects replacing slums and thus less appealing to some decision-makers.

CONCLUSIONS

I have not dealt here with the design aspects although I consider these are an integral part of treatment. I have expressed a strong bias that these should reflect the culture as well as the environment of every region.[12]

Nor have I dealt with the implementation required for administration of treatment, since few of today's measures are adequate, whether incentive or punitive. It is also true that the anonymity of the kind of professional work which must be done is rarely appealing to the architect and planner. Presently, greater aids are available for the slum clearance and total redevelopment work and undoubtedly in these the profits for owners of slum property, realtors, planners and architects are greater. However, necessary new means can be devised

[12] See my *Consideraciones Sobre la Cultura de Puerto Rico en la Planificacion*, published by the Instituto de Cultura Puertorriquena in 1961.

once a proper program is established and its values determined by both public and private sectors.[18] Furthermore, the greater profits of the quiet approach of less drastic treatments will be in the preservation of community social qualities and in the far less expenditures required of a future generation.

In a rational society these benefits should be sufficient.

[18] See my *Conservation*, published by the Metropolitan Housing and Planning Council of Chicago in 1953.

The San Francisco Community Renewal Program: A Summary

LOUIS K. LOEWENSTEIN AND CYRIL C. HERRMANN*

Six salient characteristics of this summary report should be clear at the outset:

In the first place, it is not about planning, but rather it is a plan, and specifically it is a plan designed for implementation by a city. Because it is structured to fulfill this objective, it may be considered more properly as a program or a set of criteria to achieve a desired end. Therefore, it pays more attention to the diagnosis of the problem and to the means for achieving action than is customary with most plans.

In the second place, this program is restricted to community renewal and hence does not specifically cover such aspects of urban planning as transportation or urban design. It is, however, far broader in scope than are most such studies in the sense that it is concerned with all aspects of the subject: residential, commercial, and industrial renewal and all portions of the city.

In the third place, the implementation is time-phased with a

* Louis K. Loewenstein is holder of a Ph.D. and an M.A. in City Planning from the University of Pennsylvania; he is presently a senior staff member at Arthur D. Little, Inc. He was formerly associated as an economist with the Penn-Jersey Transportation Study and as planner with the New York City Planning Department as well as the Department of City Planning at Pennsylvania. He is the author of *The Location of Work Places in Urban Areas* (New York: The Scarecrow Press, 1965) and some dozen professional journal articles.

Cyril C. Herrmann is Vice President, Urban and Regional Economics, Arthur D. Little, Inc., and formerly Associate Director of the Sloan Executive Development Program, and Assistant Professor of Marketing, Massachusetts Institute of Technology. Holder of an M.B.A. from Stanford and a D.C.S. from the Harvard Business School, he is the author of articles on operations research/simulation models in the *Harvard Business Review*.

base line of 1966 and the period of time for the action program is twelve years, which is somewhat less than is to be found in most conventional planning efforts. These dozen years are divided into two six-year periods and in this fashion the program is tied into the city's capital budgeting program.

Fourth, this program is policy oriented and, therefore, relates physical renewal to human needs. In this respect it is quite different from the more orthodox plans and programs which either pay only lip service to the notion that planning is for people or tend to compartmentalize population in one chapter and physical development in another. One reason for this integrative appearance is the fact that a systems analysis approach was used in the preparation of the study and therefore explicit consideration was given to the interdependence of such factors as housing needs, the location of public facilities, and population growth.

Fifth, this section focuses on the problems of one city, San Francisco, and draws in depth from a recent study which was made to suggest solutions to these problems in terms of tools currently available to those who are charged with urban redevelopment.

Finally, this program evolved from the development of a computer model of a residential housing market. This simulation model was designed to achieve the following purposes:

1. To identify and assess the impact of alternative long-range strategies and programs for renewal and development of the city.
2. To serve as an ongoing tool of city government to assist city officials in keeping the program which emerged up to date in the light of changing conditions and changing goals.
3. To have available on a continuing basis a method for testing the consequences of various renewal actions before they actually took place on the ground.

Community renewal is a set of tools and programs designed to eliminate blight, to preserve sound residential and non-residential areas and to improve others, in accordance with the city's goals and objectives. Thus, how these tools and programs are used depends on the purposes toward which they are directed. Based on our review of various public statements and documents, we have postulated a set of renewal goals and objectives which are both attainable and consistent. These include economic goals and residential goals.

RENEWAL GOALS AND OBJECTIVES

Economic Goals and Objectives

The best opportunities for achieving the largest total income in San Francisco, and ultimately its best distribution, appear to lie in the fields of finance, service, and related activities, and of certain types of specialized manufacturing. Therefore, such activities should be encouraged. Planning and renewal policies and programs should be designed to provide the necessary space and facilities for these specific types of activities:

• Administrative headquarters for Bay region and Northern California commercial and industrial enterprises.
• The port and port-related activities.
• Metropolitan distribution and marketing activities.
• Metropolitan specialty shopping activities.
• Government office and institutional activities.
• Cultural, entertainment, and convention facilities.
• New "incubator"-type firms and enterprises.
• Business, industrial, and professional services to support the above-listed functions.
• Local services and trades, beyond the categories listed, to serve San Franciscans.

Industrial Goals and Objectives

• In view of the benefits to be received from the growth of manufacturing activities which require a high degree of job skill, encouragement should be given to manufacturing activities which need such skills, which can operate in a centralized urban location, and which are compatible with the efforts to expand the finance and service sectors.
• To meet the needs of this type of manufacturing activity, efforts should be made to provide the job skills necessary, through job training and re-training programs aimed at upgrading the skills of the resident population. Efforts also should be made to ensure the availability of suitable industrial space by eliminating deficient buildings that cannot be economically adapted to modern manufacturing methods, by upgrading facilities that can be economically adapted, by ensuring that existing industrial facilities and areas are preserved and improved, by reducing congestion, and by providing more open space in industrial areas.

Commercial Goals

• Since San Francisco's economic future is closely tied to the proper development of its downtown district as an economic, social, cultural, and political focal point of the Bay Area, a major goal is to stimulate such development.

• Since the city must provide balanced commercial environments in keeping with the need of its residents and businesses, another goal is to develop sound, functional, and attractive neighborhood community and commercial centers, properly located so that businesses and their clientele are benefited and so that these centers do not detract from the strength of the downtown district.

Residential Goals and Objectives

• Adequate housing in a decent living environment should be provided for all San Francisco residents.

• Certain population groups have preferred and are likely in the future to prefer to live and work in a central city such as San Francisco. They are essential to the proper functioning of those activities believed most appropriate for the city as the Bay region center. Therefore, the city should be planning and renewing its housing and residential areas for these groups: immigrants from other countries and other parts of the United States including but not limited to, minority groups, whose first jobs may be semi-skilled and/or in service trades; young adults seeking employment or the anonymity of the central city; enterprising persons with new businesses to develop or new ideas to exploit or sell; senior citizens for whom a central city has special advantages; semi-skilled workers and their families; and business executives, professional men, shopkeepers, and their families.

• Each family or household should by 1978 have a safe, sound, sanitary and adequately sized dwelling unit at a cost it can afford. When new housing is not available to meet these requirements, good rehabilitated housing must be provided.

• The private market should be encouraged whenever possible to meet the needs of all the various groups.

• Sufficient public housing or rent supplementation should be provided for those who cannot afford standard private housing.

• Present overcrowding and substandard deteriorated housing (likely to threaten health and safety) should be eliminated and such possible further conditions forestalled.

· The high quality of existing sound dwelling units should be maintained.

· Maximum opportunity for choice of housing and residential location should be ensured for all people.

· Adequate community and cultural facilities, as well as adequate housing, should be provided in appropriate areas to meet the needs of people of all ages, single or married.

· Low-density, family-oriented areas and a large number of privately owned homes should remain available, to afford middle-income families alternatives within the city to the suburbs.

· A variety of higher-density accommodations should be available for young and retired couples, one-parent families, and others not needing or wanting single-family dwellings.

· Individuals, community organizations, and private groups should be encouraged to participate in the preparation as well as implementation of citywide and neighborhood renewal plans.

· It should be possible for those residents wishing to move to other areas of the city to find adequate housing, and for those with strong neighborhood ties to find in their neighborhood the housing and environmental satisfactions they seek.

· The City's diversity should be maintained. The loss of middle-income families with children is harmful to the city; the city should seek to retain its present proportion of families with children—approximately 23 percent of the total number of households.

To accommodate the anticipated population growth, the quantity and type of the city's housing supply must be changed considerably over the next twelve years. Part of the need for additional standard housing units can be met by a substantial upgrading of almost all housing units classified as substandard in 1960. There will still be a need for additional units that only can be met by new construction.

All types and sizes of housing units will be needed. Structures suitable for family living will be especially necessary to attract and retain families with children and to accommodate the population expected for this group. Most of these family-type housing units should have more than five rooms and be priced for the middle- to high-income groups. Although rehabilitation and improvement of existing structures will help, the bulk of the demand will have to be met by new construction.

The city lacks sufficient vacant land to build the increased number of new single-family dwellings needed to accommodate families with children. There are several alternatives. Ways and means must be found to divert a large portion of the households without children to other, more economic, higher-density housing, leaving the bulk of the single-family dwellings to families with children. New cooperative or rental quarters, especially the combination high-rise apartment garden and duplex block which has already proved feasible in one project, are possibilities here. New garden apartment developments with open space and other amenities are also possibilities. New building sites might be "created" on reclaimed waterfront land or other publicly owned land. City-owned properties which may be considered surplus for the uses originally intended could be considered for residential development. It would also be possible to renew (redevelop) existing non-residential surplus sites for single-family residential purposes, as well as to renew (redevelop) existing "marginal" single-family areas for higher-density family housing.

Most of the demand for single-family dwellings will be for larger units, of five rooms or more. Zoning changes in height and side-yard requirements which would facilitate addition of one or two bedrooms of existing smaller single-family structures would help in meeting the demand for family-type housing.

BARRIERS TO THE LIVING AND WORKING ENVIRONMENT AND WAYS TO OVERCOME THEM

In its efforts to achieve its housing and renewal goals and objectives, the city faces and must overcome a series of barriers which are economic or social in character. Some of the barriers are common to all central cities struggling for environmental improvement. Others, however, are unique to San Francisco, stemming from its history or topography, or special economic or social structure.

Barriers to the Improvement of the Living Environment

These include:

• Low Income. A substantial portion of San Francisco's population has income too low to enable purchase or rental of new or rehabilitated housing.

• Age of Structures. In 1960, 95 percent of San Francisco's

substandard or seriously substandard housing units were more than thirty years old and 99 percent were more than twenty years old. Not all older property is in poor condition, but keeping it in good condition requires more maintenance and repair than is required for newer housing. For this reason, the age of the city's housing units is of serious concern.

• High Percentage of Rental Households. In 1960, 65 percent of the housing units were rental units—one of the highest percentages of any major United States city. This situation poses a potential problem, since experience indicates that housing standards in rental structures tend to be lower than in owner-occupied structures. Persons who own the homes in which they live are more likely to maintain them well than are absentee landlords likely to so maintain their rental properties. The number of renter-occupied structures is likely to increase in the foreseeable future. This will require public policies designed to induce the owners—be they resident in San Francisco or elsewhere—to maintain and when necessary improve their properties.

• High Cost of Housing. Serious deterrents to the construction of new housing in San Francisco, particularly for the lower- and moderate-income groups, are the high cost of land and the high cost of construction, particularly in hilly areas. The cost of rehabilitating existing dwelling units is also high. If the city's housing and renewal goals are to be met, financial aids will have to be provided to developers of certain types of housing for specially disadvantaged groups, and to landlords of existing housing to allow them to rehabilitate their property.

• Residential Segregation of Racial and Ethnic Minorities. The tendency to segregate racial and ethnic minorities forces these groups to pay an inordinate proportion of their income for housing. The supply of housing available to minority groups is restricted, causing available structures to become overcrowded and higher-than-normal rents to be established. It also makes it possible and profitable for certain landlords to maintain substandard facilities. Minority groups are disadvantaged in their efforts to find decent housing and the number of substandard and ultimately seriously substandard housing is significantly increased. Unless the housing market is open to all racial and ethnic groups, the limited supply available to them will continue to be of poorer quality.

• Limited Concern for Housing Quality. Census information indicates that many occupants of low-rental housing pay a relatively low proportion of their income for rent. A significant number of these occupants probably could increase their rent to obtain standard housing and still not suffer financial hardship. The reason they do not is indicated by some of the findings of our special study on Renewal Attitudes. This study revealed that many people have limited concern for the quality of the physical environment and hence may pay comparatively little for housing. This limited concern hinders a continued improvement of the housing stock.

• Taxation Policies. San Francisco relies heavily on the real property tax for its revenues. The ratio of property taxes to total revenue is one of the highest in the state. Moreover, the burden of taxation is tending to fall more heavily on the improvements on the land than on the land itself. With this trend and the threat of the increasing tax rate, owners may be reluctant to improve their property, fearing that the increase in taxes will nullify the benefits of the improvements. This is particularly important in connection with substandard property, since the value of the improvements is low and the value of the land may be increasing.

• High Cost of Investment Capital in Declining Areas. Owners of property in declining areas find it very difficult to obtain the capital required to rehabilitate or remodel their property. This denies to such owners the opportunity to increase their income by upgrading their property. Consequently, many owners seek additional income by further subdividing or undermaintaining their property, or by overcrowding existing living quarters. The result is aggravation of an already deteriorating situation. If San Francisco is to be successful in maintaining and upgrading its residential environment, means must be found for property owners in these areas to obtain reasonable financing for housing improvement.

• Reluctance of Property Owners to Act Individually. Significant improvements in housing require more than individual action. Many individuals refuse to improve their property because there is no indication that others in the neighborhood will do likewise. The value of any one property depends in great part on the quality of the neighborhood in which it is located. Unless potential investors are convinced that their effort would be part of an active program to upgrade the quality of the entire neighborhood, they are unlikely to invest in any improvements to their properties, and the entire neighborhood will continue to deteriorate.

• Lack of Knowledge and Experience Regarding Home

Improvements. Many inexperienced owners need advice on how to make satisfactory and economical improvements and on how to select a reliable rehabilitation contractor. The lack of knowledge may be a sufficient deterrent to turn a general desire and willingness to improve housing into inaction.

• Environmental Deficiencies. Serious environmental and amenity deficiencies detract from the desirability of many areas and inhibit homeowners' willingness to invest in property improvement. The success of efforts to encourage homeowners and owners of rental property to invest more in housing improvements will depend in large part on the city's willingness to do its share by investing in public improvements designed to correct these environmental deficiencies.

Tools and Programs to Overcome Residential Improvement Barriers

Various tools and programs are available to deal with barriers to improvement to housing and the living environment. They will not completely eliminate the barriers, but if they are employed with vigor and imagination they can significantly lessen the harmful effects of such obstacles. Some of these tools and programs—e.g., provision of social services, the anti-poverty program, education programs, job training—have not traditionally been viewed as urban renewal measures. However, since they are designed to increase income, and thus eliminate perhaps the most significant barrier to improvement —that of limited financial ability—they must be viewed as integral parts of a renewal program.

Code enforcement is the principal tool which can be used to overcome the barriers of age of structures, high cost of investment capital, and reluctance of property owners to act individually. Housing code enforcement is the process by which city inspectors examine dwellings to determine whether they comply with the code, which sets minimum standards for physical condition, maintenance, and occupancy of all housing and which requires basic equipment and facilities. Housing code enforcement is both a regulatory activity undertaken by the city to protect public health and safety by assuring that all housing is safe and sanitary, and a service to property owners.

Many environmental deficiencies can be corrected through the city's Capital Improvement Program, through spot clearance (using powers derived from a particular urban renewal project called a Conservation and Rehabilitation Project), through amortization provisions in a zoning ordinance, through sign control ordinances and through street tree planting programs.

In some areas of the city, housing cannot be economically brought to a sound condition through code enforcement alone and environmental deficiencies cannot be corrected by the means just described. In these instances the urban renewal tool of clearance and redevelopment is appropriate.

A number of tools and programs are directed toward eliminating the barrier of inadequate earnings' capability, including: housing for low-income individuals, moderate-income private housing constructed under Section 221(d)3 of the National Housing Act, and housing for the elderly, constructed under Section 230 of the National Housing Act. Such programs as vocational training, adult education, and retraining programs upgrade earning capability; people can then earn more and thus afford better housing.

Other tools and programs operate directly to increase the amount of income available for housing. For example, rehabilitation grants to low-income homeowners, provided in the Housing Act of 1965, permit them to undertake work which they would otherwise be unable to do.

Barriers to the Improvement of the Working Environment

The major barriers to improving the city's working environment include obsolescent structures, limited room for expansion, high labor cost, high land cost and assembly problems, taxation problems, limited available financing, and environmental deficiency.

Tools and Programs to Overcome Barriers to Commercial and Industrial Renewal

The tools and programs available to overcome these barriers are, briefly: (a) clearance and redevelopment, which provide a means to eliminate obsolete structures, provide limited room for expansion, reduce high land costs, and solve land parcel assembly problems; (b) shifting the ratio of taxes to place more emphasis on land and less on buildings to possibly alleviate property tax problems; and (c) cooperation of the city in zoning, code enforcement, and provision of utilities and transportation access to eliminate environmental deficiencies. Solutions to the problems of financing include the establishment of a public or semi-public development corporation, or of a development credit corporation to increase the supply of loanable funds, and similar forms of financial assistance.

LONG-RANGE POLICIES AND PROGRAM FOR RENEWAL

The information on changes in population, housing, income, and economic activity developed as part of the CRP indicates that some changes of emphasis of policy guiding San Francisco's renewal programs will be necessary if the city is to meet its goals and objectives. Many of the CRP goals and objectives can be achieved directly through clearance and redevelopment, neighborhood conservation, code enforcement, and public housing, as well as through various financial aids for low-income and moderate-income housing. But these elements should be only part of a broader program for community improvement which includes city services, public works, and socio-economic programs. The policies recommended are designed to provide direction and focus not merely for urban renewal activity, but for such a broad program of community improvement and development.

The proposed over-all policy or strategy to provide an adequate housing supply and attractive physical environment to meet the needs of the projected population may be briefly summarized as follows:

• The needs of upper- and middle-income groups are to be met by advancing the quality of existing housing and the physical environment as incomes rise, by encouraging private enterprise to provide new housing where needed (also where necessary, using various special financial aids), and by renewal programs aimed at maintaining and improving the quality of the city's neighborhoods, particularly those deemed uniquely suited for family living.

• The needs of lower-income groups are to be met by rent supplements to lower-income persons to permit them to pay for new private housing, by providing standard housing from the existing stock, by direct public investment in new or rehabilitated low-rent housing, and by job-creating and income-improvement programs designed to enhance the earning capacity of lower-income groups so that their incomes will rise and they will thus be able to afford standard housing from their own resources.

• To improve the economic base of the entire city, it is recommended that various renewal powers be used to put underutilized commercial and industrial areas to more productive uses.

KEY ELEMENTS OF OVER-ALL POLICY

Within this over-all renewal policy, certain specific policies are considered critical to the achievement of the city's goals and objectives.

Maintaining and Upgrading Existing Housing Stock

Even if new construction is carried on at an increased rate in the years ahead, most San Franciscans in 1978 will be living in housing built before 1939. Some of this existing housing stock is already in poor condition; much of the good housing will need careful maintenance and periodic repairs if it is to remain in good condition. An important element of renewal strategy, therefore, is to make best use of the city's housing stock: to preserve what is now in good condition, to repair what can be brought to present-day standards, and to retire the obsolete and the irreparable.

To date, the city's residential renewal efforts have been directed primarily at the "bottom" of the housing quality range —the most dilapidated structures in the most seriously blighted areas. We recommend that, while work is continued at the bottom of the housing quality scale, there should be a major shift in renewal policy to arresting incipient blight. Along with this shift of emphasis to the "middle range" areas, public efforts at the top of the quality scale should be expanded by use of maintenance and surveillance programs.

Renewing Residential Areas for the Present Residents

The primary objective of residential renewal is to provide decent homes and living environments for all citizens of the community. To achieve this objective, it has been necessary or desirable in most cities, including San Francisco, to substantially change the nature and character of the land use in blighted areas. The result has been extensive clearance of houses and other buildings and the relocation of the residents. Neighborhoods programmed for clearance have usually been low-income areas which after redevelopment have generally been repopulated by higher-income groups. Similar results have been seen in many areas designated for rehabilitation;

in many instances code enforcement has had similar effects.

This approach to urban renewal admittedly meets the goal of providing decent homes and living environment, though it does so only by relocation. (According to Federal law, persons displaced by federally assisted renewal projects must be relocated in decent, safe, and sanitary dwellings within their financial means.) However, relocation, no matter how sensitively handled, has a number of disadvantages, and may often result in "pushing the blight around" to other areas of the city.

Until recently, the tools and programs available have left little alternative to heavy relocation than leaving the area completely untouched. Now, however, new urban renewal tools, especially those provided for in the Housing Act of 1965, make it feasible to adopt an alternative policy for carrying out the objectives of residential renewal: namely, rebuilding, rehabilitation, and restoring areas for the use and benefit of people presently living in the neighborhood, if they desire to remain there after renewal.

The principal tools and programs now available are:

• Rent supplements for tenancy and ownership to low-income families in 221(d)3 housing.
• Rehabilitation grants to low-income owners for repair of their homes.
• Broadening of authority of local housing authorities to buy or lease existing housing units for low-income families.
• Low-interest (3 percent) rehabilitation loans.
• Anti-poverty, manpower training and development, vocational education and other programs designed to improve economic and social well-being of low- and moderate-income households.

With these financial and other programs, it should be possible to provide decent, safe, and sanitary housing that every resident can afford. Therefore, we recommend that San Francisco adopt a policy of renewing residential areas for their present residents if those residents want to remain there after renewal. The city and residents involved would benefit from this policy because it would minimize relocation of those for whom relocation poses the greatest difficulty; help to stabilize neighborhoods and also allow for orderly transition in other neighborhoods; ease the pressure on the limited supply of low-cost housing; minimize the public resources required, not only for clearance but also for direct construction; and permit the maintenance of a viable social structure in a neighborhood.

The use of this policy should be tempered with concern that it does not result in perpetuating ghettos of racial or income classes. Renewal must be of such high quality that some different racial and income groups will be attracted into the areas being renewed.

This recommended policy should be applied to code enforcement and neighborhood conservation efforts, as well as in urban renewal projects.

Linking Physical Renewal with Human Resources Development

Social planning and physical renewal planning must function together if each is to do its job properly. Decisions made in physical planning and renewal have significant social ramifications. On the other hand, decisions about social services and social programs influence where people live and their physical environmental requirements. The quality of social services and facilities available in a neighborhood is crucial to the success or failure of physical renewal programs.

A continuous process of neighborhood improvement concerned as much with human factors as with physical factors must be established. Once a program of neighborhood improvement is initiated, increased individual pride and motivation can well follow.

The formal linking of social and physical planning will not be easy. New administrative mechanisms will have to be devised to achieve it. A formal link in renewal programs, drawing heavily on a community action (anti-poverty) program, is recommended as a central policy and approach in those residential areas requiring extensive treatment and renewal.

Renewal Treatment in Every Area—A Citywide Approach

The various parts of the city have grown, developed, and changed differently and thus have different renewal problems and needs. Some areas have so deteriorated that they no longer serve a significant economic or social purpose; they require extensive renewal treatment and possibly rebuilding. Other areas are basically sound but suffer from the abuses of time and the deterioration of the physical environment; they will require selective renewal treatment to restore them to a sound condition and improve environmental amenities. Other relatively new areas are generally sound and will require only general maintenance. When so defined, every area of the city needs some type of "renewal treatment," ranging from actions designed merely to maintain the present high quality to more extensive actions which involve rebuilding.

The achievement of renewal objectives in every area requires the programming of both private and public actions. Accordingly, the CRP considers "renewal treatment" to mean a combination of private and public actions, taken in sequence, for any given area, to maintain or restore high quality, prevent deterioration, or eliminate deficiencies.

The need for a citywide approach to urban renewal activity has become obvious as more and more communities, including San Francisco, have shown the project-by-project approach to be incapable of dealing with the huge renewal task facing them. Such an approach was not even eliminating blighted areas at the same rate at which blight was occurring in other parts of the city.

At present, legislation and administrative procedures do not reflect this expanding concept of urban renewal. State enabling legislation in California, as in other states, is still project-oriented. Federal financial assistance is largely limited to designated urban renewal projects, although under the Housing Act of 1965 provision is made for the first time for grants to cities to carry out programs of concentrated code enforcement without any specific project orientation. As part of the citywide approach to renewal, we recommend that the city not only designate specific urban renewal projects, but also use its ongoing tools and programs. The key to this approach is programmed code enforcement by means of frequent inspections and careful followups for violations, combined with the use of public improvements in a manner that promotes private investment and reinvestment. Equally essential is a citizenry informed as to the objectives of the renewal program and convinced of its usefulness. Another essential element is the integration of a variety of public services, such as law enforcement, refuse collection, and street tree planting.

Types of Treatment Areas, Policies and Approach

Because all areas require some type of renewal treatment, the city was divided into appropriate "treatment areas." Each treatment area category requires a different approach to renewal, including its own mix of tools and programs, to reflect the different physical, social and economic conditions, the severity of the problems, and the renewal and development opportunities. The categories employed for the long-range renewal program were residential rebuilding areas, residential improvement areas, residential maintenance areas, industrial-commercial rebuilding areas, industrial-commercial improvement areas, and industrial-commercial maintenance areas.

Treatment areas, it should be emphasized, are only general categories reflecting broad similarities and conditions, problems, and opportunities; even within each area conditions vary. Their boundaries should not be considered precise or fixed; they are intended to indicate general location and approaches to renewal treatment.

The recommended approaches for the various categories reflect the key elements of the over-all renewal policy described above. For example, the recommended policy for residential rebuilding areas calls for a careful coordination of physical renewal tools and social-economic programs in a time-phased plan of action.

There are five types of renewal treatment "mechanisms" available for each treatment area category. These are:

(a) Clearance and Redevelopment Project. This treatment mechanism is appropriate for many parts of rebuilding areas which cannot otherwise be restored to a sound condition. Federal financial assistance is available for such a project. Where appropriate, this mechanism should be combined and coordinated with the human resources plan.

(b) Conservation and Rehabilitation Project. This treatment mechanism is appropriate for some parts of rebuilding areas and for those improvement-type neighborhoods with a high incidence of housing and environmental deficiencies correctable without substantial clearance. This type of federally assisted urban renewal project is designed to restore the economic and social values of deteriorating residential areas which are basically sound and worth conserving and in which existing buildings, public facilities, and improvements can be economically renewed to a long-term sound condition. Clearance is confined to "spot" clearance to remove blighting influences and buildings unfeasible of rehabilitation, or to provide land for public improvements or facilities. To qualify for this type of treatment under the Federal program, the area must contain such deficiencies that public action is necessary to eliminate and prevent deterioration or blight. The use of this approach makes certain key financial and other aids available, and thus benefits owners and residents. Where appropriate, this treatment mechanism should be combined and coordinated with a human resources plan.

(c) Concentrated Code Enforcement Coupled with Environmental Improvements. This treatment mechanism is appropriate for improvement-type neighborhoods where housing and environmental deficiencies are not so serious as to require a conservation-rehabilitation approach, but are serious enough to require building-by-building compliance and a concentrated environmental upgrading effort. This treatment mechanism has been employed by the city for several years. A new provision of the Housing Act of 1965 established the authority for "programs of concentrated-code enforcement in deteriorated or deteriorating areas in which such enforcement, together with those public improvements to be provided by the locality, may be expected to arrest the decline of the area." Under this provision, the federal government will make grants to a city totaling up to two-thirds of the cost of planning and effecting such programs. These costs may include the provision and repair of necessary streets, curbs, sidewalks, street lights, tree planting, and similar improvements. Homeowners in these areas will be eligible for Section 220 FHA insured rate-market interest loans (which are generally more liberal than conventional loans), for the new 3 percent interest rehabilitation loans, and for urban renewal relocation aids.

(d) District Housing Inspection and Public Improvements through the City's Capital Improvement Program. This treatment mechanism is appropriate where housing and environmental deficiencies are minor or nonexistent, and therefore is appropriate for certain improvement type of neighborhoods as well as for "maintenance" areas of the city. Under District Housing Inspection, an inspector is assigned to a district on a permanent basis. This type of code enforcement program can prevent the deterioration of existing housing, forestall illegal conversions and overcrowding, and effect a gradual upgrading of the quality of the housing.

This type of code enforcement is best employed where housing conditions are generally good but where the age of buildings or the existence of rental buildings indicates the need for continuing maintenance. It should also be used where urban renewal projects have been completed, to encourage preservation of the values created through renewal and to prolong the usefulness of these areas. Combined with district housing inspection would be the provision of public improvements through the city's Capital Improvement Program.

(e) Reconditioning. This treatment mechanism is appropriate in neighborhoods requiring more extensive treatment but which are not scheduled for redevelopment, conservation and rehabilitation, or concentrated code enforcement to a standard just short of requiring correction of conditions which necessitate major structural changes or improvements, but do not constitute an immediate health or safety hazard or detract from the general livability of the structure. Such reconditioning would be designed to control overcrowding, eliminate hazards, and enforce sound housekeeping and maintenance practices.

THE SIMULATION MODEL

These policies and approaches culminated in a citywide action program which recommended a different type of renewal treatment for each area in San Francisco. The feasibility of this program was tested by means of a simulation model on a computer. The model was in effect a replication of a residential land and building space market in San Francisco. It was purposely designed to be sensitive to public policy decisions and city policy problems. The effects of public action controls on the market were evaluated in the program by introducing into the model alternative hypothetical public actions and goals. An analysis of these effects provided a basis for developing a long-range strategy in the program for renewal. Public actions were introduced in the model as they affected the operation of the real estate market either by interfering with, influencing, or controlling its function. These actions took the form of a zoning code which prohibited certain changes in the use of space from taking place. They also took the form of code enforcement in renewal projects which "artificially" introduced changes in the use and condition of space. Other public actions which were used included:

1) Financial measures such as tax changes or cost subsidies which affected the price and the quantity and/or quality of the available housing.

2) Public improvements which altered the relevant attraction of certain neighborhoods in the City.

This in turn affected the demand for space in the neighborhoods and thereby induced spontaneous private investment and rehabilitation construction in such areas. The result and effect of space usage was evaluated in terms of the foregoing City goals and objectives. In this way a time phase program of public actions was able to be selected in order to achieve the objectives of the renewal policy.

Each individual decision-maker was not identified and replicated in the computer. Instead, all those decision-makers who behave in a similar manner were grouped together. Consequently, the City's 1960 population was divided into 114 individual groups. Each group was selected to reflect similar income, family size, race, age, and housing preference. The groups were programmed to be living in 106 neighborhoods, defined through consideration of significant similarities. All dwelling units were grouped into twenty-seven different categories, each of which exists in a variety of physical conditions. These houses were allocated among the 106 neighborhoods indicated by the 1960 census. Investors were postulated as being willing to build new units or rehabilitate existing units whenever it became profitable to do so. The rules that govern this profitability were tied to the yield they will obtain, the price of these buildings, and the cost of such new construction and rehabilitation.

The model was programmed to be dynamic. That is, the computer was instructed so that all the decision-making groups would interact with each other in a manner that replicates their actions in the real world. The model was designed to permit the skilled planner to consider the ramifications of alternate plans before they were executed, but it was not intended to be a highly accurate forecasting tool. It is unique in that the skilled interpreter can use it to investigate all possible combinations of plans and results. It is not tied to a few statistical variables whose usefulness is restricted to specific situations. Neither is it tied to the unrealistic assumption that history will repeat itself and that projections can be made from statistically derived past trends.

Two computer runs were needed for evaluation because the model's primary strength lies in its ability to suggest the *relative* impact of public actions. That is, the most meaningful evaluation involves a comparison between a simulation of the market with the inclusion of public actions and another simulation without these actions. Therefore, one run is needed as a conditional prediction of the housing future of San Francisco under stipulated conditions that *do not* include the plans or programs we desire to evaluate.

The second public action run was identical to the base run, except that it included a simulation of a type of code enforcement, zoning, clearance, and public housing actions that were recommended in the Community Renewal Program. The public actions were simulated to test the efficacy of the recommended program items on the housing market and their ability to push it in the direction of improving the quality of housing available to the residents of San Francisco.

The analysis of these two runs provided the basis for increased confidence in the propriety of the recommended Community Renewal Program and confirmed the usefulness of a model in dealing with a complex system. For example, the public action run indicated that during the six years of the recommended code enforcement program there was a *reduction* in the number of these substandard and seriously substandard units by approximately 9 percent, while the total number of housing units was increasing. On the other hand, the increase in housing units brought with it a 3 percent *increase* in low-quality units when code endorsement was not simulated. The two runs indicated that code endorsement encouraged the private market to invest in rehabilitation at a rate 40 percent higher than in the absence of code enforcement.

This analysis also gave warning on the price or rent effects that would accompany improved housing quality. The decrease in substandard and seriously substandard units brought with it a rental increase in the remaining substandard and seriously substandard units. The runs indicated that by 1978 these units would increase in rent at a rate double that of higher quality units. Consequently, we felt that in order to avoid imposing financial hardships on low-income households, code enforcement should be accompanied by an expansion of the supply of low-cost standard housing. Therefore, additional low-cost housing units became one of the recommendations in our Community Renewal Program.

Chapter 18

THE NEW TOWNS CONCEPT

The enormous recent increase in total world population with the resultant (a) high central city density coupled with inhuman living conditions and (b) gobbling up of agricultural and other open spaces through unsatisfactory suburban sprawl, has focused the eyes of the Western world on the "hiving off" of excess and new populations into planned new towns or cities. In addition, underdeveloped nations, eager for material progress, have been forced to optimize the use of very scarce capital and natural resources by judicious balancing of newly created urban places with the magnetic attractions of the already packed few cities; moreover, creating a new national capital is a heady symbol of fresh nationhood.

Not that designed cities built from scratch are something new in history: from the Egyptians through the Greeks to the Romans to the Mongols to the medieval kingdoms of Europe, new cities for defense and trade have been a commonplace. The Incas set up new towns to strengthen their empire. There are reported to be over 150 "Newtons" in the United Kingdom and the settlement of North, Central and South America was by new towns—either planned, but more generally "happenings." Patently, the heritage of fresh capital cities does not start with Islamabad, Chandigarh and Brasilia, but reaches back through Canberra, Washington, D.C. and Petrograd to Peiping and beyond.

The British must be credited in modern times with the first burst of the current interest in new towns by their remarkable post-World War II program: some twenty-eight cities built, under construction or planned. By new town, the British mean a complete small city with dwellings, jobs, and a full complement of community facilities —including the higher culture—with a fixed area and population held firm by an encircling greenbelt. The new town is not expected to stand alone but is generally sited in some reasonable time/distance relationship with a major city or metropolis. Obviously this is no dormitory suburb. The new town is fast becoming—perhaps too naïvely and overenthusiastically—the newest ploy in American urban design. Having barely survived a nasty zig by partially coping with the devastation wrought by the National Defense Interstate Highway System, and a relatively happy zag in central city renewal, our assiduous creators of "comprehensive development plans" are now apparently ready to serve developers—public or private—in the creation of new satellite cities in a further zag. There is no national plan for urbanization even dimly sketched in the Interstate Highway scheme and only a chancy final marriage of largely haphazard renewal "projectitis" with comprehensive urban planning has taken place. At the present, there seems little likelihood, under the American federal governmental system, of making the necessary synthesis of central city development, new towns, and comprehensive transportation thinking in a national planned system, by regions, of a function/ spatial urbanization scheme for the entire country—closely linked with Canadian and Mexican equivalent planning. Merely to sketch such potentialities is to move into the twenty-first century; our new towns may merely result in new sprawl. And yet on the other hand, lacking population control, some form of ordered expansion of urbanization cannot be far ahead and Federal legislation to that effect seems to be just around the corner resting heavily on private experience and initiative—as it should—in our very mixed economy.

As the patron saint of the British new towns program, founded on the Garden Cities movement of Ebenezar Howard, Sir Frederic Osborn rightly establishes, below, Britain's place in the modern history of new settlements. I have attempted in my essay to synthesize the lessons, both good and bad, to be learned from the British program, and Frederick Gutheim has pointed out the differential experience to be garnered from continental Europe's recent undertakings in building fresh towns or parts thereof. James Rouse, as the enlightened developer of Columbia, a Maryland new city already building, speaks his piece before a congressional committee in 1966 for Federal government acceptance of the leadership in a national effort to build new communities—incidentally giving a thumbnail sketch of the level of thought and expertise that is going into his own new town. Surprisingly, Congress in 1966 made some faltering steps toward aiding by mortgage funds private builders of new communities, as well as providing planning aid to government bodies interested in developing similar towns. Charles Abrams suggests to the California governor a way out under state law which might well bear fruit, and John Rubel outlines a somewhat breathtaking marriage of space technology system analysis and economic structuring to a national new city planning system in order to realize the enormous power of the private sector of our economy in a series of combined public-private corporations exhibiting a resultant entrepreneurial strength and ingenuity far above the sum of its parts.

Britain's Place in Town Planning

SIR FREDERIC J. OSBORN*

The Industrial Revolution and its agricultural counterpart, with the consequent vast migration from the countryside to

* Vice President of the Town and Country Planning Association (London) and Vice President of the International Federation for Housing and Planning. He was for seventeen years editor of *Town and*

manufacturing towns, began in Great Britain. Whether this was historically a "good thing" many philosophers, poets, and even statesmen have questioned. But in the course of two centuries the whole civilized world has followed suit, and now the processes of industrialization and urbanization are speeding up in every continent.

The material advantages have been stupendous. The factory system, mechanical invention, the exploitation of fuels, and the development of means of transport and communications have enormously increased productivity and standards of living, and made possible huge increases of population. Unhappily from its very start the Industrial Revolution created a most unhealthy, disagreeable, and socially debasing type of town, with contrasts between the quality of environments of rich and poor that have caused grave social and political conflicts and sadly damaged human solidarity.

Much has been done during the past century to ameliorate the worst conditions in towns. But their continued growth has so intensified their disorder as largely to cancel out the benefits of detailed improvements. The "great city" appeared, and whether or not this disturbed the watching angels, civilized man saw city growth as progress; gloated over it, even boasted competitively of its speed. Only recently has the very idea of controlling town size and concentration entered the minds of authorities and governments.

Town planning, in the modern sense of public control of the form of urban development, began in Italy just 100 years ago with a law that empowered a few big cities to rationalize in some measure their new suburban extensions. The aim was to safeguard residential amenity and to promote convenience in communications, and the method was the prescription of use zones, maximum densities, minimum open space, and considered road patterns. This important break-through was followed within a decade by Sweden and Germany, and forty-four years later (1909) by Great Britain. Thus our

Country Planning and Estate Manager of Welwyn Garden City for the same length of time. He has been awarded the gold medal of the Town Planning Institute of Great Britain (1963) and the silver medal of the American Society of Planning Officials (1960). He is the author of *New Towns After the War* (1918–reissued in 1942); *Green-Belt Cities* (1946); and with A. Whittick, *New Towns: The Answer to Megalopolis* (1963). He was knighted in 1956, and was a member of the New Towns Committee of 1946. The following is reprinted with permission from *Town and Country Planning*, Vol. XXXIII, No. 11, November 1965.

country cannot claim to have been a pioneer in the field of control planning, though we can claim that by the Act of 1947 we were the first free-enterprise state to extend such control to virtually all development in both urban and rural areas.

Britain, however, can claim to be the pioneer in the creation of new planned industrial towns as distinct from statutory regulation of development. We have evolved the revolutionary concept of a general pattern of towns of controlled size on a background of green country, in which the advantages of man's achievements in science, invention, and organization can be obtained without the sacrifice of pleasure in his daily environment. The before-mentioned angels might see in this something of an *amende honorable* to the world for Britain's initiation of the "hideous town" of the industrial age. That we have long been troubled in our conscience by this responsibility is shown by innumerable passages in our literature. And a reading of the many press notices of Howard's *Tomorrow* (1898) is a reminder of how profoundly people were stirred by the picture of a new and better type of town, even though the majority of reviewers could not believe in the possibility of realizing such a vision.

It took Howard and his disciples nearly fifty years, two private-enterprise demonstrations, and incessant nattering, to get public opinion and governmental authority to accept the common-sense policy of the limitation, decentralization, and dispersal of London and other swollen cities. Lord Silkin's New Towns Act did not appear until 1946, and Mr Duncan Sandys' green belt policy not until 1955.

In the meantime, control planning as a governmental function, gradually widening in scope from suburbs to built-up and rural areas, was taken up by one country after another; in some it is now extending to regional and even national spheres. Yet, powerful as it has become, in many countries it still mainly pursues the limited purpose of sophisticating or bringing spots of order into a massive and continuing urban growth. Its laws and systems of administration have immensely advanced, essentially on the principles of the pioneer planning Acts of 1865–75. Except for public housing, which in some but not all countries is an influential factor in development decisions, the dynamic of urban growth is still mainly uncoordinated, and public planning is still primarily regulative within a municipal range of vision.

It is distressing to reflect that the overcrowding of towns, the excessive density of housing, the shortage of open space, and the exodus of the better-off to suburbs, divorcing millions of central dwellers from contact with, or even awareness of, the countryside, did not produce an effective political movement for the control of city size. Despite the efforts of the advocates of new towns it was not until the motor vehicle, which at first was welcomed as permitting infinite urban expansion, became so widely used as to threaten complete traffic strangulation that the idea that a city's size must ultimately be limited began to be seriously discussed by statesmen. And at first in Britain alone.

To this day, many states have not yet got beyond the concept of tidying up and lubricating the growth of great cities. The reason, we believe, is not that city authorities and planners are unintelligent or unimaginative. It is simply that the economic and political forces making for metropolitan growth seem to them too mighty to be stopped. At best they can be slightly deflected. In the main it is thought wiser to accept growth, and to assist it by measures to facilitate internal traffic movement; and the debate now is as to whether to go for more speedways for cars or for more public transit with limitations on private car use.

That in any very large existing city one or other or both these expedients will have to be applied in face of increasing car-ownership can hardly be denied. But surely it is utter folly to keep the tap running while you are spooning out the bath. The time has come for national policies to halt continuous metropolitan development, to reserve country land around them and between all towns, and to place the primary emphasis on providing for displaced and growing populations, and their workplaces, in smaller towns, new and old. This concept will be seen historically as Britain's great contribution to thought and practice in urban planning.

We have far to go before we can fully implement this policy. But we are on our way, and we have given a lead which other countries are certain to follow.

Lessons Learned from the British
New Towns Program

H. WENTWORTH ELDREDGE

"A Garden City is a Town designed for healthy living and industry; of a size that makes possible a full measure of social life but not larger; surrounded by a rural belt; the whole of the land being in public ownership or held in trust for the community." Garden Cities and Town Planning Association, 1919.

The most experienced, sophisticated new towns' designer-builders and administrators in the modern world are the British, although in pure bulk of new cities, they are apparently outweighed by the U.S.S.R. and in design by the Finns. While it might be rudely quipped that never have so few people spent so many pounds in Great Britain with so little idea, empirically and reliably, of what they were doing or why they were doing it, the astonishing fact remains that some twenty-eight going or about-to-be-going communities ranging from 20,000 to 100,000 inhabitants have been initiated and to a considerable degree built. Obviously, there are dozens and dozens of other modern new town examples throughout the world; the British are unique in having a national "New Towns Programme" even with its faults. If an American effort equivalent to that of the British had been carried out here—given our G.N.P., population, price level, level of living, etc.—it would amount, as a guess-estimate, to something like $9,000,000,000 in capital investment both public and private. This we have not done and are not likely to do for some time. Nevertheless, there are in the U.S.A. at this juncture at least one hundred* relatively self-sufficient new towns at various stages of planning and/or construction in a largely unthought-through macro-planning effort—despite the true excellence in isolated cases at the micro- or town-level planning. City siting seems to be largely left to pure entrepreneurial chance.

* Some experts raise this figure to two hundred. Wolf Von Eckardt, architectural and planning critic, advocated in *Harper's Magazine* (December 1965) that we build 350 new towns to aid in coping with population sprawl.

Unfortunately, sophisticated researching of goals, timing, social planning, national urbanization pattern, social infrastructure, urban design, decision-making, and public administrative setup has simply not adequately been initiated, much less carried out, for the remarkable British New Towns Programme; however, there are some very useful things to be distilled from this experience. The British have attempted to manage a population growth and urban concentration similar to ours, complicated in their case by a much sharper shortage of land in the right places. In one notable way their situation differs markedly from ours as they have been locked in an economy of scarcity since World War II, while abundance (despite miserable pockets of poverty) bubbles about our collective ears in the United States.

Here follow eighteen lessons learned from the British effort, though all critics might not agree with the entire list. These are given in no order of importance and are more or less applicable to our current situation in the United States; they are worth pondering. The British, themselves, in their newest new towns and in the recent attention paid there to regional and national space planning in conjunction with economic planning, give evidence that they too are weighing past practices carefully:

1. It is now generally understood that a new towns policy should be part of a national plan for urbanization and economic development. The planless drift of people and industry into Southeast England did not seem to have been considered at a regional scale in the siting of the original batch of new towns. New towns could be one of the key devices to forward a national development plan for urbanization in both developed and underdeveloped nations. New towns cannot be built *in vacuo;* they are integral both to central city renewal and to the agreed urbanization pattern of the country and must be founded on comprehensive national industrial and transportation plans for spatial/functional development. There certainly should be clarity in goals at the top; for example the British Board of Trade and the new towns long "competed" with little rime or reason for "good" industry.

2. A new town probably needs a population of close to 100,000 inhabitants in order to support in a lively fashion a rich urban infrastructure culturally, socially, politically and economically—especially if geographically isolated. All the truly successful British new towns are pressing toward this population figure.

3. On the other hand Great Britain has developed a variety of new town forms; a national program might profitably include a wide spectrum of types to meet varied life styles and varied regions.

4. Rather than starting afresh in all cases, developing existing towns at local invitation might very well be a less costly and more humanly desirable move. Actually many "new" towns rest heavily on existing—if chaotic—urbanization. The Town Development Act of 1952 (and subsequent acts) have attempted to do just this by the cooperation of the population-exporting city, the importing town and the financially helpful national government with some success to date. Under this scheme approximately 148,000 dwellings had been contracted for by the summer of 1965 in England and Scotland with 42,000 already built. Figures on new factory construction—necessary to a "balanced community"—were not available according to the knowledgeable *Town and Country Planning* yearly survey of 1966.

5. "Not ownership but enterprise" should characterize new town entrepreneurship. Sound private enterprise, a city corporation, a national corporation, a private foundation, or some mix of all four—given skill and imagination—can do the job well. The British have tended to stifle all but the national government corporation, although giving some recent play to city development corporations and finally to private developers within the new town limits.

6. Land ownership should remain in one hand—preferably a strong public hand. Undoubtedly, we shall err in this respect as our private developers "want out"; but possibly long-term leases with restrictive clauses, plus building codes, plus zoning, plus federal dollar carrots for good behavior, may handle this reasonably well for the U.S.A. The British have set up a national corporation to absorb the assets of each development corporation as it "finishes" building the town; profits therefrom will be devoted, one is told, for building further new towns.

7. It takes time to make a physical town; it takes even longer to make a socio-economic-political-cultural town. Perhaps fifteen years are required to form a "recognizable place"; this will be hard for hurry-hurry America to understand, much less thoroughly internalize and carry out.

8. New towns make a profit for the developer. Why then should not our national, state and local communities capture the profit for the public good—and pump back these profits

into more public good and more carefully sited and planned new towns? In a mixed economy, there is plenty of room for public enterprise too, although the great majority of our new towns are bound to be privately developed in the foreseeable future.

9. The British new town corporations, one for each city, faced impossible financial hurdles: (a) they had to borrow under unfavorable terms only from the Treasury thereby adding to capital costs, and (b) each aspect of the town had to be by itself "profitable." This latter requirement meant that all the most community-forging civic furniture waited, until years of barren residential living and bustling industry made it profitable to construct the sort of town center facilities which make a city urbane. These socio-cultural community features should have been built early at a financial loss to improve the eventual financial and human gain of the total community. Such heavy "front end costs" for social infrastructure are now accepted by private United States sophisticated builders.

10. The development corporations, be they public, private or mixed, need independence within a firm national policy "to get on with the job." The various controlling British ministries (latterly the Ministry of Housing and Local Government), and especially the Treasury, beset by many demands for very tight funds, admittedly interfered much too much in the activities of the development corporations. This may have been necessary initially, but everyone (almost) knows now that the job can be done successfully. Freedom to operate at maximum speed and effect without interminable, Pecksniffian bureaucratic checking could build better towns for less money faster—if the whole were to be couched within a framework of an unambiguous national policy as stated above.

11. The early British new town planners seemingly failed to cope with emergent technologies. Specifically they planned inadequately for private autos in the provision of garage space and in the design of pedestrian malls or precincts for multi-purpose centers, both local and central. Few, if any, imaginative prefabricated building techniques were utilized; the technology and architecture have tended to be until very recently overwhelmingly traditional—if at times mass-constructed, thereby gaining some economies of scale.

12. Clear legal powers and heavy administrative efforts are needed to hold peripheral greenbelts and to keep suburbia from slopping over the new towns. Perhaps many of the

Mark I British towns were sited too close (thirty-five miles) to London and will eventually be gobbled up by the big city.

13. A tighter urbanization pattern within each new town is in order. The British erred badly at first on this due seemingly to the romantic tradition of the wide-open Garden City. Green grass, fresh flowers and water gardens are fine; but not empty space with trite quasi-suburban villas or unimaginative dinky block apartments which do little to create "place." The Mark II newer new towns have an urbanity built in with urban density at the center. Reston, Virginia has learned this lesson as did the designers of Cumbernauld in Scotland and Runcorn on the Merseyside.

14. There were inadequate connections between intercity public transportation planning, road construction, and the location and design of British new towns. The Swedes did better with Vallingby and Forsta around Stockholm, although eventually trapped too by the increase in private automobile traffic. Washington's *Plan for the Year 2000* illustrates well this linkage of planned new cities with a road/rail network.

15. The British never have had social/community planning to equal and to complement the physical planning of the new towns. Their planning practice is heavily physical-design-oriented; the social scientists never were able to mesh well with the physical planners. And the profession of community planning simply is not well-established either in the U.K. or the U.S.A.; it should by now be fairly obvious that nowhere are the relations between physical design and social life clearly understood, much less ready yet for any "social engineering." Obviously, we had better learn a great deal more about this quickly and well, especially if we presume to build urban life from scratch in new towns. On the other hand, every opportunity should be seized to use whatever skills in social planning are available since new towns appear to be going up anyway.

16. Class mixtures envisaged by the Garden City idealists have had no striking success in new towns. The multi-class "balanced" community has not emerged; most British new towns seemingly are largely lower middle class and upper working class. Middle class and working class have not intermingled easily, although the "bourgeoisation" of the latter is patently taking place. The British upper middle class and upper class, traditional community leaders, have had little to do with the new towns as residents. Thus such a program in the United States will be no automatic cure for Negro/white

relations, although it may help to loosen up "lily-white" suburbia.

17. Once a new town's creating staff has "finished" a job, it should be heavily cadred or lured to a new job in a planful fashion. The British new towns' staffs tended to scatter. City building is seldom skill which only develops to full maturity with hard experience and we shall all need more of these people.

18. Unquestionably new towns are an economic asset (a) in themselves as large-scale real estate development schemes, but more importantly (b) as the center of sophisticated new industrial and commercial development backed by a reliable, highly skilled work force. No country, and especially Britain can survive without some such national nodes for economic growth.

Continental Europe Offers New Town Builders Experience

FREDERICK GUTHEIM*

What Europe has to offer the new town builder is experience. In the United States some two hundred new towns are in various stages of promotion. This means that land is being acquired, assembled—optioned at least. Planners and architects have been commissioned and given some limited assignments.

New town proposals are appearing with increasing frequency on metropolitan area plans. A few hundred families may be living in houses on the new town site, as at Reston, Virginia, but these are still too few, too sketchily equipped, too lacking in town centers and other significant urban features to begin to evidence their soundness. Much of our slow progress can be attributed to our lack of the experience that Europe has had.

If Europe is approached with the British definition of a new

* Independent practice as consultant on urban affairs. He has had extensive experience in housing, planning and architecture and on behalf of the UN recently advised Zambia on a housing and planning program. From 1960 to 1965 he was president of the Washington Center for Metropolitan Studies and earlier served with several of the federal housing agencies, the New York *Herald Tribune* and the American Institute of Architects. The following article is reprinted with permission from *Public Management*, April 1966, published by the International City Manager's Association.

town, little will be found that corresponds to this model. But it has been pointed out that the "contributions of the British new towns do not lie in the particular type, size, economic activity or other characteristics of the towns developed in Britain. . . ."[1] Thus the British experience has prompted the use of other measures to control physical development, to direct new urban settlement away from congested metropolitan centers, and to stimulate economic and urban development. And it is these objectives, not the formal characteristics, that attract American interest.

EUROPEAN STUDY TOURS

In the summer of 1965 two groups of Americans made impressive study tours to the principal European new towns. One group was organized by the University of Pennsylvania and included some of the most notable experts of that distinguished faculty as well as some experienced developers. The other, organized around new towns promoters mainly from the West Coast, large building supply companies, and a few discriminating journalists, had a more practical orientation. Both covered the same territory, the former in a more leisurely and penetrating fashion, the latter more brisk and hard-nosed.

What were they hoping to find? How can it be applied to the efforts under way at home?

If one expects to graft the town-building techniques of European socialism to the laissez faire building economy of the United States, the result will surely fail. The success of most European new town building efforts is not measured by their profits. In the same way, higher incomes and living standards in the United States, greater numbers of automobiles and the way they are used, and more leisure and different recreational habits prevent the adoption of new towns experience elsewhere without considerable modification. It should be easy for Americans to understand, therefore, why almost equally great differences between Great Britain and Europe prevented any replication of the British new towns on the continent.

Think of Paris or Vienna. Such centralized cities are markedly different from the sprawling, low, British towns with their

[1] Lloyd Rodwin, "Economic Problems in Developing New Towns and Expanded Towns," Background Paper No. 4, Round Table Conference on the Planning and Development of New Towns, Moscow, U.S.S.R., August 24–September 7, 1964 (mimeo). United Nations Bureau of Social Affairs, Research and Publications Section.

abundant open spaces. In these compact and overcrowded cities we find the high-density slum composed of multistory flats. In this difference, which the Danish planner Steen Eiler Rasmussen has analyzed, "the cooperation of many circumstances" has led to profoundly different urban patterns and expressions of need, and these have stamped themselves on national housing and town planning programs.[2]

British insistence on access to open country for sport and recreation and their horror of the evils of their nineteenth century cities led directly to their distinctive conception of the new town. The Europeans reached quite different conclusions, however.

EUROPEAN CHARACTERISTICS

While the British new towns program is inseparable from greenbelts, and their principal advocate of new towns is called the Town and Country Planning Association, almost no European program calls for a ceiling on central city growth and the direction of such growth into free-standing and wholly new settlements beyond commuting distance. Indeed, it is difficult to imagine that British cities themselves would have reached this conclusion had it not been imposed on them by the central government's town planning theories.

The European equivalent of the new towns program is therefore something other than Britain's favorite remedy for urban ills. It is rather close to larger American redevelopment projects—or rather what our urban renewal agencies could create if they were not shackled to the slums. (The requirement of our housing legislation that redevelopment and renewal be linked to the improvement of housing once caused the late Hugh Pomeroy to expostulate, "Either you have to start with a slum—or end up with one.")

This conception of large-scale increments of urban growth as being organic parts of older cities is deeply rooted in such classic urban forms as Amsterdam or Venice. The Italian architectural historian, Bruno Zevi, gave a clear account of this process in the expansion of Ferrara. When the d'Este family in the sixteenth century decided the town had to be enlarged they commissioned the architect Biagio Rosetti to lay out an extension of a size nearly equal to the area of the

[2] Steen Eiler Rasmussen, *London: The Unique City* (London, 1934); see also, Daniel R. Mandelker, *Green Belts and Urban Growth* (Madison, Wisconsin, 1962).

original city. When this had been accomplished, he then re-developed and modernized the older city and unified it with the new part.[3]

The organic expansion of Edinburgh (one of Britain's last remaining walled towns) in 1752, following the end of the long period of hostilities with England, when James Craig laid out the "new town," is a similar example.

Furthermore, in our times the cities of Europe have only recently emerged from their postwar reconstruction efforts. They have been intensely preoccupied with the reconstruction of older sections of cities to the exclusion of newer conceptions of urban growth.[4]

To the American observer European cities seem headed for catastrophe as the forces of economic expansion collide with equally powerful forces of urban growth. This is perhaps most keenly recognized in the handling of that universal municipal problem, the automobile, but it is equally a consideration as higher personal incomes yield new kinds of housing demands, as new investment in industrial plant seeks new locations, and as the office building boom rocks the older pattern of congested city centers. A blind and often fumbling response to these naked forces rather than any comprehensive planning to guide them seems most characteristic of the cities of Europe.

Let us look briefly at some of the developments on the continent.

SOUTHERN AND EASTERN EUROPE

This part of Europe offers several interesting examples of new towns created incident to economic development. The coal mining center of Velenje, Jugoslavia, or the steel center of Nowa Huta in Poland, are socialist "company towns." Another illustration is Anic-Gela in Sicily. Matera and several other new settlements in southern Italy are the result of land settlement or agricultural development plans.

Soviet thinking about housing and city planning has influenced the postwar reconstruction of eastern European cities,

[3] Bruno Zevi, *Biaggio Rosetti* (Milan, 1962).

[4] Leo Grebler, *Europe's Reborn Cities* (Urban Land Institute, Technical Bulletin No. 28, 1956). Also the same author's "Urban Renewal in European Countries," in the special issue on "City Planning in Europe," *Journal of the American Institute of Planners*, Vol. XXVIII, No. 4 (November, 1962), pp. 229–38.

but a closer look at developments there is required before this influence can be evaluated. The showcase city of Mamaia on the Black Sea is Rumania's effort to win tourist exchange and provide a holiday center for its own people, but that does not explain its considerable architectural interest—almost as great as similar seaside towns in Israel.

At least these can be described as town-building efforts. More typical, unfortunately, are the plans in Italy for the new Ligurian industrial center of Rivalta, which aims to relieve the congested port of Genoa. This bold scheme will relocate both industry from Genoa and the nearby ports, and the industrial overspill of Turin and Milan, in a new "development pole" with fast direct connections to the port about 50 miles distant. Had this industrial initiative been matched by an equivalent town building and housing effort, something outstanding would have resulted.

An equally missed opportunity is the industrial development of the Terneutzen Canal in the upper estuary of the Scheldt in Belgium. The economic development program in Belgium, stimulated by the Common Market and national economic planning, has not begun to grapple with social, cultural, and urbanistic problems inseparable from it.

Another distinctively European development akin to "new towns" is the creation of new town centers, often at a considerable distance from the traditional core. Such subcenters have appeared in such American cities as Pittsburgh, in response to market forces, or have been deliberately planned (but not realized in New York and Chicago).

Between Rome and Ostia a large office building complex is now being developed. Hamburg's City-Nord, some 10 miles north of the old center, is an office building concentration of 35,000 workers. An even larger office building center, replacing an older residential district, is rising at Pont de Neuilly, some 10 miles from the center of Paris, at the terminus of the Metro.

DEVELOPMENTS IN FRANCE

France is another sad story of missed opportunities. A trip through the booming new northern industrial suburbs of Paris, with its miles of new housing, is about as inspiring as a tour of the Bronx. This "termitarium" as the French critics have called it, denies any humane values of urban growth except in the crudest terms of housing supply and demand. Comprehensive planning of housing and industry, schools, and even shopping centers; provision for the automobile and even the bus; to say nothing of recreation and culture, all are lacking.

The notorious concentration of French life in Paris has depleted the more promising efforts elsewhere. Some outstanding small new towns are found in the reconstruction of Normandy. But the outstanding French idea is the "cité parallel," of which Le Mirail, near Toulouse, with its spiny plan, is the prime example. This is the most characteristic and promising urbanistic theory to emerge from Europe since the war, but there is unfortunately little to show for it thus far.[5]

DEVELOPMENTS IN GERMANY

Germany's preoccupation with urban reconstruction has received lengthy and expert criticism from Professor Grebler, whose warning that a narrow concern with housing and low standards would lead to rapid obsolescence has come true with blinding speed in the postwar economic boom that has left Germany almost the most prosperous part of Europe.

High engineering standards, competent administrators, strong local governments, and national prosperity have not succeeded in providing German answers to universal problems of urban growth.

The open space and recreation needs of an increasingly leisured people, the space to move and park the flood of automobiles, the historic but inefficiently rebuilt civic centers—these were not thought of when housing at tolerable standards and extensive production facilities were built. What is most depressing in Germany, however, is the crushing burden of materialism, the stodgy bureaucracy, the aimless waist-high prosperity.

There are exceptions, like Beilefeld, the attractive northern suburbs of Bremen, and Frankfurt's Nordweststadt. But the nearest approach to a German new town is probably Wolfsburg, the Volkswagen city, a sodden mass of industrial efficiency and good municipal intentions, complete with a cultural center and beautiful churches and good housing—but even when the sun is shining you couldn't call it a success as a town. It takes more than hard work and prosperity.

Nordweststadt is a successor to Romerstadt, Frankfurt's ad-

<hr/>

[5] *L'Architecture d'Aujourd'hui*, No. 101 (April, 1962), is a special issue on new towns and urban centers in which the idea of parallel cities is elaborated.

jacent housing colony that set the international pace for housing between the wars. It has equivalents in Cologne's "Neue Stadt," in Düsseldorf, and in other German cities, but none of them has coupled the industrial rationalization of mass housing with a reasonably attractive and humanistically oriented community plan.

Located only four miles from the center of Frankfurt, Nordweststadt will be connected by a new subway and a special expressway. There is one off-street parking space for every two families, in a locked garage. The total population of about 50,000 will be served by a two-level civic center with underground parking and a transit station.

Three other commercial centers, a carefully worked out school building plan, a single incinerator, district heating, and other sensible provisions mark the plan. But Nordweststadt is most significant because of its internal circulation plan (17 footbridges over streets), its green spaces, and its mixture of high and low buildings.[6]

SCANDINAVIA

And so to the smaller northern European lands whose accomplishments in new town building have been the most impressive and which are the despair of wistful Americans because of their socialistic implications.

These dilemmas are illustrated in Holland, where the Amstelveen settlement, at the density typical of a good American suburb, shows that excellence in urban planning which has been natural to the Dutch for three centuries. But even the creation of southern Amsterdam, with its great park, or the reconstruction of Rotterdam to provide Europe's best example of modern city planning, appear to escape our grasp.

Why can't such urban standards be realized when we develop the Tennessee or Columbia River valleys? Or in the reclamation projects in the arid western states? Or in urban renewal?

Perhaps the reason can be suggested in Sweden, where the growth of Stockholm shows a deliberate municipal strategy in application. In anticipation of its expansion, the city of Stockholm acquired some 50,000 acres of land in the environs where it was proposed to accommodate the future population.

Pending such use, the land was managed as a recreation

[6] Walter Schwagenscheidt, *Die Nordweststadt* (Stuttgart, 1964); *Der Aufbau* (Vol. XX, No. 6, June, 1965), pp. 329–35.

area or for summer camp sites. As it has been required, the city has undertaken comprehensive new town building works; coordinated with such development the city has extended the rapid transit service to such new communities.[7]

The first large postwar community to be built was Väl-lingby, where some 50,000 persons now live west of the capital city. South of Stockholm the new towns of Arsta and Forsta have been completed. The last is architecturally and sociologically the most interesting. North of the city is Grind-thorpe, with its staggering high-rise complex Taby, which is the most recent example of this continuing process of city building.

These residential communities are certainly an improvement in their comprehensiveness over the housing projects designed before the war, but their residents must still commute to central city jobs or to employment in some nearby industrial suburb. This burden has been eased by the splendid system of commuter trains, which appears to provide the model for most North American transit planning. But a better relationship of housing and work place is possible, and even excellent transit is threatened by rising automobile ownership and car pooling.

In short, these suburban new towns are dormitories. They are not really more significant than other first-class housing developments like Albertslund, outside Copenhagen. Nor do they seem likely to provide metropolitan structure. The suburban rail lines are no more successful in providing a strong line of radial development than Copenhagen's finger plan, where the green wedges between development corridors are gradually disappearing.

TAPIOLA, FINLAND

For Americans, Europe's most convincing effort in new town building is Tapiola, lying six miles west of Helsinki. The closest approach to a private enterprise undertaking, it is a paradox that Tapiola has also led to the most promising proposal for planning the metropolitan area of Finland's capital city. Although only 15,000 people live in Tapiola thus far, its

[7] Of numerous descriptions of this activity the best seem to be Sven Markelius' essay in G. E. Kidder Smith, *Sweden Builds* (New York, 1957), and the masterly account by Yngve Larsen for the International Federation for Housing and Town Planning.

international recognition has been instantaneous, and more than 100,000 visitors were registered there last year.

It has a splendid natural setting in the archipelago, delightfully varied and charming housing, a sound industrial base, and a population almost evenly divided between white collar and blue collar classes, thanks to the application of national housing subsidies.

When such seasoned observers as Commissioner Marie McGuire or private new towns developers from California have looked at it, they have seen something that could be recognized as ideal by American standards. Tapiola is not only a success with the experts and the foreigners, but foremost with the nature-loving Finns, who most appreciate its character as a true garden city.

Tapiola is the work of the National Housing Foundation, a non-profit organization created during the postwar housing shortage by a group of welfare and labor organizations who subscribed its initial capital. Since then it has been self-financing, although receiving the same housing subsidies as other nonprofit organizations that provide low-income housing.

Most of the initial money was invested in land, and building operations have required what by American standards are large down payments from the home owners and loans at high interest rates. The high standards of planning, livability, appearance, and amenity have greatly strengthened Tapiola's appeal, and this strong demand has surmounted these and other formidable difficulties.

Developed over a period of nearly 15 years, the community has grown by increments sufficiently small and varied in design to owe much of its distinctive character to this circumstance. A sound comprehensive plan has also maintained unity and assured such system-wide features as district heating and an outstanding park plan.

The prime reason for Tapiola's success, however, resulted from the leadership, perseverance, and imagination provided by its managing director, Heikki von Hertzen, a lawyer and banker who has been given international recognition for a housing achievement that ranks with the famous social service programs of his country.

By itself Tapiola would not make much impression in the sprawling form of metropolitan Helsinki, to which is being attracted by far the largest share of the national employment and population gain. To deal with those problems von Hertzen has proposed the most imaginative use of the new towns, a program that can be matched only by Britain's Southeast Plan as a bold urban strategy at a national scale.

For the Helsinki area von Hertzen has formulated the "Seven Towns" plan, directing much of the future urban growth into a series of economically balanced communities varying in size from 50,000 to 200,000.

For the rest of the nation he has proposed that new towns be used in conjunction with economic development plans to secure a more advantageous national distribution of settlement.[8] The National Housing Foundation has already acquired land for the first of the "Seven Towns" and is leading a consortium that is buying land for the second.

AND IN THE UNITED STATES

These developments have by no means gone unnoticed in the United States. As conditions favoring new towns construction ripen, there is every chance their lessons will be applied by municipalities and private real estate developers here. Indeed, they are already evident in the physical planning of such developments as Reston, Virginia, which is as close to Tapiola as we are likely to come.

But American private developers generally will be unable to respond to the qualitative challenge of European experience if we are to accept the conclusions of those who conducted their study tours of the new towns.

Mrs. Ada Louise Huxtable, the architectural critic of the *New York Times,* who accompanied the group, reported that they saw little prospect under present economic conditions that the features they admired in the new towns of Britain and Scandinavia could be incorporated in our planning. To redeem this bleak prospect should be an early goal of national housing legislation.

The lines of such new legislation were described by William L. C. Wheaton of the University of California, a former president of the National Housing Conference, following a visit to Tapiola last summer.

Everywhere planning for metropolitan regions like Helsinki requires stimulation from the national authorities to overcome the conservatism of small local govern-

[8] Heikki von Hertzen, "Framtidens Nyland," *Stadsbyggnad* (Journal of the Swedish Association of Municipal Technology), No. 6, 1964, pp. 1–12.

ments, which do not appreciate the speed of metropolitan growth, and which lack the resources needed to build new communities.

It is clear that private initiative here, with the active aid of government, can set new standards which later and broader government-sponsored programs can follow as rapidly as the authorities can assemble the required skill and resources. We in the United States have already applied this principle in the renewal of older areas, but we are only beginning in new planned towns like Tapiola.

The idea of a private development corporation is a strong one. It can direct its efforts toward the solution of major problems of urban living and urban form. It might appropriately receive government support in the form of such powers as eminent domain or some local government authority. Where it enters the field of public welfare, as in providing subsidized housing, it should also receive financial aid. This pattern, strongly supported by European experience, is an alternative to unabridged private cream-skimming from the metropolitan housing market on the one hand, or the morass of timid, boring, too-little-too-late actions of many government agencies that have attempted new town building.

The City of Columbia, Maryland
JAMES W. ROUSE*

A NATIONAL NEW COMMUNITY POLICY

May I begin by saying that I am aware of the fact that this legislation is opposed by the U.S. Conference of Mayors, by the National Association of Home Builders and by the Mortgage Bankers Association of America, and, that while I have great respect for these organizations, I believe that they misunderstand the need for and the purpose of this legislation

* President, Community Research and Development, Inc. (builders of Columbia) and the Rouse Company, which has financed over $750 million of real estate development in Baltimore, Washington, Pittsburgh and Chicago. The latter company owns and operates $100 million in real estate projects, including eight enclosed regional shopping centers throughout the country; it is now developing five additional ones as well. Mr. Rouse was a member of President Eisenhower's Advisory Committee on Housing and Chairman of the Sub-Committee that recommended the urban renewal program embraced in the Housing Act

and misjudge what the results will be, if it is passed. It is very much in the best interests of the cities of America, the home building industry and our country as a whole for this legislation to be enacted.

The simple fact is that, with the powers and processes that now exist in local government and in the home building industry, it is impossible to provide, in an orderly and intelligent way, for the metropolitan growth which we know lies just ahead.

Our cities grow by accident—by whim of the private developer and public agencies. A farm is sold and begins raising houses instead of potatoes—then another farm—; forests are cut; valleys are filled; streams are buried in storm sewers; kids overflow the schools—here a new school is built—there a church. Then more schools and more churches. Traffic grows; roads are widened; service stations, Tastee Freez, hamburger stands pockmark the highway. Traffic strangles. An Expressway is cut through the landscape—brings clover leafs—which bring shopping centers, office buildings, high-rise apartments. Relentlessly, the bits and pieces of a city are splattered across the landscape. By this irrational process, non-communities are born—formless places, without order, beauty or reason; with no visible respect for people or the land. Thousands of small, separate decisions—made with little or no relationship to one another, nor to their composite impact—produce a major decision about the future of our cities and our civilization—a decision we have come to label "suburban sprawl."

Sprawl is dreadfully inefficient. It stretches out the distances people must travel to work, to shop, to worship, to play. It fails to relate these activities in ways that strengthen each and, thus, it suppresses values that orderly relationships and concentration of uses would stimulate. Sprawl is ugly, oppressive, massively dull. It squanders the resources of nature—forests, streams, hillsides—and produces vast, monotonous armies of housing and graceless, tasteless clutter. But worst of all, sprawl

---

of 1954. One of the founders of ACTION (American Council to Improve Our Neighborhoods), he has served as its past president and chairman of its Board of Directors and is now a member of the Board of Trustees of *Urban America,* the successor to ACTION. He has lectured at Harvard, Johns Hopkins and the University of California on planning and has held many civic positions in his native Baltimore and in Washington, D.C. The following is Mr. Rouse's statement, slightly abridged, before the Housing Sub-Committee, House Banking and Currency Committee on HR 1296, Title II, Land Development and New Communities, March 25, 1966.

is inhuman. It is anti-human. The vast, formless spread of housing, pierced by the unrelated spotting of schools, churches, stores, creates areas so huge and irrational that they are out of scale with people—beyond their grasp and comprehension—too big for people to feel a part of, responsible for, important in. The richness of real community—in both its support and its demands—is largely voided. Variety and choice are reduced to a sort of pre-packaged brand-name selection of recreation, culture and education. The individual is immersed in the mass. What nonsense this is. What reckless, irresponsible dissipation of nature's endowment and man's hopes for dignity, beauty, growth.

This Sub-committee can plan better than we are building the American city. It requires no vast program of research, no technological breakthrough, no huge subsidy, no army of technicians or crusading volunteers to build better American cities. We know the rough measurements of our future growth—how many people we must provide for; what they will require in houses and apartments, schools and colleges, churches, hospitals, offices and factories, retail stores, lumber yards and service stations. Our task is simply to provide now for what we can calculate will be required to accommodate our future growth; to provide rationally now for what we know is going to occur; to arrange the pieces in a constructive way with a decent respect for man and nature instead of improvising frantically and impulsively with each new thrust of growth as if it were a gigantic surprise beyond our capacity to predict or to manage.

Why, in a nation with such enormous capacity for organization and production, is there such bewilderment about producing the environment in which we grow our people? The answer is easy but frightening. We simply have no machinery, no process, no organized capacity in the United States to put to work the knowledge that exists among us about planning for the future growth of our cities. Is there any other aspect of American life in which the gap is so wide between our knowledge and our performance as in the growth of the American City?

The building of the city is nobody's business—neither government nor industry. We have assigned a vague responsibility to local government to provide for orderly growth but have given it neither the power, the processes, nor the financial capacity with which it can fulfill that responsibility. The most advanced planning and zoning concepts in America today are inadequate to preserve our forests and stream valleys and maintain open spaces. They cannot produce well formed communities with a rich variety of institutions and activities and a wide range of choice in housing density, type, price and rent. As a matter of fact, zoning has become almost a guarantee of sprawl rather than protection against it. Frightened communities, with no alternative process available, leap to the illusion that low density zoning will preserve a way of life and protect against rising taxes. The one to three acre zoning that results simply extends a thin coat of suburban sprawl over an ever widening area.

Nor have we developed the capacity in the home building industry for producing well planned large scale urban development. Although the business of city building is the largest single industry in America, there is no large corporation engaged in it. City building has no General Motors or General Electric—no IBM, no Xerox; no big capital resources to invest in the purchase of large land areas; no big research and development program unfolding new techniques to produce a better environment. There are no large corporations engaged in the end-product production of the American City. City building—the development of houses and apartments, stores and offices—is the business of thousands of very small corporations, no one of which has within its own resources the financial capacity to invest millions of dollars in land holdings to be planned and developed over, say, 10–15 years. Thus, except for the occasional accident of a large land holding remaining in single ownership on the threshold of urban growth, there is no vehicle, public or private, by which planning and development occurs on a scale sufficiently large to provide sensitively for nature or for man.

We face the addition of 70,000,000 people to our cities over the next 20 years—a new Toledo each month or a Denver, a Dallas and an Atlanta each year. Yet, not one single metropolitan area in the United States has plans to match the growth it knows it must face; and, if it had the plans, it would lack the powers and processes to execute them. This is the state of our nation and the prospect of our civilization as we convert over 1,000,000 acres of land each year from agricultural to urban use; as we move forward to produce, over the next 40 years, in our urban centers, the equivalent of everything we have built in our cities and suburbs since Plymouth Rock. Urban growth should be our opportunity, not our enemy. It invites us to correct the past; to build new places that are infused with nature and stimulating to man's creative sense of beauty; places that are in scale with people and so formed as to encourage and give strength to real community which will enrich life; build character and personality; promote concern, friendship, brotherhood.

Is it too much for such a nation to expect that we will substitute, for aimless sprawl, places of scale and beauty that are felicitous for the growth of our people? Certainly not, but to do it we must equip our severely undercapitalized home building industry to acquire, plan and develop land on a larger scale than is now possible. That is the purpose of the FHA Insurance Program. Furthermore, we must equip our local governments to assemble land for large scale planning and development; to serve it with public utilities and roads; and then market it to private developers for construction of houses, apartments, stores, offices, industry and all the components of a sound community. That is the purpose of the loans to local land development agencies.

THE CITY OF COLUMBIA

May I illustrate what such a local land development agency might accomplish by sketching what we are doing in Columbia. And we are doing here what in many, if not most, metropolitan areas of the United States can only be done by local government.

We have assembled, at a cost of $23 million, 165 farms and parcels into 15,600 acres of land lying midway between Baltimore and Washington in Howard County, Maryland. Here we have planned the City of Columbia, which begins development this fall and is scheduled by 1980 to have a population of over 100,000 people. It will not be just a better suburb, but a complete new city.

It will employ 30,000 people in its plants, offices, stores, and institutions; provide housing for 31,000 families ranging from high-rise apartments to 10-acre lots, and priced to serve the company janitor as well as the company president. It will have 70 schools, 50 churches, a college, a hospital, a library system. It will be a city consisting of nine small towns of 10,-000 to 15,000 each with their own schools, churches, stores, and services centered at a village green. The towns will be separated by 3,500 acres of permanent open space. —Five lakes (which we will build), stream valleys, forests, 26 miles of riding trails, parks, and recreation areas will interlace the entire city.

At the center will be a lively downtown with department stores, offices, hotels, restaurants, theatres, concert halls, galleries, central library, college, hospital. Downtown will have an 80-acre lake as its front yard and a 50-acre forest at its side. The towns will be connected to one another, to downtown, and to employment centers by a bus system running on its own right-of-way.

And will Columbia hurt the City of Baltimore? Why, of course not. Would the City of Baltimore be better off with irrational, piecemeal, inefficient sprawl reaching out from its borders than it will be if the same growth is accommodated within complete, well-planned new communities? Baltimore has enormous opportunities that are not available to Columbia or any other outlying new community. It has a massive employment center at its core, strong retail facilities; the graduate schools of the University of Maryland, the Peabody Conservatory of Music, the Central Branch Library, the center of Government, a magnificent harbor. The center of Baltimore is, and always will be, closer to more people in the metropolitan area than any single outlying location. Baltimore's task, and that of every other American City, is to correct its obsolescence; get rid of its slums; to address itself to the urban renewal opportunity through comprehensive planning large enough to re-form the center of the City into a beautiful, efficient, powerful economic force, and to reshape the older areas around downtown into a system of healthy, slum-free communities. Any new community developer would be off and running if he had the advantages that are now held by the central city. A city's job is to make itself work for its people and its purposes. It cannot benefit by aimless, irrational, sprawling suburbs, nor will it be hurt by the encouragement of well-planned, well-formed new communities.

The Mayors have been misled and they will see that this is so. But the country cannot wait these precious years, when the growth is rolling in on our cities, and stand aimlessly wringing our hands in anguish about our inability to handle the demands of urban growth. We owe it to our country to make our civilization the best that we know, and not hold it back to something much less than the best, in order to avoid unhappy contrast with the worn-out, old inner cities which we know we must renew.

And what about the home builder? The home building industry is one of the largest industries in America, and yet there are no large corporations engaged in it. It is a proliferation of small enterprises that, individually, lack the capital to engage in large-scale development. There are very few, if any, home builders in America who could have, out of their own resources, invested $23,000,000.00 to acquire the land that will be Columbia. And without such large-scale land assembly, comprehensive planning and good community development is almost impossible. Let me illustrate:

1. We were able to preserve the three major stream valleys in our area—and over 3,000 acres of forest—because our land holdings were large enough to transfer development out of these areas on to the land most suitable for development. We have thus been able to establish lakes, bridle paths and an open space system which will serve the entire City of Columbia. Our first two lakes will cost over $1,500,000. A builder acquiring a few hundred acres or even a thousand acres could not possibly have absorbed this cost. But spread over 15,000 acres it adds only $100 per acre to our land cost—less, we believe, than the value added.

2. We have provided for a public transportation system in Columbia—a bus system, running on its own right-of-way, separated from the roads and the pedestrian walkways; connecting all the village centers, downtown, and major employment centers. 40% of the population will live within a two-minute walk of a bus stop. Buses will run every five minutes at 10 cents a ride for adults and a nickel a ride for kids, and, according to our engineering projections, be fully economic. But the success of this system depends upon a wide variety of uses—major employment centers, retail stores, offices, hotels, schools, etc., and a large population of prospective users. A development of a few hundred, or even a few thousand acres, could not hope to provide such a system.

3. We have been able, in Columbia, to relate the schools to the communities they serve—an elementary school at the heart of each neighborhood; a junior high school and a high school at the heart of each village. All kids will be able to walk or ride a bike to school. At the present cost of school busing in Howard County, it is possible that the County will save more than a million dollars a year in school busing alone. And the schools will be part

of the communities where the kids and their parents live. We have been able to lay out, with the approval of the School Board and the local Planning Commission, more than 50 school sites to meet the school needs in Columbia over the next 15 years. All of this is only possible because of very large land holdings and large scale planning.

4. We were able to acquire the ugly commercial islands along US 29, where it runs through the heart of Columbia, and we will be able to extinguish these commercial uses. Thus, instead of having these ugly beginnings of commercial blight extend like a cancer along the main road through our town, we have been able to establish Columbia Pike (US 29) as a landscaped parkway for the five miles it passes through Columbia. We will strengthen the commercial use and the service to customers by concentrating business in attractive, well-planned business centers off the Parkway. We paid premium prices for some of this land, as high as $75,000 an acre in some instances, and we could afford to do it only because we could spread the excess cost over our large land holdings. A developer of a few hundred, or even a few thousand acres, could not have assumed this burden.

5. Washington's National Symphony has reached an agreement with us to provide 30 concerts a season in a Summer Music Festival in Columbia each year for the next 20 years. Thirteen Protestant denominations have joined together to form a Religious Facilities Corporation and a cooperative ministry. The Catholic Archdiocese and the Jewish faith are represented as participant observers on this Church Committee and are working closely with the Protestant churches to achieve the maximum interfaith cooperation. This is one of the most remarkable demonstrations of cooperation among the churches that we have seen in our country. The State Department of Education has obtained a grant and completed a study for a library system for Columbia that contemplates resourceful use of modern technology, including computers and information storage and retrieval systems. The C & P Telephone Company has made a special study of communications systems in Columbia and has proposed the most advanced system of community-wide communications that has been made available to any community

in America. All of these developments and many others in which we are involved are possible only because we are planning a complete new community on a large enough scale to spread individual cost items that would otherwise be unacceptable, and to support education, cultural, health, recreation and business systems, that small, piecemeal, unplanned growth could not justify.

6. Most remarkable—and perhaps most important of all: we obtained our zoning. Howard County is essentially rural. It has resisted urbanization because it despises the bits and pieces of sprawl, as do nearly all rural counties that are perched on the edge of urban growth. Zoning was the major issue in the 1962 election for County Commissioners. The winning ticket promised to protect Howard County against the ravages of urban growth. You can imagine that the announcement, one year later, of our assembly of 15,000 acres of land for the purpose of building a city was greeted with skepticism, anxiety, and perhaps a touch of hostility. It must be significant to you, as elected representatives of your people, to know that when we completed our plans for a whole new city, presented them to the people of Howard County and requested a change in the County zoning laws to create a new zoning classification known as a "New Town District," not a single person in Howard County opposed this zoning request. The same people who abhorred and fought the invasion of urban sprawl, accepted, and supported the development of a whole new city that would preserve the stream valleys and the forests; provide recreation, culture, entertainment, convenient, well-planned business, and public transportation. They were willing to accept high-rise apartments, garden apartments, townhouses, the very land uses they were fighting when they were gathered together in a rational, beautiful, human, well planned new city.

But now, surely, you are asking: "If you have been able to do this at Columbia and finance it privately, are the Federal programs proposed in Title II necessary?" Clearly, I think they are, or I would not be here now.

Let me remind you that I am a private developer and a private mortgage banker. I believe in the private enterprise system. The home building industry in America is the most productive in the world. But there are some things it cannot do without assistance—the very assistance it now resists. There is absolutely no means whatsoever by which the home building industry, as it is now constituted in America, can develop the sensibly organized new communities that America needs to accommodate its future growth. The special vitality of the home building industry derives from its enormous number of individual operators, and this very fact guarantees—unless some new form of assistance is provided—that we will continue to build our cities in little bits and pieces, irrationally, unrelated to one another. The home building industry lacks the capital among its individual enterprises to undertake large-scale land assembly, planning, and development. It lacks the financial capacity and organization required to attract financial investment from life insurance companies and savings banks on the scale required to handle the growth of the American metropolis. Of course, there are exceptions. There is a handful—perhaps two handsful—of developers around the country who can attract the capital to undertake a Columbia. And such new towns will unfold. But the overwhelming preponderance of American home builders are left to the limitations of piecemeal development.

The hope of the FHA Insurance Program is that small builders will be able to undertake middle-size developments, and that middle-size builders will undertake larger developments than would otherwise be possible. And we must stimulate planning and development over larger land areas if we are to preserve our natural resources and provide communities that serve and dignify a man, his wife, and family.

The FHA financing program has provided the underlying support for the growth of the home building industry in America. It has raised housing and subdivision standards and pointed the way to steady improvement in the quality of new housing.

It is specially appropriate that its insurance program now be used to permit the private banking and building industries to improve the neighborhood—the environment—in which our housing is built. The enormous growth of our Cities calls for the planning and development, not just of houses, but of new communities. This FHA Insurance Program will be an important aid to private industry in making it possible.*

But in addition to enlarging the capacity of the home builder, we must make it possible for local government to

* Passed as Title IV, "Land Development and New Communities", of the Demonstration Cities and Metropolitan Development Act of 1966.

take the initiative in acquiring land and planning community development, in the path of urban growth, where, but for such action, piecemeal, fractured suburban sprawl is the alternative. This is no threat to the private home building industry but an asset. It means that local government by initiating, planning and development over a larger area than the small builder could possibly handle on his own, can create an environment in which the small builder has a vastly improved opportunity to compete with the large community developer. We are performing exactly this role in Columbia and will make the land available to home builders to build individual houses for sale to the market. But we will have supplied parkways, lakes, open spaces, community halls, school sites, swimming pools, tennis courts, employment centers, stores and offices to strengthen his environment and support his market.

The Country needs to enlarge the application of the process by which a Columbia is built. It cannot afford to rely on the capacity or the whim of the private developer alone. We have a national interest in seeking better communities to accommodate our urban growth. A program of loans to local land development agencies can be an important, perhaps indispensable, stimulant to the growth of this process.

A Land Development Program for California
CHARLES ABRAMS*

In a previous section, reference was made to the need for a federal loan program at nominal interest rates to facilitate land acquisition for private development and public services through state-chartered corporations. Whether such federal legislation is passed or not, it seems incontrovertible that the State should be empowered to develop its own programs for making land available for urban and suburban expansion. It can neither wait on federal assistance or depend on its small advances. Even were the program authorized tomorrow, the

* Chairman of Columbia University's Division of Urban Planning and Director of its new Institute of Urban Environment. He has been on the faculties of the University of Pennsylvania, M.I.T., City College of New York and the New School for Social Research. Identified with the housing field since 1933, he was recently described by *Architectural Forum* as the foremost housing consultant in the United States. He has served on UN housing missions or in a private capacity as consultant in Ghana, Kenya, Turkey, Puerto Rico, Israel, Barbados, Vene-

State would have to assume the initiative as well as greater responsibility to make the program meaningful. The bearing down of 15 million people on a fragmented but tightly held land supply rising in price daily makes this manifest and mandatory.

Publicly sponsored acquisition for land development is not new in the United States and the nation's capital city, laboriously undertaken by George Washington, was a "new town." Many other countries, developed and undeveloped and including England, have engaged in large-scale land acquisition operations to provide planned towns for industry, trade and housing. In 1956, Alberta, Canada, passed a New Towns Act empowering the government to declare any area of the province a "New Town" and set up a corporation to plan and finance it. After providing the necessary site improvements, the land is to be disposed of to private developers for industrial, residential and commercial development. Powers of condemnation and issuance of debentures to finance the operations are authorized as well as government advances to cover preliminary costs. After development, the town is given the status of a municipality. As of December 1959, six applications for the creation of new towns had been granted.

The record in the United States is a mixed catalogue of suburban and self-contained ventures large and small, sparked by private speculation, employer interest, public experimentation and utopian contemplations. Private "new town" operations include such differently concerned communities as Radburn (New Jersey) and Pullman (Illinois). Dozens of others have been undertaken for simple profit and they have sprung up from coast to coast as large-scale mortgage financing made them profitable and possible.

The most ambitious federal new towns effort was launched during the Roosevelt administration when, after studying 100

zuela, Jamaica, the Province of Quebec, Pakistan, India, the Philippines, Bolivia, Ireland, Japan, Nigeria and Singapore. He has held several important New York State positions as well as acting as a housing columnist for the New York *Post* from 1947 to 1950. Author of the *Revolution in Land* (1937), *The Future of Housing* (1946), *Urban Land Problems and Policies* (1953), *Forbidden Neighbors* (1955), *Man's Struggle for Shelter* (1964), he recently wrote *The City is the Frontier* (New York: Harper & Row, 1965). The following is excerpted from the report by the California Governor's Advisory Commission on Housing Problems, 1963, for which Mr. Abrams was chief consultant and author of the report itself. It is published with the permission of Edward Eichler, former chairman of the commission.

sites for new cities, the Resettlement Administration bought land in several states including Maryland, Wisconsin, Ohio and New Jersey and proceeded to build three towns as part of the economic recovery effort. After visiting Greenbelt (Maryland), President Roosevelt described the new towns effort as "an experiment that ought to be copied by every community in the United States."

Co-operation was secured from the localities but the program ran afoul of the constitutional question at a time when the Supreme Court had not yet extended federal power. By the time the Supreme Court had liberalized the welfare power and validated public housing, federal home loan bank and FHA operations, the program had been abandoned. Federal town building has continued since then, but has been confined to incidents of dam, atom plant and other federal installations.

The logic of building new towns still prevails as it did in Washington's day but new towns in California develop today mostly through the sporadic operations of unconcerted private developments which fortuitously grow into towns. Where there are still a few large estates in single ownership (the Irvine and Janss estates for example), planned developments have been built or are in process. Where the land is held in smaller parcels, development takes place fitfully, wastefully and at great cost to the taxpayer.

In both California and Texas, where operators have been able to acquire land in sufficiently large parcels, they encounter problems in financing the land and utilities and have formed special districts which have issued tax-exempt bonds at double the conventional rates for tax-exempt issues. These have become the oddities of the municipal investment market and have not enhanced the reputation of California or Texas local public issues in Wall Street circles.[1]

Sponsorship of new towns by the states and cities has flagged, partly because it is novel, partly because it is misunderstood, and partly because the state's right to sponsor such developments has not been indisputably established.

Not the least of the obstacles is that new towns programs have been too often associated with the romanticized conceptions of the "city ideal" instead of resting on the realistic need for assembling fragmented land and providing well-placed schools, streets and utilities in advance of homebuild-

[1] *Wall Street Journal*, March 14, 1962.

ing rather than after the fact. The notion that it is "socialism" (derived from some foreign programs where the state continues owning the land) is absurd—it is anything but that when implicit in the plan is the withdrawal of the public from land ownership and the reservation in public ownership only of the schools, streets and other traditional public services. If anything, its main premise is "desocialization." One of its primary aims is making land available for industry and private development, but in the right areas and where traffic snarls, excessive public works costs, distant enclaves, long work journeys and regional chaos can be avoided. In a state in which 5 million homes will be built by 1980, many new towns are inevitable and the key question should be less who stimulates their formation than that they develop and develop well and in the best places.

Proper development of a new city means that there be enough land for the schools, roads, homesites, shops and utilities essential for the city's functioning; that there be enough reserve land for growth and green space for recreation; that the industries settling in a new area have access to the space they need and to a work force of varying skills and wage levels that can reach their workplaces without the fatigue of protracted journeys from home. For the workers it means the right to choose homes close enough to their work to enable them to see their children and enjoy the maximum rest and leisure after their labors. Freedom of opportunity does not exist when there is no equal access to jobs; equal access to opportunity in turn means that all who qualify for work also qualify for a home within reach of it.

The current urban renewal programs in the older cities are the efforts to win release from the deeply-vested errors of the past, to provide for a greater diversity of population, industry and commerce after the fact and to regain some semblance of social and financial solvency after the mistakes had been made. The communities in embryo need not clear builtup land and evict their citizenry—the land is already clear. They are not tied down by existing investments that exact costly compromises and enforce half-measures—the land can be planned from the start and will be built by private builders who will play the main role in creating the city.

As for the legal question, whatever doubt may still exist as to the federal government's right to build towns within states, there is no doubt that the use of public power to assemble land in sufficiently large parcels is authorized. It is warranted certainly in connection with water installations, preservation of prime agricultural and scenic lands, and as incidents of road and transportational development. Where water lines are laid is where industry will go and where people will settle. Where the state opens up roads is where access is opened to a previously barren hinterland. It can install access roads and utilities as an incident to opening the backlands. Acquiring land incidental to traditional federal or state public improvements has been upheld in a long line of cases. Attracting industry would be a by-purpose.

It is unnecessary, however, to confine public land purchase and resale to these restricted operations. There should be little doubt in California that such right exists to prevent urban sprawl or to provide a better formula for town development than through the ubiquitous privately promoted improvement district. All the approved public purposes are wedged into it —slum prevention, housing, relocation needs, city planning, recreational and public facilities and preservation of scenic resources. It is no less a public purpose to assemble land in open areas to prevent blight than it is to remove it. Cities could be the main beneficiaries of state aid.

In *San Francisco* vs. *Hayes,* 122 Cal. App. 2d 777 (1954), cert. denied 348 U.S. 897, the City of San Francisco was authorized to acquire 325 acres of which only 15 percent was developed or occupied. The standards of blight set forth in the California statute were (a) an economic dislocation, deterioration, or disuse, resulting from faulty planning, (b) the subdividing and sale of lots of irregular shape and inadequate size for proper development, (c) the laying out of lots in disregard of the contours and other physical characteristics and (d) the existence of inadequate streets, open spaces and utilities. The new development in the *Hayes* case was carried out (after assemblage by the renewal agency) by private enterprise—as would be the case in any new towns programs.

The finding of the California Legislature in 1959 in the open space statute along with numerous legislative reports on the impact of encroachments on agricultural land and the problems of "slurb" should prove persuasive in any court test. California, moreover, has had a long background in the development of irrigation districts provided with the eminent domain power (*Fallbrook Irrigation District* vs. *Bradley,* 164 U.S. 112 [1896]). The *Hayes* case has cited with approval the case of *People of Puerto Rico* vs. *Eastern Sugar Associates,* 156 Fed. 2d. 316 (1946), cert. denied, 329 U.S. 772, which authorized eminent domain to "facilitate the utilization of the land for the best possible benefit . . . and to take all action leading to the most scientific and economic enjoyment of the land by the people of Puerto Rico." Statutes in other cities have also authorized the acquisition by state boards, of land for sale or lease as farms to qualified applicants.[2] The California Supreme Court has recently upheld a program of public acquisition for the construction of a marina for small boats which would be leased to private individuals.[3]

A program called a "new towns" program, or something else, but which seeks to avoid land misuse and stimulate proper use gets down to issues of fact and necessity evidenced by present conditions in California. Though there are some decisions to the contrary,[4] there is strong supporting precedent in other states.[5] Acquisition of land through state-chartered corporations has been undertaken in Pennsylvania where the Philadelphia Industrial Development Corporation has been given the eminent domain power. As the United States Supreme Court has put it:

> It is within the power of the legislature to determine that the community should be beautiful as well as healthy, spacious as well as clean, well-balanced as well as carefully controlled. . . . Here one of the means chosen is the use of private enterprise for redevelopment of the area. Appellants argue that this makes the project a taking from one businessman for the benefit of another businessman. But the means of executing the project are for Congress and Congress alone to determine, once the public purpose has been established. . . . The public end may be as well or better served through an agency of private enterprise than through a department of government, or so the Congress might conclude. We cannot say that public ownership is the sole method of promoting the public purposes of community redevelopment projects.[6]

---

[2] *State Reclamation Board* v. *Clausen,* 125 Wash. 525 (1920).

[3] *Ventura Port District* v. *Taxpayers,* 1 Cal. Rep. 169 (1959).

[4] *Hogue* v. *Port of Seattle,* 54 Wash. 2d, 799 (1959); *Opinion of the Justices,* 152 Md. 440 (1957); and *Opinion of the Justices,* 332 Mass. 769 (1955).

[5] *City of Frostburg* v. *Jenkins,* 215 Md. 9 (1957), where a statute was upheld authorizing the city to build industrial plants to be sold to manufacturing corporations agreeing to locate there.

[6] *Berman* v. *Parker,* 73 Sup. Ct. 98 (1954).

The test is whether the eminent domain power is used to avoid a "real hindrance" (*Hayes* case)—a hindrance which cannot be eliminated or improved without public assistance. The *Hayes* case pointed up the court's readiness to accord great weight to legislation and administrative findings of a compelling need and it is this which will be decisive in the long run. If the factual need is shown, the power is available.

The building of new towns could be undertaken first on a pilot basis through the new Housing and Development Agency. The agency should be provided with a revolving fund which can be reused as the agency disposes of any land it acquires and as the new municipality finances the purchase of the public facilities. Loans might be granted to counties for the purpose of developing new communities in this area. Cities with open land should qualify for loans enabling them to expand in a natural manner. In cases where there are no qualified local agencies, the Housing and Development Agency should be able to proceed directly or through corporations chartered by the new agency to carry out the works. The first new town might be built in connection with a state improvement such as water, a university development or road building, but this is not mandatory.

The Aerospace Project Approach Applied to Building New Cities

JOHN H. RUBEL*

It is the purpose of this paper to examine new approaches to overcoming barriers to urban betterment, especially those barriers which interfere with the fullest and most effective participation of the private sector. This discussion is based on the following principal premises:

* Director, Fast Deployment Logistics Ship Project, and formerly Vice President and Director of Technical Planning of Litton Industries, Inc., established "to convert the advanced technology of our times to practicable and marketable use, and to a commercial success, within the private enterprise system." A graduate of the California Institute of Technology, he has been associated with the Research Division of the General Electric Company, the Lockheed Aircraft Company, the Hughes Aircraft Company and the Department of Defense with the final position, 1961–63, as Assistant Secretary of Defense, Research and Engineering, and Deputy Director Defense Research and Engineering prior to joining Litton Industries. A member of the President's Task Force

1. The population of the United States is increasing at the rate of approximately three million persons per year and will continue to do so for many years into the future.

2. Most of the American people already live in cities but the trend toward urbanization is continuing and in some parts of the country accelerating.

3. Most urban growth takes place in and around metropolitan centers that are already in existence. Many of the most pressing problems associated with the American city arise because existing facilities and even the atmosphere above the city are already overloaded.

4. Since it is not likely that the American population will stop growing or that migration patterns into and around major cities will change sharply, it is to be expected that urban problems will continue to become more pressing. The physical problems will multiply—air pollution, problems of waste disposal, traffic flow, the steady erosion of recreational open space and facilities, etc. The human problems will continue to grow, also—the socioeconomic stratifications that are sharpened as land values increase and housing costs skyrocket; the tensions that stem from too little psychological elbow room; the slow decay of the living environment that results from the absence of adequate mechanisms for harnessing or even creating a sense of community and the mechanisms for community action in huge megalopoli, etc.

5. Finally, the point is made that the solution lies, at least in part, in the creation of new cities. The paper describes ways in which mechanisms might be established that would make it possible to create new cities rapidly. The objective is to create new cities that offer more advantages and fewer drawbacks, and at the same time lessen

for War on Poverty, he is Chairman, Scientific Advisory Board of the National Security Agency, as well as a member of other top federal or private research-oriented committees. He was the Regent's Lecturer at the University of California (Los Angeles) in 1962–63, the Sperry-Hutchinson Foundation Lecturer, Law School of the University of Illinois (1964), and Visiting Lecturer, Department of Engineering, University of California (Los Angeles) from 1950 and thereafter. He is the author of a number of published professional articles as well as holding responsibility for certain important classified reports including one co-signed by Secretary McNamara and Administrator Webb (NASA) proposing the inauguration of the manned lunar space program. The following article was based on ideas included in a talk given at the ACTION Symposium (1965), "Defining the Role of the Private Sector in Overcoming Barriers to Urban Betterment."

the problems of existing ones by drawing off some—say, one-third—of the approximately three million additional people who are otherwise going to add to the population of the cities already in existence in the United States every year.

RESOURCES

There can be no question about the fact that our national wealth and industrial powers are more than adequate to create new cities at an ample rate to meet the objectives set forth above—to accommodate at least one-third of the three million new Americans every year. In fact, this process is already going on under a different guise; the approximately three million new people are being housed mainly in the existing metropolitan areas. Schools are being constructed for the children; streets are being widened to accommodate traffic; commissions are meeting to attempt to solve the smog problems. Police forces are being deployed to attempt to preserve order in those sections such as Watts where the socio-economic consequences of current practices in the evolution of cities have reached the boiling-over point.

So the question is not whether or not the resources are available. The chief question is whether or not a mechanism can be devised for harnessing those resources to create a new pattern that will lead to the purposeful creation of new cities designed in a way to diminish or even eliminate the problems of existing ones.

TECHNICAL PROBLEMS

There are no purely or merely technical problems in the way either. It should be obvious that if it is possible to send a satellite to land softly on the surface of the moon and send back pictures that can be viewed by millions of Americans in the comfort of their homes, there is no merely technical or technological problem affecting everyday life that is not readily solvable in planning for and creating new cities. There is nothing about the technologies of road building, waste disposal, the construction of buildings, providing ample means for transportation and communication and the other public and private services required in a city that is not already at hand.

Furthermore, we have the means to make whatever improvements are called for. Old technologies can be modified, newer ones applied, wholly new approaches can be developed expressly tailored to better urban design, better administrative and management arrangements and more efficient use of resources, materials and space. The barriers to innovation are not technical. The important barriers are institutional—cumbersome and overlapping political and administrative jurisdictions; the codification of conventional techniques that forbid innovation; the fragmentation of markets for urban betterment that foreclose it.

CREATING NEW MARKETS

The key to creating the new cities that are needed is to start by creating a market for them. A "market" is a mechanism that provides for the purchase and sale of goods and services. Private industry and business serve markets. There is no market that is not served by an industry. There is no industry in existence that does not serve a market. If a new market is created, the industries necessary to serve it will spring up rapidly. If, therefore, one wishes to create new cities from scratch, one way—and it will be the quickest and probably the best way—is to create a market to which the private sector can respond. A new city market will create a "new city" industry.

The evolution of space technologies serves as a useful illustrative example of this process. The Surveyor satellite that is even now sitting on the surface of the moon transmitting television pictures and data back to earth was designed and built by the Hughes Aircraft Company. The rockets that launched it were engineered and constructed by the General Dynamics Corporation. The Mercury and Gemini space capsules used by our astronauts for in-orbit experimentation were designed and built by the McDonnell Aircraft Company.

Each of these is an example of some of the most advanced technological achievements in the history of the world. Nothing like these machines and the splendid achievement they represent has ever been accomplished by any nation before. All of them are new. None of them was even started more than a few years ago. The Hughes Aircraft Company succeeded in creating a successful Surveyor satellite because there was a market for it, a customer who would buy it. The McDonnell Aircraft Company was enabled to make its major contribution to space technology because there was a market for its talent and its expertise. The aerospace industry was created precisely this way: by creating a market for space projects.

America is a leader in the exploration of space, in televising pictures from the moon, in the creation of worldwide global satellite communication systems—in virtually every aspect of advanced technology and the applications of the advancing frontiers of scientific knowledge. But America is not a leader in the solution of urban problems. We are not renowned for the beauty of our cities. We are not world famous for the happy design of our neighborhoods. There has probably been more research done and more papers written and more knowledge gathered about the reaction of men to the conditions they will face in space and about means for solving problems to insure the success of space missions in just the past few years than has ever been done to understand people in cities and the design of the urban environment to satisfy human needs and improve the human conditions here on earth.

We have the science. We have the scientists. We have the technology. What is lacking is the market.

WHY NOT USE SPACE TECHNOLOGIES?

Our missiles embody and our space projects symbolize our greatest power and some of our highest technological and organizational achievements. No technology is more advanced. No achievements are more spectacular. No efforts have ever required such a marshaling of resources and genius on a national scale. None more clearly signal our capacity to harness national resources for national purposes: missiles in case of war, the conquest of space in cold war and in peace. Nobody doubts for a moment that we will reach the moon. No one questions that we could establish a base there on which men could live and work.

Perhaps it is not surprising, therefore, that people have begun to wonder if the new technologies that are conquering space might not work in our cities here on earth. At first the idea seems ridiculous. What could be more useless in your town or mine than a ten-story rocket—or a thousand of them! The million-dollar precision guidance system that puts a spaceship into an exact orbit would not guide a city council or a mayor or a real estate operator or an oil lobby. The computer that sends photographs from Mars won't even make out the week's payroll for school system employees. The sterile fa-

cilities for assembling payloads to land on the moon are useless to anyone needing surgical treatment. No: the longed-for,
looked-for "fallout" or "transfer" from space technologies to
city needs is simply not there.

The notion that it should stems from a misconception about
the origins of technologies in the first place. Technology is
developed to meet felt human needs that are expressed by
demand in some public or private marketplace. Space technology arose through that familiar process. It did not spring
forth unasked. It was not there, ready and waiting, before the
space age dawned. It did not come as spillover or fallout from
the technologies of everyday life. It was created on purpose
to fulfill specific needs established by the NASA and the Department of Defense. These agencies (plus, in a small way,
the Comsat Corporation) make the "space market." They
decide on the projects. If further technologies are needed to
make the projects go, they are developed. They are developed
to meet needs in space; it would be wholly accidental if technologies valuable to space projects should turn out to be
economically valuable in cities.

But what about the methods for creating the technologies,
if not the technologies themselves? Missile and space projects
use "systems analysis"; they require multidisciplinary teams;
the problems of space are very complex. Likewise, cities and
city problems are complex, in many ways much more so.
Surely they, too, call for multidisciplinary teams. Ergo, runs
this argument, why not use the "systems approach"? Since
the systems approach usually means using big computers to
simulate and calculate things, why not try that for cities? If
that is the approach that works for space—if that is the touch-
stone that has given man the power to fly free from the very
earth itself for the first time in human history—why not use it
to solve those problems of our cities about which every knowledgeable and feeling person is at once so concerned and so discouraged? Why not, in fact, hire the aerospace companies to
apply their computers and their systems techniques to urban
problems?

This idea stems from an equally incorrect misreading of
how science works and how technologies grow. It assumes
that there is a sort of secret formula that accounts for our
spectacular success in the development of weapons and space
systems. This is a common misconception about science and
technology in general. The popular imagination thrives on
stories of malevolent enemies wresting a secret formula from

the martyred but loyal scientist. Our personal exposure to science and mathematics, if we are not scientists, tends to reinforce this image of science as the formula, the key, the last piece in the puzzle. It is a short step from such notions to the hope that the new science, the new technology, will turn out to be the new key that will unlock the solution to the stubborn and often worsening problems of our cities. It is a futile hope.

CREATING PROJECTS

But if this is not the answer, what is? Must we be content to watch science and technology burgeon in space while we do no more than assure ourselves that space technology or systems analysis is not a panacea? How can we marshal and harness our resources and our genius to attack urban problems the way we have done in space? Certainly there must be a way.

The answer, it seems to me, is to start handling the creation of new cities or new towns the way we handle the creation of new, never-before-attempted projects in space. This means: making ad hoc projects out of the development, creation and administration of new cities. It means creating a market-place, a wholly new marketplace, one that does not now exist and never has, where private industry can come and sell the development, creation and administration of new cities. That is how we built our bombers. That is how we created the Atlas, the Titan, the Polaris and a host of incredibly complex, wholly new, never-before-attempted missile systems. That is how we have put men and machines into space. And that is how we are going to send men on a round trip to the moon. Each new undertaking was specified, authorized, funded and administered as a "project." Families of projects—bombers, missiles, space—were and are given the benefits of common administration that provides a framework of scientific, developmental and administrative support. Rocket developments, for example, need not be sponsored exclusively by each particular missile or space project, even though many have been. Continuing rocket developments can be made available to succeeding generations of missile and space projects. If there are no projects in the offing, it is still possible for the space agency and the military departments to sponsor complementary programs of rocket development in anticipation of future needs. The same is true for a vast number of interrelated technological developments that are destined to fit in with specific project needs in the future. *In short, not only do the projects themselves establish a marketplace for the evolution of the methods and the technologies needed to get them done,* the very existence of a continuing series of projects creates a market for the corresponding continuing evolution of the technologies that are likely to be needed to support them and to permit the creation of new and as yet impossible projects.

There is a profound interaction between means and needs in this process. Projects that are clearly impossible—that is, economically and technically unrealistic—are rarely started. They are not written up, funded, put out to bid. They do not become an immediate factor in the project marketplace. But they may be contemplated. They may be foreseen. They may be wished for. As technologies relevant to such projects develop further, the barriers to success are lowered. Then the time will come when the once dreamed-of project is economically and technically feasible. Then it can be undertaken, and whatever pieces of method or design are needed to complete the job will be worked out to satisfy the needs of the now new market for precisely those solutions. That new market is: the project. It is through such processes that missile and space technologies were created.

HARNESSING THE NEEDED SKILLS AND POWERS

The methods for combining and using the evolving technologies were developed in the same context and in response to the same set of market needs. By methods, I mean particularly the methods for organizing to do the jobs, especially the very large missile and space project jobs. Those methods of organization were essential to success.

There have been many changes in the arrangements and procedures over the years, but it has been apparent for a long time that at any point in time they represented important innovations in at least two fundamental ways: (a) they called for a novel articulation of public purposes with private means —it was this that led to the creation of the aerospace industry in the first place; and (b) they evoked the accelerated development and swift refinement of "systems engineering," "systems analysis," the "integrated systems management approach," "operations research." Under whatever heading, these are the methods and technologies of large-scale decision-making. They became necessary when it became possible to design large-scale, complex "systems." They became possible as soon as projects were set up which created a market which could and would support the organizations within which the systems approach could flourish.

If there is any key to the unprecedented elaboration of modern large-scale technologies and the sciences with which they are allied, the creation of these special project mechanisms is that key. We must be clear, too, that these are not ordinary projects, in the sense that a dam or a bridge or a road is a project. These are projects for the creation of solutions to tasks for which the objectives, but not all the needed technologies or methods, are known.

Whatever solutions there may be will be derived by assaulting the problem, not by looking for a formula. Whatever formulations there may be will reflect solutions uniquely applicable to the problems being solved. In order to get such solutions, in order to evolve such formulations, one must do much more than attempt to borrow the solutions or formulations that apply to a different situation. To get the solutions that apply to city problems, the markets must be created that will stimulate the evolution of the organizations that will, in turn, create the centers of motivated expertise necessary to obtain the solutions which that marketplace rewards.

DYNAMIC EVOLUTION OF NEW INSIGHTS AND TECHNIQUES

In short, if one could set up a project for the creation of a new city from scratch, and offer the job to private industry, and set up project goals in terms of the performance of a dynamic system, new industries would spring up within the framework of existing firms to meet the new needs. Soon the multidisciplinary teams would be assembled. The relevant analytical techniques would be applied. The new methods, the new technologies, the new insights would begin to emerge. The new insights and the new technologies would include wholly new species of engineering and technology. Social engineering, the applied counterpart of social science, would take form. The social sciences, increasingly linked to agencies for action, would develop more swiftly and with greater certainty than before. Now they would have new experimental situations at their disposal and the means to test and to compare hypotheses and concepts. One can predict that they would begin to shift away from the descriptive phase with which all sciences begin. They would become increasingly manipulative, as the physical sciences have. Wind tunnels and airplanes are needed in order to design the next airplane, and after that the next, in a never-ending series in which the products of an advancing technology become the tools used by scientists and technologists to make further advances. Likewise, it is necessary to be able to design and construct cities under the aegis of city-specifying, city-building project auspices so that the next city project will reflect the changed objectives and the more certain insights evolved during the first experience, all this in a never-ending series. For it is out of such a series that a "city technology" will be created analogous to "space technology." Again, it will be done not by borrowing the technologies or methods intact from the weapons or the space field, but by (a) imitating the applicable features of the organizational approaches that have given us modern, large-scale technology, and (b) creating a market in the form of projects in a framework which encourages the evolution of a new articulation of public purpose with private means. If there is a key to drawing forth the swift evolution of a "city technology" that might some day inspire a measure of that same awe inspired by our burgeoning achievements in space, this may be that key.

REQUIREMENTS FOR ESTABLISHING NEW CITY PROJECTS

One may identify at least four principal requirements that must be met in establishing new city projects. These include the following:

(1) A mechanism to set goals and specifications each time a new city project is to be undertaken,
(2) A mechanism for continuing research,
(3) Mechanisms for insuring or at least aiming at designs for dynamic evolution,
(4) The effective articulation of public power with private means.

Each of these elements is discussed briefly in subsequent paragraphs.

A MECHANISM TO SET GOALS AND SPECIFICATIONS

Unless we are to be satisfied with the evolution of cities in response to the market mechanisms that now exist, we must seek the creation of a mechanism capable of setting goals and specifications for the evolution of new cities and towns. To some degree, and in some cases a substantial one, this is already done. Government mortgage guarantees available for some kinds, but not for other kinds, of housing developments have the effect of specifying important aspects of development, especially suburban development. Their aggregate effect amounts to specifying many characteristics of the resulting megalopolis that includes what once were suburbs.

What is really desired is a mechanism for establishing specifications backed up by authority and funds to sponsor the job. The starting point ought to be specifications describing what the city is supposed to do, how it is to perform, what its objectives and characteristics will be. Writing such specifications is sure to involve a host of policy judgments. They are bound to reflect a philosophy—indeed, a large set of philosophies—about what the city is to be all about.

A government agency or group of agencies must become involved in this process one way or another. Precisely how that is to be done or could be is beyond the scope of this paper. But just as the Manhattan District of the forties was empowered to write and to implement the specifications for the atomic bomb; just as the Polaris project of the fifties and sixties was in charge of the specifications for the work to be accomplished; so must some agency have responsibility for establishing specifications for the new cities.

Performance specifications must be the starting point for the process of new city development. They will define what is to be sought and achieved but not how the job is to be done. It is this approach that will set the preconditions essential to the development of the sort of "urban technology" that is a further prerequisite for the continued evolution of urban development in America. The performance specifications are not designs. They are not specific plans. They need not specify precisely how the city will be managed, its officials elected, its administration carried out.

Design and planning come in at the point where specifications are translated into specific physical and administrative alternatives. Specific city layouts, particular administrative set-ups, the city-unique architectural objectives and standards evolve as each project evolves. When design tasks are approached this way, it is possible to use modern analytic techniques to weigh alternatives and assess one in relation to another. The advanced technologies developed out of our aerospace experiences, particularly the technologies of large-scale systems analysis, can begin to play a part when it becomes possible to stimulate the impact of this alternative or that, predicting with increasing certainty the consequences of particular decisions.

However the project is set up, the organization responsible for setting goals and specifications must exercise some kind of enduring power. If it does not have the money to spend on the project directly as it would if the project were a new airplane or missile or spacecraft, it must nevertheless have a suitable form of equally effective authority. Governmental credit mechanisms suitably administered by an adequate central authority might meet these requirements. Perhaps the manner in which the government is now contemplating sponsorship of the development of the supersonic transport—an airplane to be developed and constructed by private firms for operation by other private firms but with development costs in effect guaranteed by the Federal government—might be used to set up specifications for new cities and to provide the funds that will get them started in the first place.

A MECHANISM FOR CONTINUING RESEARCH

Neither the development of a single new city or town nor even a succession of them will fully meet the needs. It will be necessary, too, that the research-like investigative undertakings associated with the beginning of each project shall be coupled through the project organization with the engineering and application part of the job. This coupling of science and application on modern large-scale weapons and space projects has been a key factor in the development of the wholly new engineering and quasi-scientific skills so essential to the new technologies. Without that coupling, the projects could not have succeeded and the new skills necessary to make still further progress could not have been developed.

The project marketplace creates a market for the skills needed to make the projects go; many skills are then developed to meet the new needs. If anyone needs to be convinced on this score, he only needs to compare the advertisements for scientists and engineers ten or fifteen years ago with those today.

Even beyond this, however, one requires provisions for interrelating the research activities conducted on one project with those conducted on others. It is in this way that a succession of new city projects would infuse an analogous development in a variety of socio-economic areas. Forms of social engineering would arise that do not even exist today. We need them.

We need the kind of link between the social scientist and the building mechanic that the engineer has been between the physicist and the world of applied technology. That link will be—should be—the "social engineer." With continuing projects employing social scientists at one end and builders at the other end of the occupational spectrum, the social engineer will find a place to work and tasks to do in between. With time, he will become increasingly sophisticated and lean more toward science. With time, the scientists will begin to break away further from their nearly exclusive academic base. Some, just as has happened in the hard sciences in the past few decades, will fill the role of scientist-administrator-engineer for which no proper title has been invented. It is through such an evolution that bridges will be built from the social sciences to the field of action, and back again. The insights of social scientists will be translated more swiftly and systematically into the shape of real things. The results, the pitfalls, the unforeseen problems, the vital data so usually lacking will be fed back through normal project mechanisms to the academic world where they will serve as the basis for still further development of science method and art.

DESIGN FOR DYNAMIC EVOLUTION

An important by-product of research conducted in the course of each project and, over the years, at higher levels of complexity and abstraction will be methods to better insure the dynamics of city evolution. The goals and specifications for a city cannot be merely static. They must describe not only the conditions to be met in the first year of the city's life, but in the twenty-fifth year, and in the fiftieth, and in the one-hundredth. The specifications must attempt to take account of exceptional developments and unforeseen circumstances. What would happen to the city if this condition or that one were to change? How sensitive are its leading characteristics to comparatively small changes in, for example, the general economic situation or changes in methods of production or the introduction of new technologies?

Socio-economic technologies are presently unprepared to deal fully with matters of such complexity. The dynamics of a missile flying through space is complex enough, but the dynamics of urban development and evolution are far less deeply studied, are considerably more complex and are correspondingly much less well understood.

Consider the question of land ownership and its impact on the long-range prospects for dynamic evolution. How can one plan the long-range future for any city, new or old, unless the planner has effective control of land use in the city? And how can control be accomplished without ownership? To some, it seems almost obvious that there is no use talking about planning or any sort of purposeful long-range dynamic evolution for big cities as long as urban land remains one of the most attractive commodities to speculators, large and small.

This particular choice concerning the ownership and control of land is only one, albeit the most important one, of a long series of judgments that must be made in setting up the city project. These judgments require a choice between the possibilities for public good and their potential conflict with private interests. Will each individual be free to add to air pollution by driving a motor car? If so, the city designer has some calculations to make. How much air pollution is acceptable from the standpoint of the "public good"? How often can maximum levels be tolerated? What will the sources of pollution be? How much will motor vehicles account for? For a given configuration of neighborhoods, industrial centers, commuting patterns, roads and other transport systems, how do physical arrangements and population densities translate into automobile traffic and the corresponding distribution of pollution in time and space? Given the taxes, land rents and other charges against private interests conformal with the particular configuration and assumptions entered in the analysis, will the standards set for air pollution be met? Are the charges against private interest out of line? Will the "public good" be adequately served, with ample margins for safety and for error in the analysis and projections? If not, the problem needs to be redone making other assumptions and postulating different physical configurations. *Iterations of this sort are familiar to designers of complex systems. They are at the heart of the design process.* In this case, as in all other important cases, the application of such processes to urban design and betterment must confront and resolve fundamental questions of how the public good is to be served by levies against private resources and private interests and how private interest is to be served without undue charges to the public good.

Landowners will and can take nothing less than the market value of their land. Given the market mechanisms at work, this is every reason why they should and no "reason" why they should not. "Eccentric" old ladies in nineteenth-century houses may sometimes block progress by refusing to sell at inflated prices. But the "normal" owner is glad to see higher prices for his land. He, too, knows that higher land values mean bigger buildings which mean higher density which means more people in automobiles on freeways buying gasoline on which taxes are collected to build more freeways carrying more vehicles, all adding further to pollution and congestion. But pollution and congestion are beyond individual control. The natural pressures that chronically form public actions in directions which magnify private gain are largely beyond real public control. Thus, even the most superficial overview of a single confrontation of the public good versus private interest, in this case the private right to drive cars and the public need to breathe fresh air, raises the same issue in a variety of forms. Of these, none is more dominant than the need to alter the market mechanisms that govern the values and thus the uses of urban land.

The object here, and this is true for the city as a whole, ought to be to find ways to align private interest with the public good. These will often conflict when private owners hold land that affects the public good. But there is nothing fixed about the magnitude or importance of that conflict: the task is to align private interest with public interest through sound market and administrative mechanisms. The challenge is to identify the problem, to analyze its implications, to devise solutions, all with a view to purposefully creating the dynamic characteristics desired in the new city. When the task is viewed this way, the city is seen as a complex system. The ownership and control of land are system parameters. Studying and designing the desired city requires one to see these parameters as subject to change. The systems approach calls for examining many alternatives. The scientific attitude that governs the process insists on the objective analysis of alternatives. Out of such procedures come innovation and the solution to long-standing problems.

THE EFFECTIVE ARTICULATION OF PUBLIC POWER AND PRIVATE MEANS

New city projects of the sort our country needs most are not likely to succeed without the proper articulation of public power and policy with private means. Most of the talent and vigor needed for the job is to be found in the private sector. There is no better way to harness those energies and to mobilize the political consensus necessary in any case than to use private business and industry as the mechanism for the accomplishment of the public ends our society requires. Without that articulation, the projects will fail for lack of the necessary political support in any case. With it, the industrial might and organizing genius of American industry will be turned in the new direction of creating a better urban America.

It is not possible to describe in detail at this point how these arrangements should be set up, or could be. Perhaps the Congress could charter a new company, modeled somewhat after the Comsat Corporation, authorized to acquire the necessary large blocks of land and to develop it in accordance with certain objectives, very broadly stated. Some of the land might be purchased; some might be acquired in large blocks from large holders under special negotiated arrangements. For example, holders of large tracts might be willing to exchange most of their holdings for the right to hold relatively small, but highly profitable, parts of it for long-range development and exploitation, somewhat the way residential developers often hold on to shopping centers. In such cases, the owners would, in effect, pay with undeveloped land for the unearned increment of value they would expect to get from the city-building they could not hope to finance on their own. Or some of the vast Federal lands might be converted to urban use, a possibility presently being considered by the Bureau of Land Management.

The pattern of land acquisition would be varied to fit the requirements of each locale. The corporation could be required to relate itself with certain Federal agencies, chiefly the new Department of Housing and Urban Development, much as Comsat works with and through NASA, the Department of State and other Federal departments and agencies already established for functional responsibilities that ought not be duplicated. That would be a key here—the city development corporation would be responsible for the development of the new city on a project basis. Functional responsibilities in certain areas, chiefly Federal finance, would be handled by existing agencies.

Such a scheme would make it possible to admit individual and corporate residents of the new city to stockholder ownership in the corporation which, over time, would become the city itself. Perhaps there could be ways to take some profit out of the unearned increment in land values that would arise from the growth of the city, short of selling land. Increased rentals for higher-value land uses; land rentals geared (as many private leases are) to a percentage-of-sales formula; one-time assessments against large users who are willing to pay extra for the privilege of using land longer, or turning it to approved high-value uses, and so on. If some dividend payment scheme could be worked out, shares in the city corporation might be made to acquire a slowly rising value. Shareholders would thus be given a private incentive for policies and actions that increase values citywide. Perhaps closer analysis would show that some such combination of mechanisms and incentives would promise to work in the direction of greater private support of the public good.

POTENTIAL PROBLEMS—MECHANISMS AND THE SUPPORT FOR THEM

What is needed is an invention or a series of inventions leading to the creation of market mechanisms and mechanisms for the articulation of public power with private means to enable full participation by the private sector in the city-designing, city-conceiving, city-building, even city-managing business.

The would-be inventor faces a number of serious obstacles and problems. Almost any workable scheme will require legislation. Suppose, for example, that some of the vast public lands owned by the Federal government could be made available for the development of new cities. They would cost the American taxpayers nothing. If new successful cities were built on these lands, new wealth would be created. The investment necessary to create it would probably be less in the long run than the cost of urban renewal projects necessary to undo the blight that would otherwise take place in the already existing metropolitan centers whose growth is too rapid and too uncontrolled, partly because our increasingly urbanized population has no place else to go. But before legislation could be successfully proposed, the detailed arrangements for setting up the city development corporation would have to be worked out. The extent to which such legislation would be supported or opposed would depend heavily on where the new city or cities were to be located and on the forms of ownership and administration proposed for the development of the new towns and cities.

Thus, the fullest participation by the private sector might be assured if leading American firms could form consortiums specifically for the purpose of creating new cities. On the other hand, the arrangements for dealing with such consortiums and avoiding the opposition of firms not included in them could add complexities and obstacles. A newly chartered company similar in principle to the Communications Satellite Corporation might be set up for the first city and after that, a succession of similar ones for future developments. It must not be forgotten, however, that the Communications Satellite bill was filibustered for several weeks. The objections of the opponents were based on socio-political views that happened to center about the undesirability of the allegedly monopolistic role of AT&T. One might expect that corresponding objections would be raised to the establishment of an analogous corporation for the creation of new cities. The particular objections might be different and the specific grounds for objection might not be identical but the opportunity for a clash of political and social viewpoints is even more likely in the case of city building than in the case of satellite launching.

One may anticipate problems wherever state, county or other local authorities are involved. If the private firm responsible for developing the new city is, in fact, given "systems" responsibility, how will local laws and the application of local regulations in detail be made to fit with this plan to create new cities on a national scale? Nearly any specific mechanism will also face criticism, if not outright opposition, from any one of a variety of quarters. Suppose that the specifications call for a city that fulfills a variety of socio-political objectives which many consider of vital and basic importance to the American future. The desegregation of public accommodations and of residential neighborhoods and the destratification of schools and neighborhoods on economic lines are examples. The "ideal" solution from this point of view will be attractive to some but it will be attacked by others as impractical and unworkable. The converse is also true. Suppose, for example, that the new city was to be located near an existing metropolis or midway between two growing ones. Suppose, further, that it was clearly designed to solve the chief problems affecting the existing cities—the overcrowding, the sprawl, the growth of slums, the social stresses and strains, the tax burdens imposed by the influx of the poor, the erosion of the school system from an influx of poorly prepared students.

The new city could offer a solution to most of these problems to the most mobile elements of the existing ones—the middle and upper-middle classes. But that would scarcely be a "solution" from the standpoint of the administrators of the existing cities, representatives of the less privileged classes or the same architects of new urban patterns whose ideal city would be something quite different.

All such problems further highlight the most fundamental and difficult one of all: Who will move to the new cities? How will one get them to move?

A CONCEPTUAL PROBLEM

This question is not merely one of mechanisms. It is not a question of establishing a market for the creation of new cities. It is really the point at which the analogies that have been drawn thus far between aerospace programs on the one hand, and the creation of new cities on the other, break down. The government could create markets for community development. It can create markets for the development of a city-developing, city-building, even city-administering industry. It could provide programs aimed at inducing consumers to buy.

But in the end, people will decide where they are going to live and the kind of community to which they wish to move entirely on their own. The new cities that might be created by one or more of the mechanisms touched on in this paper are only a few among the many choices that could be made by the "city consumer." That consumer is the individual who is going to buy a home or rent an apartment or construct a factory or rent office space in the new city—or someplace else.

True, private builders have already found that cities for retired people can succeed. Cities of trailer homes are succeeding. Resort suburbs are succeeding. There certainly is a market for new communities.

But none of these are cities or towns in the sense intended by this paper. Some of them create new socio-economic problems, even as they appear to satisfy certain of the requirements of at least some of their inhabitants. They demonstrate that demands exist for new patterns. But they do not demonstrate the extent to which demands exist or can be created for the better and more ideal cities of the future. Will the ultimate consumer buy the product designed by architects of a better urban America—better as they, the architects, see it? Can the premises on which a new city is to be created be tested in advance? Can projects be begun with the foreknowledge they might fail or with serious doubts about their chances for success? Would that be politically viable? These, too, are questions that must be carefully examined.

It is not difficult to pose many more tough questions, but at this stage it is not very useful. The important thing to do is to re-examine the argument and the premises on which it is based. Recapitulated in somewhat changed order, it goes like this:

(1) We stand at the pinnacle of man's technological achievements in America today. No nation was ever more powerful; none ever moved with greater certainty or promise toward still greater power and fulfillment.

(2) Our missile projects embody and our space projects symbolize our highest technological achievements and our power to harness national resources for national purposes. There is nothing to equal them in the history of the world.

(3) By contrast, prospects for our cities are bleak. Public needs are served with increasing difficulty, and often with declining effectiveness.

(4) But it is futile to look for panaceas or even useful, economical fallout or transfer from missile and space technologies. Neither the technologies nor the methods that have proved so spectacularly successful in space will help much in our cities.

(5) What would work would be the introduction of a new way to make new cities. It is the project way; it is the way missile and space undertakings are organized, authorized and funded on an ad hoc, project-oriented

basis. Such projects would furnish the vehicle for the rapid development of the technologies that would be directly relevant and useful in the cities of the future.

(6) At the same time, other barriers would be removed in the framework of the project organization. Thus, three preconditions for success would be established:

    (a) A marketplace for the development of the new city patterns that are needed,

    (b) A new articulation of public purpose with private means, and

    (c) The corresponding evolution of the industrial means to fill the needs of the new markets created by the formation of the new city projects.

(7) The "new city projects" would provide a truly unique opportunity not just to plan or to analyze, but to apply the results of planning and analysis—actually experimentation—and to modify these in the light of actual results. It is precisely such feedback that makes the concept of the "systems approach" meaningful when applied to socio-economic matters of such magnitude and gravity.

(8) The "new articulation of public purpose with private means" will enlist the talents, the enthusiasms and the support of major elements of the industrial sector in the search for better solutions to the problem of American urbanization. They would be the "systems contractors." They would become responsible, under contract, for meeting project objectives. Reputation, profits and future contracts would be their incentives. Their involvement would guarantee their interest. Their interest would assure their support. The value of that support and the importance of harnessing those talents are not easily overstated.

Chapter 19

SOCIAL PLANNING

Symptomatic of the new realization of the importance of social planning by urban planners as well as political and private decision-makers are these three recent developments: (1) *The Demonstration Cities Program* proposed by the Johnson administration with a budget of $2.3 billion over six years. It is now temporarily stalled in Congress, but this imaginative mix of a wide spectrum of welfare programs with massive physical development in a coordinated effort for approximately fifty selected cities will undoubtedly be implemented, barring international catastrophe, within a year or two. It could prefigure an eventual marriage of the Poverty Program (Office of Economic Opportunity) with HUD for a coordinated attack on the total urban environment. (2) Washington, the national capital, following the leads of Philadelphia, New Haven and to a lesser extent Boston, has linked its social welfare program with physical planning and development. (3) Following in the footsteps of a planner and a political scientist, Daniel Patrick Moynihan,* dynamic sociologist, politician and author of the much-discussed and outspoken government paper "The Negro Family: The Case for National Action," was appointed in the summer of 1966 head of the Joint Center for Urban Studies of Harvard and M.I.T. Founded in 1959, it is certainly one of the most respected research centers of its kind in the country; it has moreover been significantly blessed by the Ford Foundation for its good works.

The powerful writing of persons such as Michael Harrington (*The Other America*; New York: The Macmillan Company, 1964) and the characteristic "long hot summers" of the later 1960's with their dead, injured and extensive destruction have focused public attention on the fearsome human ills of our great urban places from Los Angeles to New York with the Negro ghettos as the most noisome exhibits. The citizenry is increasingly aware that something beyond physical redevelopment, often for patent economic gains, is required to provide the sort of life America is capable of giving to its population. Jobs, education, recreation, welfare, health, community are needed beyond mere bricks and mortar; traditional city planning simply can't deliver.

Perhaps unfortunately, the present concentration is on remedial measures; that is, negative devices to aid the disadvantaged. This quite simply is not *social planning* but is *social welfare*. It is not

* See the New York *Times* Magazine, July 31, 1966, for an analysis of this dedicated and colorful figure.

personality development for the average and superior individual in a challenging amount; it is attempting merely to dredge out the disadvantaged from the morass. Admittedly, a necessary and awesome task in itself, good works—no doubt needed as a preliminary exercise to launch us into the twenty-first century with a civilization of "style and quality." American social planning tends to be like American private medicine—curative rather than, as public health medicine—preventive. Finally, the aim should be to maximize social health, but as yet frankly no one knows quite how to do this. Harvey S. Perloff, economist and planner, gives below a comprehensive overview of social planning cooperation with economic and physical planning in an idealized model still geared wisely to the possible. He sets up a fourfold pattern of (a) organizational considerations (b) substantive considerations (c) informational and planning tools (d) process and implementation. This is essentially a community social welfare approach and does not seek to optimize the total environment. Curiously, he does not dwell on family planning, one obvious method of getting at the roots of poverty. Herbert J. Gans, sociologist and planner, slaps the physical planners sharply for their overweaning pretensions in thinking that by their three-dimensional constructs they can cure mental ills and positively promote mental health. He points out that no one knows very much about mental health and traditional city planners even less. He reiterates, moreover, that the relation between physical environment and "sound human beings" is by no means clear. There is a fourth dimension *inside* people that is important—concrete and tar do not get at that. Gans is pleased that the redevelopment Federal bulldozer is out—his work had much to do with stopping this creator of human ills—and he exhibits the current egalitarian sociological ethos in his fear of designed neighborhoods even as a convenience principle. Upper middle class folkways, so often motivating city plans, unquestionably do not fit most of our citizens and cannot be rationally sanctified; the slum dwellers must participate in their own salvation in their own fashion as the Poverty Program attempted, but to date has failed to accomplish, specifically in *Community Action Programs*. Gans suggests that people, anywhere, should themselves decide what their "good environment" should be; which is clearly in the democratic tradition, even if wide open to some philosophical questioning. The Reiners, socially oriented planners, have canvassed the literature on *poverty*, much in today's news, with specific orientation toward the dynamic, if admittedly chaotic, efforts of the Office of Economic Opportunity. The OEO like a lava flow is slowly moving up to and around traditional urban political activity and physical planning. The Reiners produce four implications for urban planning from their survey: (a) the planner must rethink the premises and findings of ecological and of economic determinism; (b) the complexity of *poverty*; (c) programming—even physically—for *poverty* is much more involved than is presently understood; and (d) further clarification of what *poverty* means and what we actually propose to do about it. Maurice Broady, an English sociologist closely associated with planning in Britain, has split social planning into *social welfare*, remedial, and *social development* or positive horizon-stretching. Building on new town and central city English experience and research (much of it quantified), his paper is the suggested *social planning* section to go along with the economic and the physical design plan for the orderly expansion of the Hampshire town of Basingstoke from thirty thousand to eighty thousand by the 1980's under the Town Development Act of 1952. He foresees a richer life for all as the goal of social planning; it is noteworthy that workingmen's groups participated with him in the study. In the long run, horizons must be lifted; this is of far greater importance than costly and very complex cures, much needed as they are.

New Directions in Social Planning

HARVEY S. PERLOFF*

The United States is going through profound changes in its handling of social problems. Characteristic of such changes are the national government's direct involvement in problems such as those of poverty, race and discrimination, chronic unemployment, juvenile delinquency and mental health, and a proliferation of pilot projects in communities throughout the country testing new approaches to social welfare. All this is certain to be reflected in a changed approach to social planning. The challenge is to devise an effective form of social planning, building on those traditional features which have withstood the test of time and introducing newer features embodying the more recently recognized needs.

This paper seeks to analyze these various features and to suggest how they might be blended together. It portrays an idealized approach to social planning, essentially a "model" to highlight the overall requirements, suggesting a core around which practical, acceptable versions might be evolved.

The suggested new directions are derived from considerations of *one*, the nature of the social problems which are of increasing concern to U.S. communities, *two*, the characteristics of the institutional milieu within which these problems are handled, and *three*, the lessons to be derived from the

* For a biography, see Chapter 15. The following was reprinted with permission from the *Journal of the American Institute of Planners*, Vol. XXXI, No. 4, November 1965.

experience with planning, not only in the social sphere but in the physical, and other realms as well, since there are certain principles of planning which seem to be of extremely broad applicability.

EXISTING STRENGTHS AND NEW REQUIREMENTS

Social planning in the United States has been associated largely with Community Health and Welfare Councils. This has generated certain problems. While voluntary welfare activities (financed by United Funds or Community Chests) have been expanding within recent decades, by far the greatest growth has taken place in governmental social welfare activities.[1] Local Councils have made serious efforts to serve as overall community planning organizations, but because of resistance from outside and limitations from within (including very serious financial limitations), they have had to restrict themselves largely to concern for the activities of the voluntary agencies and have been involved only peripherally with governmental, tax-supported social programs.

In spite of this and other equally serious handicaps, our social planning has developed certain strengths, or at least potentially useful directions and traditions. Among these are the following:

1. Voluntary and democratic processes have been built into social planning operations; broad citizen involvement has been sought; a pluralistic approach to the definition and solution of social problems has been accepted.

2. The value of a broad information and research base for planning activities has been appreciated and, to the extent permitted by extremely limited resources, has been developed. Councils have launched a wide variety of studies to deepen understanding of social problems as well as to find improved methods for coping with them. They have attempted also to develop regularized flows of needed information.

3. The need for continuous evaluation of agency and Council activities has been accepted and, to some extent, implemented. (This is rare among planning activities in other fields,

---

[1] These developments and their implications for social work as well as social planning are analyzed in Harold L. Wilensky and C. N. Lebeaux, *Industrial Society and Social Welfare: The Impact of Industrialization on the Supply and Organization of Social Welfare Services in the United States* (New York: Russell Sage Foundation, 1958).

where emphasis tends to be on program development, with little evaluation of the results of existing programs.)

4. There has been a concern for *both* functional coordination and impact by geographic units. While the actual integration of the functional and the geographic aspects of social services has been limited, the dual view of community needs has given a broad dimension to social planning.

5. The desirability of planning on a metropolitan-wide basis has been accepted. Recognition of the metropolitan region as the major form of settlement in the United States suggests that social planning must be concerned with the problems and potentialities of all parts of the metropolis.

These are significant and valuable features. As social planning is both broadened and deepened to meet the very demanding social needs of modern urban communities, there is every reason to make a serious effort to retain and strengthen these features. They should not be lost as new approaches are evolved.

With this as background we examine the existing inadequacies and the new requirements for social planning to meet our rapidly changing situation with regard to welfare concepts and activities. These are discussed under four major categories: *one,* organizational considerations, *two,* substantive considerations, *three,* informational and planning tools, and *four,* process and implementation.

ONE. ORGANIZATIONAL CONSIDERATIONS

The present compartmentalization of voluntary and governmental welfare activities, as well as the inadequate planning of the two, must be squarely faced. The great growth in the importance of both underlines the need for *joint* governmental-and-voluntary planning in order to achieve an effective welfare *system* within the community. This is no simple matter for it will require a widespread appreciation of the need for such joint planning as well as a good measure of social invention. Mixed activities of this type are uncommon in the United States and the early experimental efforts are likely to encounter difficulties.

If such joint planning is to function effectively several requirements must be met. Possibly the most important need is to strengthen planning *within* each sphere. In the governmental sphere, social planning needs to become an integral part of staff planning under the chief executive, at least in the central city, but ideally in suburban governments as well. This would permit the guidance and coordination of governmental social service activities more or less in the same way that city planning agencies attempt to guide and coordinate physical development activities. Because of the severe financial pressures on cities, this is likely to take place in the near future only if the federal government provides local grants for social planning as it currently provides grants for physical development planning. A direct precedent for such federal social planning aid are the current grants under the Community Renewal Programs which supply financial assistance for broad community studies, including investigation of social problems and conditions, as a background for preparing communitywide renewal programs.

In the voluntary sphere there is also need for substantial improvements in planning by the Health and Welfare Councils if joint governmental-voluntary planning is to be effective and meaningful. Here the most immediate need is for the allocation of greater resources for planning; in most communities, Councils have received very little for this purpose. Also, planning personnel within Councils often need updating on modern planning techniques, such as those involving the use of computers, and new programming and budgeting methods.

Another requirement for effective joint governmental voluntary planning is a clearer definition of the appropriate role of each sphere in welfare activities. For example, it is conceivable that over time the voluntary approach may be used mainly to handle experimental, non-homogeneous kinds of problems (such as new kinds of comprehensive family services during their experimental stages), as well as activities requiring substantial citizen involvement (such as in certain kinds of neighborhood programs). The governmental agencies on the other hand, might be expected to handle the larger, more routinized services after they have been tested and adjusted and their merit has been proven. Developments in the mental health field have more or less followed this pattern. If this division of functions were implemented, it would also be conceivable that governmental grants might be made available to voluntary groups to carry out experimental activities that the governmental agencies felt were needed. Social planning within the Health and Welfare Councils would then be essentially concerned with probing the changing nature of social problems, discovering new approaches for dealing with these problems, setting up additional social experiments that seem useful, developing means for transferring functions from voluntary groups to governments as they become largely routinized, and improving approaches for integrating plans and activities along functional and geographic lines.

With improvement in planning in both spheres and a clearer definition of functions, joint governmental-voluntary social planning could be expected to function both naturally and effectively.

Other organizational requirements need to be noted. Because of the nature of the social problems which are of major concern, social planning must involve forces in the community other than those directly represented by the governmental and voluntary agencies. This is particularly true of the economic forces. Chronic unemployment and underemployment and inadequate income among certain groups underlie many of the most difficult welfare problems, as well as some of the thorniest issues in the provision of social services. In the past, social planning contacts with the major business and labor groups in the communities have been relatively limited. Programs touching on jobs and income have been typically the concern of chambers of commerce and economic development groups—with their own special, and generally limited, points of view—and have been related only peripherally to social services. Training and vocational guidance, relief support, human relations programs, or anti-discrimination efforts on one hand; and economic development activities, industrial promotion, and labor-management activities on the other, tend to remain in operationally separate realms even though they are closely interrelated in fact and in impact. In the future, social planning must directly involve the major economic forces in the community so that local attacks on problems of unemployment, underemployment, poverty, economic discrimination, and the like, can be carried out in a planned and coordinated fashion.

The present chasm between social and physical planning must also be bridged. Many of the decisions made in physical planning and development have significant social ramifications. This is true, to cite only a few examples, of the decisions made with regard to housing, urban renewal, and relocation which directly affect community living patterns,[2] plant loca-

---

[2] On this point, see the various articles on housing and urban renewal in *The Urban Condition, op. cit.* Also see Eunice and George Grier "Human Needs and Public Policy in Urban Development," a paper delivered before the annual meeting of the American Orthopsychiatric

tions and transportation which influence access to jobs, and standards of eligibility for public housing.[3] On the other hand, social services and social policy decisions—for example, the level of support provided to various low income groups—have an important impact on where people live and their physical requirements. Similarly, the quality of the social services and facilities available in a neighborhood is a key factor in the success or failure of neighborhood renewal and rehabilitation programs. To be sure that such important interrelationships are fully considered, physical planners might well be directly involved with the boards guiding community social planning.

If all of the above elements are important, as clearly seems the case, social planning might well be organized as a *community coalition* directly aimed at involving the broad spectrum of community forces in planning an integrated and continuing attack on the major social problems. This would call for a new type of overall planning organization, including representatives of the Community Health and Welfare Council, of all local governments, business and labor groups, physical planning and development agencies, and citizen groups.

The inclusion of representatives of citizen groups is suggested because of the possibility that the other categories might not adequately cover the community power structure or adequately represent some important groups, such as the Negro community or particular consumer groups. In the case of the first community in the country to organize such a broad-scale social planning effort on a metropolitan basis, the Washington, D. C. region, it was deemed essential to include presidential appointees on the board of the planning organization because of the importance of the federal government in the affairs of the region. In general, representation within a given community should be geared to its particular institutional milieu.

Association, March 9, 1963, for an excellent statement on the importance of combining human-behavior and physical considerations in city planning decisions.

[8] A valuable analysis of the importance of standards of eligibility in social services in general is provided in Janet S. Reiner, Everett Reimer, and Thomas A. Reiner "Client Analysis and the Planning of Public Programs," *A.I.P. Journal*, XXIX (November 1963) 270–82.

TWO. SUBSTANTIVE CONSIDERATIONS

The breadth and difficulty of the social problems that communities face today strongly suggest that social planning should include all pertinent socio-economic and human-behavior considerations which are of central significance in governmental and voluntary agency decisions. It would thereby provide the human resources counterpart to physical city planning. Thus, between the social and physical planning the community would have the capacity to study all major developments within the metropolis and to provide guidelines for desired social change and future development.

The appropriate scope for a community planning effort raises many difficult questions. Such an effort can be ineffectual either because it includes too little or because it attempts too much. The obvious criteria for coverage are significance (particularly in terms of the community's values) and relevance; but these must be defined. Drawing on major recent community studies and programs, it would seem that the logical core of a social planning effort in a metropolitan region today might be expected to extend to factors that influence:

1. *Jobs and incomes of families.* It is increasingly recognized that the most effective approach to the solution of many current social problems is to increase the number of families that are self supporting. This would involve actions to strengthen the job-getting and income-earning capacities of individuals, and includes adjusting the educational system to meet the special needs of disadvantaged groups, and to minimize school drop-outs, as well as training and retraining of adults, and improving vocational guidance programs. It is also increasingly recognized that the job situation itself is a matter of community concern and that economic development programs to strengthen the regional economy and to broaden employment opportunities particularly for the less skilled groups are of great significance in social planning. Social planning should be in a position to provide guidelines to community groups working on both the supply and demand sides of the manpower equation.

2. *Financial support to those who cannot become economically self-supporting.* Examples are the indigent aged, the disabled, and families without fathers. Public and voluntary wel-

fare programs should be jointly designed and coordinated so that no one is eliminated because of thoughtless or prejudiced eligibility rules. Also, the levels of support should be in line with changes in the costs of living and the special needs of the various disadvantaged groups.

3. *Emotional support for individuals and family groups who need it.* There should be a continuing effort to define the kinds of people needing some form of outside emotional support and to tailor community efforts to the different needs. These would range from full-time psychiatric help to temporary forms, as through counselors in school and family services. Also, a major effort should be directed at finding ways of *preventing* mental problems, by building mental health approaches into school, hospital, and social service procedures so that early diagnosis, "caretaker" support for individuals (particularly at times of crisis), and post-treatment assistance become normal parts of a widespread system to strengthen mental health.

4. *A high level of social services, particularly education and health.* This is a desired end in itself for many people. Problems which stand in the way of achieving it—such as in- adequate tax base to support education and health programs and facilities in central cities or in small communities, or out- moded schools and hospitals in older sections of the metropolis —are seen as top priority problems for social planning and ac- tion.

5. *Decent housing and a satisfying physical environment for all families.* This is a declared national objective and federal financial assistance is already provided to localities to help achieve it. If the goal is to be realized, however, the local community itself must take direct actions such as by helping to achieve policies of "open occupancy" in housing, estab- lishing sensible housing and zoning regulations, encouraging widespread rehabilitation, and providing good public services in the older, poorer neighborhoods as well as in the newly- built ones. Social planning—jointly with physical planning— must provide guidelines for such local programs.

6. *Elimination of racial discrimination.* While each com- munity in the country is split on the issue of racial discrimina- tion, increasingly the leadership groups in them recognize the desirability of carrying out positive programs to break down racial barriers at the fastest possible rate. Clearly social planning must seek for effective means to achieve the broadly

FIGURE 1. SUBJECTS OF MAJOR CONCERN TO SOCIAL PLANNING

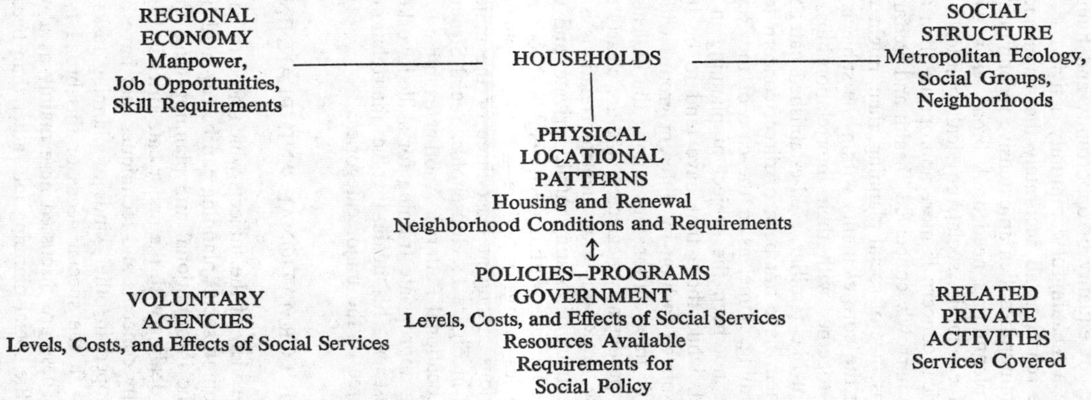

REGIONAL ECONOMY
Manpower,
Job Opportunities,
Skill Requirements

HOUSEHOLDS

SOCIAL STRUCTURE
Metropolitan Ecology,
Social Groups,
Neighborhoods

PHYSICAL LOCATIONAL PATTERNS
Housing and Renewal
Neighborhood Conditions and Requirements

POLICIES—PROGRAMS
GOVERNMENT
Levels, Costs, and Effects of Social Services
Resources Available
Requirements for Social Policy

VOLUNTARY AGENCIES
Levels, Costs, and Effects of Social Services

RELATED PRIVATE ACTIVITIES
Services Covered

held values of equality of opportunity and human dignity if it is to be a meaningful community activity.

If these reflect at all accurately the major social problems of our communities then an extensive redefinition of the scope of social planning is needed. A broad view which includes aspects of economic, social, physical, political, cultural, and psychological concern is more appropriate than a view which deals with narrowly conceived "health and welfare" problems.

The substance of social planning, then, might well be taken to include the core elements within the subjects indicated in Figure 1, together with their interrelationships. While these might seem like familiar, well-established categories, to date most of them have not been of direct concern to community social planning. Some, as in the case of the Regional Economy, have not been the subject of planning in a significant way at all, while those that have tend to be treated in essentially isolated fashion by different groups within the community. The interrelationships among the indicated categories have been particularly neglected, and are clearly of very great importance. An example of such interrelations is the question of the adequacy of existing public, private, and voluntary social service facilities within given neighborhoods as population characteristics change over time—a question which involves interconnections among at least three of the major categories mentioned in Figure 1: Households, Social Structure, and the Physical-Locational Patterns. Another example is the problem of devising appropriate training for skilled workers in anticipated industries. This, again, involves interrelationships among at least three of the major categories.

THREE. INFORMATIONAL AND PLANNING TOOLS

A deeper view of the subjects which need to be the concern of metropolitan social planning can be revealed by examining some of the informational and planning tools that might be utilized in dealing with the major categories in Figure 1. Such tools employ concepts and techniques that have been successfully developed in other kinds of planning tasks but can be adjusted to fit the special needs of this broad type of social planning. These are discussed here mainly as a way of characterizing the social planning job rather than because of their inherent worth as planning tools, particularly since several are original proposals that have never been tested.

Households: A Focus on Objectives

To ensure that the long-term welfare of the individual and the family are the main concern of social efforts, it would seem appropriate to make the Household the central focus and key testing ground of social service activities (recognizing that good measurement of effectiveness is likely to remain fairly elusive for some time). The Household is the unit best reflecting the key decision-making, income-sharing, home-sharing, child-rearing functions. This focus would call for a regular flow of information and annual reporting on the condition and needs of the households of the region, attempting to get measurements bearing as closely to end objectives as possible.

This might be approximated through a series of measures—Household Welfare Indices—aimed at evaluating the extent of realization of community objectives, such as self-support, more jobs, better income situations, and provision of a support floor. Such a focus would seem to be appropriate in the face of our widely held view that in most things the individual family is itself best able to judge where its welfare lies and that, given decent jobs and an adequate income, it can acquire the goods and services and do the things it values most. This does not diminish the importance of certain collective activities, such as the provision of education through taxes, but permits a social planning philosophy basically consistent with national values.

The reporting should, then, provide year by year an account of how the Households of the region are progressing. The self-support index should show the number of families who are financially self-supporting, partially self-supporting, and totally supported by the community. In addition, it would attempt to provide an estimate of the number who are potentially self-supporting (totally or partially), as against those who will always have to be supported. It would also show the number actually receiving financial aid, and the levels of aid, as against those needing aid, given agreed-upon income standards.[4]

The job-holding positions of the households should also be recorded, including the extent of multiple breadwinners,

---

[4] Much more difficult is the design of measures to reveal the number of persons receiving various types of emotional support against those needing this type of support. This is a subject that deserves serious research attention.

"moonlighting," steady as against periodic employment, and other significant characteristics. Household income information would be a natural corollary of the job data.

In addition, an estimated *lifetime earning-power index* as an average for the community as a whole and averaged also for each major group in the community, would provide a significant test of social progress over time. This would be a valuable overall measure of "end-value," since the income earned over a total lifetime signifies how the society values individuals' services and the extent to which individuals can achieve a high level of self-development. Most social services have a direct impact on lifetime earning power, which is influenced by raising levels of education, by improving mortality and morbidity experience through health measures, by preventing mental illness, by providing useful work for the handicapped and the aged, and by many other types of actual or potential social measures. Thus, the lifetime earning-power index can provide a general indication of the effectiveness of the entire social system taken as a whole. Such an index can be used to compare social improvement in a community over time, as well as the relative standing of different metropolitan regions at one point in time.

If the changing situation of the households in the community were clearly portrayed in an annual "State of the Region" report, summarizing through welfare measures of the type proposed here, it would serve to focus attention on major objectives and goals and help keep the community—as well as the planners—from getting lost in the details of social service operations. Planning, to do its job well, must have these clear directional signs, longer-range community objectives, or it can easily lose its way.

In addition to providing a meaningful focus on community objectives, social planning must develop a clear picture of changing conditions in the community and the emerging social problems and potentialities that result. This calls for a detailed view of key economic, social, and physical factors.

The Regional Economy

Given the central role of jobs and income in the total social affairs picture, problems and potentialities of the regional economy, as suggested earlier, must be of direct concern to social planning. From time to time ad hoc studies have been sponsored to probe the problems of the local economy and to examine ways of improving the job situation. Recently there has been an increasing appreciation of the need to put economic studies on a regularized basis to strengthen decision-making in the economic realm. Pressures in this direction have also been generated by federal government regulations concerning urban renewal and area redevelopment grants to localities which require that information on the local economy be available as background for development programs.

There are many ways in which such regularized economic studies can be organized, but whether they are part of a community's social planning operation or prepared under different auspices, it is extremely important that at least the manpower elements of such studies be carried out with the needs of social planning in mind. Without this, a key prop of social planning will be missing.

If the basic information is to be available, *regional accounts* must be developed which highlight changes in regional economic activities and the resulting job and income situation.[5] Each industry and each economic activity has its own requirements for employees, and each pays a certain level of wages and provides other forms of income. By projecting industrial patterns, even with all the uncertainties that would inevitably surround such projections, a basis is provided for anticipating changes in the job and income situation, and therefore in the resulting nature and scope of the economically-influenced social problems to be faced by the community. Beyond this, such information can provide a basis for changes in social and economic policy which can help prevent certain kinds of problems. For example, existing policy which may be forcing out older industries employing lesser skilled workers from the central city may be changed in keeping with the social objective of increasing job opportunities for such groups. The information may show that such industries cannot survive in the community under present tax, zoning, and other public policies.

The development of *manpower accounts,* as an integral part of regional accounts, is, then, a high priority activity for

[5] A group of scholars have organized themselves into a Committee on Regional Accounts associated with Resources for the Future, Inc., to promote the development of such accounts as systems of information flows for public and private decision-making in urban communities. Various aspects of the subject are discussed in papers given at two recent conferences. See Committee on Regional Accounts, *Design of Regional Accounts,* edited by Werner Hochwald (Baltimore: Johns Hopkins Press, 1961) and *Elements of Regional Accounts,* edited by Werner Z. Hirsch (Baltimore: Johns Hopkins Press, 1964).

social planning. Given the availability of such accounts, and projections based on them, the annual "State of the Region" report could provide a firmer basis for social policy decisions and social service activities.

Social Structure

The design of effective social policies and activities depends on good information not only about the sources of the social problems but on the actual or potential strengths that can be built on to prevent their occurrence or to deal with them if they do occur. Since both the problems and the strengths tend to be associated with various identifiable groups in the society, social planning needs information about such groups. Although in our present state of knowledge definition of the meaningful groupings for this purpose is itself an analytical variable, improvements and refinements in information can be expected over time with cumulative experience.

As a beginning, good use could be made of "Group and Neighborhood Profiles" which would attempt to get at the changing characteristics, major unfulfilled needs, and actual and potential strengths of *one,* various groups in the community, for example, those with less than a designated annual level of income; youths at certain critical age levels;[6] older persons; Negroes and other minority groups; and so-called "problem families," and *two,* of the various neighborhoods of the metropolis. In the latter case, this would involve viewing more or less similar characteristics and needs as in the first, but here seen as they are gathered within given areas, influenced both by the community life and by the physical environment. Both the social-group and the geographic profiles should help to reveal the sub-cultural patterns of behavior, patterns of social relations and emotional supports (or lack of them) within peer and community situations.

[6] The types of "profiles" which are likely to be of value in deepening understanding of the social problems and in indicating possible ways of solving them can be illustrated with reference to the youth groups. For example, a sharply focused picture of youth in the community might be obtained by getting information on how youths use their time. Such a Time-Use Profile, obtained through questionnaires on a stratified sample basis, would indicate how youths are influenced by their particular situations and by the forces around them. This would be helpful in understanding, for example, when and under what circumstances youths are willing to "invest" time and effort in their futures, get into trouble, relate fruitfully or harmfully to each other and to outside groups.

Such "profile" information—joined with the Household information described earlier—would provide a valuable framework for social research in depth. While the "profiles" themselves cannot provide policy and program guidelines without additional research (no more than the economic accounts can provide answers without detailed economic analysis), they can serve to highlight the questions that need further probing and help provide useful linkages between research on the one side and policy and program design on the other. In economics this is well established; national economic accounts have long been used as a framework for economic policy analysis. Such an approach could be equally valuable in the social realm. The "group and neighborhood profiles" could serve the same general "organizing" purpose as the economic accounts have served in the economic field.

The neighborhood "profiles" could serve as background information for the preparation of Neighborhood Betterment Programs, which could be developed as a valuable tool to join social planning and physical planning.

Physical-Locational Patterns

Social planning has many natural points of contact with physical city planning so that the two must function in concert if each is to do its job properly. There are many things that might be done to promote coherence between the two. It would be sensible to encourage joint studies of the social aspects of housing supply and demand, of urban renewal (here the proposed "group and neighborhood profiles" could be employed to good advantage), as well as industrial location and transportation studies. The increasing recognition of the need for such study is likely to be one of the most important forces promoting a broader type of social planning.

The integration of social and physical planning is extremely difficult, and powerful new tools will have to be devised to achieve it. The "Neighborhood Betterment Program" is suggested as a potentially important tool for this purpose. It would draw on the progress made through the community development movement, as well as the increasing concern with the neighborhood in physical city planning due to experience with urban renewal and the problems that have arisen because of the breakup of community ties.

From the standpoint of family welfare, the "micro-environment" of the neighborhood is extremely important. It is here that the youth receives much of his developmental "support" in terms of his schooling, his playmates, and the adult standards provided. Here the family receives (or does not receive) many of the needed social services and the help and companionship of friends, neighbors, and informal "caretakers." The houses, the streets, the social service facilities, the recreational facilities, and the general physical environment can be important positive factors in family welfare, or can be contributing factors in social pathology. The joining of social and physical planning could provide a *continuous process of neighborhood improvement.*

Specifically, attention might be focused on helping neighborhood groups to devise "Neighborhood Betterment Programs," working toward a gradual upgrading (less gradual in those portions designated for redevelopment) of both the physical environment and the social services and facilities within the neighborhood. Such programs would have to be revised periodically to meet changing needs.

This approach would involve the provision of extensive technical assistance in neighborhood planning by the central planning bodies as well as the more co-ordinated provision of social services by public, voluntary, and private agencies. The neighborhood planning must be over a large enough area to permit the modernization of the physical environment as well as to permit the generation of sufficient political interest to get governmental assistance and to be able to recruit adequate local leadership. This joining of professional planning skills and concentrated assistance from city departments with neighborhood participation in a concentrated activity could not only provide the kind of powerful organizing focus that a successful "community development" movement requires, but also significantly encourage the integration of social and physical planning.

Policies and Programs

The various elements discussed above would provide a view of how the individuals and families of the community were faring as well as a broader picture of changing local conditions. Social planning must also provide a continuing overview of existing social programs, expenditures, and policies, permitting a periodic evaluation of the adequacy of existing social policies and programs and providing a basis for designing improvements (assuming also a flow of information from pilot projects probing new program possibilities).

The information on programs should cover all the pertinent

social services provided throughout the metropolitan region and should show expenditures on the pertinent major functions, such as education, health, welfare, recreation, housing, and law enforcement. Ideally, the expenditures would be directly related to program objectives and stated in terms of meaningful "work units" rather than of agency outlays, thus coming as close as possible to the information for providing a "program budget" which focuses on major program objectives rather than merely on the details of agency activities. The revenue picture also needs to be recorded, with projections made of anticipated resources for social programs, so that practical plans can be prepared.

Given a foundation of this information, as well as a broadly representative social planning organization, it becomes possible to develop common strategies and policies for social service activities and firmly-based long-range programming of such activities. One of the planning tools that might be used is a *Community Policy Plan* as a guideline for governmental, voluntary, and private activities setting forth the agreed-upon common objectives, common projections of situations and requirements, and an agreed-upon system of priorities. This would enable individual agencies to prepare both long-range and short-range programs in keeping with the common strategy, rather than operating entirely within the specialized sets of reference points of today's individual agencies.

Another potentially valuable planning tool is a common *Capital and Operating Budget for Social Services* covering all the social expenditures and the revenues available to them over a three- or four-year period. The emphasis would be on the governmental and voluntary services, the private category being covered only to provide a comprehensive picture of the total effort involved. The purpose of the common budget would be to provide guidelines for governmental and voluntary budgeting, not only giving reality to the social planning but furnishing a valuable framework for decisions on emphasis and priorities in social activities.

Table I provides a summary of the various planning tools which have been suggested. As stressed earlier, these tools are concerned mainly with providing meaningful connections among the many elements with which social planning is concerned; in administrative terms this means providing focal points for coordination among separate activities which otherwise might not compose programs capable of achieving the major community objectives.

FOUR. PROCESS AND IMPLEMENTATION

In discussing the organizational and substantive elements needed for effective social planning, there have been many references to process, as critical for social planning as it is for any type of planning. The major features of the social planning process can be said to include the following:

a) Metering and reporting to highlight the problems that need attention, the progress made toward their solution, and program gaps.

b) Suggesting, financing, and/or designing research projects (and getting appropriate groups to carry them out) to deepen understanding of social problems and to suggest possible solutions. A sensitive informational funnel from research to policy and action is needed. Techniques must be evolved for creatively "translating" research findings into increasingly effective programs.

c) Designing and evaluating experimental pilot projects to find improved ways of preventing or solving social problems; again, getting appropriate groups to carry them out.

d) Examining alternative programs aimed at achieving community objectives, making estimates of anticipated relative costs and benefits, and choosing among such alternatives so that the most useful things *at a given level of expenditures of time and money* are accomplished.

e) Preparing programs and budgets of overall services to encourage coherence among the programs and to permit priority choices, within financial limitations.

f) Recruiting skilled personnel, including, among others, social workers, economists, sociologists, anthropologists, psychologists, psychiatrists, physical planners, lawyers, and functional experts in fields such as education and health.

g) Enlisting broad public participation at every level, ranging from the metropolitan leadership to the neighborhood groups. Determination of goals and priorities and the general nature of programs is best done through the cooperation of technically competent central planning units with citizen organizations and neighborhood groups.

h) Strengthening of planning and programming within constituent agencies concerned with social problems, since the effectiveness of the overall social planning depends on the soundness of planning done within the constituent organizations. Methods employed might include providing basic community information, lending personnel, training personnel in improved methods, and financial aid.

i) Preparing overall and individual program evaluation reports to provide guidelines for improved approaches.

j) Keeping the public informed of problems and progress at every stage through a wide variety of communication media.

TABLE I. PROPOSED SOCIAL PLANNING TOOLS

Major Purpose	Category	Tools
1. To permit a sharper focus on objectives and achievement	Households	*Annual State-of-the Region Report:* showing Household Welfare Indices
2. To permit a periodic review of changing conditions and emerging social problems and to suggest possible ways of dealing with the problems	Regional Economy	*Annual State-of-the Region Report:* showing (a) major changes in regional economy and in job situation (b) *Regional Accounts* including manpower and income accounts
	Social Structure	*Group and Neighborhood Profiles*
	Physical-Locational Patterns	*Neighborhood Betterment Programs*
3. To permit improvements in social service programs and better coordination among activities	Policies and Programs	*Community Policies Plan Long-term Capital and Operating Budget for Social Services*

The important role of social planning is to focus the community's attention on the critical social problems and issues, on major community objectives, and on ways of achieving them in the face of the inevitable diversity and conflict. To be effective, it has to help key decision-making units ranging from the individual family and business firm to the social agency, the local Health and Welfare Council, and the municipal governments, so that these various units can see where the common interest lies and how they might advance the broad community goals while advancing their own ends. Any activity that contributes to this objective is a logical component of the social planning process.

CONCLUSION

What has been presented here is an idealized version of social planning, concerned much more with long-range requirements than with immediate practicality. It seems likely that a community embarking on a comprehensive region-wide social planning effort would require at least five or six years to develop the kinds of planning tools and processes described. Each community is likely to develop its own "style" based on its special needs and institutional arrangements. Given the many forces in any community that might feel threatened by a comprehensive type of social planning which would imply many changes in existing approaches and institutional arrangements, the social planning evolved is hardly likely to attain a "model" form. Yet it is useful to focus attention on the more ambitious form so that a "plan for planning"—a step-by-step construction of the needed organization, tools, and processes—can be achieved.

Recent developments suggest that it will be difficult for most communities to launch a broad type of metropolitan social planning without financial help from outside, mainly from the federal government and from private foundations.[7] With this type of assistance available, however, there is every reason for those who see the advantages in a broad and humanistic form of community social planning to interest community leaders in taking the necessary steps for launching such an effort.

[7] The Ford Foundation has been making an enormous contribution to the stimulation of more effective forms of social planning, as have been various groups in the federal government, such as the President's Committee on Juvenile Delinquency and Youth Crime, and the Office of Economic Opportunity.

Author's Note: This paper was prepared for the Twelfth International Conference of Social Work, Athens, Greece, September 1964. The paper involves a development and extension of materials presented in an earlier article: Harvey S. Perloff, "Social Planning in the Metropolis," in Leonard J. Duhl, editor, The Urban Condition (New York: Basic Books, Inc., 1963), *pp. 331–47. Certain of the ideas presented here were formed, or at least deepened and sharpened, in discussions with a number of individuals who took part with the author in the establishment of the United Planning Organization of the National Capital Area, a new region-wide social planning agency with a very broad mandate.*

Planning—and City Planning—for Mental Health
HERBERT J. GANS*

Planning for mental health can be approached in at least two ways. One, which I call the goal-oriented or problem-oriented approach, sees planning as a general method for achieving goals and solving problems. In bare outline, this method begins by inquiring into the conditions necessary to reach the goal—or into the causes of the problem—and then develops empirically the programs best able to attain the goal or eliminate the problem, drawing on a variety of professions and techniques for these programs.[1]

The second approach is traditional city planning, which begins with a set of programs and methods accepted by the profession as exemplifying city planning, and inquires whether and how their application will produce better mental health. Perhaps it is wrong to call this approach traditional, for in

* Senior Research Sociologist, Center for Urban Education, 1966– ; and Adjunct Professor of Sociology and Education, Teachers College, Columbia University. An M.A. in Social Sciences from the University of Chicago and a Ph.D. in City Planning from the University of Pennsylvania, he has been associated with the American Society of Planning Officials; the Chicago Housing Authority; P.A.C.E. Associates (planners), Chicago; Division of Slum Clearance, HHFA; Institute for Urban Studies at the University of Pennsylvania; Department of Psychiatry, Massachusetts General Hospital, and Harvard Medical School as Assistant Sociologist; and the Department of City Planning as well as Lecturer in Sociology at the University of Pennsylvania before coming to Columbia University in 1964. Recipient of eight major research grants, holder of a half-dozen editorial or professional positions, and consultant to some twenty-five varied private and public planning organizations, Professor Gans in addition to forty-nine professional articles has published nine books, the best-known of which is *The Urban Villagers: Group and Class in the Life of Italian-Americans* (New York: Free Press of Glencoe, 1962).

[1] This conception was developed out of a study of community facilities planning conducted by Martin Meyerson, John Dyckman, and myself under a Russell Sage Foundation grant, now being prepared for publication. For a more detailed discussion, see Herbert J. Gans, "Recreation Planning for Leisure Behavior: A Goal-Oriented Approach," unpublished Ph.D. dissertation, Department of City Planning, University of Pennsylvania, 1957, especially Chap. 9. See also Paul Davidoff and Thomas Reiner, "A Choice Theory of Planning," *Journal of the American Institute of Planners*, Vol. 28, May, 1962, pp. 103–115, and Carol H. Posner, "Values Research in Planning," *Planning Comment*, Vol. I, Winter, 1962–1963, pp. 16–28.

years past, city planners did not find it necessary to ask whether their programs would lead to mental health. They believed that city planning was automatically conducive to this end, and that if communities permitted the city planner to apply his ideas and tools, the mental health of the population would be improved.

Today, scientific inquiry has started to replace the naive faith of our professional ancestors. Even so, there are still considerable differences between the goal-oriented and the city planning approach. The remainder of the paper will outline some of the requirements of goal-oriented planning for mental health, and then evaluate the contributions city planning can make to this effort.

DEFINITIONS OF MENTAL ILLNESS AND MENTAL HEALTH

Planning for mental health can be conceptualized either in terms of a goal, the achievement of mental health or of a problem, the existence and elimination of mental illness. This is in line with modern psychiatric thinking, which emphasizes the distinction between illness-prevention and health-seeking. In order to take the first step in the planning process, determining the causes of mental illness and mental health, it is necessary to develop some definitions. Now psychiatrists and psychologists have had as much difficulty agreeing on definitions for these two concepts as planners have had in defining planning, and my formulations should be taken only for what they are: an attempt by someone not trained in psychiatry to frame working conceptions for himself.

Although illness, mental or physical, affects individuals, it is not an entity or property within an individual. Rather, it is—as Leonard Duhl has put it—"something that is intricately tied to the individual, the host of the disease, and to the particular social setting within which both the disease and the individual's development occur."[2] Moreover, illness is a process: "diseases tend to have a natural history which often has amorphous beginnings in that many things happen within the organism which may or may not lead to what we know as disease . . . as a result of a very special combination of host, environment and the significant etiological factors, the disease

[2] Leonard J. Duhl, "The Psychiatric Evolution," Bethesda: National Institute of Mental Health, November, 1963, mimeographed, p. 9.

is said to begin. Very often, this occurs only when someone observes it."[3]

This description is especially relevant to mental illness, because whether or not an individual is mentally ill is a social as well as a clinical judgment. I would define mental illness—overly simply to be sure—as a process of internal imbalance or disturbance in the individual, which develops out of the participation of that individual in a disturbance-producing environment, and which may upset his emotional equilibrium, his physico-chemical state, his conception of himself and others, and his ability to function effectively in his various environments and roles.

The important points in this definition are the individual, disturbance and the disturbance-producing environment. Mental illness is a process experienced by an individual in his environment, and any causal analysis must take both into account. Although an environment may be disturbance-producing, it will not have this effect on everyone. Thus, of three individuals in the same environment, one may develop a mental illness, another not, and a third may even be strengthened because his distinctive personality is able to transform the disturbance-producing element into greater emotional resiliency or effort.

The emphasis on disturbance is a reaction to the traditional tendency to define mental illness on the basis of overt behavior—as an inability to function, or a disposition to act bizarrely. Lay thinking has generally assumed that an individual who acts strangely, that is, in deviation from accepted ways, is mentally ill, especially when that deviation is disapproved by the rest of society. (Conversely, if the deviant activity is approved, such people are likely to be described as entrepreneurs or geniuses.)

Ways of acting are not a useful criterion for mental illness, however, and for at least two reasons. First, individuals may be functioning perfectly well and still be disturbed, for there are some social positions which can be filled adequately by disturbed people. For example, individuals with an unusual perspective on their society, like artists, prophets, innovators, or fanatics may have developed their perspective as part of a process of internal disturbance, but are able to function and are highly rewarded for it because society needs their gift. Of course, not all—and indeed only a few—artists or prophets

[3] *Ibid.*

are emotionally disturbed, for unusual perspectives can emerge from an unusual set of experiences, without the individual suffering even a trace of disturbance.

Second, and more important for our purpose, individuals may function in ways that seem deviant or bizarre to the outside world without being at all internally disturbed, because they are living within an unusual environment which requires that they act in these ways. For example, a prisoner might turn to homosexuality in order to satisfy his sexual needs in prison without becoming disturbed, or permanently inverted. Similarly, an unemployed, poverty-stricken individual may desert his family because he can no longer support it, or that family may reject him for this reason. This enables both to survive in the environment in which they live—especially one that is more willing to support deserted wives than unemployed men—without their suffering from internal disturbance as a result.

Thus what appears to the outsider as a deviant way of behaving may be a rational way of coping with an environment, and the judgment of deviance reflects the outsider's ignorance of real conditions inside a particular environment. For instance, city planners have often criticized the unwillingness of low income people to leave slum areas, failing to see that such areas not only provide cheap housing, but also offer the kinds of social supports that poor people need to keep going in a crisis-ridden existence. Conversely, some behavior patterns may appear to be rational to the outsider, but are actually quite irrational ways of coping with the environment.

If what seems to be deviant behavior is a rational response to an environment, it usually disappears if and when the environment changes. Such a transformation is not always assured, however, for once behavior patterns are developed to respond to an environmental condition, they can become anchored within an individual's personality, and may remain even after a change in environment. Sometimes, the individual has been predisposed to a deviant activity, and the same patterns that lead a man into crime may also make him susceptible to homosexuality or drug use. But in most cases, the need to adapt to an environment in order to survive may force a person to develop feelings that create permanent disturbance within him. It is then one can speak of a disturbance-producing environment.

Also, people who act in rational but unaccepted ways may be shunned or punished by the rest of society so that they begin to view themselves as rejected, and develop emotional disturbance as a result. For example, people who use moderate amounts of alcohol to relieve tension are approved by American society, but those who use marihuana are arbitrarily rejected as drug addicts, even though the effects of alcohol are much more destructive than those of marihuana. Being punished as a marihuana user can lead to emotional disturbance, and can be traced to the role of public opinion as a disturbance-producing environment. Public opinion in turn is mainly an uncritical endorsement of a thirty-year vendetta against marihuana by the federal Bureau of Narcotics.[4]

In addition, an individual may survive in a disturbance-producing environment without disturbance himself, but be led to raise his children in such a way as to foster emotional disturbances within them. Much mental illness develops in childhood and in family interaction during childhood, but it would be wrong to argue that the cause of mental illness must therefore be sought in the family. Usually, one can trace the causal process back to the pressures that forced parents to act as they did, and these pressures come from a disturbance-producing environment.

Mental illness must thus be understood in terms of both individual and environment, that is, how a particular environment affected a particular individual. This way of putting it begins with the assumption that individual and environment are not mutually exclusive terms, for one does not exist without the other. People are not able to act without society, and society is made up of individual people. The first of these two truisms is the more important, however, for the processes that make us human beings—and those that destroy us as human beings—are to be found in society. Consequently, an individual's disturbance must always be traced back to a disturbance-producing environment, even though this may have been one in which he grew up many years earlier. Indeed, if an individual has difficulty in an environment in which others function and feel well, one can be sure that individual is still reacting to an earlier environment that produced the disturbances now interfering with his adaptation.

The central concept of the definition is therefore that of the disturbance-producing environment, that is, an environment which causes a number of people within it to come

[4] Howard S. Becker, *Outsiders*, New York: Free Press of Glencoe, 1963, Chap. 4, and Isidor Chein *et al.*, *The Road to H: Narcotics, Delinquency and Social Policy*, New York: Basic Books, 1964.

away with mental illness. Of course, no environment is purely disturbance-producing; even the worst one will also offer social and emotional supports to an individual, reducing his anxieties and draining them off in such a way as to minimize his suffering and allow him to function. Marc Fried has described the two potentials of the environment very well by pointing out that emotional breakdowns always occur within and outside the individual. A person may be suffering from an internal disturbance, but as long as the environment is supporting, he will not break down, even if he may appear to act oddly at times. If the internal disturbance coincides with a lack of support in the environment, however, a psychological breakdown is likely to take place, and this is what society calls mental illness.[5]

Every environment has some disturbance-producing and some supporting features, and probably none exists which is entirely disturbance-producing, or entirely supporting. Some environments have considerably more disturbance-producing than supporting features, however. Someday we may have the data to describe—and rank—all major human environments in terms of the proportion of disturbance-producing and supporting features. We may even be able to rank them in terms of the number of individuals who can cope only at the cost of emotional disturbance. If we can also find out what brings about the disturbance-producing features, it should eventually be possible to evaluate environments in terms of their mental health implications, eliminate those that are far more disturbance-producing than supporting, and remove at least some of the disturbance-producing features from those that are predominantly supporting. Unfortunately, given the primitive state of research on the mental health and illness potentials of environments, such knowledge will not be available soon.

Before I go into the planning implications of this definition of mental illness, some parallel comments about mental health are in order. Psychiatrists today tend to think in terms of two definitions of mental health, which might be called minimal and maximal, but are quite different in their policy implications. The minimal one emphasizes the absence of emotional disturbance in the individual—or rather, the relative absence, for no individual in any society, primitive or modern, can live

[5] Marc Fried, "Social Problems and Psychopathology," Boston: Center for Community Studies, March, 1964, mimeographed. To be published by the Group for the Advancement of Psychiatry.

without some emotional conflict. The maximal definition, also described as a positive conception of mental health, emphasizes not the prevention of mental illness, but the determination and achievement of the best, i.e., mentally healthiest, patterns of living. Thus, mental health may be defined as the ability of an individual to maximize the pursuit of his life goals—and those of the groups to which he belongs—with a minimum of emotional disturbance and within the environments of his choice. This definition emphasizes individual and group goals because I believe that there are many ways of living in our pluralistic society which are conducive to mental health, and I question the notion that only middle-class—and especially upper-middle-class—ways have this property.[6]

Both definitions of mental health assume the existence of environments which are relatively disturbance-free, and encourage most people to achieve their personal goals with a minimum of internal disturbance. Again, someday it may be possible to describe and rank environments possessing these qualities.

SOME CHARACTERISTICS OF DISTURBANCE-PRODUCING AND DISTURBANCE-FREE ENVIRONMENTS

I have been arguing that from the point of view of the planner and policy-maker, the most relevant causes of mental illness and mental health are to be found in disturbance-producing and disturbance-free environments. If this conception can be empirically verified, the first step in planning for mental health is to discover the characteristics of such environments, and the conditions which bring them into being. This is one of the tasks of a new branch of the behavioral sciences called social psychiatry, and, in years to come, planners are likely to find it a major source of the data needed for mental health planning.

Even now, there are some studies which offer clues about the nature of disturbance-producing environments. We know, for example, that concentration camps, prisons, and even traditional mental hospitals and old people's homes are of this

[6] Herbert J. Gans, "Some Notes on the Definition of Mental Health: An attempt from the Perspective of a Community Planner," Philadelphia: Institute for Urban Studies, September, 1957, mimeographed.

order.[7] Also, a number of studies suggest that certain social processes create disturbance-producing environments, among them rapid social change, downward social and economic mobility—and sometimes even upward mobility—acculturation and assimilation among ethnic groups, and migration to the city. We do not yet know, however, what it is in social change, mobility, acculturation or urban in-migration that produces the negative effects.[8]

But perhaps the clearest example of a disturbance-producing environment is poverty. The evidence for this statement comes from two recent and comprehensive research projects which show that poverty, unemployment, low socio-economic status, and life in an economically depressed area are associated with high rates of mental illness risk. Careful studies in Stirling County, a rural sector of Nova Scotia, and in midtown Manhattan both indicate the people in the lowest socio-economic level are most likely to experience mental illness.[9] The midtown Manhattan study related the likelihood of mental illness to the amount of stress encountered, and although it analyzed the mental illness potential of a large variety of stresses experienced by city dwellers, the study showed that being of lowest social and economic status was the greatest source of stress.[10] The Stirling County study discovered that people living in economically depressed communities run a greater risk of mental illness than those of similar socio-economic level living in more fortunate areas, presumably because unemployment not only adds new stresses to people's lives, but also makes them socially and individually useless, thus creating further emotional burdens.

Although all available studies show that mental illness exists at all social levels, there is general agreement that the illness

[7] Bruno Bettelheim, *The Informed Heart,* New York: Free Press of Glencoe, 1960, Chapters 7 and 8; Erving Goffman, *Asylums,* New York: Anchor Books, 1961; and Jules Henry, *Culture Against Man,* New York: Random House, 1963, Part III.

[8] Marc Fried, "The Effects of Social Change on Mental Health," *American Journal of Orthopsychiatry,* Vol. 34, January, 1964, pp. 3–28.

[9] Dorothea C. Leighton *et al., The Character of Danger,* (Volume III, The Stirling County Study of Psychiatric Disorder and Socio-Cultural Environment), New York: Basic Books, 1963, Part III; and Leo Srole *et al., Mental Health in the Metropolis* (The Midtown Manhattan Study, Volume I), New York: McGraw-Hill, 1962, Chapter 12.

[10] Thomas S. Langner and Stanley T. Michael, *Life Stress and Mental Health,* (The Midtown Manhattan Study, Volume II), New York: Free Press of Glencoe, 1963. For a careful analysis of the studies on mental illness and social class, see Fried, "Social Problems and Psychopathology," *op. cit.*

rates are inversely proportional to socio-economic level, and are highest at the lower class or bottom level. Moreover, studies also show that upper income groups typically suffer from milder illnesses like neurosis, while the low income ones develop the more serious psychoses. Not only is there clearly more stress in the lives of poor people, but they are less able to cope with internal disturbance for they get less support from their environment than do the more affluent. When the latter become mentally ill, they are helped by their families and peers, and have access to private psychiatric treatment, so that the illness is tended to early in its natural history. Lower-class people are more likely to be rejected or punished for internal disturbance by their environment. In addition, lacking the education and cultural background for the verbal and self-examination skills required by modern psychiatry—not to mention the funds for treatment—their internal disturbances are not cared for until there is a severe or psychotic breakdown, at which time they can at best expect benevolent incarceration in a state mental hospital, and often much harsher treatment.

The available evidence makes it clear that the most disturbance-producing and least supporting environment in American society is one in which poverty and deprivation create constant and ever-increasing stresses; unemployment leads to feelings of uselessness and despair, to family instability and insufficient education, and the inability to obtain access to proper treatment deprives people of the support needed to cope with these stresses. Although the existing studies have not dealt with the effect of race, data on mental illness rates among non-white populations suggest that segregation is yet another feature of this disturbance-producing environment.[11]

The same studies also make it possible to sketch the outlines of a disturbance-reducing or mentally healthy environment. In such an environment, people have stable employment, sufficient income, and the social skills needed to pursue the goals they deem most important. Moreover, economic and social conditions are such that people need not compete against or hurt each other to get their share of scarce resources—be these money or affection—and every person can perform the social functions needed to make him feel useful. In addition, people are able to obtain support to cope with inevitable

[11] Fried, *op. cit.*, and Martin M. Grossack (ed.), *Mental Health and Segregation*, New York: Springer, 1963, Part IV.

inner and external conflicts from their families and friends, from helping agencies, and from social and political institutions which can bring about social change that will do away with resolvable social problems. In short, this is an environment in which people are free to be, to belong, to help each other, and to choose those ways of living which provide them meaning and satisfaction.

The description of disturbance-producing and disturbance-reducing environments has so far been general, and I have not attempted to identify or locate such environments in the society or the community. I use the term environment loosely to include everything from a locally occurring social situation to a national institution or set of institutions, for the boundaries of the environment are determined by whatever causes the disturbance-producing elements.

The studies I have mentioned make it possible to suggest that the most crucial environments are the economic and the social: the national economic system with all its regional and local subsystems and interconnections; the national social structure—likewise with regional and local manifestations; and what might be called the micro-social structure, the set of primary groups within which people carry on most of their activities and live most intensively. These include the family, the circle of relatives, peers, colleagues, friends and neighbors they see most often, and the social, recreational and ideological outlets that matter most to them.

The economic system determines the availability of jobs and income, as well as the opportunities to acquire material and non-material tools for the pursuit of life goals. The social structure, especially its stratification and segregation systems, determines whether people are to have access to the institutions that enable them to participate in the economy, and to feel socially and personally useful. These systems set the stage for the micro-social structure. Its components can either provide support, or they can translate pressures from the economy and the national social structure into competition for scarce resources, and by setting family members or neighbors against each other in conflict, create the stresses that lead to mental illness.

Although the micro-social structure is physically located within the community or even within a neighborhood, it has little relation or relevance to the activities of the political unit called a community, or the service area for public facilities that the city planner terms a neighborhood.

PLANNING FOR MENTAL HEALTH

These very oversimplified descriptions of the causes of mental health and mental illness provide some beginning guidelines to permit planning for mental health. If the causes of mental illness I have mentioned are indeed of uppermost importance, then planning to reduce mental illness, and to achieve at least a minimal state of mental health, requires planning to reduce poverty, unemployment and discrimination, and all of the feelings of deprivation, social uselessness, and self-destruction that accompany them. Such planning means income grants—not charity or doles—to those now living beneath the poverty lines; the creation of new jobs and job training methods for people now without marketable skills; and the provision of the right kinds of educational facilities that will encourage the children of unskilled, lower-class adults not only to go to school, but to learn the kinds of occupational and social skills that will, in turn, enable them to find the jobs available in our automating society. In addition, such planning requires the elimination of racial and class discrimination so that all people will feel themselves to be equal members of society, with equal access to its basic institutions, and finally, the creation of those helping services and facilities that will provide cure, amelioration and preventive support for those now suffering from emotional disturbance, or in danger of it.[12]

Above the poverty level, planning for mental health will take different forms. In the working class, for example, one major problem is the strain between the extended family—which is valuable for the support it can give—and the development of individualism and the nuclear family which is en-

[12] A rapidly growing literature describes such needed programs in more detail. See, e.g., Michael Harrington, *The Other America,* New York: Macmillan, 1962; Robert Theobald, *Free Men and Free Markets,* New York: Clarkson Potter, 1963; Gunnar Myrdal, *Challenge to Affluence,* New York: Pantheon, 1963; and Frank Riessman, *The Culturally Deprived Child,* New York: Harper and Row, 1962. I have summarized some of these needs in "Social and Physical Planning for the Elimination of Urban Poverty," in American Institute of Planners, *Proceedings of the 1962 Annual Conference,* Washington: AIP, June 1963, pp. 176–190; and in B. Rosenberg, I. Gerver and W. Howton (eds.), *Mass Society in Crisis,* New York: Macmillan, 1964. Proposals for employment planning are discussed in my article, "Some Proposals for Government Policy in an Automating Society," *The Correspondent,* No. 30, January–February, 1964, pp. 74–82.

couraged by over-all societal trends. This is especially true among groups of European ethnic backgrounds, where the acculturation process creates strain between the generations as well. New social patterns are needed to bridge the gap between the two family types and the generations, as are incentives to encourage the non-mobile to absorb enough education to compete for available jobs.

In the middle class, where job stability is relatively assured —at least for the moment—the problem is job satisfaction for the men; opportunities for wives and mothers to take on other roles, including work; and the creation of a substitute for the no longer viable extended family that will reduce the pressure on the nuclear family to function as the sole source of affection and support. The need for job satisfaction for the men and opportunities for the woman is especially urgent in the upper-middle class, where both sexes have professional aspirations, and often have difficulty fitting into bureaucratic jobs. The professionalization of now non-professional occupations, and the creation of meaningful jobs and 4- to 6-hour workdays for women would help here.

As the ages of entry into and exit from the labor market change, adolescents and old people from almost all class levels —as well as mothers of grown children—face the problem of loss of function. Since uselessness is a major source of emotional disturbance, institutions must be developed which can use the special talents of these age groups—the youthful idealism of the teenager, and the experience and vast amount of free time of the older person—so as to give them a useful function in the society. The most difficult problem is to find such functions for young and old people without skills.

These proposals are of course much too brief to do justice to the topic, but they illustrate the kind of planning for mental health that is required at all levels of society, and the kind of data that must be available for it to happen. But data are not enough, and political power is also needed. Every citizen may be against mental illness, but even the most disturbance-producing environments offer significant supports to some people, and they will be loath to surrender these. For example, the poverty that hurts so many people also benefits others, such as slum landlords, and many of those who provide services to the poor. Without reducing their power—or finding other functions for them in the society—there can be no effective planning for mental health.

THE IMPACT OF THE PHYSICAL ENVIRONMENT ON MENTAL HEALTH

Among the environments crucial to mental illness and mental health, I have discussed so far only the economy and the social structure, but I have not mentioned the physical environment. This omission was intentional, for the available studies suggest that the role of the physical environment is much less important in mental illness and mental health.

For the low-income population, the physical environment is probably a source of additional stress, but not a major cause of mental illness. Instead, it is yet another effect or symptom of the poverty and segregation which force this population to live in overcrowded and dilapidated structures. The payment of high rents which cut into an already small income, the struggle against rats and other vermin, the inhibition of activities resulting from lack of heat and hot water, and the absence of space for social life, study and privacy due to overcrowding—all add to an already overwhelming struggle for survival.

Even so, a recent study of New York's Harlem showed that the correlation between an index of social pathologies and dilapidation was quite low, as was the correlation with overcrowding in dwelling units. Conversely, the correlation with holding low status jobs was very high. The index measured forms of outward aggression rather than emotional disturbance, but since these are also responses to stress, the correlations suggest that the physical environment is a considerably less important source of stress than being lower class. The authors of the study concluded that "Better housing, while it heightens morale, does not affect the more fundamental variables of economic status, broken homes, and lowered aspirations. Merely to move the residents of Harlem into low income housing projects without changing the patterns of their lives—menial jobs, low income, inadequate education for their children—does not remove them from the total tangle of community and personal pathology."[13]

[13] Harlem Youth Opportunities Unlimited, "Youth and the Ghetto", New York: HARYOU, 1964, pp. 158–160, quote on p. 160. The Midtown Manhattan study also found that there was no correlation between overcrowding within the dwelling and mental illness risk. Since the area studied was entirely white, however, there was little serious overcrowding, even among low-income tenants. (Personal communication from Thomas S. Langner.)

There is also no evidence to suggest that life in a poorly planned community has any significant effect on mental health. Indeed, studies of socially cohesive slum areas show that even when the housing, density, street layout and amount of open space are quite poor by middle-class standards, the social qualities of the area are more important to people than the physical conditions—or, for that matter, the better ones available in public housing. Such areas—and of course not all are socially cohesive—provide their residents with the emotional and social supports not easily obtained in most public housing projects at present.[14] Needless to say, this is no reason to reject public housing, but a spur to find ways of creating these social qualities in it.

Similarly, while planners and social critics have excoriated the post-war, mass-produced suburban subdivisions for their lack of planning, their physical homogeneity, and effect on urban sprawl, all the available evidence indicates that whatever the physical faults of these developments, they have not created the kind of stress that brings on emotional disturbance. Mass-produced housing does not lead to dulling conformity among its purchasers, any more than does the acquisition of a mass-produced car. The homogeneity of age and class that exists in some subdivisions may do violence to the city planner's ideal of the balanced community, but for the people who live in the midst of such homogeneity, it means a never before available supply of compatible neighbors, potential friends, sources of mutual aid, and suitable playmates for the children.[15] What is wrong with this homogeneity is not that it exists, but that some people, especially low-income and Negro city dwellers, have not been given an opportunity to choose it for themselves.

Moreover, a longer journey to work does not lead to emotional disturbance, and it does not take the father away from the family. If my own data, based on a single suburb near Philadelphia, are typical, increases in the journey to work are small for most people, and previous city dwellers, who report

[14] See, e.g., Marc Fried, "Grieving for a Lost Home," in Leonard J. Duhl (ed.), *The Urban Condition*, New York: Basic Books, 1963, pp. 151–171; and Chester Hartman, "The Limitations of Public Housing: Relocation Choices in a Working-Class Community," *Journal of the American Institute of Planners*, Volume 29, November, 1963, pp. 283–296.

[15] Herbert J. Gans, "The Balanced Community: An Evaluation of Homogeneity and Heterogeneity in Residential Areas," *Journal of the American Institute of Planners*, Volume 27, May, 1961, pp. 176–184.

the largest increase, also indicate that they have more time with their families than they did in the city.[16] Urban sprawl, the disappearance of the rural countryside, and the blossoming of roadside hot dog stands may reduce the esthetic pleasures of the Sunday traveller, but my observations indicate that most people derive their esthetic satisfaction not from the landscape or the architectural landmark, but from the things they own, the homes they have fixed up and altered, and from the fresh air and greenery that is available even in the most poorly planned subdivision.

The currently popular belief that life in suburbia contributes to mental illness is simply not true, and the evidence I have seen or collected suggests just the opposite. Most people who move to the suburbs report greater satisfaction with life, better morale and improved dispositions, primarily because of the pleasure derived from the house, home ownership, and the vital social life to be found among people of similar background. If satisfaction is any index to mental health, suburbia may even contribute to its betterment. Needless to say, some people are unhappy in suburbia, notably working-class families who have left urban neighborhoods in which they grew up, especially the old ethnic enclaves, and are lonely for relatives and friends they knew since childhood, but even they would not move back there.[17] In addition, some of the people who have made rapid upward strides in an affluent society and have moved to the suburbs as a result report increased emotional difficulties, but these are not caused by living in suburbia. They are the by-products of rapid mobility, which have little to do with the place of residence.[18]

The charge that suburban residence leads to boredom, loneliness, and the type of malaise that English journalists have christened the "new town blues" is also not supported by the evidence. The critics who make these charges are largely upper-middle-class people with urbane tastes who disapprove of the lower-middle-class, non-urbane culture they see in the suburbs, and justify their disapproval by hypothesizing detrimental consequences for mental health. The facts are, how-

---

[16] These findings are based on as yet unpublished data from my study of Levittown, New Jersey. Some preliminary findings appear in "The Effects of the Move from City to Suburb," in Duhl, *The Urban Condition, op. cit.,* pp. 184–198.

[17] *Ibid.*

[18] See Richard Gordon *et al., The Split-Level Trap,* New York: Bernard Geis, 1961, and my critique in *Journal of the American Institute of Planners,* Volume 28, February, 1962, pp. 47–49.

ever, that the move from city to suburb results in relatively little change either in behavior or attitudes; thus indicating, again, the relatively minor impact of the physical environment on social patterns.[19]

Conversely, there is no evidence that the kind of housing and physical planning programs advocated by city planners have a significant effect on mental health. Wilner's study in Baltimore, comparing people who moved into a new public housing project with a control group who stayed in the slums, discovered that the move to a new apartment did not affect health or mental health, although people did report increased privacy, pride in their home, and stronger feelings of self-respect.[20] Rosow's review of a number of studies of the effects of the physical environment did not deal with mental health, but it did show that what he called planned manipulation of the physical environment failed to bring about the social effects the planners had intended. He concluded that "people in general may be far less sensitive to the discrepancy between the real and the ideal in housing than are the professionals."[21]

Finally, I suspect that if the data were available, it could be shown that implementing the traditional programs of city planning, such as: the master plan, the separation of land uses, the neighborhood scheme, large amounts of open space, low density, and the isolation of car and pedestrian traffic, would not result in a measurable effect on mental health. I am not arguing that these programs are therefore undesirable, but only that they are not relevant to planning for mental health. City planners cannot honestly justify their schemes on that basis, even if it is a politically potent argument for more city planning.

[19] See, e.g., Bennett Berger, *Working Class Suburb,* Berkeley: University of California Press, 1960; Peter Wilmott, *The Evolution of a Community,* London: Routledge and Kegan Paul, 1963; William Dobriner, *Class in Suburbia,* New York: Spectrum, 1963; and Gans, "The Effects of the Move from City to Suburb," *op. cit.*

[20] Daniel M. Wilner *et al., The Housing Environment and Family Life,* Baltimore: Johns Hopkins Press, 1962.

[21] Irving Rosow, "The Social Effects of the Physical Environment," *Journal of the American Institute of Planners,* Volume 27, May, 1961, pp. 127–133, quote from p. 127. See also Alvin L. Schorr, *Slums and Social Insecurity,* Washington: Social Security Administration, 1963.

THE ROLE OF CITY PLANNING IN PLANNING FOR MENTAL HEALTH

What contribution can city planning make to planning for mental health? If the physical environment exerts only a minor impact, city planning can play only a minor role, both in the elimination of mental illness and the achievement of mental health. City planners can make sure that the physical environment does not create additional sources of stress in people's lives, and more positively, that it give them as much satisfaction as possible.

This formulation may sound no different from past definitions of the role of city planning in mental health. However, the determination of what adds stress and what provides satisfaction should not be made by the city planner—as it was in the past—but by and for the people for whom he is planning. For example, he cannot *decide* arbitrarily that high density is a source of stress; he must *discover* whether or not it is. Likewise, he cannot assume that site plans which give him esthetic pleasure will therefore provide satisfaction to their occupants; he must find out what priority people give to utility and to beauty, what their own esthetic standards are, and build them into his program.

If poverty removal is an urgent priority in planning for mental health—as I think it ought to be—the city planner can make some useful, even if not central, contributions.[22] Slum living is an additional, though minor, source of stress for the poverty-stricken, and the city planner can aid in the improvement of their housing condition.

Such improvement must, however, be aimed at the removal of stress, and not at the city planner's notion of what kind of housing is good for low-income people, or for the city's skyline. In the past, the bulldozer approach to urban renewal increased the stress for slum dwellers in a number of ways. Not only did it reduce the supply of cheap housing available to low-income people, but poor relocation methods and the

[22] Here I take issue with Nathan Glazer who argues that city planners can do little in planning for poverty removal. See his article, "Problems of Poverty and Race Confront the Planner," in American Institute of Planners, *Proceedings of the 1963 Annual Conference*, Washington: AIP, February, 1964, pp. 144–149.

virtual absence of relocation housing forced them to move into other slums or to pay much more rent than before, or both, and thus multiplied their problems. In some cases, socially vital neighborhoods which gave emotional support were destroyed, leading to the increase in emotional problems documented by Marc Fried and his associates in the study of the West End.[23]

The bulldozer approach is now on its way out, and city planners can take comfort in the knowledge that they are at least no longer adding to the stresses faced by poor people. The next challenge is to find ways of helping them, by developing methods of rehabilitation that will create livable housing without an unduly large increase in rentals, and without requiring much relocation—for even at its most humane, relocation is stressful for many people. Unfortunately, most current experiments in rehabilitation are unlikely to be helpful; they set high standards but without sufficient subsidy, so that in many cities they are forcing out the poor to provide housing for the somewhat more affluent. Perhaps current protest movements among slum dwellers, such as the rent strikes now taking place in a number of communities, will force local and federal agencies to find a way of rehabilitating housing for the present occupants, and with a subsidy that will not unduly raise their rentals. City planners can make a contribution here by supplying the research to determine what is most harmful about a slum, and then by setting up standards and priorities for a program of minimal rehabilitation so that City Hall can respond positively to the justifiable demands of the rent strikers. But more important than rehabilitation is more low-cost housing. City planners must emphasize the urgent need for such housing, supplied either through public housing projects or subsidized private housing, and located in the city, the suburbs and the projected new towns.

Since the existence of slums is ultimately determined by the inability of the poor to pay for decent housing, and since poverty is much more stressful than poor housing, the optimum solution is one which aims directly at poverty. The city planner cannot eliminate poverty or unemployment, but when he is involved in economic base planning, he can make a small contribution by orienting his plans to the creation of jobs, rather than—as at present—to the development of indus-

[23] See, e.g., Marc Fried, "Grieving for a Lost Home," *op. cit.*

trial parks, or to the growth of the city tax base. The kind of thinking that ought to go into economic base planning is illustrated by a New York City Planning Commission study of an old industrial loft district in Lower Manhattan, which showed that a proposed clearance program would eliminate from 7,000 to 13,000 jobs among predominantly unskilled and non-white workers. This analysis, a welcome reversal of the city planner's traditional bias against low-status industries and marginal firms, caused the city to reformulate the renewal project, and thus saved the jobs of a large number of people who have the most trouble finding work in today's economy.[24]

Likewise, city planners cannot do much to reduce racial discrimination, but they can make integration one priority in the location of new public facilities, and so can encourage the building of integrated schools, hospital, parks, etc. Moreover, they can re-examine, and give up, their belief in neighborhood theory, and thus deny intellectual support to those who use the theory to uphold segregation.[25] Also, city planners can revise their priorities for public facilities planning, de-emphasizing physical aspects, and making sure that the facilities will be of maximum service to those who need them. For example, school planning studies can suggest that if poor children are to be taught the skills they need to escape the trap of poverty, scarce public funds should be spent first on good teachers, rather than on expensive buildings, or 10- to 20-acre school sites. And in those communities where city planners have some voice in the formulation of capital and operating budgets, they can press for priorities that will benefit the low-income population, and improve their physical as well as social and economic environments.

In addition to removing sources of stress wherever possible, city planners can also make sure that the physical environment will give people as much satisfaction as possible, and help them live the way they want to live. This means less

[24] Chester Rapkin, "South Houston Industrial Area: A Study of the Economic Significance of Firms, the Physical Quality of Buildings and the Real Estate Market in an Old Loft Section of Lower Manhattan," New York: City Planning Commission, February, 1963.

[25] It is high time for all city planners to heed Reginald Isaacs' now almost twenty-year-old observations on this topic. See, e.g., his "The Neighborhood Unit is an Instrument of Segregation," *Journal of Housing,* August, 1949, pp. 215–219.

concern with squeezing the city into a form that is visible only in an airplane or on a map, and less attention to vistas, landmarks, and other aspects of physical structure that are of primary interest to the tourist—or to the architect-planner off on a field trip—but play a minor role in the lives of the residents. For example, some influential city planners have taken a useful urban design theory, which seeks to emphasize the main elements of physical structure to make people more aware of their surroundings and to guide them around their community, but have elevated it to such priority in the planning process that it makes city planning appear to be an adjunct of the municipal tourist promotion department.

Surely there are more urgent problems in the contemporary American city than preventing visitors or even residents from getting lost. In my opinion, city planners ought to think more about making the most important features of the physical environment, the residence and the work-place, more livable for their occupants. For instance, they ought to be determining how to plan high-rise apartment buildings, their sites and their accessory facilities so as to make these structures suitable for families with small children.

CONCLUSION

Planning for the way people live and want to live may have little direct relevance to their mental illness and mental health, but it will provide them with a more satisfying physical environment. Moreover, since there is some relationship between satisfaction and mental health, the city planner is actually making a contribution to mental health by plans that maximize people's satisfactions. I suggest that the making of such plans is the city planner's proper, and only, role in planning for mental health, and that he forego the temptation either to justify physical planning solutions as mental illness prevention schemes, or to make psychiatric judgments about those features of the community that displease him socially or esthetically.

Urban Poverty

JANET S. REINER AND THOMAS A. REINER*

The United States is a rich nation, with poverty by any number of indices afflicting only a relative few.[1] Why is there a difference of opinion as to the scope and significance of the problem?[2] Why is the nation—perhaps for the first time —explicitly confronting poverty, its reduction and possibly its elimination? Not so much, we believe, because there is now enough surplus to spare for the job, but rather because of "establishment" guilt combined with fear. The guilt grows with increasing recognition that poverty could well become a virtual anachronism, and the fear builds up as the real or imputed characteristics and behavior of the poor, particularly of the impoverished Negro, become a threat.[3]

This review first notes issues central to a definition of poverty, and refers to some research seeking to discover who is poor, commenting on the consequence of such findings. Second, it surveys the growing programs designed to help the poor directly, in both a welfare sense and as a commitment to get some of the poor out of poverty, and notes some estimates of the scope of the poverty reduction task. Third, it tries to show the relevance of this material to the work of urban planners.

* For a biography of Thomas A. Reiner, see Chapter 6. Janet S. Reiner is a Research Associate at the University of Pennsylvania. She has served as a Research and Social Planning Consultant for the Office of Economic Opportunity, the Puerto Rico Planning Board, the American Friends Service Committee, the Philadelphia Housing Association, etc. Holding an M.C.P. from the University of Pennsylvania, she is the joint author of a number of journal articles and monographs as well as publishing independently. The following was adapted from a review article in the *Journal of the American Institute of Planners*, Vol. XXXI, No. 3, August 1965, and reprinted with permission.

[1] Some international comparisons are given in Ginsburg and Berry [10] and Russett [25].

NOTE: Numbers in brackets refer to the *References* at the end of this paper.

[2] Compare e.g. Galbraith's [9] relatively sanguine evaluation with Harrington's [11].

[3] See Miller [19] and Myrdal in Shostak and Gomberg [27].

TO DEFINE POVERTY

The first problem is the definition of poverty. From the planner's viewpoint this is vital, for such a definition is necessary (a) to determine the extent of the problem, the amount of resources which must be allocated and the nature of the cure, given particular anti-poverty objectives, and (b) to identify for action purposes poverty-affected people in terms of location and other characteristics, assuming that these individuals have identity other than their poverty.

Not surprisingly, consensus on the constituents of poverty does not exist. In general terms, the question of poverty definition is approached from a subjective perspective as well as an objective direction. The analyst who stresses the need for objective thresholds or criteria set by outside specialists is challenged by writers who focus on the subject's view of himself and society. More specifically there is division among those seeking to identify poverty with respect to the relevant dimension along which to measure poverty. Finally, there is much disagreement as to the precise thresholds which separate the poor from the not poor.

Let us first note poverty from an objective direction. The most common approach is to set an annual income level below which poverty exists. This may range from one thousand dollars to three thousand dollars per family or more.[4] This type of study may be elaborated to allow more detailed calculation of appropriate poverty levels and poverty groups by allowing for family size and possibly for other factors.[5] These poverty thresholds are usually derived from estimates of consumption or "maintenance" needs: as, for example, the modest model budgets of the Bureau of Labor Statistics.[6] The purpose of such studies is to estimate the number of families and total population living in poverty, and usually to establish trends in the size of the poverty group. Among the most significant conclusions derived from such analyses are that World War II stimulated the most recent large-scale reduction in the number of poor, but that since then the incidence of pov-

---

[4] See respectively Galbraith [9], Kolko [16], Keyserling [14].

[5] For example, see Conference on Economic Progress [5] and Kolko [16].

[6] Precise sources for such estimates are given, e.g., in Kolko [16]. An illuminating comparison of the implication of several such national thresholds can be found in MacDonald's essay [18].

erty in terms of proportion of households has remained fairly stable. However, a drastic drop can be noted in the proportion of national income earned by those defined as living in poverty. The hereditary nature of poverty, so-called, has been repeatedly noted together with attempts to explain this phenomenon through a host of institutional factors.[7]

Making allowance for a range of thresholds, some onequarter to one-third of all households still exist at or below a poverty level. The concentration, as has been repeatedly observed, is highest among certain age cohorts, ethnic groups and, not surprisingly to the planners, residents of certain city neighborhoods and economic regions.[8] The multi-wage-earner family is one crucial unit in explaining certain non-poverty groups.[9] Education and, of course, unemployment are another pair of closely related explanatory variables.[10] Where an individual belongs to two or more disadvantaged subgroups, chances that he is poor increase substantially. Thus, 30 percent of non-white families are impoverished, 40 percent of the families where the head is elderly are impoverished, and 65 percent of the families headed by elderly Negroes are impoverished.[11]

Occupation and educational level have been identified as measures, largely as surrogates for the concept of class, by which poverty groups can be identified. Poverty has also been approached as a style of life: all who manifest this style are poverty-afflicted.[12] This analysis has been developed in terms of the incidence of multi-problem families or certain types of deviant behavior.[13]

A second major approach in what is labeled the "objective" category identifies poverty in terms of area of residence. The unit of analysis is spatial instead of personal. Poverty of the environment is the criterion—environment being at the scale

[7] See, for example, Harrington [11].

[8] Conference on Economic Progress [5], Keyserling [14], Kolko [16], Ornati [23].

[9] See Kolko [16] and Myrdal [22].

[10] See Kolko [16], Myrdal [22], and, especially, Morgan [20]. But, also, see Keyserling [14] who notes the surprising incidence of poverty among the well-educated: a college education is in itself no guarantee against poverty.

[11] Ornati [23]: 1960 data, $2500 poverty threshold. Harrington [11] also comments on such convergence of poverty-linked characteristics.

[12] Harrington [11] and Weaver [33] comment on reactions to the poor and to slum dwellers.

[13] See Myrdal [22] and S. M. Miller's discussion, in Shostak and Gomberg [27] of works by W. B. Miller, and Hollingshead and Redlich.

of the neighborhood.[14] However, review of the research fails to show that living in slums and an impoverished existence are synonymous;[15] neither has the causal relationship between residential milieu and life style been conclusively established. The works which seek to combine both income and area criteria to define the impoverished should also be noted. The journalists' attack on the problem is fairly representative of this group.[16]

Serious measurement problems remain even where scale and threshold have been determined. For example, a particular household might vary in size with income level and thus one might argue that the number of those poverty-affected can be underestimated.[17] What measure of wealth to use is another critical question when large families are involved. Studies generally concentrate on income flows rather than on consumption flows.[18] Thus, consumer credit is only occasionally considered. Also, usually there is no evaluation of household assets as contrasted to income.[19] Thus, problems arise which every urban planner will recognize: the subtleties involved, for example, in imputing (or the danger in failing to impute) a value to owner-occupied dwellings, or the difficulties encountered when housing markets are keyed to income alone. Differences in living costs between urban and rural areas or among various cities are encountered; these constitute yet another large area of ambiguity.[20] Finally, non-monetary income introduces another dimension. One notes that the value of public services varies from jurisdiction to jurisdiction, as does the use made of a particular mix of services by various income groups.[21]

[14] See Hunter [13] and Schorr [26].
[15] See, for example, Marris, Ryan, and Fried in Duhl [6] on the slum and its uses and users.
[16] Bagdikian [2].
[17] See Morgan [20].
[18] To the extent that earned income may be supplanted as the major device by which the economy's wealth is divided, this is a measure of declining importance; see Ad Hoc Committee on the Triple Revolution [1].
[19] The problem is posed in Miller [19] and some data are given in Kolko [16] and Morgan [20].
[20] Differences are analyzed in Thompson [29] and summary data are given in Conference on Economic Progress [5].
[21] See, for example, the research reported by Hirsch in Resources for the Future [24] and comments made by Dirks in Shostak and Gomberg [27].

Poverty as a subjective phenomenon has also been studied, though this approach has not, in the United States, at least, been used as extensively as has the objective treatment of poverty. The underlying premise of the subjective approach is that the individual is poor as long as he feels poor, rejected, or alienated from the economic or the cultural mainstream.[22] A number of works stress the dysfunctional direction of current welfare programs in confronting recipients with their inadequacies and little else.[23] A significant characteristic of the American way of life is that basic needs have indeed been met; that our "two nations," and the concept of poverty amidst affluence, arise precisely because of the possibility of a universally higher standard of living. Thus, whatever the cohort at the bottom of the income ladder (or at a low point along other dimensions of sufficiency), this group of people is a subject of interest, concern, and policy because it wants to, or is thought to want to, move out of its deprived and depressed state. This, then, is an appropriate introduction to studies of the lowest quintile or decile or other such subgroups of the population.

At this point, it is appropriate to add those works which study in depth the culture of poverty and provide a comprehensive view of the strengths and weaknesses of the poor as a cohesive community.[25]

If poverty cannot simply be expressed in dollar income terms, some other steps must be taken. But, to determine the value attached to the whole bundle of goods and services consumed requires a transformation which is extremely difficult to make, yet one which must be made if an intelligent assessment of the poverty condition is to exist. Such a transformation presumes that each individual has a value attached to each element of his consumption (and a regret value for not consuming other commodities), and that he can aggregate

[22] See Caudill in Shostak and Gomberg [27] and Miller [19], and references therein. Also see Bagdikian [2].

[23] Harrington [11], Bagdikian [2], and Caudill in Shostak and Gomberg [27] have documented the plights of the "inhabitants" of the not-so welfare state.

[24] See, for example, the extensive analyses found in Morgan [20] and in Kolko [16].

[25] Riessman, in Shostak and Gomberg [27] develops the theme that poverty creates its own antithesis in the strengths of the poor. Lewis [17] is a prime exponent of the concept of a "culture of poverty."

these into an over-all utility. A further complication arises in attempting to effect interpersonal comparisons of such subjective utilities.[26]

THE ATTACK ON POVERTY

The approach of the federal antipoverty program (Economic Opportunity Act of 1964) has been to assist in the development of a series of antipoverty measures or components coordinated through a community action agency.[27] The agency provides an umbrella of fairly strong cloth. It has its own explicit goal that is achieved through rather well-developed means: organization of community is an end in itself, though the extent to which the poor participate in decision-making is now at issue. The community development approach is used in areas populated predominantly by the poor. The warp and woof of the umbrella's cloth is "involvement of the poor," "resident participation," "neighborhood organization," "community development," and last but not least, "hiring non-professionals"—"low-income individuals and families for whom assistance is intended." The areal unit for community development may be rural, suburban or urban. The request for funds must be channeled through, but need not be made by, the lowest-level government unit containing the residences of the low-income group. It is explicitly a locally defined program; limitation on acceptable component measures are few.

While the Community Action Program (CAP) is, in its over-all direction, a modification away from the traditional social work approach with its emphasis on psychological problems,[28] the orientation and premises of the components remain those of the social worker. The unit for action and analysis of the component is not individuals, or families, or geographic areas, but rather insufficiency of behavior or condition. (But unlike public housing, great effort is made to re-

[26] Ongoing research at the Institute for Environmental Studies, University of Pennsylvania, on "Concepts and Definition of Poverty," is directed to this point.

[27] The background and scope of the legislation and program are discussed in Shostak and Gomberg [27], by Ohlin in Morris [21], and by Miller [19]. See also the OEO *Guide* [31] and OEO *Workbook* [32].

[28] On the social work approach to poverty, see Shostak in Shostak and Gomberg [27] and Titmuss [30].

duce negative and stigmatizing connotations: for example, "child development" is used in lieu of "cultural deprivation.")

The ribs of the CAP umbrella as it is now constructed are a series of components which are numerous and distinct in detail. Each component is to be directed at a particular aspect of the "network of social ills."[29] The components which are specified include but are not limited to the following programs:

Early childhood programs: pre-school and day care, and Project "Head Start."

Educational programs: remedial programs, tutoring programs, after-school study centers, field trips, and special training, design and development of material to make more effective use of facilities.

Employment programs: on-the-job training, Job Corps (residential vocational training), Neighborhood Youth Corps (work experience program), CAP employment program (work research and demonstration), training of professionals and subprofessionals in community action agencies, plus more than a dozen other training programs operated by Federal agencies which CAP can use as resources.

Programs for the aging: employment counseling for persons over sixty-five, neighborhood day rooms for senior citizens, and rural programs.

While there is also interest in programs for community service and economic development, the Office of Economic Opportunity has as yet provided no leadership.

To the extent that the poverty program focuses on insufficiency it becomes necessary to establish success indicators, targets, and causality chains; the minimum, it would appear, is a conceptual structure and organization to guarantee full reporting. With such a new program one can only anticipate extensive evaluation rather than report on any here.

Cloth and ribs do not an umbrella make. The ferrule which holds the pieces together is still missing. As the CAP administration is now structured—partly due to a non-planning approach and partly due to the hook of the complete limitation to localities—it serves as little more than a handle. Terms

[29] See OEO *Guide* [31] and OEO *Workbook* [32]. The latter contains extensive bibliographies on the program components.

such as "direction" and "coordination" remain generalizations with little substance and with few sanctions. The tone is set by local autonomy. No doubt community mobilization is the strength of the program, but—to use the metaphor once more —it is not sufficient to keep out the rain.

Though the Federal antipoverty program is the major attempt to date, it is not without critics. The investment is considered insufficient by its supporters and misdirected as well as meager by one group of its critics.

The programs are not directed to increasing aggregate job opportunity,[30] although they might (at best) increase the competitive possibilities of participating individuals.[31] Further, selective processes in any such program often benefit disproportionately the best-off among the poor who can avail themselves of particular measures.[32] Finally, wages in return for work, if ever they were sufficient, may no longer serve as adequate devices for allocation of resources and output; the job-income nexus is about to be severed.[33]

There appears to be fairly general agreement that the poverty-reduction task—no matter how poverty is defined and regardless of the scope of the effort—if it is a legitimate one for society, is beyond the resources of both the private sector and state and local governments. This conclusion is based on aggregate costs and revenues of such a task, on the inevitable migration of people, and on the inter-areal impacts of crises as well as of ameliorative efforts.[34] No study of the poverty question can thus omit reference to the macro-economic studies which set in perspective the government fiscal positions and income and expenditure trends.[35] Among the major findings are that total state and local government expenditures, rather than Federal expenditures, have significantly increased over the past decades, and that government non-military purchases have, if anything, declined as a percent of our gross national product.[36] It would therefore appear that fairly siz-

[30] See Ad Hoc Committee . . . [1], Myrdal [22], Theobald [28].
[31] Comments to this effect are made by Reagan, Gans, and Chase in Shostak and Gomberg [27].
[32] See Harrington [11], Keyserling [14], and Gans and Caudill in Shostak and Gomberg [27].
[33] Ad Hoc Committee . . . [1] and Reagan in Shostak and Gomberg [27].
[34] See Myrdal [22] and Thompson [29].
[35] See Bator [3] and Heilbroner and Bernstein [12].
[36] Bator [3].

able resources exist which heretofore have not been tapped and which could be used for a poverty-reducing effort without setting up inflationary pressures.[37]

IMPLICATIONS FOR URBAN PLANNING

1. Planning for poverty reduction should help the planner rethink the premises and findings of ecological determinism and of economic determinism. The evidence is by no means conclusive. Not all those who are impoverished are residents of slums; neither does the level of income tell the whole story of deprivation. Low-income and slum surroundings, to the best of our knowledge, certainly are not unique causes of deviant or pathological behavior. For that matter, low incomes as such are not a unique factor determining choice of slum residence.

2. Reported research helps the planner to recognize that, first, there are many types of poverty, and second, poverty afflicts people at different stages of the life cycle. There are groups in the population highly prone to poverty; others are virtually immune. Different remedial programs must be thought out, each with distinct responsiveness patterns, and each with characteristically distinct operating costs, capital investments, and physical planning features. Certain subgroups of the population can be significantly helped with simple cash grants or the provision of some other single good or service. Management of other categories of poverty (as the circumstances presented by multiproblem families) requires a frontal onslaught of a series of monetary, service, and material inputs; some categories of poverty require local capital budget inputs, others operating budget inputs, still others a mixture of the two. Poverty reduction is a classic example where timely investments forestall costly ameliorative measures, custodial care, and so forth; a stitch in time can save nine.

3. The literature suggests that relatively involved steps are needed to determine the client population of programs typical of the urban planner's concern. Anticipation of future demand for public housing, for example, is no mean task. Further, a sophisticated analysis of poverty is necessary before it is possible to identify gaps in the set of programs directed at the total population and at potential clients: gaps identified

[37] See Keyserling [14] and Myrdal [22]. These writers suggest that poverty be treated as a macro-economic employment problem and call for a balanced economy, rather than a balanced budget.

in terms of specific poor people, as these are defined by particular dimensions of poverty. It would also appear as a result of disparities in measurement techniques, that the extent and spread of subjective poverty should in part explain why clients for a program set up to alleviate poverty differ from the client population designated for the program. The varieties of subjective poverty (the extent to which the poor feel impoverished) is another area of interest, for it can provide one more way in which the planner can determine the scope of the poverty-reduction task.

4. Finally, a number of the works noted stress that the first task in the eradication of poverty is a clear specification of what precisely constitutes poverty. Each definition has a value context, and the subsequent setting of thresholds is essentially a political decision with political impacts. The planner's function would seem to be twofold: one, presentation of alternative definitions of poverty and gross consequences of the definition, leaving to the political force the choice of one definition; two, on the basis of the choice, conducting of detailed analyses as to who are the impoverished, where do they live, what responsiveness to programs can be expected and, perhaps most important, what they think they need, want, and themselves might contribute. The planner must, then, be keenly sensitive to the extent to which his municipality will go along with the war on poverty—does it seek containment, management, reduction or eradication of poverty? The general goal must be rendered specific if it is to have a meaningful role in the entire hierarchy of conflicting and complementary objectives governing the planning task. This is a necessary, if not sufficient, step in planning the good city.

CONCLUSION

Coupled with the recognition of poverty as a fact of life in America today, there has been a veritable outpouring of articles and books, material from reporting services, conference proceedings, and official reports. The interested reader might wish to refer, among others, to: Chamber of Commerce [4], Fermer *et al.* [7], and Weisbrod [34]. These three anthologies are good representatives of the literature of rediscovery, and contain many papers which build on the more empathetic works of Harrington [11], Bagdikian [2], and Klein [15].

REFERENCES

1. The Ad Hoc Committee on the Triple Revolution, *The Triple Revolution*, Washington, The Committee, 1964; reprinted in: E. Fromm, ed., *Socialist Humanism*, Garden City, N.Y., Doubleday, 1965.
2. Bagdikian, Ben H., *In the Midst of Plenty, the Poor in America*, Boston, Beacon, 1964.
3. Bator, Francis M., *The Question of Government Spending*, New York, Harper, 1960 (reprinted New York, Collier, 1962).
4. Chamber of Commerce of the U.S., *The Concept of Poverty*, Washington, Chamber of Commerce, 1965.
5. Conference on Economic Progress, *Poverty and Deprivation in the U.S.*, Washington, Conference on Economic Progress, 1962.
6. Duhl, Leonard J., ed., *The Urban Condition*, New York, Basic Books, 1963.
7. Ferman, Louis A., Joyce L. Kornbluh, and Alan Haber, *Poverty in America*, Ann Arbor, University of Michigan, 1965.
8. Duhl, Leonard J., ed., *The Urban Condition*, New York, Basic Books, 1963.
9. Galbraith, John K., *The Affluent Society*, Boston, Houghton Mifflin, 1953 (reprinted New York, Mentor, 1963).
10. Ginsburg, Norton, and Brian J. L. Berry, *Atlas of Economic Development*, Chicago, University of Chicago Press, 1961.
11. Harrington, Michael, *The Other America: Poverty in the United States*, New York, Macmillan, 1962 (reprinted Baltimore, Penguin, 1963).
12. Heilbroner, Robert L. and Peter L. Bernstein, *Primer on Government Spending*, New York, Vintage, 1963.
13. Hunter, David R., *The Slums, Challenge and Response*, New York, Free Press of Glencoe, 1964.
14. Keyserling, Leon H., *Progress or Poverty*, Washington, Conference on Economic Progress, 1964.
15. Klein, Woody, *Let in the Sun*, New York, Macmillan, 1964.
16. Kolko, Gabriel, *Wealth and Power in America: An Analysis of Social Class and Income Distribution*, New York, Praeger, 1962.

17. Lewis, Oscar, *Five Families,* New York, Basic Books, 1959.
18. MacDonald, Dwight, *Our Invisible Poor* (Sidney Hillman Reprint Series no. 23), New York, Sidney Hillman Foundation, 1963.
19. Miller, Herman P., *Major Elements of a Research Program for the Study of Poverty* (Series MR no. 14), Los Angeles, University of California, L.A., Institute of Government and Public Affairs, 1964.
20. Morgan, James N. *et al., Income and Welfare in the United States* (Survey Research Center, University of Michigan Study), New York, McGraw-Hill, 1962.
21. Morris, Robert, ed., *Centrally Planned Change: Prospects and Concepts,* New York, National Association of Social Workers, 1964.
22. Myrdal, Gunnar, *Challenge to Affluence,* New York, Pantheon, 1962.
23. Ornati, Oscar, *Poverty in America,* Washington, National Policy Committee on Pockets of Poverty, 1964.
24. Resources for the Future, Inc., Committee on Urban Economics, *Public Expenditure Decisions in the Urban Community,* Washington, R.F.F., 1963.
25. Russett, Bruce M., ed., *World Handbook of Political and Social Indicators,* New Haven, Yale University Press, 1964.
26. Schorr, Alvin L., *Slums and Social Insecurity* (Social Security Administration, U. S. Department of Health, Education, and Welfare, Research Report no. 1), Washington, U.S. G.P.O., 1963.
27. Shostak, Arthur B. and William Gomberg, eds., *New Perspectives on Poverty,* Englewood Cliffs, N.J., Prentice-Hall, 1965.
28. Theobald, Robert, *The Challenge of Abundance,* New York, Mentor, 1962.
29. Thompson, Wilbur R., *A Preface to Urban Economics,* Baltimore, Johns Hopkins Press, 1965.
30. Titmuss, Richard M., *Essays on the Welfare State,* New Haven, Yale University Press, 1959.
31. U. S. Office of Economic Opportunity, *Community Action Program Guide* (vol. I, "Instructions for Applicants"), Washington, O.E.O., 1965.
32. U. S. Office of Economic Opportunity, *Community Action Program Workbook,* Washington, O.E.O., 1965 (looseleaf).

33. Weaver, Robert C., *The Urban Complex: Human Values in Urban Life*, Garden City, N.Y., Doubleday, 1964.
34. Weisbrod, Burton, ed., *The Economics of Poverty, an American Paradox*, Englewood Cliffs, N.J., Prentice-Hall, 1965.

The Social Aspects of Town Development

MAURICE R. BROADY*

Basingstoke is presently a small town of some thirty thousand people on the main line between London and Southampton. The town-centre focusses upon the crowded high street with its old coaching inn, the open-air market and the Victorian town-hall in the square and the distinguished mediaeval church down the dip of Wote Street. The character of this old North Hampshire market town, however, is rapidly changing. For to the north and west, the new factories, warehouses and housing estates are the signs of a town development scheme under which Basingstoke will become an industrial town of over eighty thousand people by the 1980's.

This scheme was first mooted in the Greater London Plan which Sir Patrick Abercrombie produced in 1944.[1] One of its chief objectives was to relieve the population pressure and housing shortage in London, not only by building new towns but also by encouraging the expansion of smaller towns, like Basingstoke, which lay well beyond the sprawl of the metropolis. The New Towns Act of 1946, therefore, was followed in 1952 by the Town Development Act. This legislation, designed to "encourage town development in country districts for the relief of congestion or over-population elsewhere," gave the Treasury and local authorities the power to finance the development of any towns which agreed to accept people who were prepared to move out of the large conurbations.

* Lecturer in Sociology, University of Southampton, England; educated at that university and at Harvard. Member of the London Group of Project Consultants and Visiting Lecturer at the Architectural Association Planning School in London; formerly Fellow at the Salzburg Seminar in American Studies, Research Fellow at Glasgow University, and the University of Liverpool. He is the author of *Social Change and Urban Development* (Liverpool, 1961) and joint author of a forthcoming study, *Administrative Theory and Social Development*. He has published in both planning and sociological journals in Britain.

[1] *Greater London Plan 1944*, London, 1945.

Soon after the Act was passed, the London County Council opened negotiations with Basingstoke which, in November 1957, led to the borough's acceptance of a scheme under which twelve thousand Londoners would be moved into the town over a period of ten years. This initial agreement, however, was quickly overshadowed by the disclosure of the London County Council's plan to build a new town for a population of seventy thousand at Hook, only five miles away.[2] Hampshire County Council, as the planning authority concerned, opposed this project and put forward an alternative proposal to accommodate the same number of people by developing Basingstoke and two smaller towns in the county. This solution was agreed upon in October 1961 when the Hook plan was finally shelved; and it is as part of this scheme that Basingstoke will grow by the planned immigration of about twenty thousand families, most of whom will come from London.[3]

Unlike the English new towns which are developed by government-sponsored corporations using government money, town development schemes are administered jointly by the local authorities for the "exporting" and the "receiving" areas. Other interested authorities may also be associated with such schemes as "participating" authorities. The Basingstoke development is sponsored by the London County Council as the exporting authority, by the Basingstoke Borough Council as the receiving authority and by the Hampshire County Council as a participating authority; and a joint committee on which these three councils are represented administers the scheme through the Development Group, comprising the architects and other officials specially appointed for the task. It was for that committee that the following report was prepared early in 1964.

SOCIAL ENDS IN TOWN DEVELOPMENT

The object of this report is to set out comprehensively and coherently the major social issues that are likely to arise in

---

[2] See *The Planning of a New Town*, London, 1961 for an account of the Hook plan. For the history of the Basingstoke scheme, see J. H. Dunning, *Economic Planning and Town Expansion*, Southampton, 1963, Chapter 1.

[3] For an account of the Basingstoke scheme see J. H. Dunning, *op. cit.*, Chapter 2, and R. Steel and A. G. McCulloch, "Principles and Practice of Town Development—the Basingstoke Scheme," *Journal of the Town Planning Institute*, Vol. 49, No. 1 (January 1963).

the planning of Basingstoke and, within that framework, to comment in detail upon certain topics which are already being considered by the Committee. The term "the social aspects of town development" has been understood to refer not so much to tenants' reactions or demography, but rather to the *social relationships* that develop within the community. In that sense, social *planning* deals with how these relationships are affected by the disposition of *physical* amenities, while social *development* refers to the administrative policies which are designed to make the best use of *human* resources where "best" means the promotion of "a full and satisfying life in the community."

This desideratum seems to involve two very general criteria: the idea of social unity and that of social vitality. The idea of unity inspired the early efforts of many new town corporations to encourage people of different social classes to live in the same neighbourhoods. It also found expression in the egalitarian idea that the community centre should serve as the common focus of all local social activity "without distinction of political, religious or other opinions." It is now generally agreed that these particular policies do not usually succeed in overcoming differences of social class. Nor is this surprising. For such divisions are so deeply rooted in the economic structure of our society and so firmly reinforced by the educational system and by social conventions that they are likely to be influenced only marginally, if at all, by the allocation of housing and leisure-time activity. But the failure of these particular policies does not invalidate the idea of social unity, for it may still be held desirable that all residents, irrespective of social differences, should be encouraged to share some sense of identity in, and some responsibility for the town and its welfare.

Nor does it follow that nothing ought or can be done about social differentiation. What is particularly distasteful about status differences is the way in which people use them to exaggerate their own virtues and to emphasise the faults of others. This is particularly true of rapidly-growing communities where newcomers tend to be regarded with suspicion and even antagonism not only by the original residents but also by people who were themselves newcomers only a few years before. Indeed, the hostility of an existing population to newcomers may well be one of the biggest social problems involved in town development. The ideal of social unity makes it necessary to try to minimise, if it cannot be entirely avoided, the growth of social animosity within the community.

The criterion of social vitality has entailed the idea that people should participate in a wide variety of social activities. This objective has also been asserted too dogmatically. It has been rather uncritically generalised into the proposition that people can only be mentally healthy if they are actively engaged in social activities within their local society. But this is far too rash a view. For while withdrawal from social contacts is certainly one indicator of mental disturbance, it is not the only one nor is it unambiguously related to mental ill health. In any case, not everyone wishes to take part in social activities. Even in Crawley New Town, where voluntary associations are particularly vigorous, only 30 percent of the population belongs to them. But if this view will not do for *individuals,* it can still be argued that a good *town* is one that supports a wide range of social and cultural activities.

In the light of these criteria, then, the development of "a full and satisfying life in the community" seems to entail:

(a) that the townsfolk, irrespective of social differences, should feel a positive sense of identity with and responsibility in the town;

(b) that the development of acrimony and animosity between the different sections of the population should be minimised, if it cannot be entirely avoided;

(c) that every encouragement should be given to the growth of a vigorous social and cultural life.

There are three major factors that can contribute to community development: (1) people; (2) physical design; and (3) social development policy. Many local authorities are inclined to take the view that community development can be achieved by their action alone. They have tended to regard physical design and the adequate provision of social amenities as almost more important than the people themselves for whose benefit they are provided. But experience has shown that social development cannot be imposed by statutory fiat. It demands the common enterprise of both statutory and voluntary agencies. Indeed, the main assumption on which this report is based is that the major contribution to the "full and satisfying life" is made by the people themselves, and that the statutory authorities only have it in their power to establish conditions which can either hinder or encourage the townspeople to make that contribution.

I. THE PEOPLE: PROBLEMS AND POTENTIALITIES

Inducements to Move

Basingstoke has been growing rapidly for the last ten years. As its population has increased by over 50 percent since the mid-fifties, there are already a large number of newcomers in the town. They have mostly come as private individuals moving into private estates (housing developments). In the future, however, the influx of population will be on a much larger scale, much more organised and more fully under the control of the statutory authorities. In many new towns, it was hoped to get what was called a "balanced" population, that is, a population similar in age and social status to the national one. This aim was invariably scuppered by the fact that industry preferred younger people and that, in any case, it was they who were most disposed to move. The population structure that a town will get, therefore, is determined both by the kind of occupational demands that the incoming industries will make and by the readiness of people to move in order to meet them.

In the present economic situation, many more firms will be willing to come to Basingstoke than can possibly be accommodated. The Joint Committee, therefore, will be able to exercise a choice among them which will have direct effects upon the town's social structure. It seems most unlikely that, even if it wished to do so, Basingstoke will be able to avoid attracting a very high proportion of young people. But what it should be able to affect through its industrial selection policy is the class structure of the population. It is likely that a substantial proportion of commercial offices and even research organisations will be attracted to the town and this will increase the proportion of white-collar workers in the population. Thus, the incoming population may well be "unbalanced" by containing higher-than-average proportions of young families and middle-class people. Since much of the detailed planning of the town depends upon assumptions about its future population structure, and since this is directly affected by industrial selection policy, the Development Group should try to spell out explicitly what a desirable and/or probable industrial portfolio would comprise, so that the demographic assumptions on which both physical and social planning depend could be made more precisely.

How the industrial selection will work out depends, however, upon whether workers of the appropriate categories can be attracted to the town. There appear to be significant class differences in the reasons for residential movement. A study of recent movement into Basingstoke itself showed that manual workers moved mainly to improve their housing while non-manual and professional employees did so chiefly for occupational reasons. Highly skilled manual workers are likely to be reasonably well-housed in London and thus disinclined to move in order to improve their accommodation. Evidence from other expanding towns suggests that this class of labour may well be very difficult to attract. There are also grounds for expecting that skilled workers in the engineering trades will be particularly loath to move from the London area where they are in a sellers' market. Some key workers, it is true, are likely to move with their firms, but special attention may have to be given to the possibility that workers of this kind may not readily leave the London area.

This problem may not be so acute in the case of professional and managerial employees, provided that career opportunities are satisfactory. These are people, however, who are more mobile and for whom the attractiveness of the town and its environs as a place to live is especially important. It is possible, therefore, that the satisfactions demanded of a new town are much more demanding among people of this class than among manual workers. Moving, as they do, less for housing than for occupational reasons, they may well derive much less satisfaction from simply possessing a new house than do manual workers who are more likely to have moved precisely in order to improve their accommodation. Accordingly, while people of all classes are attracted by a town with good amenities, this is likely to be a particularly important factor in attracting and retaining professional and managerial employees and their families who may well constitute a higher-than-average proportion of Basingstoke's future population.

Social Adjustment

The move out from London to Basingstoke is not only a geographical transition: it is also a shift from one social milieu to another. Psychological stability tends to be fostered by social regularity. People are what they are, as persons, by virtue of the social relationships into which they enter. They are sustained as the persons they are by the conventions of the social groups to which they belong and by the assurance that comes from knowing implicitly how to conduct themselves and what conduct to expect of others in specified social situations. Any change in these conventions or any sudden move into new kinds of social situation in which they are unsure of the relevant conventions makes them feel uncomfortable precisely because the regularity of the social relationships is disturbed upon which their personal assurance is built. The move from one social milieu to another, therefore, is likely to put people under more psychological and social stress than they are usually accustomed to.

A good deal of attention has recently been given to the fact that many of the people who move out to new housing areas are leaving older urban areas in which very often they and their families have lived all their lives. It has been suggested that the social malaise and psychological disturbance experienced by newcomers to housing estates are largely due to their having been suddenly uprooted from closely knit kin groups in very stable and long-established communities. Though this may conceivably aggravate the disturbance which the transition entails, it is by no means the sole or necessarily the most important factor, since difficulties of readjustment are experienced by most people who move into unfamiliar surroundings. These problems affect the husband and children of a family a good deal less than the wife, upon whom the major burden of rebuilding social contacts in the new community chiefly falls. In a study made a few years ago of a London out-county estate, it was found that the main nervous illnesses were neurotic reactive depressions among women; and recent studies in Crawley and Basingstoke have amply confirmed that it is the women who are particularly prone to depression and dissatisfaction in new housing areas. It needs to be added that this is for the most part a temporary phenomenon and that most people in due course settle in and adapt to their new environment quite happily. Nevertheless, since these transitional difficulties will affect everyone who moves to the town, and since a minority will find themselves at least temporarily overwhelmed by them, it is useful to state briefly what is here involved.

Social readjustment is called for in two main fields. People have, first of all, to establish a new domestic regime. In moving to a new town, both the standard and the cost of living are likely to rise, especially for manual workers. The rents of new houses are likely to be higher than they were paying previously while the price of foodstuffs and other commodities is frequently higher, especially in the early phases of development when the number of shops is limited and there tends to be a sellers' market. Being young, the newcomers' families are usually growing and many are also moving into larger dwellings than they previously occupied. They are thus faced with the additional financial burdens of furnishing a new home. Since the move does not normally entail the promotion of the main wage-earner or necessarily increase his income, these increased costs are met either by credit, which in the working-class generally means expensive hire-purchase (installment buying), or by the wife's going out to work. Most people, of course, will certainly manage to re-establish a new pattern of domestic arrangements speedily enough, but there will undoubtedly be a small but less competent minority who are unable to do so.

The second area of readjustment is in the wider sphere of social relationships within the community. This involves contacts with neighbours and with local social activities. The incomers will be coming from many different parts of London; and while differences in rent levels will act as a kind of social sieve, segregating them broadly by income and social status, there will be in each new area a great variety of people from a wide variety of social backgrounds. In the intimate life of a residential neighbourhood, superficially slight variations of behaviour and social standards can cause a good deal of upset, especially to the housewife, in the initial stages of development before neighbours finally settle down into a mutually tolerable code of conduct. Furthermore, many people find it equally difficult to re-establish membership in associations like churches or darts clubs which may have given them a great deal of satisfaction in the older areas from which they came. It is important to appreciate that, for people for whom the move out to Basingstoke may well be the most momentous event in their lives, this re-establishing of social contacts may be particularly difficult.

Enough is now known about these social processes for the phases of social adjustment in new communities to be specified quite precisely. For the first six months or so, the newcomers are likely to be busy settling into and enjoying their new homes. During the next two or three years they experience the difficulties and tensions of adjusting to a new social environment, in the course of which some people either move back to where they came from or seek a transfer to another house, often on another estate. Thereafter, they begin to develop in a more stable and assured atmosphere a fresh set of social contacts and friendships. No thorough study has been done of the extent to which people return to London from the expanding towns, but in Swindon some 10 percent were said to have done so and a comparable figure was quoted by the managing director of a leading Basingstoke firm about the skilled workers who had been specially recruited in the large industrial areas of the Midlands and the North. Some such movement is inevitable. But it is clearly a substantial diseconomy and for that reason, as well as on humanitarian grounds, it is desirable that efforts should be made administratively to ease the shock of the initial transition.

Social Differences

A second major source of disturbance is the differences which exist between different sections of the community. People obviously classify themselves and others. These classifications, for example, between the newcomer and the old-timer or between the well-off and the badly-off, are not figments of the imagination. They are real and unavoidable and they may also be acrimonious. Already a slight touch of animosity can be discerned in relations between the in-comers and the older townsfolk, who are understandably resentful of the changes which the town is now undergoing. Such animosity does not need to be overt to be effective, for much subtler techniques of avoidance and rejection can make newcomers feel singularly unwelcome. In many places, indeed, the adjustment of the "overspill" population to the life of the town into which they have moved has been adversely affected in this way and given rise to "bewilderment, loneliness and sometimes fear." These antagonisms sometimes produce more obvious social tensions when divergent interests of the two groups in the population find their expression in local organisations. The existing rate-payers' (tax-payers') associations in the borough will undoubtedly be complemented by tenants' associations. These bodies may in due course come into open conflict in a way that can only exacerbate the relations between the groups they represent and hinder their mutual acceptance. In the same way, other organisations, including the borough council, can come to be divided acrimoniously between conflicting interests. It is not possible either to avoid divergent interests in a community or to cover them up. Nor is there any reason for regarding division of interests as undesirable, provided only that the conflicts which such divisions generate can be conducted in a spirit of mutual goodwill rather than mutual distrust and dislike. This, however, cannot be legislated for: it depends entirely upon the exercise of restraint and good sense by the leaders of various groups within the community.

Leadership in the Community

The number and quality of leaders which a community will produce is related to its class structure and cultural traditions. Though some ability to lead and organise is to be found in every stratum of society, it is found proportionately more among the middle-class than among the working-class. It is probable that there will be a high proportion of middle-class persons in the new Basingstoke and that their contribution to the development of the community will be proportionately great. On the other hand, these middle-class incomers may well be executives and professional men who come to Basingstoke for a few years, as one stage in a career pattern that takes them from one branch of a major company to another as they steadily ascend the spiral of managerial promotion; they may also be inclined to take houses in the villages outside the town itself. In such circumstances, it is possible that they may not be disposed to contribute substantially to the social and cultural life of a community with which their only link is that their firm happens to have an office in it and which they may, in any event, soon be leaving.

The emphasis which has been placed on middle-class leadership has often led to an under-estimation of the tradition of communal leadership within the working-class. This tradition has found its typical outlet in political and trade union activities and in sporting and social clubs. Its characteristics vary from one part of the country to another and it is difficult to discover exactly what can be expected of the London working-class in this connection. However that may be, the social development of the town clearly depends upon engaging and encouraging local leadership wherever it is to be found. Many people take on leadership responsibilities for the first time as a result of such encouragement and often acquit themselves extremely well in their posts. Some thought, therefore, deserves to be given to this whole question of how the leadership potential in the community can best be engaged.

II. SOCIAL PLANNING

Under this heading, two main questions need to be considered: (1) what social facilities should be provided in the town and (2) how they should be located. One of the major weaknesses in town planning since the war has been the inadequate or belated provision of such amenities. The reasons for this are obvious and understandable. In conditions of economic stringency, priorities have to be assigned to different kinds of development and houses and schools are clearly more urgent than community centres and playgrounds. Social amenities, however, are apt to be regarded as mere "frills" of development. But the effects of inadequate and belated provision of meeting places and other communal buildings are not easily eradicated and, as *The Lancet* remarked a year or so ago, "a few thousands of pounds spent on social amenities and social development may save hundreds of thousands used on therapeutic services and wasted in labour lost." This point appears to have been acknowledged in the recent Ministry ruling under which the new towns have been allowed to contribute the equivalent of four pounds per head of population towards the provision of social facilities. The case for such provision is now stronger than ever, for one of the main tendencies in modern living, in Britain as elsewhere, is the increase in leisure. This, together with the fact that the population of the future will be increasingly wealthy and well-educated, will undoubtedly call forth a demand for more adequate provision, particularly for leisure-time activities.

The development of these amenities as Basingstoke expands will be undertaken mainly by the statutory (governmental) authorities or by commercial interests, the one providing what is required by statute, the other what is profitable. The provision of schools by the local authority, for example, and shops, pubs, dance-halls, cinemas, and bowling alleys by commercial interests can therefore be taken for granted. What needs to be given special consideration is how the other social amenities are to be provided which are neither mandatory nor profitable: amenities that are either exclusively social, such as meeting places or community centres, or which cater for minority, and notably cultural and educational, interests.

The Town Centre

The brief for the town centre development proposes that provision should be made for a social centre and clubs. One of the chief lacunae in the town's social provision at present is a good, centrally-sited hall in which large public meetings can be held. It is to be hoped that a hall or a suite of halls of different sizes will be provided in the social centre and the new municipal buildings. It would also be desirable to provide adequate office accommodation, conveniently located either in or adjacent to the social centre, for the many branches of the voluntary social services such as the Marriage Guidance Council, the Family Planning Association, the Citizens Advice Bureau, the Women's Voluntary Service and the like which will undoubtedly develop, no doubt under a Council of Social Service, as the town grows. However well organised such bodies may be, their service to the community is often made less efficient than it could be by being carried out in unsuitable, scattered and often makeshift premises. In view of the very important social service which they provide in areas outside the range of the statutory services and of the expectation that this kind of voluntary service will grow in importance in the coming years, such provision ought to be given the most sympathetic consideration.[4] The family centre at Stevenage New Town, operated under the Stevenage Council of Social Service, in which administrative arrangements are shared among the different associations concerned, offers a useful example of what might be done.

Interest in the arts and in further education is increasing yearly. It is significant that, despite the wide diffusion of radio and television which enable people to listen to music and drama in their own homes, and notwithstanding the development of educational broadcasting, the live theatre is flourishing and attendances at evening study-courses throughout the country are now increasing more rapidly than ever before. A town that encourages "quality" activities of this kind is not only doing something intrinsically worthwhile, it is also building up its reputation as a good, lively and interesting place to live in and this, in a very real sense, is an economic asset. The borough is fortunate in having already in existence a lively Theatre Association and Concert Society, a flourishing

---

[4] This line of argument is developed more fully in my "Community Power and Voluntary Enterprise," *Social Service Quarterly*, Vol. 38, No. 3 (Winter 1964).

branch of the Workers' Educational Association, and a number of other dramatic and musical organisations. This kind of activity needs adequate accommodation, preferably in or near the centre of the town. These bodies, moreover, ought to have substantial control of their own facilities. This control is best assured by their owning, or at least leasing, the premises which they use. The rents for brand-new buildings are usually beyond the means of societies with minority membership such as these. On the other hand, they could corporately manage to rent older buildings which could be effectively converted to meet their requirements. For cultural and educational activities, two kinds of space are needed: an auditorium for dramatic and musical productions and meeting rooms of various sizes, larger ones for choir practices and orchestral rehearsals and smaller ones for discussion-groups, play-readings, small music groups and the like. For the first, the Haymarket Theatre, suitably renovated and extended so as to join onto the old town hall, would provide one useful centre. It might well be complemented by an educational centre which could make use of the present borough offices, if and when these are vacated, for such activities as require smaller rooms and a congenial and mellow atmosphere.[5] As it is intended to build at high densities on the eastern side of the town, these two buildings, lying to the south-east of the town centre, would be singularly well-sited.

Central and Peripheral Amenities

Decisions about what amenities should be provided in the peripheral areas of the town depend on judgements about the effect of the total design of the town upon social activity within it. Until six or seven years ago, the idea of neighbourhood development at fairly low densities guided the planning of most new towns and housing estates. But Basingstoke is being built at higher densities than most of the new towns and on the assumption that each family will possess a car. The road system has been designed on that basis and car parking for six thousand vehicles has been planned for the town centre. The implications of these facts are, first, that access to the centre will be easier than in a new town and, second, that about 65 percent of the population, as compared with about 50 percent in Crawley New Town, will be living within a mile of the centre. The effects of these differences upon the

[5] The municipal offices are presently housed in a delightful eighteenth-century Georgian house set in a corner of a park.

behaviour of residents are difficult to forecast, but by comparison with the new towns, there is a *prima facie* case for making a proportionally higher investment in central than in peripheral amenities. The point clearly requires much more analysis.

There are, however, good grounds for making *some* social provision in the residential areas. Of these local amenities, adequate meeting halls are essential for the development of social activities. One of the points which was most strongly recommended in the recent National Council of Social Service report on new communities in Britain was the timely provision of places in which residents could meet together. Such halls are especially needed in the early stages of development when voluntary provision in the form of church halls, for example, is limited by shortage of funds and when the need to encourage social development is greatest. Initially, some kind of tenants' common room should be provided of the kind so successfully used on municipal estates in London and Birmingham: they need not be very elaborate or costly to be effective.

In addition, land, preferably adjacent to the tenants' common room, should be allocated so as to allow for the development, as the neighbourhood grows, of a local demand for some larger facility such as a community centre. Some social activities which at first take place in the tenants' meeting rooms are likely in due course to find accommodation, for example, in church halls. But there are very often other bodies which are not adequately served either by tenants' rooms or by church halls (both of which are often booked to capacity in new estates) and which are sufficiently well-supported to justify the provision of a larger meeting-place. It is often argued on economic grounds that school buildings ought to be used for such purposes. But special provision is desirable for many activities for which school premises are inconvenient. Art and handicrafts, for example, usually require a lot of equipment and clutter which it is inconvenient to leave in a school-room: adult education classes are better conducted in an atmosphere more conducive to discussion and preferably more comfortable than the average school; while youth activities tend to be better supported if they are conducted away from school buildings. In addition, the people who engage in these various activities ought to have a say in how the premises in which they meet are conducted; and this element of self-government is much more easily established in a building specially designed for leisure-time pursuits. For the same reason, that the users ought to have some control of the premises, it is better not to provide anything more substantial than a tenants' room until there is a clear and vigorous local demand for it, which can be actively associated with the local authority in providing, running and supporting something as large as a community centre. What the planner must ensure is that sufficient space is left in the original layout of the scheme for this kind of future development.

The Location of Amenities in the Peripheral Areas

The second main issue in social planning concerns the location of amenities in residential areas and, in particular, the criteria which should guide the planner in this. One theory holds that amenities should be sited so as to foster a sense of community among the residents. This idea has been incorporated in the neighbourhood unit concept. This concept originated simply as a means of relating physical amenities systematically to the distribution of population. The size of the unit was determined by the desire to avoid small children having to cross main roads to get to school and by the fact that a population of about ten thousand was required to support a primary school. To this planning theory was then added a social theory which asserted that the neighbourhood plan and the allocation of facilities within it could also help to engender a sense of belonging and community spirit among the residents of each neighbourhood.

It is important to understand the origins of this social theory. Between the wars, the early housing estates came to be criticised not only because they were ill-provided with essential amenities, such as schools and shops, but because they lacked the neighbourliness and the sense of community which, despite bad housing conditions, people had enjoyed in the slums. How, then, could good housing be combined with neighbourliness and a sense of community? Pre-war town planning theory, tinged as it was with a rather romantic social idealism, proposed that these feelings of belonging and neighbourliness could be fostered by physical design and, in particular, by the neighbourhood unit.

The chief weakness of this theory is its assumption that social characteristics are determined by physical form. The neighbourliness of the slums, however, depended much less on their physical structure of small houses and mean streets or on the fact that they were well-endowed with pubs and corner shops than it did upon the sociological facts that the people who lived in the slums had frequently lived in the same street for one or two generations and that people who share conditions of economic hardship are prone to band together for mutual help and protection. The elements of the environment that are relevant are not physical but economic and sociological. To suppose that the physical factors are the most important, as the neighbourhood theory does, is to attribute causal significance to a purely adventitious phenomenon. But it is perfectly understandable that planners who were socially concerned should have supposed that the prime causal factor in the development of community feeling was the physical environment which it was in their power to modify.[6]

The neighbourhood unit concept, however, is open to criticism on much broader grounds. For, in the first place, it posits the village community as the social ideal when there are good grounds for believing that "community is becoming a concept which is no longer confined to a particular locality, or which, indeed, is not primarily to be identified in terms of locality." And secondly, it loses a good deal of its cogency at a time when the rapid increase of car-ownership is making people much more mobile than ever they were.

The Location of Shops

This doctrine has clearly influenced the discussions in which the Committee has been involved about the location of shops. Two divergent views are being advanced. One view holds that, in order to maximise convenience, a suite of shops should be within one-quarter mile of every resident. This would produce sixteen suites of shops of six thousand square feet: one for every three thousand people. Alternatively, it is proposed that there should be ten suites of shops of nine thousand square feet: one for every five thousand people. This proposal derives from the view that the overriding criterion in allocating shops should be "to establish focal points that will foster a sense of 'community' within the area served," and that this will be more effectively achieved in a residential unit of five thousand than in one of three thousand people.

This opinion is not tenable. The idea that a residential unit of five thousand people will necessarily be more effective in fostering a sense of community than one of seven thousand

[6] This point is more fully elaborated in my "Social Theory in Architectural Design," *Arena: the Architectural Association Journal*, Vol. 81, No. 897 (January 1966).

or three thousand is sociological speculation rather than fact; nor is there any sound reason to suppose that such minor differences of size would have any more than a marginal influence upon social consciousness. None of these figures is better than any other; and if the experience in Hemel Hempstead New Town suggests that a unit of five thousand people is the best size, then similarly impressionistic evidence, of no more but no less validity, can be adduced from Crawley to suggest that the neighbourhoods there, most of which have between fifty-five hundred and seven thousand residents, have been so successful in generating a sense of local belonging that they have actually inhibited the development of a sense of identity with the town as a whole. Accordingly, even if differences *could* be shown in the degree of community feeling in neighbourhoods of various sizes, it remains open to doubt whether such differences are causally related either to the size of the neighbourhoods themselves or to the way in which amenities are disposed within them.

But there is a further point. If the issue is the effect of the location of shops on the residents and their welfare, then economic criteria are much more tangible and significant than these "sociological" considerations. Clearly, from the point of view of the Committee and trader alike, shops must first of all give an adequate return on investment costs and rents. From the consumers' point of view, too, economy is also vital. What they want, at best, are shops that are both cheap and convenient: and it is an excessively narrow definition of the residents' welfare to focus solely upon the development of community feeling.

In general, cheapness is maximised under conditions of competition. This enjoins a layout in which shops are so grouped as to bring together a number of retail outlets in all the main trades, and this condition would presumably best be met by having all shopping facilities in the town centre. But this would clearly conflict with the other, one-quarter-mile criterion of convenience. This attempt to lay down a quantitative standard of convenience is clearly desirable since, without it, other economic factors which can be more precisely defined and which thus appear more compelling are likely to carry more weight. But two comments need to be made.

First of all, not very much information is available about what people actually regard as "convenient" distances. There is certainly some evidence, from Hemel Hempstead New Town, for example, that people prefer not to have to walk more than one-quarter of a mile to the nearest shops. Even so, the one-quarter-mile formula is a desideratum and not something objectively given in the facts of the situation. It must, therefore, be regarded less as a precise rule than as a broad guide to planning practice. A more important point, however, concerns the competitive position of the proposed shopping groups. Each of the sixteen groups would have an area of six thousand square feet which it is proposed to divide into one food store of twenty-five hundred square feet, one newsagent and tobacconist shop of fifteen hundred square feet, and two other shops each of one thousand square feet. The alternative scale of provision is for ten groups of nine thousand square feet divided into two units of twenty-five hundred and fifteen hundred square feet, plus five others each of one thousand square feet. Clearly, the sixteen groups would be more convenient. But would not commodities like groceries be dearer? The allocation of twenty-five hundred square feet for a food store allows for a number of alternative means of provision. The space could either be divided between two multiple grocers or given over to one large supermarket. If it were divided between two genuinely competing grocers or allocated for use as a supermarket to one firm sufficiently large to be able and ready to pass on economies of scale in keen prices, then, in groceries at least, convenience would presumably be matched by cheapness. But there is clearly a danger of affording one large firm a monopoly which it could exploit, for then the convenience of the one-quarter-mile principle would be countered by a marginal increase in costs to the consumer.

The Concentration of Amenities

The allocation of all social amenities in residential areas ought to be chiefly determined by similar socio-economic criteria. The first consideration in deciding whether such an amenity, be it a library or a tenants' meeting room, should be provided is what number of people are required to make it worth providing. This criterion then determines the place of the amenity in a hierarchy of areas. Within a residential district, however, it is generally more desirable to group rather than to disperse amenities. Not only is this usually more convenient but, on the principle that the more shops there are together the better will be the trade for each, the concentration of social facilities like shops, churches, clinics and meeting-halls affords a greater opportunity to residents using one amenity to make use of the others. This argument applies equally to medical provision, where a better standard of service and a more economical use of highly-trained personnel can be achieved through bringing together under one roof a number of general practitioners and ancillary workers like district nurses, health visitors and midwives. In short, the grouping of amenities is likely to maximise convenience for the residents and to ensure that they will be used to the full. If this grouping *also* serves to give a social focus to the area, so well and good.

The Distribution of Different Types of Housing

One question which is frequently raised in considering housing lay-outs is whether it is possible, and if so how, to get people of different social classes to live in the same areas. The earlier attempts to do this by building "managerial" houses in predominantly working-class neighbourhoods have clearly failed. This policy again rested upon excessively simple assumptions about how social behaviour might be modified by physical structure and unrealistic ideas about the nature of the British class system. Socially speaking, the natural thing is for birds of a feather to flock together. This applies even in working-class housing estates, where a process of transferring from one house to another in the early years of development serves to segregate tenants of different status into different areas. Housing lay-outs, therefore, must accord with the social differences in the community.

At this stage, policy decisions have to be made about the proportion of houses that should be allocated for private purchase and where they should be sited. The expectation that a higher-than-average proportion of white-collar workers will be coming to the town; the fact that this stratum is steadily growing in size as the economy changes; the knowledge that in Southampton and other English towns municipal tenants are tending to buy their own houses if only because, in a period of inflation, it is more economical to purchase than to rent a house: all these factors suggest that there will be a ready demand in Basingstoke for houses that are offered for sale. Given that, in Southampton, for example, over 40 percent of the houses are owner-occupied and that this is substantially below the proportion in Hampshire as a whole (51 percent in 1961), it may be that the Committee's allocation of

25 percent for private development, presumably for owner-occupation, is too low. This is an important matter of general policy. It would therefore be desirable to estimate more systematically than appears so far to have been done what the demand for privately-owned houses is likely to be in a town with Basingstoke's population structure.

It is inevitable that there will be different types of housing in the town, some rented and some privately-owned. Such differences of tenure are invariably associated with differences of status. Even though more and more working-class people are now purchasing their own houses, house-ownership in Britain is still predominantly a middle-class characteristic. Accordingly, the question has to be considered how far it is possible at least to inhibit the development of class animosities by the way in which housing of different kinds is allocated. As stated earlier, physical planning has no more than an indirect effect on social development. Nevertheless, it is clear that physical features are frequently used by the people themselves to emphasise existing status differences. In Welwyn Garden City, for instance, the railway line effectively segregates the pre-war from the post-war town and serves to accentuate the cleavage between the socially right and the wrong side of the tracks. Excessively sharp points of difference such as that ought, wherever possible, to be avoided. In Basingstoke, therefore, the Committee might envisage the development in *all* parts of the town of precincts of middle-class, owner-occupied dwellings, each containing perhaps two hundred to four hundred houses, distinctive enough in style and layout to attract middle-class residents and yet sharing with people of other social strata common social amenities like shops and schools so that the middle-class areas would not form completely segregated enclaves. Too many social benefits must not be expected of such an arrangement, however. There is no reason to expect that it alone would induce residents of different classes to participate in common social activities or that it would encourage the middle-class residents to act as leaders in neighbourhood organisations. Neither could it prevent the assignation of more or less favourable reputations to particular housing areas. But it might prevent the branding of any one main section of the town as better or worse than anywhere else; and that alone would clearly be worth doing.

A further source of class segregation derives from the possibility that many wealthier incomers may prefer, if at all possible, to live in the villages around the town. In a free economy, this can be no more avoided than can the acute awareness of invidious status differentials which it is likely to induce among those who might wish to do so but who simply cannot afford it. From the point of view of the borough as a whole, however, such a development would be disadvantageous, since many people who might well contribute their leadership and patronage to the well-being of the town might be ill-disposed to do so if they were living outside its boundaries.

III. SOCIAL AND COMMUNITY DEVELOPMENT

In turning, finally, to consider social development policy, a move is entailed from the field of social planning in which the statutory authorities are chiefly concerned with the *provision* of physical amenities to one in which their purpose must rather be to encourage the people themselves to contribute *their* ideas, effort and leadership to the town's well-being. Whereas in social planning the chief criterion must be social-economic, in the field of social development, it must be, in that sense, educational. For that reason, it demands on the part of the local authorities a greater sensitivity to local initiative and voluntary enterprise than is necessary, or perhaps desirable, in designing a housing layout or implementing a drainage scheme.

A Social Development Department

There are a number of reasons for setting up within the borough administration a separate department devoted to social development. In the first place, the social side of housing management will inevitably grow in importance as the size of the municipal estate increases. Not only will rent-collecting become more onerous, but the number of complaints, both frivolous and serious, the requests for house-exchanges, and the representations from tenants' associations will all grow apace. It is possible that the housing management staff can be expanded to deal with these new duties: but there are many other related matters with which it would excessively burden a housing department to have to deal and which, in any case, call for a staff more specifically trained in community development. The National Council of Social Service report noted that "most of those who have worked in new communities expressed the view that there should be, from the start, someone with a definite responsibility for social development and, it was often added, a position of sufficient status and independence to ensure that he was consulted on policy." The fact that, over the next twelve years, an average of thirty families a week and fifteen hundred a year will be moving into the town indicates statistically the importance of such an appointment.

The duties of a social development officer would begin long before the newcomers arrived. The social development officer at Harlow New Town has recently made the point that "if people are to be encouraged to put down roots quickly and play an active part in developing the life of a new community, it is absolutely essential that they should have as much information as possible about the place in which they have come to live." His initial role would be to act as the authority's information officer. But a much more important function would be to establish a staff of neighbourhood workers who would help the incomers to settle down in the town and to overcome the many social difficulties to which, especially in the early phases, they will inevitably be subject. Subsequently, he would be concerned to assist and encourage the growth of all kinds of voluntary social activity. The benefits of this kind of work accrue not only to the incomers who are helped or to the voluntary associations which need initial encouragement and support. They accrue equally to the authority, which, as the chief landlord in the town, would gain in good-will by showing itself from the start actively concerned with the welfare of its new residents, and also to industry, which would clearly benefit from a stable and contented work-force.

One further function might well be assigned to a social development department which would benefit the work of the local authority as a whole. It might take over the responsibility for intelligence and research. One of the most serious weaknesses in British local government at the present time is the absence of effective information and research departments. In British architectural practice, too, social research and the feed-back of information from the site to the drawing-board is often most inadequate. These deficiencies are particularly unfortunate in periods like the present when local authorities have taken on all manner of new responsibilities, notably in the planning field, and when social and economic conditions are changing so rapidly. The absence of a service of this kind tells especially in the early stages of town development when decisions of major importance may often be made with inadequate use of relevant social and economic data.

The Role of Voluntary Organisations

On the part of the voluntary associations in the borough, there is already a bubbling of activity which shows that some townspeople are beginning to reflect not only about how the development will affect their property or the rates but also what constructive role they can play in the expansion of the town. The establishment of the Citizens Advice Bureau a year or two ago has been followed by the formation of a social workers' group and of a study-group on town development organised by the Workers Educational Association. These are small beginnings; but they represent useful resources of local good-will, ability and leadership. At the moment, however, these initiatives are all rather ad hoc; and their sponsors, having no clear idea what the development will entail, lack a sense of direction and are uncertain about what such bodies might contribute to the town's social development.

It is in precisely this situation that the Workers Educational Association has a great deal to contribute. Its report on the social implications of the development scheme will shortly be published. It is hoped that it might be accorded some kind of official patronage as a responsible document designed to suggest how the statutory and voluntary bodies in the town might most effectively collaborate to foster the social well-being of the borough as it expands. The function of the study-group, however, is simply to make clear what the social implications of the expansion are likely to be and to put forward for discussion some ideas about what local action might be taken. The lines of development are for others to take up if they so choose. But the launching of the report might serve as an occasion on which steps might be taken to raise publicly the whole question of how the social development of the town could best be fostered.[7]

It is clear that the voluntary associations in the town urgently need some coherent idea of what their role might be and some official acknowledgement of the importance of the contribution they might be able to make. One way of achieving these objectives would be to set up a Council of Social Service with the full support of the local authority. Such an organisation would serve not only to draw the voluntary social

[7] For a fuller discussion, see my "Social Change and Town Development," *Town Planning Review* (January 1966).

services together, it would also afford them a forum for discussion and a basis for common action, represent them *vis-à-vis* the local authority in the development of social provision in the town and give them the support, so necessary in a period of very rapid growth, of the expertise and advice of the National Council of Social Service.

A second kind of organisation which would serve the same sort of function in relation to other kinds of activity is the trust. This applies particularly to sports, education and the arts. Trusts have been very effectively developed in a number of the new towns. In Harlow, for example, they have been established for both art and sport, while in Stevenage a Youth Trust was set up a year or two ago, with the support of the Gulbenkian Foundation, in order to establish a youth centre. The purpose of such organisations is to plan and co-ordinate efforts to achieve certain kinds of amenity which otherwise would not be provided and for which voluntary support is both necessary and desirable.

The Harlow Sports Trust provides a useful example of what can be done in this way. The Trust is registered as a limited company with its main object the provision of facilities for recreation, physical education and other leisure-time pursuits. It includes representatives of the statutory authorities —the County Council, Urban District Council and the Development Corporation—and two voluntary bodies—the Essex Playing Fields Association and the Sports Centre Supporters Club. It set itself to develop a sports centre costing one hundred thousand pounds, and a substantial proportion of this sum has been raised by grants from the Ministry of Education, the local authorities and national foundations, by donations from local industry and commerce and by contributions from the Sports Centre Supporters Club and a penny-a-week contributory scheme. The success of this form of organisation depends upon its being backed by a representative and influential local committee, upon the collaboration between the statutory authorities and voluntary associations and upon the elaboration of a sound and competently-drafted plan. But, in the first instance, from whichever quarter the initiative comes, what is imperative is the full collaboration of the local authorities and the voluntary bodies concerned.

The Development of Community Leadership

In this discussion of social development, it has been assumed that many more capable local leaders will be forthcoming.

But the more the importance of voluntary enterprise is acknowledged, the more exacting are the standards of competence demanded of voluntary leaders. Indeed, if local authorities are to be invited to support voluntary enterprises, they have to be assured that they are soundly conducted. Accordingly, one of the most important points which the voluntary associations now need to consider is the competence of their leadership and the efficiency of their organisation. In this connection, a local Council of Social Service could do a great deal to improve the quality of voluntary enterprise by offering advice on organisation and by setting up training-courses for local leaders as the London Council of Social Service has so successfully done in municipal housing estates in the London area.

The statutory authorities, for their part, ought to administer the facilities under their control so as to accord the maximum of responsibility to the local leaders themselves. This principle is exemplified in the relationship between the Borough Council, which owns and maintains the Haymarket Theatre, and the Theatre Association which manages it. This kind of collaboration needs to be fully developed in all manner of communal enterprises. The administration of tenants' meeting-rooms, for example, should positively encourage voluntary enterprise and responsible local leadership by devolving responsibility for their management upon the tenants' organisations themselves. This applies equally to community centres. The Moot House Community Centre at Harlow, for example, is provided by the Development Corporation and maintained by the County Education Department who pay the warden's salary and 25 percent of the running costs, but it is managed by an independent council which appoints the warden and to which he is responsible.

This principle of encouraging local enterprise by according it every support yet leaving it self-governing is of vital importance in social development policy and one which has wide application in a town development scheme. For it is chiefly through administrative arrangements of this kind that the people, who are the chief agents of social development, are likely to make the most effective use of the social amenities which the statutory authorities and voluntary associations between them will provide.

Chapter 20

CITIZEN PARTICIPATION

"Planning is for people." This tidy slogan has been part of the professional jargon for many decades. The object of the entire urban development effort, we are told, is to form a total environment maximizing life chances and returns for the citizenry. But agreeing with such vague ends does not clarify precisely who is to define them in detail, as Chapter 6 on goals evidenced, nor blueprint the design for socio-economic political structures in a pluralistic, mixed economy combined with an optimum physical infrastructure, to attain such goals.

Further, group dynamics now assures us that *means* or *process* is tangled with ends; expert definition of ends and facilities, if that is possible, does not carry the population automatically along by any stretch of the imagination. Planning, as was explored at some lengths in Chapter 17, is a process in an evolutionary world; thus the people and their city change in a reciprocal relationship—which seems on the surface a truism. The activist leaders of the rebelling inhabitants from our urban ghettos vociferously declaim that nothing can be done *for* them only *by* them and most certainly *with* them. This is merely an extreme underlining of the new mood in urban planning; the somewhat belated recognition that for *new* cities, *new* people are necessary.

Citizens show up in the planning process at three levels as: (1) individual objects; (2) individual participators or actors; (3) group participants. As objects, citizens can be the target of public relations and public education or collaborative participants in the planning process; present practice is to involve them certainly at the community level in bootstrap operations. Manipulation by experts aided and abetted by public relations types is not in vogue. Most urban decisions are private, especially in the allocation of major capital resources; only through involvement at elite, average-citizen and disadvantaged levels can private decision-making be bent toward the general welfare—especially if rewarding guide lines and pecuniary lures are set by governments. Finally citizens' organizations, action-oriented, can lead, reinforce or "louse up" professional planning; this bewilders Europeans who expect governments, even at the municipal level, to govern, but is an absolute necessity, it would appear, in the power vacuum of contemporary American jurisdictions and practice. And involvement is especially necessary if the group dynamics people perceive correctly that means and ends are inseparable.

John W. Bodine, one of the original citizen activists for Philadelphia and President of *Penjerdel*,* tells the story of how "Young Turks," prior to the power elite's attention, started the Philadelphia renaissance and now in a most planful fashion are struggling to involve the whole metropolitan area. It is pretty hard going as Bodine shows, although the earlier experience within the political city of private persons successfully pushing government is an excellent illustration of citizen, as actor and as group participant. David R. Godschalk, planner, influenced by the activities analysis technique of F. Stuart Chapin Jr. and others, applies this to the ordinary citizen to discover what he does and what he would like to do in *collaborative planning*. This system has obvious costs in time, staff, capital, diversion of effort and limited vision, but Godschalk believes that the external social economies of the operation help to guarantee the eventual success of the evolving plan in actual operation. Citizen and plan are, thereby, entangled. It is hard to see how far the "planning counsellor," a new term not unconnected with advocacy planning,† can lead the citizens in such a friction-full operation, but past experience warns us that too many advanced professional plans do not advance in the real world of recalcitrant citizens.

Stretching the concept of citizens group participation slightly, K. C. Parsons, Cornell planner, assesses the increasingly heartening story of college and university (centers or branch) involvement in their urban places as good citizens. With the enormous boom in higher education, including the community commuter colleges, such institutions cannot escape to pastoral locations even if they now wanted to. With the interest in the higher culture traced in Chapter 12, the urban institution (a non-taxpayer and non-voter) is recognized as a major amenity resource with its drama, art, music, library and potential architectural excellence—as yet not widely realized in actual construction. Good universities create a climate for urban excellence. Parson's exploration of the single or multi-institutional development corporation as a "third man" to stand between the educational complex on one hand and the city government/local community on the other is a most perceptive induction from total experience to date.

* The citizens action group working toward a Philadelphia Metropolitan Area Plan.

† See Paul Davidoff's article in Chapter 13, "Planning as a Profession."

The Indispensable One-hundredth of 1 Percent
JOHN W. BODINE*

Many observers agree that among the very largest American cities, Philadelphia has had the most notable renaissance since World War II, and that this renaissance has been notable, not only for the extent of actual physical redevelopment, but also for the vitality of citizen participation. While Philadelphia still has enormous problems, including those in the area often referred to as "social planning," it also confronts major difficulties in relation to the surrounding metropolitan region, one of the most complex in the country. The question has thus arisen in many minds as to how the business and professional leadership, which has been so effective within the city, can become equally effective in the wider metropolitan region.

To answer this question requires some analysis of the stages by which the power elite became involved in Philadelphia's problems. In developing my ideas on this, I would like to start with a few generalizations. The first is that a massive citizen effort such as we have had in the last twenty-five years within the city limits of Philadelphia has two distinctive stages, only the second of which brings into play the power elite. The people who are active in the first stage are not members of the power elite at all. At least it is not their business or social influence that renders their contribution relevant or effective. But the people who are active in the first stage, and who are not members of the power elite, are the indispensable one-hundredth of 1 percent.

My next generalization is that while the power elite has been fully involved in the physical renaissance of Philadelphia for perhaps fifteen of the last twenty-five years (the city of Philadelphia having moved some fifteen years ago into this second stage) we are, on the other hand, in the metropolitan area centering on Philadelphia, still in the first of these two stages.

* President, *Penjerdel* (Pennsylvania-New Jersey-Delaware Metropolitan Project, Inc.) and Chairman, Community Leadership Seminar, Philadelphia. He was formerly President of the City Policy Committee and President of the Citizens' Council on City Planning, Philadelphia. He holds an M.A. (Oxon.). The following, as adapted, is reprinted with permission from *Planning, 1963*, published by the American Society of Planning Officials, where it appeared as "Key Issues for Human Welfare."

In the metropolitan area where we are trying to work out ways to deal with the increasingly difficult and complex problems, it is much too early to expect a contribution from the power elite. Here, I believe, we are still almost wholly dependent on the indispensable one-hundredth of 1 percent.

If we go back twenty-nine years, to 1938, we find Philadelphia deep in the doldrums for which it used to be celebrated—corrupt and contented; except that the corruption was really rather picayune, and the contentment was pretty largely confined to the Main Line. The nature and priority of important physical improvements were hammered out in the hurly-burly of councilmanic table-pounding, and the physical planning process, such as it was, was the responsibility of one or two lowly officials, who, in an obscure back office, were supposed in a vague sort of way to keep track of what was going on. The power elite was remote and uninterested. The corridors of city hall were literally offensive to the more delicate olfactory senses, and so long as the politicians had only modest ideas about the rates of taxes and of those somewhat unsavory indirect charges made for ordinances needed by businessmen, there was little need for the power elite to sully themselves with the smells of city hall.

But there were stirrings beneath the surface. In the 1939 election the Democrats and independent Republicans made a big effort to put over a fusion candidate for mayor. Many observers believe that by an honest count of votes he would have won the election; but the Republican organization candidate was officially elected by forty thousand votes.

Now at this point a significant event occurred. There had been in the fusion campaign office a group of young idealists—ignorant of urban affairs, inexperienced in politics, without prestige or power, in some cases without very demanding jobs (the Depression lifted slowly in Philadelphia), but with ample public spirit and a willingness to work. After their candidate lost the mayoralty election, they didn't do what the power elite was doing—basking in the fleshpots of the Main Line. Instead, they started to study the city of Philadelphia.

They organized an association, called the City Policy Committee, consisting of about fifty people—considerably less than one-hundredth of one percent of the city's total population. The City Policy Committee had no budget and no staff; it merely met twice a month for several years to hear presentations by anybody who could tell them about any phase of the city government and its problems—politicians, department heads, officials of all kinds, editors, social workers, school principals, and so on. After a year or two of this the Young Turks, as they are now called, concluded that the institution the city needed most was a planning commission; and they decided to concentrate on this objective.

They studied the planning process from A to Z; they visited other cities to learn how planning was done there; they drafted an ordinance to create a modern planning commission; and then it dawned on them that they needed some access to power to get their ordinance enacted. The power elite was still remote, uninterested, and completely unorganized for such an enterprise. Fortunately, however, the Young Turks had caught the interest of one member of the power elite. The senior partner of one of the principal investment banking firms in the city listened, and finally gave the proposal his support. A few other prestigious persons joined him. But the real backing for the proposal came from a variety of civic groups whose interest and activity had been carefully mobilized and directed by the City Policy Committee and by other similar citizens' organizations.

In the end the ordinance was passed. Several of the prominent citizens nominated by the City Policy Committee were appointed by the mayor to the new Planning Commission, including the head of the investment banking firm, and Robert B. Mitchell was engaged as director. The first steps toward the physical renaissance of the city had been taken.

The Young Turks, of course, continued to keep up the pressure. They organized the Citizens' Council on City Planning, consisting of representatives of some 150 citizen organizations throughout the city, to provide a two-way liaison between the public-spirited citizen and the planning process. After the war, the Young Turks had the satisfaction of seeing one of their own members—Edmund Bacon—appointed as director of the Planning Commission. But for purposes of the present discussion their next most significant step was to conceive and promote the Better Philadelphia Exhibit—a dazzling and imaginative demonstration of what the physical development of Philadelphia could be. For this purpose a greater involvement of the power elite was required, and the Young Turks persuaded several business leaders to help raise the necessary money and to arrange space for the exhibition in a downtown department store. In six weeks the exhibit was visited by 450,-000 people, and I have often heard Ed Bacon remark that the school children who saw the exhibit in 1947 are today voting on the city's bond issues for public improvements of the type first dramatized in that exhibit. But what was even more significant, the exhibit once and for all opened the eyes of the power elite to the possibilities for Philadelphia's development. Not long after the exhibit, the Greater Philadelphia Movement was born.

In other words the decade following 1939 was a seminal period when a group of able, hardworking, public-spirited people outside of the power elite educated themselves about the city and its problems; when their awareness of city problems was disseminated through an ever-widening circle of citizen associations, also outside of the power elite; and when the resulting public pressure for change made possible new governmental institutions to achieve desirable public objectives, such as the planning commission and a new breed of public official. After this first stage had been brought to full flower in the Better Philadelphia Exhibit, the idea of the physical redevelopment of the city had become sufficiently respectable so that powerful private leaders could organize for the express purpose of moving toward a greater Philadelphia.

The framework for my discussion so far has been the city limits of Philadelphia. I would now like to turn to a broader area—the metropolitan region of which Philadelphia is the center. In the last fifteen years, while the influence of our power elite was being so successfully applied to downtown Philadelphia, the focus of our urban problems has been undergoing a dramatic shift. Whereas in 1950 the population of Philadelphia constituted 50 percent of our eleven-county region, by 1960, for the first time in history, the suburban area had passed the city and accounted for 60 percent of the five million regional total. With this shift has come a tumultuous extension of our urban problems: largely uncontrolled development threatening us with suburban slums and blight in the future; demands for additional governmental services in suburban areas, with resulting upward pressures on tax rates, and often cutthroat competition for the presumed advantages of new commercial and industrial ratables; and pressing needs for a more economical and orderly suburban transportation system, for preservation of our fast disappearing open space, for improved air pollution control, for extending and rationalizing our sewage systems, and ultimately for some planning process at the intercounty level.

All over America the same tidal wave of urbanism has burst the previous limits of our cities and has engulfed in common difficulties areas which for centuries have been unconcerned with each other's problems. The inadequacy of suburban governments to deal with expanding urbanism is all too familiar. With few exceptions, they are too small, too numerous, too weak, too poor to formulate effective policies or to carry them out. Yet experience leads us to doubt in many cases that any new layer of metropolitan government will win acceptance from suburban communities in time either to avert the worst of their crises or to maximize the best of their potentials. This is particularly true in the region around Philadelphia. Three hundred and seventy-seven municipalities in eleven counties, plus several hundred school districts and other autonomous agencies, present formidable obstacles to coherent policymaking. In addition, when you consider that they lie in parts of three states, each with different constitutional powers, each with different systems of local government, and each of course with a separate legislature much more concerned with the problems of other parts of the state, then you have complexity triply compounded.

But for purposes of our present discussion, I would like to emphasize the impediments to citizen activity presented by these hundreds of local governments. Not only does this system present a bewildering array of targets for citizen action, but how can you get citizens excited about a local government with only limited powers? No wonder so many of our suburban jurisdictions drift in a sargasso sea of inertia and conformity, with relatively little political competition.

Similarly the distances and differences between suburbs result in a marked dispersal of civic leadership. In a major city center, civic institutions can be nurtured by like-minded volunteers over the lunch table; but citizens who live and work in widely separated suburban areas have no similar means to know one another and to link hands in common civic enterprise.

In addition, the complexity and vagueness of our metropolitan problems are enough to discourage the most eager of civic beavers. Our regional transportation questions, for example, are highly complex, involving a mixed group of railroads, bus and traction companies, city-owned subways, authorities operating bridges and high-speed lines, approximately one million private automobiles and a corresponding number of trucks—all subject to numerous planning and regulatory agencies of three state governments and the federal government, and supported in varying degree by subsidies from various governmental quarters. I submit that it will take years of patient study and analysis before the issues involved in planning a sensible regional transportation system for the entire region are ready for the quick and clear-cut decisions to which the elite are accustomed.

Similarly with the difficulties of designing a sensible program for preserving open space in our region, whether for recreation or for reservoirs or industrial sites; similarly with the many scientific uncertainties and the administrative complexities of a regional program for the control of air pollution. And with respect to a more fundamental problem—that of persuading several hundred governments, each jealous of its autonomy, to cooperate in a comprehensive planning program to guide regional development—few members of the elite can take the time to grasp all the factors and personalities involved so as to assume a position of power on this issue.

Then there is the difficulty, in these complicated metropolitan affairs, of actually showing any results. As the distinguished head of the Regional Plan Association has put it, "In regional affairs, it's a long time between drinks." Progress in this field takes more than vision—it takes visionaries, and few of these are found among those who wield real power.

We can, of course, see the beginnings of the process by which this power will eventually be exercised. In the first place, the elite are steadily asserting more influence on the difficult urban problems of our larger cities. The Greater Trenton Council has had a marked impact on Trenton, the Greater Wilmington Development Council has spearheaded the awakening of planning consciousness in Wilmington, the Greater Camden Movement is beginning to bring Camden's resources to bear on their city's needs. These movements are beginning to have an influence in their communities comparable to the influence in Philadelphia of the Greater Philadelphia Movement. But these centers of elite power have not so far linked hands in a concerted move on any general regional issue.

In the second place, some members of the elite are showing a concern for a few regional situations where there has been extended study and where the issues are by now clear-cut and demonstrably affect our economic security. Take for example the problems of the Delaware River: evening out the alternation of floods and droughts, reducing pollution, improving navigation, providing for water-based recreation. These have at last become the responsibility of a federal-interstate commission, seemingly with adequate powers and budget. In attaining this result the power elite played a significant part. But we have come this far only after at least thirty years of haggling and frustration, a Ford Foundation grant of $175,000 to the Maxwell School for a study of feasible methods of organizing the basin, and the establishment of a basinwide citizens' organization with over twenty thousand addressograph plates.

Notwithstanding these beginnings, I submit that, so far as our general metropolitan situation is concerned, the difficulties of geographic dispersal, the complexity of intergovernmental problems, the frequently shifting variables, the obscurity of the feasible alternatives, the impossibility of showing quick results, and above all, the difficulty of visualizing the costly consequences of inaction—all these are formidable hurdles to citizen effort.

In this situation where do we turn for civic leadership? My thesis is that, just as in the first stage of the renaissance of Philadelphia twenty-five years ago, we must look to the indispensable one-hundredth of 1 percent, to some five hundred out of our five million population, to the public-spirited, non-prestigious workers in the civic vineyard, the people who have the time and the patience to study through these vexing questions, to sort out the alternatives, to make the solutions they arrive at respectable and even commonplace, and thus to prepare the way to usher in the second stage when the power elite can take over.

The members of the indispensable one-hundredth of 1 percent differ in several respects from what one would expect to find in the typical power structure. In the first place, while most of the men are reasonably successful in business, they do not include many top executives, even of small-town businesses, nor do they include many real leaders of the professions. In the second place, the group includes far more women than would be included in any usual definition of the power elite. These are mostly public-spirited housewives, usually college graduates, who have become attracted to public issues through their Leagues of Women Voters, for example, and who have applied their talents and relatively freer time to greasing the wheels of citizen organizations. Thirdly, the typical individual in the group has been much more closely tied over a long period to the community where he lives than is necessarily the case with the members of the power structure, even in an old city like Philadelphia. It follows that the members of our Penjerdel constituency do not include many employees of large corporations operating on a national scale, who would be subject to an abrupt move to another part of the country.

Another major contrast between the members of the power elite and our suburban constituents results from the vastly different scale of the business or professional responsibility assumed by the members of each group. The central city business leader is in the habit of dealing with very large matters, involving large amounts of money and the policies of large organizations. His problems may be varied and complex, but because of the scale of the operation it is possible, indeed necessary, for alternatives to be largely predigested by subordinates and presented to the top executives for speedy and clear-cut decision. The members of our suburban constituency, on the other hand, are not under such pressure of large responsibility and are not so much in the habit of relying on subordinates. They have the patience and the time to consider a vexatious public question from many angles and to go through the often laborious process of sorting out the important from the unimportant. Furthermore, while our suburban friends are secure in their environment, and may have prestige in local circles, they are not, because of differences of scale, exposed to so numerous or so varied a group of potential critics as the downtown business leader. Accordingly, they are less concerned about risking their more limited prestige on some novel public issue than their big-city counterparts.

In one important respect, however, the members of the one-hundredth of 1 percent have something in common with the members of the power elite. While a few members of both groups have been elected to public office, in general the members of both these groups are not active in practical politics. In part this is because the members of both groups shrink from the unpleasant notoriety and public controversy which may be associated with running for and holding public office. In part it is also traceable to the security enjoyed by the members of both groups, which they do not wish to sacrifice for the uncertainties of a political career.

On the other hand, when it comes to working out means of close cooperation with those who do get elected to public office, there is again a difference between the non-prestigious suburbanite and the downtown power elite. In Philadelphia, and increasingly in our other central cities, the power elite has learned how much can be accomplished by working with and often pressuring city officials. Our indispensable suburban friends, however, have only limited influence on the suburban officeholders. Basically I believe this is because, unlike the power elite in Philadelphia, they are limited to a multitude of small governments, which often lack the power or the economic resources to deal with the problems confronting their communities, and which are frequently run by persons of quite different social values and a different order of ability.

Of course there are some persons of wealth, social position, and business power who do take the trouble to concern themselves with even our complex metropolitan questions, and their contribution is invaluable. But I submit that they do so from an unusual measure of conviction and dedication, that their present effectiveness is based far more on these qualities than on their position or power, and that their hands are linked at this stage, not with their fellow members of the power elite, but with their more lowly fellow citizens.

I have tried to show from our experience over twenty-five years in Philadelphia why a group of dedicated, non-prestigious amateurs is indispensable to initiating civic progress in a complex situation. I have tried to describe how the members of this group differ from the power elite in their aptitude for this indispensable initial task. I would now like to describe how the organization we know as Penjerdel sought throughout our eleven-county region to arouse the interest of the indispensable one-hundredth of 1 percent, and to bind them structurally into the Penjerdel organization. It may be that the peculiar complexities of our region, possibly exceeded only in the New York metropolitan area, make our program of less general application; but I venture to describe it nevertheless, as we believe that it provides perhaps the longest, but what may well be the surest road to sorting out regional issues and mobilizing support for their solution.

Penjerdel is a regionwide civic agency. It is one of the metropolitan projects which the Ford Foundation has supported in different parts of the country. It is a tribute to Paul Ylvisaker's patience and daring that he has encouraged each of these to seek a different road toward metropolitan progress. Penjerdel was not created to make plans for our region nor even to advocate specific solutions. Its more limited objective has been twofold—to gather facts and insights about the region, and to disseminate this and other information about the region as widely as possible. This twofold program is reflected in Penjerdel's structure, as we are sponsored by fifteen colleges and universities in the region and by over one hundred citizen organizations of great variety and from throughout our eleven counties.

I leave aside, as not central to our present discussion, the work our college and university friends have been doing to study the massive problems of our area, and turn instead to the second part of our activities. This public information program has included the usual techniques of issuing a newsletter, holding regionwide conferences on important interjurisdictional problems, publicizing these problems through the mass media, and publishing reports on regional questions for our non-technical audience.

There is, however, one part of our public information program which we believe has never been tried before on such a large geographical scale—namely, our deliberate effort to organize a regionwide apparatus of citizen organizations.

To this end we first inventoried all of the citizen organizations throughout the region, and found that there were several thousand of them. We then tried to develop criteria for identifying those most likely to be concerned with interjurisdictional problems. These were the countywide organizations—chiefly associations of farmers, labor unions, leagues of women voters, and elected officials; the stream valley associations, which were accustomed to dealing with the numerous municipalities in a single watershed; and a very few general-purpose, countywide improvement associations. Then there were the organizations, largely in the central cities, which by virtue of long establishment and competence of staff offered additional potential for assisting and guiding our program. We found that there were about a hundred organizations which met these and similar criteria.

Our first step was to ask each of these groups to designate one of their number as a member of the Penjerdel corporation. In this way we vested the control of the entire Penjerdel operation directly in the hands of persons designated for that purpose by these hundred citizen groups. These hundred designees were the first members of our indispensable one-hundredth of 1 percent.

Our next step was to make our staff available, where we were invited to do so, to help these hundred groups get more dependable information about the regional setting in which they find themselves, and to direct their attention to the problems of the future. In a very tentative manner we have used a small part of the money received from the Ford Foundation to make a few grants to some of these citizen groups, to help them pay staff and other expenses so as to strengthen their own programs of citizen education.

We then started creating regionwide committees on important regional issues, drawn for the most part from the public-spirited, but generally non-prestigious persons who make up these citizen organizations. Two of these committees became fully operative—one on regional open space problems, and one on regional transportation problems. These committees met monthly in Philadelphia; they rarely decided anything; their principal function was to exchange ideas and news about what was going on in different parts of the region, and to hear presentations of current programs of governmental agencies. The value to the participants was demonstrated by the regularity of their attendance, often in spite of the substantial travel required, into and out of Philadelphia. The analogy is striking to the early meetings of the City Policy Committee two decades ago.

These committees were not composed primarily of persons with technical skill in these fields of open space and transportation. For the most part they were representatives from citizen organizations which themselves have open space or transportation committees. They represented the beginning of what could become a full array of regional citizen's committees, drawn from throughout the metropolitan area, meeting regularly in Philadelphia, getting to know each other and the regional problems each has, and forming the nexus of patient, informed, hard-working citizenry which we believe is the most dependable basis for eventual progress on regional problems.

We set up several other regionwide committees which act in an advisory capacity to the various research projects we have sponsored. For the most part these committees were composed of persons who are already experts in some aspect of the subject being investigated; but for purposes of our present discussion it is significant that we have been able to interest a number of members from citizen organizations to participate in these research advisory committees as well.

In all this work we have been trying to create the conditions in which citizen organizations will grow from their inner convictions and will reach across boundaries to share a concern for regional questions. In this effort to create a regionwide citizen structure the most ambitious and yet the most delicate part was the encouragement of new countywide citizen groups. We chose the county as the framework for this effort, not because of the present powers of county government. In New Jersey and Pennsylvania these are considerably inferior in range and relevance to urban problems to the powers of the local governments. Rather we picked the county because the counties include both "have" and "have not" municipalities and thus can straddle the major economic inequalities of the smaller units. Also the counties can afford competent staffs and, in Pennsylvania at any rate, have been increasingly active in physical planning and in the encouragement of regional developments such as the program of subsidizing our commuting railroads. Furthermore, the population of each county—hundreds of thousands of people in the case of ten out of our eleven counties—includes a wide variety of social attributes and values. Our reasoning was that if we could get the civic leaders of the many communities in a particular county to make common cause, we were well on the way to regional civic organization.

Before Penjerdel began its program there were of course numerous, well-established, countywide organizations in Philadelphia (the city and county of Philadelphia being coterminous); and two of our suburban counties had the beginnings of countywide organizations of the type I am about to describe. Since that time Penjerdel assisted the two existing organizations in suburban counties and acted as midwife at the establishment of such organizations in three more suburban counties.

These new organizations have four principal characteristics. None is particularly novel, but whatever innovation is involved inheres in the combination of all four factors. To begin with, each such organization is truly countywide, drawing its membership from all parts of the county, however varied and disparate. The framework of organization thus clearly recognizes, even dramatizes, the fact that many public problems are increasingly intermunicipal in their scope. Secondly, each such organization is widely representative. It makes a deliberate attempt to embrace all interests in the county—businessmen, labor leaders, farmers, social workers, representatives of women's organizations—in general, all types of people who are concerned for the future of the county. Third, these organizations are non-partisan and non-political, so as to keep their membership open to all, and so as to be able to deal impartially with whatever elected officials happen to be in power.

Finally, these organizations have a quite flexible program. They are general-purpose organizations, able to devote their attention to whatever problems facing the county seem most important. Most of them have been attracted to the questions of physical planning, but some have committees working on social planning, or reform of the county prison, or research into county fiscal questions. These new organizations thus differ from the established special-purpose county organizations, such as the county Boards of Agriculture or the county Chamber of Commerce or even the Health & Welfare Council. The new organizations are at once more widely representative and more flexible.

There are two features of their programs which deserve mention. In the first place, they consider themselves as a two-way line of communication between concerned citizens in the county and the county agencies which are increasingly responsible for encouraging orderly development. And they strive to keep important county issues under continuous study so that when a public question arises, often in an acute and pressing form, they will be prepared to act in a constructive and well-informed manner. Usually this is done by establishing committees on such intermunicipal issues as transportation, air pollution, industrial development, open space reservation, and so on.

Our experience with these organizations indicated that they encounter two principal difficulties. First, there is their relationship to the existing organizations. The usual criticism is that there is only so much money and manpower to go around and a new organization will weaken those already in existence. Our response to this was to encourage these new organizations to work wherever possible with the existing groups, to divide areas of interest between them in a cooperative spirit, and to exchange information to their mutual advantage. Curiously enough, it was also our experience in some of these counties that the emergence of a new countywide organization actually produced new people not previously active in civic affairs who are attracted by the importance of the new organization's objectives and program.

A second principal difficulty encountered by these organizations is that in bringing together widely different interests from throughout the country, they have exposed themselves to serious disagreements on issues on which the different parts of the country are badly divided. Our advice was that for the time being, until they have much deeper roots, these tender saplings should not buck the winds of controversy, but should confine their activities to issues on which there is considerable countywide agreement. The citizen viewpoint on highly controversial matters can be adequately presented by the presently existing local or special purpose organizations. The new countywide groups must eventually practice the art of reconciling widely differing viewpoints, but this is more likely to be a function of their increasing maturity than of their early stages.

Penjerdel was the midwife, not the parent of these new organizations. We could not direct or even supervise. But sooner or later there could be such organizations in each of the ten suburban counties of our region, each with a frame of reference and structure reasonably parallel to the others, and each eventually with an office and a competent professional staff. Our present structure permits each such organization to have a vote in our affairs and to send from its committees on special intermunicipal topics representatives to Penjerdel's region-wide committees on those topics at the center. We have thereby sought to underscore the fundamental responsibility borne by these groups for regional progress.

Lest you suspect that we were seeking to build centers of political activity, let me promptly disabuse you. It is my firm belief that it will be years and years, if ever, before we will see in a region as complex as ours any steps toward political activity on any truly regional level. But no doubt the piles we drove into the intellectual mud will some day bear a more durable civic structure, and this may become a shelter or a platform for local politicians willing to move toward new forms of intergovernmental cooperation.

So far as our results are concerned, we involved in these regional activities several hundred citizens from all parts of our region, and we were thus on the way toward mobilizing the five hundred volunteers who would constitute one-hundredth of 1 percent of our region's population. It was to the care and feeding—you might say—of this indispensable fraction of our citizenry that Penjerdel devoted a great deal of its effort—supplying them with information on regional questions; inviting them to regional conferences and forums, where they can become better informed; making them members of regional study committees on open space and transportation; giving them an opportunity to participate in an ongoing regional citizen effort.

Beyond this, our staff work was directed toward strengthening their organizations in all their variety. We have no weapons except persuasion and ideas, with here and there a little money from the amounts made available to us by the Ford Foundation. Our greatest satisfaction came from cross-fertilization of the different interests from different parts of the region. It was not merely that our staff, flying like bees from the civic flowers in one part of the region to those in another, carried news or ideas from one area to receptive groups in another. We also succeeded, despite the impediments of geographic dispersal, in encouraging fruitful contacts between our constituents. For example, much of the time at one of our open space committee meetings might be taken up with the members of citizen organizations from one part of the region telling their counterparts from another part, perhaps seventy-five miles away, about programs which they have found to be successful. And when we have encouraged citizen groups in one part of our region to invite planning officials from some other part to make a presentation at one of their meetings, this has resulted in a quite novel advance in planning interest by cross-fertilization from that distant, yet interrelated source.

If this structure, based not on direction from above, but on grass roots interest and conviction, can grow across our region, we will be far along toward building a vigorous source of support for our new regional institutions, such as our Regional Conference of Elected Officials, a possible Regional Data Service, Regional Planning Commission, Regional Air Pollution Council, and even a possible regionwide social planning group in the private sector.

But far more important than these consequences will be the one to which this paper addressed itself in the beginning. The patient work of these citizen organizations can sharpen the issues, clarify the alternatives, make regional affairs commonplace and respectable, and perhaps most important, give visibility to those officials among our hundreds of suburban officeholders who are alert to the hazards of spreading urbanism and responsive to citizen suggestion. Then at last we will have reached the second stage, when the power elite can join hands throughout the region and give their decisive support to new techniques, already on the horizon, for institutionalizing our approach to regional questions.

In other words, the process of getting the power elite involved in key issues for human welfare is like a two-stage rocket. The most dependable way to get the gilt-edge capsule that holds the power elite into really effective orbit is to put it there with a first-stage rocket powered by the indispensable one-hundredth of 1 percent. Academic research will help to chart the voyage; professional staffs will tighten the bolts and screws; a marked receptivity to new ideas will certainly be required of our civic cosmonauts. But the fuel for that first indispensable stage must come, not from pressure, but from patience; not from prominence, but from humility; not from wealth, but from vision; not from power, but from dedication.

The Circle of Urban Participation

DAVID R. GODSCHALK*

"And if provision for dialogue and drama, in all their ramifications, is one of the essential offices of the city, then one key to urban development should be plain—it lies in the widening of the circle of those capable of participating in it, till in the end all men will take part in the conversation."[1]

Advances in communications technology conceivably could make possible two-way television hookups vast enough to permit town meetings at the metropolitan scale. However, the successful working of such mass-decision processes would be doubtful, since the unitary social structure which underlay the old New England town meeting has splintered like a kaleidoscope image in the contemporary metropolis. In addition to problems of massive scale and complexity, metropolitan decisions are complicated by disturbing awareness of the inevitability of change. Still, in a democracy it should be both possible and desirable to devise means of participation by all citizens, regardless of race, influence, or income, in the shaping of urban policies and plans.

Existing political and electoral processes have proven ineffectual as channels of citizen involvement in urban develop-

* Assistant Professor of Urban and Regional Planning, Florida State University, Tallahassee; formerly with Milo Smith and Associates, Inc., Planning Consultants in Tampa and Planning Director, 1964–65, of Gainesville, Florida. Holder of a Dartmouth B.A., he received an M.C.P. from North Carolina in 1964 as a Pittsburgh Plate Glass Foundation Fellow, and an A.I.P. Student Award winner. He is the author of several professional journal articles and numerous published planning reports for Florida communities.
[1] Lewis Mumford, *The City in History* (New York: Harcourt, Brace & World, Inc., 1961), p. 117.

ment. What is needed is a *modus operandi* which brings governmental planners face-to-face with citizens in a continuous cooperative venture. Such a venture could not only educate and involve the community in planning, but could also educate and involve the planners in their community.

There is heartening evidence that the seeds of such ventures, which could be broadly identified as *collaborative planning,* are being sown in progressive planning programs. This paper will introduce the concept of collaborative planning, develop a method of operationalizing the concept through activities analysis techniques, describe an example from a pilot application in a medium-sized community, and discuss some pros and cons of the approach.

THE COLLABORATIVE PLANNING CONCEPT

Toronto, bold in its metropolitan government innovation, has also been bold in creating a planning process which directly involves citizens. When staff members of the City of Toronto Planning Board complete a set of proposals for one of the City's twenty-five planning districts, these are distributed in summary form to every district household and business establishment. Before these proposals become part of the official city plan, they are discussed at small group meetings within each sub-area of the district, amended in the light of citizen comments, and reviewed by elected officials along with scrupulously recorded reports of all citizen suggestions. Within a viable program, citizens take part in planning for their district at the same time as politicians, planners, and public officials are made conscious of district needs and desires.[2]

Toronto furnishes an excellent example of collaborative planning in action. All of the critical elements are included. First, the approach itself is geared to recognize and involve entire subcommunities. The client is clearly the public rather than special interests or the power structure. Second, the spirit is obviously one of planning *with* the people of the district rather than planning *for* them. Staff ideas are considered proposals for citizen discussion rather than master plans to be

[2] W. Harold Clark, paper delivered at "Public Consultation in the Planning Process Panel," American Society of Planning Officials and Community Planning Association of Canada Joint Planning Conference (Toronto, Canada, 1965). See also City of Toronto Planning Board, *Plan for the Don,* 1963, and other area proposals.

sold to the public. Third, the communications techniques employed are two-way discussions and dialogues. The care with which citizen suggestions and reactions are recorded and reported implies concern for a genuine interchange between the people and the planners, far beyond the hollow formalities of the typical "public hearing."

Collaborative planning, as used here, is thus similar to the collaborative marketing approach which assumes that the consumer is unsure of his specific desires but would be interested in defining them with the help of a knowledgeable counselor. Nelson N. Foote has contrasted this collaborative marketing approach with early "persuasive" or hard-sell marketing, and the more recent "listening" or poll-taking approach.[3] Planning has followed a parallel course, from the historic "music man" consultant selling package plans across the land, through the current attitude surveys awkwardly tacked onto standard planning programs. Now, some programs such as Toronto are evolving into full-fledged collaborative planning, where citizens are routinely consulted as an integral part of the process.

In addition to putting the planner into the role of a counselor, the collaborative approach opens many lines of communications with groups not usually represented through governmental channels. It can serve as a kind of early-warning system for impending social crises and changes. Here the approach is necessarily concerned with human activities, in addition to the traditional planning emphasis on land use patterns.

ANALYSIS OF URBAN ACTIVITIES

In a comprehensive study of cities, human activities are inseparable from urban facilities and institutions. For instance, without stockbrokers and market activities, Wall Street, as we visualize it today, is meaningless. Similarly, all urban areas are animated by human activities, both at the individual level and joined in organizations. A city may even be thought of as a collection of linked and interdependent activity systems through which individuals and establishments seek objectives within a particular physical setting. Activity systems refer to identifiable behavior patterns of people and organizations. Compared to the static urban image provided by maps of land use, the activities image is dynamic.

[3] Nelson N. Foote et al., *Housing Choices and Housing Constraints* (New York: McGraw-Hill, 1960), p. 308.

This dynamic image may be analyzed in terms of the linkages between establishments, the activities of various types of establishments, and the relationship between establishment activities and land use. The most complete analyses of these factors to date have been the metropolitan transportation studies. Aided by computers in processing vast amounts of data from interviews with people and from measurements of travel and land use characteristics, these transportation studies have produced workable theoretical models of urban movement systems.

Much information about the quantity of an activity can be obtained from statistical measurements, such as deriving the average number of daily automobile trips per acre of low-density, middle-income, single-family residential land use. However, it has been necessary to talk directly with people for other information, especially that concerning the quality of activity. Only the participant can furnish descriptions of his sensations, reactions, and motivations, which may be the more important long-run aspects of activities. Thus all types of activities analysis make extensive use of interviews.

Activities studies to date, like theories of urban behavior, have tended to specialize. In addition to transportation, studies have been made of central business district firms and of household leisure activities. Rannells explored the relationships between central business district activities and their physical setting in a pioneering effort using combined graphic and statistical techniques.[4] Experimental studies by Chapin and Hightower have attempted to identify and measure existing activity patterns and to explore possible future changes in household activity systems.[5] Concentrating on leisure activities, they asked people to describe their time budget of major activities and their locations for the previous twenty-four-hour period, to discuss their attitudes and satisfactions with present activity patterns, and to participate in a game aimed at discovering

[4] John Rannells, *The Core of the City: A Pilot Study of Changing Land Uses in Central Business Districts* (New York: Columbia University Press, 1956).

[5] F. Stuart Chapin, Jr. and Henry C. Hightower, "Household Activity Patterns and Land Use," *Journal of the American Institute of Planners*, XXXI (August 1965), pp. 222–31. See also: F. Stuart Chapin, Jr., *Urban Land Use Planning*, (2d ed.; Urbana: University of Illinois Press, 1965), pp. 69–106, and pp. 221–53; and Henry C. Hightower, "Recreation Activity Analysis: Toward a Spatial and Aspatial Methodology for Urban Planning" (unpublished Ph.D. dissertation, Department of City and Regional Planning, University of North Carolina).

possible future changes in the use of leisure. As research efforts the primary goals of these studies were to advance urban theory and to improve planning predictive tools. A long-range hope is the formulation of a general theory of urban activities.

ACTIVITY ANALYSIS AS A COLLABORATIVE PLANNING TECHNIQUE

In addition to use in research, activity analysis can be a useful tool for operational planning agencies. It furnishes a possible bridge between planner and citizen around which a collaborative planning process can be organized. This bridge is the community dialogue, a continuous process of give-and-take based on activities interviews and discussions.

In this process the planning agency begins public consultation in the early stages of its research, and continues through various plan-making and implementation stages. As in cybernetics, there is an integral feedback mechanism which controls and adjusts the continuing planning process. This feedback, in the form of information about citizen attitudes, values, and activities patterns, tells about actual versus expected performance of plans and actual versus stereotyped life styles and activity patterns. In an operational context in which planning is a participant in social change, as well as an observer and predictor, the use of activities analysis will necessarily be broader than in specific research studies.

An example from a pilot household activities analysis conducted in Gainesville, Florida illustrates the potential of the collaborative process.[6] A conflict between the needs and activities of two subcommunities was discovered through household interviews and field observations by the planning department. The problem was brought to the attention of the decision-makers involved, and a policy was evolved to minimize future conflicts in the area.

In Gainesville, which has developed around a state university, a general shortage of rental housing coupled with a climbing enrollment had caused a sizable invasion of rural working-class neighborhoods by university students. Because of their

[6] For a more complete description of the Gainesville study, see David R. Godschalk and William E. Mills, "A Collaborative Approach to Planning through Urban Activities," a manuscript accepted for publication in the *Journal of the American Institute of Planners* for February 1966.

greater financial power, the students were displacing working-class residents from older single-family rental dwellings as well as creating a demand for new apartment groups on land formerly occupied by old houses. Not only were working-class residents displaced downward in the housing market, but also their previously socially supportive neighborhoods were disrupted. These were major problems for working families whose incomes were stretched tightly by the costs of necessities such as food, clothing and rent, and whose friendly neighbors helped out in time of trouble.

Located between a major thoroughfare and an industrial area, these neighborhoods were part of a working-class residential district which had experienced considerable pressure for change from existing single-family residential zoning. Their informal and somewhat rural appearance would have earned them ratings of rundown or even blighted in the usual planning "windshield" survey, but their residents found them comfortable and pleasant places to live. Unaesthetic and inefficient by middle-class standards, they were considered prime targets for rezoning for apartments and commercial uses by real estate speculators.

Without some policy which recognized the needs of the working people as well as students and speculators, the majority of working-class residents would have been forced to seek new locations. Those remaining would have faced increasing social stress.

As this issue emerged from the activities analysis it was passed on to the Plan Board, who studied interview results and neighborhood field reports in working out planning objectives for the area. The one neighborhood which had clearly become primarily a student neighborhood was identified and designated for high-density apartment use. Those still predominantly working-class single family parts of the district were maintained as single-family areas. These proposals were incorporated in a district land use plan which was approved by the City Commission.

In addition to recognizing the needs of working-class neighborhoods, the question of accommodating off-campus student housing in the over-all city plan was also involved. As a joint city-university problem this was studied in a public forum with the Plan Board and university housing officials. It was recognized that significant factors included transportation between housing and the campus, as well as the cost, quantity and quality of dwellings. There was need for provision of housing and related facilities for shopping and recreation in groupings large enough to allow the development of community spirit. Among the preliminary conclusions were: student housing should be encouraged in concentrations near the campus rather than scattered in outlying low-income areas; and land use plans should be developed accordingly.

The particular outcome is not as relevant as the way in which a community issue was discovered and transmitted through planning channels. Without household interviews this issue would have received little attention, since the students and working-class people involved did not have established communications linkages with city government. This issue, along with others discovered during the Gainesville activities analysis, has been incorporated into an "activities base," which serves as a kind of urban intelligence file for continuing planning.

PROS AND CONS OF COLLABORATIVE PLANNING

In light of universal difficulties with planning programs, it may seem that involving the public will only cause more complications in an already complex task. However, if planning effectiveness is measured in terms of improving opportunities for human activities and development, rather than solely in terms of efficiency of plan-making, then collaboration is justified. Toronto stands out as a city with both an impressive record of effective planning and an active collaborative process.

One obvious problem is the additional staff required for collaborative planning. The Gainesville activities analysis used graduate students and social workers as interviewers, under the direction of a trained planner. Another way to provide the necessary public contact would be to use retired persons or those not presently in the labor force as participant observers in various sub-communities. Training for these local "planning agents" could be handled through adult education or extension courses. Not only would this reduce the demands on scarce planning personnel, but participant observers could also provide a stronger and more continuous linkage than repeated interviews. One further way to handle research and citizen participation would be through an urban institute which could serve as a local communication center. The institute could channel information to the planning agency, while serving as a focus for citizen participation.[7]

Another problem results from the difficulty of synthesizing large amounts of complicated activities data. Computers can be expected to help out. However, the tendency of computers and statistical techniques for handling massive data to suppress individual irregularities will require careful programming if the results are not to be homogenized. It seems that new social science analytical techniques will need to be developed to handle activities data.

There is also the problem of the apparent political nature of the collaborative process. However, it has long been recognized that planning and politics are inseparable parts of the democratic process of government. To bury the head of a planning agency in the sands of purely technical operation is to deny the creative responsibility of planning.

Finally, the question arises as to how much time the planning agency can take away from administration and comprehensive plan preparation for collaborative work. This will vary according to the depth of commitment to citizen involvement. As Chapin points out, activities analysis can be considered as another tooling up study for planning.[8] However, in a deeper sense the collaborative process could also be considered an alternative to the comprehensive planning process as it is practiced today. Garrison suggests that with increasingly good information and methods of feedback, the 1975 transportation planning model ". . . should be less of a long-range forecasting device and more of a guiding device to keep development on course in light of a high level of information."[9] Similarly, urban planning could be freed from historical forecasting techniques which often produce plans that are obsolete when implemented. By substituting a vigorous collaborative planning process, planning would become a guidance device, firmly rooted in actual human activities and values.

In summary, the collaborative planning process described

---

[7] A regional institute which has structured its program to serve as a nerve center is the Urban Research Center of Florida State University at Titusville, Florida. An institute has been suggested for inclusion in the development program of the new town of Columbia in Maryland, with the rare opportunity of observing and participating in an urban community from inception.

[8] F. Stuart Chapin, Jr., *Urban Land Use Planning*, p. 221.

[9] W. L. Garrison, "Urban Transportation Planning Models in 1975," *Journal of the American Institute of Planners*, XXXI (May 1965), p. 157.

here puts the planner in the role of public development counselor. Rather than attempting to impose his own values and life style, he seeks to know the values and life styles of his client community. Activities analysis is one useful tool for gaining this understanding, especially when used as a two-way communications device as well as an analytical technique. Although usually employed separately, there is much to be gained by combining the collaborative planning process as used in Toronto with the activities analysis as used in recent urban research. Planning under this approach could ultimately become a guidance device which evolved not only better plans but also better planners and better citizens until finally all men were capable of joining the circle of urban participation.

The Role of Universities in City Renewal

K. C. PARSONS*

THE BEGINNINGS OF UNIVERSITY RENEWAL

The rural-small town image of university environment fades slowly in America. While there are scholarly uses of isolation, our urban civilization and our universities are gradually trading pieces of agrarian mythology for the realities of the world.

There are difficulties as well as advantages for universities and colleges in the city. Land is expensive, and expansion generates struggles with local government and neighbors. Blight

* Professor and Chairman, Department of City and Regional Planning, Cornell University. He was with the Cleveland City Planning Commission from 1953 to 1957, ending his service there as Head, Community Planning Section. He has acted as consultant for Cleveland; Lakewood, Ohio; Auburn, N.Y.; Ithaca, N.Y.; Wayne State University; New York State University Construction Fund (on-campus plans for twenty-two branches of the State University); U. S. Department of State/A.I.D. campus plans for the University of Ife, Nigeria; among others. He has published a number of journal articles on campus planning and *Cornell: A History of Campus Planning and Development* (Cornell University Press, 1966) as well as *An Annotated Bibliography on University and Medical Center Planning Development* (Oakland, California: Council of Planning Librarians Exchange Bibliographies, No. 22, September 1962). The report that follows is a revised and updated version, published with permission, of his two articles for the *Journal of Higher Education* "A Truce in the War between Universities and Cities" (Vol. 34, No. 1, January 1963, pp. 16–28) and "Universities and Cities—The Terms of the Truce between Them" (Vol. 34, No. 4, April 1964, pp. 205–16).

often threatens the maintenance of an academic community near the institution, and crime endangers the staff and students. City institutions have all too often jumped at the first opportunity to flee these difficulties.

Nevertheless, urban universities are beginning to stand their ground in the city. They are beginning to make substantive contributions to urban life. Urban studies are as advanced in this country as they are anywhere in the world. What seems more significant is the action of many institutions of higher education to preserve and enhance their city surroundings. There are indications of a truce in the war between universities and cities.

When did the truce begin? When did American universities become aware of the city as a place of potentials as well as threats? When did these universities begin to become part of the answer to city problems instead of, in their flight and isolationism, part of the problem? There were early stirrings in New York and elsewhere; some of the more obvious recent accomplishments have been in Chicago, Philadelphia and Cleveland.

Chicago's pioneer in terms of action for neighborhood improvement was the Illinois Institute of Technology (I.I.T.). There a private redevelopment program began in South Side Chicago in the mid-thirties. The Institute, after considering a move to the suburbs or purchase of a downtown hotel, concluded that the site of its parent Armour Institute, except that it was situated in the midst of South Side Chicago's slums, came closest to an ideal location. The Institute's part-time students lived and worked in Chicago. Most of its full-time students were from the Chicago area; the South Side had good transportation access. Research operations would be close to Chicago industry.

The initial assumption was that the Illinois Institute of Technology could create a city within a city and ignore the surrounding neighborhood. This concept of an inward-turning "island in a sea of blight" was short-lived. Raymond Spaeth, who was Vice President in charge of Development during the period of great expansion, describes the Institute's decision to embark on a program of community improvement as essential to the development of its long-range educational program.[1]

[1] American Society of Planning Officials, *Planning 1958* (Chicago: The Society, 1959).

I.I.T., along with Michael Reese Hospital, played a major role in establishing the South Side Planning Board, shaping Chicago's redevelopment program and preparing a plan for redevelopment of the South Side. It carried out its own land-acquisition program, buying the bulk of the 110 acres needed for campus expansion, including the notorious "Mecca," a slum warren almost beyond belief. Recently the higher land-price increases, generated in large part by I.I.T.'s efforts at neighborhood improvement, have forced it to depend on the acquisition of city land and write-down under redevelopment.

The campus, staff, and student housing designed by Miss van der Rohe and the improved neighborhood environment, including the expanded facilities of Michael Reese Hospital, new housing, stores, schools, and recreation areas, assure the Institute's future in the area. They constitute a substantial contribution to the renewal program in Chicago. While its campus is only a small part of the total renewal effort on the South Side, the participation of the Institute and the part played by Michael Reese Hospital in the total effort have been as important to their future as their own expansion. Seven square miles of the South Side, what was once Chicago's worst slum, are now in various stages of redevelopment, and these institutions can claim the major credit for initiating the program. In the late sixties, as the last blocks of deteriorated housing and commercial buildings between the I.I.T. campus and the Lake Meadows Redevelopment project south of Michael Reese Hospital are rebuilt, one wonders what the chances of successful rebuilding would have been without the continued efforts of these institutions. As developers, as organizing and coordinating forces and as attractors of other developers, the institutions have demonstrated the power of "healthy urban tissue" in regenerating the inner city.

Similar efforts in the area around Columbia University in New York began in 1947 with the founding of Morningside Heights, Inc. Again, a number of institutions in the area recognized the potentials of joint action in matters of neighborhood conservation and improvement. By 1956, Morningside Heights, Inc., had stimulated commitment of $136,000,000 to construction projects. But this was not part of an overall neighborhood plan and the issues and program objectives were not as clear-cut as they were on the South Side of Chicago. The area was not a slum, but there were slums nearby. Land costs were high, and the officials were at first committed primarily to a program which emphasized expansion of the institutions they represented rather than neighborhood improvement.

Nevertheless, the results, while not as dramatic as those on Chicago's South Side, laid the basis for an unusual type of university-community program. The Morningside Gardens housing project was carried through in spite of substantial neighborhood opposition. The importance of institutional concern for neighborhood needs was now more clearly recognized. Crime-prevention programs, including recreational activities supported by the institutions, efforts to improve area schools, work with the major property owners to maintain environmental standards, and liaison with city officials have been strengthened in an effort to build co-operation with the neighborhood. Still, a relative lack of vigorous and responsive leadership from officials of the institutions on issues of neighborhood renewal early in the program placed a severe handicap on future efforts. The city's early redevelopment policies, notably a disdain for planning on a scale larger than was necessary for the individual project, were not conducive to the best results in Morningside Heights. And, although the characteristics of the neighborhood did not lend themselves to the easy organization of citizen participation, no special effort was made to generate extensive participation in or support for a renewal program.[2] Now, with more enlightened policies in effect, a more comprehensive approach to renewal in Morningside Heights is under way.

A plan for the community around Columbia University is being prepared, and more extensive neighborhood-renewal activity is programed. Expansion room for Columbia still figures as a major element of the program, but it is complemented and complicated by increased concern for the neighborhood. The job to be done is difficult, partly because so few Columbia faculty and staff live in Morningside Heights. More recent efforts in citizen participation have at least served to prove that opposition to the University is a powerful organizing force in the community. The Morningside Renewal Council, initiated with the assistance of the city's Housing and Redevelopment Board in 1964, includes representatives from all community organizations. The fact that each local organization may have a representative on the Council is said to have stimulated the formation of several new organizations. By late 1965 one of

---

[2] Peter Rossi and Robert Dentler, *The Politics of Urban Renewal* (New York: Free Press of Glencoe, Inc., 1961).

the Council's leaders noted that they were so well organized that she could bring people out to a meeting or protest by pulling a switch. While the conflict between neighborhood and university continues, Morningside Heights, Inc. has also added strength. James Feldt, formerly Chairman of the New York City Planning Commission, became president of Morningside Heights, Inc. in 1965, and the staff has been supplemented by the addition of a planning unit. The city's renewal policies now recognize the importance of neighborhood planning, and efforts to establish a community of interest may lead to the positive attitudes necessary to renewal of life as well as environment.

Faced with similar problems as regards city policy on renewal planning but possessing greater potential for local citizen organization, the University of Chicago and its neighborhood have acted more vigorously. Shortly after the South Side renewal program started, a need for similar action became apparent five miles south in the neighborhood around the University of Chicago. With the organization of the Hyde Park-Kenwood Community Council in 1949 and the South East Chicago Commission in 1952, a new and quite different effort to join university and community action in neighborhood renewal began to take shape. Here, to a greater extent than in the district around Columbia University, conservation was the principal environmental objective. The establishment of the community on a stable interracial basis was the main social objective.

The existence of two mediating organizations and vigorous leadership in both the community and the university make the Hyde Park-Kenwood-University of Chicago renewal activity much more complex than the Chicago South Side or the New York-Morningside Heights efforts. Organizational relationships and approaches to institutional expansion and neighborhood improvement have been strikingly different.

The South-East Chicago Commission represents the institutions, primarily the University. Its executive director, Julian Levy, described the organization as the "political action arm of the University." The idea of organizing the Commission came from within the University, and its planning unit prepared the over-all Hyde Park-Kenwood renewal plans under contracts with the city. The Commission acted vigorously at city, state, and national levels to secure legislative and financial support for renewal in the area. It also operated in various direct ways to improve the environment: to obtain better po-

lice protection and housing-code enforcement; to further rehabilitation; to encourage faculty, staff and student residence
in the neighborhood; and to acquire land for university expansion through the Illinois redevelopment-companies law. It
has been a powerful force working in the University's broad
interest in the neighborhood.

The Hyde Park-Kenwood Community Conference represents the neighborhood. It is a mass-membership, "grass-roots"
organization with a sizable professional staff. It has worked
to build confidence in a future for the area while operating
with other forces to determine just what that future would be.
It has helped organize street and block clubs, helped interpret
planning proposals to the residents, and spoken clearly for
the interests of the people who live in the area. In its own
program and in assisting numerous area organizations in
their programs, the Conference has operated through a number of committees as well as through its own staff. These committees have such diverse concerns as planning, schools, block
organization, legal problems, real estate, public relations, personnel, budget, membership, and the maintenance of an interracial community. The Conference's orientation was primarily
toward social action in the neighborhood until renewal plans
involving city action with state and federal support were
evolved by the Planning Unit of the South-East Chicago Commission. The emphasis then shifted to the interpretation of
plans to the neighborhood and criticism of plans in the interest
of the neighborhood.

In their thorough case study of the Hyde Park-Kenwood-
University of Chicago renewal effort, Rossi and Dentler conclude that the University's emphasis on the deterioration of
its total environment and underemphasis of its own needs for
expansion "heightened the perception of the institution as performing a role in defense of the general public interest." This
in turn has permitted the resolution of plans for neighborhood renewal. Rossi and Dentler also believe that "the sources
of heaviest strain . . . were those stemming from poor community relations and socially insensitive practices of the University of Chicago."[3]

The Hyde Park renewal program has achieved substantial
success. Expenditures for residential rehabilitation in 1965 exceeded nine million dollars. New private construction between
1959, when the plan was approved, and the end of 1965 ex-

[3] Peter Rossi and Robert Dentler, *The Politics of Urban Renewal*,
pp. 280, 281.

ceeded fifty-five million dollars. In addition to elegant new housing and a shopping center designed by I. M. Pei, more modest improvements have been provided: a local shopping center owned and operated by displaced merchants and a not-for-profit artisans plaza for artists and others who cannot pay economic rents.

It is doubtful that much could have been achieved if the Hyde Park-Kenwood Community Conference had not provided a means for conducting a dialogue between the University and the community. Elsewhere, the lack of effective citizens' organizations has left a vacuum into which ad hoc opposition groups have rushed. The result has often been the stalemate of renewal programs. Indeed, the "South Campus" proposals of the University of Chicago have stirred a hornet's nest of opposition in the Woodlawn Community south of the Midway. Here, in a transient neighborhood, the vigorous efforts of the South-East Chicago Commission to launch a program that would provide room for the University to expand by clearing large areas was fought by the citizens' organization of the community which invited the Industrial Areas Foundation, headed by Sol Alinsky, to help organize militant opposition. The community group favored conservation, "a minimum of clearance, and the remaking of Woodlawn strictly for its present people and by their own . . . determination." The community organization was opposed to "planning for" the community instead of "planning with" the residents and other institutions. The University and the Commission apparently limited their immediate objectives to expansion of the University and related institutions.

It is interesting to note that the difference in Commission policy in Hyde Park-Kenwood and Woodlawn has been one of the major issues in the conflict between the University and Woodlawn neighborhood groups. The "truce" was breached. A program of renewal for the entire Woodlawn area was not opposed by the Commission, but neither did it support one as it did in Hyde Park-Kenwood. Perhaps this is the chief reason the University and the Commission were attacked so vigorously by Woodlawn neighborhood organizations.

By late 1965 the city, the University and the Woodlawn community organizations managed to develop a program and approach satisfactory to all the participants. The Chicago City Council approved early land acquisition in the 60th-Cottage Project which includes expansion of the University to the south, housing rehabilitation, a new Veterans Administration

Hospital and new middle-income housing. Priority will be given to the hospital and to housing in order to ease relocation problems to the greatest extent possible. The Woodlawn Organization and other groups in Woodlawn supported the project in various public hearings.

Compatibility with the immediate neighborhood is a crucial aspect of university and college life in the city and involvement in urban renewal. Institutions do not vote and they do not pay taxes. The value of the institution to the city and the neighborhood is often not appreciated by the citizens, sometimes for good reasons: lack of college and university interest and participation in community affairs, the effect of large-scale clearance projects, and the walling off of the institution from the community.

At Illinois Institute of Technology, Columbia, and the University of Chicago, new organizations were created to perform the tasks of joining city, neighborhood and university policy in reshaping the environment. The organizational tools and patterns of action of these new institutions were forged in New York and Chicago. They are being employed with variations in Cleveland, Philadelphia, Pittsburgh, Syracuse and elsewhere to reconcile university, neighborhood, and city objectives and programs in urban renewal.

In the decade of the fifties, many urban universities decided that life in the city is one of the assets of civilization. Some of them began developing new attitudes toward the potentials of their city sites, toward neighborhood environment, and toward local urban-renewal policies. Then in 1959, *rapprochement* between universities and cities was assisted by the passage of Section 112, an amendment to the National Housing Act. This legislation encourages a limited partnership between the city and the university in urban-renewal projects of direct concern to both.

SECTION 112 OF THE HOUSING ACT OF 1959

In the ten years before the adoption of Section 112, many urban universities had benefited directly or indirectly from urban-renewal programs. Land cleared in urban-renewal projects was sold for campus expansion to New York University, Pratt Institute of Technology, Fordham University, Illinois Institute of Technology, Drexel Institute of Technology, Temple University, the University of Pennsylvania, and the University of Pittsburgh. Columbia University, Massachusetts Institute of

Technology, the University of Chicago, and Yale University stimulated or supported renewal projects in their vicinity.

City governments now had an incentive for entering into serious discussions with university officials regarding the mutual benefits of joint renewal programs. They had seen little to gain in good will, tax revenue, or improved living conditions from university-oriented renewal until it was harnessed to general neighborhood improvement. Section 112 of the housing act added luster to such a harness. For every dollar an educational institution or its non-profit agent spends "for acquisition of land, buildings or structures within, adjacent to or in the immediate vicinity of, an urban renewal project, for demolition . . . for relocation of occupants and for rehabilitation of buildings," the city may receive two to three dollars of federal urban-renewal assistance. The land and the buildings acquired, and demolished or rehabilitated, must be used for educational purposes and in accordance with the renewal plan and an approved development plan proposed by the institution or its non-profit agent.[4] The cost of building new university facilities is not eligible for credit.

By late 1961 universities were proposing to spend twenty-eight million dollars to acquire nearly one thousand acres of land from local renewal agencies for urban-renewal projects.[5] By mid-1962, thirty-four separate renewal projects involving Section 112 credits from thirty-eight institutions of higher education or from hospitals were in project development; another fifty-one projects were being planned or discussed. Section 112 credits for institutional land purchases and relocation expenses were estimated at $32,000,000 for the approved projects and $112,000,000 for the projects in some stage of planning or discussion, a total of $144,000,000.[6] If the usual ratio between local financing and Federal assistance prevails and if the present financing plans are carried out, over $430,000,000 in Federal renewal matching funds could be secured for the cities in which these projects are located.

By 1965 at least seventy-seven renewal projects involving Section 112 credits were in the execution or advanced plan-

[4] For a detailed description of the provisions of Section 112, see B. T. Fitzpatrick, *Assistance for Colleges and Universities Located in or Near Urban Renewal Areas* (Washington, D.C.: American Council on Education, 1961).

[5] At a meeting sponsored by the West Philadelphia Corporation in Philadelphia on September 20, 1962.

[6] Unpublished data from a survey conducted by the Program Planning Branch of the Urban Renewal Administration in July 1962.

ning stages. Credits for these projects were estimated at $70,-000,000.[7] An unpublished 1965 survey by the Department of Housing and Urban Development listed 198 "educational institutions and hospitals with anticipated or approved Section 112 credits."

In effect, if not in so many words, Section 112 of the National Housing Act has established a national policy of strong encouragement to joint city-university renewal programs. The assumptions seem to be that growth and improvement of urban institutions of higher education are in the national as well as the local interest, that improvement of university environment is an important part of improving city and neighborhood environment, and that university participation in urban-renewal projects will strengthen non-university aspects of the projects.

National concern for higher education is not a new policy, but the idea that the Federal government should encourage universities and cities to cooperate in the mutual improvement of their environment is new and the 1959 Housing Act amendment was only its first manifestation. For example, the Higher Education Act of 1965 authorizes grants "to strengthen community service programs of colleges and universities so as to assist the solution of community problems such as housing, poverty, government, recreation, employment, youth opportunities, transportation, health and land use."

In the instance of renewal there are powerful arguments for joint university-city action. Renewal programs permit universities to acquire land for expansion at a write-down in cost after the city has used its power of eminent domain to acquire and clear sites. Vacation or improvements of city streets and utility replacements or increased capacities are needed to accommodate institutional expansion. Renewal can be a remedy for the neighborhood deterioration which makes it difficult for students and faculty to live near the university in good housing, in a locality with schools, recreation, and shopping

[7] Housing and Home Finance Agency. "Urban Renewal Project Characteristics—December 31, 1964." Tables 6, 6a, 6b and 10. None of the data covers projects in the early planning stage or contemplated actions which have not been given final approval. The prototype Section 112 project in Chicago still show none of their contemplated $12,000,-000 credit even though everyone concerned is fully aware that they will be claimed.

facilities that meet their standards. The cities will benefit, too. More and more young city residents are attending college, and increasing numbers of older city residents are returning to college for further education or are attending adult-education classes or occasional lectures, concerts, plays and exhibitions at the university. The research and teaching programs of universities, colleges and institutes of technology are important assets in local economic and cultural development. In many cases, new buildings cannot be provided for their needs unless land is made available through urban renewal. In some instances, without the institutions as agents in the development of project land and as active forces in encouraging higher standards in housing and neighborhood facilities, city-sponsored renewal projects would be doomed to failure.

It was argued that the federal inducements to city-university joint action were justified because the cities and the universities were not sufficiently motivated to action by the potential rewards I have outlined. A strong incentive was needed to unite the cities and the institutions in a program of renewal in spite of the many issues on which their respective needs and policies were likely to be divergent. Section 112 of the National Housing Act has provided the incentive as indicated above.

Section 112 credits reduce city cash requirements for urban renewal, thereby releasing funds for city improvement or renewal outside the university district. But since the provisions of Section 112 contribute only money solutions, the social and political conflicts over renewal in a university community remain to be resolved by some other means. There appear to be three broad areas of potential conflict among the university, the neighborhood, and the city: (1) the institution's concepts of its needs in the neighborhood of which it is a part are likely to be at odds with those of a substantial number of the residents; (2) the city's judgment concerning its commitments to a large-scale renewal program in addition to the usual citywide municipal functions is often at odds with the university's notion of the importance of its urban problems; and (3) residents outside the university area are likely to view the relocation of families from clearance projects in university districts as potential threats to the stability of their neighborhoods.

UNIVERSITY VERSUS COMMUNITY OBJECTIVES

Some bitter battles have been fought because the urban university's ideas about the right kind of neighborhood environment often vary from those of the residents. Both groups are in favor of better housing, better schools, better parks and playgrounds, and traffic and parking improvements. The battles therefore center principally on the amount of land clearance necessary for university expansion and the type of housing to be provided. Differences of opinion run primarily along social, economic, and racial lines. Although the same debate takes place elsewhere in the city, it is intensified in the university neighborhood because the university is an easy target for criticism. The following compares university neighborhood objectives with those likely to be valued by the residents. The lists include only objectives which conflict. There are, of course, many which both groups share.

Typical Goals of the University in Neighborhood Improvement

• Room for university growth.
• Maximum provision of middle-income housing and upper middle-income housing, emphasizing more housing for university faculty.
• Housing for minority groups, with maintenance of a stabilized, racially integrated neighborhood.
• Modern shopping districts, implying the acceptance of chain stores and high rents for new buildings.

Typical Goals of Residents in Neighborhood Improvement

• Minimum demolition of housing for non-residential use.
• Maximum provision of low-income housing and lower middle-income housing, emphasizing housing for the present residents (some of whom may be university families).
• More good housing for minority groups—with the likelihood of opposition to the use of quotas.
• Small, scattered, owner-operated stores at low rents.

If neighborhood conditions are unsuitable or if university expansion displaces them, some residents of university districts can move to the suburbs. Others, especially Negro families and poor families, have no such alternative. Because of exclusion policies in the suburbs, they must stay in the city, whether they like it or not. So must the universities. Julian Levy, executive director of the South-East Chicago Commission in the University of Chicago area, noted in 1961 that the habitual retreat of urban-university faculty members to suburbs by late afternoon is increasing the tendency of higher educational institutions to become collections of scholarly commuters rather than communities of scholars. Optimum cross-fertilization of disciplines, he adds, is possible only when the university community exists as a place of residence. Levy's concise statement about the possibility of the physical university's following its scholars to the suburbs has a ring of finality: "The market for second-hand universities is non-existent."[8] So it would appear that the urban university has a substantial interest in neighborhood improvement and will have to work out the means of bringing it about with the minority-group and low-income families of its district as well as with its resident faculty and student body.

When an urban university decides it will take positive steps to improve its neighborhood environment, two opposite channels of action are open. At one extreme, the university can attempt to enlist the urban-renewal forces of the city to supplement its efforts to expand its facilities and create or maintain a residential academic community, limiting itself to programs which help achieve these objectives. At the other extreme, it can lend its efforts only to programs which seek to improve the neighborhood for all those who live and work there. Exclusive concentration on either of these strategies is likely to have unfortunate results. If the university adopts the first course of action—and commands enough influence in the city—it may obtain dramatic results for its community of scholars in a short time, but they will come about at the expense of lasting improvement in the neighborhood and city environments. If the second strategy is employed, the university's needs for space and a residential academic community may go unrealized, while only minimal improvements are achieved in the neighborhood.

The presence of a vigorous, growing university is a neighborhood asset, but one that cannot be turned to account unless the university speaks clearly and effectively about it and acts to achieve its internal goals. On the other hand, single-mindedness (or narrow-mindedness) of purpose may result in the grounding of expansion programs on political shoals. The achievement of short-term institutional objectives may

---

[8] "The Influence of Environment on Urban Universities," *Educational Record*, XLII (April 1961), p. 138.

eventually be canceled out by failure to deal with the total problem of neighborhood environment.

Clearly, then, the urban university must steer a course through the conflicts between university and neighborhood objectives, guided not merely by its own needs but by recognition of the needs of its neighbors. Realizing that the advancement of research and education is contingent upon the development of a favorable climate, it must give concrete expression to its concern for the neighborhood life around it.

Most of our major cities are committed to large-scale urban-renewal programs which involve dozens of projects. While these programs are generally well staffed and well established, renewal procedures are complex, and renewal politics are rough-and-tumble. Joint city-university renewal plans compete with many other projects for the attention of city government and renewal agencies. The university's special problems of expansion and neighborhood improvement are minuscule when compared with the total demands on municipal government.[9]

The city's willingness to assume its share in the task of university-area renewal and its ability to commit funds for this purpose are quite different matters. Expensive public improvements are needed everywhere in the city. Money is limited, and universities do not vote. The general public may be aware of the value of educational institutions, but many square miles of blighted areas wait to be rehabilitated or cleared and basements may be regularly flooded in other areas. The city may look unfavorably on the expenditure of millions on improvements which seem to benefit only those dry, comfortably housed university people "who don't pay taxes."

Under such circumstances, the leverage of Section 112 credits is seldom enough in itself to launch a university-city renewal program. The institution must enter the arena of urban-renewal politics. But to do so directly and individually is inadvisable and usually unsuccessful. Some powerful lubrication is needed to move the forces of city policy in concert with the forces of the neighborhood and the institution. This

[9] The West Philadelphia Corporation makes the point that its $250,-000,000 investment in facilities and its 46,000 jobs (in the West Philadelphia area) are an important economic asset to the city. But in 1956 the assessed valuation (less than the market value) of industrial and residential real estate in the city of Philadelphia was over $3.7 billion, and there were 965,000 persons employed in the city.

is being provided most effectively by a number of university area-development corporations.

Coalitions of outer-city groups and disenchanted university-neighborhood residents have launched vigorous attacks on "ivory-tower proposals" for university expansion and renewal. The political power of such aroused citizen groups is impressive. City executives and city councils are likely to respect it and sometimes to act and vote accordingly. If the university's policies show signs of racial or economic prejudice, they are assailed on all sides. The sometimes invisible line between policies intended to achieve racial balance and policies intended to exclude minority groups entirely, makes the institution's actions vulnerable to unjustified emotional as well as to reasoned attack.

UNIVERSITY AREA DEVELOPMENT CORPORATIONS

The efforts of the urban university to expand its facilities and to maintain or establish an academic community in its neighborhood depend greatly on citywide as well as neighborhood support. This support is forthcoming from watchful citizens only when the university's motives unquestionably include the betterment of the city and the neighborhood as well as its own immediate environment. For example, by its active support of numerous neighborhood organizations and programs, the West Philadelphia Corporation has shown clearly that the five institutions* it represents are genuinely concerned for the needs of the neighborhood. The Corporation's policy is to keep everyone in the neighborhood well informed about institutional plans and neighborhood-renewal plans, and to assist local groups with staff and financing when these are needed.

The functions which university area-development corporations perform can be grouped under three headings: (1) research and planning for individual institutions and management of common services for groups of institutions; (2) research, planning, and active participation in neighborhood activities, including urban-renewal programs; and (3) communication and co-ordination of policies and programs with city officials and neighborhood organizations. The emphasis

* The University of Pennsylvania, Drexel Institute of Technology, Presbyterian Hospital, The Philadelphia College of Pharmacy and Science, and the Philadelphia College of Osteopathy. The Editor.

these organizations place on these functions varies, but their work usually includes all of them.

In addition to conducting their own programs, the corporations are often forced to mediate disputes between the institution and the city, the institution and the neighborhood, or, in some cases, between the neighborhood and the city, on issues such as housing-code enforcement, crime prevention, renewal plans and priorities, zoning changes, relocation policies, and municipal services. The organizations may also provide direct services to the institution, to the neighborhood, and occasionally to the city, including planning for expansion of institutions, youth programs, intercampus police protection, crime-prevention programs, off-street parking, shuttle-bus service, land acquisition, loans for rehabilitation, technical and financial assistance for residential rehabilitation, programs to increase utilization of institutional facilities by neighborhood residents, technical services for neighborhood renewal, and negotiations with potential renewal-project developers.

The University Circle Development Foundation in Cleveland has probably done the most effective work in interinstitutional planning and management of common services for a group of institutions. Western Reserve University, Case Institute of Technology, the University Hospitals, and over thirty smaller institutions, including churches, hospitals, museums, and institutes which serve metropolitan Cleveland, are clustered in a five-hundred-acre area four miles east of downtown Cleveland. In 1952, nine of the institutions organized a conference committee to discuss common concerns and develop programs of joint action. In 1956, they agreed that further unplanned growth and change in the district were undesirable and retained two firms to prepare a twenty-year physical-development plan for the area.[10]

The plan assigned space for the growth of existing and anticipated institutions, and for public recreation, housing, and shopping, with minimum dislocation; gave each function its best possible location; integrated the proposed development area with surrounding neighborhoods; proposed an improved system of circulation and parking; and phased the changes over a twenty-year period.

But how could all of these changes involving thousands of

[10] Adams, Howard, and Greeley, *University Circle: Technical Report on a General Plan for the Future Development of the Area* (Cambridge, Massachusetts, 1957).

institutional, public, and private decisions be co-ordinated? Many of the proposals involved development of privately held land. Many transfers of land between institutions were necessary. City-financed improvements—new roads, modified underground utilities, public parking, and public parks—had a bearing on most of the proposals. Many of the proposals were for facilities that could not be classed as public improvements although they were to be used by all of the institutions: a common building, joint parking facilities, small private parks, and vehicular and pedestrian circulation. The effects of these changes on the surrounding neighborhoods and the city had to be reassessed daily, and there was pressure for swift action.

To carry out the plan, an effective organization operating at a level between the various institutions, and between the institutions and the neighborhood and city, was a necessity. It was essential for the institutions to empower a single agency to act in their common interest. Funds for the joint projects of the institutions were needed, and the many problems incident to moving the institutions, the neighborhood, and the city through the process of remodeling their environment had to be solved. The University Circle Development Foundation was established to assist in all of these matters. Its institutional membership grew from nineteen to twenty-nine between 1957 and 1962 and to thirty-four in 1965.

The Foundation co-ordinates planning and capital-funds campaigns of area institutions; acquires land reserves for them well in advance of need; builds and operates parking facilities and parks; directs a sixteen-man area police force; represents area institutions in negotiations with the city and federal agencies on urban-renewal projects; and provides liaison with citizens' organizations in surrounding areas. Its operations are financed from contributions made by the area's institutions and from funds raised in independent campaigns. The Foundation's 1961–62 fund drive raised $6,000,000. More than $10,000,000 in cash and firm commitments have been received since 1957. These funds are used for administration and planning, land acquisition, parking construction, landscaping, a faculty center, and other facilities for common use. The parking program is designed to be self-supporting. A 350-car, $670,000 parking garage was completed in 1962. The cost of the area police force is shared by the institutions on a pro rata basis.

All participating institutions sign agreements which commit them to a centralized land-acquisition program. The Foundation acquires the land needed for institutional expansion and the sites for new institutions. The only land that will be acquired from the city under urban renewal will be for a research park. Initial exploratory costs of this project were borne jointly by Case, Western Reserve, and the Foundation. Staff housing will also be developed on project land, but by private developers. The city condemns land for institutional expansion only when negotiation by the Foundation fails. The city has also co-operated in providing parking facilities and a ring road, and will provide over $4,000,000 in capital improvements as part of the Euclid-University Renewal Project.

The Foundation is, in effect, an area-redevelopment corporation. Area institutions delegate to it substantial responsibility in the planning and development of services and facilities, in the co-ordination of interinstitutional planning and development, and in the maintenance of relations with adjacent neighborhood agencies and the city government. This delegation of responsibility places the Foundation, as mediator, at the focus of all negotiations between institution, neighborhood and city.

The solid accomplishments of the University Circle Development Foundation in the last eight years mask the substantial job before it. The interinstitutional police force has been effective in helping the city police protect the residents of the area and the staff and visitors in area institutions. The joint parking program is a successful model for other multi-institution areas. A loop shuttle-bus service that serves a growing number of fringe parking lots has eased area traffic problems. The land-acquisition program has proved its merits (by mid-1963 forty-four acres of land had been acquired at a cost of $4,700,000; land valued at $1,200,000 had been resold for institutional building sites). The successful capital-funds drive promises continued expansion of services to area institutions. Total construction expenditures during this period amount to more than $74,000,000. There is an increased spirit of co-operation among member institutions.

Co-ordination with neighborhood groups outside the Circle area has developed at a slower pace. Because of its concentration on the affairs of its member institutions, the Foundation has not until recently devoted as much attention to developments in the surrounding neighborhoods as it would have liked. Large-scale renewal in some of them which have reached an advanced stage of deterioration, and the encroachment of the institutional area on others, present serious cultural problems, recognition of which is bringing about increased participation of the institutions and the Foundation in neighborhood activities.

The staff of the Foundation has worked closely with city-renewal officials in the project-area office of the Euclid-University Renewal Project and with neighborhood social agencies and citizens' organizations on matters not directly associated with institutional expansion. Participation of the University Circle group in the renewal project with the city has also added materially (through Section 112 credits and joint planning efforts) to the feasibility of city financing of an extensive renewal program in the area west of the institutions. The Foundation and the institutions seem to be growing in awareness of the importance of their need for commitments to neighborhood programs.

In contrast to the institutional emphasis of the University Circle Foundation program, that of the West Philadelphia Corporation, in the area around the University of Pennsylvania, has focused mainly on the neighborhood environment. While it plays a part in co-ordinating the expansion plans of its member institutions, its aid to the public schools and its support of residential rehabilitation and construction programs have claimed the major share of its efforts. Early in the West Philadelphia program it was decided that the institutions' interest in the future of the neighborhood should be separated from their interests in expansion. The board of the Corporation represents the founding institutions and the community at large. In public and private the Corporation regularly announces its "dedication to the renaissance of the community," invites the help and counsel of all interested individuals and organizations, and states its belief that "with united and enlightened efforts of residents, businessmen, institutions and public and private agencies, the trend towards blight can be reversed."

The first issue of the community newspaper, *University City News,* launched two years after the program began, stated that its purpose was "to create a community atmosphere that [would] permit University City to become one of the world's largest cultural, educational, and science research centers." The effort to emphasize University City's unity seems to be successful. A group of businessmen who formerly called themselves "The 40th and Market Business Association" changed their name to "The University City Business Association." Renewal projects are named "University City" projects.

The Corporation has been active in fulfilling its public commitment to work with the neighborhood. Early projects included surveys of market factors in the area, a study of local public schools, securing regular attendance at meetings of some dozen neighborhood groups, employment of staff to work with home owners on rehabilitation problems, and close liaison with city officials on the new Philadelphia zoning ordinance. The Home Improvement Information Service provides free advice on cost of financing, contractors, city regulations, and design. The Corporation has remodeled several demonstration houses, and is assisting in financing a major effort to rehabilitate houses in one section of the district. It has helped several builders who wished to remodel area houses or build new houses on vacant parcels. At the same time, the Corporation has been active in fighting the illegal practices of "slumlords" who were illegally converting old houses into small units.

In its six years of operation, the Corporation has become heavily involved in all aspects of neighborhood revitalization. Several schools in the area have been designated "university-related schools." Here the resources of area institutions are brought to the aid of school programs and improved health care. The University of Pennsylvania has assigned fifteen scholarships to area students as part of a high school motivation program. The Corporation provides mimeographing and mailing services to neighborhood organizations and has worked as unpaid consultant to the Philadelphia Redevelopment Authority on an eighty-three-acre renewal project which will include a large scientific research park.

It has worked with the City Planning Commission in the development of a long-range plan for the area. Through the University Science Center in which Penn is associated with fifteen academic and medical institutions in the Delaware Valley, it is contributing to building up the industrial and economic health of a wider region.[11] The influence of university-city renewal activities in West Philadelphia is both subtle and dramatic. The latter effect can be seen in the new buildings of the University, the progress of the science center, new private apartment and townhouse construction, extensive renovation of older houses and a new private swim

[11] Gaylord Hanwell, "Annual Report of the President . . ." (1965).

club in one neighborhood. The subtle changes "include the revitalization of many neighborhood organizations, the steady rise in private residential values and the possibility that sufficient stimulus has been given to countervailing forces so that [there is hope for] an integrated neighborhood that is both balanced and stable . . ."[12]

CITY, NEIGHBORHOOD AND UNIVERSITY MUTUAL GAINS

In 1951, the University of Pennsylvania was still seriously considering a move to the country. The University and the other institutions that support the West Philadelphia Corporation are now deeply committed urbanites. Their involvement in urban renewal, beginning with the purchase of project land in the mid-fifties, has increased until it has become one of the principal means by which the institutions and their neighborhood strive for a social *modus vivendi* and improvement of the environment. Three urban-renewal projects involving 180 acres of land in West Philadelphia are being planned. The West Philadelphia Corporation has been involved in over one hundred citizens' meetings where these plans were discussed.

Such extensive university area-renewal efforts also require extensive and effective communication and co-operation with city planning agencies, renewal departments and authorities, and public-works, building, and welfare departments. The management of the development corporations through which institutional liaison with city government and the neighborhood is achieved requires the services of a full-time staff and numerous consultants. The effective university area-development corporations representing the universities and other institutions in the competition for city urban-renewal funds, and settling differences between institutions and between institutions and their neighbors, are vigorous, well-staffed, well-financed, and diversified. They wield substantial power to achieve their goals.

The development of a local program for university-neighborhood-city co-operation in urban renewal is a specialized job. The university area-development corporations in a number of major cities are the mediators in a limited truce

[12] Comments by Harold Taubin, Director, University of Pennsylvania Planning Office (1966).

in the war between universities and cities. The acute problems of social change, neighborhood deterioration, and procurement of land for expanding institutions will continue to generate controversy. Institutions, city, and neighborhood are bound to disagree on the nature of the problems, the best solutions, and the timing of action. The success of several of these organizations in bringing about a good measure of understanding and co-operation between the disputants increases our hope that a new era has begun for the city as a place of learning.

These new types of institutions stand in pivotal positions between universities and the power centers of the cities and between the universities and adjacent neighbors. There is no ideal type of "third party"; no single example which embodies all of the inventiveness characteristic of these emerging institutions, but an examination of their collective objectives and performances indicates that organizations of this type play important roles in the reconciliation of conflicts and the realization of greater potentials between universities and cities. Their success is a hopeful sign of a truce in the war between universities and cities. They represent only one aspect of the university's changing role in our society, but an important one.

The concept of strong mutual interests between universities and cities has come a long way in the United States in the last decade. The Irvine campus of the University of California is the basic building block for the new community of Irvine. The new campuses of the University of Illinois in Chicago and Cleveland State University are being built on renewal cleared land in the hearts of those cities. The University of California is contemplating a new campus in San Francisco and the universities in Cambridge, Boston, St. Louis, Milwaukee and dozens of other cities are actively involved in the renewal efforts of these cities. A British writer commenting on the excellence of the planning program at the Tufts-New England Medical Center in Boston under the direction of Herman H. Field, provides a sidelight on the situation in Great Britain:

Medical and university institutes . . . are unable to expand to the size required by the present work let alone look forward to satisfaction of their future needs. In the absence of a massive urban renewal effort it is probable that for our institutions the only way that they will get enough room will be to leave their historic sites completely.[13]

So we in the United States have come a long way. But we still have some distance to climb before we achieve the level of Leyden's desire for higher education in the city. When the States General of Holland gave the citizens of Leyden a reward for their bravery in war, they were offered a choice between exemption from taxes or a university. They chose the university!

[13] *Architectural Design* (November 1965).

Chapter 21

THE URBANIZATION OF DEVELOPING NATIONS

Western experience—whether directly applicable or not—is being drawn on heavily in developing countries to alleviate the fantastic urban messes created as their expanding populations rush to where "the action is." Though fewer in number, urban places in developing areas are growing faster than urban places in the West. William Alonso has tentatively advanced the thesis that the ecology of cities in such areas is not dissimilar from that found by decades of research on American cities, although a patchwork pattern is more pronounced. Within pie-shaped sectors fringe slums compete with the mounting suburbanization of the rising middle class. Slums, generally squatter colonies, tend to be peripheral rather than central as in the West and to result from group colonization movements—in some cases connected with declining tribalism. Slums may also be in the eye of the observer—especially the observer from the urbanized old nations—slums may turn out to be way stations once social mobility starts up.

Urbanization may precede *industrialization* and there may be industrialization without heavy urbanization; both could conceivably occur without *modernization* or the internalizing by millions of people of the clock and a money economy in a secular society with ordered political power and administration. Some of these interrelations were considered by Gideon Sjoberg in Chapter 3, a short summary of existing knowledge in comparative urban sociology. Here some planning facets of this urbanizing surge engulfing all of mankind are considered.

Sam Schulman, sociologist, reacts in a strongly written description of a Colombian *turgurio* or squatter slum. This is no Mexican *ranchero* slum of hope as that studied by Lisa Peattie but a human cesspool from which there seems to be no escape. Just how can such fetid human encampments be planned into civilization; Schulman is not hopeful and sees the situation worsening in these places where human *dignitad* is broken. Lloyd Rodwin, planner and economic geographer, looks hard at such slums in developing nations and advocates extreme moderation in slum clearance. He sets up three measures for determining what housing "needs" actually are in a major national program for housing production: (1) comparative national data on housing stock and adequacy, (2) gearing housing to productivity, (3) gearing housing to consumption levels. In some such a fashion only by weighing these variables differentially can sophisticated programs of housing production be programmed and adjusted to the spatial needs of the entire society. Failure to cope with dwelling requirements can bring explosions within the body politic and the deep wounding of future generations. But housing supply in developing nations will have to stand in line with other pressing demands for capital. No housing, no matter how deficient, should be cleared—every bit of the existing dwelling supply must be conserved and bettered; he foresees continuing shortages as a result of urban population growth and "undoubling" as aspirations increase. Alfred P. Van Huyck, Calcutta renewal planner, echoes Rodwin's plea for the conservation of existing housing stock and he is for the elimination of grandiose major mass housing programs with impracticably high standards. There is neither the skill nor the capital to engage in such enterprises. Van Huyck advocates temporary shelter coupled with general environmental improvement for so great is the immediate need. He counsels against the common error in India of concentrating too much capital in a relatively few projects; this has occurred in new town development, in industrial complexes and in many other physical development projects as well as in mass housing schemes.

Charles Abrams, planner and international housing expert, covers the regional front and proposes for developing countries United Nations Development Corporations able to finance, build, aid and administer as a method of coping with the scale of activity required. His *region* goes beyond the often miniscule, non-functional new nation itself. This analysis indicates once again that the management of urbanization is beyond city boundaries, to regional boundaries, to national boundaries, even to international areas. Lawrence D. Mann, research and field planner, proposes a systems analysis technique for programming national urban development within a national budgeting process to decide the allocation of investment priorities within a nation. The national development corporation would have subordinate regional and "city" equivalents carrying on the same process within the system of central guidance. Undoubtedly, Abram's U.N. Development Corporation could be fitted into such a scheme. Mann's proposal is, of course, applicable to developed countries also and makes an interesting connection with the two chapters that follow: Chapter 22 on socialist (Communist) planning and Chapter 23 on macro-planning above and beyond the urban limit.

Latin American Shantytown
SAM SCHULMAN*

In Brazil it is called *favella;* in Argentina, *banda de miseria;* in Peru, *barriada.* In Colombia it is *tugurio.* But whatever the name, its characteristics are the same: It is the rudest kind of slum, clustering like a dirty beehive around the edges of any principal city in Latin America.

In the past two decades poor rural people have flocked to the cities, found no opportunities but stayed on in urban fringe shantytowns, squatting squalidly upon the land. In modern Caracas or cosmopolitan Lima, as in tens of other Latin-American cities, a glance at the surrounding hills is a view of misery at its worst. Death is easy and often. Hunger and pain are facts of everyday life.

Traditional living patterns undergo intense strain and often give way in these slums. Living almost like animals, the *tugurio's* residents are overwhelmed by animality. Religion, social control, education, domestic life are warped and disfigured.

For more than nine months my wife and I studied and worked in such a slum—the "Barrio of 65" ("the 65th Street Neighborhood")—a hillside shanty settlement in Bogotá. The barrio clings to the rounded knobs and slopes of the small foothills at the base of the Andes along the eastern edge of the city. A wide dirt path, an extension of Calle 65 (65th Street), winds through the area and gives it its name. There are about 250 individual dwelling units and about 1,200 residents.

Throughout Latin America, extensions of the central city have been traditional living areas for the poor. Squatting has

* Professor of Sociology, Colorado State University; formerly teacher at *Instituto Chileño–Norte Americano de Cultura,* Santiago, Chile, lecturer in comparative government at Mexico City College, Mexico D.F., and graduate Visiting Professor of Sociology, *Facultad de Sociologia, Universidad Nacional de Colombia,* Bogotá (1965). He was the Director of the Organization of American States' Annual Course, Inter-American Center for Agrarian Reform (1963–65). He has been on the faculties of the University of Florida and Oklahoma State University. In addition to professional articles, he has published a number of pieces of a non-scholarly nature. His graphic "Latin American Shantytown" appeared in the *New York Times Magazine,* January 16, 1966 © 1966 by the New York Times Company. Reprinted by permission.

always been an accepted mode of life, and even at the turn of the century, small isolated squatters' holdings began to spring up around Bogotá. With the beginning of national strife after the assassination of the Liberal party leader, Jorge Elíecer Gaítan, in 1948, thousands ran for safety to Bogotá. The city could not absorb them. It had neither industry nor services to provide places for the illiterate and untrained country people.

They spilled over into the uninhabited or sparsely settled hills bordering Bogotá's poor sections and remained, building hovels. In the lower part of the Barrio of 65, property owners expanded their facilities, adding a few more rooms facing a courtyard, building additional shacks nearby, and renting these out for nominal fees to the newcomers. As the newcomers kept coming, spaces between shacks and more permanent dwellings were filled: a few more scraps of cardboard, a few more rolled-out oil cans, a few slabs of corrugated iron for roofs. These, too, were soon rented.

About four years ago, several of the tenants of the lower barrio, tired of paying rent, began an invasion of a large municipally held hill above them. With the settlement upon the hill a new phase of the barrio's growth began, and, month by month, a few more shacks crept upward. In 1966 they are still creeping.

And they are still creeping up most of the other hills bordering the poor areas of Bogotá. At present, one in every 10 residents of this city of more than 1.7-million lives in a hillside *tugurio*. Seven out of 10 urbanites in Colombia are poor, but the *tugurio* is the worst face of urban poverty.

There is no real water supply in this *tugurio*. Women and children fetch water in old oil or lard cans from a municipal hydrant at the base of a hill. Only a few homes have electricity —illegally secured by tapping the electric company's power line. A few houses have one- or two-burner bottled-gas stoves; most residents cook over small wood fires around each of which are placed three large stones supporting a cooking pot.

The barrio has about 20 latrines. A few belong to special families, and their doors are secured by padlocks. Others are not so exclusive; they belong to groups of people or to compounds. In every case, foul water carrying human excrement floats from under the privies and runs in black rivulets down paths of the barrio. Children play alongside and in the contaminated streams.

It is no surprise that endemic and epidemic diseases run

rampant. Children are the chief victims. A measles outbreak may kill large numbers of youngsters. Infant diarrheas, upper respiratory infections, malnutrition also take a high toll.

Diets are typically protein-low, if not completely protein-absent. The average daily fare is built largely around potatoes, rice and a hot drink made from unrefined sugar. When it is possible—and it rarely is—a heavy soup is made from scraps of meat or fish that have been classified as unsalable in local food markets. Perhaps a chicken that has been carefully raised among the children and debris of the barrio is added.

Sheep, hogs, a few cows are seen, but they are usually raised for sale. A burro or two are the prized animals of only a few, and these are used to aid in the dull and heavy tasks associated with slum life—hauling water, firewood, or clothes to be laundered in a ravine a few blocks away.

Living space is extremely limited. In the lower area of the Barrio of 65 a family usually has a single room and a small lean-to for cooking. Houses of the upper barrio are larger. They, too, may consist of only a single room, or the space may be partitioned into several rooms of minimal dimensions. Most of the barrio's residents live close to one another. A child being spanked is heard by 50 neighbors. The total effect is that of masses of tightly packed shacks ringing small common patios. Here clothes are hung to dry, garbage is accumulated, a hog and some chickens are enclosed, and here the children pass most of their day.

A typical house has a low ceiling and a dirt floor. A rustic door or curtain at the entrance shields the residents from wind, rain and passersby. Windows are rare. In this dingy room, a family sleeps, dresses, eats and attends to its personal necessities.

One or two narrow beds—usually handmade cots or their cheap, poorly made commercial equivalents—are placed against the walls. One bed is usually reserved for adults, who often sleep with the youngest child. Other children sometimes crowd five to a bed. More hardy youngsters roll up in blankets and sleep on the earth floor.

A wooden trunk, containing most of the family's possessions, is placed alongside a bed. Atop the trunk is the family's washbasin. A chair or two and a small table may be wedged in among the other things. Clothes, especially "Sunday" clothes, are hung on the wall, the door, the headboard of a bed, or may dangle down from the ceiling. Beneath one of the beds is the dwellers' chamberpot. Profusely ornamenting the walls are religious pictures and a photograph or two: the bride at marriage, the husband doing his stint in military service, the baptism or confirmation of a child.

This can be home for a dozen people. Privacy is unheard of, and all know the extreme intimacies of human contact. Only darkness hides the nakedness of this contact.

The home has no real facility for bathing. And washing is not a cherished custom. Faces and hands of children and adults may be cleaned, hair combed or brushed for receiving visitors, attending mass or going to the local church. But usually the living area smells heavily of continued, unwashed occupation, and is usually in disarray. The chamberpot often is not emptied after each use, but only when it is full. Then it is dumped into one of the few latrines, a drainage gutter or the paths that serve as streets in the barrio. Children grow up with the sounds of sleeping, eating, evacuation and sexual relations—of their own family, and their neighbors—in their ears.

In this setting, traditional norms of family life are challenged. Most of the barrio's residents still have their roots in the country. But Colombia's rural poor still retain their basic peasant dignity. There are free spaces and clean air beyond their shacks; there is a tiny garden growing products for home consumption; there is no sharp comparison between peasant life and the affluence of many others. Close by, perhaps, is the master's fine home, but it is a singular jewellike exception to those of his peasants. In the city, whole neighborhoods of fine homes and vast numbers of "better" people are only blocks away from the *tugurio*. There is no longer free space and tiny gardens. And the peasant's dignity is buried in urban poverty's abyss.

In such a setting, there is little feeling of community. True, when outside authorities seek to exert control within the barrio, residents may come together in common defense. But generally they are tied only by the bond of misery, and do not help each other.

Violence is common. A weekend seldom passes without some explosive episode. The men, whose chief recreation is playing a rustic pitch-and-toss game called *tejo* and drinking beer, may dispute a point and fall into a drunken fight with fists or knives. A backyard rivalry or sexually based competition among women may result in a stabbing. Habitually, men castigate both their women and their children by beating them, and a mother's reprimand to a child is often a hard slap or a switch across the face or bottom. Brutality is part of life, and is accepted.

Unemployment is another fact of life. Economic need is so great in the barrio that young people try to obtain jobs as soon as they can, if jobs are available. It is easiest for young girls to secure positions as beginners in domestic service: They earn between $3 and $4 a month, and are supplied uniforms, sleeping quarters and food. The relatively few men in the barrio are employed at simple tasks—when they can find work —such as gardening and construction.

But squatters, never an integrated part of the greater community of Bogotá, face the employment dilemma of most other deprived peoples: "Last to be hired, first to go." And unemployment has soared in the city. In late 1965 it amounted to almost 20 per cent of the labor force. Those who have suffered most are the unskilled people of the *tugurios*. Mothers and children are often seen in better neighborhoods begging. Idleness, extreme poverty and need have forced some of the men to become petty sneak thieves; some of the women have turned to prostitution; many of the children have become street gamins.

Unemployment and disrupted family structures go hand in hand. More than half, perhaps as many as two-thirds, of the family units in the barrio are quasi families, lacking a permanent father. A few have no mother or father, and children live with grandparents, aunts, godparents or friends. Abandoned women with children are commonplace. A man feels little obligation to the woman he lives with and seldom participates in guiding the development of children. In an almost totally Roman Catholic country, people of the barrio do not have time, money, or ambition to indulge in the requisites of the church. A "free union," a condoned form of sexual alliance, is the dominant form of marriage in the slums. Partners are married as long as they wish to remain married.

There are, of course, some couples in the barrios who are both legally and religiously married, but they are rare exceptions. Their marriage is not seen as something "better." In the eyes of other residents, they have had "more luck," "more money" or "more pull."

Outside the barrio, however, a religious marriage is thought to have greater prestige and slum couples will invent such an event to keep from being humiliated. In a recent series of interviews, a field worker reviewed the details of their "marriage" with a pair from the barrio, speaking to each member individually. Both said they had been married in the church, but each gave the name of a different church and even a different date for the event.

But any man and woman who live together in the barrio are considered "married," and the woman is addressed as "*Señora.*" It is also custom to call an unmarried mother by the same term: She is a *señora,* though she is single. Children born to any "married" couple will bear their father's surname; those born to a single woman will bear hers.

Barrio women have many children. Contraception, even the simplest kind, is not understood. It is not unusual for a married woman to have had 10 or 12 pregnancies. Many babies die at birth. But the death of a child is not a horrible event. There is grief, but also a feeling that the "tiny angel" goes directly to heaven. There is also the feeling the child is fortunate to meet God without having to endure the hardship of adult life. It is a rare family in the barrio that does not have one or more *angelitos.*

Even in homes where the husband or male partner is seldom present, he is the undisputed source of authority. A husband's needs are met before those of any other member of the family. He eats first, and the best of what little there may be. Children do not disturb him when he is resting. Spending money for beer while his children beg for food is not considered wrong.

Even the health of others is subordinated to his needs. Children are not taken to the local clinic when they are ill because their mothers must spend most of their mornings preparing lunch for working husbands. It would have angered the men if lunch were not brought to the job on time. Women make long treks on foot or in overcrowded buses with freshly cooked food to keep their men in good spirits. A seriously ill child might die for lack of attention on one hand; a woman might face a beating, social castigation and possible desertion on the other.

All important decisions are made by men. The role of a woman is simply caretaker of the home and children. Children are brought up by their mothers and seldom have an adequate example of an adult male on which to orient their lives. When a man is not working, he spends his time with his cronies, not with his youngsters.

Some mothers will lock their children in shacks for hours on end while doing day work. The money earned is quickly given to the husband. One completely happy young man, living in his mother's house with his wife and child, felt extremely fortunate: His mother had a steady job and his wife worked several days a week. He did not work. He would periodically look for a job, but he was not driven to finding work. There was no need to do so while his women were employed.

Family life in a *tugurio* is based upon simple, uncluttered, primitive norms. It reflects the attitude of people who know and expect only harshness. Yet there are few ugly children. They are beautiful, with the smooth skins and large dark eyes of the Colombian mestizo; they are joyful, playing along the dirt paths and in the contaminated waters of the barrio. But life's harshness bends them. Women age while still young, and men are content to be brutes. The barrio, in the end, makes its people as ugly as itself. Families cannot help but mirror the harsh and ugly total social milieu that encompasses them.

Each year, the barrio forces itself more and more on its residents. Few can leave, for there is really no place to go. Gradually fear of the "outside" develops.

In mid-1965 two families were offered the opportunity to leave and start new lives with adequate financial support from an agency of the municipal government. Both refused: the first, because the barrio had always been "home" and its members wanted their roots to be maintained; the second, because of intense fear of all the unknowns of an inimical big city.

The *tugurio* is a deep intellectual and spiritual crevice filled with constant misery and peopled with depressed and passive human lives. Escape is virtually impossible and, when a way out is allowed a select few, they do not understand. They suspect it, and remain in the depths. And the depths will remain for decades. The *tugurio* is firmly rooted in Colombian urban life.

There are some men—their numbers are small, but they are growing—of goodwill and insight who are profoundly disturbed, and passionately concerned with the eradication of these subhuman clusters. Msgr. Ruben Isaza, Bishop Coadjutor of Bogotá, has called them "malignant tumors that have grown upon my city" and, along with others of his countrymen, is working for their displacement and for the betterment of the social and economic factors which have created them. There is much planning, and there are the beginnings of action programs. The Mayor of Bogotá is dedicated to a platform of slum clearance, and has given first priority to the *tugurios.* The Colombian Army has established labor battalions to help construct low-cost homes for *tugurio* inhabitants. The Alliance for Progress has given substantial sums—and will continue to give them—to assist the Colombian Government's urban resettlement agencies in the diminution of the *tugurios.* High-school and university students, religious groups, citizens' organizations, the major newspapers of Bogotá and other cities—all have voiced concern and are urging development programs to remedy a condition which they admit is abhorrent, dangerous and shameful to their national pride.

But the Colombian economy is too weak to support a full-scale "war against poverty." The fight against the *tugurios,* the scores of barrios like the Barrio of 65, moves at a slow pace, and the problem is large—growing a little bit larger every day.

Measuring Housing Needs in Developing Countries

LLOYD RODWIN*

A mathematician once observed that all problems are divided into two classes: soluble questions which are trivial, and important questions which are insoluble. If so, measuring housing needs has some of the earmarks of an important question. For the kinds of housing available in developing countries and the varying needs for housing on the part of millions of people in those countries are surely not commensurable. But do these difficulties inhibit us from producing estimates of housing needs? Not at all! Practicing social scientists and their ilk perform, indeed must perform, such alarming feats every day. Still it is salutary occasionally to

* Professor, Department of City and Regional Planning at the Massachusetts Institute of Technology and Chairman of the Faculty Committee of the Joint Center for Urban Studies of M.I.T. and Harvard. He is an associate editor of *Daedalus* and has consulted widely both here and abroad. The author of numerous professional articles, he published *The British New Towns* (Harvard University Press, 1956), an influential work in that field. He is presently engaged on a study of national policies for urban and regional development. The following article is adopted from "Measuring Housing Needs in Underdeveloped Countries," edited by Burnham Kelly, the Report of a Conference sponsored at the Massachusetts Institute of Technology by the A. F. Bemis Foundation, 1953, and reproduced with the permission of the M.I.T. Department of City and Regional Planning.

shudder about the difficulties, if only because this may caution us to mind the tenacity with which we hold our opinions.

There are several criteria one can employ to arrive at first approximations of housing needs. Four of the more important are: (1) housing which satisfies some socially determined set of standards; (2) housing which contributes directly to added production or output; (3) housing as a consumption good—as a self-justifying human preference; (4) housing to suit political requirements. Though these criteria are not mutually exclusive, we gain insight by keeping them separate.

The *first measure* is the most well-known, the most employed and the least useful, at least for developing countries. This is because even on the basis of the most minimum standards, needs are so far in excess of resources. Still, the measure continues to be employed partly out of custom, partly for the purpose of shocking sensibilities, although in almost all other respects it leaves much to be desired. For example, comparative national data and studies on housing needs are collected by UN. They are the best data now available and are perhaps helpful for occasional references and other equally limited purposes. Even for these requirements, there are serious gaps and limitations.[1] Data are often inadequate or nonexistent on crucial items, such as households; family formation and dissolution; family size and characteristics; development plans and migration; income and ethnic distributions; the number, location, quality and other characteristics of the existing stock of housing. The same holds true for information on production capacity, tenure, prices, rent levels, demolitions and the like. Averages obscure crucial distinctions, and differences in standards, definitions, dwelling types, collection periods, reliability, etc. render comparisons futile. Unless skillfully interpreted, the data provided are misleading and have little use in this form.

Instead of efforts to establish national averages or to develop international comparisons, it might be wiser to concentrate more attention on improvements of analytical tools and methods of data collection so that the housing specialists in different countries could do a better job of analyzing their country's, or region's, or locality's housing requirements. This might ultimately provide more usable data, and avoid the frittering away of resources in meaningless studies.

---

[1] Most of the limitations are not the fault of the analysts. Indeed, they often draw the readers' attention to the unavoidable inadequacies of their studies.

The *second measure,* which is now slowly coming into vogue, is geared to productivity. It is limited to the same goals which now generally dominate national development policy, i.e., raising output and income. It is one thing, however, to cite such a rule, and quite another thing to apply it. The closest experience we have had in the United States with such programming occurred during the past war, and the lessons of that experience would repay more careful examination—for they are clearly pertinent. In estimating the housing essential for defense, efforts were made to examine housing requirements on a locality basis and to determine the amount of housing necessary for immigrant war workers to prevent turnover or any curtailment of essential war or defense production. The resources programmed for housing during the war were based on these studies. The rule about productivity is based on the same principle. What it says in effect is that in the campaign for economic development all resources including those available for housing must be allocated for the support of those activities which will add most to the output and income of the country. This in effect presupposes that developing nations would have to scale the importance of their productive activities and make rough first approximations of the amount of housing that would be needed to maximize the expansion of these activities. A more adequate allocation may be slowly approximated as experience with development programs and further studies disclose the nature of the need.

This is not the place to spell out the details. But it should be clear that the better we understand the major variables and techniques of analysis of the components of housing need and of housing supply and production, the more reliable will be our programming of these requirements. Only by detailed examination of the local and regional housing market can one determine whether additional housing will be needed for development programs; and if so, where, how much, and what type, i.e., whether temporary, mobile or permanent, for ownership or for rent, the sources and terms of financing, the private and public building mechanisms, the price and rent range and the related community facilities and services. Failure on most of these details is tantamount to waste.

Moreover, estimates of housing requirements will be a function of policy decisions affecting important components of this housing market. Let me cite a few illustrations:

1. *Slum Clearance.* In most Western nations a significant proportion of housing needs, ranging approximately from one-fifth to one-half of the total estimates, is based on replacement requirements. Only housing of defined standards is considered adequate. The existing stock of substandard housing is scheduled for eventual elimination. These standards vary, of course, for different periods, countries and regions. However, even in advanced countries no knowledgeable houser insists on physical clearance when there is a serious shortage. Regardless of the deplorable conditions of existing housing in underdeveloped areas, it would be unwise to eliminate almost any utilizable housing space until the quantitative and *price* requirements are satisfied. There are many families in both the richer and the poorer countries who need inexpensive housing more than they need housing of higher standards. To forget this is to forget one of the most important criteria of a sound housing policy.

2. *Existing Stock of Housing and New Construction.* In fact, one of the most difficult and crucial questions is not how much new housing, but what proportion of the scarce resources available for housing should be applied to improvements of the existing stock of housing. There is no easy or single answer. But it is worth remembering that in most communities the amount of new construction is picayune compared with the total stock of housing. Aside from self-help schemes with locally available materials, there are many measures unrelated to the provision of new housing, such as programs for road building, improved water supply, and repairs, maintenance and improvements which can directly or indirectly extend the life, effect significant improvements in the quality, and even enlarge the total housing capacity of the existing stock of housing. Concentration *only* on new housing may be equivalent to missing the forest for the trees. Housing needs growing out of neglect of the existing stock of housing may be enormous, as the housing experts in France and more recently in Britain have discovered. Just because the total amount of new housing will be so limited, it may be dangerous to invite hardships by ignoring possibilities for more adequate and complete utilization of existing housing.

3. *Location of Economic Activities.* The unutilized capacity of the existing stock of housing and community facilities may also serve as a reminder to economists and housers that indispensable, or in economic jargon "complementary" housing needs may be wastefully generated, albeit for productive en-

terprises. Such a situation can occur if a choice of sites is possible for new economic activities and the sites with existing suitable housing resources and community facilities are overlooked. This factor may be a more important argument for regional planning than for dispersal. Another way of stating this point is that there is no *a priori* case for economic development in new areas; if anything the contrary is true, especially where short-term benefits happen to be more important. Indeed, if the British New Towns experience affords any lessons at all, it should be the huge, staggering requirements that development in virgin or in relatively undeveloped areas generates on materials, utilities and services, all of which constitute frozen capital until growth has proceeded to the point of reasonable utilization of these facilities. Particularly in situations where immediate benefits are of paramount importance, this fact should not be overlooked. And, though these observations may give that impression, this is not an argument against new towns or village development. Many such towns and villages will and should be built in expanding metropolitan regions and new growth zones in the hinterland. But new towns in developing areas should be strategic necessities: they will be most successful when they take into account the existing physical development and available resources and when they fulfill an inescapable regional function.

The *third measure,* housing for consumption, is also relevant for undeveloped countries and it is not necessarily inconsistent with the second criterion. It might be inconsistent if it cut out activities likely to add more to output than housing would. But it appears far more likely that self-help programs could tap human and physical resources, a large part of which might not otherwise be used. Indeed, if the housing needs or potential housing preferences could be determined and served, the catalytic effects—on effort, on savings, perhaps even on education and birth control—might ultimately be of tremendous significance. Here is a real frontier for evaluations of past experience, for sample surveys and other techniques of analysis. In developing such studies the assistance of cultural anthropologists and sociologists might be very valuable. Arriving at some estimate of total needs is clearly less important than fathoming what these people might want, or need, or respond to. Pilot projects might be of real value if they help to present a choice of alternatives which could give the vital clues.

The *fourth criterion* is political. For even if the resources available for housing are committed only where indispensable for maintaining or adding to highly productive activities, and even if self-help is resorted to as a device to get additional and otherwise untapped resources allocated to housing, there will still be a large residue of housing needs which cannot be satisfied for a long time. What is more, the discontent with housing will be aggravated because housing demands during periods of relatively successful economic development often rise faster than supply. The explanation for this apparent paradox is not simply that population and family growth will continue, but that rising income often generates demand for space and housing, promotes "undoubling," accelerates family formation and raises social standards of demand. These pressures may well affect almost the entire stock of housing and may, because of the inflationary impact, worsen the situation, particularly for those who have not shared the rise in income. Since existing housing resources leave narrow margins for economizing on space, prices are likely to soar and there will be bitter discontent.

If such a situation develops, certain public measures may be warranted to avoid exploitation and undesirable effects on morale. Indeed, whether we like it or not housing will be promised and even provided in some measure to avoid political instability. Unfortunately for the politician and the economy, this measure is vague and difficult to apply; and surveys may not be too helpful although some day our opinion polls may give us some useful clues. Yet crude and vulgar as this objective may be, in some situations clearly it would be dangerous to ignore. Indeed, recent experiences in Britain, France and the USSR have provided interesting evidence that discontent with housing could play a significant role in forcing a change of policies and perhaps even in toppling a government. Conceivably the effects might be more unsettling elsewhere. In fact I venture to suggest a very tentative and imprecise proposition for exploration. Food and education probably give "the biggest payoff" in terms of productivity; but to what extent, I wonder, do social explosions come from disproportions as well as deficiencies. That is, if our efforts are too distorted and the disproportion between achievements in one field compared to another becomes too wide e.g., possibly between food and education on the one hand, and shelter and other necessities on the other, might there not be far greater discontent and instability?

To sum up. If economic development is to be accelerated, in most cases a grave housing problem cannot be avoided. That alas, so far as I can judge, is the peculiar logic of development of primitive economies; and it seems to have been the experience for all countries regardless of the type of economic system. But at least economic development in the twentieth century need not be callous, if the needs are sensed, if exploitation is minimized, and if major efforts are evident. Possibly only those governments which begin to ponder and explore the "important" insoluble question of needs and show serious evidence of taking vigorous measures to deal with them can create the faith indispensable for the progress we are trying to achieve.

An Approach to Mass Housing in India: with Special Reference to Calcutta
ALFRED P. VAN HUYCK*

India faces the greatest problems of urbanization the world has ever known. Never before has so vast a population faced the immense tasks of building a modern urban environment. Furthermore, India is determined to accomplish this feat without totalitarianism or subjecting its people to the social abuses of the industrial revolution. Figuratively speaking, the nation is trying to jump from the eighteenth to the twentieth century in one leap.

To accomplish this lofty goal, India has been utilizing the planning technique of Five-Year Plans. Such plans are made up of targets with projects and procedures for their achievement. Slum clearance and low-cost housing have had a relatively small, but for urban areas important place in the overall planning procedure. The objective of this paper is to

* President, PADCO (International Planning and Development Cooperative). Formerly Chief Planner, Urban Renewal, Ford Foundation Advisory Planning Group, Calcutta, India, and prior to that Director of Planning and Urban Renewal, Herbert H. Smith Associates, West Trenton, New Jersey. Co-author of the book: *The Citizens Guide to Urban Renewal*, he holds an M.R.P. from the University of North Carolina. Much of this material was first presented to the Belgrade Congress of the International Union of Local Authorities on June 23, 1965.

analyze in broad terms this aspect of national policy with special reference to Calcutta, West Bengal. This aspect of housing is only one part of the total housing program in India, and is oriented to the bottom of the economic ladder.

I. THE URBAN FRAME OF REFERENCE IN INDIA

The selection of a mass housing strategy should be made within the context of the pattern of urbanization in the country. In India surprisingly enough, the process of urbanization is occurring at a relatively leisurely pace.[1]

Nonetheless the figures involved are still tremendous. Over eighty million people already live in India's urban areas. Here they maintain a rate of natural increase of between 1.5 and 2.0 percent per annum, which suggests approximately forty million births in the next twenty-five years.[2] With a declining death rate, this will undoubtedly result in a large net increase in the urban population by natural increase alone.

The predictability of migration is always difficult. Its eventual rate is very much dependent on the future of agriculture. It has been pointed out that when agricultural development will reach a level at which productivity begins to rise per unit of labor instead of unit of land, then the "big flood will break" in rural migration hitherto largely determined by the growth of population alone.[3] In 1961 only 18 percent of the population lived in urban areas. Allowing for a relatively modest increase to 19.3 percent by 1976 it can be estimated that 120 million people will live in urban areas.[4]

TABLE I. POPULATION PROJECTIONS FOR INDIA 1961–86

Year	India Population (million)	Per Cent Urban in India
1921	251	11.4
1931	279	12.1
1941	319	13.9
1951	361	17.3
1961	439	18.0

[1] Kingsley Davis: "Urbanization in India: Past and Future" in Roy Turner, ed., *India's Urban Future* (1962), pp. 3–7.

[2] Leo Jakobson, "Housing Note" (1965), unpublished.

[3] Sachin Chaudhuri: "Centralization and Decentralization" in Turner, *op. cit.*, p. 239.

[4] Calculated by the author from projections in Table I.

Projections	I	II
1966	492	18.1
1971	555	18.7
1976	625	19.3

PROJECTIONS: I 1961 Study Group of the Planning Commission (Third Five-Year Plan—Notes on Population and Employment, Table I, Column 4, p. 750).
II Estimated urbanization rate of Logistic Curve.

The distribution of this vast increase in urban dwellers is in itself a problem of great concern to the planners of India. At the moment approximately one-fourth of the total urban population of India (21.5 million people) is located in the eleven largest cities.[5] Furthermore, the class of cities over one hundred thousand population (the largest class) make up the fastest-growing of the six classes of cities set forth by the Census of India.

TABLE II. POPULATION GROWTH OF MAJOR METROPOLITAN
CITIES IN INDIA DURING 1931–61*

Name of City	Population		(add 000)		Variation
	1931	1941	1951	1961	1931–61
Calcutta Metropolitan District	2485	4054	5253	6575	4090
Greater Bombay	1303	1695	2839	4152	2849
Madras	647	777	146	1729	1082
Delhi	447	696	1437	2344	1897
Hyderabad	667	739	1086	1251	784
Ahmedabad	314	607	828	1206	892
Bangalore	311	411	786	1207	896
Kanpur	244	487	708	971	727
Poona	263	350	600	737	474
Lucknow	275	387	497	656	381
Nagpur	242	329	485	690	448

SOURCE: Census of India 1931–61.
* Population Growth and Urban and Regional Planning—A Background Paper Contributed to the Asia Population Conference: 1963. Town and Country Planning Organization, Government of India, Ministry of Health, Table VII.

Nowhere in India is this problem more strikingly illustrated than in the case of Calcutta. Calcutta dominates a four-state

[5] Calculated by the author from figures in Table II.

hinterland where there is not another city of over four hundred thousand people. Out of a total population of 111 million persons only 14.4 million live in urban areas, and of those, 6.5 million live in the Calcutta Metropolitan District. It is not surprising that Calcutta is the eventual destination of the migrant in Eastern India. The Calcutta Metropolitan Planning Organization estimates that by 1976, the total population will have increased to between nine and ten million people. This represents a net increase of between 2.5 and three million persons.[6]

A brief analysis of the settlement pattern of the recent urban migrants within the Calcutta Metropolitan District shows that older core areas, such as the city of Calcutta itself, are being bypassed in favor of the fringe areas. The greatest rates of growth are to be found in the non-municipal and rural areas. In short the mass of the urban area is rapidly increasing in size and density outside of the center. This situation is further complicated as these areas are the least prepared to handle growth and are generally lacking in all facilities and services.

II. EXISTING URBAN CONDITIONS IN CALCUTTA

Calcutta's reputation as an overcrowded and noxious city is well known. In the words of Kipling, it is "chance-erected, chance-directed." The reason for the problems are mainly: the aftereffects of World War II, when Calcutta was a military supply base; the Bengal Famine of 1945; and the partition of the country in 1947, with consequent influx of displaced persons from East Pakistan.[7] It is now one of the ten largest urban areas of the world and the largest in India. Settled in the mid-eighteenth century, Calcutta grew up lineally, north and south along the banks of the Hooghly River as the industrial hub and major port of Eastern India. Its east–west expansion was restricted on either side of the river by marshy land. Its growth was uncontrolled and without plan. It is still today the financial, manufacturing, administrative and distribution center for all Eastern India and by consensus a city whose problems are among the worst in the world.

The World Health Organization, surveying the city's water

---

[6] Estimated by the Calcutta Metropolitan Planning Organization.

[7] "Drafting a New Blueprint for India's Largest Urban Centre" The Ford Foundation, New Delhi, India (1964), p. 1.

and sanitation situation in 1959, made it clear that the low standard or absence of basic environmental health amenities was an undoubted cause for the continued prevalence of cholera and other epidemic diseases; and that to eliminate such pestilence, safe water and adequate sewerage and drainage must be provided for the entire population.

Almost any type of urban amenity known is lacking either wholly or in part in the city. Huge deficiencies in open space, education, mass transit and road construction await workable programs along with the environmental health problems of water, sewerage and drainage. It is not surprising that the city also is faced with a chronic housing shortage and great problems of dilapidation and overcrowding in the existing housing supply.

Various estimates of the housing shortage in Calcutta as of 1961 range over half a million units on the basis of the difference between the total number of families that normally need houses and the number of families that are in actual occupation of a dwelling.

According to the census figures, the situation in the Calcutta area is probably worse than elsewhere in India. For instance, the average occupancy ratio for urban India is 2.7 persons per room, 78.4 percent of all dwellings are in the one- to two-room category and the average dwelling size is 1.9 rooms. The corresponding figures for Calcutta City are three persons per room, 85 percent one- to two-room dwellings and 1.6 rooms per average dwelling. Furthermore, in the urban areas of West Bengal only 65 percent of the housing units are of permanent, usually brick construction; the other 35 percent are of mud, bamboo or other similar materials.[8]

The slum problem which has received the most attention to date in Calcutta is that of the bustees. Bustees are areas upon which are built one-story huts. Usually a hut will contain eight little cubicles each of which is rented to a separate family. In Calcutta City alone, there are over three thousand such bustees containing about thirty thousand huts on a total of seventeen hundred acres of land. The population of the bustees is approximately seven hundred thousand people. These areas are all of slum character, but some are much worse than others.[9] Many have no sewer connection, and night soil is manually collected in earthenware bowls from

[8] Census of India, 1961, Vol. XVI, Part IV.
[9] CMPO . . . "A Note on a Massive Bustee Improvement Programme for Calcutta and Howrah," unpublished (1964).

time to time. The drains are all open and usually clogged, resulting in vile odors in summer and flooding during monsoon. The water supply is usually grossly inadequate. The over-all condition is of great overcrowding in particularly noxious surroundings. It is no wonder that great concern is expressed for these areas.

The bustees are not the only slum areas in the city. So-called pukka slums, because they are multistoried buildings of brick, also exist. In some ways these are even worse, as they do not have the light and air of the bustees and when the sanitary facilities break down, which is often, the confined nature of the building makes conditions unbearable. Little is known statistically about the pukka slums, but it is roughly estimated that another two hundred fifty thousand persons live in such quarters. The remainder of the housing supply is for the most part better, but still not very satisfactory with the exception of some opulent quarters for the very rich which stand in marked contrast to the mass.

It is to this congested and deficient city that the masses of in-migrants will come in the next decade seeking work and shelter. And it is precisely this relationship between the migrant and the existing urban structure which possess the key problem for the future of Calcutta and urban India.

III. A CRITICISM OF CURRENT APPROACHES

Most plans for existing cities propose very large urban-renewal-type programs for slum clearance rehousing, and land development. The success or failure of current approaches rests on the design standards used, time, cost and social acceptability to the entire urban population. The standards used invariably affect all three of the other criteria, yet so often the standards chosen have been extracted from planning and housing literature of the West. Kindleberger and Spengler in the evaluation of the World Bank reports made this point:

Essentially, however, these are essays in comparative statistics. The missions bring to the underdeveloped country a notion of what a developed country is like. They observe the underdeveloped country. They subtract the latter from the former. The difference is a programme. Most of the members of the mission come from developed countries with highly articulated institutions for achieving social, economic and political ends. Ethnocentricity leads inevitably to the conclusion that the way to achieve the comparable levels of capital formation, productivity and consumption is to duplicate these institutions . . .[10]

This tendency is not just the error of the international consultant. Local planners seem equally determined to develop plans and programs using the same inappropriate standards and scale. In India, which generally has a well-educated planning profession as well as a large number of foreign consultants, these problems still appear.

To borrow standards in such a manner is all too widespread a practice in Indian planning. There is a need to develop meaningful standards which are indigenous to the Indian situation. Standards that are borrowed have little applicability and can result in a serious waste of resources. Standards set too high in this manner mean that a few projects built at this level will be relatively lavish and benefit the few, but the many will have even less than before.

The use of high standards is, of course, only one factor for the basic shortfall in housing construction and urban renewal activities. During the third Five-Year Plan, approximately nine thousand slum clearance rehousing units were sanctioned for Calcutta. At the end of 1964 only three thousand had been completed and during 1965 another one thousand units should be finished. The estimated shortfall will be around five thousand units of the target.[11] The fourth Five-Year Plan calls for another nine thousand units of slum clearance housing. From these figures, it is obvious that no major slum clearance urban renewal can be undertaken before 1971. Furthermore, the administrative machinery to develop a more massive program is not available.

Actually this slow pace in slum clearance is probably a good thing if the views of Charles Abrams are correct. He has written:

> In the long run, the most blighting influence on a city is not the one-storey shack, however bad, but the tall crowded tenement with its small cubicles for masses of

[10] C. P. Kindleberger: "A Review of the Economy of Turkey; The Economic Development of Guatemala; Report on Cuba," *Review of Economics and Statistics*, Vol. 34, No. 4 (November 1952), as quoted in Jakobson, *op. cit.*

[11] Interview with Wayne Daugherty, Ford Foundation Consultant on Housing, April 1965.

people. Planners exhort nations to build well and permanently. The nations that can afford to do so should but in the poorer countries not only is the choice narrow and the time short but the stakes are large and the mistakes enduring. If compromises must be made because of emergency, the planners who make them should weigh both the immediate by-products and the future means of rectifying them.[12]

The social acceptability of the rehousing estates has also been of only limited success. Sidhendu Mukherjee of the Calcutta Metropolitan Planning Organization suggested some of the reasons why this is so:

The occupations of slum-inhabitants such as rickshaw pullers, corporation sweepers, scavengers, hand-cart pullers, hawkers, shop assistants, office peons, factory workers and domestic servants all have to depend on the peculiarities of the city social life. Consequently, such low paid workers are forced to find their residence in the slums. The overwhelming number of these slum-dwellers have their place of work within a mile of their residence.

This fragmentation into slum-pockets is one of the major hindrances towards treatment of the slum problem. There are more than 3,000 slum-pockets in Calcutta. In essence they may be considered "service pockets" as the inhabitants serve the people of the adjoining areas. It would not be wise to remove such slum-dwellers to distant areas in the conurbation. Without suitable employment opportunities, they would probably migrate back into the city to swell the number of squatters or pavement-dwellers. The failure of some of the refugee rehabilitation programmes and the subsequent squatting by the refugees in railway stations or pavements are sharp pointers in this respect.

It is also significant to note that even though the scope of slum clearance programmes is not very great because of the inadequacy of requisite funds, the actual state of affairs within the existing programme is far from satisfactory. Studies have revealed that after clearance, only about 20% to 30% of the genuine slum-dwellers go over to the Bustee Rehousing Estates. The rest chose to go to

[12] Charles Abrams, *Man's Struggle for Shelter in an Urbanizing World*, M.I.T. Press, Massachusetts (1964).

other slums in the adjoining areas, thereby increasing congestion or join a third group which took shelter on pavements or under bridges or even inside railway wagons or large diameter sewer pipes of the Corporation.[13]

Even if such social considerations can be set aside, there is still a strong case to be made against present slum clearance practice in India on purely economic and financial grounds.

Professor Wellisz, who was formerly with the Ford Foundation in Calcutta, did extensive work on the subject of the real costs of slum clearance and rehousing, and the following paragraphs have been summarized from his papers.[14]

For slum clearance and rehousing schemes the Government of India grants direct subsidies and low-interest loans to the state governments. They also stipulate specifications for redevelopment schemes, suggest tenant classifications and set maximum rents. At present the program (now being considered for upward revision) sets the ceiling for construction at Rs 6,600* per family in Calcutta, in units of 232 square feet. The maximum income of an eligible family is set at Rs 250 per month and the maximum rent is Rs 21.50 per month. In short, the Government of India stands ready to shoulder part of the slum clearance and rehousing costs provided that the costs are kept within reasonable limits. The housing must conform to decent standards, so that old slums are not replaced with publicly built new slums. Ceilings are set on income of the families and rents to insure that poor people benefit from the program.

Subsidization of housing involves a transfer of income from taxpayers to those who obtain space in the subsidized projects. It means putting more resources into housing than would occur in the absence of the subsidy. Resources are, therefore, transferred to housing from consumption of other goods or investment. It is implied that this should be the best use of the funds. The use of subsidies in urban renewal and rehousing programs is justified on the grounds that slum clearance

[13] Sidhendue Mukherjee, "Studies on Slums in the Calcutta Metropolitan District; An Outline of the Principles and Perspectives of the Slum-Areas' Programme," unpublished (July 1963).

[14] Stanislaw H. Wellisz, "India's Slum-Clearance Policy: An Economic Evaluation," unpublished (1963).

* Approximate equivalents: One Rupee (R) equals 21 cents; one Lakh (100,000 Rupees) equals 21,000 dollars; one Crore (100 Lakhs) equals 2.1 million dollars. The Editor.

should benefit the poor members of society, it should not harm the people living in the slums, and the programs should seek to reduce economic inequalities.

Professor Wellisz undertook an analysis to determine the approximate size of the real subsidy involved per family per year. He started with the cost of the unit set at Rs 6,600 the upper limit, and assumed a vacancy of 2.5 percent, a sixty-year life to the structure, the cost of the thirty-year loan at 4.5 percent as well as the opportunity cost of alternative investments, which in India could pay a return of at least 13 percent. His conclusion was that the actual social cost of housing each family was Rs 938 per year not counting the cost of city services. Subtracting the maximum rent, the net cost was determined to be Rs 680 per year per family. The failure to pay rents would, of course, greatly increase this figure and the experience in Calcutta has been that substantially less than 100 percent of the rent is actually collected. Various studies suggest the maximum rent a family can afford is 15 percent of their income; therefore, only those making Rs 173 per month can afford to live in the subsidized projects.

Wellisz then determined who paid the subsidies and concluded that the range of families all over India making between Rs 100–150 would make an annual contribution of Rs 226 per subsidized family, and the category of families making less than Rs 100 would contribute another Rs 68 to the subsidy because of indirect taxes. The result is that "middle-income" slum dwellers receive the benefit and the poorer slum dwellers do not. The latter often attempt to sell their occupancy rights to unauthorized persons.

It is obvious from the record to date and the conceivable amount of new construction to be undertaken during the next ten years that the present slum clearance program will not eradicate the slums of Calcutta. There are 189,000 bustee families alone in the core city. It would require an expenditure of 124.7 crores of rupees or approximately 262 million dollars to build the housing required. It would then consume another 12.8 crores of rupees or some 26 million dollars for annual subsidies.[15] The expenditure of such sums of money on one city for slum rehousing alone is clearly impossible.

Finally, the magnitude of India's housing problem becomes evident when one realizes that the average income of Calcutta's slum dwellers is approximately equal to the per-capita

[15] CMPO, *op. cit.*

income in the state as a whole. The average bustee dweller is not the exceptionally ill-fortuned person. If the city slum dweller receives special treatment, he will be raised above the average. The city slums are fed by the migration of people from the country. This occurs largely because of the poverty of the rural areas. Thus city slums are the result of the nation's poverty, and not merely isolated islands of poverty in the city.[16]

IV. NEW APPROACHES

Some 27,700 dwelling units a year must be constructed by the government in the Calcutta Metropolitan District merely to keep pace with projected population growth. The present proposals for the fourth Five-Year Plan included in the state's request is for twenty-seven thousand dwelling units of all types, or less than is required for a single year of construction if full demand is to be met.[17] It is obvious that new and drastic proposals must be sought and successfully applied. Such programs must recognize the following conclusions about the current slum clearance and housing situation:

1. Vast amounts of new low cost housing must be built for new urban in-migrants.
2. Urban renewal, which involves only slum clearance and rehousing, cannot be undertaken at a large scale because of the costs to the public and the minimum addition to the housing stock above mere replacement.

From these two conclusions a basic strategy for housing and slums begins to take shape:

1. EXISTING HOUSING STOCK EVEN IN SLUMS MUST BE CONSERVED WHEREVER POSSIBLE SO THAT NEW HOUSING RESULTS IN A MAXIMUM NET GAIN.
2. ENVIRONMENTAL IMPROVEMENTS TO DEAL WITH THE GREATEST SLUM HEALTH HAZARDS SHOULD BE UNDERTAKEN TO MAKE SLUMS LESS INTOLERABLE.
3. STANDARDS FOR NEW HOUSING MUST BE LOWERED TO THE POINT THAT IT IS POSSIBLE TO BUILD SHELTER FOR THE URBAN MIGRANT WITHOUT DIRECT SUBSIDY. THIS WOULD MEAN GIVING UP RIGID OBSOLETE STANDARDS AND NOT REQUIRING PERMANENT PUKKA CONSTRUCTION.

[16] Wellisz, *op. cit.*
[17] Jakobson, *op. cit.*

4. DEVELOP NON-PERMANENT CONSTRUCTION TECHNIQUES
WITH LIFE SPANS OF BETWEEN 15 TO 25 YEARS FOR
SHELTER IN NEW URBAN AREAS.

A program developed on these policies would of necessity
involve massive slum improvement for existing areas and the
control of new urbanization in projects such as non-permanent
open lot developments. This viewpoint is also expressed by
Charles Abrams in his recent book:

A city built today should, therefore, take account of the
essential expansion tomorrow. Yet cities built under the
pressure of industrial fluctuations and population pressures will hardly reflect careful planning. They may have
to be rebuilt when occasion permits. Therefore, while
the wealthier nations are now engaged in urban renewal,
the underdeveloped ones must plan for urban renewability. In the sense, the building of dispensable (low-cost,
not temporary) buildings is preferable to lasting medioc-
rity and blight. Zoning should limit density and height
until the area is ripe for renewal. The lot layouts and the
replacement of utilities and roads are the principal conditioning factors in rebuilding. If the houses are simple,
they are improvable or dispensable.[18]

Non-permanent construction can be of several types and
lends itself to a variety of design solutions. In many ways it
is similar to the type of construction that is already occurring
on the periphery of the large urban areas. Essentially it attempts to introduce urban living patterns yet permit a continuation of village activities such as handicrafts and minor
farming operations near enough to the city so that the population can be employed in urban jobs. The difference between current uncontrolled development and controlled non-
permanent housing areas is that the latter will be according to
a set plan which looks ahead to the convertibility to permanent construction at a later date by designing the water system, sewers, drainage and roads accordingly. Furthermore,
by careful organization net densities of four hundred persons
per acre can be achieved which will be fully compatible with
the densities required for permanent urban construction
later on.

[18] Abrams, *op. cit.*, p. 240.

The non-permanent housing area would be provided with the necessary urban amenities such as water taps, sanitary latrines, lighting, paving and filtered water supply. The housing units would be of mud and bamboo or equally light and cheap construction. The entire development of this nature should be without Government subsidy for the shelter units themselves as the average income for slum dwellers is presently Rs 120/- a month and it can be assumed that the new migrants would be able to achieve a similar level and this would permit the full amortization of an initial investment of Rs 1,520 in each dwelling unit.[19]

Government subsidy in the form of land and infrastructure, while substantial, will be transferable to new permanent construction in the future.

For the last few years, the Calcutta Metropolitan Planning Organization has been evolving a concept of slum improvement which would neutralize some of the worse aspects of the bustees. This program recognizes the reality that these slum areas cannot be cleared in the near future, though it optimistically keeps total clearance as the ultimate goal. The program calls for the installation in each bustee area of an adequate, safe water system, community water taps and baths, a sanitary sewerage system connected with sanitary latrines, a storm drainage system, pavement of the alleys and paths, outdoor lighting and the filling of tanks. (In order to fill areas to build in Calcutta the procedure has been to dig holes which then fill with water. These become stagnant and unsanitary because of the human waste which drains into them from unsanitary privies located on the edges.) The net result of this program will be a startling improvement in living conditions for over four hundred thousand bustee dwellers in Calcutta.[20]

Estimates worked out for pilot areas indicate the cost of the improvements for areas presently sewered will be Rs 120 per capita and for the unsewered areas Rs 150 per capita. The cost of administration and planning, etc., brings the total figure to an estimated Rs 187 per capita or less than Rs 1,000 per family. This amounts to less than two years of subsidy of a rehoused family under the existing slum clearance program.

An important by-product of the program is the proposal to buy the land upon which the slums are located to facilitate

[19] Wellisz, *op. cit.*
[20] CMPO, *op. cit.*

clearance and redevelopment at a future date. Financing of this aspect of the program will be handled through government bonds.

V. CONCLUSIONS

This paper has attempted to deal realistically with the problem of mass housing in the urbanizing process of a developing country beset with extreme poverty. It has pointed out the futility of the present program which, by using too-high standards applied at too high a cost, restrict all possibility of achieving a massive result.

This basic strategy error, discussed here in the context of mass housing, can be found in new town developments, industrial complexes and in fact, many of the physical development projects so far undertaken. Essentially, the problem lies in the concentration of a disproportionately great amount of capital in a relatively small number of projects which means that the vast majority of the country will be no better off than before. As a result the country's standard of living gap is actually widening even though showpiece projects are successfully completed.

The concentration of resources on environmental improvement programs such as the bustee program and temporary housing projects discussed here are illustrative of an alternative approach. This policy could be the first step on a long-range program of renewal for the cities of India.

Regional Planning in an Urbanizing World: Problems and Potentials

CHARLES ABRAMS*

The subject of regional planning in an urbanizing world is a mouthful which is easier to introduce orally than to digest. One is immediately confronted with definitions of terms—the nature of a region, the meaning of planning, and the bewildering problems of the less-developed nations.

The dictionary definition of a region affords us only a clue. It defines a region as:

* Delivered before the Town Planning Summer School, Exeter University, England, September 9, 1964. For a biography of Mr. Abrams, see Chapter 18.

1. a more or less defined portion of the earth's surface, especially as distinguished by certain natural features or climatic conditions; or
2. an area, space, or place, of more or less definite extent or character; or
3. an administrative division of a city or district.

The city planner is apt to be confronted by any one of nine types of regions. They include:

1. An already defined jurisdictional unit such as a county, state or province.
2. A large metropolitan complex like London and New York, or the Chicago region containing one thousand disparate governments.
3. A group of smaller municipalities, a solution to whose common problems is sought by creating an integrating regional plan.
4. Two or more states, cities or other bodies voluntarily delegating some powers over common problems (water, port, sewage, parks, housing, etc.) to an autonomous body formed specially for these purposes.
5. A section of a country whose physiographical features make regional planning desirable.
6. An international waterway, form of communication, or power governed by two or more countries.
7. A new city whose expansion will necessarily affect the surrounding area.
8. An existing city with undeveloped land stirring at its periphery.
9. A number of rural areas concerned with flood control, water, transportation, or some other common problem.

Impetus has been given to regional planning by the increase not only in world population but in the mobilities—mobility of transport, power, industry, goods, and people. The compass within which man once lived and worked has enlarged. With power and workers transportable over longer distances, the old jurisdictional limits are no longer realistic. Planning today may often embrace a single city or a region of which the city is a part, as in the case of Rangoon, Cairo, Djakarta, Amman, Beirut and Karachi.

So, too, bringing in water can make the desert a bustling suburb or re-create an area like Israel's Beersheba region. The settlement of industries on outlying land can spawn new cities as well as new regions. Regional rationalization may also be a device for bringing land owned by competing jurisdictions into rational control.

Another perplexing problem arises when we try to define planning or master planning in a world in which the planning process is being conditioned by the nature of the particular society and the pressure of a particular need. In the non-democratic society, the regional good of the greater number is determined by a smaller number, while in a democracy, what is the greater good of the greater number is conditioned by respect for the individual. Democratic city planning is a subtle and difficult compromise in which the quest for order is tempered by the respect for rights.

The increase in government power over city development and housing has better enabled government to influence the emerging scene and to guide development. Government's expanded powers and functions are now main influences in the location of industry, the flow of housing and the manipulation of environment. At one time, private improvements came first and impelled public improvements as a sequel. Today, what the government builds directly or allows to be built is the primary influence; private investment is more apt to follow after the public policies and improvements are made. Public programs and improvements can induce people to remain in the city's center or induce them (through subsidies or other inducements) to move outside by the thousands.

Master planning can be one of the tools of regional planning but has limitations as well as values. By aligning perspectives, goals, laws and procedures and assigning a time schedule to them, developmental aspirations are set on course. It educates the citizens and officials, may win their commitment and help preserve policy against the fitful decisions of public works departments or the vapory fancies of dreamers. But a main limitation of the master plan is that it is subject to constant discomposure by intruding events.

Another obstacle is that when a plan is set down at one time, all the opponents are brought out simultaneously, threatening the plan as a whole. Planners in democratic countries therefore prefer to present the master plan in stages, while others label it as a guide only.

The problems of master planning were illustrated in Dublin when that city hired Sir Patrick Abercrombie to prepare its master plan in 1936. Abercrombie projected new traffic routes for a future population of 750,000; he proposed a greenbelt of 120,000 acres around Dublin and anticipated a number of self-contained satellite towns on the fringe, should his population estimate be exceeded. The Abercrombie plan was an inspiring blueprint, enlivened by rhetoric, exhortation and hope. But it was relegated to the archives because it proposed too much, appeared too costly, and because there were too many vested interests to be disturbed at once; immediate housing programs, moreover, had more political appeal than city planning.

The rock on which regional planning is either shattered or to which it is firmly secured is jurisdiction. Two conflicting forces at work in our world are becoming more and more difficult to accommodate. On the one hand there is the spatial revolution which has dissolved the tyranny of distance. With the greater mobilities of transportation, power, communication, industry, goods and people, the old lines of jurisdictional authority are no longer realistic and the pressure is to cross jurisdictional lines to favor the true needs of people and industry.

At the same time, however, home rule, local autonomy, decentralization and deconcentration are still asserting their claims. They are being re-enforced by the assertion of loyalties—tribal, customary, racial, local or provincial. These ties tend to confine regions to areas that may make little sense from a planning standpoint but they make considerable sense for the politician looking for public support.

In democratic countries, one is often confronted by regional plans which are nothing more than advisory or exhortatory. Or they may be coordinative, in which a plan attempts through financial inducements to win over competing jurisdictions to a regional consensus. Compulsory features, however, have been added in some of these cases to prevent unwise industrial settlement, deforestation, deruralization, or some other undesirable development. Whether compulsion, inducement, or persuasion is used often depends on the urgency of the need or the political complexion of the government.

The most important (and potentially the most constructive) regional plan is one in which there is an actual improvement of major proportions which brings inevitable consequences in its wake. The harnessing of the Volta River in Ghana will not only turn bauxite into aluminum but alter the lives and ways of a rural-tribal society. It will disenthral its economy from its major dependency upon cocoa; inspire secondary industries, shipping and trade; improve health. It may also have political, social and economic consequences, including an alteration of the relationship between government, private investment, local agencies and people.

The harnessing of a river in East Pakistan will reduce flood damage, maintain and extend the area of cropped lands, swell their yields, provide navigation and improved fishing and multiple other blessings.

The control of the Jordan in the Middle East would not only affect the physical and economic patterns of the two countries concerned but might ultimately have a beneficial impact on the political relationships between the countries involved if not on their neighbors as well.

The development of India's Damodar Valley through an organization similar in some respects to the Tennessee Valley Authority has aimed to prevent the costly floods of the Damodar River and latterly to spur a full development of the river, including irrigation, navigation and electric power projects.

The Bhakra-Nangal project, India's largest multipurpose undertaking, diverts water into the Nangal Hydel canal supplying two completed hydroelectric plants; ultimately, the 108-mile Bhakra irrigation canal will be included as well.

When there is this type of improvement, the prospects are better for the assertion of national sovereignty and the subordination or accommodation of conflicting local interests. The task becomes more difficult, however, when there are vested political interests such as a city or region with defined political authority. This is true not only in the United States but in a number of the less-developed countries and in those with recently formed governmental structures.

An example is Nigeria, a federation of three regions, with its national capital in Lagos, a small island carved out of the tip of the western region. The Moslem northern region holds half the federation's population, the eastern region has the Ibo tribe and the western region the Yorubas. The tripod form of government was designed to prevent any one region from dominating the other two. Lagos, however, in the western region, has a growing population and is really part of a Lagos region in which more than 40 percent of the region's people commute between Lagos and the suburbs of the western region. The Lagos worker is unconscious of the burdens which separate the capital from the western region but the west is nevertheless conscious of the fact that Lagos ends at its borders and is jealous of any intrusions by the central government. When one political party dominated the central government as well as Lagos and another political party controlled the western region, regional expansion struck a serious political snag and a United Nations mission was requested to evolve some form of autonomous corporation that would be acceptable to both. Of course, a shift in political control in which the same political party controls both the west and the central government might help resolve the problem.

The separation between Kampala and the surrounding urban area of Uganda is accentuated by the traditional and political differences between the central government and Uganda. Here, too, a United Nations mission was invited to help solve the development problem affecting a large part of the African urban population and a number of constituent authorities within the regional zone.

Another example is Japan's Hanshin metropolitan region embracing Osaka, Kobe, Kyoto, Nara, Sakai, and Wakayama. As an industrial and financial center, this putative region ranks second only to Tokyo, but its growth has not kept pace with Tokyo. Two serious handicaps are water supply and soil subsidence. Better coordination is needed to improve flood control, sewage disposal, river basin development, soil conservation, port development, land reclamation, air purification, transport and general land use for industrial expansion and housing.

As in the United States, however, a regional solution of the problems is deterred by competition and jealousies among the governmental units. Japan is an infant democracy with a grown-up's productive potency. It is a democracy by constitution but tradition has not yet encrusted its precedents and the process of regional rationalization is slow and cumbersome. Hanshin's problem dramatizes the dilemma in the regional planning process of other democratically structured systems. On the one hand, localization of function provides competitive stimulus among communities, local initiative, and more intimate contact between citizen and city. Without regional cooperation, competition heads toward chaos. The challenge to Japan as well as to other democratic systems is whether they are capable of fashioning the right tools to win such cooperation while preserving some of the values of local autonomy.

There are numerous devices which can be employed without excessive arrogations of power and if these fail, central authority has to be asserted in essential cases, i.e., where the problems cross local jurisdictions, are national in scope or in financial involvement, or touch the national welfare power. The requirements of commerce, defense, transport, or an economic crisis will spur intervention. But central intervention need not always mean lasting intervention, for once the problem is resolved, considerable local authority can be restored. The central authority should try to induce before it regulates, regulate before it takes over, and, when it centralizes, it can thereafter decentralize. Nor, when it socializes, need it continue to own and operate what has been socialized. One of the great surviving political illusions is that what the government takes over, it must also operate. Unlike generals, however, states rarely fade away. When they keep accumulating power, they never wither away because they have no place whither to wither to. Public acquisition of land for planning, for example, is justified but it can yield to private development and home ownership after the plan is made.

One of the dangers of which the planner should be warned is that of generalization. Though there are common denominators in the world such as industrialization, migration to the cities, slums, outward expansion from the central cities, and an increase in power over land operations, there are also vast differences between one country and another as well as between the more-developed and the less-developed nations. No regional planner, for example, would recommend to a nation the American pattern under which fifty states possess sovereign power over land, the boundaries of which make no regional sense and were often demarcated by straight lines drawn more than a century ago for an agricultural society. Britain's new towns program is still unacceptable in the United States today. Nor would self-contained new towns be relevant in many underdeveloped countries, which may have no alternative to the enlargement of already existing industrial concentrations in their big cities. Despite the desirability of industrial decentralization, a nation's desire that industry settle where it is good for the nation is not always what the industrialist thinks is good for his business, and where capital investment is at a premium, the investor's inclinations are apt to have more weight than those of the planning officials. The investor often finds the metropolis the area with the banks, universities and the better newspapers; where the executives can meet face to face; where the distributors and buyers are located; where foreign businessmen are most likely to visit; where the best professional and skilled workers are available; where there are secondary service industries; where air and rail service is best; and where a ready-made consumer market already exists. In the big city, approaches can be made more easily to tax officials and men of influence. Finally, in a world in which executives are at a premium, the executive's wife is a potent factor in industrial location; because the big city offers better schools, department stores, doctors, dentists, psychoanalysts, safer water, bridge clubs and first-rate beauty parlors, her decision may tip the scales in the decision of an industry to locate.

Tokyo, for example, the world's largest city, is also the most overcrowded. It would seem logical for Japan to foster the building of new free-standing cities elsewhere, or at least to encourage the growth of secondary areas such as sparsely settled Hokkaido, or Hanshin, which has a good port and other facilities. The obstacle is that too many Japanese industrialists find that the advantages of Tokyo outweigh the disadvantages. In a bank-note world, it is better to be as near as possible to the bank notes.

Yet, if the big city must inevitably grow bigger, what will happen when a city like Calcutta reaches twelve to sixteen million in 1970 or a conceivable fifty million by 2000? While not every city is Calcutta, there are in India some 106 cities with populations of one hundred thousand or more that might form the basis for extension and for industrial expansion in the ensuing decades. In fact, enlarging existing cities into regional formations offers less risk than building isolated new towns.

There are, nevertheless, many developing areas where new towns offer an important opportunity. Singapore, for example, would have difficulty expanding its existing borders but because the island is small, it offers an opportunity to plan a number of cities on the waterways, reserving the central area for the common needs of the whole region such as water, airports, a greenbelt, connecting arteries between cities and open space.

If new towns are set up on land distant from the large city, it is best that they be sufficiently varied in their industries, opportunities and interests to have their own polar influences. It is best, too, that a regional site have a surrounding agricultural area. This would not only allow room for expansion but make food available and add to the economic base of the industrial complex.

In all cases involving the less-developed areas, however,

regional planning should be viewed in the context of their over-all problems. These countries are experiencing their revolutions—industrial, social and political—all at once in contrast to the sequential developments in the more-developed ones.

Thirty-five years from now, the world's population will have increased by some three billion, and the day when the earth must hold seven billion is no farther away than World War I is from today. The impact will be felt most in the cities of the less-developed world, for although total population in these regions will grow by 40 percent in fifteen years, urban population will double. The urban population of Africa will probably grow from 58 million in 1960 to 294 million by the year 2000; that of Asia from 559 million to 3,444 million; and that of Latin America from 144 million to 650 million.

This population surge is confronting the less-developed countries with enormous housing problems which are becoming worse rather than better with the years. These nations lack capital to finance industries, squatters are overrunning both their public and private lands, and it should be a sobering fact for the planner to know that the planned city of Ankara now has a population 45 percent of which are squatters; the planned city of Manila likewise has a 25 percent squatter population; and the squatter population of cities in Latin America is often 25 percent or more. Santo Tome in Venezuela, a new regional steel town, had twenty thousand squatters when the steel mill was only employing its first thousand workers. Regional planning in the less-developed areas should anticipate and prepare for these squatter movements or the best-laid plans may fail. In Santo Tome, I recommended a "squatters welcome" policy under which areas would be reserved for such squatters in the planning of the region; land and utilities were laid out for them in advance and they were permitted to put up whatever houses they wished. A small loans program was made available to them for the purpose.

Often such planned slums may be better in the long run than unplanned slums, and when ownership is given the squatter, the houses tend to improve remarkably. The sites selected for squatters must be close to work or they will disregard the assigned sites and squat in the central area. With their growing political strength, it may be ultimately impossible to dislodge them.

In the development of regions, planning, in short, may have to be taken in two steps—the first anticipating substandard houses on planned sites, and the second stage (urban renewal) when the country is ready for it. Regional planning, instead of laying down an unalterable plan, may have to be flexible and be devised for future urban renewability instead of immediate slum clearance.

I should also like to emphasize the universal housing default as a bar to regional development. The technical genius that has broken the secrets of speed, sound, space and light still cannot build a house cheap enough for the rank-and-file. A Soviet cosmonaut today can orbit the world but the state that launched him cannot establish a good housing program on the ground. A Negro laborer's family in New York and a squatter in Caracas may both have television sets but neither can afford a decent house.

The anomaly is that, in a primitive village, the housing problem is not critical and human waste disposal is manageable. But the moment a nation embarks on its industrial development, its housing problem looms large. When the breadwinner moves from village to city, he finds the land staked out into small lots to be bought or rented. He no longer has the time to build, and often his meager diet provides him with too little energy to do so after his daily exertions and his long journey to work. He must buy materials from manufacturers or middlemen and, to buy or rent a home, he must have a constant flow of money from a steady job.

Complicating the housing problem in the less-developed areas is land speculation, which has been intensified by population increase, freedom from land taxation, by provision of roads and utilities by governments, by inflationary trends, and by the dearth of alternative investments. There is actually no shortage of land for urban use, for man is small and his needs for urban workspace and homes are relatively insignificant. In the highly industrialized United States, for example, urbanized land occupies only about 1 percent of the entire land supply, while Europe averages eighty-five people to every square kilometer, Asia averages only sixty, and the world in general only twenty-one. The real problem is not space shortage for cities but the intense competition for sites within the fermenting urban areas. If the urban radius within each country can be stretched by proper land policy and by the addition of transportation and utilities, the land for homes and workplaces should be more than ample, even by the year 2000.

The less-developed countries face not only a lack of skills but a lack of financing mechanisms for home building. Land transfer and registration systems hardly exist. The lag and discontinuity in construction activity has discouraged many workers from training for the building trades. The local materials industries remain underdeveloped, too. All these problems must be resolved before regional plans can be consummated.

I should like to mention one other aspect of the regional planning process that has been ignored, and it concerns the role of the United Nations. Regional alliances to achieve economic cooperation among nations constitute one of the United Nations' cardinal purposes and offer the prospect of peaceful adjustment of interboundary differences. The transition from force to contract achieved by man seems long overdue for the world's governments. There are many projects which can create international river valleys and make water, power, communications, transport, and industry a multinational dividend of compact and cooperative effort.

An identification of the problems which can yield to contract is needed and thereafter the formulation of legal instruments and devices which can serve to convert fears, jealousies or disagreements into definable accords. There is a record of tens of thousands of international agreements, but few that rationalize the problems of an international region.

From the time of the informal Concert of Europe to the much more powerful European Economic Community, intergovernmental bodies have been increasing in political, economic and social regions in Europe and elsewhere. The Organization for European Economic Cooperation, with seventeen states, is an example. A number of regional agencies, political and economic, also operate under the United Nations Charter and still others function outside the United Nations.

Unfortunately, most of the international agencies concerned with regional problems are separated from actual development. As with national regional planning, it is the proximity of the improvement that gives the plan life and impact.

What are needed are:

1. Up-to-date surveys of potential projects (international waterways, dams, transport, industry or communications) and the development of an inventory of those undertakings in which good sense would dictate the making of regional arrangements.

2. Initiation of a few viable undertakings with a constructively contagious quality.

3. Development of a pool of experts equipped to aid in the planning, development and management of the enterprises.

4. Enrollment of private investment through limited guarantees or other inducements.

5. Provision of ample funds as an inducement to undertake the projects.

6. Refinement of the corporate, contractual, managerial and administrative mechanisms for building and operating international regional enterprises so as to give proper representation to the nations concerned, effect a reasonable distribution of costs and dividends and win the confidence of the participating nations.

While the World Bank and other international agencies are making loans for such projects, they are not engaged in construction and operation. This leaves a challenging gap to be filled.

The least explored and most fruitful potential would be a regional development corporation set up by the United Nations itself. Possessing technical skills, it would not exact a predatory price for harnessing them. It would not demand a military alliance in return for the loan. To gain this objective, however, a transition must be made by the United Nations from "consultation," "research," "study," "advice" and "recommendations" to actual financing, building, aiding and operating.

The development of new devices for regional planning presents a challenging frontier for improving conditions within countries and between them. But no government and even less so can an international government ever acquire sovereignty or even influence without a spending power. Oddly, the United Nations was granted the war power (in Korea and the Congo) but no funds for developing its influence for peace. In this respect, the potential for using the United Nations as an instrument of regional progress highlights the international vacuum and perhaps the most challenging regional frontier of all.

Research for National Urban Development Planning

LAWRENCE D. MANN*

AUTHOR'S NOTE: The discussion here is based less on academic research as to how national planning for urban development should be done than on extended experience in trying to help do it in one country: Chile. The approach that has evolved through many months of constantly revised experimentation in the Chilean situation is here stated in a form as general as possible. It is to be expected that some of the elements would not be so feasible or useful in other countries. In particular, no pretense is made that the Chilean approach has much to teach such highly developed nations as the United States in the practice of planning there—though some contribution need not be logically excluded. The bibliography cited in the notes that follow is not claimed to be exhaustive. It is given only to credit direct sources of ideas. The concepts that make up the scheme could not all belong to a single author, and in fact many of them were developed in brainstorming sessions with the Chilean planners Juan Astica, Guillermo Geisse, and Gastón Maturana, as well as John Friedmann. Other names could also be mentioned.

Urban planners trained for practice in the United States are often cast in quite different roles when working in the less-developed countries of the world. They generally work for a national government rather than a local authority. Frequently they find themselves highly placed in the more powerful ministries. The typical weakness of the market economy, of private initiative generally, in most developing countries implies that governments, through their officials, effectively decide what is going to happen in the cities and towns, just as elsewhere in the society and economy. It is the basis for such urban development decisions that concerns us here.

The international reputation of American city planning is that it is much richer in ideas than in accomplishments. This perhaps not totally unfair evaluation can be understood as partly a response to the relatively weak position enjoyed by the United States planner at home. His proposals rarely have

* Planning Advisor to the Chilean Government, Ford Foundation Planning Team, Santiago, Chile. Holder of an M.C.P. and a Ph.D. in city and regional planning from Harvard, he has enjoyed wide research experience both here and abroad in physical and in social planning, including work with Peter Rossi, Martin Meyerson, the Centre for Urban Studies (University of London), and EKISTICS. He has been on the planning faculties of both the University of North Carolina and Harvard and has published in professional journals.

a dramatic and lasting impact on the development of urban areas where he works, yet his professional ideology says they should. The power of local free enterprise and of active local politics in deciding how urban development shall take place are simply the facts of professional life. These circumstances have led the American planner to think through a number of urban economic and policy problems that his counterparts in other parts of the world have neglected. This is particularly true for methods of urban study and the relation of research to policy. In these fields, United States planners would seem to have a special contribution to make in international technical assistance.

Besides providing a very real opportunity to help where professional help is most needed, American technical assistance in urban planning has become something of a proving ground for ideas untested (and perhaps untestable) in their native setting. Where such assistance works well, therefore, it can be very much a two-way proposition; improvements can be witnessed in both planning methods and in the situation with which the planning is concerned. At the same time, new approaches may be confronted with reality and modified as necessary for possible later application. One such case, that of national policy and programming, is the theme here.

NATIONAL URBAN STRUCTURE AND DEVELOPMENT

In a number of countries there is much talk, and some progress, concerning national physical plans and their coordination with economic and social plans. Such national plans, except when agricultural in focus, are also sometimes called urban development plans.[1] The basic idea underlying such

[1] There has been much thought along these lines in Britain, especially in the writings of the geographer, Dudley Stamp. The French *aménagement du territoire* may be seen in this light, and this has spread to a number of French-speaking countries. (See my "French Regional Planning," *Journal of the AIP*, May 1964.) The Israel case is well documented. Russia and most East European countries have such planning going. (See Jack Fisher, "Planning the City of Socialist Man," and, with Zygmunt Pióro and Nilos Savić, "Socialist City Planning: A Reexamination," *Journal of the AIP*, November 1962 and February 1965, respectively.) Also relevant here are: Britton Harris, "Urbanization Policy in India," in *Papers and Proceedings*, Regional Science Association, Vol. V, 1959; and Ibrahin Hilimi Abdel-Rahman, "Relations between Urban and National Planning," in Monroe Berger (ed.), *The New*

proposals comes from geographic and economic studies of patterns or structures of urban influence within a nation. An extensive international literature exists on this matter.[2]

It is well established that larger cities serve larger surrounding areas, generally, than do smaller ones and that they do this through productive, commercial, administrative, social, and cultural facilities located centrally. Based on impressive evidence, it seems quite proper to speak of a *hierarchy* of urban service areas in any country. Moreover, where such a structure is not clearly formed, it seems to evolve over time in mutual causation (or at least in correlation) with socioeconomic development. This would be one way of looking at the subject matter of national urban structure and its development.

There is another aspect of national urban structure and development, one on which the bulk of the discussion usually centers. Given the fact that most developing countries have one urban center that tends to dwarf all others, there is much dispute over the economic and social correlates of bigness or smallness—both positive and negative. There are proponents, advocates arguing highest advantage, for each of the following: a single large metropolis,[3] two or more smaller provincial metropoli,[4] medium-sized provincial cities,[5] and the small semi-rural town or village.[6] When economic arguments are emphasized, larger cities are evidently favored, though not

---

Metropolis in the Arab World, New Delhi, Allied Publishers (for the Congress for Cultural Freedom), 1963. See also Richard Meier's comments in his "Rationalizing Urban Development," Chapter 21 in his *Developmental Planning*, New York, McGraw-Hill, 1965. For Chile, the best works are Juan Astica's paper (see note 21) and Guillermo Geisse, "Información Básica de una Política de Desarrollo Urbano-Regional," *Cuadernos de Economía*, No. 6, May–August 1965.

[2] The extent of this literature can be quickly appreciated in the annotated bibliography by Brian Berry and Allen Pred, *Central Place Studies*, Philadelphia: Regional Science Research Institute, 1961 and 1964.

[3] See Walter Isard and Thomas Reiner, "Regional Science Techniques in Regional Planning," *Papers and Proceedings* of the Regional Science Association, Volume IX (1962).

[4] See Lloyd Rodwin, "Metropolitan Policy for Developing Areas," *Daedalus*, Winter 1961.

[5] The implication was taken by some from the widely influential early work of Colin Clark. See also P. Sargent Florence in Robert M. Fisher, *The Metropolis in Modern Life*. New York: Doubleday, 1955.

[6] See Richard Waverly Poston, *Democracy Speaks Many Tongues: Community Development around the World*. New York: Harper & Row, 1962.

entirely conclusively. Smaller cities and villages seem more desirable from the vantage of certain social considerations, but this argument has not been very rigorously reasoned. Given such confusion on a theoretically optimum urban structure for a nation, the wisest course is probably to begin with the urban structure as it exists, project the tendencies of its change to gauge the probable future situation. Then the present, and especially the probable future, urban structure may be evaluated carefully in terms of accepted national objectives.

Planning analysis sometimes bogs down as soon as the question of goals or of objectives is posed. For national urban development policy, we may suggest, goal-specification is not an insurmountable problem. One way of simplifying the goals of national urban development is suggested below.

PROGRAMMING NATIONAL URBAN DEVELOPMENT

A basic essay on urban development planning for the economically less-advanced countries a few years ago pointed to the need of a national urban development plan *plus* regional capital investment budgets.[7] This approach, developed by Lloyd Rodwin in earlier work,[8] still has much validity. Since it was written, the emphasis in American urban planning thought (as opposed to practice) has, with few exceptions, sharply veered in the direction of short- and medium-range programming rather than long-range planning.[9] The new emphasis has much to do with mathematical manipulation of models for short-run optimization in public decisions and has some valuable indications for capital investment decisions in developing countries that will be developed below. However, it would be an error to lose sight of the value of a national urban development plan as a way of setting the framework for such programming. Given the pace of change in many developing countries, one should at least have a view of how

[7] Benjamin Higgins, Charles Haar and Lloyd Rodwin, "Coordination of Economic and Physical Planning in Developing Areas," *Journal of the AIP*, 1958.

[8] Lloyd Rodwin, "National Urban Policy for Developing Countries," *Papers and Proceedings* of the Regional Science Association, Volume III, 1957.

[9] See Melvin M. Webber, *Process Planning: Symposium on Programming and the New Urban Planning*, a special issue of *Journal of the AIP*, November 1965. Note especially articles by Webber, Donald Michael and Ira Robinson therein.

several times the present population, at a multiple of the present per capita income, could be beneficially accommodated in the national territory. Without such a view, including relationships as much as a physical end-state, incremental decisions could lead as likely to the infernal as to anywhere else.

Programming itself will be geared to the national budgetary process in most countries. If there are to be subnational capital budgets, these will need to be ultimately reconciled at the national level. The scale of the "region" may be highly variable from country to country. Some small nations are no larger than a major United States or European metropolitan area in terms of population. The reason for subnational capital budgets would appear to be twofold: provide information (including local preferences) not easily collectible at the national level, and stimulate local participation in the decision process. If this view of the functions of regional capital budgets is correct, the "regions" should be as small as may be found to be feasible for national coordination and no larger than required for efficient decisions on the investments involved.

It is highly important to recognize, and the programming approach implies, that one cannot change a national urban structure radically in a few years. There are documented analyses of experience in Czechoslovakia[10] and in Israel[11] that probably set effective limits on what may be done even in circumstances somewhat more special that can be realistically expected to occur in most developing countries. It does not follow, however, that nothing can be accomplished in this field.

Urban planners in a number of developing countries will be responsible for deciding where and what types of housing, community facilities, utilities, streets and other infrastructure are to be budgeted for public construction. Something like half of all national public investment may be included. Even given the regulatory powers of economists (national economic planning guide lines, budgetary veto powers), engineers, politicians and others, this will be no mean undertaking. For

[10] Emanuel Hruska, "Towards a New Pattern of Settlement-Structure in Czechoslovakia," *Bulletin* of the International Federation for Housing and Planning, 1964–65.

[11] Eliezer Brutzkis, "Planning for a New Settlement Structure in Israel," *Bulletin* of the International Federation for Housing and Planning, 1964–65.

such "social infrastructure" will almost certainly double, and it may triple, during the professional lifetimes of the present generation of planners. Thus a substantial impact on the urban development structure of these countries is effectively going to be decided by planners already identifiable.

How are the planners going to decide these important issues? There exists in practically every country a stock of traditional or conventional methods for so deciding, a combination of political porkbarreling mixed with some technical imitation and a bit of native innovation. On the technical side, there are engineering and welfare approaches, based on standards and criteria taken from a limited sampling of international literature plus, in some cases, training in the United States, or some European country. The same applies for urban planning approaches, which may range from City Beautiful through Corbu to urban systems design, from master plans to capital budgeting, from slum clearance to urban rehabilitation. Fortunately, in most developing countries, there are a few planners who have opted for the most modern ideas they have been exposed to—sometimes becoming self-educated in important subjects that their formal education neglected. There are cases where, building on such men and their ideas, coherent and effective methods for programming urban infrastructure can be developed. It is with such a possibility in view that the approach outlined below is elaborated.

In any case, national urban development planning will proceed from an understanding of the present situation and from some appreciation of probable future tendencies. Hopefully, we insist, it will also consider where the country is going in the long run. But the short- and medium-range programming will be strongly grounded in present physical, economic, social and political reality. Where it is not, urban planners are unlikely to long hold responsibility for such decisions; for mere dreams cannot be afforded in a climate of acute and pervasive problems. The view of such reality must be convincing enough for both bureaucratic and quasi-political dialogue.

A RESEARCH FRAMEWORK FOR URBAN DEVELOPMENT PLANNING

What was just said about urban development programming implies a special need for sound information on which to base annual and multi-year investment program proposals. Research soundly executed and carefully interpreted will be the keystone of urban development planning. The relation between research and policy decisions needs to be carefully examined and understood.

Looking back on the role of research in urban and regional planning one observes, from the beginning, the importance of a kind of "social survey" and of various density measures. If there has been an identifiable field of research for planning, it has centered on these two kinds of investigation: a general study and diagnostic of the situation, and special attention to the number of people residing or number of buildings existing per unit of space. Land use and various traffic studies came later. There have of course been a number of refinements and elaborations to these.

Much of what is actually done in modern urban and regional planning agencies is frankly research. Design of studies, collection of data, analysis of information collected, and interpretation of its meaning occupy most of the personnel most of the time in such offices. Planning *per se*, the formulation of proposed actions, depends on research but takes less time and personnel.

Second-rate research has sometimes passed as first-rate planning. Much of the work done in planning offices would not fare well if compared to the research criteria of the scientific disciplines most closely related to its subject matter. Officials responsible for evaluating studies and analysis have had scant acquaintance with research standards generally, let alone the finer points of demography, economics, sociology and other relevant fields.

This problem has tended to correct itself, especially in the larger planning offices of the United States, by the employment of substantial numbers of trained social scientists in planning offices. At the same time, even more markedly, sociologists, economists and political scientists have participated in the training of planners and in carrying out research that might provide useful guides to planning offices.

New problems have arisen in this corrective process. A growing gap between academic approaches and professional practice has developed. Communication between the "frontiers of knowledge" and the "beachheads of action" has been neglected. But, even if this difficult obstacle could be overcome, a still more thorny one would remain. The increasing elaborateness in study of existing and probable future situations, achieved by the input of social science approaches and people into the planning process, has sometimes muddied that basic process of proposing actions which is planning. The means become the end. The reasons for doing land use studies, population projections, economic base studies, and transportation analyses get lost in the details of research technique. And a series of academically excellent studies, by disciplinary criteria, may result in weak action proposals—or no proposals at all.

It may now be worth trying to think through the relation of research to planning with a view to developing a framework for the research function of professional planning offices. This attempt would be of some importance if urban and regional planning as practiced in large agencies of the United States were to be applied to other situations. Apart from the relatively more powerful role of planning agencies in the less-developed countries, the scarcity of human and material resources for planning is severe. In these circumstances the urgency of obtaining the highest possible efficiency out of research for planning is in clear focus.

There have been some partial efforts to provide a framework relating research to planning. The Lynch-Rodwin "theory of urban form" may be seen in this light, as it tries to relate environmental categories directly to socio-economic goals.[12] Two approaches of Chapin and his North Carolina associates may be similarly regarded: the "goal-forms" are precisely parallel, though simpler, than the Lynch-Rodwin formulation; and the "activity systems" promise a necessary link between physical forms and socio-economic goals, though their importance in this respect has not been fully discussed.[13]

[12] See their paper of that title in the *Journal of the AIP*, 1958.

[13] One presentation of the "goal-forms" approach, which impressed the late Catherine Bauer Wurster, will be found in the final chapter of *Urban Growth Dynamics in a Regional Cluster of Cities*, New York, Wiley, 1962. The "activity analysis" approach is set forth in Chapin's revised *Urban Land Use Planning* (Chapter 6 especially), Urbana, University of Illinois Press, 1965. Other similar efforts are listed in Chapin and Henry C. Hightower, "Household Activity Patterns and Land Use," *Journal of the AIP*, August 1965. See also David Godschalk and William Mills, "A Collaborative Approach to Planning through Urban Activities," *Journal of the AIP*, March 1966. My own early thinking on human activity intensity has remained largely unpublished. Some of it was developed in a processed memorandum in 1961. (At the Center for Urban Studies, University of North Carolina.) This was further developed in "Toward Land Use Planning," *Proceedings*, Southeast Chapter, AIP, 1962. The fullest presentation was in an unpublished paper, Southeast Section, Regional Science Association, Roanoke, Virginia, 1963. That both the concept and the empirical use of

In the framework relating research to planning that we have in mind here, the urban planner makes *proposals for change*. These proposals will refer largely to *the physical environment* (especially certain kinds of buildings and other works), but there will be some *"institutional"* elements of the proposals that cannot be strictly related to the physical. His proposals, whatever their focus, imply, and if implemented would make possible and/or likely, the *facilitation* of certain *activities*, of various *types* (at several possible levels of consideration), at various *intensities* in time and *densities* in space. All this would have a variable but potentially knowable impact on *individual people* (both psychologically and physiologically) and on "organizations" (economic, social, political and cultural). These impacts in turn would, to variable but potentially knowable degrees, coincide or conflict with *values, goals and objectives* of the society which should be expressed operationally in *norms and standards* at a technical level. The challenge of research for planning, in this view, lies exactly in fleshing out and quantifying the relationships just given. (See Figure I.) It is a much taller order than may be at once apparent.

Many of the kinds of information implied, especially those related to human activity intensity of various kinds, have not been fully developed academically or in the richest and largest United States urban planning offices. Yet all parts of the outline do seem necessary to make sense out of the research-planning relationship. Certainly activities are a necessary bridge from forms to goals, and intensity patterns would be more sensible than simple categories or density as a concept of how plans influence people and organizations.

In developing countries, such a framework can play only the role of an orienting scheme. If parts of it are non-researchable in the affluent setting, with highly trained personnel, the gaps are bound to be even more marked in situations where these prerequisites are lacking. Yet it may provide

---

"intensity" in human activities and land use have far to go should be evident from Marion Clawson and Charles L. Stewart, *Land Use Information*, Washington and Baltimore, Resources for the Future and Johns Hopkins Press, 1965. In the scheme relating research to planning in the following section, the term "institution" is used in the abstract or sociological (Weberian) sense; and the concept "organization" is also abstract in the sense of modern administrative and organization theory. As for methods of research, the best general guide remains Russell Ackoff, *et al., Scientific Methods Optimizing Applied Research Decisions.* New York: Wiley, 1962.

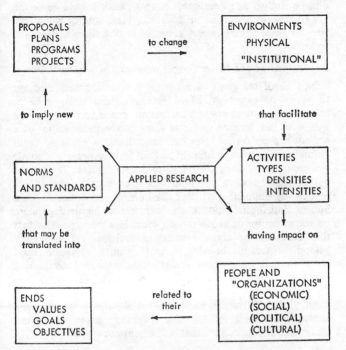

FIGURE 1. Relation of Research to Planning

useful reference points for a research program for national urban development planning. To see the extent that this may be so, let us examine the kind of a research program that may prove feasible in some of the developing countries.

RESEARCH FOR A BASIC NATIONAL POLICY OF URBAN DEVELOPMENT[14]

It was argued above that, though much of the importance of national planning for urban development would be related to short-range programming, it is essential that a basic policy

[14] The material in this and the following sections is directly based on unpublished material developed in Chile during the period 1964–66. The original scheme of research for national urban development plan-

also be studied and developed. Such a policy should guide the programming. To arrive at it, certain basic studies would appear to be necessary in any country, among them at least the following:

1. *Analysis of the Goals Sought through Urban Development*

Not all of the goals of a society are immediately relevant to urban development. More precisely, how well or badly urban development may be carried out could turn out to be a matter of indifference as far as some of the basic values of a society are concerned. But two main lines of goals do seem germane and influenceable by urban development: *economic development* and *equalization of opportunities*. It can be demonstrated that an optimum rate of economic development is logically impossible without maximizing economies of scale and minimizing transport costs, both factors highly dependent on the structure of urban development in a country. The fact that much of the actual investment decisions for urban development are for housing, schools, clinics, recreation and other facilities—and these are effective means of facilitating equal levels of opportunity. We may assume that these two goals provide the core of those that may guide urban development planning. But, in each national situation, some special study should be given the way they may apply and other, more specific, objectives that will orient such planning.

2. *Analysis of Existing Urban Structure*[15]

It is essential to know the point from which one starts. Any attempt at a national urban development policy that does not

ning comes from my 1965 memo "Suggested Work Program for an Urban Development Planning Directorate." A fuller discussion of these and related administrative framework, prepared by Guillermo Geisse and a work team of Chilean planners, is: Chile, Ministerio de Vivienda y Urbanismo, Dirección de Planeamiento del Desarrollo Urbano, *Programa de Trabajo*, 1966. As adviser to the work team, I contributed three appendices to this document, the rough translations of the titles being: I: "The Urban Structure of Chile: A Proportional Model and Its Projection"; II: " 'Economic Growth Poles' and 'Social Development Foci'—Their Synthesis for Locational Programming of Urban Investments"; and III: "International Approaches to Local Short-Range Investment Programming." In later references these will be referred to simply as Appendix I, Appendix II and Appendix III.

[15] Material in this and the following section are based on Appendix I of the *Programa de Trabajo*. See note 14.

begin from a penetrating analysis of the urban structure as it exists, is doomed to be unrealistic and probably useless. Certain key elements will be needed in such an analysis:

- Specification of the major urban areas of the country;
- specification of the influence areas of each of these, at various levels of analysis, with proportions of national population and activities found in each;
- analysis of the interconnectedness and flows between these urban influence areas.

In this analysis, one must be clear about the hierarchy of urban influence areas of a country. In most developing nations, as already indicated, a single urban area or "core" urban region has dominant influence over the whole national territory. But at a second level of consideration the regional dominance of certain metropolitan areas, and of several cities in less focused provincial regions, may be evident. The content of urban influence at this level may be administration, cultural activities, banking and major manufacturing and wholesaling. At another level of analysis, including virtually all of the major provincial cities and concentrating on a more frequent interchange of goods and services between city and surrounding area, zones of influence may be identified for provincial cities in relation to each other, to the major provincial metropoli, and to the "core" urban area—for adjacent cities. Other levels of analysis, considering successively smaller urban areas and more intermediate and frequent interchanges, can also be undertaken. In any case, the structure of urban influence areas implies a flow of goods, services, information and people between urban foci and the areas that surround them. The latter generally provide raw materials, people and the cultural folklore in this exchange; the former provide a whole range of finished goods, services, jobs and money, and relatively more "modern" or national (or often international) culture.

There are no pat guidelines for identifying the various levels of analysis that may be relevant in a given country. But it is to be highly recommended that the structure at each level be expressed as percentages of national population, employment, commerce or of other data. The use of the proportions in describing existing urban structure of a country fits well with the needs of investment programming as outlined below.

3. *Projection of the Urban Structure*

No modern planner believes that the analysis of the existing situation automatically provides obvious answers to appropriate policies. (The proponents of the social survey approach to urban planning apparently used to think so.) This is no profound technical discovery but rather a belated acceptance of what wise men have long known. It was Lincoln, a hundred years ago, who observed: "If we can but know where we are and whither we are tending, then we can perhaps know what to do."

For national decisions on appropriate urban structure, it is basic to understand what the recent and long-term trend has been in this matter. A twenty-year projection of proportions of national population and activities in each of the country's urban influence areas, at each selected level of analysis, seems a reasonable basis and is technically quite feasible. The interconnections and flows between the various urban influence areas could be either projected or derived from projections of population and socio-economic activities. It would be convenient for some purposes to have the population projections by age and sex cohorts. These data are particularly relevant to the programming to certain specific kinds of social infrastructure: housing (family formation), schools and health facilities are examples.

4. *"Implicit Urban Structure": The End-State in Flux*

A twenty-year projection of the trends in urban development structure may not, for purposes of basic decisions, bring the "whither we are tending" into an entirely clear focus. An even longer-term view of the probable future could serve as a useful heuristic device in this respect. Such a quasi-utopian vision has been dubbed a "caricature of the future" by Martin Meyerson, who has thought through the utility of the approach in planning. However, Meyerson,[16] along with the

---

[16] Martin Meyerson, "The Utopian Tradition and the Planning of Cities," *Daedalus*, Winter 1960. A similar position on the function of utopian thinking seems to be the net message of Thomas Reiner in his *The Place of the Ideal Community in Urban Planning*, Philadelphia, University of Pennsylvania Press, 1963. The direct link between the two works is pointed to by William Wheaton in his introduction to the latter.

Goodmans,[17] combine such views of future states with goals; the approach here is somewhat different.

What we seek in implicit urban structure of a country is the logical situation that would emerge if present tendencies were to continue over a long, but unspecified, time. It is the "end state" of forces at work now and in the recent past. But it is not a static end situation: There is no implication that nothing else can happen once it is reached, and flows and activities will be at least as important as physical objects. Abstract goals do not enter into the content of the implicit urban structure, except as they are implicit in present trends. In this sense it is like the results of a projection. Yet we avoid the definite time and pretense at rigor of method that "projection" implies. Rather, we may try to answer this question:

> If present trends were to continue, what would the urban structure of the country be like with three times the present population at four times the present per capita income?

5. Evaluation of Projected and Implicit Urban Structure

Based on the goal analysis and on the analysis of projected and "implicit" urban structure (which are both founded on the existing structure), it is then possible to arrive at an informed evaluation of the situations implied by the latter. Specifically, one may attempt an intelligent answer to the following question:

> What, if anything, is there in the emerging urban structure of the country that would tend to work against national economic development, increasing equality of opportunity and other relevant national objectives: and how much of this is apt to have relatively short-run manifestations?

It is on the answer to this question that a sound national urban development policy may be developed. It will be a policy based on "preventive planning" since it reacts to likely problems rather than proceeding from positively stated goals. But

[17] Paul and Percival Goodman, *Communitas: Ways of Livelihood and Means of Life* (revised edition), New York, Vintage Books, 1960. See also David Riesman's comments on the original edition of this work in several articles, including "Some Observations on Community Plans and Utopias." *Individualism Reconsidered.* Glencoe: The Free Press, 1954.

this need no more be a defect than is the "negative hypothesis" in statistical inference. And, in its dynamic application to the annual and middle-range programming, the positive face of the policy may be exposed. (See Figure 2.)

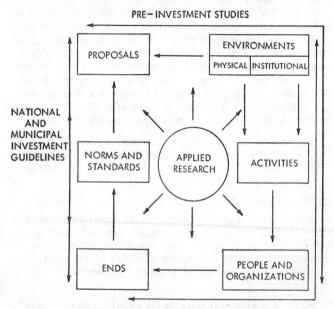

FIGURE 2. Relation of Research to National Urban Development Planning (See Figure 1.)

RESEARCH FOR MIDDLE-RANGE AND ANNUAL PROGRAMMING

The brave new world of local capital budgeting that opened to the American city planning profession a generation or two ago only hints at the work of investment programming that urban planners are and will be undertaking in some developing countries. At the national level, a number of much more elaborate instruments of programming are being promoted by an international corps of economists, finance men, and administration specialists. These new and complex methods must be adapted to the needs of a sector of the economy that is constantly under attack: housing and related social overhead. The urban planner is *engagé* in promoting sound project development and evaluation, for investments the benefits of which are definitionally non-economic in the main—although they may have or produce external economies of considerable magnitude. He wants to see that these get a fair shake when compared (in the national processes of economic planning and capital budgeting) with projects of the more directly productive economic sectors. All this must be accomplished using methods developed for, and thus somewhat biased toward, manufacturing, mining or other extraction and agriculture. Yet this is only half the problem. The social overhead investments that are the guts of urban development are also the traditional refuge of political porkbarreling. The substitution of technical criteria for political ones, which is really what national planning in this sector is all about, is understandably met with resistance.

The urban planner venturing into this can of worms needs to be very sure of his facts and of the methods by which these are collected and analyzed. And that implies good research.

The Problem of Urban Development Programming.[18] Before turning to the appropriate supportive research, we should first consider more fully the nature of the programming itself. In the urban development-social overhead sector, we may think of middle-range programs as being of about five years' reach. These have an annual program that must be fitted into the national budgetary calendar. And, in keeping with good public administration and budgetary practice, both must be broken down into specific projects. But what is a meaningful project in the area of housing and urban development? It obviously cannot be every single building, nor even every grouping of buildings on specific sites, however reasonable a definition this latter might seem in terms of common usage, e.g., "a housing project." There are two reasons why this is true: First, there are too many projects of this kind every year in an active development program to make the accepted standard

[18] The problem of defining projects is partly developed in my paper, "Los Proyectos de Inversión en el Sector Vivienda-Equipamiento Comunitario-Desarrollo Urbano," Chile, Ministerio de Vivienda y Urbanismo, Dirección de Planificación del Desarrollo Urbano, April 1966. Many of the matters in the following sections are elaborated in the same document, which is essentially an adaptation of the World Bank approach to programming through project development.

"project development" and "project evaluation" procedures feasible. (Sixty man-days per project would not be outlandish for project development and evaluation, plus substantial costs for investigation. Any small country with an active development program would have several hundred such projects per year.) Second, the relative advantages and disadvantages ("benefits" and "costs") of projects of this kind would be difficult to estimate; for there are locational and functional "linkages" between these, and other projects at the same level, nearby or even in the broader urban area. For these reasons, one is tempted to suggest treating each urban area's social infrastructure investments over a middle-range period as indivisible "projects." But this may be too radical a proposal for most situations. Rather it seems advisable to think of perhaps five or six multiproject projects for each urban area or major part thereof. The following kinds of urban development projects suggest themselves: (1) new housing—community facilities-utilities developments that signify expansion of existing urban area; (2) comprehensive urban renewal efforts of various kinds, including facilities and utilities; (3) provision of community facilities for an urban area, apart from expansion and renewal efforts; (4) utilities work, apart from comprehensive expansion or renewal; (5) street works, apart from comprehensive expansion or renewal. A final kind of project might be included in some situations: the creation of essentially new urban areas such as satellite cities. These have broad implications for other economic sectors and would deserve special treatment if they are being considered. There would thus be a maximum of five projects per existing locality over a medium-range program period.

This concept of "projects" would bring the total number confronting the programmers in the housing-urban development sector well within manageable limits. And the urban focus would facilitate consideration of most of the linkages. The more specific subprojects that make up each of these "multiple projects" still have to be specified, it is true; but these can be handled internal to the sector, and their treatment may be more flexibly and rapidly organized than is appropriate in multi-sectoral decision-making. What the kind of project definition suggested does do is to help urban development programmers get on with the business of making decisions on what kinds of infrastructure are to be built, in which year, and especially in which urban areas of the country.

Locational Programming.[19] The key question in urban development programming is that of allocating investment priorities to the localities of a nation. The application of the national policy for urban development comes in here with force, but in the real world there is apt to be a timing problem. For the basic studies for national policy will be going on while some priority decisions of lasting significance have to be made. The budgetary calendar has a cosmic-like force and waits for no man to get his basic policies straight.

There are three apparently quick ways to set priorities for localities. One is to use population, say, on the percent of national population living in each urban area. This has a ring of basic justice about it and can provide the basis for dialogue with politicians. But since we will know the urban structure is changing, we would need at least to use projected rather than actual (or census) population. A second is to concentrate on economic factors, favoring those localities with apparently most to contribute to national economic development. This is the European "growth pole" approach in essence and, while having much to recommend it, the criterion suffers from the widespread pretense that the only legitimate national objective is economic development. A third way would be to concentrate on deficiencies, allocating most to the most "needy" localities, those most lacking in social infrastructure and suffering most from problems whose solution might be aided by it. This welfare or community development or social development approach has much of merit, but it could easily lead urban development programming astray.

[19] The approach in this section has been developed in some detail in Appendix II of the *Programa de Trabajo* cited in note 14. The elaboration there is in terms of Chile's three hundred-odd *comunas* (townships) and leads to tentative six-year investment targets for the sector in each. The same is done for two higher levels of urban influence areas: thirty "broad intercommunal urban influence zones" and the more inclusive six "sub-national major urban influence zones"—covering the entire national territory at each level. The estimated proportional contribution to national economic development is based largely on market potential, following Vining's assumption about long-term randomness of natural resources in development. (See his "Outline of a Stochastic Model for the Study of the Spatial Structure and Development of a Human Population System," *Papers and Proceedings*, Regional Science Association, Vol. XIII, 1964.) The social development measure is based on a series of assumptions relating infrastructure investments of existing social marginality and problems of local areas. The reasoning is too involved to detail here, but the basic data are from Armand Mattelart, *Atlas Social de las Comunas de Chile*, Editorial del Pacífico, 1965.

Some combination of these three approaches is necessary for locational programming for urban development. Somehow projected population, estimated contribution to national economic development, and estimated contribution to increasing equality of opportunity (to *people,* not to physical *areas* in the national territory) must be synthesized to arrive at sound criteria for such decisions. Preliminary efforts at such synthesis seem promising, though substantial problems remain.

Based on general investment objectives for each urban area, targets should be set for a five- or six-year period, perhaps as percentages of total urban development investment during the period. Then annual programs are successively compared with this target, in terms of *cumulative* proportion of the sector's investment in each urban area. The trick is to get the cumulative proportion in the fifth or sixth year of the program to approximate, for each urban area, the original (or modified) target.

The Spectrum of Pre-Investment Studies:[20] There is emerging international agreement that projects to be financed by public funds should pass through a series of increasingly finer filters before finally making their way into the national capital budget. These filters consist of (1) studies of various aspects of

[20] See note 18. The Chilean experience in broad urban pre-investment studies is now confined to nine important provincial cities, but will probably move into the metropolitan areas during 1967. The studies were in large part designed by an urban planner, Gastón Maturana, then working in the Project Evaluation Office of the Budget Bureau. The instructions for carrying out the studies are highly detailed, about the same length as the text of the present discussion. Carried out by private consultant teams, the studies are supervised and controlled by the Urban Development Directorate of the Ministry for Housing and Urbanism and financed by the Budget Bureau, in part by foreign aid. Here, as elsewhere, we have avoided detail of research methods. Of key importance in these studies, however, were the method used in population projection and the employment of a well-constructed sample survey to get at the dynamics of housing and community facilities demand. A cohort-survival method, using *locally* calculated survival rates and modified by socio-economic data that would influence migration was found most suitable. (*Cf.* my processed memos "Un Método de Proyectar la Población de Comunas" and "Sugerencias sobre Control de Proyecciones de Población.") The type of data needed for "market analysis" of community facilities is far from fully understood. (*Cf.* Russell Ackoff, "Towards Quantitative Evaluation of Urban Services," in Howard Schaller, *Public Expenditure Decisions in the Urban Community,* Washington, D.C., Resources for the Future, 1963; also my processed memo "Cómo Medir los Beneficios de Infraestructura Local"). Yet it has been possible to design questionnaires that do throw much light on the matter.

the project at various levels of detail, and (2) decisions based on these studies. The latter are rather straightforward: *exclude* from lists of projects, or *include* in list and, if included, *increase* priority, *retain* priority, or *decrease* priority. The former, the pre-investment studies, require more attention here.

The name "pre-investment" studies may be new to many planners, even though the contents of some of them will be quite familiar. In terms of the kinds of project definition and programming for urban development discussed above, we may indicate several types of pre-investment studies for the housing-urban development sector.

Project Identification Studies. It has been noted in the public administration of many countries that the traditional methods of identifying possible projects frequently neglect many potentially excellent ones. In response there have developed special studies to identify a broad cross-section of potentially sound projects, together with enough basic information on each so that appropriate decision-makers can decide which of these to develop further.

Applied to the urban-based multiple-project concept developed above, these project identification studies become broad analyses of situations in specific urban areas or urban influence zones. Work to date on this kind of study shows that, moving from a diagnostic-in-depth through a sort of market-analysis to project identification and preliminary indication of justification and feasibility, it will be possible to get a much more complete picture of the initial content of various kinds of projects for each urban area. Moreover, for projects that get an initial green light, it will be generally possible to develop, from data generated in these same studies, a key document on each project known as the "comprehensive basic report." Such studies would be required for each of a country's major metropolitan areas and regional cities, including in each case information on the smaller urban areas within their respective zones of influence, though generally at a somewhat lower level of detail.

It should be made clear that project identification studies for the housing-urban development sector cannot be confined only to the kind of social infrastructure for which a particular ministry or other agency may be responsible. The very justification of the kinds of urban projects discussed above depends on projects in other sectors of the economy. To the extent that schools and health facilities are separated out, administratively, from other kinds of community facilities (as they frequently are), they need to be recognized or suggested in the same urban development project identification studies. Industrial development projects tend to be urban, and many transportation and energy projects are based on urban demands. In some regional cities, agricultural development projects may have great bearing on urban development in the "service center." Social overhead investment for mining or other extractive centers clearly cannot be well programmed without knowledge of the basic productive sector. For these reasons, the urban development project identification studies will need to take cognizance of projects being considered by each of these other sectors. Nor is that all. Urban development programmers should also communicate the results of their broad urban studies to programmers in other sectors, providing tentative suggestions for projects to be developed by each of them, together with specification of relation or linkage to projects being developed in the housing-urban development sector. Such "coordination by communications" will never have perfect results, but it is far better than no coordination at all.

Feasibility Studies. Though this term is sometimes used as the generic name for all pre-investment studies, it is probably best reserved for a later, more detailed study of projects surviving two earlier screenings by housing-urban development programmers. These are initial inclusion, and (after the "comprehensive basic report") decision to submit for intersectoral evaluation by the budget bureau and the national economic planners. Feasibility studies should be designed to aid these decision-makers to answer three explicit questions: (1) Can the project described in fact be carried out? (2) Will the project actually accomplish what is sought by it? and (3) How important are the objectives sought by this project in a national perspective? For, should decision-makers at this level attempt to get involved in more detailed and technical questions, they would never get their annual workload accomplished.

The first of these questions will depend in part from data already developed in the urban project identification studies. (Availability of materials and labor and entrepreneurs.) Other data on sources of funds and detailed financing arrangements would be needed from the finance office of the housing-urban development agency. And such information would be complemented by other agencies, regarding the over-all financial situation of the national budget, international credits, etc. One of the key aspects of this question will be *organizational* feasibility of the projects; and, in centralized countries at least, this would depend only partly on studies carried out locally. Much of it would have to come from national administrative studies.

The second question, whether or not the project will attain the intended, can be based largely on data obtained from the project identification studies. Some additional investigations may be necessary, and results from prior research on the same subject matter will doubtless be in play. For this question needs to be answered at the level of precision provided by benefit-cost analysis to fulfill its purpose in multisectoral project evaluation. The extent of the challenge is evident from the meager progress in applying benefit-cost analysis to urban development social overhead projects in the international literature. Yet the development of some such tool is just what national decision-makers are going to be asking of urban development programmers in the years ahead.

The third question, on the basic national priority of the objectives sought through the various projects, will (at the technical level) largely depend on the quality of answers to the second question. If the benefits pretended for social overhead projects generally, and those of urban development in particular, are not made meaningful to the economists and engineers of budget bureaus and national planning offices, the strain will be to relegate them to a residual lump of "non-evaluable" projects. Such projects, in effect, are largely, left to the play of political forces. But economic planners may well be concerned that the residuum becomes the bulk of the budget. And where they are intelligent, it should be possible to convince them that strictly economic development objectives, especially in urban development cannot exhaust the legitimate aims of any national government. The rigorous development of a second major objective such as "increasing equality of opportunity" in project evaluation would go far toward providing an objective basis for evaluating projects in the social overhead sectors. And such development will have to rely on a combination of basic and applied research, part of which will fall within project identification and feasibility studies.

Design Studies. These will be the engineering and architectural studies necessary prior to any construction. They will probably be undertaken largely by operating rather than programming agencies. Yet programmers will need to be concerned especially with the costs of alternative site and buildings designs, which are of special implication for programming and feasibility of projects in the less-developed countries.

Evaluation Studies. Over time, a series of results-analyses from typical kinds of projects needs to be built up. Such data is necessary to guide preliminary project identification and also to support some of the claims to be put forth in feasibility studies. In some cases urban development programming agencies will have to carry out such studies themselves. In others, they must be intelligent consumers of evaluation studies done by other agencies and institutions. (See Chart II.)

RESEARCH FOR LOCAL-TO-NATIONAL PROGRAMMING[21]

In many developing countries local decision-making on local investment projects is no more than a myth. The control of the investment decisions of importance to municipalities is almost entirely in control of the national government. Local governments have few funds of their own and often even less technical capacity to decide wisely on how to spend them. Their role is largely limited to petitioning for the things they want, either through political channels or technical ones, or both.

For small countries with urgent development problems, it could be argued, such an arrangement need not be all bad. A centralized scheme is probably more efficient than a decentralized one, especially when the key scarcity is that of trained technicians. Any sharp decentralization of responsibilities and funds to intermediate and local government would probably result in more serious setbacks than appreciable advances to socio-economic development.

On the other hand, there are two remarkable inefficiencies in the centralized approach to deciding on investment with

[21] The basis for much of this section can be appreciated from Juan Astica's paper, "The Use of Urban Policy and Local Planning in the Process of Comprehensive National Development," Cornell Conference on Urban Development and Modernization in Latin America, Ithica, 1965. Some parts were also developed in Appendix III of the *Programa de Trabajo.* See generally the conclusions of Harold Alderfer, *Local Government in Developing Countries.* New York: McGraw-Hill, 1964.

largely local impacts. First, there is no sound way that a central government can efficiently collect good and up-to-date information on distant localities. Experience shows that many decisions taken in this way work out badly simply because technicians in the capital city could not know what was common knowledge to local residents. Apart from the complexities of local habits, tastes, and preferences, which are obvious keys to relative priorities of one kind of local project compared to another, there are always special conditions of a local environment that can never be appreciated from a distance. It is clear that petitions reaching national agencies often favor special interest groups locally. Nor can short-term visits by national functionaries fill in the picture for adequate national decisions. Urban project identification studies could not provide complete and up-to-date coverage. The second inefficiency has to do with the petitioning process itself in a country that seeks social as well as economic development. It has been remarked that the institution of petitioning a national government is not much more than a modern manifestation of the feudal dependency relationship between serf and lord. If social development in modern society means anything, it means increasing participation of individuals and smaller groups in matters that most directly affect them. Without this, one has a constant or increasing "margination" or even "alienation" of a mass with respect to the total society and the elite having immediate access to or control over it. It is worth noting that totalitarian forms of national government have recognized, and reacted to, both of these aspects of inefficiency in centralized government more forcefully than have some democratic states.

For these reasons, if for no others, it is advisable that something be done by a number of developing countries to stimulate the participation of municipal governments in the national urban development planning process. A realistic approach would seem to be that of setting up a system of national-municipal covenants regarding capital investments to be made in the localities. These would be based on comprehensive municipal development programs, something like local capital budgets but with the sources of funds left partly open and the presumption being that many of the actual investments would be made through the national rather than the local government. It would be required that projects financed by the municipality itself be included in the same document. Also the selection and assignment of priorities to projects would be based on an open hearing of local interest groups before the final document was prepared and passed upon by the municipal council.

The role of the urban development planning agencies at the national level would be threefold. First, it would provide technical assistance to the municipalities through loaning planning officials from the national agency to the municipalities over reasonable periods of time. These functionaries-on-loan would live and work in the local community during the preparation of the comprehensive investment plans. Second, the national agency would prepare manuals and guide lines to aid the municipalities in sound development of the programs. Included would be norms and standards of housing, community facilities and utilities, by size and type of community, that would seem initially reasonable based on the present stock in various parts of the country and in terms of apparent financial feasibility. Such standards would be generally in terms of construction (such as floor space) and land area per capita or per family. Third, and most importantly, the national urban development agency would study the municipal investment programs; and, once approved in all or in part, projects included would be committed to the annual programming for the sector. Thus a more powerful tool for influencing and guiding urban development would be placed in the hands of the municipalities, and national programming for the same purpose would be placed on a surer basis.

The research required for the national agency is essentially that of arriving at solid guide lines and standards to guide the municipalities in preparing their investment programs. Technicians to be loaned to the municipalities must be well-trained in applying such standards, as well as in carrying out local interviews and surveys. The ideal would be for national technicians to train local officials to continue the programming work on an annual basis. (See Figure 2.)

CONCLUSIONS

The aim of the above discussion has been to sketch one framework for the content of national planning for urban development in the economically less advantaged countries—although with possible implications for more developed societies. Emphasis has been on the research content of basic national policy formulation, annual and middle-range programming, and intergovernmental collaboration. United States planners have a potentially valuable contribution to make in international technical assistance on these matters during the years ahead.

Chapter 22

URBAN PLANNING IN THE SOVIET UNION AND EASTERN EUROPE

Jack C. Fisher is the West's foremost student of urban planning carried out within the parameters of Communist doctrine. In the Communist nations, urban physical planning is dovetailed into national over-all planning, albeit in a somewhat different fashion in the Soviet Union and in each of the Eastern European and other Communist countries. But all of them appear to share a common set of problems in setting goals, in administrative forms, in the allocation of scarce resources and in implementation, which differ in kind as well as in degree from the difficulties faced by "capitalist-democratic" planners. Communist pastures may even look greener upon occasion to Western planners, frustrated as they are in the democratic maze and by the resultant proto-planning techniques, which seem at times to be reduced to simple persuasion of the reluctant private sector by an inadequate public sector based on piecemeal data. Actually, Communist planners have their own particular awkward doctrinal burdens to shoulder and special sorts of rigid administrative barriers to overcome.

Unfortunately, no up-to-the-minute analysis of the Chinese People's Republic's urban-oriented planning based on open sources could be unearthed to complement the analysis of Soviet and Eastern European experience. It should be noted that in Yugoslavia at Ljubijana an active window to the West has been opened in 1966 by the foundation of the Cornell-Yugoslav Urban and Regional Planning Center, mutually financed by the Ford Foundation, the Department of State, and Yugoslav sources. The Center is staffed and backed by the Cornell University Graduate Department of City and Regional Planning in cooperation with the University of California at Berkeley, The University of Chicago and the University of Southern California. The long-run aim is to have this institute form a center for the meeting on common professional grounds of East European planners with Western planners for the mutual benefit of both.

Urban Planning in the Soviet Union and Eastern Europe

JACK C. FISHER*

There is a fundamental difference between the philosophy and practice of city planning in the United States and the USSR. As a result of growing complexity within our urban agglomerations, city planning in this country is increasingly stressing socio-economic analysis rather than relying upon the more abstract, or perhaps, visionary design solutions. Here, the spatial solutions, the design component of the plan, is the result of detailed socio-economic investigation which itself sets the limits and dictates the nature of the visual solution. This may well be, of course, the result of the increasing complexity and diversity of our metropolitanized society.

The institutional nature and role of central authorities has also been a conditioning factor in the differing approaches to city planning in our two countries. In the Soviet Union, the State (Economic) Planning Commission provides the basic inputs into the system requiring only of the city planner the automatic implementation of existing norms based upon the so-called "city-forming population" base of any given city. Once this figure is established (by GOSPLAN, the State Planning Commission), the settlement's physical layout, density, street pattern, utilities network, etc., become "knowns" by simple reference to a basic book of standards.[1] American city planners, lacking a higher administrative source of economic development data, have been forced to acquire at the local level, a socio-economic perspective. Thus income dis-

* Member of the Department of City and Regional Planning at Cornell University. Speaking Serbo-Croat, Polish and Russian, he has spent three years professionally in Eastern Europe and the Soviet Union. He edited *City and Regional Planning in Poland* (Ithaca: Cornell University Press, 1966), and is author of *Yugoslavia: A Multinational State: Regional Variation and Political Response* (San Francisco: Chandler Publishing Company, 1966) as well as a number of articles on Soviet and Eastern European planning in both Western and Communist journals.

[1] See: *Regulations and Norms for the Planning and Construction of Cities—USSR*, translated by U. S. Joint Publications Research Service from *Pravilia i Normy Planirovki i Zastroyki Gorodov* (Moscow, 1959) JPRS, No. 9891 (September 4, 1961) and *Handbook for Designers—City Planning* [*Spravocnik proektirovshika-gradostroitelstvo*] (Moscow, 1963).

tribution, probable changes in consumer preferences, detailed traffic flow studies, etc., characteristic of an American city planner's attention, are completely alien to his Soviet counterpart.

When viewed within the context of the Soviet Union alone, this static, design-oriented perspective is not inconceivable, nor perhaps, even out of place given Soviet priorities. Long years of neglect of urban needs as a result of the complete preoccupation with industrialization, the effect of war destruction, coupled with the traditional low standard of living, have recently forced Soviet planners to seek rapid increase in the quantity of residential space to the neglect of any qualitative improvement. Given, therefore, the level of development, the existing demand, and the relatively small proportion of GNP allocated, currently or in the foreseeable future, for investment in housing and urban services, the nature of the Soviet city and regional planning operation may be made to appear more rational. Not so, however, with the countries of Eastern Europe.

In the East European countries a radical change is now, in 1965, under way in all facets of spatial planning. These countries, with significantly smaller land areas, varying population densities, and different urban settlement patterns realize they must seek new approaches to constrain and condition the increasing problems apparent within their urban complexes. The methods, goals, and institutional relationships among the various planning agencies and administrative levels, inherited from an earlier period of greater Soviet influence, are undergoing change. The process and the goals vary from country to country. We shall examine the nature of city planning in Eastern Europe and look somewhat more sharply at differences from Soviet practice.

It should be noted that the term "spatial planning" is used to denote those areas traditionally described by the term "physical planning." The term "physical planning" may well become an obsolete term reflecting past practice when the methods of economic analysis were not applied to the solution of urban and regional physical planning problems. The historical tradition associated with the term "physical" planning implies a contradiction between economic and physical planning. The distinction does not and should not exist as it may often restrict realistic and comprehensive solutions to regional problems. A clearer distinction may well be that between topical types of planning—economic, social, political and areal scales of planning—international, national, regional, metropolitan and local. "Seeking a common denominator for all planning activities which stress an areal dimension, we may use the term 'spatial' planning."[2]

PART I: PLANNING THE CITY OF SOCIALIST MAN[3]

The ideals expressed for socialist utopian cities during the late forties and early fifties appear today to be in sharp contrast with the existing reality of urban life in most East European cities. This difference did not signify a change of policy until the most recent time: questions concerning the proper land use structure for a socialist city and the nature of the urban center have never ceased to occupy the thoughts of planning theoreticians. It is clear, however, that economic priorities of industrialization during the fifties necessitated the imposition of minimal housing standards and other measures designed to maximize the impact of very limited investments. Concern for the ideal was relegated to the background in order to make the best use of the meager resources available for housing and urban development. During the entire period of the cult of the personality (the Stalinist Period), the belief persisted that there is a difference, or at least that there should be a difference, between socialist cities and those of the non-socialist world.[4] The lack of adequate resources made

[2] Antoni Kuklinski, manuscript article prepared for a United Nations Conference on New Towns in Moscow, August–September 1964. Kuklinski is a Polish specialist working in regional planning and applied geography.

Kuklinski's position is interesting and worthy of further study. Caldwell may well be suggesting the term "environmental planning" to include both topical and spatial dimensions of developmental considerations. See L. K. Caldwell, "Environment: A New Focus for Public Policy?" *Public Administration Review,* 1963.

[3] These sections are based, with changes, upon my 1962 article, "Planning the City of Socialist Man," *Journal of the American Institute of Planners,* November 1962, and the comments on that article made by a Polish and Yugoslav representative with my rejoinder, which appeared in the February 1965 issue of the *Journal.* These articles have been reprinted and are available as reprints 1 and 1a of the Division of Urban Studies, Center for Housing and Environmental Studies, Cornell University, Ithaca, New York.

[4] "The composition and pattern of the city is established with the social means of production, with the character of the productive relations and social structure. *The plans of cities will express . . . the class nature of society.* This law runs as a red thread through the history of the origin and development of cities:" Ljubo Ilic, "O urbanistickoj metodi," *Urbanizam i Architektura,* XXV–XXVII (1949), p. 95.

it almost impossible to construct cities that would in any way approximate the philosophical dreams of the early postwar years.

Increased industrial production, the easing of the Cold War, the gradual negation of the worst features of Stalinism, and increasing independence from Soviet control achieved by the individual East European countries, stimulated increased investments in housing and urban facilities and made possible a re-examination of the theoretical basis of socialist city planning. Russians, to a more limited extent, but especially Poles, Czechoslovaks and Rumanians, are beginning to re-examine the philosophical tenets of Marxist-Leninism and its implications for operational city planning and future urban development.[5] This statement is not intended as a criticism: for, just as it is necessary for us to measure our continuing urban expansion against increasing physical mobility, improved technology and the resulting social and administrative problems, so socialist planners must examine their planning mechanism and urbanization process in the light of their social goals, improved investment possibilities, and increased national independence.

Three operational factors contributed to deficiencies in city planning in Eastern Europe during the 1950's:

One, planning and design proposals were rarely related to the economic realities of the urban area or its region. The spatial aspects of projected economic programs were neither properly studied nor adequately anticipated.

Two, city planning, due in part to its isolation from economic planning, consisted more or less of a set of formal alternatives or a series of sporadic plans. One contributing factor was the time variation between physical and economic plans; most city plans were for twenty to thirty years, while economic plans were for a maximum of seven years, and usually for far shorter periods with much revision and occasionally total alteration of the plan.

Three, even where there was an urban master plan, a capital investment program for its implementation was often lacking. In many cases, the city planning authorities would draw

[5] See B. Michael Frolic's examination of the newest utopian ideals of Soviet planners: "The Soviet City," *Town Planning Review,* XXIV (January 1964), pp. 285–306.

up the plan without either the financial resources or administrative apparatus necessary to carry it out.[6]

The difficulties arising from these three factors were recognized and gradual corrective action began to be applied at least by 1959 in most countries. In Yugoslavia, city planning developed as a serious professional discipline concerned with more than urban design only after 1959. Though city planning offices existed prior to 1959, they were generally composed of architects or, at best, urban designers. Governmental legislation in 1959 and 1961 provided the necessary legal basis and stimulation for the evolution of sound city planning practice in Yugoslavia.[7] In Poland, though the years 1960 and 1961 introduced new and important measures, subsequent economic difficulties and the failure of many high officials to recognize the importance of spatial planning tended to minimize the intended goals of the Physical Planning Act of 1961. It need only be noted that the Committee for Construction, Architecture, and Town Planning—the main Polish administrative and coordinative body—was eliminated without replacement in October of 1963.[8] In Czechoslovakia, the fields of spatial planning, construction and architecture were centralized in October 1963, with the creation of the Commission for Investment Construction. With the establishment of this Commission, planners, architects and builders received the authority and financial backing to carry out long-range programs aimed at renewing and developing the country's environment. Major modifications are currently under consideration that will eventually modify and modernize planning administration and practice in that country. In Rumania, a remarkable improvement in local planning has occurred since provincial offices were first established between 1957

[6] This is obviously in contrast with American city planning practice which has, since the 1930's, been increasingly concerned with capital-budgeting and long-range financial plans: "It is essential that long-range financial planning go hand in hand with preparation of the master plan for physical development of the city." "Long-Range Financial Planning," *Local Planning Administration*, Third Edition (Chicago: The International City Managers' Association, 1959), p. 370.

[7] For a discussion of the administrative system see: Jack C. Fisher, "The Yugoslav Commune," *World Politics*, April 1964, and my forthcoming book: *Yugoslavia: A Multinational State—Regional Variation and Political Response* (San Francisco: Chandler Publishing Company, 1966).

[8] For a comprehensive discussion of city and regional planning in Poland see: Jack C. Fisher (ed.), *City and Regional Planning in Poland* (Ithaca: Cornell University Press, 1965).

and 1959. As a result of the increased competency of local planners and the increased local autonomy of regional officials much discussion is currently underway as to the future role of the central State Committee for Construction, Architecture, and Standardization. A much less administrative or directive role for central authorities may well be the outcome.

PART II: THE OPERATIONAL PRINCIPLES OF SOCIALIST CITY PLANNING

Though the existing urban reality in Eastern Europe does not appear as yet to have been directly influenced by Marxist philosophy (as interpreted by the Russians), nevertheless, the influence on practical planning objectives was clear, at least until most recently. There are four general, but basic, elements traditionally characteristic of socialist urban planning:

1. *Standardization:* The establishment of norms for the standardization of housing or "living space" has become an operational part of socialist city planning. In order to achieve urban uniformity and, perhaps even more important, to maximize the effectiveness of limited investments, "it is necessary to regulate, in a socially correct way, the standard of satisfaction of housing needs."[9] Thus, "in accordance with the discussed ordinance, the average size of apartments in houses constructed by housing cooperatives of the tenant type cannot exceed fifty square meters, and the maximum [referring to other construction types] seventy-one square meters of floor space . . ."[10]

All housing constructed in Poland at the present time must conform to the legally established norms. The size of apartments assigned to new projects depends upon the number in the family. Single people and married couples without children are segregated into special units containing the legally delimited living space for one or two persons. Apartments for larger families are in units clustered together adjacent to service areas for the families. Specifically, the writer has found that new apartments for families with children in cooperative developments in Warsaw average about forty-two square meters of total floor area. Out of this, thirty-four square

[9] Robert Marowski, "Normatyw projektowania mieszkan i budynkow wielorodzinnych spoldzieni mieszkaniowych," *Miasto*, XI, No. 2 (February 1960), p. 17.
[10] *Ibid.,* p. 18.

meters is the "living space" area (living room, bedroom, dining room).[11]

In all socialist countries, standardization has increased. This refers not only to the application of uniform standards of "living space" but also to an increasingly larger industrialized, or prefabricated, component within the construction industry. Prefabrication has become a dominant element in construction over the last few years. The net effect of standardization on general living conditions is difficult to evaluate, but a substantial improvement in housing norms does not appear to have taken place. Standardization has meant governmental distribution of an increasingly scarce commodity to an increasing number of consumers. "Sanitary norms," the desirable minimum space-requirement per capita officially set down by each regime, have been steadily revised downward, to minimize the increasing gap between the desired norms and the actual living conditions. The effect, therefore, of strict regulation of housing has been a gradual equalization of per capita "housing space"—an equalization which, due to faulty construction methods, particularly the initial inefficiency of prefabricated construction and the lack of sufficient investments in housing, has generated year-by-year a decrease, until most recently, in the average per capita "living space." In Warsaw, from an estimated "living space" per capita average of seven square meters in 1955–57, the average fell to a current (1962) 5.5 square meters.[12]

The net effect of uniform housing regulations has not been positive, but it must be underlined that the respective countries

[11] The over-all density of current residential construction is high. Computation of total residential built-up area multiplied by the number of stories, divided by the total ground area of any given Warsaw complex, averages over .90 and usually .92 or .93, exclusive of all areas occupied by services, commercial, and recreational structures. A further operational norm which the architects attempt to fulfill is that apartments should be so constructed that on the twentieth of October each apartment will receive at least 2½ hours of sunlight.

[12] Though my information would continue to support this statement, Zygmunt Pioro took issue with it in his commentary to my 1962 article: "This statement is erroneous, as it concerns the provisional measure of Warsaw's Council to regulate space allocation in new state buildings. The aim of this regulation was to liquidate substandard, slum dwellings. This norm will be obligatory up to 1965. This administrative measure does not, however, in any way support Fisher's conclusion. The quality of housing cannot be measured by spatial indices only. It is necessary to take into account such factors as dwelling equipment, spatial layout, and external service facilities": *Journal of the American Institute of Planners* (February 1965), p. 34.

did not place housing high on their list of investment priorities. The last few years indicate a slight trend toward greater investments in housing. Prefabricated construction has improved, especially in Czechoslovakia, and supply, though far from meeting demand, is increasing. The past has not been noteworthy but current trends may gradually—though slowly —reverse, and per capita "living space" throughout the course of the next decade or so may reach the minimum standard of the official desired "sanitary norm" (in general, nine square meters of "living space" per capita).

Yugoslavia differs most sharply from this general picture. Almost no industrialized construction components exist and housing is administered and financed entirely different than in any of the other East European countries. As a result of an administrative reform enacted in 1959–60, a special institution, the Fund for Housing Construction, was established at the local level in each of the communes or townships. These agencies represented a significant advance over the earlier system. They were based upon the economic success of each commune and were thus intended to stimulate economic development. A tax of 4 percent on the salaries and wages of all workers and employees formed a stable financial base. With the creation of the Funds, there was at last a local agency concerned with long-range housing policy backed by a constant source of financial resources. This concentration of decision-making authority and resources within a single agency eliminated one of the greatest institutional barriers to an effective housing policy, characteristic of Eastern Europe. Previously the responsibility had been divided among a number of administrative organs, resulting in the collective dissipation of responsibility. There was now an agency of local government responsible for the coordination of all housing development in the area of the commune. In contrast to the marked improvements in the quantity of housing constructed each year since 1956, one only has to observe the continuing lack of adequate commercial services in new residential areas; there is no agency directly responsible for the planning, coordination and construction of these local services.

A major goal of standardization, however, emanating from the Soviet Union, has been a desire to industrialize construction work by performing construction tasks in plants rather than on actual construction sites. The rapid increase of prefabricated materials, particularly precast concrete, results in a reduction in the use of the major conventional building materials (lumber, construction steel and brick) per unit of construction. The industrializing of construction has, in the Soviet Union, reduced the need for skilled construction laborers which were in very short supply, allowed production to continue during the long and severe winters, and provided for the more efficient control and allocation of scarce building supplies and equipment.

In particular, the Soviet Union has placed great stress on the prefabrication of large wall panels for residential dwellings. The cost of traditional construction averages around 131 rubles per square meter compared to 102 to 105 rubles per square meter for dwellings made of prefabricated wall panels. The funds for construction are allocated directly by GOSPLAN and supervised by STROIBANK (Construction Bank). It appears that the concern of these central agencies is only that the designated volume of housing be constructed within any given period. Costs for new construction are calculated by GOSPLAN at 141.50 rubles per square meter. The greater, therefore, the proportion of prefabricated construction (at the much lower cost of 102 rubles per square meter) the larger the surplus of funds left to the disposition of the city councils.[18]

Prefabrication has led to a number of negative tendencies in the USSR. The great stress on quantity which industrialized methods allow is most certainly at the cost of quality. Of all the socialist countries, drab, monotonous and poor internal design is nowhere more apparent than in the Soviet Union. Large tracts of multistory dwellings of similar style and form, arising in cities throughout the Soviet Union, characterize the "success" of the industrialized methods. Yet the Soviets have achieved their major goal: massive production of low-price, standardized, multifamily housing units. Is this pattern of Soviet industrialized housing construction relevant to the East European countries as was initially assumed? Much discussion now centers on this question throughout these countries.

Czechoslovakia, of all countries, including the Soviet Union, has made the greatest strides in perfecting the industrialized process for producing large wall panels. Is this emphasis correct?

A number of factors influence the cost of production. Clearly, production costs decrease with increasing manufacturing capacity as well as capital expenditure per unit of an-

---

[18] Based on figures supplied by the Leningrad City Planning Commission and a construction enterprise in Leningrad.

nual production. However, assuming continuous demand for structural elements, the market district grows, as does the cost of transportation and capital outlay for the means of transportation.

My calculations would suggest that for Poland, Rumania and perhaps Hungary, excessive stress on a nation-wide program of prefabricating large panel units is not economical. Limited use of prefabrication may be made in the one or two larger cities of the country. Population density, land area, and the structure of the urban network would significantly increase costs in these three countries. For Czechoslovakia, the model would suggest that a network of prefabrication plants to serve the entire country would be economically efficient. An optimum plant capacity of 125,000 cubic meters per year with an average transport distance of 33 km for thirty plants or 38 km for twenty plants is possible due to the size, average population density and structure of the urban network. If capacity increases as a result of increasing demand as expected, the average transportation distance would remain theoretically constant. The function reads:

$$d = \frac{1}{-2} \sqrt{\frac{a}{n}}, \text{ where}$$

$a =$ the marketing area

$n =$ number of manufacturing plants, and

$d =$ average distance plus 30 percent for deviation of roads from the straight line.

In my opinion, the current trend toward improved economic efficiency will limit, with the exception of Czechoslovakia, any significant increase in massive industrialized construction techniques in Eastern Europe.

2. *Proper Size of a City:* Another planning assumption is that the growth and size of cities will have definite restrictions. The critical element in determining the limits of any particular urban agglomeration is "the size of the productive substance"—the labor force—within it. Thus, urban size is to be determined by the ratio of employed population in basic industries to total population:

Proper size of a town depends, first of all, upon its productive function and upon the number of people employed in its establishments and institutions. . . . Proper proportion between the size of the city's creative groups, the size of the servicing groups, and the total number of inhabitants should always be maintained. Subsequently, any further development of the town should be adjusted proportionately to the increase of its productive substance.[14]

Any increase in the size of the urban complex depends, first of all, upon calculation of the "city-forming" segment of the population:

> The computed population total is determined in city planning projects on the basis of the share of the city's population employed in enterprise and institutions of city-forming importance, according to the formula:
>
> $$N = \frac{K.100}{P}$$
>
> where N is sought-for computed population total for the city; K is absolute-figure total of workers in enterprises and institutions of city-forming importance; P is share of city-forming group in the population total of the city, in percent. . . .
>
> The share of the workers of enterprises and institutions of city-forming importance in the city's population total should be for the period of calculation, assumed at 27 to 35 percent according to concrete conditions.[15]

According to a Soviet definition, "city-forming" includes employees of all basic industries, transportation and construction enterprises, administrative units above the city level, educational, scientific, and medical institutions.

Throughout the Soviet Union, planners express the conviction that large cities must be contained to their present size, that increased growth "would produce all the inherent evils so apparent in American, Western European and Japanese cities." One possible measure in hand to create the desired response is to build a series to new towns and satellite cities around large urban agglomerations. Potential satellite cities are currently conceived as existing settlements within a radius of 30 to 50 km from the central city which, though having a

[14] Juliusz Gorynski, *Nowa Kultura* (Warsaw) August 20, 1950.

[15] *Regulations and Norms for the Planning and Construction of Cities—USSR* [translated by U. S. Joint Publications Research Service from *Pravila i Normy Planirovki i Zastroyki Gorodov* (Moscow, 1959)]. JPRS, No. 9891 (September 4, 1961), 11.

distinctive set of functions, will be dependent for many needs upon the central city. Thus, these cities are to be satellite or dependent, presumably for cultural amenities and employment opportunities, upon the central one. "New towns" are located at greater distances (100–250 km) and are envisioned as totally independent settlements with their own basic industrial and service components. The basic principle is to locate these new settlements, where possible, on existing transportation routes near sites of major resource deposits.

The "optimum size" of cities, new towns and satellite cities is a topic of continuing discussion in the Soviet Union. Satellite cities range in size today from two thousand or three thousand inhabitants to over 100,000. A distinction appears to be made between satellite cities around urban agglomerations under one million population and those over one million. Optimum size for those under one million is suggested as from 60,000 to 120,000 while for those of "million" cities from 200,000 to 250,000.[16]

It appears, however, that most of the arguments for limiting urban growth are ideologically based, derived in part to counter the "bigness" and thus unhumane conditions supposedly characteristic of major Western cities as well as the belief that, by means of size limitation, one somehow can equalize the differences between the city and the countryside—perhaps by having a greater number of smaller cities. Whatever the philosophical justification, concrete conditions suggest detailed socio-economic analysis is not one of the determining elements.

Despite the planners' concern in restricting population growth, they have generally been unsuccessful. In fact, there has been an extreme disproportion between the growth of the various sizes of cities: excessive growth of large complexes and little expansion of smaller settlements. Budapest, Lublin and Skopje are examples of extreme growth in Eastern Europe. Despite almost fifty years of socialist planning attempts to restrict population growth, these attempts have been remarkably unsuccessful in the Soviet Union.[17]

It is clear, however, that despite Soviet city planners' concern for the optimum size of the city, they really are powerless

[16] B. A. Kamenski, et al.; Prigorodne Zone Krupnih gorodov [Suburban Zones of Large Cities], Leningrad: 1963; pp. 111–13.

[17] B. Svetlichnyi, "Soviet Town Planning Today," Voprosy Ekonomiki, No. 7 (1960), appeared in translation in Problems of Economics, III, No. 8 (December 1960), pp. 30 and 32.

to accomplish this goal. GOSPLAN sets the increase in industrial employment which is the basic input into the physical planning process. It is on the basis of these figures that cities are designed for a twenty or thirty-year perspective period. But, as so often happens, GOSPLAN is forced to increase the industrial capacity of a given city far above the original estimate. Thus, cities planned for 60,000 to 100,000 people have been forced to contain populations double or triple that number. Until such time that economic analysis figures heavily into the physical planning procedures and urban complexes are viewed as urban systems rather than individual entities, continuation of such gross errors can only be expected.

3. *The City's Center:* The earliest postwar Communist pronouncements stressed that the distinctive character of the socialist city's center should be its political-cultural-administrative function rather than as an area of retail concentration. The center receives priority in programming; it is the vital part necessary to coordinate the entire complex. The usual center in reconstructed cities has a large square designed to provide room for parading troops and for throngs of people on holidays. The center also serves as a setting for the principal public buildings and monuments. The only commercial elements programmed for the socialist center are the hotel for tourists, the single department store, and perhaps a restaurant and coffee shop.[18]

The more closely the socialist center approaches the above-outlined concept, the more radically will it depart from the traditional capitalist concept of the central business district. Land costs and the prices of goods are uniform throughout the entire socialist urban complex. The center is an area where, theoretically, the needs of the population of the entire regional complex, as set by the state, are administered, but in which the masses of the population have little need to venture except for state holidays and occasional visits to the one department store, the restaurant, and the coffee shop.

The above discussion characterized the concept of the theoretical socialist urban center described throughout the fifties. There is no question that a non-commercial urban center was initially considered necessary for a socialist city; in Soviet Union today, this concept is still maintained. Zygmunt Pioro offered strong protest to this characterization of Polish cities though he admitted that nothing has been offered in its place.

[18] *Regulations and Norms, op. cit.,* p. 166.

Discussion on this subject declined and is only become a major subject of study among planners at the present time. The character of the center of a socialist city is a fundamental problem which is as yet unresolved for the East European countries. It is equally true that most Polish (as Czechoslovak) cities do not correspond with the stated ideal of a cultural, administrative, and political functional center. This did not, however, result from a desire on the part of Polish or other East European planners to create a central business district in our sense of the word, but rather from the need of supplying cheaply and efficiently the commercial services planned, but never constructed, in the new residential districts. By the late 1950's, the lack of adequate services in these districts created pressures for an immediate solution. It was considered more economical to concentrate the services in one central area rather than disperse them through the neighborhood units. The resulting commercial developments may well give the urban centers of smaller cities a permanent commercial character which will prove financially and functionally impossible to eliminate.

4. *Neighborhood Unit Concept:* The basic tool of socialist planners in their attempt to create "urban uniformity" is today the division and construction of cities by neighborhood units. All the preceding features of socialist planning have gradually merged to support an elaborate division of the city into self-contained units. The planned structure of the population defines the ultimate size of the city, and thus indicates the size and number of neighborhood units and the relationship of each unit's center to the administrative core.

Polish sociologist Zygmunt Pioro highlights the features of socialist planning and implies the importance of the neighborhood unit concept:

> The principles of social justice in Polish town planning are realized by using the official norms and standards which determine: per capita living space, population density, quantity of social services adjusted to projected population limits within particular neighborhood units, without class distinctions. The only basis for differentiation of available physical environment among urban families are biological characteristics of families and their social-cultural positions. In that way, while making master plans for new towns, the necessary urbanized area is computed according to: 1 hectare for 300–500 inhabit-

ants, 12 square meters of floor space for one person. The dwelling structure should correspond to the structure and size of families; the number of service utilities: kindergartens, schools, playgrounds and clubs, are computed according to the planned number of children (a proportion of the prospective population) and an accepted frequency; the network of shops and other services is established by normative indices based upon the number of inhabitants per neighborhood unit. Functional and spatial structure of new residential areas and towns corresponds, due to the development of functionally similar neighborhood units, to the social conception of a socialist urban community.[19]

The idea of a city consisting of neighborhoods with uniform social mixtures is an interesting one, for many American planners have urged a related policy for our cities ("the balanced community").[20] I believe, however, that it is safe to assume that the neighborhood, particularly as a social entity is dead in the United States. Mobility, ubiquitousness of appliances, and changing social patterns have invalidated this traditional concept for that 80 percent of the metropolitan population living outside the ghettos and blighted areas around the core. It is interesting to speculate whether East European pre-occupation with the neighborhood unit concept is a function of the level of development or only ideological whim.

Though the layout and construction of neighborhood units is a major feature of planning in every socialist country, its recognition as an operational administrative unit varies from country to country. In Poland, examination of the layout of new cities and new residential areas clearly reveals the existence of spatially cohesive neighborhood units. Though the neighborhood unit is a planning concept in Poland, Polish planners do not as yet stress the sociological unity of the area. Administrative recognition of the neighborhood unit is lacking

[19] Zygmunt Pioro, "Some Social Aspects of the Development of New Towns in Poland," report to the Sociological Institute of Utrecht, Holland, 1961. For analysis of existing characteristics of neighborhood units in a single city see: Zygmunt Pioro, "The Social Environment of Two Housing Estates in Lublin," *The Society of Housing Managers Quarterly Bulletin*, IV, No. 18 (April 1960), pp. 7–16; a more detailed discussion by the same author is *Ekologia Spoleczna w Urbanistyce* (Warszawa: Wydawnictwo "Arkady," 1962).

[20] See Herbert Gans, "The Balanced Community: Homogeneity or Heterogeneity in Residential Areas?" *Journal of the American Institute of Planners*, XXVII (August 1961), pp. 176–84.

in Poland. There are signs that the organizational hierarchy of the building co-operatives (building co-operatives are financed in part by private shareholders as distinct from state construction enterprises) will gradually emerge to provide two distinct administrative units between the citizen and the large city districts.

Yugoslav experience is of particular interest in this regard. As a result of the increasing tendency toward administrative decentralization in Yugoslavia, a new intermediate unit between the citizen and the local urban district developed: the *stambena zajedica* (housing community, or the neighborhood unit). The neighborhood (community) is a self-managing, independent unit which theoretically acts as an association to look after local affairs. The representative body of the unit is the Neighborhood Unit Council, though administrative functions are in the hands of an executive body—the Management Board. The term *stambena* (housing) *zajednica* was changed to *mesna* (local) *zajednica* by the new Yugoslav Constitution of April 1963. The "local community" (the technical translation) is "a self-governing community of citizens of rural and urban settlements," in which "the citizens directly participate in self-government in activities that satisfy the basic communal, cultural, health, social, and other needs and desires of the community."[21] Kardelj has observed that *mesne zajednice* (local communities), have primarily three functions: "first, the *mesna zajednica* is a unit of the city plan; second, it is a unit and form of self-government in the commune; and third, it is a means of widening the material-technical base for the everyday life of the family and the individual."[22]

In the Soviet Union we find the basic city planning unit fundamentally similar to the *mesna zajednica*, the *microrayon* or neighborhood unit. Frolic adequately summarizes the service sectors relationship to the construction of the residential *microrayons*:

> A fundamental principle of *microrayon* construction is the integration of service areas within the residential district. If commercial and cultural facilities are located

[21] *Mesne Zajednice u kommunalnom sistemu i zadaci Socijalistickog Saveza* [The Local Communities in the Communal System and the Goals of the Socialist Alliance], Subotica (December 1962), p. 1.

[22] Edvard Kardelj, *Samoupravljanje u komuni* [Self-government in the Commune], Materijali sa godisnje skupstine Stalne Konferencije Gradova Jugoslavije, Nis, 30 Oktobar—1 November 1961 (Belgrade, 1961), p. 19.

close to the dwelling area, then the inhabitants will not have to converge on the city centre in search of services.

It is envisaged that the needed facilities will be provided at three geographical levels, thus providing superior service to the population. In each microdistrict with 6,000–12,000 people, schools, day nurseries and kindergartens, small stores and restaurants, apartment house kitchens, repair shops, parks and athletic fields will be provided immediately adjacent to apartment houses. In a residential neighborhood consisting of several microdistricts, there will be a neighborhood centre with club houses, cinemas, libraries, dispensaries, department stores, markets, headquarters of civic organizations, and area-wide parks and squares for meetings, demonstrations and festivals. (M. Frankland, "Moscow Cliff Dwellers," London Observer Service, Moscow, Toronto *Globe and Mail*, October 26, 1962.)

This is the ideal hierarchy of services which the Soviet planners would like to see constructed. Of course, as has been shown in the examples of the New City of Sciences and of Kryukovo, this pattern does not always occur. There has been a tendency to "save" the construction of service areas for the last, and then a hasty attempt had been made to provide them to people "stranded" in a serviceless area. Eventually these services will be provided, though there may be a considerable time lag. In fact, so great is the need to get people into new homes that families move before the pavements, gardens and sometimes roads around the block are completed.

Theoretically, three types of public and commercial service centres must be provided for the inhabitants: primary, secondary and everyday. The primary level of services is designed for a group of from 1,500 to 3,000 inhabitants (there is no consensus on an established standard). These services include the following: communal kitchens, small shops, bakery, dairy, children's playgrounds, dining rooms; these are to be located at little more than an eighth of a mile from the living area. Everyday services are located approximately half a mile from living areas and include: shops of a larger size for bread, milk, meat, baked goods, a delicatessen, restaurant, cafe, shoe-repair shop, haberdashery, small goods shop, laundry, cleaner, and hairdresser, as well as a cultural-administrative centre with a housing maintenance office. This level of services is designed for a population of 6,000. Secondary services supposedly are located no more than a mile away from living areas, but the example of the New City of Sciences indicates that this may not always be the case. At this level (which is designed to service between 12,000 and 18,000 inhabitants) there are department stores, supermarkets, dining rooms, cafe-restaurant, *kombinat* of domestic services, sports base, non-essential repair shops, savings bank, post office, hairdresser and so on.

Moscow's *microrayons*, therefore, are in a great state of flux. It is impossible to determine standards for the proper size of these areas, the heights of buildings, the living space per capita, and provision of services. There are several reasons for this. Firstly, Moscow's projects are of immense size, and land is relatively scarce in the city. The problem is partly one of trying to fit an enormous number of people into a limited area, and under these circumstances, something must give way. If the *microrayon* survives the enormous building pace in the city (and it appears to be doing so), then, despite the lack of resources which increases the heights of buildings, lowers living standards, chops away at green spaces, and provides imperfect integration of services, the *microrayon* concept will have definitely taken root and will provide Moscow with a socialist basis, when more resources will be devoted to housing construction.[23]

A glimpse into the future was provided by an April 1961 article in *Borba* concerning a newly developing area of New Belgrade, Yugoslavia. The *mesne zajednice* units are to be self-contained units, each with a school, nurseries, stores, services, pharmacies, health centers, and playgrounds. Above this level will be the *stambena cetrvt* (housing quarter), with higher-level commercial and service establishments. A city region (*gradski rejon*) is a third administrative level with still more refined establishments: a radio-TV store, fish market, department store, furniture store, bank, and people's home. The top of the pyramid will be the city's center consisting of administrative and cultural institutions. In Yugoslavia, there is evolving an administrative system which will

[23] B. Michael Frolic, "The Soviet City," *The Town Planning Review*, XXXIV, No. 4 (January 1964), pp. 300–2. Available as Reprint Number 7, the Division of Urban Studies of the Center for Housing and Environmental Studies, Cornell University, Ithaca, New York.

conform to even the most ambitious desires of current socialist planning theory.

Against the backdrop of anticipation, so briefly described above, exist the present urban complexes of the Soviet Union and Eastern Europe. Are the contemporary cities attempting to conform to theory, or is there still that traditional land use differentiation which appears familiar to most Westerners? Setting aside dogmatism, we can view the nature of the present urban evolution of selected cities against the imagined "final" pattern which the socialist planner has envisioned. We should understand not only the pattern of today, but the anticipated pattern which an analysis of the city's present evolution indicates will exist within the predictable future.[24]

PART III: THE CITIES OF SOCIALIST MAN

As a simple conceptual device for observation and analysis, I postulate for Eastern Europe today the existence of three types of urban pattern. Each corresponds in a different degree to the goals of socialist urban planning theory: (1) the urban complex which apparently conforms in broad terms to the tenets of socialist theory; (2) the complex which has retained the urban pattern or format developed during the capitalist era but has, by the substitution of a few institutions, transformed one of the urban components; and (3) the city in which both the format of the complex and the structure of each component part have remained unchanged. These three

---

[24] Some words of caution are necessary. The architectural appearance of the new postwar buildings in socialist countries does not constitute, in and of itself, a complete break with the past and a confirmation of socialist planning theory. The function of the dwelling and its relationship to the past land-use format of the city is of major significance. Radicalism in the architectural form of the new construction, the most striking aspect of modernity, obscures but does not obliterate a continuity in trend of urban development.

Warsaw, as well as the other major Polish cities, regardless of the "correctness" in our estimation of its current layout, was built during the last twenty years under unfavorable economic conditions and political diversity. In 1945, Warsaw was 85 percent destroyed. There was no Marshall Plan, and, on the contrary, for a number of years an unfavorable trade exchange existed even between Poland and the Soviet Union, which further strained Poland's economy. Vast areas of the country were devastated and population migrations out of, across and into the area within Poland's redrawn postwar frontiers numbered over ten million people. The situation in most of Eastern Europe, though far less drastic, was nevertheless comparable. When we analyze what is, we must clearly remember how little there was.

existing types of complexes are the result of the interaction of two basic factors: one, the size and nature of the original, pre-revolutionary (which, of course, refers to the period before the Communist take-over) urban pattern; and second, the planned population increase under socialism.[25]

1. *The "Socialist" Urban Complex:* Throughout Eastern Europe and the Soviet Union, thousands of fields and meadows have been transformed into urban complexes to house the rapidly growing working class. These genuinely new cities—constructed on previously non-urbanized sites—should represent the utopia of urban planning in socialist design. These are the "new socialist cities."

The new cities' departure from the traditional capitalist layout, in terms of urban design, should be complete, as there was no existing urban complex to condition the planner's pencil. Each country has its new socialist city, its showcase where socialist theory should be visible in spatial terms: Nowa Huta and Nowe Tychy in Poland, Sztalinvaros in Hungary, Dimitrovgrad and the new resort cities along the Black Sea in Bulgaria and also in Rumania, the new com-

---

[25] Milos Savic, Director of the Novi Sad City Planning Commission, made the following remarks in his commentary in regard to this section of my 1962 article: "The rapid economic development which occurs in Yugoslavia and the countries of Eastern Europe has brought consequences other than increased urbanization. Nevertheless, in the article [of Fisher's] the existence of three types of urban complexes is correctly presented. It is important for all these three types to be developed according to a plan which entails the describing principles of city planning. The first type—the new cities—most easily satisfy this condition. The second type, which is the expansion of an existing city so that both a quantitative and qualitative change takes place, involves the most difficult problems resulting from the city's heritage. The third type which Fisher calls "cities which experience no change" is, in reality, rather rare. If, by this type, we mean cities which have not had an explosive development but which nevertheless have expanded, then they are, of course, developing according to some plan, although more gradually.

"The most common is the second type of city. This type is the expression in one sense of the natural development of society. Here implementation of elementary planning measures requires major intervention in the growth of the city. In the first place, transportation routes, the location of railroads, and new streets must satisfactorily connect the various zones within the city and the city with the region. The construction and expansion of the city's center demand new space. Since the center includes buildings of historical and cultural value, these objects must be incorporated and preserved in the new plan. In such conditions, economic considerations are less important than preserving historic areas": Milos Savic, "Comment" *Journal of the American Institute of Planners,* XXXI, No. 1 (February 1965), p. 37.

plexes of Gavirshov and Poruba in Czechoslovakia, Tito-
grad and Velenje in Yugoslavia and Kryukovo and Sumgait
in the Soviet Union. Over eight hundred new towns and cities
have been built in the Soviet Union since the revolution.

The cities were often built to accomplish a single specific
purpose: to house the workers of a large steel complex or
mine, to relieve congestion in an adjacent industrial area, or
to serve as a regional administrative center. The site of each
new city is usually determined by the location of required
raw materials and ease of transportation.

The format of the new cities is usually simple and direct.
The entire complex centers on a square of administrative-
cultural composition, from which radiate streets lined by massive residential units. The residential dwellings are usually of
two types: large, five- to nine-story apartment buildings consisting of two- to three-room apartments for families; and
dormitories for unmarried workers. Adjacent to the entire
complex is located the enterprise in which most of the residents are employed.

Let us turn briefly to four new cities. Each was built in a
particular locality in response to a regional plan based upon
certain economic considerations. Each city began construction
in a different time period, with resulting differences in quality
and functional layout.

Nowa Huta in Poland has long symbolized the very essence
of a socialist new city. Located ten miles from Krakow in
Southern Poland, the city houses the workers employed in
the major steel mill in Poland, with an annual steel production
of over 1.5 million tons. A city of 100,000 now stands where
a few years ago there were only open fields. The city was
planned to balance Nowa Huta's residential area against the
vast layout of the industrial complex. The urban center is
composed of the main administrative buildings: town hall,
Party headquarters, and the trade union. Residential complexes encircle the city's center. The visible results were far
from successful at first. Construction proceeded slowly; temporary dwellings for laborers multiplied, while permanent
construction lagged. The Polish press was full of articles
which indicate the depressed social conditions which existed
in Nowa Huta, including the lack of promised cultural and
entertainment facilities. Though, during the last few years
some of the failings have been eradicated, Nowa Huta today
portrays in the monotony of her skyline the scars of the

Stalinist era and the architectural eclecticism of the earlier phases of socialist realism.

Eighty percent of Nowa Huta's population is of rural origin. They have come directly from backward peasant villages to highly urban conditions. They did not know how to use modern technical and sanitary installations. At first they wished to adopt their new urban surroundings to their former country-life style. The newcomers wished to cultivate gardens and maintain livestock. They found in Nowa Huta no place for these activities, and administrators soon found coal in washbasins and pigs on balconies. The former villagers could not find in the new shops the kind of furniture to which they had been accustomed. They brought, therefore, to Nowa Huta their parents' old beds, tables, and shrines which were too big for the small Huta rooms. Previously, family life had been concentrated in and around the kitchen, but the new kitchens were too small to preserve the old pattern. The process of adaptation and integration was not as easy as town planners had thought.

Nowe Tychy, south of Katowice in Silesia, was designed solely as a residential area for the overcrowded Upper Silesian Industrial Complex. Though Nowe Tychy shared many of the same problems of Nowa Huta, a distinctly "Silesian" difficulty developed. Sharp antagonism grew between miners of Silesian origin and the new miners from other regions of the country. It was below the honor of the old Silesian miners to be treated on the same basis as the newcomers. Many acts of assault indicated the grave resentment existing between these two population segments.

According to the plan, Tychy's center is to consist of the tallest buildings in the complex, a main square (not yet completed), and the main railroad station. In characteristic fashion, clustered residential units are to surround the center. Nowe Tychy represents a major break in the theory of Nowa Huta's development. The latter's center was constructed first, with intensity of construction decreasing from the center. In contrast, Nowe Tychy was built from the outskirts toward the center, so that when the entire complex was completed, the planners would be better able to provide for the needs of the existing population. A major flaw in design, however, placed the main railroad station too far from the urban complex for walking convenience. Silesian residents have hesitated to leave their more crowded but convenient Silesian flats to seek residence in the more distant Tychy.

Neither Nowa Huta or Nowe Tychy successfully implemented the operational guide lines of socialist planning.
Population limits have in one case (Huta) not been contained
within "planned" limits, while in the other, improper location
of the railroad station tended to restrict population growth.
In both, services were initially neglected, though in Nowe
Tychy's case the prudent policy of not constructing the city's
center during the earlier era of political rigidity did provide
later the opportunity for a more rational distribution of
services within neighborhood units. Huta and Tychy illustrate a universal property of socialist construction to date:
the more recent the implementation of the plan, the more
laudable are the results.

Sumgait, a new satellite city located 35 km north of Baku on
the Caspian Sea, may serve as our example of a Soviet new
town. The city is developing by microrayons, each in theory
to be self-contained, related to a district center which
focuses on the administrative-cultural center of the city.
Originally planned for 80,000 people, Sumgait now has over
100,000 and is expected to grow to 180,000. One can thus
imagine the difficulties as a result of overtaxing a utility system originally designed for less than half of the existing population. The birth rate in the city is now one of the highest in
the Soviet Union: 48 per 1,000, compared to 33 per 1,000
for the country as a whole. Though Sumgait provides the
expression of a vigorously growing community, the initial
inflexibility of the master plan, combined with GOSPLAN's decision to create a major new factory in the area, is producing
problems which can only provide greater inconvenience for
the city's population.

It is in Yugoslavia, however, that, at the moment, the model
of a city which conforms in broad terms to the tenets of socialist planning is found. In the north, in the Republic of
Slovenia, lies Velenje, center for a coal district. The planned
population is set at 30,000 and, at the present time, the city
has attained somewhat more than half of that figure. The
average density of the residential area is 183 inhabitants per
hectare—relatively high due to the apartment-house nature of
the complex. The residential area is divided into four small
neighborhood units equipped with school, shopping center
and local public buildings. The entire residential complex is
located around a large open square for pedestrian use where
civic, cultural and educational buildings have been placed to
serve the whole district. The center itself offers the impression,

not of a potential area of high concentration of retail goods and services, but as a point of orientation, a muted centripetal force which provides a subtle unity to the entire complex. The standardization of residential construction, gradual population influx, distinct neighborhood units—each with corresponding services—located around an administrative-cultural center, and a high quality of construction and design suggest that Velenje today takes first place in both the planning and realization of a "socialist" city. One can, with proper insight, envisage Velenje as an ideal urbanistic and architectural expression of socialist realism.

As a final note, it should be mentioned that Skopje, Yugoslavia—destroyed by earthquake on July 26, 1963—is now developing a new central core and greatly expanded residential area under an advisory committee and permanent resident staff established by the United Nations.[26] During 1965, the plan for the central area was selected from among those submitted to an international competition. The international character of the project, the attention and interest already given the project, suggests that new Skopje's evolution should be given continuous attention in the years to come.

2. *The Socialist Planning Impact on Existing Urban Patterns:* The majority of the cities of Eastern Europe were not created under socialism, but have had a long history of development. These cities provide the greatest problems for planners as they attempt to achieve their socialist goals. Here the policies of the new regimes are publicly put to their most decisive tests.

One of the classics of postwar construction was the rebuilding of the old city of Warsaw. In 1945, this part of the city, as most remaining sections, lay in ruins. As socialism began to make itself felt in Polish architectural circles, reconstruction of the city began in conformity with somewhat vaguely worded notions of socialist planning.[27]

[26] See Jack C. Fisher, "The Reconstruction of Skopje," *Journal of the American Institute of Planners,* XXX (February 1964), pp. 46–48.

[27] "The plan of spacing in a socialist city must provide all necessary clues as to the socialist relationships of the respective parts of the city and should find its expression in the common link and not in the division of buildings into isolated islands": Juliusz Gorynski, *Nowa Kultura* (Warsaw), August 20, 1950. Thus, there was to be no sharp division or distinction among the various parts or components; the quality of the residential areas and their social composition is to be everywhere the same. No part of the city should ideally attract or repel certain classes —wealthy people living in exclusive residences, the poor in low-rent

To the Polish peasant as to the Polish intellectual, the old city core was the symbol of the Polish nation itself: Therefore, to let it remain in ruins or to rebuild it along modern lines would have symbolized that the traditional, "true" Warsaw, would never rise from the ashes of German destruction. Thus, regardless of political creed or position, to each and every Pole the reconstruction of the old section of Warsaw exactly as it once existed would represent the reincarnation of the Polish nation, a monument to the endurance and courage of the Polish people. Socialism gave priority to Polish nationalism, and after great expense and long periods of extended research, each building of the old city reappeared, and each element of the design, each frieze, was a masterful representation of the original. Polish desire to recreate the traditional old center was not limited only to Warsaw, but was a characteristic feature of early reconstruction throughout Poland. The old cores of Lublin, of Poznan, of Gdansk and the village of Kazimierz are typical examples.

"Socialist" planning was given due consideration in other parts of Warsaw. Most striking of all was the massive Palace of Culture, symbol of the new political order, constructed in the center of the city on the site of some of the most extensive ruins. The building is a classic example of traditional Soviet "wedding-cake" design, common to the Stalinist era of socialist realism. At the other extreme, the most completely devastated section of the city was, of course, the ghetto. Here, the systematic demolition of each and every building (except for a single Catholic Church) by the Germans, made rubble clearance impossible. Newly designed apartment houses were placed on top of the rubble, some three or four feet above the former ground level.

In another of the newly created People's Republics, Bulgaria, the country's capital was altered under the guidance of socialist planners with entirely different results. The socialist concept of the city's center is expressed in a decree of the Presidium of the Bulgarian National Assembly, November 30, 1951, issued by the Council of Ministers:

The reconstruction of the center of Sofia;
To build in the center of Sofia:

a. Building for Council of Ministers
b. Building for the State Opera

---

burned-out industrial areas. All parts of the city of socialist man was to be composed, in theory, of all people—a truly classless potpourri.

   c. Building for the Ministry of Heavy Industry
   d. Building for the Ministry of Electrification
   e. Club of the Soviets
   f. Edifice of a sample State Hotel
   g. Building for the Central Universal Department Store.

This decree was realized; the center of Sofia does consist of these buildings grouped around a large square. Note the distinct character of the district, which functions, not as the city's core of retail concentration, but as the political-cultural-administrative center. Beyond this administrative core were concentrated, particularly in recent years, local shopping centers to serve specific areas. Between the neighborhood shopping centers and the city's core have gradually emerged district centers with mixed administrative-commercial functions.

Zagreb and Split in Yugoslavia are two cities which the writer has extensively studied. The following discussion, though directly referring to Zagreb and Split, could well describe a number of other Eastern European cities, all of which have had a long period of historical development. The city's center is and has always been an indicator of each city's trend of evolution. In Zagreb's case, the center has gradually migrated south since 1850 under the attraction of the railroad and resulting industrialization. Characteristic residential land use differentiation developed with three clearly recognizable zones of first class, average, and poor residential areas which emerged north-south across the complex. The present planners have continued the southward movement of the city's center south of the main urbanized area. Thus, the postwar planners responded to the traditional land use trends and established a new center on a site where the prewar planners had once envisioned it. The selected area was to function as the city's center, but because it had been relatively vacant, the site provided an opportunity to produce a new composition for the center—one which would correspond to socialist concepts. Thus, Zagreb's planners were able to construct a new socialist component while the remaining sections of the city were unchanged.[28]

---

[28] "In summary, the city has more than doubled its population and yet retains a remarkable conformity to a past urban pattern or format despite numerous declarations to the contrary. The capitalistic heritage is too strong a factor for the socialist planners to overcome. They were able, in Zagreb's case, to introduce a distinctly socialist urban component into the traditional format of the city when past tradition allowed the incorporation of a new, previously non-urbanized area.

Throughout the centuries of Split's evolution, the city's center had never migrated from its shore location adjacent to the original and existing site of Diocletian's palace. The present socialist planners of Split have decreed the incorporation of an adjacent area—to provide for the needs of the rapidly expanding population—with the traditional urban center to form one enlarged center. In Split's case, tradition had restricted the city's center throughout the centuries to the proximity of the palace-shore location—a tradition respected by the present planners.

A more detailed explanation of the urban evolution of each city lies beyond the scope of this article. But it is clear that the location of the city's center in relation to the other parts of the city continues to reflect the way in which the city traditionally developed, despite more "rational" planning policy. The land use of the remaining urbanized area, i.e., industrial and residential, remains essentially unaltered. Thus, *at the present stage of socialist development,* Zagreb and Split are examples of the two possible types of urban complexes having continued existence under socialism. These may be considered as (1) a complex which conforms completely to the former urban arrangement and (2) one which concentrates significant elements of a socialist society in one part of the city, while leaving the remaining urbanized area unmodified in its traditional over-all arrangement.

The planners of Zagreb, Split and most of the other cities of Eastern Europe began the postwar reconstruction of their cities in conformity with the existing land use of each complex; they have not as yet come to terms with the idealized dictates of Marxist-Leninism. Practical planning principles applied by Socialist planners are noteworthy. It is true that

---

Nevertheless, the layout of Zagreb in 1970 or 1980 will show, in its overall format, the capitalistic nature of the past.

"Each historic period has contributed an ingredient to the urban complex. There was no qualitative change but one continuous evolution from point of origin to the present time. Feudalism produced a concentrated urban complex with but slight expansion. Capitalism under the drive of a dynamic technology expanded the urban pattern, doubled and tripled the population, and established an urban format and land-use pattern which restricts the free exercise of subsequent planning. Socialism has produced, in a short time, remarkable expansion of the urban pattern under the impulse of increased industrialization. But there is no qualitative difference in the nature of the resultant pattern; there is only compression of the time of development": Jack C. Fisher, "Urban Analysis: A Case Study of Zagreb, Yugoslavia," *Annals,* Association of American Geographers (September 1963), pp. 283–84.

Eastern Euorpean cities are undergoing a rapid expansion of their industrial base with a corresponding population increase. Yet the predictable pattern of the future city appears to be more in conformity with the individual city's past evolutionary trends than with the present theory of planning. Each city's past evolution conditions today's and tomorrow's complex.

PART IV: SUMMARY

The aspirations of the planners to create distinctly socialist cities—cities which in their format and internal population arrangement would reflect the classless nature of their society —were muted, diluted, and redirected during the course of fluctuating political conditions and economic difficulties. This ideal arrangement appears to be the least feasible and yet it is in *one* sense an area where planners may have some success.

If we interpret "urban uniformity" to mean a truly classless dispersal of the population throughout the urban complex without regard to economic or political status, then clearly, this is not and will not be obtained during our lifetime. If, however, "urban uniformity" refers to the spatial characteristics of the urban pattern, then its realization may be more plausible.

In all socialist countries the role of the neighborhood unit in planning has increased; the delimitation and construction of self-contained units with local service areas based on an estimated norm of service personnel per thousand is a major yardstick. It should be remembered, however, that though the potential is there, the network of internal service centers is currently weakly developed. The neighborhood center will consist of retail stores, medical station, schools, and recreational areas, usually centrally located within the complex. In the newest cooperative developments, apartments for families (as distinct from separate dwellings for single persons and married couples without children) are situated nearest to the schools and recreational areas. Major transportation routes form the boundaries of the respective neighborhoods but do not pass directly through them. The planners maximize the projected use of public transportation and attempt to make it as convenient as possible for the maximum number of inhabitants, while discounting (except in Yugoslavia) a greatly expanded use of private automobiles.

The newest Yugoslav projects conform to the neighborhood unit approach, and as indicated previously, the Yugoslavs may well have anticipated the entire socialist camp in the development of an administrative system incorporating the neighborhood (*mesna zajednica*) as the basic unit. The early postwar "socialist" cities were for many reasons far from successful, for despite intent or declaration, neighborhood arrangements and corresponding services were neglected. Newer projects, however, in Warsaw, Sofia, and other major cities, are being built block-by-block, neighborhood-by-neighborhood. The co-operative construction in Warsaw is particularly noteworthy, as is the new regional plan for the development of the Rybnik area south of Katowice in Poland. Rybnik is to be developed as a new industrial and mining area south of Silesia. The master plan for the area is just completed. In Rybnik the planned enlargement of existing villages and the construction of new towns are all based upon the neighborhood unit concept. In the Soviet Union all planning and construction within the major urban centers is done according to neighborhood (*microrayon*) layouts.

In the writer's opinion, the next twenty years will increase the "structural uniformity" of the city; uniformity is interpreted to refer to an urban complex with neighborhood units of corresponding size provided with similar services located around an administrative center which serves the needs of the entire region. More difficult, if not impossible, to attain will be "classless" or social uniformity.

In this regard, Zygmunt Pioro's comments are most interesting:

> One of the characteristics of the socialist city, according to Fisher, is urban uniformity in its social and physical aspects. Fisher supposes that the norms and standards necessary to realize this rule are widely applied in Polish town planning practice. I would rather define the rule as the "principle of equal possibilities." This meaning is much nearer to the ideology of socialism which predicates social justice on the basis of a classless society and equal chances of opportunity for every working man. Of course, this principle should be considered as one which will be accomplished gradually. Thus, if Mr. Fisher looked for urban uniformity, he would not find it. But he could easily, if impartially minded, find the principle of equal possibilities at a certain stage of realiza-

tion. The postwar development of Polish cities is the expression of the national endeavor to meet differentiated and constantly growing human needs. If, as the result of spontaneously working ecological forces, there are internal migrations in the city that bring about concentrations of people in particular social categories, nevertheless housing equipment, services, and transportation facilities are equal or are intended to be equal. (Zygmunt Pioro, "Comment" *Journal of the American Institute of Planners* [February 1965], p. 33.)

The development of socially distinct areas has been intensified in still another way. State enterprises constructed residential complexes for selected *social groups,* groups with special abilities desired by the state. Professional groups with similar educational backgrounds and economic status were selectively concentrated into isolated units. Building co-operatives, previously discussed, are also furthering group segregation. The net effect of co-operative construction has been that the better paid strata in socialist society pool their resources to construct suitable housing with generally higher "living space" per person than the rest of society. State construction serves currently to supply housing (usually with somewhat lower "living space averages") for the lower end of the urban economic scale.

The degree to which the term "urban uniformity" can be interpreted to refer to the spatial characteristics of the future socialist urban pattern offers itself, as suggested by Pioro, as an element for further research during the ensuing years. The use of the term in reference to demographic and social characteristics has been made valueless as practical political and economic pressures have demanded pay-offs to select groups, and as economic criteria played a decisive role in shaping the social structure of the city.

Have the present planners failed? The answer is a qualified "NO." There are, however, four main reasons for their comparative lack of success to date: (1) the devastation of most of their cities and the high cost of bringing them up to minimum livable conditions; (2) political rigidity of the Stalinist era and its effect on architectural form and planning concepts; (3) lack of detailed knowledge and skill regarding sound construction techniques, resulting from the emphasis on prefabrication, and understanding of the implications of the new architectural forms; (4) the persistent emphasis of each regime's investment policy on priority projects such as heavy industry, with small percentages of investment in housing and urban development. The contemporary cities fall far short of the ideal socialist goal. Housing is inadequate and extreme overcrowding exists. The skills and experiences of the planners, however, have consistently increased; yesterday's mistakes have not been forgotten. New apartment houses, improved streets, and cultural facilities are coming in for a greater share of investment.[29]

Throughout Eastern Europe and the USSR, well-planned cities with attractive and comfortable residential units are being built today. It is yet to be seen whether these cities will achieve the ideal socialist planning goals in their internal urban structure and population distribution. This is prerequisite to their identification as truly the cities of *socialist* man.

[29] I offer without comment, Pioro's comments on this section: "In concluding his observations, Fisher poses the question, 'Have the present (socialist) planners failed?' and answers with a 'No' followed by a series of reasons for failure which nearly cancels this 'No.' Polish town planners cannot accept his view of the situation, however. There is no clash between physical and economic planning in Poland. As a rule, city plans are realized according to the accepted standards and modern pattern of city structure. If specific parts of our city plans were not fully realized, the main reason was economic difficulties resulting from the 'cold war' and other international economic forces such as the common market. Impartial observers should understand this background in order to have a comprehensive picture of such an extremely complex activity as town planning." *Ibid.*

Chapter 23

MACRO-PLANNING: FUNCTIONAL
AND SPATIAL

Cities can't plan cities. Urbanization is much too universal a phenomenon; it is of too large and complex a scale to be managed at the
political city level. The functional city extends beyond political
boundaries to include the hinterland in a reciprocal relationship. The
scale of the system can increase further to include the region, which
has meaning as part of the relatively closed national system. Quite
possibly metro governments might plan metropolitan areas, but there
are no adequate METROS. To catch and tame a metropolis, a large
net is needed and the net must be on the scale of a national land use
plan or "national environmental plan" as the French have named it.
But merely to control and program space is insufficient without
matching plans and programs for the multiplicity of functional areas
of the economy and of social life. To quote from the *British National
Plan,** a functional plan, the following aspects of the socio-economic-
political system are included: *Industrial Sectors*—engineering and allied industries; construction; energy; transport; and other industries.
The Use of Resources—consumer expenditures; housing; public expenditures; defense; health and welfare services; education; benefits
and assistance. As the *Basis for Growth* consideration must be given
to output; productivity and the demand for labor; manpower; industrial efficiency; investment; prices and incomes; balance of payments; and regional planning. All this to be accomplished by *An
Action Programme* encompassing: Government overseas spending;
private investment abroad; reallocation of Government spending; industrial policy to improve efficiency and balance of payments; manufacturing investment; productivity, prices and income policy; active
labor market policy; regional policy. The only facet lacking, by the
way, is a *population policy* on both quantity and quality. This detailed list has been included to indicate that such a plan would affect
the open system of every city, town and rural area in Britain and
that only through the addition of a coordinated land use or spatial
system could the totality be controlled and programmed for—not to
mention budgeted and funded. The French General Commissariat
for Planning, organized in 28 industrial functional sectors was joined
in the Fifth Plan (1966–70) by the *National Commission for Integrated Development* signaling the marriage of the complementary
concepts of economic planning and environmental (spatial) planning

* H.M.S.O., CMND. 2764, London, 1965.

in regional form. Thus in the case of both Britain and France, there is "indicative" or "collaborative" national planning (as differentiated from the "directed" Communist style), broken down into regions as the key managing concept. The English, essentially spatial or territorial, regional plans have come tumbling out one after the other preceding and contemporary with *The National Plan: The North East, Central Scotland, The South East Study,* etc.

In the open system of the city with massive input variables of central government policy, how can anyone "plan" adequately at the local level? This is the lesson of the book: city plans depend on national plans, both spatial and functional, programmed and budgeted through time. Urbanization is too complex and too extended to be managed at the micro level, even though information must be fed up to macro regional and national levels, and be administered in practice at the micro level with the national government providing the bulk of the funds. The policy, multi-faceted program, and funding must be national. The United States has not reached this stage yet by any stretch of the imagination. The Department of Housing and Urban Development has some policies, programs and funds for coping with urban places; these schemes are often connected with transportation macro-planning emanating from the Department of Commerce; sometimes hopefully connected with actions of the Department of Health, Education and Welfare and the enthusiastic gyrations of the Office of Economic Opportunity. The Army Engineers have their say about the urban environment as do the Departments of the Interior and of Agriculture. But there is no Economic Development Plan, no Natural Resources Plan, no Social Development Plan and no overarching National Plan to put all these together—much less any adequate political mechanisms to program and fund such an endeavor. Perhaps the rudiments are to be found in the Bureau of the Budget serving the President directly—but only the rudiments. In actual fact there are no clear integrated policies existent, on which a national planning effort might be started, only some vague statements about goals. Imaginative persons are, however, slowly beginning to collect ideas for the *year* 2000 in the study of *futurism* by the sophisticated extrapolation of trends and even to consider long range programming by the use of mathematical models. This endeavor is going on principally in universities and research institutes; our sister Western nations are already operating to a greater or lesser degree at this level of planning sophistication as a national government function. Communist nations have been at this for years in their own fashion. American planning is piecemeal, remedial or negative. We have little positive and practically no national macro-scale operations outside of the limited sectors of Defense and Space.

John Dyckman, who is as ready as the next planner to venture intellectually, comes flatly to earth in his paper on the new wave of state planning, borne in on the incoming tide of federal dollars. State planning is an anathema to the purist thinker, as contrary to the concept of functional areas; a state is merely happenstance hallowed by history. But the reality is that states might in the long run be the instruments of national development policy, as it is implemented through regions. In the short run, state development of amenities and the educational infrastructure may turn out to give a solid boost toward advancing balanced urbanization. Myles Wright has synthesized European, including British, experience with regionalism concluding; first, that balanced development for a country-wide common level of wellbeing seems to be a universal goal. Second, Western nations are developing other parts of their countries as counter attractions to the overurbanization of the great capital cities, such as London or Paris. The use of regional development agencies, separate from existing local governments and national ministries, appears to be the most efficient device. Wright advocates concentrating on six or seven cities by liberal national programmed funds as specific counter attractions to the capital region; this is somewhat reminiscent of Arthur Row's method of *guiding* the growth of the New York Metropolitan area by nodes of mixed public development —patently on a much smaller scale.†

Cornelius de Cler, Dutch planner, explains the advanced pattern of land planning law in his country. That society has had local planning required by law for sixty-five years; in addition today there are a national land use plan and an economic development plan with social development portions already in operation. Land in Holland is not regarded as a commodity but as a precious national heritage. Moreover, a democratic people like it; let government govern (although amply protected from bureaucratic dictate) and recognize that the general welfare stands above private needs and gain. My concluding short piece on Total Environmental Planning speaks for itself.

State Development Planning in a Federal Economic System

JOHN W. DYCKMAN*

INTRODUCTION

The increase in state planning activity since 1959, which parallels the rash of planning activity stimulated by the National Resources Planning Board in the period 1935–43, has been funded by the Housing and Home Finance Agency,

† See Chapter 8.
* For a biography, see Chapter 6. This paper was presented at the Cornell Conference on State Planning, "Existing State and Future Trends," Ithaca, New York, March 22–24, 1966.

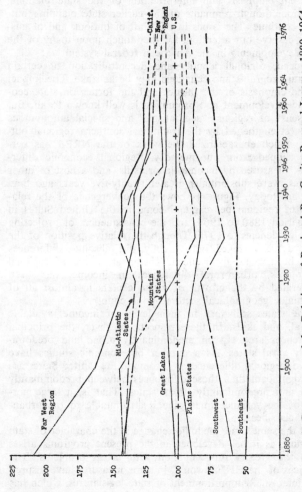

FIGURE 1. Convergence of the Relatives of Regional Per Capita Personal Income, 1880–1964, with Projections to 1976

now transformed into HUD. The change in auspices of state planning activity has had the effect of producing a somewhat different emphasis and interpretation of the state planning function, though remnants of the earlier state planning outlook continue. The issues in this shift of outlook and of auspices deserve our attention, for they touch upon many of the key developments in the American federal system.

Indeed, regional identity and decentralization of certain federal programs and functions may be at stake. The impact of the emphasis of the thirties and the forties on state economic development and promotion is well known to all. But the sense of regional "separatism," and special autonomous goals, strengthened by the traditional southern regional outlook, which characterized the work of the NRPB has perhaps slipped from our memory. Regional economic differences, measured by income, labor skills, and a host of other indices, were substantially greater twenty-five years ago than they are today. Figure 1 shows the convergence of the relatives of regional per capita income in the United States in the period 1880 to 1964, and the consequences of projecting these tendencies to 1976. Though the relative position of the regions has changed only slightly, the absolute differences have been markedly reduced. The great source of regional differences, urban-rural differences in income, has been moderated by the growth of urban centers in almost all of the major geographical sectors of the country.

The states still vary in their levels of income, available capital, and skills. In these respects, however, the principal differences are between predominantly urban and predominantly rural states. As a number of economic studies have shown, regional differences in income in the United States are less significant than those differences between predominantly rural and predominantly urban states. That is, a large portion of the variance in income is attributable to the urban-rural classification.

At the same time, the major change in the character of state planning as it has developed in the present programs arises from the greater preoccupation with urban problems. The auspices of the HHFA would, in some measure, have insured that interest. Reapportionment of state legislatures, which has begun in earnest, guarantees it. But other factors are at work as well. Some economists have been calling for an overhaul of the federal regional character of many of our economic institutions. For example, Eli Shapiro, professor of Finance at Harvard, has recently recommended that the regional structure of the federal reserve system be abolished. In his argument, the national credit market is essentially a single market, and regional banks "seem to have little power to effect their regional interest and can no longer expect their actions to have primary effects in their own regions."[1]

If regional Federal Reserve Banks have little power to effect the course of regional economies, one may well ask what impact state governments can have on the growth of their economies. Certainly, if we consider *economic stabilization* to be a primary state economic goal, state governments have very little effective scope.

State economic promotion has been marginally effective at best. The development agencies have struggled with inadequate tools, employing advertising, resources research, and a variety of promotional concessions, in taxes and in plans, to secure economic development. These efforts, though they have succeeded in attracting the more marginal enterprises for whom taxes and building concessions might be decisive, have not succeeded in effecting major structural changes.

STATE ECONOMIES IN A FEDERAL SYSTEM

One may tentatively list five principal reasons why state economic development activities and state economic interventions are not decisive in shaping the economic fortunes of the states.

1. In the United States federal system, the states are open economies in a relatively closed system;

2. In that federal system, states have ceded the bulk of stabilization powers to the federal government, which operates both fiscal controls and independent public works programs;

3. The economic resources of the state, particularly as they depend upon a sales tax base, are cyclically perverse, and in the national monetary economy, states are not permitted the latitude of substantial deficit financing available to the national government;

4. The absolute scale of federal expenditure is very large compared to that of any individual state, so that small federal shifts can have large effects in the state's economy;

5. State economic interests have been difficult to identify,

[1] Eli Shapiro, *Business Week*, March 5, 1966, p. 78.

due to rural-urban legislative splits within the state, and the tendency for urban areas of states to spill over state lines.

Indeed, one must carefully consider the scope of action available to states in our federal economic system. The states do not have the ordinary economic controls available to national governments.

The states are *open* economies; open to the national investment system, to the shift in national markets, national technical change, and above all, national policies.

Moreover, in the American system, states, like other regional economies, operate in a system of free factor movement. When the regional economies are growing rapidly, resources may flow into the state, and when the growth is influenced by structural shifts, factors may flow out. Thus, when the federal government makes large purchases from defense producers in the state of California, skilled technicians and other resources flow into the State from other states. Similarly, when technological developments shift factor requirements, as was the case in the cotton agriculture of Arkansas, unskilled labor (field labor in this case) may shift out of the state. Both types of development may be viewed as a kind of growth, though neither is controlled at the state level. The nationally induced shift from traditional forms of production to advanced electronics and missile systems appreciably raised the *average* wage in manufacturing in California, while the out-migration of unskilled labor was an important influence in raising average personal and household income in the state of Arkansas.

The states, of course, vary enormously in the extent to which they are relatively self-contained economies. The state of New Jersey is an outstanding example of a state whose major economic activities are located in metropolitan areas centered in other states (New York and Pennsylvania). Governor Hughes sounded a perceptive note in his inauguration speech this year when he called for the state to search for its identity. Functionally, at least a quarter of the metropolitan residents of the country are living at any time in more than one state. Interstate commutation, on a daily basis, is not accurately measured, but a sizable portion of workers in the New York, Philadelphia, Chicago, St. Louis, Boston and Washington, D.C. metropolitan areas cross state lines daily. In the course of these journeys, they earn money in one state, spend it in another, and possibly pay taxes in a third. For these areas, the sheer accounting of economic contributions of in- and out-of-state residents is a formidable task. A state government cannot be assured, further, that a policy contributing to the development of an economy in one of its major metropolitan areas will not incidentally contribute as much or more to a neighboring state.

But perhaps most important from the standpoint of economic planning and policy making, the states have ceded many of the traditional economic controls to Washington in our federal system. In this open economy, fiscal stabilization is a difficult goal for state planning. Control of exports and imports is meaningless. By any count, the states are dependent on national economic decisions which they do not directly control.

On the other hand, many federal purchases of the social overhead and public forming variety are funneled through state agencies. Thus, for example, the massive federal highway building program is substantially under the local direction of state departments of highways. State agencies may directly and indirectly manage a host of federal programs which are locally administered. The role of the state in developing its land and its resources is, moreover, substantial. The pattern of development of the land of the state is greatly influenced by locational decisions on highways, dams, recreation conservation areas, and a host of other decisions which may be made in state agencies. The long-run economic development impact of these state programs, though marginal, may prove to be substantial.

Unfortunately, the states are relatively unequally equipped to carry out these programs. Federal grant programs which are organized on a matching, rather than an equalization basis may be beyond the means of the poorer states.† And since the federal system makes programs available to all states, the relative advantage of the more prosperous states may be enhanced by these programs rather than diminished. This tendency is reinforced by the disposition of Congress to fix maxima, or "close" the grants.

† Two-thirds of the programs set up before 1963 contained no equalization provisions. The amount distributed under equalization provisions in 1962 was only 18.6 percent of federal grants funds. James A. Maxwell, *Financing State and Local Governments,* Brookings Institution, Washington, D.C., 1965, p. 60.

STATE ECONOMIC PLANNING

Despite an unequal endowment, all states are involved in planning and development activities to promote economic growth. The total amount spent on these activities probably exceeds forty million dollars annually. (The Commerce Department estimate for 1960 was thirty-nine million dollars.)[2] More than 11 percent of the total in 1960 was for "planning," and subsequent State Development Planning efforts under 701 program grants have had an inevitable economic development perspective, though these latter have by no means been "promotional."

Some of the problems faced by state governments planning economic development have emerged from the studies in these recently funded State Development Plans. All of these plans show more or less detailed economic analysis of conditions in the respective states, and some contain forecasts of major economic indicators. Few have been so bold as to state development targets quantitatively.

If such targets were stated, they might take the form of traditional objectives of state income, employment, wage levels, and per capita or family income. It is difficult for states to attack these problems, for it is difficult for state governments to know the extent of discretionary action available to them to effect the desired outcomes. To some extent, the general level of activity in the United States economy acts as a constraint upon the prospects of the states. But what does a 4½ percent rate of growth in the United States GNP mean for state opportunity? The simplest way to approach a state's prospect is to hitch it to a national expectation. The task then becomes that of forecasting the state's share in a national pie. National growth rates may be taken as boundary conditions limiting state or regional growth rates.

Aside from its engaging simplicity, this method has certain pitfalls. For one, there is no national plan which specifies the desired balance of regional or state "shares." Nor is there a national purchase plan—even for the Department of Defense— by state or region which specifies the probable level of federal demand for state output. All national forecasting models are essentially "one-region" models.

[2] See David K. Hartley, "State Expenditures on Planning and Development in 1960," Area Trend Series No. 6, Department of Commerce (February 1961).

In a related way, no particular spatial structure is specified for the national forecasts, so that a state may maintain a roughly equivalent "share" in the national economy while experiencing decisive internal shifts in some of the component accounts. These shifts may take place in the industrial structure of the state, in the employment mix, or even in the total population over which a given income is to be distributed. As we have seen, migration changes can be responsible for a large portion in the shift in per capita income between states.

Differences in personal income between states may be produced by (1) regional variation in the proportion of total population employed—a factor dependent upon age distribution of the population and labor force participation rates; (2) on equal regional distribution of high and low wage or earning industries; (3) differences from state to state in the level of wages and salary paid for work in the same industry group. To change these distributions, state governments must overcome not only inertial forces, but must set up equilibrating movements as well. In this respect, the openness of the United States economy may be seen as an advantage as well as a threat to the planning by states. Unfortunately for the states, they have shown little ability to manipulate the incentives which bring about these shifts.

Typically, states seek to improve per capita income by attracting capital investment. In the national system of private finance and ownership, there may be a tendency for capital in place to be "used up" before being replaced. This exerts an inertial effect on a given distribution of industrial investment. At the same time, out-migration of workers is an individual decision, presumably influenced by work opportunity.[3]

In the case of Arkansas, which has pursued a vigorous economic development program, in which a number of attractive incentives have been held out to industry, one must conclude that the gains in per capita income realized by the state in the period 1950 to 1960 were more profoundly influenced by the out-migration of low income agricultural workers, predominantly non-white, than by the influx of capi-

---

[3] According to Saben, reporting a sample of three million workers in 1962 and 1963 by the BLS, about half the migrants in the sample moved for work related reasons, and unemployed workers were more likely to migrate than those who were employed. Samuel Saben, "Geographic Mobility and Unemployment Status, March 1962–March 1963," *Monthly Labor Review* (August 1964).

tal. In the decade 1940 to 1950, the rate of net migration for Arkansas was −21.3 (expressed as a percent of the population at the beginning of the period), and for the decade 1950 to 1960 was −22.7.[4] The percentages of non-white population represented by this out-migration were 32.4 and 35.0 respectively for these decades. McDonald[5] has documented that such out-migration is necessary to maintain and increase the relative position of the southwest in national per capita income averages. He observed ". . . when out-migration from the region was negligible, as during the '20s, the southwest's per capita income fell relative to the national average. Only when out-migration was substantial, as during the '40s, did the southwest experience gains in relative per capita income. Analysis of migration rates by states and counties supports the contention that differential rates of migration are very helpful in explaining the pattern of change in the southwest's relative per capita income since 1920."

The formidable technical problems which beset the economic analysts and forecasters in state development plan studies are symptoms of the relatively uncontrolled paths of state economic development. In the California Development Plan studies, in which we played the role of researchers charged with forecasting responsibilities, we encountered these difficulties in an acute form. In forecasting the statewide and regional employment, wages, and income and in analyzing shifts in the California economy, the structurally most important "exogenous" factor in any quantified model proves to be government demand for military, aerospace and related goods and services.[6] But no adequate forecast of defense demand, by the necessary components (and certainly not by location of contractor) was available to us. No Federal policy, other than a generalized, not too-fast "low-bid" policy has been articulated to guide the regional forecaster, despite the size of the defense demand in the national economy, and its overwhelming importance to the economy of certain states.

Similarly, in forecasting the population of California—particularly when the forecasts are required in great age-sex and

[4] Stephen L. McDonald, "Economic Development and Population Shifts in the Southwestern States since 1920," *Texas Business Review*, April 1965, p. 97, Table 1.

[5] *Ibid.*

[6] Richard Burton and John Dyckman, "Defense Expenditures in Forecasts of California's Economic Growth," *Western Economic Journal*, Spring 1965, pp. 133–41.

regional detail—migration estimates are crucial. (For about a decade, net in-migration to the state has averaged from 300,000 to 350,000 per year.) But migration depends on developments in other states as much as upon developments in California, for there are two or more sides to every "differential opportunity." Our analysis of a recent, an unexpected, slackening in the rate of net migration to California hints that the phenomenon may be produced more by the Vietnam war-boom labor shortages in midwestern and Great Lakes states than by any fall in economic growth rate in California. In the short run, fluctuations in employment conditions in traditional recruitment grounds may be beyond the forecasting art of California planners, but if Federal actions which might cause such fluctuations are not guided by any regional allocation policy, the task is virtually hopeless.

STATE ACTION PROGRAMS

How does a state government affect economic development in a federal system? Despite the dependency of state government in the economic development sphere, one should not conclude that it is powerless. The traditional techniques of "publicity, promotion, and research" have probably had some desired effect, though these are difficult to measure, and one cannot stifle the suspicion that they have been modest beyond any belief of their proponents. Where the major obstacle to economic growth is *information* about a given area which is mysteriously not at the disposal of some "free" decision-maker, the problem can clearly be solved by communication. But at best, these processes require a highly selective communication. At times, this selection becomes dangerously close to deception, a deception which may grossly miscalculate the real needs of the client.

In general, there are two alternative tacks to the public relations approach. One is direct and short-range, the other indirect and long-range. The former seeks to attract capital, the latter concentrates on its deployment. Richard Siegel, currently with the California State Office of Planning and recently with the Bank of America, has summarized the direct, short-run, operational devices as follows:

1. Provision of plant sites and buildings on favorable financial terms.

2. Provision of loans or equity capital to firms ordinarily unable to obtain money at "normal" market rates and terms.
3. Provision of public services free or at reduced rates for a specified time period.
4. Provision of technical or management services.
5. Favorable tax treatment for a specified time period.
6. Financial aid to cover moving or expenses incurred in locating or relocating.
7. Formation of development organizations.[7]

In one or another form, some or all of these devices have been used by development corporations in Georgia, Tennessee, Rhode Island, Pennsylvania and other states. Siegel urged the institutionalization of certain of these development activities in the state government. Further, he recommended a series of interlocking state, regional, and local development agencies which could go further in the provision of loans, acquisition of funds through market sources, real estate services, and promotion. A number of other writers have recently analyzed experiences of the development corporations, all of which are aimed at attracting capital rather than shifting human resources or reallocating available capital.

The disposition of academic economics has been to treat such promotional efforts as distortions of market forces. Some economists, perhaps the majority in our universities, would consider these efforts to be perverse, at least in part, for they would see the most efficient solution to be the migration of human resources. In view of the ill-defined state role in the federal economic system, and our implicit political commitment to a competition between states in the economy, I would be reserved about them on other grounds—particularly that they have shown such low yield for the expenditure involved.

Here, I prefer to focus on the long-range, more roundabout efforts of the state which may, in any event, prove to be the most important influences both for economic development and for the general welfare of the citizens of the states. These more round-about steps are variously described as "provision of social overhead," or as "creating a favorable environment for economic growth." Because of the difficulty in measuring the impact of these factors on the actual devel-

[7] R. A. Siegel, "Organization for Regional Economic Development," Bank of America, mimeographed (October 1964).

opment decisions, there is a tendency to relegate them to second place in the industrial development agencies, if not in the long-range planning.

SOME FUNCTIONS OF A STATE DEVELOPMENT PLAN

Given the limitations of states in securing reallocation of national resources or redeployment of private capital, what should a state development plan try to do? First, and foremost, it can make a careful assessment of the condition of the state, its prospects for change, and its probable future conditions, given all the difficulties of forecasting that obtain for the states in our federal system. On the basis of this assessment it can turn to the important task of setting goals and targets for the state, expressed, so far as possible, in quantitative terms. "Goal setting" has become a *pro forma* activity in planning, recognized both as necessary and perfunctory obeisance to little-tended household gods.

Goal statements fall into disrepute partly because they may be distant, vaguely well-intentioned clichés, and partly because they are spuriously concrete, setting global aims that cannot be achieved in the reasonably near future. I favor setting ambitious goals, but goals that can be framed in terms of target variables realizable in two, five, or ten years. That is, I favor goals that, if never absolutely attainable, are approachable in stages. For example, a state development plan might set up such goals as "human resource development," "full use of capital in the service of human resources," "reduction of obstacles to choice in occupation, place of residence, and place of work." These in turn might be converted into targets for educational programs, for the spatial allocation of investment in the state, for reduction of discrimination in jobs and housing, etc. In each case the targets would be set in quantitative terms. Public programs may then be mobilized, and coordinated, in the service of these targets. An audit of progress, and public performance, can be conducted with relatively good measures. (I am not for a moment so naive as to think that this notion will be appealing to most political leaders.)

What kinds of goals should be set by states? No blanket answer can be given to this question, but in view of what has been said about the powers of states, and of the requirement that goals be approachable, some observations are in order.

Some goals become attainable by redefining others. That is, goals are interdependent. We have seen that the goal of increasing per capita income may be more easily achieved by accepting slower, or even negative population growth. In a changing national system of activity, with a shifting geographic division of labor, one might expect the historic roles of some geographic subdivisions, including states, to change. Such changes have been notable throughout our history, though it must be admitted that states have been slow to accept the realities of change. The struggles of a Massachusetts legislature caught between an independent yeomanry in the West and the merchant capital of the colonies in the East is charmingly archaic when neither longer exists, but residues of this struggle have left their archaic dust on contemporary state politics. Setting meaningful targets for state planning will mean adapting priorities to the realities of the contemporary American economy.

Looking back on the experience of state development planning, we can find a number of specific actions which states can meaningfully take today. Most obviously, states may make the most of the discretionary allocation of capital now at their disposal. Some of this spending power stems from the increase of state revenues, another portion comes from the growing volume of the federal pipeline to state treasuries. The case of highway expenditures illustrates this point. Of some 11.3 billion dollars spent on highways by all governmental levels in 1963, over 7.4 billion were spent directly by states. Another 1.4 billion was turned over by state governments to local governments. Some 95 percent of all federal expenditure on highways was intergovernmental—usually in the form of grants to state highway departments.[8] These figures dramatize the key role of the state agency in funneling highway funds to local governments, and to various areas of the state. One need not belabor the importance of route choice and alignment in the local development of areas of the state. One may well ask, however, how much state goals of full employment, resource use, regional income equalization, etc. govern the decisions of highway departments.

The coordinative role of the state government with respect to its own programs is dramatized by the 701 development

[8] Maxwell, *op. cit.*, p. 172.

plan studies. A glance at the summary Figure 2 shows the relative importance of certain expenditures in state government in recent years. The growth of education, highways, and welfare functions, at least as reflected in expenditures, has been dramatic. Coordination of these programs is, however, still primitive. Testifying to the Advisory Commission on Intergovernmental Relations of the House of Representatives in

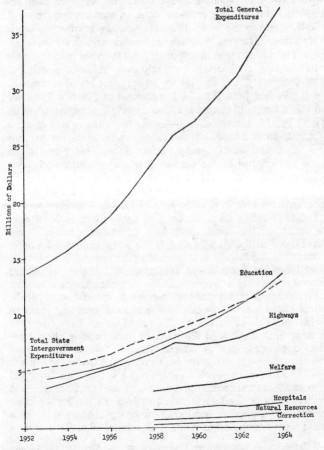

FIGURE 2. Trends and General Expenditures of State Governments for Selected Functions

1962, the late Catherine Bauer Wurster observed that, "In connection with the proposal for review of federal-aid projects, however, no mention is made of the state's need to coordinate its own heavy expenditures and multifarious programs (many of which involve federal aid) on both a statewide and regional basis. . . . If the states would begin to exercise their inherent powers and direct responsibilities with respect to planning and coordination of their own activities, wouldn't this provide some of the missing links?"[9] At the state house level, this coordination is often difficult. Education, highways, welfare, and other agencies have their independent empires, traditional constituencies and "symbiotic" groups, civil service entrenchment, legislator protectors, etc. Ultimately, the key agency in securing coordination will be the Budget Bureau or the Department of Finance. For only in this stronghold can adequate countervailing power be mustered by the executive. Such an agency must approve state contracts and financial transactions, set salaries for exempt positions, and audit agency performance. This gives it the powerful control of the purse-strings and through such control, coordination might be achieved.

Coordination at the state agency level is but a part of the coordinative task in development planning. A sizable portion of state spending takes the form of subventions to local governments, and in some areas, local government budgets may rival those of the state in size. If the long-range development strategy of the state is to be served by strategic deployment of social overhead investment and program budgets, which are aimed at creating a favorable long-range climate for economic development, or for the realization of specific state goals, some coordination between state and local spending must be achieved. The key areas of this coordination have been the metropolitan regions of the state. In these regions, there have developed ecologies of special interests which have been fiercely competitive for funds, services, industries, and other benefits. In the metropolitan areas one also finds the principal problems of transportation confusion and friction, air and water pollution, and recreational deficits. In the earlier cited testimony, Catherine Wurster went on to observe that "if a state were committed to prepare an interim plan for a metro-

[9] Catherine Bauer Wurster, "Government in Metropolitan Areas, Commentaries on the Report by the Advisory Commission on Intergovernmental Relations," U. S. House, 87th Congress, 1st, 1962, p. 121.

politan region in the absence of local initiative, simply as a necessary basis for its own and federal decisions about highways, water, parks, housing, etc., wouldn't this be a powerful incentive to unified local action?"[10]

In the San Francisco Bay Area, the *threat* of state action has been an adequate spur to creation of a voluntary association of bay area governments. Whether these governments will in fact succeed in forming a genuine limited-purpose metropolitan government remains to be seen, but the state action has at least created that possibility. In a similar vein, the role of the states, and of inter-state compacts, in bringing order out of the chaos of metropolitan transit and transportation may be increasingly important. While the city of Philadelphia created, with its initial subsidy, the Southeast Pennsylvania Transportation Authority, the state has taken over the major responsibility for its funding. A similar authority has been created for Massachusetts Bay, and more may be expected.

If Jean Gottman is correct that amenities have become the prime force in the localization of economic activity in our society, the role of the states in fostering metropolitan amenities may be an important contribution to the long-range infrastructure so essential to economic development. Obviously, natural amenities are not equally available to all states. Some attractions given by nature have been obliterated by past economic development. Others were unequally distributed from the start. But if history can be created in the service of the tourist trade, it is not too much to ask that physical amenities be provided in the service of economic activity. The state programs in parks, hospitals, and higher education can all contribute to such outcomes, and deserve great care and coordinated planning of state and local authorities.

In this connection, a major emphasis has been placed on the role of higher education in fostering economic growth and development. The prime examples of this cause-effect relationship have been the Route 128 Boston Development, related to MIT, and the Stanford-Menlo Park electronics development, related to the Stanford Research Institute and University. Both of these examples may be overdrawn and oversimplified in their popular form. Recent studies of the origins of the aerospace industry in California, and the genesis of its expansion and contract strength, including the one done at Stanford Research Institute, suggest that the role

[10] *Ibid.*

of the universities in the development of the California scientific economy has been overstated. The real strength of California, one may infer, is in the pool of scientific manpower which it has been able to attract. In part this manpower is attracted by the great university system, including the opportunity of sending one's children to strong state universities. But to some extent, the climate attractive to scientists and technicians is a more subtle blend of amenity, contained urbanity, recreational and cultural opportunities, and incidentally, formal education. The strength of the university as an amenity may well be the result of its ability to attract certain peripheral activities and to foster a consumer culture.

In any event, whatever the instrumental power of urban amenities and metropolitan attractions, state planning may wish to create these conditions for their own sake. For as we have noted, the state development plan will wish to set targets for the people of the state which represent, in some rough fashion, the welfare of the people. Measures such as per capita income have no other attraction for us. In the similar way, more subtle measures of real per capita income in the form of "social accounting," which has not yet developed, may become targets for future state plans.

In the long run, the states may become the agents of national planning changes. One might expect the states to agitate for national regional planning. Certainly the states, in their own planning efforts, would benefit from the development of an explicit national manpower policy. That policy will need some quantitative targets on employment levels, mobility of labor, education and skilled development, and differentials in wages. (A national minimum wage has considerable regional consequences which become increasingly sharp as the minimum level is increased.)

Eventually, the states may seek the federal support in developing regional economic intelligence, organized around regional labor market boards. The states will wish to share in intelligence on changing technologies, on some pooling of information of opportunities for capital, on the impacts of technical changes on skill and career obsolescence. This intelligence can form the basis for "indicative planning" or control by information of the type being developed by the French national economy. At the state level, control by direct government powers is likely to be less important in planning in any event.

If, as Professor Shapiro suggested in an earlier quote, the nation is in fact one big capital market, there might well be a national policy of regional capital allocation. In such a policy, a deliberate effort might be made to secure sharper, rather than reduced, differentials in regional interest rates. The principle of equalization in federal programs is growing. It can be extended to a host of public goods in which there is at present great differential in consumption. Certainly education is a first round target. Without a national program to equalize educational opportunity by region, it is doubtful that the economic development potential of some regions can be realized, unless a national manpower policy effects rapid transfer of personnel.

In summary, I believe that state development planning, as it has been pursued in the United States, has been hampered by (a) the essential disabilities of the states as autonomous economies, (b) an obsession with the attraction of industry and capital flows from private sources, (c) the lack of informing federal policy and plans. A contemporary strategy for state development planning might include, in addition to more sophisticated planning techniques, (a) an operational statement of goals, (b) flexibility in abandoning old targets in the service of new priorities, (c) a disposition to accept some present costs in the service of long-range targets, (d) the nerve to force rationalization and coordination on state agencies and on local recipients of state aid, and (e) pressure to secure a clarification of federal regional policy.

Regional Development: Problems and Lines of Advance in Europe

MYLES WRIGHT*

In the past decade almost every country in Europe has adopted in part a regional approach to national investment and development problems. Belief has grown that the new approach promises something of value, and the organizations to enquire into or promote regional development in Western European countries are now very numerous.

* Lever Professor of Civic Design, University of Liverpool, since 1954; Planning Consultant to the University since 1957; and Associate Editor of the *Town Planning Review* (U.K.). Formerly Assistant Editor of the *Architects' Journal,* he was a partner in Sir William Holford's

A number of summaries of regional development problems and policies in Europe are available and are listed at the end of this article. These show that the broad objectives are the same in every country, and so are many of the approaches to solutions of particular problems. The basic aim of all regional policies has been and is to promote the fullest development of the country's total resources by suitable guidance of investment, region by region, over a period of years. The phrase 'balanced development' is often used: this implies a need and duty on the part of central governments to correct disparities in living conditions and opportunities and employment that now exist between one region and another.

These disparities are the main reason why regional policies have come into existence. That acute shortage of labour in one region should co-exist with unemployment in another is felt to be wasteful as well as unjust. Governments are unwilling to wait until 'market forces' correct these inequities, and have indeed grave doubts whether they ever would or could. In addition, the new mobility arising from the increased use of motor vehicles is changing most local problems into regional problems, while at the same time the huge cost of modern physical investments—motor roads, power stations, housing estates and the like—makes it essential that their location and relationships should be the subject of skilful forethought and decision. The proper scale for such guidance today is clearly regional.

On the other hand, Governments in Europe still have doubts about the validity and proper extent of a regional approach to national development problems: on how much guidance or aid should be given to less favoured districts, and about new administrative machinery that may be needed. There is a good deal of evidence that the central governments of most countries hoped, to begin with, that Ministerial declarations of intention to help less developed regions, backed by

firm from 1948–54, principally engaged on planning proposals for Cambridge (England) and Corby New Town. Planning consultant for a number of redevelopment schemes in British cities, he also worked with the Minister of Local Government, Republic of Ireland, on the planning of the Dublin region. He is the author of *The Planner's Notebook* (1948); *Corby New Town,* with Sir William Holford (1952); *Land Use in an Urban Environment,* Editor and contributor (1961) and *The Dublin Region, Preliminary Report* (1965) as well as a number of other technical publications. This article is reprinted with permission by the Liverpool University Press, copyright holder, from the *Town Planning Review,* Vol. 36, No. 3, October 1965.

some simple system of grants to new factories established therein, would do all that was needed. These hopes have not been fulfilled.

THREE KINDS OF PROBLEM REGION

In terms of national development and regional 'imbalance' there are in all countries two, and in most three, quite different kinds of region. These are:

1. Poorly developed rural regions, having relatively primitive living conditions and few opportunities for employment, which are losing population.
2. Urban regions that contain a large proportion of the country's total population, are still growing, and increasingly reveal national and local disadvantages of overgrowth.
3. Urban industrial regions that are in decline or are growing much more slowly than the more prosperous industrial regions.

The E.F.T.A.[1] and P.E.P.[2] publications state that the characteristics of problem regions are the same in all countries. Those of types 1 and 3 are unemployment, outward migration of the young, low incomes, poor services and often apathetic local administrations who feel that the whole problem is too much for them. The introduction of the most modern techniques in agriculture, forestry and fishing may lead to a further decline of population in rural regions, despite a rise of average income; and modern growth industries established in such regions have tended to become 'islands', drawing staff from, and transmitting dividends to more prosperous regions.

Remedies for the stagnation in older industrial regions are no easier to find. The main assets of such regions are underemployed labour, a long industrial tradition and existing transport networks. On the other hand, craft divisions may have become somewhat rigid during economic depression, and low standards of housing and services and much derelict land may discourage new immigrant enterprises. Unresilient industrial

---

[1] European Free Trade Association. *Regional Development Policies in Efta.* Geneva, 1965.

[2] Political and Economic Planning. *Regional Development in the European Economic Community.* Prepared by B. C. Robertson. Published by P. E. P. and Allen and Unwin. London, 1962.

regions of this kind exist in Germany, France and Britain. They are of special importance in the formulation of British regional policies. Their populations could not possibly be moved elsewhere, they contain fixed assets of great value for many years to come, and they are obvious candidates for choice as 'counter-attractions' to London and Birmingham by reason of their transport networks, status as regional capitals and labour reserves. Above all, they provide the most challenging test for theories of 'balanced' regional development: how much aid the country can or must give to less favoured regions; the proportions in which such aid should be divided between direct provision of new industrial employment and general improvement of 'infrastructure'; and whether new administrative machinery is needed for the effective guidance of regional development.

The drawbacks and potential dangers of overgrowth within one or a very few urban regions have been a cause of disquiet for many years; first in France in relation to Paris, but for more than 30 years in Britain and smaller countries.[8] This is a world-wide phenomenon, irrespective of the country's economic circumstances or technological advance. Usually it is the capital city that has grown excessively. Easy access to central government and to capital for new ventures, a large market for talent, labour and produce, and cross-fertilization between new processes, are obvious causes of metropolitan growth. One might also add that, since Roman times, it has proved expedient for central governments to shield the populations of their capitals from the worst of current economic stresses.

In the last decade however a new urgency has come into discussions of how to slow down the growth of Europe's largest cities. The cause of this has been the demand for much more urban space which has been generated by rising prosperity and the huge space demands of motor vehicles. European governments now fully realize that there comes a point where the economic advantages of a concentration of population and activities begins to be demonstrably off-set by difficulties of movement, and by deterioration of other aspects of social and

[8] *Au Foras Forbartha Teoranta. Regional Planning Conference Dublin 1965.*
J. V. Curtin: Regional Problems and Possibilities in Ireland.
Pierre Viot: Economic Planning and Physical Planning in France.
U.N. Economic Commission for Europe: Regional Physical Planning and its relation to Economic Planning.

physical environment. They have also been clearly warned that the inevitable and rapid increase in the use of motor vehicles may soon raise these disadvantages to a dangerous level. It seems certain that central governments' appreciation of the threat to metropolitan regions has added impetus to regional development studies and acceptance of the idea of developing centres of 'counter-attraction'.

* * *

The existence of problem regions of these three kinds in western European countries, coupled with much increased demands for space for urban purposes, may thus be regarded as the common origin of regional studies and policies. Ideas of social justice impelled governments to try to aid backward regions; the labour reserves in such regions provided a second incentive; and the motor vehicle threat to overgrown, and particularly metropolitan, regions clinched the matter.

Governments have however been cautious in adopting ideas of a regional approach to the solution of national economic and development problems. The transformation in the last decade of at least major local problems into regional ones, has pushed governments to the half-way house of a central appraisal of regional problems, but progress has been cautious. Certainly British Governments (of both political parties) have disliked the implications of the change; the main reason being their unwillingness to upset any further a long-established and recently somewhat shaky local government structure. This attitude is understandable, though not necessarily wise on a long view. The detached observer may be convinced that the effective guidance of regional development —in a co-ordinated pattern of costly investments in particular projects at chosen places—will soon be found incompatible with a local government system which makes a sharp distinction between town and countryside, and often takes a parochial view of development. Yet suitable machinery for the guidance of region-wide physical development has not been the subject of much serious study, and certainly is not agreed. Holland has probably made the most progress in this difficult field. But measures of guidance of physical development that are essential in a country whose survival, and in part creation, has depended on them, are not necessarily suitable for application elsewhere.

APPROACHES TO SOLUTIONS

The publications listed disclose some agreement among European countries on how best to try to solve the problems of the three kinds of region. There should be a long term programme extending over 20 to 40 years. Help for less developed regions should be of a 'pump-priming' type and not a charitable dole. Aid should be concentrated on the places and projects that offer the best chance of economic success, in the hope that prosperity will spread outwards from the chosen points in concentric ripples. Larger centres, including some in older industrial regions, should be deliberately developed as counter-attractions to over-developed metropolitan regions. Some 'relief of pressure' is essential for overgrown regions in terms of land, but (in a way not clearly seen as yet) this relief should be provided in a manner that will not halt the renovation and development of regions of counter-attraction. One or more of these ideas may be emphasized or left unmentioned in a particular country according to its special circumstances or political pressures, but so far as there is a European consensus of opinion on the strategy and tactics of regional development, it seems to be along these lines.

In carrying out these aims all governments have moved cautiously. In particular, they have been unwilling to make changes in the relationships and responsibilities of central departments and local government. Before making such changes they have tried to test the validity of 'regionalism', and of regional development policies, by means of special agencies. The number of special agencies, funds or committees now wholly or partly concerned in the furtherance of regional policies in Europe is very large, and their methods of operation appear almost infinitely diverse. Moreover, it is almost impossible for a foreigner to judge the results of an agency's work, even though this work is described in plain terms in his own language: for the results will depend on the influence of the agency's work on other authorities or attitudes of mind in the country concerned, and of these he has no knowledge of the convincing kind that only comes from experience.

Two tentative conclusions however do emerge from study of European regional policies so far. The first is that a considerable fog overlies the boundary between the economic and physical components of regional development, and that the latter have received so far very little attention. The economic and social aspects are summarized lucidly, both as regards problems, alternative remedial policies and the general lines along which these might be implemented. But when description of implementation approaches the boundary of topography, land use, and physical relationships of the various works—which it rarely does—then the fog begins to gather. There is the suggestion that these things are second stage processes: and this is quite true. There is also however, some implication that the location and relationship of needed physical works within a region may be left for 'local' decision: and this is surely untrue. The renovation or further development of a region will demand—if maximum benefit and economy are to be achieved—that major physical works should be coordinated for the region as a whole, both in location and in accordance with a regional programme and budget over a period of years. Effective machinery to secure this co-ordination is certain to be needed.

The second conclusion that emerges from a study of European regional policies is that actions taken so far are broadly divisible into four groups, each of which is worth brief description. These groups may be called employment aids; declarations of policy; regional economic studies; and studies of physical feasibility. Description is confined to actions taken in Britain, but readers of the publications listed in the footnotes will probably agree that actions in Britain have been paralleled broadly, and sometimes almost exactly, by those of other countries.[4]

EMPLOYMENT AIDS

By the phrase 'employment aids' is meant the whole range of legislation and grants which was and is intended to encourage the provision of additional employment in particular areas. In Britain the Special Areas Act of 1934 may be said to have established these aids as part of a continuing policy.

The seeming merit of these aids is that they go straight to the heart of the matter. Given more employment and so more money in circulation, it was hoped that backward regions would soon catch up with the rest; and there need be no interference with the normal working of local government. At one time (1960), the desire for simplicity in giving such aid—

[4] Republic of Ireland. *Second Programme for Economic Expansion.* Stationery Office. Dublin, Pr. 7239, 1963 and 7670, 1964.

or desire to escape political lobbying—led to legislation that a district with more than a certain percentage of unemployment should automatically qualify for aid. It thus became possible for small and widely dispersed districts to slide in and out of eligibility for aid over quite short periods of time and rendered a long-term policy extremely difficult to put into effect.

Up to 1939 comparatively little was achieved in Britain by employment aids. Since 1945, a great deal of new employment has been created in less favoured regions wholly or partly by means of such aids. Yet this success has been accompanied by growing doubts whether concentration on the provision of new industrial employment could halt the continuing (though diminished) migration to the Midlands and South East. The steady increase of office and service employment, as opposed to manufacturing, increased these doubts, which were not greatly diminished by the removal from London to the provinces of portions of Government departments concerned with routine work. By 1955 it was being argued that the 467 factories and large extensions provided on Merseyside in the previous decade were, many of them, placed in districts from which, on valid social grounds, there should be a sizeable removal of population. In come cases it could be demonstrated that the policy of the Board of Trade was directly opposed to that of the Ministry of Housing and Local Government, which was responsible for town and regional planning.

From 1955 onwards two views on regional policies gained ground in Britain. The first was that the less-favoured industrial regions should each be examined as a whole, so that major aspects of its economic and social life and its potentialities could be seen in relation to one another. This view thus advocated a return to studies begun in the period 1943–50 and later abandoned. The second view flowed from the first. It was that the whole physical environment of certain northern urban regions should be upgraded and if need be renewed, so as to enable them to act as counter-attractions to London and Birmingham.

These views were slow to gain Government support, but they may be said to have ended belief that employment aids alone could correct Britain's regional imbalance.

* * *

In 1963, the National Economic Development Council stated that underemployed labour in northern regions should be regarded as a national resource, and not merely a social burden. This had been preceded (1960–63) by a considerable change in Government opinion towards much more positive and broadly based regional policies. The first steps to give effect to the change of view were the setting up of inter-Departmental study groups or special committees. Their aim was mainly to examine the inter-Departmental aspects of demands for land and projects for development in the largest urban regions. A change towards a co-ordinated programme for renovation or extension of such a region would plainly affect the policies, local programmes and relationships of five or more Ministries, and it was these matters which the study groups set out to examine, against a somewhat fragmentary background knowledge of regional circumstances and trends.

It seems fair to say that by 1963 the British Government (then Conservative) had concluded that a much broader and more vigorous approach was needed to correct regional imbalances, but that they were not agreed on the forms, scale and co-ordination of the remedial measures that would prove practicable. In this situation of agreement on broad objectives and reasonable doubts over means, the Government decided to arouse and test public support by declarations of policy.

POLICY DECLARATIONS

The first two of what are here called policy declarations were published in the autumn of 1963. Both Central Scotland[5] and The North East[6] were described as programmes for growth and development, and were accompanied by diagrammatic maps, showing main roads, new towns and areas of intended growth. The documents were short and carefully written. They expressed determination to act, sketched a programme of co-ordinated actions and promised Government support. On the other hand, they avoided discussion of new administrative machinery that might be needed to ensure effective guidance of the location, relationship and timing of the various widely spaced and costly proposals. The omissions were noted at the time, and may at the time have been prudent. For new machinery would almost inevitably affect local

[5] Scottish Development Department. *Central Scotland: a programme for development and growth.* Cmnd. 2188, H.M.S.O. Edinburgh, 1963.

[6] Secretary of State for Industry, Trade, and Regional Development. *The North East, A programme for regional development and growth.* Cmnd. 2206 H.M.S.O. London, 1963.

government structure and powers, and these were and still are under examination by a Local Government Commission —the second since 1945. There was good reason for not adding to the Commission's already extremely difficult task by speculations about possible new administrative needs that lay outside the Commission's terms of reference.

The brevity, simplicity of aim and perhaps the impact of the first two reports were all diminished in their three successors. The South East[7] report has been criticised as declaring a policy of defeatism by accepting the need to provide for a large increase of population within 60–70 miles of London, though it made plain that most of the increase forecast would arise from natural increase rather than by immigration.

The two most recent reports, for the North West[8] and West Midlands[9] are included under 'declarations of policy' more because that is what they were expected to be than for their contents. They have suffered by being ordered by the Conservative Government and published by its successor, which has ideas of its own on how the foundation for regional policies should be prepared. The groups of civil servants—from various Departments—who produced the reports were therefore probably left without firm policy directives during crucial months. As a result, the North West and West Midland reports are long, and mainly descriptive of what is. Both contain cautious indications of new centres of growth. In the West Midlands, new centres are advocated mainly to avoid the evils of expansion closely around Birmingham. In the North West, the reason given for proposing new centres of growth is partly the difficulty of finding places near the older cities that would be attractive to new enterprises or as places to live.

* * *

It may be held that only one recommendation is common to all five 'declarations of policy' reports in Britain—Central Scotland, North East, South East, North West and West Midlands. This is that 'growth' should be spread over a considerable area around big cities, based on a much expanded

[7] Ministry of Housing and Local Government. *The South East Study, 1961–1981*. H.M.S.O. London, 1964.

[8] Department of Economic Affairs. *The North West a regional study*. H.M.S.O. London, 1965.

[9] Department of Economic Affairs. *The West Midlands a regional study*. H.M.S.O. London, 1965.

framework of communications, employments and places of residence. In view of the growth of motor traffic and enormous cost of providing for it in older and densely developed cities, this recommendation may be seen as recognition of the inevitable for all urban regions. But it is a recommendation that raises two separate problems. In the South East and West Midlands the new growth points are intended as a relief of intolerable pressures, present and to come, within existing built-up areas. But their designation carries the threat that it will not lead to a thinning out of people and employments from nearby big cities but rather to the attraction of immigrants from other parts of the country.

In the North, the problem is different and perhaps smaller, but one to which it is equally difficult to find the right answer. The danger there is that new growth points, on pleasant sites 30 miles from older and somewhat grimy cities, may attract too much capital, brains and youthful energy, and so leave the older central cities in an even worse state, economically and physically, than they are now.

Declarations of policy do however seem a simple means of promotion of regional growth, though their effectiveness may depend on the firmness with which they are supported, and specially on their being restricted to a few chosen areas. Development and renovation have in fact taken place on a large scale in Central Scotland and the North East in recent years. Much of it must have been in preparation long before 1963 and so would have taken place in any event. Yet the increase of optimism and self-confidence in both regions in the last two or three years has been marked. There are therefore grounds for holding that policy declarations by central Government, backed by a reasonable increase in Exchequer grants, are potentially powerful instruments towards correction of regional disparities. But they are instruments that are readily blunted. There cannot be growth everywhere, and managements and investors know it well. A succession of policy declarations—especially long ones—which suggest growth areas in many different parts of a country, will inevitably lessen confidence in the central Government's will or capacity to correct regional disparities that have been obvious for 30 years. In this connection, Chapter 4 of *Depopulation in Mid-Wales*[10] seems relevant.

[10] Minister of Housing and Local Government and Minister of Welsh Affairs. *De-Population in Mid-Wales*. H.M.S.O. London, 1964.

REGIONAL ECONOMIC STUDIES

The phrase 'regional economic studies' is used to cover a wide range of enquiries that are intended to enable central government to compare the social and economic circumstances and prospects of different regions. Their aim is to enable government to decide the best practicable long-term 'balance' between the various regions, and the forms and scale of investment needed to achieve it. Such studies should desirably be inclusive, covering all regions, and be completed within a relatively short period. If enquiries are confined to regions where action is allegedly most urgent, the government will not have the means to make an informed comparison between prosperous and backward areas, and will be liable to be assailed by a variety of pressure groups whose arguments will be difficult to refute. It is also becoming much more widely held that these regional reviews should be repeated at suitable intervals. Major weaknesses of past studies of this kind have been, first, that their findings and recommendations were regarded as of permanent value, requiring no later review, and, secondly, that too little attention was paid to the machinery needed to implement the recommendations. The publications referred to in this article suggest that governments in Western Europe have now come to regard regional development as a continuing process of readjustments and renewals over a period of 40 years, and subject to review on the basis of a new survey every five or seven years.

This attitude is broadly that of the present British Government, who have set up regional economic planning boards and councils covering a large part of England. Each region has an executive board of civil servants and an advisory council drawn from industry and universities. It is expected that a report will be prepared and published for each region during the next two years. It may be that the reports published in July for the North West and West Midlands foreshadow the form of the coming regional economic reports; or the former may be seen as a bridge between the earlier Policy Declarations (with which they have been grouped in this article) and future reports of the regional economic boards, who may adopt a new approach to the same group of problems.

* * *

The general European acceptance of the need for a regional balancing process is emphasized by what has happened in Britain's near neighbour, the Republic of Ireland, whose 1961 population was 2,800,000. A variety of employment aids have been offered in Ireland since 1952—in addition to tariffs since the 1930s—and a number of them have been intended to help districts that were losing population most heavily. In the past year, the Republic has accepted the need for a broader approach, and the country has been divided into nine regions and a series of comparative studies of resources and development prospects have been put in hand. It is intended to entrust these studies to private consultants and three firms have already been appointed.

The recent Irish approach to regional problems is of interest for two reasons.

The studies begun this year may be regarded as a combination of the broad economic enquiries described above, and the 'feasibility studies' that are briefly examined later in this article. The small size of the Irish regions (with a population range from 923,000 to 87,000) is a sensible explanation of this combined approach. All economic programmes must eventually be expressed in physical terms, and in a small region investment possibilities are so closely tied up with topography, communications, the relationship of settlements, and infrastructure generally, that economic, social and physical circumstances are most suitably considered together.

The second aspect of the Irish approach to regional problems that is of special interest is the quite strong political pressure for growing prosperity to be widely diffused, and that some special consideration should be shown to the more remote districts. This impulse to help historic and often very beautiful districts and to re-invigorate traditional ways of life commands sympathy in all countries. It is evident in Scandinavian and Scottish and Welsh regional policies, and in the help given to Southern Italy. It is, however, an attitude which the central Government of each of the countries concerned has to try to reconcile with compelling duties and modern economic facts: their responsibility for economic growth in the country as a whole; the fact that growth is most rapid in a few highly populated centres: that aid for less favoured regions is most economically rewarding if concentrated in a few most promising centres; and the plenitude of evidence that most of the traditional rural livelihoods—agriculture, fishing, forestry—would be probably most economically rewarding (in the narrow sense) if they were changed into capital intensive rather than labour intensive enterprises of large size. That none of the countries concerned has much enthusiasm for the changes of the latter kind has some economic justification. Modernization would not only greatly change ways of life which many would wish to retain, they would almost inevitably call for change in the appearance of large districts whose present beauty and ancient landscape and settlement forms are a great and growing tourist attraction. There seems no answer to this problem save in slow and cautious changes carried out with skills that are scarce and expensive.

* * *

Another view of British regional needs should be mentioned here as an introduction to the fourth and last method of approach to the solution of regional problems.

This view is difficult to summarize, but seems mainly to arise from anxiety over timing and machinery. Physical planners—with a background in the land-using professions and skills—have seen that regional development must mainly take place through a series of building and civil engineering projects at particular places, arranged in a programme and subject to a budget. These men are aware that pre-war and post-war 'regional plans' foundered because they were just a series of aspirations in pictorial form. There was no programme and no machinery for execution. Moreover, these earlier plans lacked the essential base of economic studies of the resources and strength and failings of the region, and considered suggestions for a mutually supporting series of remedies and new investments.

This essential economic base is now being supplied. It is however felt by some physical planners that the new regional boards and councils are examining regions that are far too large to be of practical assistance in guiding regional redevelopment—at least for some years. Although the broad national comparisons that will emerge from study of the English regions will be of value in determining strategy for 40 years ahead, they will be of little immediate use in the places where action is most needed. To summarize the second view somewhat crudely, it is that the places where regional guidance is most needed in Britain is in the six or eight urbanized regions which are obvious candidates for choice as counter-attractions to London and Birmingham. It is argued that a concentration of effort upon these regional capitals presents the greatest opportunity to establish real counter-attractions, and centres from which, by outward spread of prosperity, regional unbalance may be permanently redressed. It is further held that the shortage of time available to prepare for mounting motor traffic, the land shortage, administrative sub-division and other local problems in these urban regions, confirms the demand for a concentration of effort. The relatively small size of the urban regions concerned would enable economic and physical problems to be considered together, and firm recommendations made for a programme of action and the machinery needed to carry it out.

This alternative view has been over-simplified in this summary. There does however appear to be some real difference of opinion concerning the best use of economic manpower in Britain for the solution of regional problems in the next few years. At one extreme, there is the need for a long-term strategic view, dealing in broad comparisons. At the other, there is a demand for economists to help solve immediate and extremely complex problems in a few very important areas: problems of the comparative value of investment in communications, infrastructure generally, new employments, redevelopment, and regional programmes and budgets. Until recently economists have been uneasy colleagues in this more limited field. Their training, like that of many geographers and sociologists, has been concentrated upon accurate description of what is—or was; and appeals for help to determine what should be, in a particular locality and within ten years, have been received with something like alarm. Yet few questions could be more important than where Britain places works which Dr P. A. Stone has estimated to cost about £200,-000 millions before the year 2004, and occupy 1½ million acres of additional land.

British Governments of the past five years have been aware of the opinion just described. It was indeed obvious that the land use and development problems of the larger urban regions were growing more and more complex, and could not be solved by a planning system under which each local authority in an urban region prepared its own independent plan. A radius of 10 miles from the centre of Manchester embraces in whole or part the territories of nine such planning authorities, who are by no means agreed on the best future pattern of development for their region. The need for unbiased examination of the problems of land use problems in urban regions of this kind led to investigations that are here called feasibility studies.

FEASIBILITY STUDIES

Feasibility studies, as now being undertaken in Britain, are in part an extension of the housing needs and land availability studies begun by the Ministry of Housing and Local Government's own staff about five years ago, and in part an extension of the New Towns' procedure of preparing an outline plan for the rapid growth of a new settlement. They comprise a coordinated study of the economic, social and physical possibilities of a limited area with the aim of achieving specific objectives within a limited period of years. The objective may be a large extension of an existing town (Peterborough, Ipswich, Runcorn); the creation of virtually new towns (Skelmersdale, Mid-Wales); or the renovation and further development of an older industrial region which also contains progressive chemical industries (Teeside). The areas and objectives vary greatly in size and complexity, but all these studies are alike in two respects. They have all been commissioned by central government, and they will result in proposals for physical developments of great size, together with a suggested programme and some estimate of costs.

These larger feasibility studies have special interest in that they will require joint consideration of the economic, social, physical and administrative aspects of urban regional development on a larger scale, and probably more realistically, than has taken place in Britain hitherto. Up to now, regional economic studies, actual construction projects (such as the building of a new town) and questions of changes in local government boundaries and powers, have been examined or carried out by separate bodies and on greatly differing scales. A decision to proceed with the renovation of further development of Portsmouth-Southampton or Teeside would however require an integrated solution to be found for problems in all three fields, in relation to a particular area and within a few years. Such solutions will be essential if urban regional development is to be effectively guided, and the manifest difficulty of achieving them suggests strongly that some new administrative machinery will be necessary. The huge cost of motorways, new housing schemes and other major units of investment, coupled with scarcity of resources, will require—as has been stated earlier—that the location and timing of each new investment should be the best that is practicable from the point of view of the region as a whole. It is very unlikely that the necessary firmness of control could be achieved by the existing system of relationships between Government and local authorities.

THE MAJOR PROBLEMS

Regional problems and approaches to their solution in Western Europe may thus be summarized as follows:

The regions that are causing most concern are of three kinds: 'underdeveloped' (mostly rural); 'overdeveloped', usually including the capital city; and declining or unresilient industrial regions, some of which contain much derelict land or are otherwise unattractive in physical environment and general living conditions.

The solutions to these problems that have been or are being tried are very numerous but fall broadly into four groups: employment aids; declarations of policy; regional economic studies on a national and comparative basis; and feasibility studies of how to carry out, in physical terms, desirable changes in selected areas where action is most urgently needed.

Two further generalisations seem valid. All governments have been reluctant to disturb the existing pattern of central and local government responsibilities and relations. They have therefore examined regional problems by means of special committees or agencies, in the hope that the problems could be solved by a limited number of special aids or projects, combined with improvements in liaison between central and local government authorities. This general approach—extremely diverse in its detailed forms—has had some successes, but has brought no conviction that it offers more than a temporary solution for problems that continue to grow.

The second generalisation follows from the first. No vigorous examination seems to have been made of interrelated economic, physical and administrative problems that would have to be solved in order to guide a programme of regional development over an extended period, and of how this could be done. It is easy to see why this examination has not been made. Men and women with the necessary skills are few and busy; such a study might miss some of the biggest difficulties unless it was related to a particular region; and if it were so related there would be much opposition to its being put in hand on the grounds, *inter alia,* of the damage it might do to the work and recommendations of the Local Government Commission.

It may be that in Britain the nearest politically acceptable substitute for such a study would be an impartial examination of the proposals in the Teeside feasibility study in relation to the future local government structure proposed for the same area.

FUTURE LINES OF ACTION

In trying to foresee future lines of action towards solving regional problems, it is useful to begin by noting the most powerful and seemingly permanent forces making for regional changes. Two of these seem dominant and are interconnected. The first is the normal human desire for a better job, a better home, schools and hospitals and more opportunity for popular forms of leisure activity. The second force is the demand for more space in and around almost every kind of building and—above all—much more space for moving and storing motor vehicles. The first attracts, as it always has attracted, young people from isolated communities towards big cities. The second diminishes, and is now doing so at an accelerating rate, the advantages of living in a big city and produces a counterflow outwards.

These are very obvious facts. The two forces have been at work in Europe for several centuries and probably since cities existed and migration became reasonably safe. But until the last 30 or 40 years they have been at work at a leisurely pace. It is their rapidly increasing strength and rate of operation that has been underestimated by Governments.

A publication from Sweden[11] has usefully summarized recent data on the two forces. In all countries, irrespective of their economic structure, the largest cities have grown fastest. Mobility of employees in search of jobs has grown greatly, and is not confined to movement from less to more favoured areas, and in broad terms this mobility is regarded as economically beneficial. As average income rises each individual,

[11] International Conference of the International Federation for Housing and Planning. *Growing space needs in the urbanized region,* Orebro, Sweden, 1965.

family and firm, demands more space, and to this personal or industrial demand there has been added in the last 20 years the huge land demands of motor vehicles. Demand for space in an urban region grows more than proportionately to the increase of population.

In Sweden the land area per head in urbanized districts is growing by 3.25 per cent per year. This is the same rate of growth as that of the gross national product and almost the same as the annual increase in goods carried by road (3.8 per cent). In the U.S.A. the land area per head in urbanized areas now exceeds a quarter of an acre and is expected to rise to half an acre by 1980. Figures are given for the increase in floorspace per user for most types of building. These figures, and the fact that every country in Europe expects a continuing increase in motor traffic, have obvious implications for those who frame regional policies.

One of these is that for those who have or soon will have the use of a motor car, most economic and social activities have become regional in scale: since the area within reach in an hour's journey—given favourable conditions—is about 50 times what it was half a century ago. A second implication is that the advantages of living and working in a low density area are substantial for those who travel to work by car. For example, 62 per cent of those who travel by road to Bishops Stortford (population 20,000) and Maidenhead (40,000) between 7 and 10 a.m. travel by car; for Watford (76,000) the percentage is 48; for Leeds (309,000), 27. Third, the advantages of living in big cities of the normal densely developed kind are growing less, and will inevitably continue to do so. The twofold demand for extra space within each building and for the movement and storage of vehicles, cannot be fulfilled. The difficulty of providing for the movement of people and goods at reasonable speed and cost is now the major anxiety in big cities. It has led to a ban in Greater Paris on new buildings likely to increase employment and to the recent ban on new office buildings in Central London. In Britain, proposals have been made for restricting traffic on urban roads by imposing a charge on vehicles, and it is probable that some such restriction will have to be introduced.

Low density development on new land is far less costly than redevelopment of existing cities, less disturbing and far quicker. It follows that demand for more urban space will be supplied, in the main, by large new developments at low density.[12] The key question for regional policy makers in all countries is where the extra land should best be provided. The answer should try to meet the needs of 40 years ahead so far as these can be foreseen: it must also have regard to the present location of employments, the need to keep the country as a whole prosperous and to the limited resources available for new developments.

The physical solution is to enlarge the framework of every urban region, so as to relieve damaging pressures and facilitate movement, while seeking to divert to new or old centres in less favoured regions an appreciable proportion of new growth. As a general aim, this is what European governments are trying to do, but there is little agreement on methods, timing or administrative machinery. Moreover, there are grounds for the same complaints as were made by those in high command in the Allied forces in World War II: that they could rarely obtain a clear statement of the resources that would be made available for a given operation, and that too little attention was given to the machinery needed to carry out a complex plan.

There is some agreement on methods for the carrying out of regional development policies in under-developed and usually rural areas; and the physical problems are relatively simple. These areas have the assets of plenty of land and usually of a reserve of labour. As a bus service, or a car of some kind, comes within the reach of most families, some disadvantages of isolation can be removed at a relatively cheap cost. A larger school, churches, clinic and perhaps tourist camping grounds or hotels could be concentrated at 'key' villages, where piped water and electricity and domestic sewerage also become practicable.

The next order of magnitude of 'growth centre' is the rural regional centre to which many countries are paying attention. This is seen as a single larger town, or a group of smaller ones close together, which would become a focus for the communities within 25 or 30 miles. In general, such a centre is seen as the smallest unit to which substantial centre government aid would be given. Roads, electricity and sewerage would be provided, and economic hopes pinned to a slow growth of rurally based enterprises: forest products and fish and dairy processing, veterinary and agricultural service stations, tech-

[12] Robert Grieve. *Regional Planning*. Town Planning Inst. Journal. June 1965.

nical training, and regional craft centres. In addition, it is hoped that the probable huge future demand for tourist holiday accommodation will provide rural regional centres with opportunities for profitable development and a substantial summer income. This particularly applies to centres near the sea or other large water areas, as these are specially attractive to the modern holiday maker. There are doubts whether it would be desirable to try to establish in such rural centres branches of modern industry that are not closely tied to local resources. The availability of labour may not be a great enough advantage to off-set the drawbacks of a lack of a local network of sub-contractors and industrial linkages, and difficulty in attracting able managers. Industrial development may also discourage tourist and holiday development and some of the older people who often retire to centres of this kind. The general approach to the establishment of rural regional centres is supported by the settlement hierarchy studies from Christaller onwards.

In physical terms, the growth of rural centres will depend for its progress on the right kind of plan, which need not be elaborate, and on implementation that manages to avoid the ill effects of local authority rivalries.

* * *

Enlargement of the framework of larger urban regions and choice of growth centres in or near them are problems of an entirely different order of magnitude: equally great, though different, for 'unresilient' and 'overdeveloped' regions.[13]

The key factor, already stated, is that the growth of motor traffic is markedly reducing the overall advantages of big cities for living and working. The best position now for the go-ahead family and firm is a position near but not in a big city— where the twofold advantages of regional concentration and local spaciousness may be enjoyed. The physical solution, diagrammatically, is to bring into existence a grid of communications (mainly roads) which will link new and old settlements in the region in mutual support and spread the traffic load. This grid or network pattern has developed on a large scale, largely unplanned, in the United States, and exists in Europe in more rudimentary forms.

It is clear that if it were possible to plan and guide the de-

[13] Myles Wright. *The Dublin Region: Preliminary Report*. Stationery Office, Dublin, 1965.

velopment of such a new pattern of communications and settlements, the advantages would be very great. In broad terms this is what European governments would like to do, but the process is slow and fumbling, mainly from doubts as to the extent of guidance that will prove practicable— politically, financially and administratively.

The present position in Britain is probably as complex as any in Europe. The biggest urban regions contain about half the country's population, a high proportion of economic activities and very costly traffic networks, mostly radial. Two of these (London and Birmingham) are overloaded, and threaten severe congestion and general deterioration of environment. The most obvious solution is to try to spread future growth and development more equally between 8 or 10 existing urbanized regions. Indeed, this may be called the only solution, since mass migration would create impossible conditions both at the receiving and exporting ends. It is the solution adopted—again in very broad terms—by the Government.

A decision to implement it more forcefully would cause acute controversy over two major questions that have long been obvious.

To what extent will it prove practicable to repress further development in the South East and West Midlands and divert new enterprises elsewhere? Judged by Government action so far the answer seems to be: not very much. It has been held, rightly, that there must be some relief of intolerable pressure on urban space in the South East and West Midlands. The easiest way to relieve pressure on London is to make more use of medium-sized towns within 60 to 100 miles, which could take a large increase of population without serious deterioration in their present traffic and living conditions. This is being done, but apart from the movement of some Government departments (to Worthing, Basingstoke, Southend, Hastings, etc.) it is doubtful how much relief of pressure in London will be achieved by these means. It is probable that London and its peripheral towns will both continue to grow and to continue to attract population from elsewhere. The suggestion of growth areas in an arc 30 miles to the west and north of Birmingham may have similar results. These may either attract enterprises from Birmingham (and thus contribute to relief of pressure in Birmingham but do nothing for less favoured regions), or new enterprises from other parts of the country which are anxious to gain a foothold near Birmingham. The effect of 'relief of pressure' decisions near London and Birmingham on potential areas of counter-attraction should receive study and may demand some hard decisions, as does the extra aid for development in these other regions that would be economically practicable.

The second major problem concerns the scale of the new regional framework of communications and settlements that is needed to spread the traffic load, and to provide a large part of 1½ million acres of extra urban land likely to be needed during the next 40 years. These frameworks should be no larger than will provide for easy movement and good living and working conditions for an expanded population, for they will be very costly. The danger is that a wealthy region with easy topographical conditions will treat itself to a super-grid that will add to its attractive power. A super-grid of this type—approximately 100 miles square is already emerging in the South East, fortified by expansion proposals from Southampton round to Ipswich, and even Peterborough, and may fill in rapidly. Its attractive power is likely to become very great.

In the North of England and in Scotland a grid on the same—or at least a large—scale may be suggested by difficult topography, derelict land and unattractive living conditions in major cities, but the difficulties of creating it and the diffused prosperity needed to justify it, would seem enormous. It would appear preferable in the North to concentrate aid on a few chosen areas, and to hope for an outward spread of prosperity concentrically. The Northern grids, to begin with, should therefore be no larger than is likely to be needed for 20 years ahead, though they might well be open-ended. The 15 mile radius from Liverpool, suggested by proposals for Skelmersdale, Runcorn and Warrington, appears about right for Merseyside. It promises mutual support rather than rivalry between old cities and new settlements: and mutual support of towns and enterprises on the basis of an expanded but not too large grid would seem the best recipe for renovation and development of unresilient urban regions. The scale of the desirable framework for expanded urban regions would therefore be a rewarding field for study.

* * *

It is possible to suggest some certain conclusions concerning the future development of the urban regions of Europe.

These conclusions are very general and mainly concern physical arrangement.

1. Each country will try to spread growth over a number of urban regions and to slow down the rate of growth in present dominant regions.

2. It will be essential to provide for a considerable expansion at low density to take place in urban regions in order to relieve the pressure on space in large cities. A redevelopment plan for a large city that is not integrated with a plan for the surrounding region is likely to be of little practical value and may prove harmful by advocating solutions that can never be fulfilled.

3. The need for a great increase in urban space will require an enlarged framework of communications, of a grid type rather than radial. The framework would encourage 'loosening up' by bringing into existence new places for residence and work, which would be linked with one another as well as with older cities and towns.

4. The size of the enlarged framework chosen for a particular region will be of great importance. The balance of arguments suggest that it should be as small as is consistent with easy movement by road and reasonably quiet living and working conditions. This would be more economical and encourage cross-linkages which make an important contribution to growth. Provision could be made for later expansion of the framework. All countries favour concentration of aid upon relatively few urban regions.

5. New administrative machinery will be needed to choose the urban regions of growth, prepare the framework and guide their fabrication. The investments required will be so costly that their location, relationship and timing will require guidance for the whole urban region. In general, the new machinery will be concerned with the translation of economic plans for the region into physical plans for particular projects at particular places.

Dutch National Land Use Planning

DR. CORNELIUS DE CLER*

The Netherlands, in the northwest corner of Europe, with an area of 40,000 square kilometers, of which actually an area of 7,000 square kilometers is water, is a small country about the size of Maryland, one of the smaller states in the U.S.A. However significant agriculture and cattle-breeding in the Netherlands may have been—and still are today—the most important sources of livelihood have always been commerce and shipping and added to this since the nineteenth century there has been an industrial development, which in the twentieth century has assumed very considerable proportions. At the present time, therefore, the agrarian population is definitely in the minority, since no more than 10 percent of the male working population is engaged in agriculture, a figure which by the end of the present century will have dropped to only a few percent. Hence, the majority of the population, lives in towns. The Netherlands is and will continue to be one of the most highly urbanized countries and it is probably no exaggeration to say that this flat, densely populated and almost fully cultivated country is one vast urban region.

The Netherlands in its limited area accommodates some twelve million people, which amounts to no less than approximately 360 inhabitants per square kilometer or ca. 900 inhabitants per square mile. It is, therefore, one of the most densely populated countries in the world and more densely populated than, for example, Japan or Puerto Rico and certainly more densely populated than any other European country. What does such a population density imply? It implies that within his national frontiers the Dutchman has at his disposal on an average 3,000 square meters, that is a piece of land measuring about 100 by 100 feet. A high population density is in itself not so remarkable in this part of Europe. It is here that we find the large delta of the rivers Rhine,

* Head of the Town Planning Section, Central Directorate of Housing and Building Industry; advisor to the Council of State, The Netherlands. Formerly associated with the Municipal Town Planning Bureau, City of Rotterdam, and the Reconstruction Bureau, Isle of Walcheren, he is a graduate of the Technical University of Delft.

Meuse and Scheldt, which flow through regions where and around which there are various large agglomerations and densely populated areas, such as the industrial areas along the Ruhr in West Germany and those of Belgium and the north of France. There are some twenty million people in these areas alone. Hence, as regards population density the difference between the Netherlands and its neighboring West European countries is only marginal. The same applies to the natural growth of the population. It is true that on account of the favorable birth and death rates this growth is greater in the Netherlands than in any one of the neighboring countries, viz. between 1.3 and 1.4 percent yearly. Consequently, the twleve millions increase at a rate of one million every seven years, but then, after all, the life expectancy of man is relatively good in all the West European countries.

If in these respects the Netherlands is not really different from its neighboring countries, the question arises whether there is anything in which it can claim to be unique. There certainly is one not very favorable aspect—namely the very low level of the greater part of the country relative to the sea and the rivers. On account of this situation the Netherlands has lived for many centuries under the threat of flooding by high tides and high river discharges. A large part of the country—roughly half—is maintained artificially and protected by a close defense system of dikes, a finely divided discharge network of ditches and canals and thousands of pumping units. For centuries the people in large parts of the Netherlands have lived at often more than ten feet below sea level and nobody thinks this strange or disquieting. It is just part of everyday life to find yourself at that often subtle point of equilibrium between land and water. This situation is so exceptional that the Dutch language has an absolutely untranslatable term to describe all the activities relating to the art of preserving this equilibrium that affords protection against the water outside the dikes and the control of the water inside the dikes. This word is *waterstaat,* the nearest translation being perhaps "water control." Thus, there is in the Netherlands a Ministry of Transport and *Waterstaat,* legislation relating to *Waterstaat,* special administrative bodies such as *Rijkswaterstaat* (national *waterstaat*) and *Provinciale Waterstaat.*

The Dutch knew quite well what they were doing when they settled on this muddy, low-lying land. The soil deposits in the delta are very fertile indeed and the yield per hectare attains fabulously high figures, especially in the horticultural districts.

An even more important reason is that the lower reaches of the rivers and the sea inlets into which the rivers discharge offered natural harbors and that the digging and constructing of new docks, watercourses and quays in the soft soil was often a relatively simple matter. The fact that the erection of buildings on the other hand presented considerable difficulties —in the west of the country practically every building stands on a foundation of from sixty- to eighty-foot-long piles—was just taken into the bargain. Owing to the fairly mild sea climate it was fortunately not necessary to make the buildings of heavy construction to keep out the cold. Relatively thin brick walls and large window openings, which together make for a light construction, are characteristic of Netherlands building.

In their struggle against water the Netherlanders were not always on the defensive. In the course of the centuries they developed unique new methods of land reclamation. A large part of the land below sea or river level was reclaimed by surrounding it with dikes and subsequently draining it by means of simple sluices and by pumping, depending on the level of the land in question. The reclamation of land from the water is an old process, which was applied as far back as the early Middle Ages, originally on a modest scale. The use of windmills and, later still, steam engines for pumping out the water increased the possibilities of land reclamation even further, until in the end it was possible to drain fairly large lakes. The process of land reclamation is still being continued even today, using up-to-date aids and techniques, including plastic sheeting to stabilize the sandy bottom of the sea inlets. Ever since 1918 this has led to the gradual reclamation of the Zuiderzee, whereby the firm land within the boundaries of the Netherlands in an entirely peaceful manner has been increased by approximately 10 percent.

Even in the earliest times such drastic and such important matters as the construction of dikes, the digging of drainage canals and the reclamation of new land, could not be undertaken by the individual. Joint consultation is essential even to determine the location of a dike; its construction requires the manpower of many, while its maintenance involves the cooperation and vigil of just as many people. Is it perhaps on account of these special circumstances that in the Netherlands it has been accepted for many centuries that in matters of land use joint action is desirable and in some cases even essential. Is this perhaps the reason why the Netherlander—despite the great value he has always attached to his personal freedom as a seaman, a merchant and an entrepreneur, thus as a free citizen—is inclined to accept curtailment of this freedom as soon as the problem of land use arises? This might well be made the subject of interesting historical and socio-psychological studies.

In planning its towns and villages, and the open country in between, the Netherlands has created sound and effective legislation enabling the twelve million inhabitants to be saved from spatial chaos, despite the scarcity of land and despite many and varied land uses. The Netherlands is still an orderly country, a country like a large, well-kept garden. This legislation passed through a process of development and initially—in 1901 when the Housing Law was introduced, which for the first time put urban planning on a legal basis—was undoubtedly of much simpler form and with much more modest aims than those of present planning legislation. The title "Housing Law" is a clear indication that originally the principal aim was "housing" and that urban planning, insofar as this was provided for in the Law, was regarded as little more than simply an aspect of good housing. Hence, at the beginning of the twentieth century the Law did not go further than the requirement that municipal councils of more than twenty thousand inhabitants and those which showed a rapid rate of expansion—of more than 20 percent in five years—should draw up a plan for laying on streets, squares and canals. In that initial stage land use, other than for roads, and especially the use of land for building purposes had not been provided for. Thus these early efforts were still far removed from the ideal of integrated land use planning.

The first seeds fell in fertile soil, however, and after some drastic revisions in the twenties and the thirties, planning legislation developed into an effective system of legal provisions. Just before World War II the need was felt for a third far-reaching modernization, but this could not go through because of the war. It was not until 1945 that planning legislation was brought up-to-date—admittedly with a little patchwork here and there.

As the situation gradually got back to normal after the war, there was a growing need for sound, modern legislation in the sphere of planning, quite separate from the Housing Law, of which it had always formed part. Thus, after many years of preparation a new law was introduced on the 1st of August 1965, which provides for all kinds of refinements and improvements in the planning machinery. Since in the meantime planning activities had come to include far more than just the building of new and the expansion of existing villages and towns and since all land use was regulated by the law—also if this did not involve any building activity—a title for this legislation such as "the townplanning law" was considered incorrect. Thus, the law was called "Physical Planning Law" or, perhaps even more to the point, "Town and Country Planning Law." The system of legal provisions as it developed in the years after 1901 and as again laid down in the new law in 1965 contained these main points:

1. Building, regardless of its purpose, is only allowed after permission has been obtained from the municipal authorities.
2. A building permit may only be granted if the building plan is in conformity with the town plan for the area where the building is to take place.
3. Each municipality must draw up a town plan for its territory outside the built-up area, indicating for all the land whether it will be open for building and, if so, *what* may be built. For the built-up areas the municipalities are free to draw up a plan if they wish to do so. All town plans—whether compulsory or otherwise—have the same legal consequences.
4. Supra-municipal interests must be regulated in regional plans, which are drawn up by the provincial authorities.
5. The municipal authorities are entitled to apply a system of permits to any activities—other than building plans—causing a change in the land, such as excavations and reclamation projects.

This direct coupling of all building activities and—if necessary also other activities—to town and country planning at municipal level, together with the fact that practically every Netherlands municipality of any importance has a plan laying down land use within its territory, has resulted in land use being nicely under control, while the land itself makes a very orderly impression. Despite the high population density, the country does not make the impression of being "full up" and at a fairly short distance from the large cities it is still possible to find agrarian districts that have escaped urban sprawl.

The Netherlands can consider itself fortunate that the administrative setup controlling the planning machinery is fairly simple. The central government—a parliamentary democracy—exercises authority over eleven provinces and under these provinces there are about 950 municipalities, which—large or small—all have the same powers and together cover the whole of the territory of the Netherlands. The highest authority in the municipal sphere is the municipal council, which represents the legislative power. In addition, the municipality has an executive power, which is vested in the burgomaster and aldermen. Similarly, the province has legislative power—vested in the Provincial States—and executive power—vested in the Deputed States. Since 1901 the planning system has operated in such a way that the power to take the initiative is placed at the bottom, which means that the municipalities make the plans for their territory. The fact that local initiative, if not strong enough in itself, can be stimulated by the higher authority on the strength of the legal obligation to make plans, does not detract from the principle that the plans are not imposed from above, but are first and foremost drawn up at the local government level. Considering the historical development, in which town-planning originated in the local housing legislation, this is readily understandable, but the phenomenon is more than just a mere historical peculiarity, since it also means that planning stands close to the citizen, since the plans are drawn up by those who are acquainted at close quarters with the local needs.

Planning without the necessary expert knowledge is inefficient and this has been fully realized also in the Netherlands. Moreover, local interests can clash with the interests of neighboring local units. Hence, the system cannot operate properly without a certain amount of quality control and the coordination of divergent local interests. The law provides for this by stipulating that all municipal plans must be approved by the provincial authorities—thus by the executive body, the Deputed States—before they can come into force and prior to implementation. As regional planning is in the hands of the provincial authorities, this guarantees that local plans are checked against the regional plans. The primary object of provincial supervision is—insofar as the municipalities are not already so inclined themselves—to promote the orderly growth of the settlements and to counteract wild developments. Moreover, the province has a means of "timing" otherwise entirely acceptable developments by rejecting, wholly or in part, any plans which—in the opinion of the provincial planning authorities—tend to be too large. Thus development can be kept fairly well under control both in time and place. There is a reason for using the phraseology "fairly well under control," because on this point the local and the provincial planning authorities often disagree.

Supervision from above—by the provincial authorities—may give rise to conflict between authorities at different levels. If this occurs, the central government decides the issue. This is referred to as "the Crown," which means that the decision is taken by Royal Decree, the responsibility of the Minister of Housing and Physical Planning. The Crown does not only decide in disputes between the various authorities. Private persons also can lodge any objections they may have to a plan with the Crown. It is not so, however, that the central government can only take action in those incidental cases where there is conflict between authorities or to objections from citizens. Apart from the line from bottom to top, along which the municipal plan moves up for approval to the provincial authorities and, if necessary, to the Crown, the Netherlands planning machinery also has a line from top to bottom. In the first place there is a Physical Planning Council, a special body within the Cabinet, of which all ministers who are concerned with the planning in some way or other are members. It is here, at Cabinet level, that the government planning policy is decided. Naturally, the Physical Planning Council is mostly concerned with the broad planning policies but it is not at all impossible that from time to time it will also deal with some important detail. There is no rule which restricts the task and scope of the Physical Planning Council and it cannot be denied that the interest of Ministers sometimes also extends to details. This special body within the Cabinet characterizes the important place which physical planning occupies in the Netherlands.

Whereas the Physical Planning Council lays down broad policy outlines, the implementation and the "daily care" of the planning are the responsibilities of the Minister of Housing and Physical Planning. It is he who is responsible for guarding the interests of sound physical planning and for working out new ideas in this sphere. In this task he is assisted by a Government Physical Planning Service, an expert body with a highly qualified staff. The Minister of Housing and Physical Planning is empowered by law to issue binding directives to the next lower government level—that of the province—in regard to the drawing up of regional plans. Hence, the government planning policy has a direct effect downwards. Similarly, the provincial authorities can—in their turn assisted by the experts of the Provincial Planning Services—issue binding directives to the municipalities for drawing up municipal plans. Their directives must be based on the regional plans. Ultimately all this results in the detailed municipal plans, which are binding upon the citizen: if he wants to build something, his building plan must fit in the municipal plan; if it does not, he will not get a permit. The line from top to bottom, therefore, descends from main principles and policies—at national and provincial levels—to details determined in the local sphere.

Hitherto, reference has only been made to authorities, government plans and procedures. The question which arises is that part the ordinary Netherlander plays in all this. After all, these plans are drawn up in his interests and for his benefit. Can he influence these plans and can he oppose them if he should wish to do so? It would not be in keeping with the historic character of the Netherlander and it would not satisfy his sense of justice, if the greatest attention were not devoted to his rights and desires.

There is a characteristic difference between a country like the Netherlands—and many other West European countries—and a country like the United States; that in the Netherlands direct interference by the citizen with and his direct influence on matters of public interest are much smaller than on the other side of the Atlantic Ocean. The Netherlander seldom participates in actions aiming at the promotion of some public interest. He seldom forms citizens' committees or similar bodies. His influence works almost exclusively via the governmental representative bodies—municipalities, provincial councils and parliament—which he has elected himself. As political life in the Netherlands has a certain stability and the average Netherlander has confidence in the representatives of his choice—and rightly so—he leaves a lot to the discretion of these representative bodies. Apart from this political world there is the civil service, which operates independently of the political tides, since it changes neither at the top nor at the bottom, except for the highest of offices—the ministers—when the political situation changes. The service moreover has an old tradition of expertness, integrity and loyalty towards the highest in office, irrespective of political color. Consequently, the civil service enjoys in general the confidence of the citizen; thus the public does not as a rule get very excited about initiatives in the public sector, in municipal or regional planning.

But even though the public collectively does not as a rule feel particularly concerned, the private individual can have all kinds of interests that can be seriously affected by planning.

It is at this point that the Netherlands legislation in the sphere of physical planning contains a number of safeguards, which ensure that the private and public interests must be weighed one against the other during the planning process. For example, the citizen has three opportunities to state his opinion, make known his objections and defend his interests in regard to the plans. The first opportunity occurs when the plan is drawn up in the local sphere, when he can address himself to the municipal council after the plan has been laid open to public inspection during a period prescribed by law. At the risk of encouraging speculation, the planning process must be public. The people concerned cannot be kept dangling in the air, because the municipal council must give its decision on the objections raised within a certain period after the plan has been laid open to public inspection. In regard to objections and in regard to the question as to whether they should be sustained or not the municipal authorities usually seek the advice of their own townplanning service—if a large or medium-size municipality is concerned—or the advice of a private planning consultant if the municipality is too small to have a planning service of its own.

If the citizen is not satisfied with the decision—which is given in the form of a substantiated resolution of the council—he can lodge his objections a second time at the level of the provincial authorities. There his private interests are once more weighed against the public interests and here also the objections are dealt with on the strength of advice obtained from an expert civil service department, the Provincial Planning Service. If the citizen is then still of the opinion that he has not obtained justice, he has yet a third chance: he can appeal to the Crown. Again the interests are weighed and again the government body giving the decision is advised by experts. The decision of the Crown—at least if the case gets as far as the Crown, otherwise the same applies to the provincial government—is then final and this makes the plan binding. If the complaining citizen suffers substantial damage, the law demands that he should receive compensation. Hence, if necessary, three opportunities of being heard, three investigations, three times advice from different experts and three times a decision from different government bodies.

After this description of the superior qualities of the Netherlands planning machinery it is necessary to restore equilibrium somewhat by mentioning a drawback of the system. It must be admitted that the care taken is great, but the duration of the procedure is proportional to that care. Hence, speed of action is certainly not the most striking characteristic of Netherlands planning policy. It takes time to lay the plans open to public inspection and it also takes time to hear the objections. The same applies to the compilation of expert advice, not to speak of administrative resolutions. But how can it be otherwise? Anyone who wants to have his plans accepted—both by the individual and by the community—must make a sacrifice somewhere. And in the Netherlands the choice has been for the meticulous care taken in guarding the interests of all concerned and the sometimes rather slow rate of progress is taken for granted. The carefulness has yet another aspect: the plans usually go into fairly great detail, both for the residential areas and for other types of land use. There are a number of reasons for this. Netherlanders attach considerable value, for example, to good design for towns and villages. Furthermore, an effort is made legally to arrange the planning in such a way that not a single owner can be surprised by unexpected—and to him harmful—initiatives being put into effect on land in the vicinity of his property. The vast amount of detail, together with the sometimes time-consuming procedure for drawing up and amending plans, has introduced a certain amount of rigidity into planning as a whole. In recent years especially these long lean times were felt to be a considerable drawback and one of the gains in the 1965 revised law—is that it is possible to deviate to some extent from established detailed plans according to an accelerated procedure. It has also become possible to start with a rough plan drawn up according to normal procedures, which can be worked out in greater detail according to an accelerated procedure. Thus, these two methods introduce flexibility into the system as a whole, without detracting in any way from the essential requirements of legal security, efficiency and good design.

In the Netherlands, therefore, tradition and national character have led to the development of the habit of planning as a continuous process of research, design, implementation and checking to see whether the results fulfill the expectations. Municipal plans have now been practically joined up to cover the whole national territory; many regional plans have already been drawn up or are in preparation. These are the plans, but will they remain paper plans? Is there any certainty that they will be effectuated? In the past, there have certainly been times that many plans were no more than mere possibilities that would probably never be realized. Especially since World

War II influence by the substantial population growth and by the housing shortage, a plan is now not only an arrangement for land use on a legal basis, but is in effect a short- or long-term implementation program. This applies especially to the residential areas, of which the realization is often a matter of great urgency. An important point is, the availability of the necessary land for such purposes but in this respect also the Netherlands is in a unique position: land can be expropriated according to a procedure laid down by law for the implementation of town plans, irrespective of whether they concern the building of residential neighborhoods, the laying on of industrial estates, recreational areas or of a new network of roads, etc. The unique aspect does not lie so much in the legal provisions available for this purpose—many other countries have a similar arrangement—but rather in the very wide use made of these facilities. Public acceptance of expropriation is so widespread that in carrying out town plans at the municipal level, expropriation is the rule rather than the exception, be it that a settlement by agreement often follows after the onset of the expropriation procedure. Perhaps it is also the result of the centuries long struggle against the water, namely in the sense that the Netherlander has a deep-rooted understanding of the fact that the free disposal of the often threatened land had to be restricted in the general welfare involved in the planning, construction and maintenance of the system of dikes, sluices and watercourses. In addition, this state of affairs is also a practical necessity, since in many cases the weak (water-threatened) soil must first be raised or turned into fully serviced building land which can only be done if ownership of the land has been brought under one strong hand—that of the municipal authorities. Expropriation is effected according to very carefully arranged procedures, which protect the party whose property is expropriated in all kinds of ways and which guarantee that his capital position is not affected. He will lose his land, but for this land he receives a reasonable compensation in money, down to the last cent.

As mentioned above, planning in the Netherlands extends to practically every kind of land use, irrespective of whether it concerns residential areas, industrial estates, provisions for active or passive recreation or the infrastructure. The Netherlands believes in comprehensive planning, in which the association between the various kinds of land use is recognized and expressed. This applies both to regional and to municipal plans. The plan recently developed by the municipality of

Amsterdam for the large expansion project to the southeast of the city, the "Bijlmermeer" plan is illustrative: It involves first and foremost a network of main roads from the new part to the existing part of the city, as well as access roads and roads for internal traffic in the new sector, to which end public and private transport has been studied relative to each other, both in regard to moving and stationary vehicles. Thus, the parking problem has also received full attention. The residential areas have been located, building densities fixed and the building height determined in the various parts of the residential areas. Land has been earmarked for shopping centers, churches, schools, cultural and medical facilities, for police supervision, for municipal services; thus for all the buildings required to form a complete, modern, residential neighborhood. The plans also provide for playgrounds for infants and older children, sports grounds, public gardens and the necessary parks. Special attention is also given to water, this indispensable element in Netherlands town-planning. It will be appreciated that all this was preceded by extensive research and programming.

Has this elaborate planning machinery enabled the Netherlands to solve all its problems? If this were only true! It is after all by no means a simple matter to keep developments in hand in such a densely populated, reasonably prosperous and active country. There is first of all industrial development, which tends to concentrate round the port areas in the west, including industries which have no immediate need for deep navigational water. Will the concerns who are indeed in need of deep water still be able to find this in the future? Much will depend on whether the government will have succeeded in diverting the industries not tied to the seacoast elsewhere in good time. Every effort is made to promote the spreading of industry by granting premiums, but it is a moot point whether this attempt will be entirely successful. Another source of anxiety is the accumulation of the population around the port areas in the west and in the western provinces in general. The high population density here—appreciably higher still than the national mean, which is high enough as it is—actually forces a very careful use of the land with fairly high buildings, but the public prefers the one-family house in garden surroundings. Plans which would take up too much space or would spoil areas of great scenic beauty still have little chance of being approved by the authorities. The demand for the one-family house as elsewhere in Europe and America and the desire for a house somewhere "in the country" are strong, however, and it will be very difficult in the face of this pressure to control a steady process of suburbanization and the accompanying urban sprawl. It will be *essential* to aim at a certain amount of concentration. Perhaps "concentrated deconcentration"—the formation of closely linked up chains of settlements—will be the solution.*

The growing demand for the summer cottage and "the second house" for the week-ends make all this even more difficult, since in a country where space is at a premium the interests of the masses will soon be hard pressed if too much is done to satisfy the recreational desires of the more affluent few. If this trend were to be allowed to develop freely, all lake banks, borders of woods, briefly all beauty spots would in no time be crowded with private cottages. Something similar is happening on the water: wherever the scenery is beautiful, it does not take long for houseboats to appear—floating summerhouses. Hence, the municipal authorities are constantly busy imposing all kinds of restrictive measures, which often hit out hard at owners and speculators, and which therefore are not very popular. This is accompanied by a constant battle waged by the authorities against all kinds of evasions. It will not be long before it will be necessary to establish new public recreational areas at a reasonable distance from the large cities in the west by transforming certain parts of the flat country into parks.

Plans have already been made for developing ten large park areas, where gardens, play-grounds and water will alternate, in the western provinces. To ensure that in due course, when the funds for these expensive projects will become available, there will still be space, it will be necessary even at this stage to counteract any development that would stand in the way of their realization. This is no simple matter in a country where many farmers are turning their dairy farms into much more lucrative market gardens.

The rapidly increasing number of cars adds to the difficulties. Compared with the U.S.A., but also compared with the European countries such as Sweden, Great Britain or Belgium, the Netherlands is not highly motorized. The number of inhabitants per passenger car is about twelve. A substantial increase in the number of cars is most likely and it is expected

* See Professor Jac. P. Thijsse, "Conurbation Holland," in Chapter 8 of Volume I.

that by about 1970 the number of cars will have doubled. Where in this densely populated country will it be possible to find the space for the roads that will be needed to carry all these vehicles with safety. Yes, with safety and convenience, because the largest increase is found in the category of cars bought for recreational purposes. Thus, the Netherlands faces the future with a number of difficult and complicated problems in the sphere of physical planning, problems that cannot be solved solely with more or less perfect planning machinery, but the solution to which is subject to two widely divergent conditions: money and especially power of administration.

There is one major circumstance which will assist the Netherlands in solving these problems: the decision taken in 1918 to reclaim the large inland sea, the Zuiderzee. At first the aims of the reclamation plans were very limited. The principal aim was the considerable shortening of the coastline, protected by dikes and dunes against high flood tides, by sealing off the Zuiderzee with the approximately fifteen-mile-long barrier dam. Since then this tidal mass of salt water has been transformed into an enormous constant-level fresh-water reservoir. The high tides swept up by the north-westerly gales, which in former times formed the Zuiderzee and right into the twentieth century caused periodical flooding, now spend themselves against the straight new dam in the north of the country. A second aim was—since it had been made clear by World War I how dependent the country was on food imports—to increase the agricultural acreage, so as to be more or less self-sufficient as regards food production in times of danger. After completion of the barrier dam in 1928, a start was therefore made with the reclamation of the area of water captured behind it, which was to take place in five phases that is five large *polder* areas. Two of them have now been completed and two more are in different stages of construction. But much has changed since the projects were started. Improving the defense against the sea is still the first aim, but increasing the agrarian acreage is no longer of such great importance, seeing that the rising population of the Netherlands can now no longer be fed with homegrown products anyway. On the other hand the reclaimed areas present entirely new possibilities, which could not have been foreseen in 1918, such as the shortening of road communications, laying on recreational woods on land which is less suitable for agriculture, and especially the development of new industrial, residential and recreational areas so as to relieve the crowded west and the Amsterdam agglomeration in particular. A large new town, called Lelystad—after the famous engineer Lely, who made the reclamation of the Zuiderzee his lifework—will establish itself roughly in the middle of the Zuiderzee, amongst the smaller new towns and villages. The central part of the former Zuiderzee, where it is deepest, will remain water. This will be the "IJssellake" (*IJsselmeer*). Small lakes will also remain between the reclaimed areas and the "old land." Together, these waters form both a recreational area and a stock of fresh water. The latter is especially important for the drinking-water supply and to force back the salt seawater penetrating through the weak soil or entering the land via sluices and open river mouths. Thus, a land reclamation project, originally purely intended for agricultural purposes, has now become the subject of integrated land use for a complete and adequate environment for modern man.

Is there anything wonderful about what is being undertaken in the Netherlands? Certainly not. A modern, industrialized country, of which there are so many, seeks specific solutions to its specific problems by effective planning. Furthermore, it is considered that ways have been found along which agreement can be reached on a plan: expert preparation, adequate publicity and legal security for the citizen. There are also ways that can be followed if there is no agreement about land-use with the owner: then expropriation must be possible. There is no secret about it; on the contrary it is quite clear what all this means: the Netherlander realizes that under the present circumstances the creation of a truly human environment for the general welfare demands effort and sacrifices and he is fully prepared to accept this along with a continuing improvement of his planning legislation and the plans themselves.

Total Environmental Planning

H. WENTWORTH ELDREDGE*

The conservation, rehabilitation, and development of both natural and man-made environment is a massive task clearly calling for the upgrading of our planning technology, or re-

* Adapted from *Beauty for America, Proceedings of the White House Conference on Natural Beauty* (Washington, D.C., U. S. Government Printing Office, 1965), pp. 606–7.

source allocation for agreed-on goals, from a micro- to a macro-scale level in three specific ways to match the ever-growing increase in the socio-economic complexity and extent of the rapidly expanding American scene. Specifically, considerations of (1) area, (2) function and (3) time are all too limited in our planning capabilities.

First, the amount of area covered by plans should be continually enlarged. There is a distinct need for a national urbanization pattern or locational strategy for the entire United States; moreover, this should be co-ordinated with Canada and Mexico on a continental level. *Second,* the number of functions that are bundled in comprehensive plans must be broadened to include all major sectors of the economy (the rationalization of the steel industry and agriculture, for example) as well as sectors of social, aesthetic, and political import and action—not necessarily of immediate economic consequence—in a unified approach. Aesthetic and humanistic values and institutions must be in a planned relationship to economic and political values and institutions. Thus all such activities must be designed as a unit both physically and as social structures. Clearly both the public and private sectors must be meshed. The poverty program and urban/rural redevelopment are cases in point. Population planning is a precise and absolute base for the entire macro-planning endeavor. *Thirdly,* the United States seems strikingly incapable of planning long-range macro-scale programs in time. We seemingly can't get much further ahead than next year's administrative budget on a national scale—except in some specific areas of defense, space, and resource planning of relatively limited scope. Planning-in-time we do well enough for a micro-space or for a micro-function, but ten-, twenty-, fifty-, and one hundred-year national plans are still beyond us. Lead time must be stretched.

The amount of capital needed for these massive operations both public and private, will run into many tens, even hundreds of billions of dollars and demand a driving, expanding, planned, mixed economy; there is no cheap way out. Unless this country can think big in area, function, and time, worthy of our resources, power, and vision, there will be neither man-made nor natural beauty for a potentially Great Society.

INDEX